INTRODUCTION
MANAGEMENT
ACCOUNTING

C000147979

Introduction to Management Accounting Online

A wide range of supporting resources are available at:

MyAccountingLab

Register at **www.myaccountinglab.com** to create your own personal account using the access code supplied with your copy of the book,* and access the following **student** learning resources:

- **A dynamic eText** of the book that you can search, bookmark, annotate and highlight as you please

- **Self-assessment questions** that identify your strengths before recommending a personalised study plan that points you to the resources which can help you achieve a better grade

- **Guided solutions** that take you step by step through solving a problem

- **Flashcards** to test your understanding of key terms

* If you don't have an access code, you can still access the resources. Visit **www.myaccountinglab.com** for details.

IN MEMORIAM

Charles T. (Chuck) Horngren, Edmund W. Littlefield Professor of Accounting, Emeritus at Stanford University, passed away on 23 October, 2011. Over the course of his academic career, Chuck was honoured with the most distinguished accolades that can be granted to an accounting scholar. He wrote some of the globe's best selling textbooks in management and cost accounting. He blessed all who came to know him with his deep insight, his vibrant personality and his sharp wit. Chuck was an international treasure to the accounting world.

INTRODUCTION TO
MANAGEMENT
ACCOUNTING

Alnoor Bhimani
London School of Economics

Charles T. Horngren
Stanford University

Gary L. Sundem
University of Washington, Seattle

William O. Stratton
Dixie State College of Utah

David Burgstahler
University of Washington, Seattle

Jeff Schatzberg
University of Arizona

PEARSON

Harlow, England • London • New York • Boston • San Francisco • Toronto • Sydney
Auckland • Singapore • Hong Kong • Tokyo • Seoul • Taipei • New Delhi
Cape Town • São Paulo • Mexico City • Madrid • Amsterdam • Munich • Paris • Milan

Pearson Education Limited
Edinburgh Gate
Harlow
Essex CM20 2JE
England

and Associated Companies throughout the world

Visit us on the World Wide Web at:
www.pearson.com/uk

Original edition, entitled *Introduction to Management Accounting* published by Prentice Hall,
One Lake Street, Upper Saddle River, New Jersey, USA
Copyright © 2002 by Prentice Hall, Inc.

First published by Pearson Education Limited in 2012

© Pearson Education Limited 2012

ISBN 978-0-273-73755-1

British Library Cataloguing-in-Publication Data
A catalogue record for this book is available from the British Library

Library of Congress Cataloguing-in-Publication Data
A catalog record for this book is available from the Library of Congress

10 9 8 7 6 5 4 3 2 1
15 14 13 12

Typeset in 9/11.5 pt ITC Charter by 75
Printed and bound by Rotolito Lombarda, Italy

BRIEF CONTENTS

Introduction to Management Accounting Online

A wide range of supporting resources are available at:

MyAccountingLab

Register at **www.myaccountinglab.com** to create your own personal account using the access code supplied with your copy of the book,* and access the following teaching and learning resources:

Resources for students

- **A dynamic eText** of the book that you can search, bookmark, annotate and highlight as you please

- **Self-assessment questions** that identify your strengths before recommending a personalised study plan that points you to the resources which can help you achieve a better grade

- **Guided solutions** that take you step by step through solving a problem

- **Flashcards** to test your understanding of key terms

Resources for instructors

- **Instructor's manual,** with complete and fully worked solutions

- **PowerPoint slides**, containing exhibits from the book

- **Testbank** of question material

For more information, please contact your local Pearson Education sales representative or visit **www.myaccountinglab.com**.

* If you don't have an access code, you can still access the resources. Visit **www.myaccountinglab.com** for details.

Learning objectives

When you have finished studying this chapter, you should be able to:

1 Describe the major users and uses of accounting information.
2 Describe the cost–benefit and behavioural issues involved in designing an accounting system.
3 Explain the role of budgets and performance reports in planning and control.
4 Discuss the role accountants play in the company's value-chain functions.
5 Identify current trends in management accounting.
6 Explain why ethics and standards of ethical conduct are important to accountants.

Learning objectives introduce topics covered and summarise what you should have learnt by the end of the chapter.

Starbucks

If you had asked most people a decade or two ago whether consumers around the world would pay a premium price for a 'better' cup of coffee, few would have answered yes. Nevertheless, the expansion of Starbucks since its founding in 1971 in Seattle's Pike Place Market has been nothing short of phenomenal. In 2010, Starbucks' total revenues – the amount the company received for all the items sold – were $10.7 billion, compared with only $700 million in 1996. Net income – the profit that Starbucks made – was

$1.4 billion, up from only $42 million in 1996. Total assets – the recorded value of the items owned by Starbucks – grew from less than $900 million in 1996 to more than $6.3 billion in 2010. These numbers are accounting measures of the cumulative success of numerous managers of Starbucks stores in many countries. Managers use these figures, and more detailed accounting numbers, to make day-to-day decisions and to measure performance.

Starbucks has established a worldwide reputation to match its financial success. It was ranked seventh among *Fortune* magazine's '100 best companies to work for'. *Business Ethics* magazine placed it ninth in its list of '100 Best corporate citizens'. Interbrand ranked Starbucks among the best 100 global brands for 2010. Finally, in 2010 *Fortune* named Starbucks

Starbuck's coffee shops have strategic locations throughout the world, including this one in Shanghai.

Chapter-opening vignettes help you understand accounting's role in current business practice, with examples from real companies, such as Starbucks, McDonald's, Dell and Nike.

MAKING MANAGERIAL DECISIONS

It is sometimes difficult to accept the proposition that past or sunk costs are irrelevant to decisions. Consider the ticket you have to a major football game in December. After getting the ticket, you learn that the game will be on TV, and you really prefer to watch the game in the comfort of your warm home. Does your decision about attending the game or watching it on TV depend on whether you were given the ticket for free or you paid €80 for it? What does this tell you about a manager's decision to replace a piece of equipment?

Answer

The amount paid, whether it be €0, €80 or €1,000, should make no difference to the decision. You have the ticket, and you have paid for it. That cannot be changed. If you really prefer to watch the game on television, it

may have been a bad decision to pay €80 for a ticket. But you cannot erase that bad decision. All you can do is choose the future action that has the most value to you. You should not suffer through a less pleasant experience just because you paid €80 for the ticket.

A manager must make the same analysis regarding the replacement of a piece of equipment. What the company spent for the old equipment is irrelevant. Keeping equipment that is no longer economical is just like using a ticket for an event that you would rather not attend. Additionally, keeping the equipment creates an opportunity cost because the company forgoes the disposal value of the old equipment, in the same way that keeping the ticket prevents you from reselling it to another fan (which is a relevant item in this scenario).

Making managerial decisions boxes give examples of business decisions in practice, helping you to apply accounting theory to the real world.

Exhibit 5.7 Marginal revenue and cost in perfect competition

Exhibits provide visual presentation of accounting concepts to illustrate key points and aid your understanding.

Exhibit 5.8 Marginal revenue and cost in imperfect competition

BUSINESS FIRST
Sony lowers break-even point during economic recession

One might think that break-even is a term that is not often used in business. However when economic conditions result in declining sales, companies are keenly aware of the break-even point.

In 2002–2003, many high-technology companies reported on their attempts to achieve profitability in spite of declining sales. The situation repeated itself for many types of companies in 2008–2009. They often focused on how their efforts to control costs reduced their break-even points. If a company faces rapidly falling sales, it must restructure its costs to be able to break even at a lower volume. Restructuring costs can involve reducing both fixed and variable costs.

Consider Sony's PlayStation 3. It costs Sony about $500 to make a PS3 but the sales price is about $300 and with the recession of 2008–2009 coupled with competitive pressure from Nintendo Wii and Microsoft Xbox 360, raising price was not an option. So how could Sony lower its costs to breakeven? The two actions Sony considered were reducing variable

cost and fixed cost. To lower its variable cost, Sony reduced the number of parts and the cost for the console's central processing unit. Reducing the number of parts also lowered Sony's fixed costs, such as assembly equipment and salaries of purchasing agents responsible for vendor negotiations.

In June 2010, Sony Computer Entertainment Worldwide Studios' Head, Shukei Yoshida reported: 'We aren't making huge money from hardware, but we aren't bleeding like we used to.' However, in April 2011, Sony issued a warning to 77 million users that the PS network had been hacked into, leading to its shutdown which was to last three weeks. A news report stated: 'Playstation network hack could cost Sony €318 per account claims research firm.' (Reported in www.psu .com27/4/2011.)

Sources: 'Sony PS3 costs less to make, but still a money loser,' *Techweb*, 30 December 2008; 'Sony finally turns a profit', www. Techrader.com30/6/2010.

Business first boxes provide insights into operations at well-known organisations, including Sony, Walt Disney and Johnson & Johnson.

Summary problem for your review

PROBLEM

Exhibit 6.5 looks beyond 1 year. Examining the alternatives over the equipment's entire life ensures that peculiar nonrecurring items, such as loss on disposal, will not obstruct the long-run view vital to many managerial decisions. However, Exhibit 6.5 presents both relevant and irrelevant items. Prepare an analysis that concentrates on relevant items only.

SOLUTION

Exhibit 6.6 presents the analysis with relevant items only – the cash operating costs, the disposal value of the old equipment, and the acquisition cost of the new equipment. To demonstrate that the amount of the old equipment's book value will not affect the answer, suppose the book value of the old equipment is €500,000 rather than €4,000. Your final answer will not change. The cumulative advantage of replacement is still €2,500. (If you are in doubt, rework this example, using €500,000 as the book value.)

Summary problems for your review provide step-by-step solutions, helping you to practise and master accounting techniques.

(continues overleaf)

Highlights to remember summarise and recap the key points of the chapter, providing a useful revision tool.

Highlights to remember

1 **Explain step- and mixed-cost behaviour.** Cost behaviour refers to how costs change as levels of an organisation's activities change. Costs can behave as fixed, variable, step, or mixed costs. Step and mixed costs both combine aspects of variable- and fixed-cost behaviour. Step costs form graphs that look like steps. Costs will remain fixed within a given range of activity or cost-driver level, but then will rise or fall abruptly when the cost-driver level is outside this range. Mixed costs involve a fixed element and a variable element of cost behaviour. Unlike step costs, mixed costs have a single fixed cost at all levels of activity and in addition have a variable cost element that increases proportionately with activity.

2 **Explain management influences on cost behaviour.** Managers can affect the costs and cost behaviour patterns of their companies through the decisions they make. Decisions on product and service features, capacity, technology and cost-control incentives, for example, can all affect cost behaviour.

3 **Measure and mathematically express cost functions and use them to predict costs.** The first step in estimating or predicting costs is measuring cost behaviour. This is done by finding a cost function. This is an algebraic equation that describes the relationship between a cost and its cost driver(s). To be useful for decision-making purposes, cost functions should be plausible and reliable.

4 **Describe the importance of activity analysis for measuring cost functions.** Activity analysis is the process of identifying the best cost drivers to use for cost estimation and prediction and determining how they affect the costs of making a product or service. This is an essential step in understanding and predicting costs.

Assignment material includes a wide range of exam-style questions, critical thinking exercises, problems and case studies.

CRITICAL THINKING EXERCISES

3.26 Mixed costs and the sales force

Wysocki Company pays its sales force a fixed salary plus a 5 per cent commission on all sales. Explain why sales force costs would be considered a mixed cost.

3.27 Committed and discretionary fixed costs in manufacturing

Among the fixed costs of Howarth Company are depreciation and research and development (R&D). Using these two costs as examples, explain the difference between committed and discretionary fixed costs.

3.28 Cost functions and decision making

Why is it important that decision makers in a corporation know the cost function for producing the company's products?

3.29 Statistical analysis and cost functions

What advantages does using regression analysis have over the visual-fit method for determining cost functions?

EXERCISES

3.30 Step costs

Which of the following are step costs? Why?

(a) Rent on a warehouse that is large enough for all anticipated orders.
(b) Teachers for a private elementary school; one teacher
(c) Sheet steel for a producer of machine parts; steel is pu
    where each carload contains enough steel for 1,000 p

CASE STUDY 2

Siemens Electric Motor Works (A) (abridged)

Ten years ago our electric motor business was in real trouble. Low labour rates allowed the Eastern Bloc countries to sell standard motors at prices were unable to match. We had become the high cost producer in the industry. Consequently, we decided to change our strategy and become a specialty motor producer. Once we adopted our new strategy, we discovered that while our existing cost system was adequate for costing standard motors, it gave us inaccurate information when we used it to cost specialty motors.

Mr Karl-Heinz Lotte, director of Business Operations, EMW

Siemens Corporation

Headquartered in Munich, Siemens AG, a producer of electrical and electronic products, was one of the world's largest corporations. Revenues totalled 51 billion deutschmarks in 1987, with roughly half this amount representing sales outside the Federal Republic of Germany. The Siemens organisation was split into seven major groups and five corporate divisions. The largest group, Energy and Automation accounted for 24% of total revenues. Low wattage alternating current (A/C) motors were produced at the Electric Motor Works (EMW), which was part of the Manufacturing Industries Division of the Engery and Automation Group. High wattage motors were produced at another facility.

GUIDED TOUR OF MyAccountingLab

MyAccountingLab is an online assessment and revision system that puts you in control of your learning through a suite of study and practice tools tied to the online eText.

Why should I use MyAccountingLab?

With more than 300,000 registered students in 2010 doing four million assignments, MyAccountingLab is the most effective and reliable learning solution for accounting available today.

We polled 10,000 student users of MyAccountingLab from around the globe in 2010:

- 92% of students said that MyAccountingLab learning aids helped them while completing homework and/or preparing for exams

- 89% of students said that MyAccountingLab helped them earn a higher grade

- 92% of students would recommend MyAccountingLab for future courses

How do I use MyAccountingLab?

The **Course Home Page** is where you can view announcements from your instructor and see an overview of your personal progress.

View the **Calendar** to see the dates for online homework, quizzes and tests that your instructor has set for you.

Your lecturer may have chosen MyAccountingLab to provide online **homework**, quizzes and tests. Check here to access the homework that has been set for you.

Practice tests for each chapter of the textbook enable you to check your understanding and identify the areas in which you need to do further work. Lecturers can customise and assign the practice tests or students can complete the tests on their own.

Course Home Page

Practice Test

(continues overleaf)

Keep track of your **results** in your own gradebook.

Work through the questions in your personalised Study Plan at your own pace. Because the **Study Plan** is tailored to each student, you will be able to study more efficiently by only reviewing areas where you still need practice. The Study Plan also saves your results, helping you see at a glance exactly which topics you need to review.

Study Plan

Additional instruction is provided in the form of detailed, step-by-step **solutions** to worked exercises. The figures in many of the exercises in MyAccountingLab are generated algorithmically, containing different values each time they are used. This means that you can practise individual concepts as often as you like.

There is also a link to the **eText** from every question in the Study Plan, so you can easily review and master the content.

View supporting multimedia resources such as links to the eText and Glossary Flashcards.

Help Me Solve This

Lecturer training and support

Our dedicated team of Technology Specialists offer personalised training and support for MyAccountingLab, ensuring that you can maximise the benefits of MyAccountingLab. To make contact with your Technology Specialist please email **feedback-cw@pearson.com**.

For a visual walkthrough of how to make the most of MyAccountingLab, visit **www.myaccountinglab.com**.

To find details of your local sales representatives go to **www.pearsoned.co.uk/replocator**.

PREFACE

Now more than ever, managers have to understand how their decisions affect costs.

Management accounting is an essential tool that enhances a manager's ability to make effective organisational decisions. *Introduction to Management Accounting* describes both theory and practice so students understand how to produce and use information in day-to-day decision making. From the first chapter, we encourage students to think about the advantages and disadvantages of various approaches.

Introduction to Management Accounting deals with all business sectors – nonprofit, retail, wholesale, service, selling, and administrative situations – as well as manufacturing. The focus is on planning and control decisions, not on product costing for inventory valuation and income determination.

■ Our philosophy

Introduce concepts and principles early, then revisit them at more complex levels as students gain understanding, and provide appropriate real-company examples at every stage.

Management accounting entails an understanding of costs, benefits and context. Students begin their understanding of managerial decisions by asking 'How will my decisions affect the costs and revenues of the organisation?'. Students then progress to more complex questions: 'What is the most appropriate cost-management system for the company?', 'What products or services should we emphasise?', 'What do our budget variances mean?'.

Our goals are to choose relevant subject matter and to present it clearly and accessibly, using many examples drawn from actual companies. Companies such as Starbucks, Haier, Dell, Siemens, Haribo and others set the stage for chapter material and are revisited throughout to help students understand management accounting concepts in a real-company context.

■ Supplements for instructors

INSTRUCTOR'S SOLUTIONS MANUAL Comprehensive solutions are provided for all end-of-chapter questions.

POWERPOINT SLIDES Complete PowerPoint presentations are provided for each chapter. Instructors may download and use each presentation as it is or customise the slides to create tailor-made slide shows.

TESTBANK of question material for each chapter, which can be downloaded and assigned to students.

■ MyAccountingLab for students

Students may visit **www.myaccountinglab.com** to find valuable learning material. See page i for further details.

ACKNOWLEDGEMENTS

We have received ideas, assistance, miscellaneous critiques, and assorted assignment material in conversations with and by mail from many students, academics, and business leaders. Each has our gratitude, but the list is too long to enumerate here. We wish to thank the following reviewers whose feedback was helpful:

Thomas Ahrens, University of UAE
Jim Carroll, Georgian Court University
Christopher Chapman, Imperial College
William Creel, Herzing College
Stan Davis, Indiana University – Purdue University Fort Wayne
Victor Franco, ISCTE
Chris Gilbert, Glendale Community College
Valerie Goodwin, Olean Business Institute
Lawrence Grasso, Central Connecticut State University
Henry Huang, Butler University
Agatha Jeffers, Montclair State University
Cody King, Georgia Southwestern State University
Roman J. Klusas, University of Indianapolis
Chuo-Hsuan (Jason) Lee, Plattsburgh State University of New York
Teemu Malmi, Aalto University
Lisa Martin, Hampton College
Maureen Mascha, Marquette University
Jerold R. Miller, Chaparral College
David Mona, Champlain College
Julian Mooney, Georgia Southern University
Behnaz Quigley, Marymount University
Bill Rankin, Colorado State University
Patrick Rogan, Cosumnes River College
Walter Smith, Siena College
Ken Snow, Kaplan University & Florida Community College at Jacksonville
John Stancil, Florida Southern College
Vic Stanton, Stanford Graduate School of Business
Holly Sudano, Florida State University
Diane Tanner, University of North Florida
Geoffrey Tickell, Indiana University of Pennsylvania
Michael Tyler, Barry University
Karen Wisniewski, County College of Morris
Carsten Rohde, Copenhagen Business School

We also thank Farah Ahamed for help with research, pedagogical assessment, proofing the manuscript and checking the instructor's solutions manual. Finally, students in our classes have provided invaluable feedback on previous editions, for which we are grateful.

Many people at Pearson also earn our deepest thanks for their thoughtful contributions, including Katie Rowland, Gemma Papageorgiou, Joy Cash, Philippa Fiszzon, Jenny Oates, Robert Chaundy, Summa Verbeek, Louise Hammond, Sarah Flint, Colin Reed, Michelle Morgan and Geoff Chatterton.

Alnoor Bhimani
Charles T. Horngren
Gary L. Sundem
William O. Stratton
David Burgstahler
Jeff Schatzberg

■ Publisher's acknowledgements

We are grateful to the following for permission to reproduce copyright material:

Text

Case Study on pages 26–7 from The ethical dilemma at Northlake, *CMA Magazine* (Grant Russell 1993); Box on page 49 from Disney Sues Top Video Chain, *Los Angeles Times*, 03/01/2003; Case Study on pages 73–4 from *'Electronic Boards plc' by Innes, J. and Mitchell, F. in Case Studies in Management Accounting*, Philip Alan Publishers (Otley, D., Brown, D. and Wilkinson, C. (eds) 1988); Case Study on pages 110–1 from *'Permaclean Products plc' by Otley, D. in Case Studies in Management Accounting*, Philip Allan Publishers (Otley, D., Brown, D. and Wilkinson, C,(eds) 1998), Reprinted by permission of David Otley; Case Study on page 170 from *Siemens Electric Motor Works (A) (Abridged)*, Harvard Business School Case (Robert S.Kaplan 1990), Copyright © 1990 by the President and Fellows of Harvard College. Reproduced with the permission of Harvard Business School Publishing; Case Study on pages 168–9 based on a case written by Ken Bates, Victoria University of Wellington; Case Study on pages 221–2 from La Grande Alliance, *Harvard Business School Case* (Malone, C. and Baldwin, C. 1988), Copyright © 1975 by the President and Fellows of Harvard College. Reprinted by permission of Harvard Business School Publishing; Case Study on page 275 from Hereford Steak Houses, Ahrens, T. and Chapman, C., Reproduced with permission of Professor Thomas Ahrens and Professor Christopher Chapman; Case Study on page 372 from *Zeros plc by Mitchell, F., in Case Studies in Management Accounting* Philip Allan Publishers (Otley, D., Brown, D. and Wilkinson, C. 1988); General Displayed Text on page 380 after Hyundai Smokes the Competition, *Fortune Magazine*, 18/01/2010 (Taylor, A.), "Hyundai smokes the competition" from Fortune Magazine, 1/5/2010 © 2010 Time Inc. Used under licence.; General Displayed Text on page 420 adapted from www.thetimes100.co.uk, © The Times/ nisyndication.com. Reprinted with permission.; Case Study on page 436 adapted from Transfer Pricing with ABC, *Management Accounting* (Kaplan, R., Weiss, D. and Desheh, E. 1997), From Kaplan, Weiss, Desheh. http://college.cengage.com/accounting/resources/students/readings/kaplan.htm. ©, a part of Cengage Learning, Inc. Reproduced by permission. www.cengage.com/permissions; Case Study on pages 459–60 from *Empire Glass Company (A)*, Harvard Business School Case (Hawkins, D. 1964), Copyright © 1964 President and Fellows of Harvard College. Reprinted with permission of Harvard Business School Publishing.

Photographs

Alamy Images: Aerial Archives 232, David Lyons 642, DB Images 77, Holger Burmeister 630, Imagebroker 176, Mauritius Images GmbH 1; **E M Clements Photography:** 278; **Getty Images:** 416, 518, AFP 477, Bloomberg 30; **The Advertising Archives:** 375; **Press Association Images:** 114; **Reuters:** Thomas Peter 580; **Rex Features:** Chris Martin Bahr 329; **Cover image:** *Front:* **Getty Images:** Asia Images Group.

In some instances we have been unable to trace the owners of copyright material, and we would appreciate any information that would enable us to do so.

Managerial accounting and organisations

Learning objectives

When you have finished studying this chapter, you should be able to:

1 Describe the major users and uses of accounting information.
2 Describe the cost–benefit and behavioural issues involved in designing an accounting system.
3 Explain the role of budgets and performance reports in planning and control.
4 Discuss the role accountants play in the company's value-chain functions.
5 Identify current trends in management accounting.
6 Explain why ethics and standards of ethical conduct are important to accountants.

Starbucks

If you had asked most people a decade or two ago whether consumers around the world would pay a premium price for a 'better' cup of coffee, few would have answered yes. Nevertheless, the expansion of Starbucks since its founding in 1971 in Seattle's Pike Place Market has been nothing short of phenomenal. In 2010, Starbucks' total revenues – the amount the company received for all the items sold – were $10.7 billion, compared with only $700 million in 1996. Net income – the profit that Starbucks made – was

$1.4 billion, up from only $42 million in 1996. Total assets – the recorded value of the items owned by Starbucks – grew from less than $900 million in 1996 to more than $6.3 billion in 2010. These numbers are accounting measures of the cumulative success of numerous managers of Starbucks stores in many countries. Managers use these figures, and more detailed accounting numbers, to make day-to-day decisions and to measure performance.

Starbucks has established a worldwide reputation to match its financial success. It was ranked seventh among *Fortune* magazine's '100 best companies to work for'. *Business Ethics* magazine placed it ninth in its list of '100 Best corporate citizens'. Interbrand ranked Starbucks among the best 100 global brands for 2010. Finally, in 2010 *Fortune* named Starbucks

Starbuck's coffee shops have strategic locations throughout the world, including this one in Shanghai.

the third most admired company in the food services industry and 26th in its ranking of the world's most admired companies.

How did Starbucks accomplish all this? As we embark on our journey into the world of management accounting, we will explore what it takes for a company such as Starbucks to ensure that when Mei-Hwa Zhang walks into a Starbucks in Beijing, she has much the same quality experience as Mohammad Kumar does in a Starbucks in Kuwait or Franz Mueller does in Zurich. All Starbucks' managers, from baristas to store managers to the chief executive officer, use accounting reports to assess how well their unit meets corporate goals and objectives. Accounting provides a common language to help managers around the world communicate and coordinate their actions. By the time you finish reading this book, you will be comfortable with the accounting information managers use to make their decisions. You will better understand how to use information to develop plans, make short-term and long-term decisions, assess performance and, in general, be a better manager.

Managerial accounting can help managers with all sorts of decisions. For example consider decisions you might face as a manager in the following situations:

- Suppose you are a Boeing engineer preparing manufacturing specifications for a component of its new 787 Dreamliner airplane. There are three possible ways to organise the assembly of the component. Which is the most cost-effective approach?

- Suppose you are a product manager at Nestlé and you are designing a new marketing plan for Kit Kat. Market research predicts that distributing free samples at supermarkets will increase annual sales by 4 per cent. Will the cost of producing and distributing the free samples be more or less than the profits from the added sales?

- Santander offers a 'preferred overdraft rate' account with a zero per cent annual equivalent rate on overdrafts up to £5,000 for 12 months for switching customers. How much does it cost the bank to provide this free service?

- Perkins School for the Blind offers a variety of training and educational programmes. As Head, you must set a goal for the group's annual fund drive based on the estimated cost to support its planned activities.

- Hyde Park Café currently is open only for dinner, but the owner is considering opening for lunch. The average lunch is priced at about £9 and the café expects to serve about 40 lunches per day. Can the chef produce a luncheon menu that meets the café's quality standards at an average cost that yields a reasonable profit?

- Amazon.co.uk offers free one-day delivery on all orders for subscribers to Amazon Prime that pay a single £49 annual fee. Does the fee plus the profits from increased sales to subscribers exceed the cost of providing free delivery?

In making decisions such as these, managers turn to management accountants for information. The Chartered Institute of Management Accountants (CIMA) in the UK states that 'Management accounting combines accounting, finance and management with the leading edge techniques needed to drive successful businesses.'

In this chapter, we consider the purposes and roles of management accounting and accountants in different types of organisations, as well as some of the trends and challenges faced by accountants today. Information is useful only if decision makers can rely on it. Therefore we place special emphasis on the ability of management accounting information to reflect wider operational and strategic enterprise concerns including ethical issues. ∎

Accounting and decision making

Objective 1
Describe the major users and uses of accounting information.

The basic purpose of accounting information is to help decision makers – company presidents, production managers, hospital or school administrators, investors and others. **Decision making** – choosing from among a set of alternative courses of action designed to achieve some objective – drives the need for accounting information. Regardless of who is making the decision, understanding accounting information allows for a more informed basis for action.

◼ Users of accounting information

Both internal parties (managers) and external parties use accounting information, but they often demand different types of information and use it in different ways. **Management accounting** produces information for managers within an organisation. It is primarily concerned with the process of identifying, measuring, accumulating, analysing, preparing, interpreting and communicating information that aims to help managers pursue organisational objectives. CIMA states that chartered management accountants advise managers about the financial implications of projects, explain the financial consequences of business decisions, formulate business strategy, monitor spending and financial control, conduct business audits and explain the impact of the competitive landscape. In contrast, **financial accounting** produces information for external parties, such as stockholders, suppliers, banks and government regulatory agencies. We list the major differences between management accounting and financial accounting in Exhibit 1.1. In this book we focus on management accounting.

	Management accounting	Financial accounting
Primary users	Organisation managers at various levels	Outside parties such as investors and government agencies but also organisation managers
Freedom of choice of accounting measures	No constraints other than requiring the benefits of improved management decisions to exceed information costs	Constrained by financial reporting standards
Behavioural implications in selecting accounting measures	Choice should consider how measurements and reports will influence managers' daily behaviour	Choice based on how to measure and communicate economic phenomena; behavioural considerations are secondary, although executive compensation based on reported results may have behavioural impacts
Time focus of reports	Future orientation: formal use of budgets as well as historical records. Example: 20X2 budget versus 20X1 actual performance	Past orientation: historical evaluation. Example: 20X2 actual performance versus 20X1 actual performance
Time span of reports	Flexible, varying from real time to 10–15 years	Less flexible; usually one year or one quarter
Types of reports	Detailed reports: includes details about products, departments, territories, etc.	Summary reports: primarily report on the entity as a whole
Influence of other functional areas	Field is less sharply defined; heavier use of economics, decision sciences and behavioural sciences	Field is more sharply defined. Lighter use of related disciplines

Exhibit 1.1 Distinctions between management accounting and financial accounting

What kinds of accounting information do managers need to achieve their goals and objectives? Good accounting information helps answer three types of questions:

1 *Scorecard questions*. Is the company doing well or poorly? **Scorekeeping** is the classification, accumulation and reporting of data that help users understand and evaluate organisational performance. Scorekeeping information must be accurate and reliable to be useful. For example, Starbucks produces numerous reports to evaluate results for stores and divisions.

2 *Attention-directing questions*. Which areas require additional investigation? **Attention directing** usually involves routine reports that compare actual results to before-the-fact expectations. For example, a manager who sees that a Starbucks store has reported profits of €120,000 when budgeted profit was €150,000 will look for explanations as to why the store did not achieve its budget. Attention-directing information helps managers focus on operating problems, imperfections, inefficiencies and opportunities.

3 *Problem-solving questions*. Of the alternatives being considered, which is the best? The **problem-solving** aspect of accounting often involves an analysis of the impacts of each alternative to identify the best course to follow. For example, Starbucks experiments with adding various items to its menu. After an analysis of how a new product will affect revenues and costs, management decides which items to add and which to delete.

The scorecard and attention-directing uses of information are closely related. The same information that helps a manager understand and evaluate performance may also serve an attention-directing function for the manager's superior. For example, by pinpointing where actual results differ from plans, performance reports show managers how they are doing and where to take action. Companies produce most scorecard and attention-directing information on a routine basis every day, month, quarter or year.

Problem solving sometimes relies on routine information used for scorekeeping and attention directing. However, when organisations make long-range plans or nonrecurring decisions, such as whether to make or to buy parts, replace equipment, or add or drop a product, specially prepared information is often required. For example, Starbucks uses problem-solving information when deciding whether to run expensive advertising campaigns.

MAKING MANAGERIAL DECISIONS

Managers use accounting information for many different types of decisions. Accountants must make sure that they produce information that is useful for these various decisions. What type of information – scorekeeping, attention-directing or problem-solving – would managers use for each of the following decisions? Why?

1 Deciding whether to replace a traditional assembly line with a fully automated robotic process.

2 Evaluating the performance of a division for the preceding year.

3 Identifying which products exceeded their budgeted profitability and which ones fell short of their budgets.

Answers

1 *Problem solving*. This is a one-time decision for which managers need information about the potential impacts of each of the alternatives under consideration.

2 *Scorekeeping*. This is a routine evaluation of an organisational unit for which managers want systematic data on a regular basis.

3 *Attention directing*. To identify products that need attention, managers want information that highlights deviations of actual results from pre-specified expectations in the budget.

▨ Influences on accounting systems

An **accounting system** is a formal mechanism for gathering, organising and communicating information about an organisation's activities. In order to reduce costs and complexity, many organisations use a general-purpose accounting system that attempts to meet the needs of both external and internal users. However, as outlined in Exhibit 1.1, there are important differences between management accounting information and financial accounting information.

There are three categories of requirements imposed on accounting systems designed to meet the requirements of external users. First, public companies' financial reports for external users must adhere to a set of standards known as **generally accepted accounting principles (GAAP)**. In the UK, the chief body which establishes standards is the Accounting Standards Board, which issues Financial Reporting Standards. The Financial Accounting Standards Board (FASB) determines US GAAP. Across more than 100 countries worldwide, companies must comply with **International Financial Reporting Standards (IFRS)** set by the International Accounting Standards Board (IASB). Second, every company is also subject to various taxes and therefore subject to various reporting requirements specified by tax rules and regulations. Finally, many companies are subject to other government regulations.

There are many other governmental regulations that influence accounting systems. For example, the UK Corporate Governance Code 2010 is a set of principles aimed at companies listed on the London Stock Exchange. It is a consolidation and refinement of a number of different reports and codes relating to concerns over the existence of 'good' corporate governance practices. The original intent was to address financial scandals, including that of Polly Peck, a major UK company which went insolvent after years of falsifying financial reports and led to the setting up of a committee which produced the Cadbury Report in 1992. In the US, in 2002, the **Sarbanes-Oxley Act** encompassed several levels of regulation. Driven by corporate bankruptcies blamed in part on accounting lapses (as well as deficiencies in corporate governance, lax securities regulation and executive greed), the act requires more top-management oversight of a company's accounting policies and procedures. By requiring chief executive officers to sign a statement certifying the accuracy of the company's financial statements, the act makes accounting numbers the concern of all managers, not just the accountants. Sarbanes-Oxley requires external auditors to examine and prepare a separate report on a company's system of **internal controls** – policies to protect and make the most efficient use of an organisation's assets. While some managers insist that the extra costs of compliance with the act exceed the benefits, others believe the regulations provide stronger controls and more informative reports whose benefits exceed the costs.

The requirements of external reporting should not constrain the scorekeeping, attention-directing and problem-solving information that can be generated to meet the needs of internal users. In later chapters, we will see many examples where information needed for a decision is not being generated by the general-purpose accounting system designed to meet external reporting requirements. As a decision-maker, you must recognise when information from the existing accounting system is not appropriate for your decision and be prepared to ask for additional information to be generated. Your requests for more information should be balanced against the cost of obtaining the information. But, the organisational and environmental context of the usage of accounting information must also be considered. As explained in the following section, ideally you should only acquire additional costly information when the expected benefit of an improved decision exceeds the cost of the information. However, such costs and benefits are rarely readily quantifiable. For this reason, judgement and an assessment of the information's source of derivation and its deployment should be present.

Cost–benefit and behavioural considerations

Objective 2
Describe the cost–benefit and behavioural issues involved in designing an accounting system.

Managers should bear two important ideas in mind when designing accounting systems: (1) cost–benefit balances and (2) behavioural and contextual issues.

The **cost–benefit balance** – weighing estimated costs against probable benefits – is the primary consideration in choosing among accounting systems and methods. Throughout this book, we will refer repeatedly to cost–benefit considerations. Accounting systems are dynamic organisational entities as well as economic goods – such as office supplies or labour – available at various costs. Which system does a manager want to buy: a simple filing drawer for amassing receipts and cancelled cheques, an elaborate budgeting system based on computerised models of the organisation and its subunits, or something in between?

The answer will be partly affected by the buyer's perceptions of the expected benefits in relation to the costs. For example, consider a manager of a group of Finnish university hospitals who is considering installing a Cosmic, which is a suite of e-health applications from Cambio Healthcare Systems – a provider of healthcare IT solutions in Scandinavia. Users enter a piece of information only once and the system automatically integrates it with billing, insurance claims and patient history records. Such a system is efficient and subject to few errors, but should it be purchased? That depends on whether its expected value to the clinic is greater than its cost of €300,000. While comparison of costs and benefits is conceptually simple, it is often difficult to estimate both costs and benefits, a point that will be illustrated repeatedly in later chapters.

Managers should also consider behavioural and contextual issues. This refers in part to the system's effect on the behaviour and actions of managers. For example, consider a performance report that a manager's superiors use to evaluate the operations for which the manager is responsible. If the report is too complex or difficult to use, the manager may ignore the report in making decisions. If the report unfairly attributes excessive costs to the manager's operations, the manager may lose confidence in the system and not let it influence future decisions. In contrast, a system that managers understand and believe in can greatly influence their decisions and actions. Likewise, if the organisation has several sub-cultures with one group of employees being very receptive to making decisions using financial information – say engineer-trained personnel; but another group – say marketing professionals – prefer to use alternative sources of information in determining managerial options, then senior managers need to be cognisant of these differences in decision-making information sources.

In a nutshell, think of management accounting as a balance between costs and benefits of accounting information coupled with an awareness of the importance of behavioural effects and contextual factors. Therefore, management accountants must understand the many factors within organisations which may affect information generation and usage.

The management process and accounting

Accounting information helps managers plan and control the organisation's operations. In practice, planning and control are so intertwined that it seems artificial to separate them. In studying management, however, we find it useful to concentrate on either the planning phase or the control phase to simplify our analysis.

▇ The nature of planning and control

The left side of Exhibit 1.2 demonstrates the planning and control cycle of current operations that could be used by a particular Starbucks store. **Planning** (the top box) refers to setting

Exhibit 1.2 Starbucks store – accounting framework for planning and control

objectives for an organisation and outlining how it will attain them. Thus, planning provides the answers to two questions: What objectives does the organisation want to achieve? When and how will the organisation achieve these objectives? For example, the Starbucks store's management may want to increase profitability and to achieve it by adding new drinks and increasing advertising.

Control refers to implementing plans and using feedback to evaluate the attainment of objectives. Feedback is crucial to the cycle of planning and control. Planning determines action, action generates feedback and the control phase uses this feedback to influence further planning and actions. Timely, systematic reports provided by the internal accounting system are the chief source of useful feedback. The control section in Exhibit 1.2 shows the actions that are intended to increase profitability and how Starbucks will evaluate the actions. The Starbucks store will implement its plan to expand the number of drinks on its menu and increase advertising. Management will evaluate these actions based on three performance measures, the increase in drinks sold, increase in advertising expenditures and the increase in revenue. Performance evaluation results will in turn be used for further planning and implementation.

■ Management by exception

Objective 3
Explain the role of budgets and performance reports in planning and control.

The right side of Exhibit 1.2 shows that the accounting system formalises plans by expressing them as budgets. A **budget** is a quantitative expression of a plan of action. Budgets also help to coordinate and implement plans. They are the chief devices for disciplining management planning. Without budgets, planning may not get the front-and-centre focus that it deserves. The Starbucks store expresses its plan for product growth and improved marketing through revenue and advertising budgets.

The accounting system records, measures and classifies actions to produce performance reports (the last box in Exhibit 1.2). **Performance reports** provide feedback by comparing results with plans and by highlighting **variances**, which are deviations from plans. Organisations use performance reports to judge managers' decisions and the productivity of organisational units. Performance reports compare actual results to budgets, thereby motivating managers to achieve the objectives. For example, managers of the Starbucks store evaluate the effectiveness of its advertising plan by comparing the increase in revenue and profits to the increase in advertising costs. Based on their evaluation, managers at Starbucks make corrections and revisions to their plans.

Exhibit 1.3 shows a simple performance report for a hypothetical Starbucks store, the Mayfair Starbucks. The first column of Exhibit 1.3 is the budget for March 20X1. It is based on a predicted level of sales and the estimated costs needed to support that level of sales. After managers and their superiors agree on a budget, it becomes the managers' target for the month. As the store sells its products and incurs costs, Starbucks' accounting system collects the revenue and cost information. At the end of each month (or more often if managers need more frequent feedback), the accounting department prepares a store-level performance report, such as the one in Exhibit 1.3. Managers use the performance report to help evaluate the store's operations.

The Mayfair store report shows that the store met its targeted sales, but the £2,500 unfavourable variance for ingredients shows that these costs were £2,500 over budget. Other variances show that store labour costs were £400 under budget, and other labour was £50 over budget. At the Mayfair store, management would undoubtedly focus attention on ingredients, which had by far the largest unfavourable variance. However, it may also be worthwhile to investigate the £400 favourable labour variance. By investigating favourable variances, managers may find better ways of doing things.

Performance reports spur investigation of exceptions – items for which actual amounts differ significantly from budgeted amounts. Managers then revise operations to conform with the plans or revise the plans. This process is **management by exception**, which means concentrating on areas that deviate from the plan and, in the absence of other evidence, presuming that areas that conform with plans are running smoothly. Thus, the management-by-exception approach frees managers from needless concern with those phases of operations that adhere to plans. However, well-conceived plans incorporate enough discretion or flexibility so that the manager feels free to pursue any unforeseen opportunities.

Notice that although budgets aid planning and performance reports aid control, it is not accountants but operating managers and their subordinates who use accounting reports

	Budget	Actual	Variance
Sales	£50,000	£50,000	0
Less:			
Ingredients	£22,000	£24,500	£2,500 U
Store labour (baristas, etc.)	12,000	11,600	400 F
Other labour (managers, supervisors)	6,000	6,050	50 U
Utilities, maintenance, etc.	4,500	4,500	0
Total expenses	44,500	46,650	2,150 U
Total operating income	£ 5,500	£ 3,350	£2,150 U

U = unfavourable – actual cost greater than budgeted; actual revenue or profits less than budgeted
F = favourable – actual cost less than budgeted; actual revenue or profit greater than budgeted

Exhibit 1.3 Mayfair Starbucks store – performance report for the month ended 31 March 20X1

to plan and control operations. Accounting assists the managerial planning and control functions by providing prompt measurements of actions and by systematically pinpointing trouble spots.

Planning and control for product life cycles and the value chain

Many management decisions relate to a single good or service, or to a group of related products. To effectively plan and control production of goods or services, accountants and other managers must consider the product's life cycle. **Product life cycle** refers to the various stages through which a product passes: conception and product development; introduction into the market; maturation of the market; and, finally, withdrawal from the market. At each stage, managers face differing costs and potential returns. Exhibit 1.4 shows a typical product life cycle.

In the planning process, managers predict revenues and costs over the entire life cycle – however long or short. Then accounting systems track actual costs and revenues throughout the life cycle. Periodic comparisons between planned costs and revenues and actual costs and revenues allow managers to assess the current profitability of a product, determine its current product life-cycle stage and make any needed changes in strategy.

For example, suppose Sanofi-Aventis is developing a new drug to reduce high blood pressure. There will be substantial development costs and no revenue during the product development stage. Most of the revenues from the product will be received during the introduction and mature market stages when there will also be production costs. During the phase-out of the product, there will be little revenue but Sanofi-Aventis will need to keep the drug on the market for those who have come to rely on it. Thus, the product pricing strategy must recognise the need for revenues during the introduction and mature market stages to cover both development and phase-out costs as well as the direct costs of producing the drug.

Product life cycles range from a few months (for fashion clothing or faddish toys) to many years (for automobiles or refrigerators). Some products, such as many computer software packages, have long development stages and relatively short market lives. Others, such as Airbus A380 airplanes, have a market life many times longer than their development stage. Many companies are working to shorten the product development phase, both to reduce the time during which a product generates no revenue and to bring products to market on a more timely basis.

■ The value chain

Objective 4
Discuss the role accountants play in the company's value-chain functions.

In addition to considering a product's life cycle, managers must recognise those activities necessary for a company to create the goods or services that it sells. These activities comprise the **value chain**, the set of business functions or activities that add value to the products or services of an organisation. These functions include the following:

Exhibit 1.4 Typical product life cycle

- *Research and development*: the generation of ideas related to new products, services or processes.
- *Design of products, services or processes*: the detailed design and engineering of products, services or processes.
- *Production*: the coordination and assembly of resources to produce a product or deliver a service.
- *Marketing*: the manner by which individuals or groups learn about the value and features of products or services (for example, advertising or selling activities).
- *Distribution*: the mechanism by which a company delivers products or services to the customer.
- *Customer service*: the support activities provided to the customer.

Not all functions are of equal importance to the success of a company. Senior management must decide which of these functions enables the company to gain and maintain a competitive edge. Design, innovation, service, ease of access and cost leadership can be crucial to a firm's ability to maintain competitive superiority.

Accountants play a role in supporting all the value-chain functions. They do so at the production stage, where accountants facilitate cost planning and control through the use of budgets and performance reporting and help track the effects of continuous improvement programmes. Accounting can also have a great influence on the two pre-production value-chain functions. For example, accountants provide estimated revenue and cost data during the research and development stage and during the design stage of the value chain. Managers use these data to decide which ideas will move to the production stage and which will be dropped. These data also enable managers and engineers to reduce the life-cycle costs of products or services by changing product and process designs. Accountants can give managers feedback on ideas for cost reductions long before the company must make a commitment to purchase expensive equipment.

Accountants also play a role in post-production value-chain functions. For example, marketing decisions have a significant impact on sales, but the cost of marketing programs is also significant. Accountants analyse the trade-off between increased revenues and costs. In addition, accounting information can influence decisions about distributing products or services to customers. Should a company sell its products directly to a chain of retail stores, or should it sell to a wholesaler? What transportation system should be used – trucks or trains? Accountants provide important information about the costs of each alternative. Finally, accountants provide cost data for customer service activities, such as guarantee and repair costs and the costs of goods returned. Managers compare these costs to the benefits generated by better customer service. As you can see, cost management is important throughout the value chain.

Each value-chain function should focus on activities that create value for the customer. Successful businesses never lose sight of the importance of maintaining a focus on the needs of their customers. For example, one of the main principles in Starbucks' mission statement is to 'develop enthusiastically satisfied customers all of the time'. Digital technologies have affected the organisational focus of many enterprises in important ways. A.G. Lafley, the president and CEO of Procter & Gamble noted over a decade ago that 'the consumer is boss', arguing that firms need to move away from a mass marketing push model towards pull, noting that consumers are becoming more demanding and engage with organisations more. Today, executives such as Rich Green, Nokia's Chief Technology Officer, notes 'The big a-ha moment is when enterprises finally realise that their digital existences are being defined by the consumer world, not the reverse.' (Quoted in www.bryaneisenberg.com/2011/05Theconsumerisboss/.) Customers are also the focus at Wal-Mart, as explained by Sam Walton, founder and former chairman:

> *There is only one boss – the customer. Customers can fire everybody in the company from the chairman on down, simply by spending their money somewhere else.*

MAKING MANAGERIAL DECISIONS

Measuring costs at various stages of the value chain is important to Starbucks. Suppose that you are a Starbucks manager or accountant. For each of the following activities, indicate the value-chain function that is being performed and what accounting information might be helpful to managers in the function:

1 Process engineers investigate methods to reduce the time to roast coffee beans and to better preserve their flavour.

2 A direct-to-your-home mail-order system is established to sell custom-blended coffees.

3 Arabica coffee beans are purchased and transported to company processing plants.

4 Focus groups investigate the feasibility of a new line of Frappuccino drinks.

5 A telephone hotline is established for mail-order customers to call with list items and comments on the quality and speed of delivery.

6 Each company-owned retail store undertakes a campaign to provide information to customers about the processes used to make its coffee products.

Answers

1 *Research and development or design.* Both the generation of ideas for new processes and the design of new production processes are important parts of the value chain. Managers need the costs of various possible production processes to decide among the alternatives.

2 *Distribution.* This provides an additional way to deliver products to customers. Managers need information on the costs of a mail-order system to compare to the added profit from mail-order sales.

3 *Production.* Starbucks purchases only premium beans, but the company is still concerned about the purchase price of beans and transportation. These are part of product costs incurred during production.

4 *Research and development or marketing.* These costs (mostly wages) are incurred prior to management's final decision to design and produce a new product. Predicted revenues and costs from the Frappuccino market can help managers design a drink that is both marketable and profitable.

5 *Customer service.* These costs include all expenditures made after Starbucks has delivered the product to the customer; in this case, Starbucks obtains feedback on the quality and speed of delivery. Managers will trade off the cost of the hotline and the value of the information generated from the calls.

6 *Marketing.* These costs are for activities that enhance the existing or potential customers' awareness and opinion of the product. Like many advertising expenses, it is easy to estimate the costs of such a programme but hard to quantify the benefits.

The value chain and the concepts of adding value and focusing on the customer are essential for success. Therefore, we will return to the value chain and use it to guide some discussions in this book.

Accounting's position in the organisation

The role of management accountants in organisations has changed rapidly over the last decade or so. Consider the following four work activities of management accountants:

- collecting and compiling information;
- preparing standardised reports;
- interpreting and analysing information;
- being involved in decision making.

Trends revealed by recent surveys show that management accountants are spending less time on the first two activities and more time on the last two. In essence, the management

BUSINESS FIRST
The accountant's role at Alghanim Industries

Ranked along with Deloitte & Touche, Microsoft, Proctor & Gamble and Marriott, Alghanim Industries of Kuwait is one of the best employers in the Middle East. A multibillion dollar conglomerate with strongholds in the Middle East and Turkey, the company manages more than 300 global brands and agencies in Eastern Europe, Africa and east and southeast Asia. Operations need to be segregated not only geographically but also by products, which include automotive sales, consumer electronics, home furnishings and the manufacturing of construction materials together with associated supply chain services from shipping to distribution and delivery. Managers use a complex and intricate accounting information system to provide information which is essential to decision making.

The role of the management accounting teams is to tailor the provision of relevant and reliable information to the needs of the decentralised management teams and still provide the board with timely analysis of ongoing commercial activity. Alghanim recruits many professional accountants and MBA graduates who gain line experience so that they are part of a process that translates transaction records into the strategic planning process. This enables managers at different levels to measure performance against corporate targets, identify strengths and weaknesses immediately, and take actions that are appropriate to achieving corporate profitability and growth targets. The process relates activity and costs on a timely basis so that managers become aware of the cost impact of their decisions.

The sophisticated accounting information system also incorporates more than one cost method for many operations so that management receives more than just the pure financial data. Costs can be combined for the full supply chain and combined with non-financial activity-based data. This provides managers at many levels with the ability to consider and understand the full functional analysis of activity and provides a continuous improvement programme for products and services.

Sources: http://www.alghanim.com/home.asp; http://www.hewittassociates.com/Intl/AP/en-ME/AboutHewitt/Newsroom/PressReleaseDetail.aspx?cid=6704

accountant is becoming an internal consultant on information-related issues – that is, an advisor for managers about what information would be useful, what information is available, and how to analyse the information and use it in decision making. Decision making is the core of the management process. Decisions range from the routine (making daily production schedules) to the non-routine (launching a new product line), and accountants are information specialists who aid the decision makers.

Adaptation to change

Objective 5
Identify current trends in management accounting.

Businesses in the twenty-first century differ from those in the twentieth century. Markets have become more competitive, and access to information has become more important. Many companies today derive their competitive advantage from their information, not their physical facilities. Companies such as Amazon.com pride themselves on managing the information obtained from their customers and suppliers. Such companies must continually improve their accounting information. The information that supported traditional companies in the 1980s and 1990s does not adequately support the modern business environment.

Four major business trends are influencing management accounting today:

1 Shift from a manufacturing-based to a service-based economy in many developed countries.

2 Increased global competition.

3 Advances in technology.

4 Increased management flexibility.

◼ Service sector

Accountants in manufacturing organisations developed many of the basic ideas of management accounting. These ideas, however, have evolved so that they apply to all types of organisations, including service and nonprofit organisations. **Service organisations**, for our purposes, are organisations that do not make or sell tangible goods. Accounting firms, law firms, management consultants, real estate firms, transportation companies, banks, insurance companies and hotels are examples of profit-seeking service organisations. Most nonprofit organisations, such as hospitals, schools, libraries, museums and government agencies, are also service organisations.

The characteristics of service organisations include the following:

1 *Labour is a major component of costs*. The highest proportions of expenses in service organisations, such as schools and law firms, are typically wages, salaries and payroll related costs, not the costs relating to the use of equipment and physical facilities.

2 *Output is usually difficult to measure*. Because service outputs are intangible, they are often hard to measure. For example, the output of a university might be defined as the number of degrees awarded, but many critics would maintain that the real output is what is contained in the students' brains.

3 *Service organisations cannot store their major inputs and outputs*. Services cannot usually be stockpiled. For example, an airline cannot save an empty airline seat for a later flight, and a hotel's available labour force and rooms are either used or unused as each day passes.

The service sector now accounts for almost 80 per cent of the employment in the United States, Canada and western European countries. Sixty-five to eighty per cent of the gross national product of these countries also derives from the service sector. Service industries are extremely competitive, and their managers increasingly rely on accounting information. Many examples in this book are from service companies.

Managers and accountants in service companies, whether profit-seeking or nonprofit organisations, have much in common. They raise and spend money. They prepare budgets and design and implement control systems. They all have an obligation to use resources wisely. Used intelligently, accounting information contributes to efficient operations and helps organisations achieve their objectives.

Simplicity is the watchword for accounting systems in service industries and nonprofit organisations. Why? Because many of the decision makers using these systems, such as doctors, professors or government officials, are too busy to try to grapple with a complex system. For them to use the information, it must be in a form that is easy to understand. In fact, simplicity is an important consideration in the design of any accounting system. Complexity generates costs of gathering and interpreting data that may exceed prospective benefits.

◼ Global competition

Global competition has increased in recent years as many countries have lowered international barriers to trade, such as tariffs and duties. In addition, there has been a worldwide trend toward deregulation. The result has been a shift in the balance of economic power in the world. To regain their competitive edge, many companies redesigned their accounting systems to provide more accurate and timely information about the cost of activities, products or services. Improved cost information helps managers better understand and predict the effects of their decisions.

While globalisation has integrated world economies, societies and cultures to a degree via trade, transport and communication, it has also increased competition and the size of markets. The sourcing of cheaper materials and parts and access to lower-cost labour has decreased costs for many firms.

Advances in technology

The dominant influence on management accounting over the past decade has been technological change, affecting both the production and the use of accounting information. The increasing capabilities and decreasing cost of computer processing and storage has changed how accountants gather, store, manipulate and report data. In many cases, databases allow managers to access data directly and to generate their own reports and analyses. Today managers and accountants work together to assure the availability of the data needed for decisions and to be sure managers know how to assemble and use the data.

One of the most rapidly growing uses of technology is **electronic commerce** or **e-commerce** – conducting business online. While the internet boom that focused on business-to-consumer (**B2C**) transactions ended in 2001, e-commerce focusing on business-to-business (**B2B**) transactions continued to grow at nearly 50 per cent a year. B2B creates real savings to the companies involved. For example, some companies have reduced procurement processing costs by as much as 70 per cent by automating the process.

A major effect of technology on accounting systems has been the growing use of **enterprise resource planning (ERP)** systems – integrated information systems that support all functional areas of a company. Accounting is just one part of such a system. For example, Oracle describes its JD Edwards EnterpriseOne ERP system as one that 'helps you integrate all aspects of your business – including customer relationship management, enterprise asset management, enterprise resource planning, supply chain management and supplier relationship management'. Other well-known ERP system providers are SAP, Microsoft Dynamics and The Sage Group. Accountants must work with managers throughout the organisation to ensure that the ERP system provides the financial information that managers need.

The adoption of computerised technologies such as computer-aided design, testing and manufacturing, has altered the cost structures of firms. Investing in flexible manufacturing systems and robotics has increased possibilities for firms as they develop new products. But this has made more complex the costing activities of firms which can use the same technologies to produce a wide variety of products.

Because management accounting supports business decisions, accounting systems must adapt to changes in management practices. Some companies implement sweeping changes in operations through **business process reengineering**, the fundamental rethinking and radical redesign of business processes to improve performance in areas such as cost, quality, service and speed. Companies reduce process time by redesigning, simplifying and automating the production process. They use **computer-aided design (CAD)** to design products that can be manufactured efficiently and **computer aided manufacturing (CAM)** to direct and control production equipment. **Computer-integrated manufacturing (CIM) systems** use CAD, CAM, robots and computer-controlled machines (see Bhimani 2012). The costs of such a system are quite different from those of a less-automated system. Companies that install a full CIM system use very little labour. Instead, they acquire the robots and computer-controlled machines needed to perform the routine jobs that were previously accomplished by assembly-line workers. Accounting systems of the last century designed primarily around the accounting for labour are not useful in CIM environments.

Increased management flexibility

One management change leading to increased efficiency and flexibility in business processes has been the adoption of a **just-in-time (JIT) philosophy**. Originally, JIT referred to an inventory system that minimised inventories by arranging for materials and sub-components to arrive just as they were needed for production and for goods to be made just-in-time to ship them to customers – no sooner and no later. But JIT has become the cornerstone of a broad management philosophy. It originated in Japanese companies such as Toyota and Kawasaki. Now many large companies use JIT, including Hewlett-Packard, Porsche, General Motors, Tata and Xerox, as well as many smaller firms. The essence of the JIT philosophy is to eliminate waste. Managers try (1) to reduce the time that products spend in the production process and (2) to eliminate the time that products spend in activities that do not add value (such as inspection and waiting time).

Another management approach focused on efficiency and flexibility is **lean manufacturing**, which applies continuous process improvements to eliminate waste from the entire enterprise. For example, Matsushita Electric's Saga plant on Japan's Kyushu Island decreased the time it takes to produce a finished product from 2½ days to 40 minutes by replacing conveyor belts with clusters of robots. As with JIT, lean ideas are now being extended beyond manufacturing to other business processes.

A focus on quality is also important in today's competitive environment. A decade or more ago, many companies undertook **total quality management (TQM)** initiatives. TQM minimises costs by maximising quality. It focuses on continuous improvement in quality and satisfying one's customers. Recently, the focus on quality has shifted to **Six Sigma**, a disciplined, *data-driven approach* to eliminating defects in any process. Six Sigma is essentially a continuous process-improvement effort designed to reduce costs by improving quality. Pioneered in the 1980s by Motorola, Six Sigma has also been implemented by companies such as General Electric in the United States and Samsung in Korea to transform their business. Six Sigma seeks to ensure that internal processes are running as efficiently as possible.

Why do these business process changes affect management accounting? They all directly affect costs, and accountants often measure the actual cost savings, predict anticipated cost savings, and develop costs for products or services for different production environments. For example, a British company reduced the time to manufacture a vacuum pump from 3 weeks to 6 minutes by switching from long assembly lines to manufacturing cells that accomplish all production steps in quick succession. Accountants measured the benefits created by the reduced production time. In general, when companies change their production processes to accomplish economic objectives, accountants predict and measure the economic impact.

MAKING MANAGERIAL DECISIONS

Suppose you are a manager of a BASF chemical plant. The plant has just undertaken a **business process reengineering** project and, as a result, has substantially changed its production process. It is much more automated, with newly acquired equipment replacing labour-intensive operations. The plant is also making more use of electronic commerce and moving toward a JIT inventory policy. You have a meeting with your accountant to discuss possible changes in your accounting system. What types of accounting-system changes might be warranted?

may have focused on accounting for labour, while the new system should focus on the use of the automated equipment. This will direct attention to the most important costs in the process and make sure that they are monitored and controlled. Problem-solving needs will also be different. Initially, the plant's managers will probably want comparative data on the cost of the new process versus the cost of the old. In the future, they will need information about how best to use capacity that the plant owns (the equipment) rather than how much labour to use for the planned level of production.

Answer

Major changes in production processes generally lead to different information needs. The old accounting system

Ethical conduct for professional accountants

Objective 6
Explain why ethics and standards of ethical conduct are important to accountants.

Business processes and accounting systems change. However, the need for accountants to maintain high ethical standards of professional conduct will never change. The Institute of Management Accountants says that ethics 'deals with human conduct in relation to what is morally good and bad, right and wrong. It is the application of values to decision making. These values include honesty, fairness, responsibility, respect and compassion.' Business processes and accounting systems change. However, the need for accountants to maintain high ethical standards of professional conduct will never change. The International Ethics Standards Board has as its aim to 'serve the public interest by setting high quality ethical standards for professional accountants and by facilitating the convergence of international and national ethical standards'. The UK professional body, The Chartered Institute of Management Accountants (CIMA) has aligned its code of ethics with those issued by the international body.

We like to think of ethics as simply doing what is right. One way to decide whether an action is unethical is to ask yourself whether you would be embarrassed to read about your action in the newspaper the next day. Another warning sign that an action may be unethical is when the justification for the action is 'Everybody else is doing it', the phrase Warren Buffett has described as 'the five most dangerous words in business'.

Why is integrity so important to accountants? Think of it this way: If you buy a car, you can see many of the quality details. Further, if something goes wrong with the car, you will certainly know it. But accounting information is different. You can't see its quality. You might not notice for years that something is wrong – probably not until it's too late to do anything about it. Thus, you rely on the integrity of accountants to assure yourself that the information about a company is correct. If you cannot trust the accountant, then the information is nearly worthless.

In the remainder of this section, we discuss ethical standards and formal codes of conduct and the difficult issue of ethical dilemmas, situations where conflicting values make it unclear which is the ethical action.

■ Standards of ethical conduct

Ethical standards require accountants to adhere to codes of conduct regarding objectivity, confidentiality, integrity, credibility, professional behaviour and competence. Professional accounting organisations have procedures for reviewing alleged behaviour that is not consistent with the standards.

The ethical organisation also has policies in place to motivate ethical actions. Integrity and outspoken support for ethical standards by senior managers, in both word and deed, are the greatest motivators of ethical behaviour throughout an organisation. A code of conduct – a document specifying the ethical standards of an organisation – is the centre piece of most ethics programmes. (See the Business first box, 'Ethics and corporate codes of conduct', on p. 17.) But having a code is not sufficient. Actual policies and practices influence behaviour. This means that managers' evaluations must include an assessment of ethical conduct. Organisations cannot tolerate unethical behaviour, even if it appears to lead to great financial performance. For example, in the early 2000s, Enron, WorldCom, Tyco, Global Crossing, Adelphia, Xerox and others created accounting entries to make their financial reports look better than their actual performances. In some cases, accountants participated in these fraudulent activities. In other cases, they simply did not step up and challenge what they surely knew (or at least should have known) was misleading information.

Many companies make ethics a top priority. The Ethisphere Institute annually lists the 'world's most ethical companies'. In 2011 the only firm in the 'Restaurants and cafés' category was the Starbucks Coffee Company. For example, Starbucks includes ethical principles in the first line of its mission statement: 'To establish Starbucks as the premier purveyor of the

BUSINESS FIRST
Ethics and corporate codes of conduct

The Sarbanes-Oxley Act of 2002 requires companies 'to disclose whether or not, and if not, the reason therefore, such issuer has adopted a code of ethics for senior financial officers, applicable to its principal financial officer and comptroller or principal accounting officer, or persons performing similar functions'. This has created increased interest in corporate codes of conduct. However, a code of conduct means different things to different companies.

One company had only one rule: 'Don't do anything you would be embarrassed to read about in tomorrow's newspaper.' Others have detailed lists of dos and don'ts. Some companies use consulting firms to advise them on their codes. Although the codes and their development differ, the goal is generally the same – to motivate employees and suppliers to act with integrity.

Consider BBC Worldwide, which takes the position: 'For us, ethical trading means ensuring that the factories which make our products have responsible labour and health and safety practices.' Some codes of conduct are highly specific to the organisation. The International Cricket Council has a code of conduct which identifies

the following as serious offences: gambling on matches (betting); failing to perform in a match in return for a benefit such as money or goods (match fixing); inducing a player to perform one of these actions; failure to report certain incidents relating to match fixing or gambling.

While having a code of conduct is important, it is not sufficient. After all, Enron's code of conduct specified that 'business is to be conducted in compliance . . . with the highest professional and ethical standards'. Top management must set the tone and get out the message. Management must recognise and reward honesty and integrity. The corporate culture, more than codes of conduct, is the real influence on the ethical climate of an organisation. Codes of conduct can be a part, but only a part, of developing a culture of integrity.

Sources: Sarbanes-Oxley Act of 2002, HR 3763; RedHawk Productions website (http://redhawkproductions.com); Financial Executives Institute website (www.fei.org); D. Blank, 'A matter of ethics', *Internal Auditor*, February 2003, pp. 27–31; Enron Corporation, *2000 Corporate Responsibility Report*, p. 3; BBC Worldwide website May 2011; www.icc-cricket.yahoo.net.

finest coffee in the world while maintaining our uncompromising principles as we grow.' Other Ethisphere-honoured companies include Adidas, Comme Il Faut, Standard Chartered Bank, Henkel, Ricoh, Singapore Telecom and H&M.

Ethical dilemmas

The ethical standards of the profession leave much room for individual interpretation and judgement. A first step is to ask two questions: Is this action unethical? Would it be unethical not to take this action? If the answers to these questions are clear, then the ethical action is clear. A manager's ethical choice becomes more complex when there are no legal guidelines or clear-cut ethical standards. Ethical dilemmas exist when managers must choose an alternative and there are (1) significant value conflicts among differing interests, (2) several alternatives are justifiable, and (3) there are significant consequences for stakeholders in the situation.

Suppose you are an accountant and your boss has asked you to supply the company's banker with a profit forecast for the coming year. A badly needed bank loan rides on the prediction. Your boss is absolutely convinced that profits will be at least €500,000 – anything less than that and the loan is not likely to be approved.

Your analysis reveals three possible outcomes: First, if the planned introduction of a new product goes extraordinarily well, profits will exceed €500,000. Second, if there is a modestly successful introduction, there will be a €100,000 profit. You believe this is the most likely outcome. Third, if the product fails, the company stands to lose €600,000. Without the loan, the new product cannot be taken to the market, and there is no way the company can avoid a loss for the year. Bankruptcy is a real possibility.

What forecast would you make? The fundamental issue here is disagreement about the prospects for the new product. If your boss is correct, it would be unethical to make a forecast of less than €500,000, which seems to guarantee financial problems, perhaps even bankruptcy. This would hurt stockholders, management, employees, suppliers and customers. But if you are correct about the most likely outcome, a forecast of €500,000 may not be fair and objective. It may mislead the bank.

There is no easy answer to this dilemma. It is one of those grey areas where either action includes risks. But remember that a series of grey areas can create a black area. That is, a series of actions that push the boundary of ethical behaviour can add up to a clearly unethical situation. Accountants must draw the line someplace, and it is usually better to err on the side of full disclosure than to withhold important information. Enron repeatedly pushed boundaries by reporting only optimistic information. If its managers had done this once or twice, it might not have created a problem. But the pattern of exclusively optimistic projections eventually deteriorated into completely unrealistic, and unethical, projections.

Summary problem for your review

PROBLEM

Yang Electronics Company (YEC) developed a high-speed, low-cost copying machine marketed primarily for home use. However, as YEC customers learned how easy and inexpensive it was to make copies with it, sales to small businesses soared. Unfortunately, the heavier use by these companies caused breakdowns in a component of the equipment that had been designed only for light use. The copiers were guaranteed for two years, regardless of the amount of usage. Consequently, YEC began to experience high costs for replacing the damaged component.

As the quarterly meeting of YEC's board of directors approached, the CFO asked Mark Chua, assistant controller, to prepare a report on the situation. It was hard to predict the exact effects but it seemed that many business customers were starting to switch away from the YEC copier to more expensive copiers sold by competitors. It was also clear that the increased guarantee costs would significantly affect YEC's profitability. Mark summarised the situation in writing as best he could for the board.

Alice Martinez, YEC's CFO, was concerned about the impact of the report on the board. She did not disagree with the analysis, but she thought it would make management look bad and might even lead the board to discontinue the product. She was convinced from conversations with the head of engineering that the copier could be slightly redesigned to meet the needs of high-volume users, so discontinuing it might pass up a potentially profitable opportunity.

Martinez called Chua into her office and asked him to delete the part of his report dealing with the component failures. She said it was all right to mention this orally to the board, noting that engineering is nearing a solution to the problem. However, Chua felt strongly that such a revision in his report would mislead the board about a potentially significant negative impact on the company's earnings.

How should Chua resolve this situation?

SOLUTION

Martinez's request violates requirements for competence, integrity and objectivity. It violates competence because she is asking Chua to prepare a report that is not complete and clear, and omits potentially relevant information. Therefore, the board will not have all the information it should to make a decision about the component failure problem.

The request violates integrity because the revised report may subvert the attainment of the organisation's objectives to achieve Martinez's objectives. Management accountants are specifically responsible for communicating unfavourable as well as favourable information.

Finally, the revised report would not be objective. It would not disclose all relevant information that could be expected to influence the board's understanding of operations and, therefore, its decisions.

Chua's responsibility is to discuss this issue with increasingly higher levels of authority within YEC. First, he should let Martinez know about his misgivings. Possibly the issue can be resolved by her withdrawing the request. If not, he should inform her that he intends to take up the matter with the company president, and even the board, if necessary, until the issue is resolved. So that Chua does not violate the standard of confidentiality, he should not discuss the matter with persons outside of YEC.

Highlights to remember

1 **Describe the major users and uses of accounting information.** Internal managers use accounting information for making short-term planning and control decisions, for making nonroutine decisions and for formulating overall policies and long-range plans. External users, such as investors and regulators, use published financial statements to make investment decisions, regulatory rulings and many other decisions. Managers use accounting information to answer scorekeeping, attention-directing and problem-solving questions.

2 **Describe the cost–benefit and behavioural issues involved in designing an accounting system.** Companies design management accounting information systems for the benefit of managers. These systems should be judged by a cost–benefit criterion – the benefits of better decisions should exceed the cost of the system. Context will often dictate choices and outcomers. Behavioural factors – how the system affects managers and their decisions – greatly influence the benefit of a system.

3 **Explain the role of budgets and performance reports in planning and control.** Budgets and performance reports are essential tools for planning and control. Budgets result from the planning process. Managers use them to translate the organisation's goals into action. A performance report compares actual results to the budget. Managers use these reports to monitor, evaluate and reward performance and, thus, exercise control.

4 **Discuss the role accountants play in the company's value-chain functions.** Accountants play a key role in planning and control. Throughout the company's value chain, accountants gather and report cost and revenue information for decision makers.

5 **Identify current trends in management accounting.** Many factors have caused changes in accounting systems in recent years. Most significant are a shift to a service-based economy, increased global competition, advances in technology and changed business processes. Without continuous adaptation and improvement, accounting systems would soon become obsolete.

6 **Explain why ethics and standards of ethical conduct are important to accountants.** Users of accounting information expect accountants to adhere to high standards of ethical conduct. Most users cannot directly assess the quality of that information, and if they cannot rely on accountants to produce unbiased information, the information will have little value to them. That is why professional accounting organisations, as well as most companies, have codes of ethical conduct. Many ethical dilemmas, however, require more than codes and rules. They call for value judgements, not the simple application of standards.

Accounting vocabulary

Vocabulary is an essential and often troublesome phase of the learning process. A fuzzy understanding of terms hampers the learning of concepts and the ability to solve accounting problems. Before proceeding to the assignment material or to the next chapter, be sure you understand the words and terms in the Accounting vocabulary section of each chapter. Their meaning is explained within the chapter and in the glossary at the end of this book.

accounting system, p. 5
attention directing, p. 4
B2B, p. 14
B2C, p. 14
budget, p. 7
business process
   reengineering, p. 14
code of conduct, p. 16
computer-aided design (CAD),
   p. 14
computer-aided manufacturing
   (CAM) p. 14
computer-integrated
   manufacturing (CIM)
   systems, p. 14
control, p. 7
cost–benefit balance, p. 6

decision making, p. 3
electronic commerce
   (e-commerce), p. 14
enterprise resource planning
   (ERP) system, p. 14
e-commerce, p. 14
ethics, p. 16
financial accounting, p. 3
generally accepted accounting
   principles (GAAP), p. 5
International Financial
   Reporting Standards (IFRS),
   p. 5
Internal controls, p. 5
just-in-time (JIT) philosophy,
   p. 14
lean manufacturing, p. 15

management accounting, p. 3
management by exception,
   p. 8
performance reports, p. 8
planning, p. 6
problem solving, p. 4
product life cycle, p. 9
Sarbanes-Oxley Act, p. 5
scorekeeping, p. 4
service organisations, p. 13
Six Sigma, p. 15
total quality management
   (TQM), p. 15
variances, p. 8
value chain, p. 9

Fundamental assignment material   MyAccountingLab

1.A1 Scorekeeping, attention directing and problem solving

For each of the following activities, identify the primary function that the accountant is performing – scorekeeping, attention directing or problem solving – and explain why it best fits that category.

1 Preparing a schedule of depreciation for forklift lorries in the receiving department of a General Electric factory in Scotland.
2 Analysing, for a Sony production superintendent, the impact on costs of purchasing some new assembly equipment.
3 Preparing a scrap report for the finishing department of a Toyota parts factory.
4 Interpreting why the Colville Timber Resource Company did not adhere to its production schedule.
5 Explaining the stamping department's performance report.
6 Preparing a monthly statement of European sales for the Ford Motor Company's vice president of marketing.
7 Preparing, for the manager of production control of a Mittal Steel plant, a cost comparison of two computerised manufacturing control systems.
8 Interpreting variances on the University of Manchester's purchasing department's performance report.

9 Analysing, for an Airbus manufacturing manager, the desirability of having some parts for the A380 airplane made in Korea.

10 Preparing the budget for the dermatology department of Providence Hospital.

1.A2 Management by exception

Student Accounting Club (SAC), the accounting society, held a party. The society expected attendance of 70 persons and prepared the following budget:

Room rental	£ 140
Food	700
Entertainment	600
Decorations	220
Total	£1,660

After SAC paid all the bills for the party, the total cost came to £1,865, or £205 over budget. Details are £140 for room rental; £865 for food; £600 for entertainment; and £260 for decorations. Eighty-five persons attended the party.

1 Prepare a performance report for the party that shows how actual costs differed from the budget. That is, include in your report the budgeted amounts, actual amounts and variances.

2 Suppose the society uses a management-by-exception rule. Which costs deserve further examination? Why?

1.A3 Professional ethics

For each of the following situations, indicate how ethical standards for management accounting may influence the manager and what the appropriate action should be:

1 At a dinner party, a guest asked a Kellogg's manager how a major new cereal was doing. The manager had just read a report that said sales lagged much below expectation. What should he say?

2 Felix just graduated from business school with an accounting specialisation and joined the accounting department of Pioneer Enterprises. His boss asked him to evaluate a market analysis for a potential new product prepared by the marketing department. Felix knows very little about the industry and he never had a class to teach him how to make a market analysis. Should he just do the best he can on the analysis without asking for help?

3 Mary Sue prepared a budget for a division of Southeastern Electronics. Her supervisor, the division manager, was not happy that she included results for an exciting new product that was to be introduced in a month. He asked her to leave the results for the product out of the budget. That way, the financial results for the product would boost actual profits well above the amount budgeted, resulting in favourable reviews for the division and its managers. What should Mary Sue do?

1.B1 Scorekeeping, attention directing and problem solving

For each of the following activities, identify the function the accountant is performing – scorekeeping, attention directing or problem solving. Explain each of your answers.

1 Estimating the operating costs and outputs that could be expected for each of two large metal-stamping machines offered for sale by different manufacturers; only one of these machines is to be acquired by your company.
2 Recording daily material purchase vouchers.
3 Analysing the expected costs of acquiring and using each of two alternate types of welding equipment.
4 Preparing a report of overtime labour costs by production department.
5 Estimating the costs of moving corporate headquarters to another city.
6 Interpreting increases in nursing costs per patient-day in a hospital.
7 Analysing deviations from the budget of the factory maintenance department.
8 Assisting in a study by the manufacturing manager to determine whether to buy certain parts needed in large quantities for manufacturing products or to acquire facilities for manufacturing these parts.
9 Preparing estimated costs for a new marketing campaign.
10 Recording overtime hours of the product finishing department.
11 Compiling data for a report showing the ratio of advertising expenses to sales for each branch store.
12 Investigating reasons for increased returns and allowances for drugs purchased by a hospital.
13 Preparing a schedule of fuel costs by months and government departments.
14 Computing and recording end-of-year adjustments for expired fire insurance on the factory warehouse.

1.B2 Management by exception

The Party Shop sells fireworks for the five weeks preceding 31 December. The outlet in Covent Garden had budgeted sales of £75,000. Expected expenses were as follows:

Cost of fireworks	£36,000
Labour cost	15,000
Other costs	8,000
Total costs	£59,000

Actual sales were £74,600, almost equal to the budget. Party Shop spent £35,500 for fireworks, £18,000 for labour and £7,910 for other costs.

1 Compute budgeted profit and actual profit.
2 Prepare a performance report to help identify those costs that were significantly different from the budget.
3 Suppose the business uses a management-by-exception rule. What costs deserve further explanation? Why?

1.B3 Ethical code of conduct

According to the Financial Executives Institute, 'corporate governance consultants and academics agree that a company needs to have a code of conduct' for its employees. Most companies, even many of those who experienced ethical breakdowns, have such a code. Answer the following questions about corporate codes of conduct.

1 What is a corporate code of conduct?
2 What types of issues are covered in a corporate code of conduct? At what level of detail?
3 In some cases codes of conduct were not effective. What, besides simply having a code, is necessary for a code of conduct to be effective?

Additional assignment material

QUESTIONS

1.1 'Who uses information from an accounting system?

1.2 'The emphases of financial accounting and management accounting differ.' Explain.

1.3 'The field is less sharply defined. There is heavier use of economics, decision sciences and behavioural sciences.' Identify the branch of accounting described in the quotation.

1.4 Distinguish among scorekeeping, attention directing and problem solving.

1.5 'Accounting principles assist the development of management accounting systems.' Do you agree? Explain.

1.6 Why is integrity so important to accountants?

1.7 'Integrity is more important for business professionals than it is for business students.' Do you agree? Explain.

1.8 Give three examples of service organisations. What distinguishes service organisations from other types of organisations?

1.9 What two major considerations affect the design of all accounting systems? Explain each.

1.10 'The accounting system is intertwined with operating management. Business operations would be in a hopeless tangle without the recordkeeping that is so often regarded with disdain.' Do you agree? Explain, giving examples.

1.11 Distinguish among a budget, a performance report and a variance.

1.12 'Management by exception means abdicating management responsibility for planning and control.' Do you agree? Explain.

1.13 Why are accountants concerned about product life cycles?

1.14 Name the six primary business functions (excluding support functions) that make up the value chain and briefly describe each.

1.15 'Accountants in every company should measure and report on every function in the company's value chain.' Do you agree? Explain.

1.16 Distinguish between the duties of line managers and staff managers.

1.17 The role of management accountants is changing, especially in companies with a 'flatter' organisational structure. What are some of the changes?

1.18 How are changes in technology affecting management accounting?

1.19 Briefly describe how a change in a plant's layout can make its operation more efficient.

CRITICAL THINKING EXERCISES

1.20 Marketing and management accounting

A cross-functional team of managers, including the management accountant, performs each of the following activities. However, depending on the nature of the decision to be made, one functional area will take the leadership role. Which of these activities is primarily a marketing decision? What would the management accountant contribute to each of the marketing decisions?

1 Porsche Motor Company must decide whether to buy a part for one of its cars or to make the part at one of its plants.
2 Airbus must decide the price to charge for spare parts it sells over the internet using its Spare Parts website.

3 St Luke's Hospital must decide how to finance the purchase of expensive new medical analysis equipment.
4 Amazon.com must forecast the impact on video sales of a new advertising programme.
5 Mission Foods, a leading producer and distributor of tortillas to retail and food service industries, must decide whether to accept a special order for tortilla chips by a large, national retail chain.
6 Target Stores must decide whether to close one of its retail stores that is currently operating at a loss.

1.21 Production and management accounting

A cross-functional team of managers, including the management accountant, performed each of the following activities. However, depending on the nature of the decision to be made, one functional area will take the leadership role. Which of these activities is primarily a production decision? What would the management accountant contribute to each of the production decisions?

1 Saab Automobile AB must decide whether to buy a part for one of its cars or to make the part at one of its plants.
2 Boeing Company must decide the price for spare parts it sells over the internet using its spare parts website.
3 St Mary's Hospital must decide how to finance the purchase of expensive new medical analysis equipment.
4 Amazon.com must forecast how a new advertising programme will affect DVD sales.
5 Mission Foods, a leading producer and distributor of tortillas to retail and food service industries, must decide whether to accept a special order for tortilla chips by a large, national retail chain.
6 Dell Computers must decide whether to spend money on training workers to perform set-ups and changeovers faster. This will free up capacity to be used to make more computers without purchasing more equipment.
7 Ford Motor Company must decide whether to keep or replace four-year-old equipment used in one of its Escape plants.

EXERCISES

1.22 Management accounting and financial accounting

Consider the following short descriptions. Indicate whether each of the following descriptions more closely relates to a major feature of financial accounting or management accounting:

1 Field is less sharply defined
2 Provides internal consulting advice to managers
3 Has less flexibility
4 Is characterised by detailed reports
5 Has a future orientation
6 Is constrained by accounting standards
7 Behavioural impact is secondary.

1.23 Planning and control, management by exception

Study the Starbucks store in Exhibit 1.2 on p. 7. Suppose that for next year a particular store budgeted revenue of €330,000, a 10 per cent increase over the current revenue of €300,000.

The actions listed in Exhibit 1.2 resulted in six new budgeted products and a total advertising budget of €30,000. Actual results were as follows:

New products added	7
Advertising	€ 33,000
Revenues	€ 326,000

1 Prepare a performance report for revenues and advertising costs using the format of Exhibit 1.3 on p. 8.
2 Suppose the remaining cost elements of net income were not available until several months after the store implemented the plan. The net income results were disappointing to management – profits declined even though revenues increased because costs increased by more than revenues. List some factors that might have caused costs to increase so much and that management may not have considered when they formulated the store's plan.

1.24 Microsoft's value chain

Microsoft is the world's largest software company. For each of the following value-chain functions, discuss briefly what Microsoft managers would do to achieve that function and how important it is to the overall success of Microsoft.

R&D	Product (service) and process design
Production	Marketing
Distribution	Customer service
Support functions	

1.25 Cost–benefit of the ethical environment

A poor ethical environment results in costs to the company. On the other hand, a good ethical environment creates benefits. List several costs of a poor ethical environment and benefits of a good ethical environment.

PROBLEMS

1.26 Management and financial accounting

Lillian Choi, an able mechanical engineer, was informed that she would be promoted to assistant factory manager. Lillian was pleased but uncomfortable. In particular, she knew little about accounting. She had taken one course in financial accounting.

Lillian planned to enroll in a management accounting course as soon as possible. Meanwhile, she asked Walt Greenspan, a cost accountant, to state three or four of the principal distinctions between financial and management accounting.

Prepare Walt's written response to Lillian.

1.27 Costs and benefits

Marks & Spencer, a huge retailer in the United Kingdom with sales of more than £9 billion, was troubled by its paper bureaucracy. Looked at in isolation, each document seemed reasonable, but overall a researcher reported that there was substantial effort in each department to verify the information. Basically, the effort seemed out of proportion to any value received and, eventually, the company simplified or eliminated many of the documents.

Describe the rationale that should govern systems design. How should a company such as Marks & Spencer decide what documents it needs and which can be eliminated?

1.28 Changes in accounting systems

In the last decade, Boeing has made several significant changes to its accounting system. None of these changes was for reporting to external parties. Management believed, however, that the new system gave more accurate costs of the airplanes and other products produced.

1   Boeing had been a very successful company using its old accounting system. What might have motivated it to change the system?
2   When Boeing changed its system, what criteria might its managers have used to decide whether to invest in the new system?
3   Is changing to a system that provides more accurate product costs always a good strategy? Why or why not?

1.29 Value chain

Nike is an Oregon-based company that focuses on the design, development and worldwide marketing of high-quality sports footwear, apparel, equipment and accessory products. Nike is the largest seller of athletic footwear and athletic apparel in the world. The company sells its products to more than 18,000 retail accounts in the United States and through a mix of independent distributors, licensees and subsidiaries in approximately 180 countries around the world. Nike contracts with more than 700 factories around the world to manufacture virtually all the company's products. Nike produces most footwear and branded apparel products outside the United States.

1   Identify one decision that Nike managers make in each of the six value-chain functions.
2   For each decision in requirement 1, identify one piece of accounting information that would aid the manager's decision.

CASE STUDY

The ethical dilemma at Northlake

The case assumes no technical knowledge of management and cost accounting but deals with ethical issues that often face accounting professionals. It engages in a discussion of how far the notion of 'different costs for different purposes' might extend.

Our story opens with an irate Jim McIntosh confronting his manager of corporate reporting: 'I thought we had an understanding on this issue, Frank. Tina tells me that you are threatening to go public with your stupid statements about the report. For Pete's sake, Frank, wake up and smell the coffee! You're about to damage all the important things in your life: your career, your friendships and your company!'

Frank sat quietly in the overstuffed sofa in his VP's expansive office. He thought that the pale green report lying on the desk looked innocent enough, but it certainly had provided the basis for some serious turmoil: Jim stood by his desk trembling with rage. His face was bright red and mottled with anger. Frank had often seen Jim upset, but never in a temper such as this.

'I'm sorry, Jim', Frank replied softly, 'I know how much this means to you, but I don't think that I have a choice in this matter. I can't sit idle while you and that twit from financial analysis allow this report to go forward. You both know that these numbers have no foundation in fact.'

The report, entitled 'Endangered species: The pulp and paper industry in the Upper Peninsula', laid out the industry's response to the new government proposals to put effluent controls on the discharge of waste water from pulp and paper mills in environmentally sensitive regions of the province. One section of the report detailed the financial consequences of the emission controls as determined by each of the five pulp and paper companies operating in the region. Amalgamated Forest Products had taken the industry lead in developing the report and the company president, Jean Letourneau, was scheduled to testify before a legislative sub-committee next week, giving the industry perspective on the proposed legislation.

Amalgamated had three major mills, located in some of the more remote locations in the province. The firm had been facing difficult financial times due to the recession and this had caused substantial hardship in the three small communities where the mills were located. Corporate offices were located in Northlake, a town of approximately 10,000 people.

The section of the report dealing with the dollar impact to Amalgamated Forest Products of installing the emission control equipment had been prepared by Tina Pacquette. Tina, a long-term employee of the firm, had risen through the accounting department to become the manager of financial analysis. While Tina and Frank were at equal levels in the organisational structure, their working relationship had not been particularly cordial. In Frank's opinion, Tina's work was barely adequate, but then, no one asked for his opinion.

'Well, Frank, your pig-headedness has really caused a problem for all of us! Wait here! I'll get Jean Letourneau and we'll see what he thinks about your efforts.' Jim left the office and slammed the door.

As he waited in the silence of his boss's beautifully decorated office, Frank looked back over his ten years with Amalgamated Forest Products. Just like his father before him, Frank started with the firm after completing high school and his first job was as a yard man sorting out damaged logs before processing. That's when Frank severely damaged his right leg on the job. He had been celebrating the birth of his son the night before and he was unable to manoeuvre his footing with the dexterity required. Surgery saved the leg and he was extremely grateful that the company had brought him inside to the accounting office. An accounting clerk's salary was low compared with being a yard helper, but in a short time his natural talent for analysis brought him to the attention of the vice-president, Finance. Within two years, Jim McIntosh had arranged for him to go to university, complete his CMA designation after graduation, and then return to Amalgamated. The financial support provided by the firm had been adequate but not lavish by any means, and Frank had done well in his studies. He was the gold medallist for his province on the CMA examinations, and he had returned to Northlake in triumph. With three young children and a proud wife, Frank had been appointed to a new position in corporate reporting. After a year of having Jim as his mentor, he rose to the position of manager of corporate reporting.

Source: Russell, G. (1993) 'The ethical dilemma at Northlake', *CMA Magazine*, March. Reproduced with permission from Professor Grant Russell.

The office door opened abruptly and Jim entered with the company president. Jean Letourneau was a distinguished man of approximately 60 years of age. He had a long history with Amalgamated and a solid reputation in the pulp and paper industry.

'What's the problem, Frank?' Jean's voice broke into the silence. 'Jim tells me that you have a few concerns about the report that we're submitting to the legislative committee.'

'Well, Mr Letourneau, I think we – the company – have some major problems here. The report indicates that we'll have severe financial problems if we're forced into building a lagoon for waste water treatment. In fact, the report says we are likely to be pushed into bankruptcy if the legislation is passed. But we all know these estimates of costs are highly inflated. There's no way that our operating costs would be raised by 30 per cent. I could see our operating costs rising by only 8–10 per cent. That's what the internal report Tina wrote a year ago predicts and there's really been no significant change. Moreover, you have to testify before the legislative committee as to the truthfulness of this report – and there's not a shred of truth in it. The other cost estimates are all high and the prediction of our product demand is based upon a further deepening of the recession. For our internal purposes, we have been using an estimated increase of 10 per cent in demand.'

'Slow down, son', Letourneau's calm voice broke in, 'We have to use different figures for different purposes. When we report to our shareholders, we give them numbers that are substantially altered from the internal documents, right? In this case, we have to make those dunderheads in the government see what all this regulation is doing to us. Besides, they know we're going to use the most effective numbers to justify our position.'

'But this isn't simply a matter of different figures', Frank spluttered. 'These numbers have been totally fabricated. And they don't take into account the damage that we're doing to the Wanawashee River. The same stuff we're dumping was cleaned up by our competition years ago. The community downstream is still drinking this garbage. We're going to be subject to a huge lawsuit if they ever trace it to us. Then, where will we be? I've got to worry about my professional obligations as well. If this blows up, you could go to jail and I could get my designation revoked.'

'We'll cross that bridge when we come to it', Jim McIntosh interjected. 'You've got to remember what's at stake here. Northlake's totally dependent on the mill for its economic survival. As the mill goes, so goes the town. It's your buddies you'd be threatening to put out of work, Frank. This legislation may not bankrupt us, but it will certainly put a squeeze on profits. If profits are gone, no more reinvestment by Chicago. Head office is putting lots of pressure on us to improve the bottom line since the takeover last year. They're talking about cutting all of that new production line equipment we requested.'

'The bottom line is this, Frank', Letourneau spoke softly. 'You're an important part of our team – we've invested a lot in you. Jim was talking about working you into a new role: V.P.-controller. We'd hate to let you go because of this small issue. However, we need to have everybody working towards the same goal. Besides, Jim tells me this isn't even your responsibility. If you hadn't picked up the copy of the report on Tina's desk, we wouldn't even have involved you. Now take the rest of the day off, go home to Cheryl and the kids and take out that new speedboat of yours. Think the problem through and I'm sure you'll see the long-term benefit of what we're doing. This pollution problem is a 'Northern problem' that we can resolve here, not in some fancy legislature in the south. Besides, we've had the problem for as far back as I can remember. So a few extra years certainly won't hurt.'

This is a general case on the design of a management and cost accounting system for a firm operating in a high-tech environment. It provides an opportunity for a broad discussion not only of the appropriateness of particular accounting techniques but also of the need to consider strategic, behavioural and organisational factors.

Question

What would you do if you were Frank?

Introduction to cost behaviour and cost–volume relationships

Learning objectives

When you have finished studying this chapter, you should be able to:

1 Explain how activity cost drivers affect cost behaviour.

2 Show how changes in cost-driver levels affect variable and fixed costs.

3 Calculate break-even sales volume in total sales in euros and total units.

4 Create a cost–volume–profit graph and understand the assumptions behind it.

5 Calculate sales volume in total sales and total units to reach a target profit.

6 Differentiate between contribution margin and gross margin.

7 Explain the effects of sales mix on profits (Appendix 2A).

8 Compute cost–volume–profit relationships on an after-tax basis (Appendix 2B).

Boeing Company

In 1915, William Boeing, a Seattle timberman, assembled his first airplane in a boathouse. In 1954 Boeing introduced its first four-engine 707. The Boeing family of jets has grown to include the 727, 737, 757, 747, 767 and 777. The company delivered its first 787 Dreamliner in late 2011. Today, the Boeing Company is the world's largest aerospace company, the second largest maker of commercial jets, and the second largest military contractor. Boeing produces 30 to 35 commercial jetliners each month and had annual revenue of $68.6 billion in 2011. The company makes planes with 100 to well over 500 seats and has more than half of the world's market share in airplane sales, and that is growing as Boeing successfully competes for the growing demand for airplanes. How will Boeing maintain its competitive edge and profitability margin? With intense competition from Airbus, Boeing knows that it can improve profits more by controlling (reducing) costs than by increasing prices to customers – especially when many of its customers have shrinking profits following the global financial crisis. So, should it build bigger airplanes or more of the existing size but with improvements in features and efficiencies that will lower customers' operating

The design and production of an airplane is a complex process. This is the first assembled Boeing 787 Dreamliner airplane at its production facility at Everett, WA.

costs? Which alternative has lower costs for Boeing and its customers? To answer these questions, Boeing has to understand its own costs as well as the costs of its customers. This chapter begins your study of costs so that you, too, can assess the costs that are important to Boeing and other companies, big and small, as they make crucial decisions about their products, services and processes.

Consider a recent decision Boeing faced regarding development and production of a new airplane. Back in 1999, the company started an R&D programme for the Sonic Cruiser. The Sonic Cruiser emphasised speed – it was designed to reduce travel time by about 20 per cent. An important part of its research was the assessment of its customers' costs – both of operating their existing fleet of planes and of the costs of the new Sonic Cruisers. In early 2001, discussions with airlines in North America, Asia and Europe confirmed the design offered exactly what airlines and passengers were looking for: the ability to fly quickly and directly to their destinations while avoiding time-consuming and costly stops at major hubs. In late 2002, after more than three years of research, the company had completed the design of the new airplane and was faced with the final decision to launch. A decision to launch would involve a huge immediate investment in costly plant and equipment resources. To pay for these assets and make a profit, Boeing had to be confident that its customers would be willing to pay more for the airplane than it cost Boeing to design, produce and sell it.

But production ultimately hinged on whether customers wanted a faster airplane that used the most up-to-date technology both in operating the airplane and producing it. Despite the years of development activities, Boeing decided not to proceed with the Sonic Cruiser. Why? The economic recession and the terrorist attacks of 11 September 2001, had changed the airline industry's needs. According to Alan Mulally, CEO of Boeing Commercial Airplanes at the time, the airlines made it clear that they wanted a cheaper plane rather than a faster plane. Therefore, Boeing management decided to dedicate its resources to developing the 787 Dreamliner – a 'super-efficient' version of its existing 777 jetliner. Boeing's managers made their decision after a careful analysis of its own production costs and the airlines' operating costs, comparing them to the predicted demands for airline travel in the next decade.

Managers need to understand costs. For example, how much would it cost Boeing to produce each Sonic Cruiser? How much for each 787? How much cost does Air France incur when it adds one more passenger at the last moment to an existing flight, or when it adds one more flight to the schedule? What does it cost Toyota to develop a new line of luxury autos, as it did with Lexus? How much does it cost to produce one more Lexus? How will an increase in Finland's population affect the costs needed to run the country's department of motor vehicles? What does it cost Nestlé Purina to meet Asda's specifications for shipments of pet-care products? What activities contribute most to Nestlé Purina's cost to serve Asda stores? These questions are really different forms of one general question: What will happen to financial results if a company or organisation changes its level of activity?

Although financial results are based on revenues and costs, we will focus primarily on costs in this chapter. As we saw in the case of Boeing, companies usually have more control over their costs than they do over their revenues. One of the main goals of management accounting is helping managers control (and reduce) costs. But managers cannot control costs unless they understand **cost behaviour** – how the activities of an organisation affect its costs. ∎

Identifying resources, activities, costs and cost drivers

Objective 1
Explain how cost drivers affect cost behaviour.

Different types of costs behave in different ways. Consider Boeing's costs of making the 737-900ER – Boeing's newest single-aisle airplane. As Boeing produces more airplanes, it buys and uses more resources, such as electrical wire, seats, aluminium and labour. Therefore, each additional airplane requires Boeing to incur more of these resource costs. In contrast, the cost of other resources such as the factory and salaries of key managers, stay the same, regardless of the number of airplanes made. To predict costs and to manage them on a day-to-day basis, Boeing managers identify:

- key activities performed;
- resources used in performing these activities;
- costs of the resources used; and
- **cost drivers**, measures of activities that require the use of resources and thereby cause costs.

Exhibit 2.1 shows how activities link resources and their costs with the output of products or services. For example, an activity that requires resources and therefore causes costs for Boeing is installing seats in the 737-900ER. This activity uses many resources, but let's consider just two: (1) the seats themselves, which Boeing purchases from a subcontractor, and (2) labour for installing the seats. One measure of activity, number of seats installed, is an appropriate cost driver for the cost of the seats. Another measure of activity, labour hours used in installing the seats, is a cost driver for the cost of labour resources.

To control costs, managers usually focus their efforts on managing the activities companies perform to make, sell and deliver products or services – not necessarily on the products and services themselves. This is why it is important to focus on the activities used to produce outputs, products or services, and the resources needed to support the activities. For example, a production manager needs to know how routine activities, such as machine maintenance and repairs, affect production costs. Likewise, a sales manager needs to know how activities, such as order processing and post-sales support, affect sales costs. Consider one of the many activities performed as part of the production function at Boeing's plant – receiving parts that production workers install on an airplane. Of course, managers want to know the cost of the parts they purchase, but they also need to know how the receiving activity affects production costs. For example, how does the increase or decrease in receiving activity affect the lease payment for renting the equipment used to move parts from the receiving area to the production floor? How does it affect the cost of fuel for the moving equipment?

An organisation has many cost drivers across the various activities of its value chain. For example, one manufacturer of pet foods has a plant that has more than 50 production activities and a total of 21 cost drivers. Exhibit 2.2 lists examples of resource costs and potential cost drivers for activities in each of the value-chain functions. How well we identify the most appropriate cost drivers determines how well managers understand cost behaviour and how well managers can control costs.

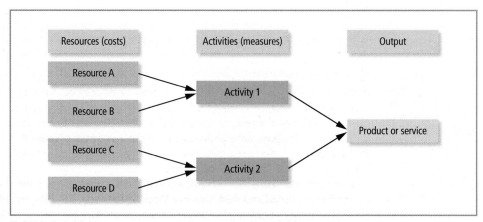

Exhibit 2.1 Linking resource costs to outputs via activities

Value-chain functions and resource costs	Example cost drivers
Research and development	
• Salaries of sales personnel, costs of market surveys	Number of new product proposals
• Salaries of product and process engineers	Complexity of proposed products
Design of products, services and processes	
• Salaries of product and process engineers	Number of engineering hours
• Cost of computer-aided design equipment used to develop prototype of product for testing	Number of distinct parts per product
Production	
• Labour wages	Labour hours
• Supervisory salaries	Number of people supervised
• Maintenance wages	Number of mechanic hours
• Depreciation of plant and machinery, supplies	Number of machine hours
• Energy cost	Kilowatt hours
Marketing	
• Cost of advertisements	Number of advertisements
• Salaries of marketing personnel, travel costs entertainment costs	Sales euros
Distribution	
• Wages of shipping personnel	Labour hours
• Transportation costs including depreciation of vehicles and fuel	Weight of items delivered
Customer service	
• Salaries of service personnel	Hours spent servicing products
• Costs of supplies, travel	Number of service calls

Exhibit 2.2 Examples of value-chain functions, resource costs and cost drivers

In this chapter we focus on a simple situation of one activity and one cost driver for the production of a particular product or service. The activity will include all aspects of the production and sale of the product or service. The cost driver will be the number of units produced and sold, which we assume drives all the resource costs. Therefore, the analysis will examine how decisions about the volume of production and sales affect costs. This simplified analysis is useful to managers who want a rough estimate of the relationship between production volume and costs.

·Variable- and fixed-cost behaviour

Objective 2
Show how changes in cost-driver levels affect variable and fixed costs.

To understand cost behaviour, it is important to distinguish variable costs from fixed costs. Accountants classify costs as variable or fixed depending on how much they change as the level of a particular cost driver changes. A **variable cost** changes in direct proportion to changes in the cost driver. In contrast, changes in the cost driver do not *immediately* affect a **fixed cost**. Suppose units of production is the cost driver of interest. A 10 per cent increase in the units of production would produce a 10 per cent increase in variable costs. However, the fixed costs would remain unchanged.

Consider some variable costs and assume that the cost driver is the volume of final goods or services produced and sold. Suppose Watkins Products, the 140-year-old health food company, pays its sales personnel a 40 per cent straight commission on sales. The total cost of sales commissions to Watkins is 40 per cent of sales – a variable cost with respect to sales revenues.

If cost-driver level increases (or decreases)		
Type of cost	**Total cost**	**Cost per unit***
Fixed costs	No change	Decrease (or increase)
Variable costs	Increase (or decrease)	No change

* Per unit of activity volume, for example, product units, passenger kilometres orders processed or sales in euros

Exhibit 2.3 Cost behaviour of fixed and variable costs

Or suppose Long Lake Bait Shop buys bags of fish bait for €2 each. The total cost of fish bait is €2 times the number of bags purchased – a variable cost with respect to units (number of bags) purchased. Notice that variable costs do not change *per unit*, but that the *total variable costs* change in direct proportion to the cost-driver activity.

Now consider a fixed cost. Suppose Sony rents a factory to produce DVD players for €500,000 per year. The number of DVD players produced does not affect the *total fixed cost* of €500,000. The *unit cost* of rent applicable to each DVD player, however, does depend on the total number of DVD players produced. If Sony produces 100,000 DVD players, the unit cost will be €500,000 ÷ 100,000 = €5. If it produces 50,000 DVD players, the unit cost will be €500,000 ÷ 50,000 = €10. Therefore, a fixed cost does not change in total, but the per-unit fixed cost becomes progressively smaller as the volume increases.

Note carefully from these examples that the 'variable' or 'fixed' characteristic of a cost relates to its total euro amount and not to its per-unit amount. Exhibit 2.3 summarises these relationships.

When analysing costs, you may find these two rules of thumb useful:

1 *Think of fixed costs on a total-cost basis.* Total fixed costs remain unchanged regardless of changes in the cost-driver.

2 *Think of variable costs on a per-unit basis.* The per-unit variable cost remains unchanged regardless of changes in the cost-driver. As a result, the total variable cost varies proportionately with the level of the cost-driver.

Now consider again the receiving activity at the Boeing plant discussed in the previous section. Exhibit 2.4 shows the relationship between the receiving activity and the costs of the fuel and equipment resources. The receiving activity requires many more resources such as labour and supplies, but we restrict our discussion to just fuel and equipment. The relationships between activities and resources used can be shown using symbols.

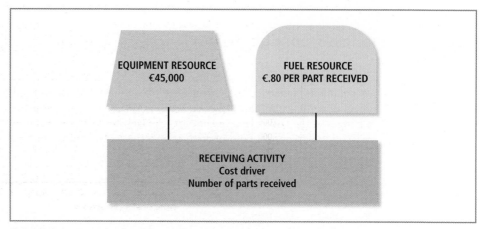

Exhibit 2.4 Receiving activity and resources used

We introduce some of these symbols here in Chapter 2 and will use these same symbols in later chapters to depict more complex business processes. We denote an activity by the symbol ▪. We use the symbol ▪ to represent a variable-cost resource and the symbol ▪ to represent a fixed-cost resource. The total fuel and equipment costs were €24,000 and €45,000, respectively, and the department received 30,000 parts. Notice in Exhibit 2.4 that we apply the two rules of thumb by showing the total fixed lease cost of €45,000 and the per-unit variable fuel cost of €24,000 ÷ 30,000 = €0.80 per part received. Both of these amounts tend to be relatively constant over the wide range of receiving activity. This is an important characteristic because we can use both of these numbers to calculate the activity costs for various levels of the cost driver.

Suppose we want to know what the total fuel and equipment cost would be if only 27,500 parts were received. We can use Exhibits 2.3, 2.4 and our rules of thumb to find the answer. Total fuel cost is variable with respect to parts received, but the fuel cost per part received does not change. Equipment lease cost in total does not change when the number of parts received decreases. So the total cost of receiving 27,500 parts would be (27,500 × €.80) + €45,000 = €67,000. Notice how we used the rules of thumb to answer the question. We used the unit cost of €.80 for variable fuel cost and the total cost of €45,000 for the fixed equipment lease cost. Exhibit 2.5 shows the total cost lines for both resources. These lines can be used to find an estimate of the total costs at any cost-driver level.

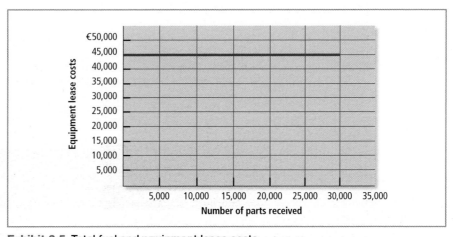

Exhibit 2.5 Total fuel and equipment lease costs

Summary problem for your review

PROBLEM

Refer to the previous discussion of the receiving activity at the Boeing plant and Exhibit 2.4. The plant manager is looking at a monthly report of plant costs and notices that the receiving activity costs vary substantially from month to month. He is interested in knowing more about why the total cost and unit costs of the receiving activity changes when the number of parts received changes. He gives you the data for parts received for the last several months and you note that the range is from 10,000 to 30,000.

1 Prepare a table that shows the cost of each resource, the total cost, and the total cost on a per-part-received basis. Use increments of 5,000 parts beginning with 10,000.

2 Prepare brief explanations of why the total and unit cost patterns change.

SOLUTION

1 The table can be developed by using the two rules of thumb that are based on the relationships shown in Exhibit 2.3. We can also quickly estimate the total costs from the cost lines in Exhibit 2.5.

(1) Parts received	(2) Equipment cost	(3) €.80 × (1) Fuel cost	(4) (2) + (3) Total cost	(5) (4) ÷ (1) Cost per part received
10,000	€45,000	€8,000	€53,000	€5.30
15,000	45,000	12,000	57,000	3.80
20,000	45,000	16,000	61,000	3.05
25,000	45,000	20,000	65,000	2.60
30,000	45,000	24,000	69,000	2.30

2 Column (4) shows the total cost of the receiving activity. The total cost increases with increases in the number of parts received due to the increase in variable costs. Whenever we see a pattern of increasing total costs, we may initially assume that it is due to variable-cost resources responding to increasing levels of the cost driver. Column (5) shows the cost per part received. The decreasing cost pattern is due to the fixed equipment cost being spread over increasing levels of the cost driver – number of parts received. For example, when the number of parts received increases from 10,000 to 15,000 parts, the cost per part decreases by €1.50 from €5.30 to €3.80. This is exactly the amount of the decrease in the equipment cost per part, which is €4.50 (€45,000 ÷ 10,000) less €3.00 (€45,000 ÷ 15,000). The variable fuel cost per part stays the same at €0.80.

MAKING MANAGERIAL DECISIONS

A key factor in helping managers understand cost behaviour is distinguishing between variable and fixed costs. Test your understanding by answering the following questions.

(continued)

MAKING MANAGERIAL DECISIONS (CONTINUED)

1 A producer of premium ice cream uses 'litres of ice cream produced' as a cost driver for the production activity. One of the main resources this activity uses is dairy ingredients. Is the cost of dairy ingredients a variable or a fixed cost?

2 The same company uses 'supervisory hours' as a cost driver for the supervision activity. The most costly resource used by this activity is supervisory salaries. Is the supervisory salaries cost variable or fixed?

Answer

The best way to determine whether the cost of a resource is fixed or variable is to ask the question, 'If the level of the cost driver changes, what will happen to the cost?' If the company increases (decreases) its production of ice cream, then the cost of dairy ingredients will also increase (decrease). Thus, the cost of dairy ingredients is a variable cost. If the number of supervisory hours increases (decreases), supervisory salaries will not change. Thus, the cost of supervisory salaries is a fixed cost.

◼ Relevant range

Although we have just described fixed costs as unchanging regardless of changes in the given cost driver, this rule of thumb holds true only within reasonable limits. For example, rent costs, which are generally fixed, will rise if increased production activity requires a larger or additional building – or if the landlord decides to raise the rent. Conversely, rent costs may go down if decreased production activity causes the company to move to a smaller plant. The **relevant range** is the limit of cost-driver level within which a specific relationship between costs and the cost driver is valid. Even within the relevant range, though, a fixed cost remains fixed only over a given period of time – usually the budget period. Fixed costs may change from budget year to budget year solely because of changes in insurance and property tax rates, executive salary levels or rent levels. But these items usually do not change significantly within a given year.

For example, suppose that the relevant range of production activity for an Osram lightbulb plant is between 40,000 and 85,000 cases of lightbulbs per month and that total monthly fixed costs within the relevant range are €100,000. Within the relevant range, fixed costs will remain the same. If production falls below 40,000 cases, changes in production processes would slash fixed costs to €60,000 per month. If operations rise above 85,000 cases, rentals of additional facilities would boost fixed costs to €115,000 per month. Exhibit 2.6 graphs the actual costs in the top figure and the assumed fixed-cost-behaviour in the bottom. The two are identical only within the relevant range.

Exhibit 2.6 shows graphically these assumptions – a given period and a given activity range. It is highly unusual, however, for monthly operations to be outside the relevant range. Therefore, the three-level refinement at the top of Exhibit 2.6 is usually not graphed. Instead, a single horizontal line is typically extended through the plotted activity levels, as at the bottom of the exhibit. Often a dashed line is used outside the relevant range.

The basic idea of a relevant range also applies to variable costs. That is, outside a relevant range, some variable costs, such as fuel consumed, may behave differently per unit of cost-driver activity. For example, the variable cost per case for the Osram lightbulb plant might increase if production activity exceeds 85,000 cases per month because of the lower efficiency of the new facilities.

◼ Difficulties in classifying costs

Is it difficult to classify a cost as exactly variable or exactly fixed? As you may suspect, it often is. Many complications arise, including the possibility of costs behaving in some nonlinear way (not producing a straight-line graph). For example, tax preparers often become more efficient

Exhibit 2.6 Fixed costs and relevant range

as they learn to process the new year's tax forms, thus processing more returns per hour. This means that total variable costs may actually behave as in panel A and not as in panel B.

Moreover, more than one cost driver may simultaneously affect costs. For example, both the weight and the number of units handled may affect the costs of shipping labour at an Amazon.com warehouse. We will investigate various facets of this problem in succeeding chapters; for now, we assume that we can classify every cost as either totally variable or totally fixed. We assume also that only one cost driver affects a given variable cost and that the variable costs change in direct proportion to the cost driver.

Whether we classify costs as fixed or variable also depends on the situation. More costs are fixed and fewer are variable when decisions for which we use the cost information involve very short time spans and very small changes in activity level. Suppose a Lufthansa plane with several empty seats will depart from its gate in 2 minutes. A potential passenger is running down a corridor bearing a transferable ticket from a competing airline. Unless the gate attendant holds the airplane for an extra 30 seconds, the passenger will miss the departure and will not switch to Lufthansa for the planned trip. What are the variable costs to Lufthansa of delaying the departure and placing one more passenger in an otherwise empty seat? Variable costs (for example, one more meal) are negligible. Virtually all the costs in this situation are fixed (for example, flight crew and maintenance crew salaries).

Now, in contrast, suppose Lufthansa's decision is whether to add another flight, acquire another gate, add another city to its routes, or acquire another airplane. Many more costs

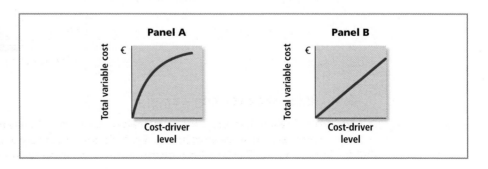

would be variable and fewer would be fixed. For example, in the case of adding a flight, the salaries of the flight and maintenance crews would now be variable. This example underscores the importance of the decision situation itself in the analysis of cost behaviour. Whether costs are really 'fixed' or 'variable' depends heavily on the relevant range, the length of the planning period in question and the specific decision situation.

Cost–volume–profit analysis

Managers often classify costs as fixed or variable when making decisions that affect the volume of output. Consider the decision about how many units of a product to produce in the coming year. Managers realise that many factors in addition to the volume of output will affect costs. Yet, a useful starting point in their decision process is to predict how the choice of production level will affect costs.

The managers of profit-seeking organisations usually study the effects of output volume on revenue (sales), expenses (costs) and net income (net profit). We call this study **cost–volume–profit (CVP) analysis**. The managers of nonprofit organisations also benefit from the study of CVP relationships. Why? No organisation has unlimited resources, and knowledge of how costs fluctuate with changes in volume helps managers to understand how to control costs. For example, administrators of nonprofit hospitals are concerned about the behaviour of costs as the volume of patients fluctuates.

To apply CVP analysis, managers usually resort to some simplifying assumptions. The major one is that we can classify costs as either variable or fixed with respect to a single measure of the volume of output activity. This chapter focuses on such a simplified relationship.

◼ CVP scenario

Amy Winston, the manager of food services for one of Boeing's plants, is trying to decide whether to rent a line of snack vending machines. Although individual snack items have various acquisition costs and selling prices, Winston has decided that an average selling price of $1.50 per unit and an average acquisition cost of $1.20 per unit will suffice for purposes of this analysis. She predicts the following revenue and expense relationships:

	Per unit	Percentage of sales
Selling price	$1.50	100
Variable cost of each item	1.20	80
Selling price less variable cost	$ .30	20
Monthly fixed expenses		
Rent	$ 3,000	
Wages for replenishing and servicing	13,500	
Other fixed expenses	1,500	
Total fixed expenses per month	$18,000	

We will now use these data in examining several applications of CVP analysis.

Objective 3
Calculate break-even sales volume in total sales in euros and total units.

◼ Computing the break-even point

The most basic CVP analysis computes the monthly **break-even point** in number of units and in sales in euros. The break-even point is the level of sales at which revenue equals expenses and net income is zero. The business press frequently refers to break-even points, especially during times of economic downturn such as in 2001–2002 and in 2008–2009. For example, a news story in 2010 read: 'Linux finally breaks even.' (www.Theregister.co.uk/2010/02/26.) Another news story stated that 'Record digital media profits and tight budgeting helped Channel 4 to break even last year – despite the worst advertising downturn in its 2-year history' (www.independent.co.uk/news/media/c4-breakeven23/6/10).

Some people call the study of cost–volume–profit relationships break-even analysis. However, this term is misleading. Why? Because CVP analysis does much more than compute the break-even point. It is often an important part of a company's planning process. It helps managers to predict how their decisions will affect sales, costs, and net income. Nevertheless, computing a break-even point is one application of CVP analysis.

BUSINESS FIRST
Sony lowers break-even point during economic recession

One might think that break-even is a term that is not often used in business. However when economic conditions result in declining sales, companies are keenly aware of the break-even point.

In 2002–2003, many high-technology companies reported on their attempts to achieve profitability in spite of declining sales. The situation repeated itself for many types of companies in 2008–2009. They often focused on how their efforts to control costs reduced their break-even points. If a company faces rapidly falling sales, it must restructure its costs to be able to break even at a lower volume. Restructuring costs can involve reducing both fixed and variable costs.

Consider Sony's PlayStation 3. It costs Sony about $500 to make a PS3 but the sales price is about $300 and with the recession of 2008–2009 coupled with competitive pressure from Nintendo Wii and Microsoft Xbox 360, raising price was not an option. So how could Sony lower its costs to breakeven? The two actions Sony considered were reducing variable cost and fixed cost. To lower its variable cost, Sony reduced the number of parts and the cost for the console's central processing unit. Reducing the number of parts also lowered Sony's fixed costs, such as assembly equipment and salaries of purchasing agents responsible for vendor negotiations.

In June 2010, Sony Computer Entertainment Worldwide Studios' Head, Shukei Yoshida reported: 'We aren't making huge money from hardware, but we aren't bleeding like we used to.' However, in April 2011, Sony issued a warning to 77 million users that the PS network had been hacked into, leading to its shutdown which was to last three weeks. A news report stated: 'Playstation network hack could cost Sony €318 per account claims research firm.' (Reported in www.psu .com27/4/2011.)

Sources: 'Sony PS3 costs less to make, but still a money loser,' *Techweb*, 30 December 2008; 'Sony finally turns a profit', www. Techrader.com30/6/2010.

We next illustrate the two basic methods for computing a break-even point: the contribution-margin method and the equation method.

Contribution-margin method

Consider the following common-sense arithmetic approach. Every unit sold generates a **unit contribution margin** or **marginal income**, which is the unit sales price minus the variable cost per unit. For the vending machine snack items, the unit contribution margin is €.30:

Unit sales price	€1.50
– Unit variable cost	1.20
= Unit contribution margin	€ .30

When do we reach the break-even point? When we sell enough units to generate a **total contribution margin** (total number of units sold × unit contribution margin) equal to the total fixed costs. Divide the €18,000 in fixed costs by the €.30 unit contribution margin. The number of units that we must sell o break even is €18,000 ÷ €.30 = 60,000 units. The sales revenue at the break-even point is 60,000 units × €1.50 per unit, or €90,000. (Note that some managers and accountants use the term **contribution margin** to mean either unit contribution margin or total contribution margin, assuming that the context makes clear which they mean.)

Think about the contribution margin of the snack items. Each unit sold generates extra revenue of €1.50 and extra cost of €1.20. Fixed costs are unaffected. If we sell zero units, we incur a loss equal to the fixed cost of €18,000. Each unit sold reduces the loss by €.30 until sales reach the break-even point of 60,000 units. After that point, each unit sold adds (or contributes) €.30 to profit.

The condensed income statement at the break-even point is:

	Total	Per unit	Percentage
Units	60,000		
Sales	€90,000	€1.50	100
Variable costs	72,000	1.20	80
Contribution margin*	€18,000	€ .30	20
Fixed costs	18,000		
Net income	€ 0		

* Sales less variable costs

Many companies sell multiple products and, therefore, have no single unit price and unit variable cost. For example, a grocery store sells hundreds of products at many different prices. In such a company, it would not be meaningful to compute a break-even point in overall units sold. Instead, we use total sales and total variable costs to calculate the variable cost percentage and the contribution margin percentage:

variable-cost percentage = total variable costs ÷ total sales

contribution-margin percentage = total contribution margin ÷ total sales

= 100% − variable cost percentage

Consider our vending machine example:

Sales price	100%
− Variable expenses as a percentage of sales	80
= Contribution-margin percentage	20%

The variable-cost percentage is 80 per cent, and the contribution-margin percentage is 20 per cent. We can also express these percentages as ratios, the **variable-cost ratio** and **contribution-margin ratio**, which are .80 and .20, respectively. Therefore, 20 per cent of sales is available for the recovery of fixed expenses and the making of net income. Thus, we need €18,000 ÷ .20 = €90,000 of sales to break even. Remember that the contribution-margin percentage is a percentage of sales. Using the contribution-margin percentage, we can compute the break-even volume in sales without determining the break-even point in units.

Equation method

The equation method is the most general form of analysis, one you can adapt to any conceivable cost–volume–profit situation. You are familiar with a typical income statement. We can express any income statement in equation form, or as a mathematical model, as follows:

$$\text{sales} - \text{variable expenses} - \text{fixed expenses} = \text{net income} \qquad (1)$$

That is,

$$\left(\begin{array}{c}\text{unit sales}\\ \text{price}\end{array} \times \begin{array}{c}\text{number}\\ \text{of units}\end{array}\right) - \left(\begin{array}{c}\text{unit}\\ \text{variable cost}\end{array} \times \begin{array}{c}\text{number}\\ \text{of units}\end{array}\right) - \begin{array}{c}\text{fixed}\\ \text{expenses}\end{array} = \begin{array}{c}\text{net}\\ \text{income}\end{array}$$

At the break-even point, net income is zero:

$$\text{sales} - \text{variable expenses} - \text{fixed expenses} = 0$$

Let N = number of units to be sold to break even. Then, for the vending machine example,

$$€1.50N - €1.20N - €18,000 = 0$$
$$€.30N = €18,000$$
$$N = €18,000 \div €.30$$
$$N = 60,000 \text{ units}$$

Total sales in the equation is a price-times-quantity relationship, which we expressed in our example as €1.50N. To find the sales, multiply 60,000 units by €1.50, which yields the break-even sales of €90,000.

You can also solve the equation for break-even sales without computing the unit break-even point by using the relationship of variable costs and profits as a percentage of sales:

$$\frac{\text{variable-cost}}{\text{ratio or percentage}} = \frac{\text{variable cost per unit}}{\text{sales price per unit}} = \frac{€1.20}{€1.50} = .80 \text{ or } 80\%$$

Let S = sales in euros needed to break even. Then

$$S - .80S - €18,000 = 0$$
$$.20S = €18,000$$
$$S = €18,000 \div .20$$
$$S = €90,000$$

Relationship between the two methods

You may have noticed that the contribution-margin method is merely a shortcut version of the equation method. Look at the last three lines in the two solutions given for equation 1. They read

Break-even volume	
Units	**Euros**
€.30N = €18,000	.20S = €18,000
$N = \dfrac{€18,000}{€.30}$	$S = \dfrac{€18,000}{.20}$
N = 60,000 units	S = €90,000

From these equations, we can derive the following shortcut formulas:

$$\text{break-even volume in units} = \frac{\text{fixed expenses}}{\text{unit contribution margin}} \qquad (2)$$

$$\text{break-even volume in sales} = \frac{\text{fixed expenses}}{\text{contribution-margin ratio}} \qquad (3)$$

MAKING MANAGERIAL DECISIONS

Managers use CVP analysis to predict effects of changes in sales or costs on the break-even point. Using shortcut formulas (2) and (3), answer the following questions. Remember that the contribution margin per unit equals the sales price per unit minus the variable costs per unit.

1 What would be the effect on the unit and money sales break-even level if fixed costs increase (and there are no other changes)?

2 What would be the effect on the unit and money sales break-even level if variable cost per unit decreases (and there are no other changes)?

3 What would be the effect on the unit and money sales break-even level if sales volume increases (and there are no other changes)?

Answers

1 The break-even level in both units and money sales would increase if fixed costs increase.

2 The break-even level in both units and money sales would decrease if variable cost per unit decreases.

3 Think before answering this question. The actual (or even planned) volume of sales in units has nothing to do with determining the break-even point. This is why unit sales volume does not appear in either equation (2) or (3).

Which should you use, the equation or the contribution-margin method? Use either. Both yield the same results, so the choice is a matter of personal preference or convenience in a particular case.

Graphing the break-even point

Objective 4
Create a cost–volume–profit graph and understand the assumptions behind it.

Exhibit 2.7 is a graph of the cost–volume–profit relationship in our vending machine example. If you fully understand the contribution margin or equation method, you do not need to also learn the graphical method. However, most students find that a careful study of the graphi-

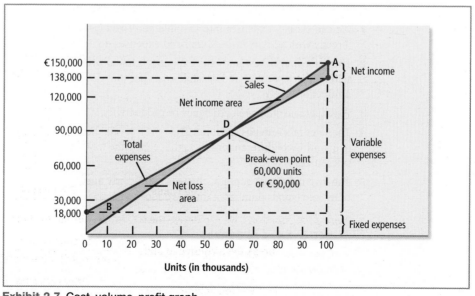

Exhibit 2.7 Cost–volume–profit graph

cal method leads to a better understanding of CVP analysis. Study the graph as you read the procedure for constructing it.

1 *Draw the axes*. The horizontal axis is the sales volume, and the vertical axis is euros of cost and revenue.

2 *Plot sales volume*. Select a convenient sales volume, say, 100,000 units, and plot point A for total sales euros at that volume: 100,000 × €1.50 = €150,000. Draw the revenue (that is, sales) line from point A to the origin, point 0.

3 *Plot fixed expenses*. Draw the line showing the €18,000 fixed portion of expenses. It should be a horizontal line intersecting the vertical axis at €18,000, point B.

4 *Plot variable expenses*. Determine the variable portion of expenses at a convenient level of activity: 100,000 units × €1.20 = €120,000. Add this to the fixed expenses: €120,000 + €18,000 = €138,000. Plot point C for 100,000 units and €138,000. Then draw a line between this point and point B. This is the total expenses line.

5 *Locate the break-even point* – where the total expenses line crosses the sales line. This is at, 60,000 units or €90,000. On the graph, this is shown where total sales revenues exactly equal total costs, point D.

The break-even point is only one part of this cost–volume–profit graph. The graph also shows the profit or loss at any rate of activity. At any given volume, the vertical distance between the sales line and the total expenses line measures the net income or net loss.

Managers often use break-even graphs because these graphs show potential profits over a wide range of volume more easily than numerical exhibits. Whether you use graphs or other presentations depends largely on your preferences. However, if you need to explain a CVP model to an audience, a graphical approach can be most helpful.

Note that the concept of relevant range applies to the break-even graph. Almost all break-even graphs show revenue and cost lines extending back to the vertical axis as shown in Exhibit 2.7. This approach is misleading because the relationships depicted in such graphs are valid only within a particular relevant range of volume. Nevertheless, for presentation purposes, most managers extend revenue and cost lines beyond the relevant range.

Regardless of the method used for CVP analysis, it is based on a set of important assumptions. Some of these assumptions follow:

1 We can classify expenses into variable and fixed categories. Total variable expenses vary directly with activity level. Total fixed expenses do not change with activity level.

2 The behaviour of revenues and expenses is linear over the relevant range. This means that selling prices per unit and variable costs per unit do not change with changes in sales and production levels.

3 We expect no change in efficiency or productivity.

4 The sales mix remains constant. The **sales mix** is the relative proportions or combinations of quantities of different products that constitute total sales. (See Appendix 2A for more on sales mixes.)

5 The inventory level does not change significantly during the period. That is, the number of units sold equals number of units produced.

Changes in fixed expenses

Changes in fixed expenses cause changes in the break-even point. For example, if we double the €3,000 monthly rent of the vending machines, what would be the monthly break-even point in number of units and sales?

The fixed expenses would increase from €18,000 to €21,000, so

$$\text{break-even volume in units} = \frac{\text{fixed expenses}}{\text{unit contribution margin}}$$

$$= \frac{€21,000}{€.30}$$

$$= 70,000 \text{ units}$$

$$\text{break-even volume in euros} = \frac{\text{fixed expenses}}{\text{contribution margin ratio}}$$

$$= \frac{€21,000}{.20}$$

$$= €105,000$$

Note that a one-sixth increase in fixed expenses altered the break-even point by one-sixth: from 60,000 to 70,000 units and from €90,000 to €105,000. This type of relationship always exists between fixed expenses and the break-even point if everything else remains constant.

Companies frequently lower their break-even points by reducing their total fixed costs. For example, closing or selling factories decreases property taxes, insurance, depreciation and managers' salaries. When demand for cars fell because of the slumping economy in 2008, big car companies made structural changes to reduce fixed costs. If they had merely produced fewer cars and lorries with the same fixed/variable cost structure, their volume would have fallen below its break-even point. By reducing fixed costs, the companies lowered their break-even points and reduced their losses.

Changes in unit contribution margin

Changes in variable costs also cause the break-even point to shift. Companies can reduce their break-even points by increasing their unit contribution margins through either increases in unit sales prices or decreases in unit variable costs, or both.

For example, assume that the fixed rent for the vending machines is still €3,000. (1) If the rental charge includes €.03 per unit sold in addition to the fixed rent, find the monthly break-even point in number of units and in sales. (2) If Winston reduces the selling price from €1.50 to €1.35 per unit and the original variable expenses per unit are unchanged, find the monthly break-even point in number of units and in sales.

Here's what happens to the break-even point:

1 The variable expenses would increase from €1.20 to €1.23 per unit, the unit contribution margin would decline from €.30 to €.27, and the contribution-margin ratio would become €.27 ÷ €1.50 = .18. The original fixed expenses of €18,000 would stay the same, but the denominators would change from those previously used. Thus,

$$\text{break-even point in units} = \frac{€18,000}{€.27} = 66,667 \text{ units}$$

$$\text{break-even point in euros} = \frac{€18,000}{.18} = €100,000$$

2 If Winston reduces the selling price from €1.50 to €1.35 per unit and the original variable expenses are unchanged, the unit contribution margin would fall from €1.50 − €1.20 = €.30 to €1.35 − €1.20 = €.15, and the break-even point would soar to €18,000 ÷ €.15 = 120,000 units. The break-even point in euros would also change because the selling price per unit and contribution-margin ratio change. The contribution-margin ratio would be

€.15 ÷ €1.35 = .11111. The break-even point in euros would be 120,000 units × €1.35 = €162,000 or, using the formula,

$$\text{break-even volume in money sales} = \frac{€18,000}{.11111} = €162,000$$

You can see that small changes in price or variable costs can lead to large changes in the unit contribution margin and, hence, to large changes in the break-even point.

■ Target net profit and an incremental approach

Objective 5
Calculate sales volume in total money sales and total units to reach a target profit.

Managers also use CVP analysis to determine the total sales, in units and euros, needed to reach a target profit. For example, in our snack vending example, suppose Winston considers €1,440 per month the minimum acceptable net income. How many units will she have to sell to justify the adoption of the vending machine plan? How does this figure 'translate' into money sales?

To compute the target sales volume in units needed to meet the desired or target net income, we adapt the basic break-even formula (equation 1 on p. 42):

$$\text{target sales} - \text{variable expenses} - \text{fixed expenses} = \text{target net income} \qquad (4)$$

or

$$\text{target sales volume in units} = \frac{\text{fixed expenses} + \text{target net income}}{\text{unit contribution margin}}$$

$$= \frac{€18,000 + €1,440}{€.30} = 64,800 \text{ units} \qquad (5)$$

The only real difference from the normal break-even analysis is that here we use a positive target net income instead of a break-even net income of €0.

Another way of getting the same answer is to use your knowledge of the break-even point and adopt an incremental approach. The phrase **incremental effect** refers to the change in total results (such as revenue, expenses or income) under a new condition in comparison with some given or known condition.

In this case, the given condition is the 60,000-unit break-even point. We would recover all expenses at that volume. Therefore, the change or increment in net income for every unit of sales beyond 60,000 would be equal to the unit contribution margin of €1.50 – €1.20 = €.30. If €1,440 were the target net profit, €1,440 ÷ €.30 would show that the target volume must exceed the break-even volume by 4,800 units; it would therefore be 60,000 + 4,800 = 64,800 units.

To find the answer in terms of money sales, multiply 64,800 units by €1.50 or use the formula:

$$\text{target sales volume in euros} = \frac{\text{fixed expenses} + \text{target net income}}{\text{contribution-margin ratio}}$$

$$= \frac{€18,000 + €1,440}{.20} = €97,200 \qquad (6)$$

To solve directly for money sales with the incremental approach, we would start at the break-even point in money sales of €90,000. Every sales euro beyond that point contributes €.20 to net profit. Divide €1,440 by €.20. Money sales must exceed the break-even volume by €7,200 to produce a net profit of €1,440. Thus, the total money sales would be €90,000 + €7,200 = €97,200.

The following table summarises these computations:

	Break-even point	Increment	New condition
Volume in units	60,000	4,800	64,800
Sales	€90,000	€7,200	€97,200
Variable expenses	72,000	5,760	77,760
Contribution margin	€18,000	€1,440	€19,440
Fixed expenses	18,000	—	18,000
Net income	€ 0	€1,440	€ 1,440

Multiple changes in key factors

So far, we have seen changes in only one CVP factor at a time. In the real world, managers often make decisions about the probable effects of multiple factor changes. For example, Boeing may cut the price of its airplanes to stimulate a larger volume of sales. Mars might decrease the size of its Snickers chocolate bar, saving variable costs and increasing the unit contribution margin, but also decreasing sales volume. Or Medtronic might automate the production of its insulin infusion pump, replacing variable costs of labour with fixed costs of equipment.

Consider our vending-machine example. Suppose Winston is considering locking the vending machines from 6:00 pm to 6:00 am, which she estimates will save €2,460 in wages monthly. However, the cutback from 24-hour service would hurt volume substantially because many nighttime employees use the machines. Should the machines remain available 24 hours per day? Assume that monthly sales would decline by 10,000 units from the current sales level. We will perform the analysis for two months representing the lowest and highest predicted sales volume: (1) 62,000 units and (2) 90,000 units.

We will consider two approaches. The first is to construct and solve equations for conditions that prevail under each alternative and select the volume level that yields the highest net income.

Regardless of the current volume level, be it 62,000 or 90,000 units, if we accept the prediction that sales will decline by 10,000 units, closing from 6:00 pm to 6:00 am will decrease net income by €540:

	Decline from 62,000 to 52,000 units		Decline from 90,000 to 80,000 units	
Units	62,000	52,000	90,000	80,000
Sales	€93,000	€78,000	€135,000	€120,000
Variable expenses	74,400	62,400	108,000	96,000
Total contribution margin	€18,600	€15,600	€ 27,000	€ 24,000
Fixed expenses	18,000	15,540	18,000	15,540
Net income	€ 600	€ 60	€ 9,000	€ 8,460
Change in net income	(€540)		(€540)	

A second approach – an incremental approach – is quicker and simpler. Simplicity is important to managers because it keeps the analysis from being cluttered by irrelevant and potentially confusing data.

What does the insightful manager see in this situation? First, whether the vending machines sell 62,000 or 90,000 units is irrelevant to the decision at hand. The issue is the decline in volume, which is 10,000 units in either case. The essence of this decision is whether the savings in fixed costs exceed the loss in total contribution-margin in money terms.

Lost total contribution margin, 10,000 units at €.30	€3,000
Less savings in fixed expenses	−2,460
Prospective decline in net income	€ 540

The incremental analysis also shows that locking the vending machines from 6:00 pm to 6:00 am would cause a €540 decrease in monthly net income. Whichever way you analyse it, locking the machines is not a sound financial decision.

■ CVP analysis and computer-based spreadsheets

The use of spreadsheets simplifies the examination of multiple changes in key factors in a CVP model. Managers in a variety of organisations use a personal computer and a spreadsheet-based CVP modelling program to study combinations of changes in selling prices, unit variable costs, fixed costs and desired profits. Many nonprofit organisations also use computerised CVP modelling. For example, some private universities have models that help measure how decisions, such as raising tuition, adding programmes and closing dormitories during winter holidays, will affect financial results. The computer quickly calculates the results of changes and can display them both numerically and graphically.

Consider our vending machine example. Exhibit 2.8 is a sample spreadsheet that shows what the sales level would have to be at three different fixed expense levels and three different variable expense levels to reach three different income levels. The computer calculates the 27 different sales levels rapidly and without error. Managers can insert any numbers they want for fixed expenses (column A), variable expense percentage (column B), target net income (row 3 of columns C, D and E) and the computer will compute the sales level.

	A	B	C	D	E
				Sales required to earn	
1				annual net income of	
2	**Fixed**	**Variable**			
3	**expenses**	**expense %**	**€ 2,000**	**€ 4,000**	**€ 6,000**
4					
5	€4,000	0.40	€10,000*	€13,333	€16,667
6	€4,000	0.44	€10,714*	€14,286	€17,857
7	€4,000	0.48	€11,538*	€15,385	€19,231
8	€6,000	0.40	€13,333	€16,667	€20,000
9	€6,000	0.44	€14,286	€17,857	€21,429
10	€6,000	0.48	€15,385	€19,231	€23,077
11	€8,000	0.40	€16,667	€20,000	€23,333
12	€8,000	0.44	€17,857	€21,429	€25,000
13	€8,000	0.48	€19,231	€23,077	€26,923

* (A5 + C3)/(1 − B5) = (€4,000 + €2,000)/(1 − €.40) = €10,000
(A6 + C3)/(1 − B6) = (€4,000 + €2,000)/(1 − €.44) = €10,714
(A7 + C3)/(1 − B7) = (€4,000 + €2,000)/(1 − €.48) = €11,538

Exhibit 2.8 Spreadsheet analysis of CVP relationships

BUSINESS FIRST
Did Blockbuster violate Disney contract? Accounting disagreement or ethical issue?

In early 2003, the Walt Disney Company sued Blockbuster, claiming that Blockbuster had violated a 1997 agreement between the two companies. Prior to the agreement, Blockbuster purchased videos from Disney for about $65 each and kept all the rental revenue. Under the pact, Blockbuster agreed to purchase movies from Disney for $7 a copy and then pay the studio a portion of the revenue from each rental.

The contract allowed Blockbuster to buy more copies of each video, which led to the guarantee that customers could rely on Blockbuster to have a copy of any movie they wanted or else the rental was free. With this policy, Blockbuster increased its market share of the video rental market from 28 per cent to 40 per cent. Essentially, Blockbuster turned a fixed cost, $65 per tape, into primarily a variable cost, with a small $7 fixed-cost portion and a larger variable-cost portion that depended on how much revenue Blockbuster generated from its rentals.

The arrangement was similar to that between the owners of shopping malls and many of their retail store tenants. Each store pays a monthly rental fee plus a percentage of its sales. Just as shopping mall owners rely on their tenants to truthfully report their sales, Disney relied on Blockbuster to correctly account for its video rentals.

In addition, Blockbuster and Disney also agreed on when Blockbuster could sell old rental tapes. Since these were so inexpensive for Blockbuster, selling them could be a lucrative business. But Disney did not want these low-cost tapes competing with its own videotape sales. Thus, it placed restrictions on when Blockbuster could sell them.

In the suit, Disney claimed that Blockbuster improperly deducted 'promotional' credits from its gross rental fees, failed to account for 'hundreds of thousands' of missing videos and sold videos prematurely. Disney had to rely on Blockbuster to correctly account for its rental revenues and inventory of tapes. Blockbuster claimed that its accounting was in accordance with the original agreement.

This is an example where good ethics and good accounting are both important. The original agreement promised benefits to both companies – more rental income for Disney on hit movies and more cost-structure flexibility for Blockbuster. But such a contract will not work if each party cannot trust the other. It's not clear who is right in this case, but both companies were hurt by the allegations. At a minimum, both will need to include better monitoring provisions in future contracts because other companies will suspect Disney of trying to get more than it deserves and Blockbuster of playing accounting tricks to minimise its payment to Disney.

Source: 'Disney sues Blockbuster over contract', *New York Times*, 4 January 2003; 'Disney sues top video chain', *Los Angeles Times*, 3 January 2003.

In addition to speed and convenience, computers allow a more sophisticated approach to CVP analysis than the one illustrated in this chapter. The assumptions we listed on p. 44 are necessary to simplify the analysis enough for most managers to construct a CVP model by hand. Computer analysts, however, can construct a model that does not require all the simplifications. Computer models can include multiple cost drivers, nonlinear relationships between costs and cost drivers, varying sales mixes and analyses that need not be restricted to a relevant range.

The use of computer models is a cost–benefit issue. The reliability of these models depends on the accuracy of their underlying assumptions about how revenues and costs will actually be affected. More complex models often require fewer assumptions and, thus, are more reliable. However, sometimes the costs of modelling exceed the value of the improved quality of management decisions. In small organisations, simplified CVP models often are accurate enough; more sophisticated (and more expensive) modelling may be unwarranted.

Additional uses of cost–volume analysis

■ Best cost structure

Analysing cost–volume–profit relationships is an important management responsibility. Managers are well advised to gain a thorough understanding of the organisation's cost structure – the combination of variable- and fixed-cost resources. For example, purchasing automated machinery may raise fixed costs but reduce labour cost per unit. Conversely, it may be wise to reduce fixed costs to obtain a more favourable combination. Thus, a company may decide to compensate its sales force via sales commissions (variable costs) rather than pay them salaries (a fixed cost). Another example of exchanging a fixed cost for a variable cost is a contract Blockbuster signed with Disney and other major studios. Instead of buying video tapes for $65 each, a fixed cost for each tape, Blockbuster paid only a $7 fixed cost and an additional variable cost equal to a percentage of the rental revenues. You can see one result of this contract in the 'Business first' box above.

Generally, companies that spend heavily for advertising are willing to do so because they have high contribution-margin percentages (e.g., airlines, cigarette and cosmetic companies). Conversely, companies with low contribution-margin percentages usually spend less for advertising and promotion (e.g., manufacturers of industrial equipment). As a result, two companies with the same unit sales volumes at the same unit prices could have different attitudes toward risking an advertising outlay. Assume the following:

	Perfume company	Janitorial service company
Unit sales volume	200,000 bottles	200,000 square feet
Sales at €10 per unit	€2,000,000	€2,000,000
Variable costs	200,000	1,700,000
Total contribution margin	€1,800,000	€ 300,000
Contribution-margin percentage	90%	15%

Suppose each company can increase sales volume by 10 per cent with the same expenditure for advertising:

	Perfume company	Janitorial service company
Increase in sales volume, 20,000 × €10	€200,000	€200,000
Increase in total contribution margin, 90%, 15%	180,000	30,000

The perfume company would be inclined to increase advertising considerably to boost the total contribution margin by €180,000. In contrast, the janitorial service company would be foolhardy to spend large amounts to increase the total contribution margin by only €30,000.

Note that when the contribution margin as a percentage of sales is low, great increases in volume are necessary to generate increases in net profits. On the other hand, decreases in profit are also small as volume decreases. High contribution-margin ratios have the opposite effect – large increases in profits as sales grow but also large decreases in profits if sales fall.

◼ Operating leverage

In addition to weighing the varied effects of changes in fixed and variable costs, managers need to consider their firm's ratio of fixed to variable costs, called **operating leverage**. In highly leveraged companies – those with high fixed costs and low variable costs – small changes in sales volume result in large changes in net income. Changes in sales volume have a smaller effect on companies with less leverage (that is, lower fixed costs and higher variable costs).

Exhibit 2.9 shows cost behaviour relationships at two firms, one highly leveraged and one with low leverage. The firm with higher leverage has fixed costs of €14,000 and variable cost per unit of €.10. The firm with lower leverage has fixed costs of only €2,000 but variable costs of €.25 per unit. Expected sales at both companies are 80,000 units at €.30 per unit. At this sales level, both firms would have net incomes of €2,000. If sales fall short of 80,000 units, profits drop most sharply for the highly leveraged business. If sales exceed 80,000 units, however, profits also increase most sharply for the highly leveraged concern.

The highly leveraged alternative is more risky. Why? Because it provides the highest possible net income and the highest possible net losses. In other words, net income is highly variable, depending on the actual level of sales. The low-leverage alternative is less risky because variations in sales lead to only a small variability in net income. At sales of 90,000 units, net income is €4,000 for the higher-leveraged firm but only €2,500 for the lower-leveraged firm. At sales of 70,000 units, however, the higher-leveraged firm has zero profits, compared to €1,500 for the lower-leveraged firm.

◼ Margin of safety

CVP analysis can also help managers assess risk by providing a measure of the margin of safety. The **margin of safety** shows how far sales can fall below the planned level of sales before losses occur. It compares the level of planned sales with the break-even point:

margin of safety = planned unit sales − break-even unit sales

The larger the margin of safety, the less likely it is that the company will have an operating loss, that is, operate below the break-even point. A small margin of safety may indicate a more

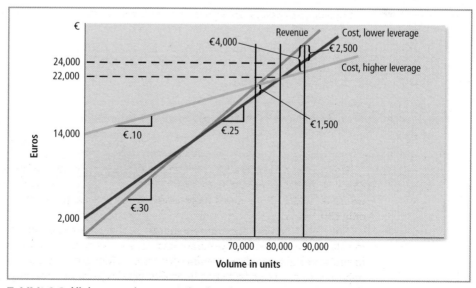

Exhibit 2.9 High versus low operating leverage

risky situation. If Amy Winston in our vending machine example had predicted a sales volume of 80,000 units, the margin of safety would be 20,000 units:

$$\text{margin of safety} = 80{,}000 \text{ units} - 60{,}000 \text{ units} = 20{,}000 \text{ units}$$

▉ Contribution margin and gross margin

Objective 6
Differentiate between contribution margin and gross margin.

This chapter has focused on the contribution margin. However, accountants also use a similar term, *gross margin*, to mean something quite different. Too often people confuse the terms *contribution margin* and *gross margin*. **Gross margin**, also called **gross profit**, is the excess of sales over the cost of goods sold. **Cost of goods sold** is the cost of the merchandise that a company acquires or produces and then sells. Compare the gross margin with the contribution margin:

$$\text{gross margin} = \text{sales price} - \text{cost of goods sold}$$
$$\text{contribution margin} = \text{sales price} - \text{all variable expenses}$$

Exhibit 2.10 shows costs divided on two different dimensions. As shown at the bottom of the exhibit, the gross margin uses the division on the production or acquisition cost versus selling and administrative cost dimension, and the contribution margin uses the division based on the variable-cost versus fixed-cost dimension.

In our vending-machine illustration, the contribution margin and the gross margin are identical because the cost of goods sold is the only variable cost:

Sales	€1.50
Variable costs: acquisition cost of unit sold	1.20
Contribution margin and gross margin are equal	€ .30

Now, suppose the firm had to pay a commission of €.12 per unit sold:

		Contribution margin	Gross margin
Sales		€1.50	€1.50
Acquisition cost of unit sold	€1.20		1.20
Variable commission	.12		
Total variable expense		1.32	
Contribution margin		€ .18	
Gross margin			€ .30

Exhibit 2.10 Costs for gross margin and contribution margin

Nonprofit application

Consider how cost–volume–profit relationships apply to nonprofit organisations. Suppose a city has a €100,000 lump-sum budget appropriation to conduct a counselling programme for drug addicts. The variable costs for counselling are €400 per patient per year. Fixed costs are €60,000 in the relevant range of 50 to 150 patients. If the city spends the entire budget appropriation, how many patients can it serve in a year?

We can use the break-even equation to solve the problem. Let N be the number of patients, substitute the €100,000 lump-sum budget for sales, and note that sales equals variable expenses plus fixed expenses if the city completely spends its budget.

$$\text{sales} = \text{variable expenses} + \text{fixed expenses}$$
$$\text{€100,000 lump sum} = \text{€400N} + \text{€60,000}$$
$$\text{€400N} = \text{€100,000} - \text{€60,000}$$
$$N = \text{€40,000} \div \text{€400}$$
$$N = 100 \text{ patients}$$

The city can serve 100 patients. Now, suppose the city cuts the total budget appropriation for the following year by 10 per cent. Fixed costs will be unaffected, but service will decline.

$$\text{sales} = \text{variable expenses} + \text{fixed expenses}$$
$$\text{€90,000} = \text{€400N} + \text{€60,000}$$
$$\text{€400N} = \text{€90,000} - \text{€60,000}$$
$$N = \text{€30,000} \div \text{€400}$$
$$N = 75 \text{ patients}$$

The percentage reduction in service is $(100 - 75) \div 100 = 25\%$, which is more than the 10 per cent reduction in the budget. Unless the city restructures its operations, the service volume must fall by 25 per cent to stay within budget.

A graphical presentation of this analysis is in Exhibit 2.11. Note that lump-sum revenue is a horizontal line on the graph.

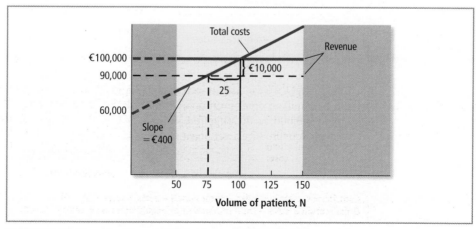

Exhibit 2.11 Graphical presentation of nonprofit application

Summary problem for your review

PROBLEM

A summary of the budgeted income statement of Williams Irish Gift Shop follows:

Net revenue	€ 800,000
Less expenses, including €400,000 of fixed expenses	880,000
Net loss	€(80,000)

The manager believes that an additional outlay of €200,000 for advertising will increase sales substantially.

1 At what sales level will the shop break even after spending €200,000 on advertising?

2 What sales level will result in a net profit of €40,000 after spending the €200,000 on advertising?

SOLUTION

1 Note that all data are in euros, not units. Most companies have many products, so the overall break-even analysis deals with euro sales, not units. The variable expenses are €880,000 − €400,000 = €480,000. The variable-cost ratio is €480,000 ÷ €800,000 = .60. (Remember to divide variable costs by sales, not by total costs.) Therefore, the contribution-margin ratio is .40. Let S = break-even sales in euros. Then

$$S - \text{variable expenses} - \text{fixed expenses} = \text{net profit}$$
$$S - .60S - (€400,000 + €200,000) =$$
$$.40S = €600,000$$
$$S = \frac{€600,000}{.40} = \frac{\text{fixed expenses}}{\text{contribution-margin ratio}}$$
$$S = €1,500,000$$

2
$$\text{required sales} = \frac{(\text{fixed expense} + \text{target net profit})}{\text{contribution-margin ratio}}$$

$$\text{required sales} = \frac{(€600,000 + €40,000)}{.40} = \frac{€640,000}{.40}$$
$$\text{required sales} = €1,600,000$$

Alternatively, we can use an incremental approach and reason that all euro sales beyond the €1.5 million break-even point will result in a 40 per cent contribution to net profit. Divide €40,000 by .40. Therefore, sales must be €100,000 beyond the €1.5 million break-even point to produce a net profit of €40,000.

Highlights to remember

1 **Explain how cost drivers affect cost behaviour.** A cost driver is an output measure that causes the use of costly resources. When the level of an activity changes, the level of the cost driver or output measure will also change, causing changes in costs.

2 **Show how changes in cost-driver levels affect variable and fixed costs.** Different types of costs behave in different ways. If the cost of the resource used changes in proportion to changes in the cost-driver level, the resource is a variable-cost resource (its costs are variable). If the cost of the resource used does not change because of cost-driver level changes, the resource is a fixed-cost resource (its costs are fixed).

3 **Calculate break-even sales volume in total money sales and total units.** We can approach CVP analysis (sometimes called break-even analysis) graphically or with equations. To calculate the break-even point in total units, divide the fixed costs by the unit contribution margin. To calculate the break-even point in total sales, divide the fixed costs by the contribution-margin ratio.

4 **Create a cost–volume–profit graph and understand the assumptions behind it.** We can create a cost–volume–profit graph by drawing revenue and total cost lines as functions of the cost-driver level. Be sure to recognise the limitations of CVP analysis and that it assumes constant efficiency, sales mix and inventory levels.

5 **Calculate sales volume in total sales and total units to reach a target profit.** Managers use CVP analysis to compute the sales needed to achieve a target profit or to examine the effects on profit of changes in factors such as fixed costs, variable costs or cost-driver volume.

6 **Differentiate between contribution margin and gross margin.** The contribution margin – the difference between sales price and variable costs – is an important concept. Do not confuse it with gross margin, the difference between sales price and cost of goods sold.

Appendix 2A: Sales-mix analysis

Objective 7
Explain the effects of sales mix on profits.

To emphasise fundamental ideas, the cost–volume–profit analysis in this chapter focused on a single product. Nearly all companies, however, sell more than one product. Thus, they must be concerned with sales mix, which you will recall from p. 44 is the relative proportions or combinations of quantities of products that comprise total sales. If the proportions of the mix change, the cost–volume–profit relationships also change.

Suppose Ramos Company has two products, wallets (W) and key cases (K). The income budget follows:

	Wallets (W)	Key cases (K)	Total
Sales in units	300,000	75,000	375,000
Sales @ €8 and €5	€2,400,000	€375,000	€2,775,000
Variable expenses @ €7 and €3	2,100,000	225,000	2,325,000
Contribution margins @ €1 and €2	€ 300,000	€150,000	€ 450,000
Fixed expenses			180,000
Net income			€ 270,000

What is the break-even point for each product? The typical answer assumes a constant mix of four units of W for every unit of K. Therefore, let K = number of units of product K to break even, and 4K = number of units of product W to break even:

$$\text{sales} - \text{variable expenses} - \text{fixed expenses} = \text{zero net income}$$
$$[\text{€}8(4K) + \text{€}5(K) - \text{€}7(4K)] - \text{€}180,000 =$$
$$\text{€}32K + \text{€}5K - \text{€}28K - \text{€}3K - \text{€}180,000 = 0$$
$$\text{€}6K = \text{€}180,000$$
$$K = 30,000$$
$$4K = 120,000 = W$$

The break-even point is 30,000K + 120,000W = 150,000 units.

This is the only break-even point for a sales mix of four wallets for every key case. Clearly, however, there are other break-even points for other sales mixes. For instance, suppose Ramos Company sells only key cases and fixed expenses stay at €180,000:

$$\text{break-even point in units} = \frac{\text{fixed expenses}}{\text{contribution margin per unit}}$$

$$= \frac{€180,000}{€2}$$

$$= 90,000 \text{ key cases}$$

If Ramos sells only wallets:

$$\text{break-even point} = \frac{€180,000}{€1} = 180,000 \text{ wallets}$$

We can see that the break-even point could be 180,000 units (of wallets), 90,000 units (of key cases) or 150,000 units (30,000 key cases and 120,000 wallets).

Managers are not interested in the break-even point for its own sake. Instead, they want to know how changes in a planned sales mix will affect net income. When the sales mix changes, the break-even point and the expected net income at various sales levels change also. For example, suppose overall actual total sales were equal to the budget of 375,000 units. However, Ramos sold only 50,000 key cases.

	Wallets (W)	Key Cases (K)	Total
Sales in units	325,000	50,000	375,000
Sales @ €8 and €5	€2,600,000	€250,000	€2,850,000
Variable expenses @ €7 and €3	2,275,000	150,000	2,425,000
Contribution margins @ €1 and €2	€ 325,000	€100,000	€ 425,000
Fixed expenses			180,000
Net income			€ 245,000

The change in sales mix has resulted in a €245,000 actual net income rather than the €270,000 budgeted net income, an unfavourable difference of €25,000. The budgeted and actual sales in number of units were identical, but the proportion of sales of the product bearing the higher unit contribution margin declined.

Profitability of a given product helps guide executives who must decide to emphasise or deemphasise particular products. For example, given limited production facilities or limited time of sales personnel, should we emphasise wallets or key cases? Other factors beyond the contribution margin can affect these decisions. Chapter 5 explores some of these factors, including the importance of the amount of profit per unit of time rather than per unit of product.

Appendix 2B: Impact of income taxes

Objective 8
Compute cost–volume–profit relationships on an after-tax basis.

Thus far we have ignored income taxes. In most nations, however, private enterprises must pay income taxes. Reconsider the vending machine example in this chapter. As part of our CVP analysis, we discussed the sales necessary to achieve a target income before income taxes of €1,440. If income tax is payable at a rate of 40 per cent, the new result would be:

Income before income tax	€1,440	100%
Income tax	576	40
Net income	€ 864	60%

Note that

net income = income before income taxes − .40 (income before income taxes)

net income = .60 (income before income taxes)

income before income taxes

$$= \frac{\text{net income}}{.60}$$

or

$$\text{target income before income taxes} = \frac{\text{target after} - \text{tax net income}}{1 - \text{tax rate}}$$

$$\text{target income before income taxes} = \frac{€864}{1 - .40} = \frac{€864}{.60} = €1,440$$

Suppose the target net income after taxes was €864. The only change in the general equation approach would be on the right-hand side of the following equation:

$$\text{target sales} - \text{variable expenses} - \text{fixed expenses} = \frac{\text{target after-tax net income}}{1 - \text{tax rate}}$$

Thus, letting N be the number of units to be sold at €1.50 each with a variable cost of €1.20 each and total fixed costs of €18,000,

$$€1.50N - €1.20N - €18,000 = \frac{€864}{1 - .4}$$

$$€.30N = 18,000 + \frac{€864}{.6}$$

$$€.18N = €10,800 + €864 = 11,664$$

$$N = €11,664 ÷ €.18 = 64,800 \text{ units}$$

Sales of 64,800 units produce an after-tax profit of €864 as shown here and a before-tax profit of €1,440 as shown in the chapter.

Suppose the target net income after taxes was €1,440. The volume needed would rise to 68,000 units, as follows:

$$€1.50N - €1.20N - €18,000 = \frac{€1,440}{1 - .4}$$

$$€.30N = €18,000 + \frac{€1,440}{.6}$$

$$€.18N = €10,800 + €1,440 = 12,240$$

$$N = €12,240 ÷ €.18 = 68,000 \text{ units}$$

As a shortcut to computing the effects of volume on the change in after-tax income, use the formula:

$$\text{change in net income} \left(\begin{array}{c} \text{change in volume} \\ \text{in units} \end{array} \right) \times \left(\begin{array}{c} \text{contribution margin} \\ \text{per unit} \end{array} \right) \times (1 - \text{tax rate})$$

In our example, suppose operations were at a level of €64,800 units and €864 after-tax net income. The manager is wondering how much after-tax net income would increase if sales become 68,000 units:

$$\text{change in net income} = (68,000 - 64,800) \times €.30 \times (1 - .4)$$
$$= 3,200 \times €.30 \times €.60 = 3.200 \times €.18$$
$$= €576$$

In brief, each unit beyond the break-even point adds to after-tax net profit at the unit contribution margin multiplied by (1 – income tax rate).

Throughout our illustration, the break-even point itself does not change. Why? Because there is no income tax at a level of zero profits.

Accounting vocabulary

break-even point, p. 39
contribution margin, p. 40
contribution-margin
   percentage, p. 41
contribution-margin ratio, p 41
cost behaviour, p. 31
cost driver, p. 32
cost of goods sold, p. 52

cost–volume–profit (CVP)
   analysis, p. 39
fixed cost, p. 33
gross margin, p. 52
gross profit, p. 52
incremental effect, p. 46
margin of safety, p. 51
marginal income, p. 40

operating leverage, p. 51
relevant range, p. 37
sales mix, p. 44
total contribution margin, p. 41
unit contribution margin, p. 40
variable cost, p. 33
variable-cost percentage, p. 41
variable-cost ratio, p. 41

Fundamental assignment material   MyAccountingLab

2.A1 Fixed- and variable-cost behaviour

Consider a particular Boeing plant. Maintaining a clean working environment is important to Boeing. Cleaning the plant is the responsibility of the maintenance department. Two of the resources needed to clean the plant are labour and cleaning supplies. The cost driver for both resources is square feet cleaned. Plant cleaning labourers are paid the same wages regardless of the number of times the plant is cleaned. Cleaning supplies is a variable cost. The 40,000 square foot plant is thoroughly cleaned from four to eight times a month depending on the level and stage of production. For the most recent month, March, the plant was cleaned four times. The March cost of labour was $24,000 and cleaning supplies used cost $9,600. The production schedule for the next quarter (April through June) indicates that the plant will need to be cleaned five, six and eight times respectively.

1 Prepare a table that shows how labour cost, cleaning supplies cost, total cost and total cost per square feet cleaned changes in response to the square feet cleaned. What is the predicted total cost of plant cleaning for the next quarter?
2 Suppose Boeing can hire an outside cleaning company to clean the plant as needed. The charge rate for cleaning is $5,900 per plant cleaning. If the outside cleaning company is hired, Boeing can lay off the workers who are now cleaning the plant and will spend nothing for cleaning supplies. Will Boeing save money with the outside cleaning company over the next quarter? Prepare a schedule that supports your answer.

2.A2 Cost–volume–profit and vending machines

Enriquez Food Services Company operates and services snack vending machines located in restaurants, gas stations and factories in four southwestern states. The machines are rented from the manufacturer. In addition, Enriquez must rent the space occupied by its machines.

The following expense and revenue relationships pertain to a contemplated expansion programme of 40 machines.

Fixed monthly expenses follow:

Machine rental: 40 machines @ €53.50	€2,140
Space rental: 40 locations @ €38.80	1,552
Part-time wages to service the additional 40 machines	2,008
Other fixed costs	300
Total monthly fixed costs	€6,000

Other data follow:

	Per unit (snack)	Per €100 of sales
Selling price	€1.00	100%
Cost of snack	.80	80
Contribution margin	€ .20	20%

These questions relate to the given data unless otherwise noted. Consider each question independently.

1 What is the monthly break-even point in number of units (snacks)? In euro sales?
2 If 40,000 units were sold, what would be the company's net income?
3 If the space rental cost was doubled, what would be the monthly break-even point in number of units? In euro sales?
4 Refer to the original data. If, in addition to the fixed space rent, Enriquez Food Services Company paid the vending machine manufacturer €.02 per unit sold, what would be the monthly break-even point in number of units? In euro sales?
5 Refer to the original data. If, in addition to the fixed rent, Enriquez paid the machine manufacturer €.05 for each unit sold in excess of the break-even point, what would the new net income be if 40,000 units were sold?

2.A3 Exercises in cost–volume–profit relationships

Barkins Moving Company specialises in hauling heavy goods over long distances. The company's revenues and expenses depend on revenue-miles, a measure that combines both weights and distance. Summarised budget data for next year are based on predicted total revenue miles of 800,000. At that level of volume, and at any level of volume between 700,000 and 900,000 revenue kilometres, the company's fixed costs are €120,000. The selling price and variable costs are:

Per revenue-kilometre	
Average selling price (revenue)	€1.50
Average variable expenses	1.30

1 Compute the budgeted net income. Ignore income taxes.
2 Management is trying to decide how various possible conditions or decisions might affect net income. Compute the new net income for each of the following changes. Consider each case independently.

(a) A 10 per cent increase in sales price.
(b) A 10 per cent increase in revenue miles.
(c) A 10 per cent increase in variable expenses.
(d) A 10 per cent increase in fixed expenses.
(e) An average decrease in selling price of €.03 per revenue mile and a 5 per cent increase in revenue miles. Refer to the original data.
(f) An average increase in selling price of €.05 and a 10 per cent decrease in revenue kilometres.
(g) A 10 per cent increase in fixed expenses in the form of more advertising and a 5 per cent increase in revenue miles.

2.B1 Fixed- and variable-cost behaviour

Outback Steakhouse has 970 restaurants offering steak, chicken and seafood served in an Australian-themed atmosphere. Maintaining a clean environment for customers is a key success factor at Outback. Each restaurant is cleaned regularly after closing. In addition to regular cleaning, from 5 to 20 times a month, depending on various factors including the amount of business, a special treatment is given to the floors consisting of breaking down the old wax and rewaxing. So the total number of times a restaurant is cleaned varies from 35 to 50 times a month.

The two most costly resources needed to clean an Outback restaurant are labour and supplies. The cost driver for both resources is square metres cleaned. Cleaning labourers are paid the same wages regardless of the number of times a restaurant is cleaned. Cleaning supplies is a variable cost. The cost of supplies used per square metre for regular and special cleaning is about the same. Suppose one of the local Outback restaurants in Milan has 5,000 square metres. In October, the restaurant was cleaned 35 times. The cost of cleaning labour was €30,000 for October and cleaning supplies cost €10,500. The months of November and December are typically much busier, so the restaurant manager expects to clean 45 times and 50 times in November and December, respectively.

1 Prepare a table that shows how labour cost, cleaning supplies cost, total cost and total cost per square metres cleaned changes in response to square metres cleaned. Use volumes of 35, 40, 45 and 50 times cleaned. What is the predicted total cost of cleaning for November and December?

2 Suppose Outback can hire an outside cleaning company to clean the restaurant as needed. The charge rate for cleaning is €.20 per square metre. If the outside cleaning company is hired, Outback can lay off the workers who are now cleaning and will spend nothing on cleaning supplies. Will Outback save money with the outside cleaning company over the next two months? Prepare a schedule that supports your answer. What information would you need to make a recommendation about hiring the outside cleaning company on a permanent basis?

2.B2 Cost–volume–profit at a day care facility

Beth Durham opened Beth's Corner, a small day care facility, just over two years ago. After a rocky start, Beth's Corner has been thriving. Durham is now preparing a budget for November 20X7.

Monthly fixed costs for Beth's Corner are:

Rent	£ 800
Salaries	1,400
Other fixed costs	100
Total fixed costs	£2,300

The salary is for Ann Page, the only employee, who works with Durham by caring for the children. Durham does not pay herself a salary, but she receives the excess of revenues over costs each month.

The cost driver for variable costs is 'child-days'. One child-day is one day in day care for one child, and the variable cost is £10 per child-day. The facility is open from 6:00 am to 6:00 pm week-days (that is, Monday–Friday) and there are 22 weekdays in November 20X7. An average day has 8 children attending Beth's Corner. State law prohibits Beth's Corner from having more than 14 children, a limit it has never reached. Durham charges £30 per day per child, regardless of how long the child is at the facility.

1 What is the break-even point for November in child-days? In revenue money?
2 Suppose attendance for November 20X7 is equal to the average, resulting in $22 \times 8 = 176$ child-days. What amount will Durham have left after paying all her expenses?
3 Suppose both costs and attendance are difficult to predict. Compute the amount Durham will have left after paying all her expenses for each of the following situations. Consider each case independently.
  (a) Average attendance is 9 children per day instead of 8, generating 198 child-days.
  (b) Variable costs increase to £12 per child-day.
  (c) Rent increases by £220 per month.
  (d) Durham spends £300 on advertising (a fixed cost) in November, which increases average daily attendance to 9.5 children.
  (e) Durham begins charging £33 per day on November 1 and average daily attendance slips to 7 children.

2.B3 Exercises in cost–volume–profit relationships

Each problem is unrelated to the others.

1 Given: Selling price per unit, €20; total fixed expenses, €5,000; variable expenses per unit, €16. Find break-even sales in units.
2 Given: Sales, €40,000; variable expenses, €30,000; fixed expenses, €8,000; net income, €2,000. Find break-even sales in euros.
3 Given: Selling price per unit, €30; total fixed expenses, €33,000; variable expenses per unit, €14. Find total sales in units to achieve a profit of €7,000, assuming no change in selling price.
4 Given: Sales, €50,000; variable expenses, €20,000; fixed expenses, €20,000; net income, €10,000. Assume no change in selling price; find net income if activity volume increases by 10%.
5 Given: Selling price per unit, €40; total fixed expenses, €80,000; variable expenses per unit, €30. Assume that variable expenses are reduced by 20% per unit and the total fixed expenses are increased by 10%. Find the sales in units to achieve a profit of €20,000, assuming no change in selling price.

Additional assignment material   MyAccountingLab

QUESTIONS

2.1 'Cost behaviour is simply identification of cost drivers and their relationships to costs.' Comment.

2.2 Give two rules of thumb to use when analysing cost behaviour.

2.3 Give three examples of variable costs and of fixed costs.

2.4 Why is the word *immediately* used in the definition of *fixed cost* and not in the definition of *variable cost*?

2.5 'It is confusing to think of fixed costs on a per-unit basis.' Do you agree? Why or why not?

2.6 'All costs are either fixed or variable. The only difficulty in cost analysis is determining which of the two categories each cost belongs to.' Do you agree? Explain.

2.7 'The relevant range pertains to fixed costs, not variable costs.' Do you agree? Explain.

2.8 Identify the major simplifying assumption that underlies CVP analysis.

2.9 'Classification of costs into variable and fixed categories depends on the decision situation.' Explain.

2.10 'Contribution margin is the excess of sales over fixed costs.' Do you agree? Explain.

2.11 Why is *break-even analysis* a misnomer?

2.12 'Companies in the same industry generally have about the same break-even point.' Do you agree? Explain.

2.13 'It is essential to choose the right CVP method – equation, contribution margin, or graphical. If you pick the wrong one, your analysis will be faulty.' Do you agree? Explain.

2.14 Describe three ways of lowering a break-even point.

2.15 'Incremental analysis is quicker, but it has no other advantage over an analysis of all costs and revenues associated with each alternative.' Do you agree? Why or why not?

2.16 Define operating leverage and explain why a highly leveraged company may be risky.

2.17 Suppose a company with high operating leverage is also operating at near capacity for all its fixed-cost resources. How could an increase in sales volume result in decreasing economies of scale for this company?

2.18 What is the relationship between the margin of safety and the break-even point?

2.19 'The contribution margin and gross margin are always equal.' Do you agree? Explain.

2.20 'CVP relationships are unimportant in nonprofit organisations.' Do you agree? Explain.

2.21 Study Appendix 2A. A company sold two products. Total budgeted sales and total actual sales in number of units were identical. Actual unit variable costs and sales prices were the same as budgeted. Actual contribution margin was lower than budgeted. What could be the reason for the lower contribution margin?

2.22 Study Appendix 2B. Given a target after-tax net income, present the CVP formula for computing the income before income taxes.

2.23 Study Appendix 2B. Present the CVP formula for computing the effects of a change in volume on after-tax income.

CRITICAL THINKING EXERCISES

2.24 Marketing function of value-chain and cost behaviour

Refer to Exhibit 2.2. For the two examples of marketing costs given in Exhibit 2.2, describe their cost behaviour in relation to the cost driver listed.

2.25 Production function of value-chain and cost behaviour

Refer to Exhibit 2.2. For the labour wages and depreciation of plant and machinery examples of production costs given in Exhibit 2.2, describe their cost behaviour in relation to the cost driver listed.

EXERCISES

2.26 Identifying cost drivers

The following list identifies several potential cost drivers for a manufacturing company that makes eight products. The company uses a JIT production system so it stores finished product for a very limited time. The eight products vary substantially in size from small (plastic casings for pens) to large (plastic casings for truck instrument panels). The company uses order-processing labour to process all orders from customers.

- Number of setups
- Setup time
- Square feet
- Cubic feet
- Cubic feet weeks
- Number of orders
- Number or order line items.

For each of the following situations (activity and related resource), identify the best cost driver from the list and briefly justify your choice.

1 To produce a product, production mechanics must set up machinery. It takes about the same time to set up for a production run regardless of the product being produced. What is the best cost driver for the resources used during the setup activity?
2 Instead of the situation described in number 1, what driver should the company use for the setup activity if it takes longer to set up for complex products, such as the instrument panel casings, than for simple products, such as pen casings?
3 What driver should the company use for warehouse occupancy costs (depreciation and insurance)? The company uses the warehouse to store finished products.
4 What driver should the company use for the warehouse occupancy costs if it did not use a JIT system (that is, the company maintains inventories) and, upon inspection, one of the products had a thick layer of dust on it?
5 What driver should the company use for order processing cost? All orders are similar in terms of types of products ordered and it takes about the same time to process each type of product.
6 What driver should the company use for order processing cost if orders vary substantially in terms of types of products ordered and it takes about the same time to process each type of product?

2.27 Basic review exercises

Fill in the blanks for each of the following independent cases (ignore income taxes):

	Sales	Variable expenses	Contribution margin	Fixed expenses	Net income
1	€900,000	€500,000	€ —	€330,000	€ —
2	800,000	—	350,000	—	80,000
3	—	600,000	360,000	250,000	—

2.28 Variable- and fixed-cost behaviour

Refer to Exhibits 2.2 and 2.4 on p. 33 and 34. Part of a company's marketing function is as described in Exhibit 2.2. Two of the many marketing-function activities are advertising and selling. The annual cost behaviour of the resources used to perform the advertising activity is depicted in the diagram below using the same symbolic structure as defined in Exhibit 2.4. Which of the two costs is fixed? Which cost is variable? What is the total cost of advertising if the number of advertisements is 50? 100? Does the total cost of advertising double in response to a doubling of the cost driver level? Why or why not?

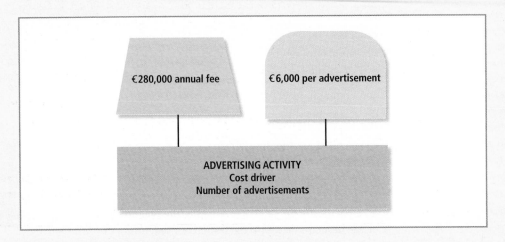

2.29 Basic review exercises

Fill in the blanks for each of the following independent cases:

Case	(a) Selling price per unit	(b) Variable cost per unit	(c) Total units sold	(d) Total contribution margin	(e) Total fixed costs	(f) Net income
1	€25	€—	120,000	€720,000	€650,000	€ —
2	10	6	100,000	—	320,000	—
3	20	15	—	100,000	—	15,000
4	30	20	60,000	—	—	12,000
5	—	9	80,000	160,000	110,000	—

2.30 Basic cost–volume–profit graph

Refer to Exercise 2.29. Construct a cost–volume–profit graph for Case 2 that depicts the total revenue, total variable cost, total fixed cost and total cost lines. Estimate the break-even point in total units sold and the net income for 100,000 units sold.

2.31 Basic cost–volume–profit graph

Refer to Exercise 2.29. Construct a cost–volume–profit graph for Case 4 that depicts the total revenue, total variable cost, total fixed cost and total cost lines. Estimate the break-even point in total units sold and the net income (loss) for 50,000 units sold.

2.32 Basic cost–volume graphs

From the following two graphs, construct two graphs that depict the cost behaviour on a per-driver-unit basis. Which of the two constructed graphs show fixed-cost behaviour? Variable-cost behaviour?

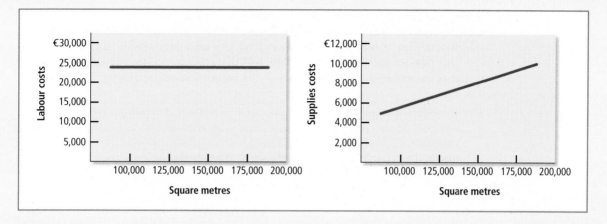

2.33 Basic cost–volume graphs

From the following two graphs, construct two graphs that depict the cost behaviour on a total cost basis. Which of the two constructed graphs show fixed-cost behaviour? Variable-cost behaviour?

2.34 Hospital costs and pricing

St Martin Hospital has overall variable costs of 20 per cent of total revenue and fixed costs of €40 million per year.

1 Compute the break-even point expressed in total revenue.
2 A patient-day is often used to measure the volume of a hospital. Suppose there are to be 40,000 patient-days next year. Compute the average daily revenue per patient-day necessary to break even.

2.35 Cost–volume–profit at a hospital

Children's Hospital predicts variable costs of 70 per cent of total revenue and fixed costs of £42 million per year for 2011.

1 Compute the break-even point expressed in total revenue.
2 In 2011 Children's Hospital expects total revenue of £150 million from 200,000 patient days. Compute (a) expected profit for 2011 if costs behave as expected, and (b) total profit if variable costs in 2011 are 10 per cent greater than predicted.

2.36 Variable cost to break even

General Mills makes Nature Valley granola bars, Cheerios cereal, Yoplait yogurt, Häagen-Dazs ice cream and many other food products. Suppose the product manager of a new General Mills cereal has determined that the appropriate wholesale price for a carton of the cereal is $48. Fixed costs of the production and marketing of the cereal is $19 million.

1 The product manager estimates that she can sell 800,000 cartons at the $48 price. What is the largest variable cost per carton that General Mills can pay and still achieve a profit of $1 million?
2 Suppose the variable cost is $25 per carton. What profit (or loss) would General Mills expect?

2.37 Income taxes

Review the illustration in Appendix 2B. Suppose the income tax rate were 25 per cent instead of 40 per cent. How many units would the company have to sell to achieve a target after-tax net income of (a) $864 and (b) $1,440? Show your computations.

2.38 Income taxes and cost–volume–profit analysis

Study Appendix 2B. Suppose Hernandez Construction Company has a 30% income tax rate, a contribution-margin ratio of 25 per cent and fixed costs of €440,000. What sales volume is necessary to achieve an after-tax income of €84,000?

PROBLEMS

2.39 Joe's Pub, cost–volume–profit analysis in a small business

Joe Bell recently opened Joe's Pub in the University District. Because of licensing restrictions, the only alcohol he can sell is beer. The average price of beer at Joe's Pub is €3.00 per glass and each glass costs Joe an average of €2.20. Joe has hired a bartender and waiter at €3,000 and €2,000 per month, respectively. His rent, utilities and other fixed operating costs are €5,000 per month.

Joe is considering selling burgers during the lunch hour. He feels that this will increase his daytime business, which is currently quite small. It will also allow him to be more competitive with other local bars that offer a wider variety of food and drinks.

Joe would like to sell the burgers for €1.25 each in order to be attractive to customers. Joe will buy buns for €1.20 a dozen and ground beef for €2.80 per pound. Each pound of ground beef will make seven burgers. Other ingredients will cost an average of €.20 per burger. Joe will also need to hire a part-time cook at €1,200 per month. Other additional fixed costs will run about €360 a month.

1 If Joe sells only beer, how many glasses of beer does he have to sell each month to make a monthly profit of €2,000?
2 If Joe sells only beer, how many glasses of beer does he have to sell each month to make a monthly profit of 5 per cent of sales?
3 Suppose Joe decides to add burgers to his menu. How many does he need to sell to break even on the burgers? Assume that there is no effect on beer sales.
4 The main reason Joe wanted to add burgers was to attract more customers. Suppose that 2,000 extra customers per month came for lunch because of the availability of burgers and that each bought an average of 1.5 beers. Compute the added profit (or loss) generated by these extra customers.

5 Joe was not sure how many new customers would be attracted by the burgers. Give Joe some advice about how many new customers would be needed to just break even on the new business if each new customer bought one burger and one beer. Include an assessment of the consequences of volume falling below or above this break-even point.
6 Joe could offer a higher quality burger if he spends 50 per cent more on the ingredients. He could then charge €2.00 for them. Explain how Joe could determine whether the higher quality burgers would be more profitable than the regular burgers.

2.40 Fixed costs and relevant range

Bridger Canyon Systems Group (BCSG) has a substantial year-to-year fluctuation in billings to clients. Top management has the following policy regarding the employment of key professional personnel:

If gross annual billings are	Number of persons to be employed	Key professional annual salaries
€2,000,000 or less	10	€1,000,000
€2,000,001–2,400,000	11	€1,100,000
€2,400,001–2,800,000	12	€1,200,000

Top management believes that the group should maintain a minimum of 10 individuals for a year or more even if billings drop drastically below €2 million.

For the past 5 years, gross annual billings for BCSG have fluctuated between €2,020,000 and €2,380,000. Expectations for next year are that gross billings will be between €2,100,000 and €2,300,000. What amount should the group budget for key professional personnel salaries? Graph the relationships on an annual basis, using the two approaches illustrated in Exhibit 2.6 on p. 38. Indicate the relevant range on each graph. You need not use graph paper; simply approximate the graphical relationships.

2.41 Comparing contribution margin percentages

Following are actual statements of operating income for Microsoft and Procter & Gamble (in millions):

Microsoft		Procter & Gamble	
Revenues	$60,420	Net sales	$83,503
Cost of revenue	11,598	Cost of products sold	40,695
Research and development	8,164	Selling, general and administrative expenses	25,725
Sales and Marketing	13,039		
General and administrative	5,127	Operating income	$17,083
Operating income	$22,492		

Assume that the only variable cost for Microsoft is 'cost of revenue' and for Procter & Gamble it is 'cost of products sold'.

1 Compute the contribution-margin percentage of Microsoft and that of Procter & Gamble. Why do you suppose the percentages are so different?
2 Suppose each company increases its revenue by $10 million. Compute the increase in operating income for each company.

3 Explain how the contribution margin percentage helps you predict the effects on operating income of changes in sales volume. What assumptions do you make in forming such a prediction?

2.42 Promotion of a rock concert

BBT Productions Ltd, is promoting a rock concert in London. The bands will receive a flat fee of £7 million in cash. The concert will be shown worldwide on closed-circuit television. BBT will collect 100 per cent of the receipts and will return 30 per cent to the individual local closed-circuit theatre managers. BBT expects to sell 1.1 million seats at a net average price of £13 each. BBT will also receive £300,000 from the London arena (which has sold out its 19,500 seats, ranging from £150 for box seats to £20 for general admission, for a gross revenue of £1.25 million); BBT will not share the £300,000 with the local promoters.

1 The general manager of BBT Productions is trying to decide what amount to spend for advertising. What is the most BBT could spend and still break even on overall operations, assuming sales of 1.1 million tickets?

2 If BBT desires an operating income of £500,000, how many seats would it have to sell? Assume that the average price is £13 and the total fixed costs (including £2,000,000 in advertising) are £9 million.

2.43 Basic relationships, restaurant

Jacqui Giraud owns and operates a restaurant. Her fixed costs are €21,000 per month. She serves luncheons and dinners. The average total bill (excluding tax and tip) is €19 per customer. Giraud's present variable costs average €10.60 per meal.

1 How many meals must she serve to attain a profit before taxes of €8,400 per month?

2 What is the break-even point in number of meals served per month?

3 Giraud's rent and other fixed costs rise to a total of €29,925 per month and variable costs also rise to €12.50 per meal. If Giraud increases her average price to €23, how many meals must she serve to make €8,400 profit per month?

4 Assume the same situation described in requirement 3. Giraud's accountant tells her she may lose 10% of her customers if she increases her prices. If this should happen, what would be Giraud's profit per month? Assume that the restaurant had been serving 3,500 customers per month.

5 Assume the same situation described in requirement 4. To help offset the anticipated 10% loss of customers, Giraud hires a pianist to perform for 4 hours each night for €2,000 per month. Assume that this would increase the total monthly meals from 3,150 to 3,450. Would Giraud's total profit change? By how much?

2.44 Changing fixed costs to variable costs at Blockbuster Video

According to an article in *Business Week*, when John F. Antioco took charge of Blockbuster Video he changed the company's strategy. Traditionally, Blockbuster had bought videotapes from the movie studios for an average cost of about $65 each, planning to rent them out often enough to make a profit. Mr Antioco replaced this strategy with one that allows Blockbuster to purchase videos for an average of $7 per tape and pay the studio 40 per cent of any rental fee received for the tape. With this arrangement, Blockbuster can afford to stock more copies of each tape and guarantee customers that the tape they want will be in stock – or the rental is free. Suppose that Blockbuster rents videotapes for $2 a day. Assume that operating costs are all fixed.

1 Under the traditional strategy, how many days must each tape be rented before Blockbuster will break even on the tape?

2 Under the new strategy, how many days must each tape be rented before Blockbuster will break even on the tape?

3 Suppose customers rented a particular copy of *Babel* for 50 days. What profit would Blockbuster make on rentals of the tape (considering only the direct costs of the tape, not the costs of operating the rental store) under the traditional strategy? Under the new strategy?

4 Suppose customers rented a particular copy of *The Departed* for only 6 days. What profit would Blockbuster make on rentals of the tape (considering only the direct costs of the tape, not the costs of operating the rental store) under the traditional strategy? Under the new strategy?

5 Comment on how the new arrangement affects the risks Blockbuster accepts when purchasing an additional copy of a particular videotape.

2.45 CVP and financial statements for a mega-brand company

Procter & Gamble Company is a Cincinnati-based company that produces household products under brand names such as Gillette, Bounty, Crest, Folgers and Tide. The company's 2008 income statement showed the following (in millions):

Net sales	$83,503
Costs of products sold	40,695
Selling, general and administrative expense	25,725
Operating income	$17,083

Suppose that the cost of products sold is the only variable cost; selling, general and administrative expenses are fixed with respect to sales.

Assume that Procter & Gamble had a 20 per cent decrease in sales in 2009 and that there was no change in costs except for decreases associated with the lower volume of sales. Compute the predicted 2009 operating income for Procter & Gamble and its percentage decrease. Explain why the percentage decrease in income differs from the percentage decrease in sales.

2.46 Bingo and leverage

Many churches sponsor bingo games, a tradition stemming from the time when only specific nonprofit institutions were allowed to sponsor games of chance. Reverend Justin Olds, the pastor of a new parish in Orange County, is investigating the desirability of conducting weekly bingo nights. The parish has no hall, but a local hotel would be willing to commit its hall for a lump-sum rental of €600 per night. The rent would include cleaning, setting up and taking down the tables and chairs and so on.

1 A local printer would provide bingo cards in return for free advertising. Local merchants would donate door prizes. The services of clerks, callers, security force and others would be donated by volunteers. Admission would be €4.00 per person, entitling the player to one card; extra cards would be €1.50 each. Many persons buy extra cards so there would be an average of four cards played per person. What is the maximum in total cash prizes that the church may award and still break even if 200 persons attend each weekly session?

2 Suppose the total cash prizes are €1,100. What will be the church's operating income if 100 persons attend? If 200 persons attend? If 300 persons attend? Briefly explain the effects of the cost behaviour on income.

3 After operating for 10 months, Reverend Olds is thinking of negotiating a different rental arrangement but keeping the prize money unchanged at €1,100. Suppose the

rent is €200 per night plus €2 per person. Compute the operating income for attendance of 100, 200 and 300 persons, respectively. Explain why the results differ from those in requirement 2.

2.47 Choosing equipment for different volumes

MetroCinemas owns and operates a nationwide chain of cinemas. The 500 properties in the chain vary from low-volume, small-town, single-screen cinemas to high-volume, big-city, multiscreen cinemas.

The management is considering installing machines that will make popcorn on the premises. These machines would allow the cinemas to sell freshly popped popcorn rather than the prepopped, prebagged corn that it currently sells. This proposed feature would be properly advertised and is intended to increase patronage at the company's cinemas.

The machines can be purchased in several different sizes. The annual rental costs and operating costs vary with the size of the machines. The machine capacities and costs are as follows:

	Popper model		
	Standard	**Deluxe**	**Jumbo**
Annual capacity	50,000 boxes	120,000 boxes	300,000 boxes
Costs			
Annual machine rental	£7,840	£11,200	£20,200
Popcorn cost per box	.14	.14	.14
Cost of each box	.09	.09	.09
Other variable costs per box	.22	.14	.05

1 Calculate the volume level in boxes at which the standard and deluxe poppers would earn the same operating profit (loss).
2 The management can estimate the number of boxes to be sold at each of its cinemas. Present a decision rule that would enable MetroCinemas management to select the most profitable machine without having to make a separate cost calculation for each cinema. That is, at what anticipated range of unit sales should the cinema use the standard model? The deluxe model? The jumbo model?
3 Could the management use the average number of boxes sold per seat for the entire chain and the capacity of each cinema to develop this decision rule? Explain your answer.

2.48 Sales compensation, variable/fixed costs and ethics

Most companies compensate their sales forces with a combination of a fixed salary and a commission that is a percentage of sales. Consider two companies competing for the same customers – for example, Kellogg's and Post cereals. Suppose that Kellogg's pays its sales force a large fixed salary and a small commission, while Post pays its sales force a small fixed salary and a large commission. The total pay on average was the same for both companies.

1 Compare the sales cost structure of Kellogg's with that of Post. Which has the larger fixed cost? Which has the larger variable cost? How will this affect each company's risk? (Focus on how the company's profits change with changes in volume.)
2 What incentives does each pay system provide for the sales force?
3 Might either incentive system create potential ethical dilemmas for the sales personnel? Explain.

2.49 Hospital patient mix

Study Appendix 2A. Hospitals measure their volume in terms of patient-days. We calculate patient-days by multiplying the number of patients by the number of days that the patients are hospitalised. Suppose a large hospital has fixed costs of €54 million per year and variable costs of €600 per patient-day. Daily revenues vary among classes of patients. For simplicity, assume that there are two classes: (1) self-pay patients (S) who pay an average of €1,000 per day and (2) non-self-pay patients (G) who are the responsibility of insurance companies and government agencies and who pay an average of €800 per day. Twenty per cent of the patients are self-pay.

1 Compute the break-even point in patient-days, assuming that the hospital maintains its planned mix of patients.
2 Suppose that the hospital achieves 225,000 patient-days but that 25 per cent of the patient-days were self-pay (instead of 20 per cent). Compute the net income. Compute the break-even point.

2.50 Income Taxes on Hotels

Study Appendix 2B. The Four Winds Hotel in downtown Lisbon has annual fixed costs applicable to rooms of €9.2 million for its 600-room hotel, average daily room rates of €105 and average variable costs of €25 daily for each room rented. It operates 365 days per year. The hotel is subject to an income tax rate of 40 per cent.

1 How many rooms must the hotel rent to earn a net income after taxes of €720,000? ~~Of €360,000?~~
2 Compute the break-even point in number of rooms rented. What percentage occupancy for the year is needed to break even?
3 Assume that the volume level of rooms sold is 150,000. The manager is wondering how much income could be generated by adding sales of 15,000 rooms. Compute the additional net income after taxes.

CASES

2.51 Hospital costs

Gother City Hospital is unionised. In 20X6, nurses received an average annual salary of €45,000. The hospital administrator is considering changes in the contract with nurses for 20X7. In turn, the hospital may also change the way it charges nursing costs to each department.

The hospital holds each department accountable for its financial performance and it allocates revenues and expenses to departments. Consider the expenses of the obstetrics department in 20X6.

Variable expenses (based on 20X6 patient-days) are:

Meals	€ 610,000
Laundry	260,000
Laboratory	900,000
Pharmacy	850,000
Maintenance	150,000
Other	530,000
Total	€3,300,000

Fixed expenses (based on number of beds) are:

Rent	€3,000,000
General administrative services	2,200,000
Janitorial	200,000
Maintenance	150,000
Other	350,000
Total	€5,900,000

Management assigns nurses to departments on the basis of annual patient-days as follows:

Volume level in patient-days	Number of nurses
10,000–12,000	30
12,001–16,000	35

Total patient-days are the number of patients multiplied by the number of days they are hospitalised. The hospital charges each department for the salaries of the nurses assigned to it.

During 20X6, the obstetrics department had a capacity of 60 beds, billed each patient an average of €810 per day and had revenues of €12.15 million.

1 Compute the 20X6 volume of activity in patient-days.
2 Compute the 20X6 patient-days that would have been necessary for the obstetrics department to recoup all fixed expenses except nursing expenses.
3 Compute the 20X6 patient-days that would have been necessary for the obstetrics department to break even including nurses' salaries as a fixed cost.
4 Suppose obstetrics must pay €200 per patient-day for nursing services. This plan would replace the two-level, fixed-cost system employed in 20X6. Compute what the break-even point in patient-days would have been in 20X6 under this plan.

2.52 CVP in a modern manufacturing environment

A division of Hewlett-Packard Company changed its production operations from one where a large labour force assembled electronic components to an automated production facility dominated by computer-controlled robots. The change was necessary because of fierce competitive pressures. Improvements in quality, reliability and flexibility of production schedules were necessary just to match the competition. As a result of the change, variable costs fell and fixed costs increased, as shown in the following assumed budgets:

	Old production operation	New production operation
Unit variable cost		
Material	€ .88	€ .88
Labour	1.22	.22
Total per unit	€ 2.10	€ 1.10
Monthly fixed costs		
Rent and depreciation	€450,000	€ 875,000
Supervisory labour	80,000	175,000
Other	50,000	90,000
Total per month	€580,000	€1,140,000

Expected volume is 600,000 units per month, with each unit selling for €3.10. Capacity is 800,000 units.

1 Compute the budgeted profit at the expected volume of 600,000 units under both the old and the new production environments.
2 Compute the budgeted break-even point under both the old and the new production environments.
3 Discuss the effect on profits if volume falls to 500,000 units under both the old and the new production environments.
4 Discuss the effect on profits if volume increases to 700,000 units under both the old and the new production environments.
5 Comment on the riskiness of the new operation versus the old operation.

2.53 Multiproduct break even in a restaurant

Study Appendix 2A. La Brasserie is a French restaurant in Nice. A simplified version of its income statement follows:

Revenues	€2,098,400
Cost of sales, all variable	1,246,500
Gross profit	851,900
Operating expenses	
Variable	222,380
Fixed	170,940
Administrative expenses, all fixed	451,500
Net income	€ 7,080

The average dinner tab at La Brasserie is €40 and the average lunch tab is €20. Assume that the variable cost of preparing and serving dinner is also twice that of a lunch. The restaurant serves twice as many lunches as dinners. Assume that the restaurant is open 305 days a year.

1 Compute the daily break-even volume in lunches and dinners for La Brasserie. Compare this to the actual volume reflected in the income statement.

2 Suppose that an extra annual advertising expenditure of €15,000 would increase the average daily volume by three dinners and six lunches, and that there is plenty of capacity to accommodate the extra business. Prepare an analysis for the management of La Brasserie, explaining whether this would be desirable.

3 La Brasserie uses only premium food and the cost of food makes up 25 per cent of the restaurant's total variable costs. Use of average rather than premium ingredients could cut the food cost by 20 per cent. Assume that La Brasserie uses average-quality ingredients and does not change its prices. How much of a drop-off in volume could it endure and still maintain the same net income? What factors in addition to revenue and costs would influence the decision about the quality of food to use?

CASE STUDY

Electronic Boards plc
John Innes and Falconer Mitchell, University of Edinburgh
This is a general case on the design of a management and cost accounting system for a firm operating in a high-tech environment. It provides an opportunity for a broad discussion not only

of the appropriateness of particular accounting techniques but also of the need to consider strategic, behavioural and organisational factors.

Introduction

Jack Watson, an electrical engineer, established Electronic Boards plc as a 'one-man' company in the early 1980s. From small beginnings, the company earned a reputation for the quality and reliability of its products and grew rapidly and consistently until, by 2011, it employed over 200 people and had achieved a turnover of £56 million and a profit after tax of £4.1 million. In addition to Jack Watson, the managing director, the board consists of a production director, a research director and a marketing director.

Market circumstances

The company produces customised batches of electronic circuit boards for approximately 15 major customers in the defence, computer, electrical goods and automotive industries. The market is highly competitive in respect of both price and quality. Market price has fallen steadily in recent years. In addition to several other independent firms both from the UK and Far East, many of their larger customers have in-house facilities for the production of circuit boards. These latter firms deliberately subcontract a portion of their circuit board requirements for strategic reasons. In a recession they can cease or reduce their subcontracting and bring the work in-house, so stabilising their own employment levels.

Operational circumstances

The production process for circuit boards is complex, multi-stage and highly automated. Production flows continuously through the various processes and any hold-up quickly affects the flow of work at all production stages. Experience has shown that a proportion of the final output contains faults and has to be scrapped. These scrap levels typically vary between 10 per cent and 25 per cent of good output, a considerable learning effect is apparent and the yield on repeat orders is usually significantly improved. At present, faulty products are identified only on completion, although action has been instigated (in the form of an investigative working party) to achieve an earlier identification of faults.

Orders are obtained in three ways:

1 By written tender for large contracts (approximately 40 per cent of business).

2 By telephone quotation for small orders (approximately 20 per cent of business) – a price is normally quoted to the caller during the call.

3 By repeat orders (approximately 40 per cent of business).

Prices are calculated by estimating the direct material cost of an order and adding on an allowance for all other costs and profit. This allowance is based on the previous year's direct material cost to sales margin. In recent years the cost structure of the firm's output has been as follows:

Cost structure of current boards	
Direct materials	65%
Direct labour	5
Production overheads	20
Non-production overheads	10
	100%

Source: Innes, J. and Mitchell, F. (1988) 'Electronic Boards plc', in D. Otley, D. Brown and C. Wilkinson (eds) *Case Studies in Management Accounting* (Hemel Hempstead, UK: Philip Allan Publishers). Reproduced with permission.

Direct materials are by far the major cost component and this importance is reflected in the high levels of materials stock which are held by the company.

Financial information

It is generally accepted by the senior members of management that the development of a management accounting system has been neglected. This has been attributed mainly to the dismissive attitude of line management to accountants. Encapsulating this view was the comment of one senior manager, 'they are "bean-counters" who know nothing about the electronics industry, the problems we face and the decisions we have to take'. The consistent success of the company in the absence of any management accounting system has reinforced this type of attitude among managers and directors in the company. No qualified accountants have been appointed to the board, and until 2010 only one qualified accountant was employed by the company. His prime responsibility was the preparation of statutory financial accounting statements for shareholders. In addition, however, since 2008 a half-yearly company profit and loss account and balance sheet has been prepared for the board.

No product costing system has been in operation. For financial statement preparation, work in progress is simply valued at an estimate of its direct material content cost and finished goods stock is valued at a discounted selling price (using the previous year's gross profit percentage). However, some managers have complained about their lack of knowledge of unit production costs and about their inability to pinpoint which contracts or types of work have been profitable for the company.

Budgets are no longer prepared. Attempts were made to produce annual budgets in 2006 and 2007 but the firm's accountant experienced great difficulty in obtaining reliable estimates from line management. His lack of authority within the firm and the absence of a finance director to provide support rendered his requests for information ineffective. Consequently, acceptance of the budgets which he prepared was not forthcoming. They were quickly viewed as unrealistic by management and after a few months ignored.

Capital budgeting decisions have been based upon the need for the firm to remain at the forefront of production technology. If new equipment became available which would improve the firm's product quality, it was usually purchased and then funds were 'found' to finance it. This had often led to the company having unexpected overdrafts and high bank charges and interest expenses.

Recession

In 2011 the firm experienced its first recession. Market share fell, sales dropped to £21.5 million, a loss of £1.7 million was made and the company's liquidity suffered considerably. The market decline was expected to continue in 2012 and the managing director of Electronic Boards plc sought ways of alleviating the effects of the recession on the company's financial performance. He found, however, that the lack of management accounting information hampered him in pinpointing problem areas and in identifying cost-reduction possibilities. Consequently, he approached a firm of management consultants to provide a blueprint for the development of a management accounting system over the next two years.

Question

Prepare a blueprint for the board of Electronic Boards plc outlining the main factors which it should consider in establishing a useful management accounting function within the company.

Measurement of cost behaviour

Learning objectives

When you have finished studying this chapter, you should be able to:

1 Explain step- and mixed-cost behaviour.
2 Explain management influences on cost behaviour.
3 Measure and mathematically express cost functions and use them to predict costs.
4 Describe the importance of activity analysis for measuring cost functions.
5 Measure cost behaviour using the engineering analysis, account analysis, high-low, visual-fit and least-squares regression methods.

Air Arabia

Air Arabia, the first Middle East low-cost airline, is based in Sharjah in the United Arab Emirates. Operating scheduled services to 67 destinations, the airline is strategically located for cargo and passenger operations. Air Arabia commands a niche market. Customers seek effective control over freight distribution and employee travel costs. Air Arabia sets prices on a customer-by-customer basis. Clients are able to streamline their supply chain; reduce operating costs; and enjoy fast, efficient user facilities.

Air Arabia supports rapid industrial development funded by the world's richest oil and natural gas resources. Sharjah provides modern purpose built and consumer friendly commercial facilities. Less congested than Dubai, air cargo distribution functionality is available to the various industries in the rapidly emerging Gulf markets. Sharjah expedites customs and immigration clearance, again lowering costs. Air Arabia has opened up new hubs for the Gulf travel market. The airline operates 25 Airbus 320-214 planes with an industry-low fleet average age under three years. Air Arabia's Annual Report 2010 identifies its vision 'to be one of the world's leading budget airlines'. It provides more frequent air services than competitors, with a fleet that operates on routes selected to ensure twice the revenue earning air miles per plane than competitors. In the 2010 report, Air Arabia notes: 'We have continued our legacy of being one of the world's most profitable airlines and registered a net profit of around AED 310 million for 2010.'

Air Arabia has opened new hubs for the Gulf travel market.

Chapter 2 demonstrated the importance of understanding the cost structure of an organisation and the relationships between an organisation's activities and its costs, revenues and profits. This chapter focuses on **measurement of cost behaviour**, which means understanding and quantifying how activities of an organisation affect its costs. Recall that activities use resources and these resources have costs. We measure the relationship between activity and cost using cost drivers. Understanding relationships between costs and their cost drivers allows managers in all types of organisations – profit-seeking, nonprofit and government – to do the following:

- Evaluate strategic plans and operational improvement programme. (Chapter 4)
- Make proper short-run pricing decisions. (Chapter 5)
- Make short-run operating decisions. (Chapter 6)
- Plan or budget the effects of future activities. (Chapters 7 and 8)
- Design effective management control systems. (Chapters 9 and 10)
- Make proper long-run decisions. (Chapter 11)
- Design accurate and useful product costing systems. (Chapters 12–14)

As you can see, understanding cost behaviour is fundamental to management accounting. There are numerous real-world cases in which managers have made very poor decisions to drop product lines, close manufacturing plants, or bid too high or too low on jobs because they had erroneous cost-behaviour information. This chapter, therefore, deserves careful study. ■

Cost drivers and cost behaviour

Accountants and managers often assume that cost behaviour is linear over some relevant range of activity levels or cost-driver levels. We can graph **linear-cost behaviour** with a straight line because we assume each cost to be either fixed or variable. Recall that the relevant range specifies the limits of cost-driver activity within which a specific relationship between a cost and its cost driver will be valid. Managers usually define the relevant range based on their previous experience operating the organisation at different levels of activity.

In this chapter, we focus on those costs for which the volume of a product produced or service provided is the primary cost driver. These costs are easy to identify with, or trace to, products or services. Examples of volume-driven costs include the costs of printing labour, paper, ink and binding to produce all the copies of this textbook. The number of copies printed affects the total printing labour, paper, ink and binding costs. We could easily trace the use of these resources to the number of copies of the text printed by using schedules, payroll records and other documents that show how much of each resource was used to produce the copies of this text.

Activities not directly related to volume also affect costs. Such costs often have multiple cost drivers. For example, the wages and salaries of the editorial staff of the publisher of this textbook are not easy to trace to outputs. These editorial personnel produce many different textbooks, and it would be very difficult to determine exactly what portion of their wages and salaries went into a specific book, such as *Introduction to Management Accounting*.

Understanding and measuring costs that are difficult to trace to outputs can be especially challenging. In practice, many organisations use a linear relationship with a single cost driver to describe each cost, even though many costs have multiple causes. This approach is easier and less expensive than using nonlinear relationships or multiple cost drivers. If we use it carefully, this method often provides cost estimates that are accurate enough for most decisions. It may seem at odds with reality and economic theory, but the added benefit of understanding 'true' cost behaviour may be less than the cost of determining it, which is consistent with the cost–benefit approach to decision making.

Accountants often describe cost behaviour in visual or graphical terms. Exhibit 3.1 shows linear-cost behaviour, the relevant range and an activity or resource cost driver. Note the similarity to the cost–volume–profit (CVP) graphs of Chapter 2.

■ Step- and mixed-cost behaviour patterns

Objective 1
Explain step-
and mixed-cost
behaviour.

Chapter 2 described two patterns of cost behaviour: variable costs and fixed costs. Recall that, within a relevant range, a purely variable cost changes in proportion to changes in its cost driver's activity, while changes in the cost-driver level do not immediately change a fixed cost. In addition to these pure versions of costs, two additional types of costs combine characteristics of both fixed- and variable-cost behaviour. These are step costs and mixed costs.

Step costs

Step costs change abruptly at different intervals of activity because the resources and their costs are only available in indivisible chunks. If the individual chunks of cost are relatively large and apply to a specific, broad range of activity, we consider the cost a fixed cost over that range of activity. An example is in panel A of Exhibit 3.2, which shows the cost of leasing oil and gas drilling equipment. When oil and gas exploration activity reaches a certain level in a given region, the company must lease an entire additional rig. One level of oil and gas rig leasing, however, will support all volumes of exploration activity within a relevant range of drilling. Within each relevant range, this step cost behaves as a fixed cost.

In contrast, accountants often describe step costs as variable when the individual chunks of costs are relatively small and apply to a narrow range of activity. Panel B of Exhibit 3.2 shows the wage cost of cashiers at a supermarket. Suppose one cashier can serve an average of 20 shoppers per hour and that within the relevant range of shopping activity, the number of shoppers can range from 40 per hour to 440 per hour. The corresponding number of cashiers would range between 2 and 22. Because the steps are relatively small, this step cost behaves much like a variable cost and we could assume it is variable for planning purposes with little loss of accuracy.

Mixed costs

Mixed costs contain elements of both fixed- and variable-cost behaviour. The fixed-cost element is unchanged over a range of cost-driver activity levels. The variable-cost element of the mixed cost varies proportionately with cost-driver activity within the relevant range. You might think of the fixed cost as the cost of having available the capacity necessary to operate at any volume within the relevant range and the variable cost as the additional cost of using that capacity to produce at the specified level of output.

Exhibit 3.1 Linear-cost behaviour

Exhibit 3.2 Step-cost behaviour

Many costs are mixed costs. For example, consider the monthly facilities maintenance department cost of the Parkview Medical Centre (PMC), shown in Exhibit 3.3. Salaries of the maintenance personnel and costs of equipment are fixed at £10,000 per month. In addition, cleaning supplies and repair materials vary at a rate of £5 per patient-day[1] delivered by the hospital.

The chief administrator at PMC used knowledge of the facilities maintenance department cost behaviour to do the following:

1 *Plan costs*. In May, the hospital expected to service 3,000 patient-days. May's predicted facilities maintenance department costs are £10,000 fixed costs plus the variable cost of £15,000 (3,000 patient-days times £5 per patient-day) for a total of £25,000.

2 *Provide feedback to managers*. In May, the actual facilities maintenance costs were £34,000 in a month when PMC serviced 3,000 patient-days as planned. The administrator wanted to know why the hospital overspent by £9,000 (£34,000 less the planned £25,000) so that managers could take corrective action.

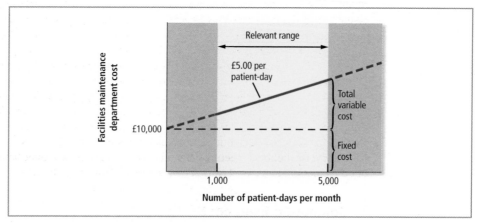

Exhibit 3.3 Mixed-cost behaviour

---

[1] A patient-day is one patient spending 1 day in the hospital. One patient spending 5 days in the hospital is 5 patient-days of service.

3 *Make decisions about the most efficient use of resources.* For example, managers might weigh the long-run trade-offs of increased fixed costs of highly automated floor cleaning equipment against the variable costs of extra hours needed to clean floors manually.

We can see that managers not only passively measure how costs behave, they also actively influence the cost structure of an organisation. Let's explore in more detail how managers influence cost behaviour.

Management influence on cost behaviour

Objective 2
Explain management influences on cost behaviour.

In addition to measuring and evaluating current cost behaviour, managers can influence cost behaviour through decisions about such factors as product or service attributes, capacity, technology and policies to create incentives to control costs.

Product and service decisions and the value chain

Throughout the value chain, managers influence cost behaviour. This influence occurs through their choices of process and product design, quality levels, product features, distribution channels and so on. Each of these decisions contributes to the organisation's performance, and managers should consider the costs and benefits of each decision. For example, Hertz, the car rental company, would add a feature to its services only if the cost of the feature – for example, GPS navigation systems in its vehicles – could be more than recovered in profit from increased business and/or extra fees it could charge for the feature.

Capacity decisions

Strategic decisions about the scale and scope of an organisation's activities generally result in fixed levels of capacity costs. **Capacity costs** are the fixed costs of being able to achieve a desired level of production or to provide a desired level of service while maintaining product or service attributes, such as quality. Most companies make a capacity decision infrequently. They consider capacity decisions as strategic because large amounts of resources are involved. An incorrect capacity decision can have serious consequences for the competitiveness of a company. However, some companies make capacity decisions so frequently that they almost become routine operating decisions, such as opening a new Starbucks or McDonald's. In this case, the decision to open a new Starbucks is still strategic, but it becomes highly structured.

Companies in industries with long-term variations in demand must be careful when making capacity decisions. Companies may not be able to fully recover fixed capacity costs when demand falls during an economic downturn. Additionally, capacity decisions can entail an ethical commitment to a company's employees. Most companies try to keep a stable employment policy so that they do not need to fire or lay off employees unless there are huge shifts in demand. In the economic downturn of 2008, news stories about companies 'downsizing' and initiating extensive layoffs abounded. But other companies managed the decrease in demand without imposing large emotional costs on their employees. Companies that plan their capacity to allow flexibility in meeting demand generally survive economic hard times better, without the emotional upheaval caused by widespread firings and layoffs.

Committed fixed costs

Even if a company has chosen to minimise fixed capacity costs, every organisation has some costs to which it is committed, perhaps for quite a few years. A company's **committed fixed costs** usually arise from the possession of facilities, equipment and a basic organisational structure.

They include mortgage or lease payments, interest payments on long-term debt, property taxes, insurance and salaries of key personnel. Only major changes in the philosophy, scale, or scope of operations could change these committed fixed costs in future periods. Recall the example of the facilities maintenance department for the Parkview Medical Centre. The capacity of the facilities maintenance department was a management decision, and in this case the decision determined the magnitude of the equipment cost. Suppose PMC were permanently to increase its patient-days per month beyond the relevant range of 5,000 patient-days. Because PMC would need more capacity, the committed equipment cost would rise to a new level per month.

Discretionary fixed costs

Some costs are fixed at certain levels only because management decided to incur these levels of cost to meet the organisation's goals. These **discretionary fixed costs** have no obvious relationship to levels of capacity or output activity. Companies determine them as part of the periodic planning process. Each planning period, management will determine how much to spend on discretionary items such as advertising and promotion costs, public relations, research and development costs, charitable donations, employee training programmes and purchased management consulting services. These costs then become fixed until the next planning period.

Managers can alter discretionary fixed costs – up or down – even within a budget period, if they decide that different levels of spending are desirable. Conceivably, managers could eliminate such discretionary costs almost entirely for a given year in dire times, whereas they could not reduce committed costs. Discretionary fixed costs may be essential to the long-run achievement of the organisation's goals, but managers can vary spending levels broadly in the short run.

Consider Marietta Corporation, which is experiencing financial difficulties. Sales for its major products are down, and Marietta's management is considering cutting back on costs temporarily. Marietta's management must determine which of the following fixed costs it can reduce or eliminate and how much money each would save:

Fixed costs	Planned amounts
Advertising and promotion	£ 50,000
Depreciation	400,000
Employee training	100,000
Management salaries	800,000
Mortgage payment	250,000
Property taxes	600,000
Research and development	1,500,000
Total	£3,700,000

Can Marietta reduce or eliminate any of these fixed costs? The answer depends on Marietta's long-run outlook. Marietta could reduce costs but also greatly reduce its ability to compete in the future if it cuts fixed costs carelessly. Rearranging these costs by categories of committed and discretionary costs yields the following analysis:

Fixed costs	Planned amounts
Committed	
Depreciation	£ 400,000
Mortgage payment	250,000
Property taxes	600,000
Total committed	£1,250,000

Discretionary (potential savings)		
Advertising and promotion	£	50,000
Employee training		100,000
Management salaries		800,000
Research and development		1,500,000
Total discretionary		£2,450,000
Total committed and discretionary		£3,700,000

Eliminating all discretionary fixed costs would save Marietta £2,450,000 per year. However, Marietta would be unwise to cut all discretionary costs completely. This would severely impair the company's long-term prospects. Nevertheless, distinguishing committed and discretionary fixed costs would be the company's first step in identifying where costs could be reduced.

Technology decisions

One of the most critical decisions that managers make is choosing the type of technology the organisation will use to produce its products or deliver its services. Choice of technology (for example, labour-intensive versus robotic manufacturing, personal banking services versus cash machines or e-commerce versus in-store sales) positions the organisation to meet its current goals and to respond to changes in the environment (for example, changes in customer needs or actions by competitors). The use of high-technology methods rather than labour usually means a much greater fixed-cost component to the total cost. This type of cost behaviour creates greater risks for companies with wide variations in demand.

Cost-control incentives

Finally, the incentives that management creates for employees can affect future costs. Managers use their knowledge of cost behaviour to set cost expectations, and employees may receive compensation or other rewards that are tied to meeting these expectations. For example, the administrator of Parkview Medical Centre could give the supervisor of the facilities maintenance department a favourable evaluation if the supervisor maintained quality of service and kept department costs below the expected amount for the actual level of patient-days. This feedback motivates the supervisor to watch department costs carefully and to find ways to reduce costs without reducing quality of service.

Cost functions

As a manager, you will use cost functions often as a planning and control tool. A few of the reasons why cost functions are important are listed here:

1 Planning and controlling the activities of an organisation require accurate and useful estimates of future fixed and variable costs.

2 Understanding relationships between costs and their cost drivers allows managers in all types of organisations – profit-seeking, nonprofit and government – to make better operating, marketing and production decisions; to plan and evaluate actions; and to determine appropriate costs for short-run and long-run decisions.

The first step in estimating or predicting costs is **cost measurement** – measuring cost behaviour as a function of appropriate cost drivers. The second step is to use these cost measures to estimate future costs at expected levels of cost-driver activity. We begin by looking at the form of cost functions and the criteria for choosing the most appropriate cost drivers.

▦ Form of cost functions

To describe the relationship between a cost and its cost driver(s), managers often use an algebraic equation called a **cost function**. When there is only one cost driver, the cost function is similar to the algebraic CVP relationships discussed in Chapter 2. Consider the mixed cost graphed in Exhibit 3.3 on p. 80, the facilities maintenance department cost:

$$\text{monthly facilities maintenance department costs} = \text{monthly fixed maintenance cost} + \text{monthly variable maintenance cost}$$

$$= \text{monthly fixed maintenance cost} + \left(\text{variable cost per patient-day} \times \text{number of patient-days in the month} \right)$$

Let
  Y = monthly facilities maintenance department cost
  F = monthly fixed maintenance cost
  V = variable cost per patient-day
  X = cost-driver activity in number of patient-days per month

We can rewrite the mixed-cost function as

$$Y = F + VX$$

or

$$Y = £10,000 + £5.00X$$

This mixed-cost function has the familiar form of a straight line – it is called a linear cost function. When we graph a cost function, F is the intercept, the point on the vertical axis where the cost function begins. In Exhibit 3.3, the intercept is the £10,000 fixed cost per month. V, the variable cost per unit of activity, is the slope of the cost function. In Exhibit 3.3, the cost function slopes upward at the rate of £5 for each additional patient-day.

In our example, we use patient-days as the relevant cost driver. How did we choose this cost driver? Why not use number of patients, or number of operations, or facility square footage? In general, how do we develop cost functions?

▦ Developing cost functions

Managers should apply two criteria to obtain accurate and useful cost functions: plausibility and reliability.

1 The cost function must be plausible, that is, believable. Personal observation of costs and activities, when it is possible, provides the best evidence of a plausible relationship between a resource cost and its cost driver. Some cost relationships, by nature, are not directly

observable, so the cost analyst must be confident that the proposed relationship is valid. Many costs may move together with a number of cost drivers, but no cause-and-effect relationships may exist. A cause-and-effect relationship (that is, the cost driver causes the organisation to incur the resource cost) is desirable for cost functions to be accurate and useful. For example, consider three possible cost drivers for the total cost of a Finnair round-trip flight from Tuurku to London: miles flown, number of passengers and passenger-miles (number of passengers times miles flown). Which of these possible cost drivers makes most sense? The answer is passenger-miles – the cost driver used by almost all airlines because both distance AND number of passengers flown impact cost incurrence.

2 In addition to being plausible, a cost function's estimates of costs at actual levels of activity must reliably conform to actually observed costs. We assess reliability in terms of 'goodness of fit' – how well the cost function explains past cost behaviour. If the fit is good and conditions do not change in the future, the cost function should be a reliable predictor of future costs.

Managers use these criteria together in choosing a cost function. Each is a check on the other. A manager needs to fully understand operations and the way accountants record costs to determine a plausible and reliable cost function that links cause and effect. For example, companies often perform maintenance when output is low because that is when they can take machines out of service. Lower output does not cause increased maintenance costs, however, nor does increased output cause lower maintenance costs. A more plausible explanation is that over a longer period increased output causes higher maintenance costs, but daily or weekly recording of maintenance costs and outputs may make it appear otherwise. Understanding the nature of maintenance costs should lead managers to a reliable, long-run cost function.

MAKING MANAGERIAL DECISIONS

A cost function is a mathematical expression of how cost drivers affect a particular cost. However, an intuitive understanding of cost functions is just as important as being able to write the mathematical formula. Suppose you have been using a cost function to predict total order-processing activity costs. The cost function is total costs = £25,000 + £89 × (number of orders processed). This formula is based on data that are in the range of 0–700 orders processed. Now, you want to predict the total cost for 680 orders. You have a few fundamental questions to answer before you are comfortable using the cost function in this situation. What does it mean when a cost function is linear? Why do managers want to know whether a cost is linear? What is the importance of the relevant range?

Answer

A linear cost function means that there are two parts to the cost. One part is fixed – that is, it's independent of the cost driver. The other part varies in proportion to the cost driver – that is, if the cost driver increases by X per cent, this part of the cost also increases by X per cent. Knowing that a cost is linear allows a manager to separate the cost into fixed and variable components – a simplification that helps you understand how decisions will affect costs. Incidentally, the predicted total cost for 680 orders is £25,000 + (£89 × 680) = £85,520. As long as the operating conditions that existed when the data were collected have not changed significantly, then knowing that the number of orders processed is within the relevant range – 0–700, in this case – gives you confidence in the predicted total cost.

■ Choice of cost drivers: activity analysis

Objective 4
Describe the
importance of
activity analysis
for measuring cost
functions.

How do managers construct reliable and plausible cost functions? Well, you cannot have a good cost function without knowing the right cost drivers, so constructing a cost function starts with choosing cost drivers – the X in the equation on p. 84. Managers use **activity analysis** to identify appropriate cost drivers and their effects on the costs of making a product or providing a service. The final product or service may have several cost drivers because production may involve many separate activities. The greatest benefit of activity analysis is that it directs management accountants to the appropriate cost drivers for each cost.

Consider Northwestern Computers, which makes two products for personal computers: a plug-in music board (Mozart-Plus) and a hard-disk drive (Powerdrive). These two products consist of material costs, labour costs and support costs. In the past, most of the work on Northwestern's products was done by hand. In such a situation, labour costs were the primary driver of support costs. Support costs were twice as much as labour costs, on average.

Northwestern has just finished upgrading the production process. Now the company uses computer-controlled assembly equipment, which has increased the costs of support activities, such as engineering and maintenance, and has reduced labour cost. Its cost function has now changed; specifically, labour cost is now only 5 per cent of the total costs at Northwestern. An activity analysis has shown that the number of components added to products (a measure of product complexity), not labour cost, is the primary cost driver for support costs. Northwestern estimated support costs to be €20 per component. Mozart-Plus has five component parts and Powerdrive has nine.

Suppose Northwestern wants to predict how much support cost it will incur in producing one Mozart-Plus and how much for one Powerdrive. Using the old cost driver, labour cost, the prediction of support costs would be as follows:

	Mozart-Plus	Powerdrive
Prior labour cost per unit	€ 8.50	€130.00
Predicted support cost		
2 × direct labour cost	€17.00	€260.00

Using the more appropriate cost driver based on the new production process, the number of components added to products, the predicted support costs are as follows:

	Mozart-Plus	Powerdrive
Predicted support cost at €20 per component		
€20 × 5 components	€100.00	
€20 × 9 components		€180.00
Difference in predicted support cost between the	€ 83.00	€ 80.00
old and new cost function	higher	lower

By using an appropriate cost driver, Northwestern can predict its support costs much more accurately. Managers will make better decisions with this more accurate information. For example, they can relate prices charged for products more closely to the costs of production.

One major question remains in our discussion of the measurement of cost behaviour: How are the estimates of fixed costs and variable cost per cost-driver unit determined? The equation on p. 84 denotes these amounts by F = monthly fixed maintenance cost and V = variable cost per patient-day. In practice, organisations use several methods of measuring cost functions and determining values for F and V. Let's look at each of these methods.

Methods of measuring cost functions

Objective 5
Measure cost behaviour using the engineering analysis, account analysis, high-low, visual-fit and least-squares regression methods.

After determining the most plausible drivers behind different costs, managers can choose from a broad selection of methods of approximating cost functions. These methods include (1) engineering analysis, (2) account analysis, (3) high-low analysis, (4) visual-fit analysis and (5) least-squares regression analysis. These methods are not mutually exclusive; managers frequently use two or more together to avoid major errors in measuring cost behaviour. The first two methods rely primarily on logical analysis of the cost environment, whereas the last three involve explicit analysis of prior cost data.

Engineering Analysis

The first method, **engineering analysis**, measures cost behaviour according to what costs should be in an on-going process. It entails a systematic review of materials, supplies, labour, support services and facilities needed for products and services. Analysts can even use engineering analysis successfully for new products and services, as long as the organisation has had experience with similar costs. Why? Because they can base measures on information from personnel who are directly involved with the product or service. In addition to actual experience, analysts learn about new costs from experiments with prototypes, accounting and industrial engineering literature, the experience of competitors and the advice of management consultants. From this information, cost analysts estimate what future costs should be. If the cost analysts are experienced and understand the activities of the organisation, then their engineering cost predictions may be quite reliable and useful for decision making. The disadvantages of engineering cost analysis are that the efforts are costly and may not be timely.

Nearly any organisation can use this approach to measuring cost behaviour. For example, Weyerhaeuser Company, producer of wood products, used engineering analysis to determine the cost functions for its 14 corporate service departments. These cost functions measure the cost of corporate services used by three main business groups. Weyerhaeuser found that its accounts payable costs for each division are a function of three cost drivers: the number of hours spent on each division, number of documents and number of invoices.

Now consider Parkview Medical Centre, introduced earlier in the chapter. An assistant to the hospital administrator interviewed facilities maintenance personnel and observed their activities on several random days for a month. From these data, she confirmed that the most plausible cost driver for facilities maintenance cost is the number of patient-days. She also estimated from current department salaries and equipment charges that monthly fixed costs approximated £10,000 per month. Using interviews and observing supplies usage during the month, she estimated that variable costs are £5 per patient-day. She gave this information to the hospital administrator but cautioned that the cost measures may be wrong because of the following reasons:

1 The month observed may be abnormal.

2 The facilities maintenance personnel may have altered their normal work habits because the assistant was observing them.

3 The facilities maintenance personnel may not have told the complete truth about their activities because of their concerns about the use of the information they revealed.

However, if we assume the observed and estimated information is correct, we could predict facilities maintenance costs in any month by first forecasting that month's expected patient-days and then entering that figure into the following algebraic, mixed-cost function:

$$Y = £10,000 \text{ per month} + (£5 \times \text{patient-days})$$

For example, if the administrator expects 3,000 patient-days next month, the prediction of facilities maintenance costs would be as follows:

$$Y = £10,000 + (£5 \times 3,000 \text{ patient-days}) = £25,000$$

■ Account Analysis

In contrast to engineering analysis, users of **account analysis** look to the accounting system for information about cost behaviour. The simplest method of account analysis classifies each account as a variable or fixed cost with respect to a selected cost driver. The cost analyst then looks at each cost account balance and estimates either the variable cost per unit of cost-driver activity or the periodic fixed cost.

To illustrate this approach to account analysis, let's return to the facilities maintenance department at Parkview Medical Centre and analyse costs for a recent month. The following table shows costs recorded in a month with 3,700 patient-days:

Monthly cost	January amount
Supervisor's salary and benefits	£ 3,800
Hourly workers' wages and benefits	14,674
Equipment depreciation and rentals	5,873
Equipment repairs	5,604
Cleaning supplies	7,472
Total facilities maintenance cost	£37,423

Recall that the most plausible and reliable driver for these costs is the number of patient-days serviced per month. Next, the analyst determines which costs may be fixed and which may be variable. Assume that the analyst has made the following judgements:

Monthly cost	Amount	Fixed	Variable
Supervisor's salary and benefits	£ 3,800	£3,800	
Hourly workers' wages and benefits	14,674		£14,674
Equipment depreciation and rentals	5,873	5,873	
Equipment repairs	5,604		5,604
Cleaning supplies	7,472		7,472
Total facilities maintenance costs	£37,423	£9,673	£27,750

Measuring total facilities maintenance cost behaviour, then, requires only simple arithmetic. First add up all the fixed costs to get the total fixed cost per month. Then divide the total variable costs by the units of cost-driver activity to get the variable cost per unit of cost driver.

$$\text{Fixed cost per month} = £9,673$$
$$\text{Variable cost per patient-day} = £27,750 \div 3,700 \text{ patient-days}$$
$$= £7.50 \text{ per patient-day}$$

The algebraic, mixed-cost function, measured by account analysis, is

$$Y = £9,673 \text{ per month} + (£7.50 \times \text{patient-days})$$

Account analysis methods are less expensive to conduct than engineering analyses, but they require recording of relevant cost accounts and cost drivers. In addition, like engineering analysis, account analysis is subjective because the analysts decide whether each cost is variable or fixed based on their own judgement.

Summary problem for your review

PROBLEM

The Reliable Insurance Company processes a variety of insurance claims for losses, accidents, thefts and so on. Account analysis using one cost driver has estimated the variable cost of processing the claims for each automobile accident at 0.5 per cent (.005) of the monetary value of all claims related to a particular accident. This estimate seemed reasonable because high-cost claims often involve more analysis before settlement. To control processing costs better, however, Reliable conducted an activity analysis of claims processing. The analysis suggested that there are three main cost drivers for the costs of processing claims for car accidents. The drivers and cost behaviour are as follows:

0.2% of Reliable Insurance policyholders' property claims
+ 0.6% of other parties' property claims
+ 0.8% of total personal injury claims

Data from two recent car accident claims follow:

	Vehicle claim No. 607788	Vehicle claim No. 607991
Policyholder claim	£ 4,500	£23,600
Other party claim	0	3,400
Personal injury claim	12,400	0
Total claim amount	£16,900	£27,000

1 Estimate the cost of processing each claim using data from (a) the single-cost-driver analysis and (b) the three-cost-driver analysis.

2 How would you recommend that Reliable Insurance estimate the cost of processing claims?

SOLUTION

1 Costs are summarised in the table here.

	Vehicle claim No. 607788		Vehicle claim No. 607991	
	Claim amount	Processing cost	Claim amount	Processing cost
Using single-cost-driver analysis				
Total claim amount	£16,900		£27,000	
Estimated processing cost at 0.5%		£ 84.50		£135.00
Using three-cost-driver analysis				
Policyholder claim	£ 4,500		£23,600	
Estimated processing cost at 0.2%		£ 9.00		£ 47.20
Other party claim	0		3,400	
Estimated processing cost at 0.6%		0		20.40
Personal injury claim	12,400		0	
Estimated processing cost at 0.8%		99.20		0
Total estimated processing cost		£108.20		£ 67.60

2 The three-cost-driver analysis estimates of processing costs are considerably different from those using a single cost driver. If the activity analyses are reliable, then vehicle claims that include personal injury losses are more costly to process than property damage claims. If these estimates are relatively inexpensive to keep current and to use, then it seems reasonable to adopt the three-cost-driver approach. Reliable will have more accurate cost estimates and will be better able to plan its claims processing activities. Reliable processes many different types of claims, however. Extending activity analysis to identify multiple cost drivers for all types of claims would result in a complicated system for predicting costs – much more complex (and costly) than simply using the total sterling value of claims. Whether to undertake an activity analysis for all types of policies depends on cost–benefit considerations. Managers can address such considerations by first adopting activity analysis for one type of claim and assessing the usefulness and cost of the more accurate information.

High-low, visual-fit and least-squares methods

When enough cost data are available, we can use historical data to estimate the cost function mathematically. Three popular methods that use such data are the high-low, visual-fit and least-squares methods. All three of these methods are more objective than the engineering-analysis and account-analysis methods. Each is based on hard evidence as well as on judgement, and they use more than one period's cost and activity information. Account analysis and engineering analysis will probably remain primary methods of measuring cost behaviour because the three mathematical methods require more past cost data. Products, services, technologies and organisations are changing rapidly in response to increased global competition and technological advances. In some cases, by the time enough historical data are collected to support these analyses, the data are obsolete – the organisation has changed, the production process has changed, or the product has changed. The cost analyst must be careful that the historical data are from a past environment that still closely resembles the future environment for which a manager wants to predict costs. Another concern is that historical data may hide past inefficiencies that the company could reduce if it could identify them.

Data for illustration

In discussing the high-low, visual-fit and least-squares regression methods, we will continue to use the Parkview Medical Centre's facilities maintenance department costs. The following table shows monthly data collected on facilities maintenance department costs and on the number of patient-days serviced over the past year:

Facilities maintenance department data

Month	Facilities maintenance department cost (Y)	Number of patient-days (X)
January	£37,000	3,700
February	23,000	1,600
March	37,000	4,100
April	47,000	4,900
May	33,000	3,300
June	39,000	4,400
July	32,000	3,500
August	33,000	4,000
September	17,000	1,200

(continued)

October	18,000	1,300
November	22,000	1,800
December	20,000	1,600

High-low method

When sufficient cost data are available, the cost analyst may use historical data to measure the cost function mathematically. The simplest of the three methods to measure a linear-cost function from past cost data is the **high-low method** shown in Exhibit 3.4.

The first step in the high-low method is to plot the historical data points on a graph. This visual display helps the analyst see whether there are obvious errors in the data. Even though many points are plotted, the focus of the high-low method is normally on the highest and lowest activity points. However, if one of these points is an outlier that seems in error or non-representative of normal operations, we should use the next-highest or next-lowest activity point. For example, we should not use a point from a period with abnormally low activity caused by a labour strike or fire. Why? Because that point is not representative of a normal relationship between cost and cost driver.

After selecting the representative high and low points, we can draw a line between them, extending the line to the vertical (Y) axis of the graph. Note that this extension in Exhibit 3.4 is a dashed line, as a reminder that costs may not be linear outside the range of activity for which we have data (the relevant range). Also, managers usually are concerned with how costs behave within the relevant range, not with how they behave either at zero activity or at impossibly high activity levels. Measurements of costs within the relevant range may not be reliable measures or predictors of costs outside the relevant range.

The point at which the line intersects the Y-axis is the intercept, F, or estimate of fixed cost. The slope of the line measures the variable cost, V, per patient-day. The clearest way to measure the intercept and slope with the high-low method is to use algebra:

Month	Facilities maintenance department cost (Y)	Number of patient-days (X)
High: April	£47,000	4,900
Low: September	17,000	1,200
Difference	£30,000	3,700

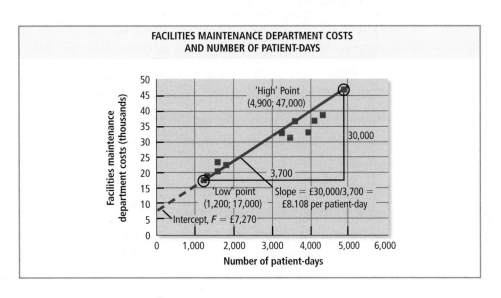

FACILITIES MAINTENANCE DEPARTMENT COSTS AND NUMBER OF PATIENT-DAYS

'High' Point (4,900; 47,000)

30,000

3,700

'Low' point (1,200; 17,000)

Slope = £30,000/3,700 = £8.108 per patient-day

Intercept, F = £7,270

Facilities maintenance department costs (thousands)

Number of patient-days

Exhibit 3.4
High-low method

Variable cost per patient-day,

$$V = \frac{\text{change in costs}}{\text{change in activity}} = \frac{£47,000 - £17,000}{4,900 - 1,200 \text{ patient-days}}$$

$$V = \frac{£30,000}{3,700} \qquad = £8.1081 \text{ per patient-day}$$

Fixed cost per month, F = total mixed cost less total variable cost

At X (high): F = £47,000 − (£8.1081 × 4,900 patient-days)

= £47,000 − £39,730

= £7,270 per month

Summary problem for your review

PROBLEM

The Reetz Company has its own photocopying department. Reetz's photocopying costs include costs of copy machines, operators, paper, toner, utilities and so on. We have the following cost and activity data:

Month	Total photocopying cost	Number of copies
1	£25,000	320,000
2	29,000	390,000
3	24,000	300,000
4	23,000	310,000
5	28,000	400,000

1 Use the high-low method to measure the cost behaviour of the photocopy department in formula form.

2 What are the benefits and disadvantages of using the high-low method for measuring cost behaviour?

SOLUTION

1 The lowest and highest activity levels are in months 3 (300,000 copies) and 5 (400,000 copies).

$$\text{Variable cost per copy} = \frac{\text{change in cost}}{\text{change in activity}} = \frac{£28,000 - £24,000}{400,000 - 300,000}$$

$$= \frac{£4,000}{100,000} = \underline{\underline{£0.04}} \text{ per copy}$$

Fixed cost per month = total cost less variable cost

at 400,000 copies: £28,000 − (£0.04 × 400,000) = £12,000 per month
at 300,000 copies: £24,000 − (£0.04 × 300,000) = £12,000 per month

Therefore, the photocopy cost function is

Y(total cost) = £12,000 per month + (£0.04 × number of copies)

2 The benefits of using the high-low method are as follows:

- The method is easy to use.
- Not many data points are needed.

The disadvantages of using the high-low method are as follows:

- The choice of the high and low points is subjective.
- The method does not use all available data.
- The method may not be reliable.

$$\text{At X (low): } F = £17{,}000 - (£8.1081 \times 1{,}200 \text{ patient-days})$$
$$= £17{,}000 - £9{,}730$$
$$= £7{,}270 \text{ per month}$$

Therefore, the facilities maintenance department cost function, measured by the high-low method, is

$$Y = £7{,}270 \text{ per month} + (£8.1081 \times \text{patient-days})$$

The high-low method is easy to apply and illustrates mathematically how a change in a cost driver can change total cost. The cost function that resulted in this case is plausible. Before the widespread availability of computers, managers often used the high-low method to measure a cost function quickly. Today, however, the high-low method is not used as often because it makes inefficient use of information, basing the cost function on only two periods' cost experience, regardless of how many relevant data points have been collected.

Visual-fit method

In the **visual-fit method**, we draw a straight line through a plot of all the available data, using judgement to fit the line as close as possible to all the plotted points. If the cost function for the data is linear, it is possible to draw a straight line through the scattered points that comes reasonably close to most of them and thus captures the general tendency of the data. We can extend that line back until it intersects the vertical axis of the graph.

Exhibit 3.5 shows this method applied to the facilities maintenance department cost data for the past 12 months. By measuring where the line intersects the cost axis, we can estimate

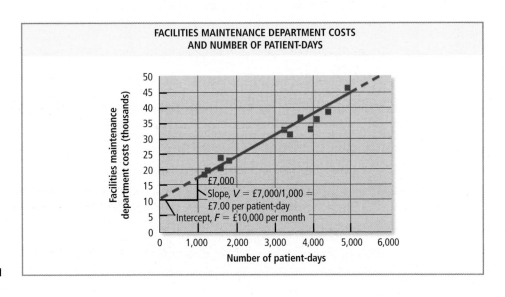

Exhibit 3.5
Visual-fit method

the monthly fixed cost – in this case, about £10,000 per month. To find the variable cost per patient-day, select any activity level (for example 1,000 patient-days) and find the total cost at that activity level (£17,000). Then, divide the variable cost (which is total cost less fixed cost) by the units of activity.

$$\text{Variable cost per patient-day} = (£17,000 - £10,000) \div 1,000 \text{ patient-days}$$
$$= £7 \text{ per patient-day}$$

The linear-cost function measured by the visual-fit method is

$$Y = £10,000 \text{ per month} + (£7 \times \text{patient-days})$$

Although the visual-fit method uses all the data, the placement of the line and the measurement of the fixed and variable costs are subjective. This subjectivity is the main reason why many companies with sufficient data prefer to use least-squares regression analysis rather than the visual-fit method.

Least-squares regression method

Least-squares regression (or simply **regression analysis**) measures a cost function more objectively and explicitly than does the visual-fit method. Least-squares regression analysis uses statistics rather than human eyesight to fit a cost function to all the historical data. A simple regression uses one cost driver to measure a cost function, while a multiple regression uses two or more cost drivers. We will discuss only simple regression analysis in this chapter. Appendix 3 (p. 96) presents some statistical properties of regression analysis and shows how to use computer regression software.

Regression analysis measures cost behaviour more reliably than other cost measurement methods. It also yields important statistical information about the reliability of its cost estimates. These statistics allow analysts to assess their confidence in the cost measures and thereby select the best cost driver. One such measure of reliability, or goodness of fit, is the **coefficient of determination, R^2** (or R-squared), which measures how much of the fluctuation of a cost is explained by changes in the cost driver. Appendix 3 explains R^2 and discusses how to use it to select the best cost driver.

Exhibit 3.6 shows the linear, mixed-cost function for facilities maintenance costs as measured mathematically by regression analysis. The fixed-cost measure is £9,329 per month. The variable-cost measure is £6.951 per patient-day. The linear-cost function is

$$\text{facilities maintenance department cost} = £9,329 \text{ per month}$$
$$+ (£6.95 \times \text{number of patient-days})$$

or

$$Y = £9,329 + (£6.951 \times \text{patient-days})$$

Compare the cost measures produced by each of the five approaches:

Method	Fixed cost per month	Variable cost per patient-day
Engineering analysis	£10,000	£5.000
Account analysis	9,673	7.500
High-low	7,270	8.108
Visual-fit	10,000	7.000
Regression	9,329	6.951

Because of their grounding in statistical analysis, the regression-cost measures are more reliable than those obtained from the other methods. Thus, managers would have more confidence in cost predictions from the regression-cost function.

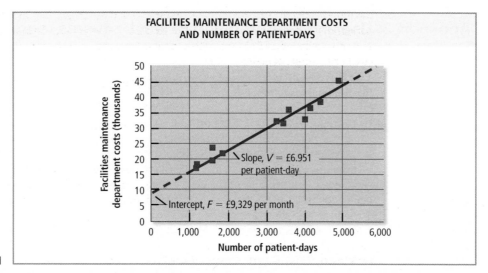

Exhibit 3.6
Least-squares
regression method

Highlights to remember

1 **Explain step- and mixed-cost behaviour.** Cost behaviour refers to how costs change as levels of an organisation's activities change. Costs can behave as fixed, variable, step, or mixed costs. Step and mixed costs both combine aspects of variable- and fixed-cost behaviour. Step costs form graphs that look like steps. Costs will remain fixed within a given range of activity or cost-driver level, but then will rise or fall abruptly when the cost-driver level is outside this range. Mixed costs involve a fixed element and a variable element of cost behaviour. Unlike step costs, mixed costs have a single fixed cost at all levels of activity and in addition have a variable cost element that increases proportionately with activity.

2 **Explain management influences on cost behaviour.** Managers can affect the costs and cost behaviour patterns of their companies through the decisions they make. Decisions on product and service features, capacity, technology and cost-control incentives, for example, can all affect cost behaviour.

3 **Measure and mathematically express cost functions and use them to predict costs.** The first step in estimating or predicting costs is measuring cost behaviour. This is done by finding a cost function. This is an algebraic equation that describes the relationship between a cost and its cost driver(s). To be useful for decision-making purposes, cost functions should be plausible and reliable.

4 **Describe the importance of activity analysis for measuring cost functions.** Activity analysis is the process of identifying the best cost drivers to use for cost estimation and prediction and determining how they affect the costs of making a product or service. This is an essential step in understanding and predicting costs.

5 **Measure cost behaviour using the engineering analysis, account analysis, high-low, visual-fit and least-squares regression methods.** Once analysts have identified cost drivers, they can use one of several methods to determine the cost function. Engineering analysis focuses on what costs should be by systematically reviewing the materials, supplies, labour, support services and facilities needed for a given level of production. Account analysis involves examining all accounts in terms of an appropriate cost driver and classifying each account as either fixed or variable with respect to the driver. The cost function consists of the variable cost per cost-driver unit multiplied by the amount of the cost driver plus the total fixed cost. The high-low, visual-fit and regression methods all use historical data to determine cost functions. Of these three methods, regression is the most reliable. ■

Appendix 3: Use and interpretation of least-squares regression

While we can perform regression analysis of historical cost data by hand, it would be unusual to find cost analysts doing so. Rather, they use computers that are much faster and less prone to error, and also produce explicit statistical analyses of the results. Therefore, we focus on interpretation of the results from a regression performed by a computer.

This appendix is not a substitute for a good statistics class. More properly, think of it as a motivator for studying statistics so that you can better interpret regression cost estimates. Recall that in this textbook we consider only simple regression (one cost driver) analysis. Incorporating more than one cost driver into a cost function via regression (multiple regression) is beyond the scope of this text, and again, you should consult a statistics textbook to learn about such an advanced regression technique.

Assume that there are two potential cost drivers for the costs of the facilities maintenance department in Parkview Medical Centre: (1) number of patient-days and (2) total value of hospital room charges. Regression analysis can assist in the determination of which activity is the better (more descriptive) cost driver in explaining and predicting costs. Exhibit 3.7 shows the past 12 months' cost and cost-driver data for the facilities maintenance department.

■ Regression analysis procedures

Most spreadsheet software available for PCs offers basic regression analysis in the Data Analysis or Tools commands. We will use these spreadsheet commands to illustrate regression analysis because many readers will be familiar already with spreadsheet software.

Entering data

First, create a spreadsheet with the historical cost data in rows and columns. Each row should be data from one period. Each column should be a cost category or a cost driver. For ease of analysis, all the potential cost drivers should be in adjacent columns. Each row and column should be complete (no missing data) and without errors.

Month	Facilities maintenance cost (Y)	Number of patient-days (X_1)	Value of room charges (X_2)
January	£37,000	3,700	£2,183,000
February	23,000	1,600	2,735,000
March	37,000	4,100	2,966,000
April	47,000	4,900	2,846,000
May	33,000	3,300	2,967,000
June	39,000	4,400	2,980,000
July	32,000	3,500	3,023,000
August	33,000	4,000	2,353,000
September	17,000	1,200	1,825,000
October	18,000	1,300	1,515,000
November	22,000	1,800	1,547,000
December	20,000	1,600	2,117,000

Exhibit 3.7 Facilities maintenance department data

Plotting data

There are two main reasons why the first step in regression analysis should be to plot the cost against each of the potential cost drivers: (1) Plots may show obvious nonlinear trends in the data; if so, linear regression analysis may not be appropriate for the entire range of the data. (2) Plots help identify outliers – costs that are in error or are otherwise obviously inappropriate.

Plotting with spreadsheets uses Graph commands on the columns of cost and cost-driver data. These Graph commands typically offer many optional graph types (such as bar charts and pie charts), but the most useful plot for regression analysis usually is called the XY graph. This graph is the type shown earlier in this chapter – the X-axis is the cost driver, and the Y-axis is the cost. The XY graph should be displayed without lines drawn between the data points (called data symbols) – an optional command. (Consult your spreadsheet manual for details because each spreadsheet program is different.)

Regression output

The format of the regression output is different for each software package. However, every package will identify the cost to be explained ('dependent variable') and the cost driver ('independent variable') in the cost function.

Producing regression output with spreadsheets is simple: Just select the Regression command, specify (or highlight) the X-dimension[s] (the cost driver[s]), and specify the Y-dimension or 'series' (the cost). Next, specify a blank area on the spreadsheet where the output will be displayed and select Go. The following is a regression analysis of facilities maintenance department costs using one of the two possible cost drivers, number of patient-days, X_1.

Facilities maintenance department cost explained by number of patient-days

Regression output	
Constant	9,329
R^2	0.955
X coefficient(s)	6.951

Interpretation of regression output

The fixed-cost measure, labelled 'constant' or 'intercept' by most programs, is £9,329 per month. The variable cost measure, labelled 'X coefficient' (or something similar in other spreadsheets), is £6.951 per patient-day. The linear cost function is

$$Y = \text{£9,329 per month} + (\text{£6.951} \times \text{patient-days})$$

As mentioned in the chapter, it is important to consider plausibility and reliability in evaluating a cost function and its estimates. Plausibility simply refers to whether the estimated cost function makes economic sense. We can assess this by examining the sign of the variable cost estimate. In the preceding cost function, this estimate is +£6.951. The positive sign in this cost function implies that as patient-days increase, facilities maintenance costs also increase (specifically, by £6.951 per patient day). We assess the economic plausibility of this positive relationship by asking ourselves whether it makes economic sense that an increase in patient-days should increase facilities maintenance costs. Based on our economic intuition, it appears that a positive relationship makes sense (that is, we would expect that increasing patient-days would increase the cost of cleaning supplies and repair materials such that total facilities maintenance costs increase). While plausibility appears to be a simple and straightforward item to assess, it is the most important element to assess in a cost function. We would not want to use a cost function to estimate and predict costs if it did not exhibit plausibility (even if it displayed good reliability) because, without plausibility, we do not fundamentally understand the cost function, which makes cost estimation and prediction suspect.

Regarding reliability, the computer output usually gives a number of statistical measures that indicate how well each cost driver explains the cost and how reliable the cost predictions are likely to be. A full explanation of the output is beyond the scope of this text. However, one of the most important statistics, the coefficient of determination, or R^2, is an important measure of reliability – how well the cost function fits the actual cost data. In general, the better a cost driver is at explaining a cost, the closer the data points will lie to the line, and the higher will be the R^2, which varies between 0 and 1. An R^2 of 0 means that the cost driver does not explain variability in the cost data, whereas an R^2 of 1 means that the cost driver explains the variability perfectly. The R^2 of the relationship measured with number of patient-days as the cost driver is 0.955, which is quite high. This value indicates that the number of patient-days explains facilities maintenance department cost extremely well. In fact, the number of patient-days explains 95.5 per cent of the past fluctuations in facilities maintenance department cost. Such a regression is highly reliable.

In contrast, performing a regression analysis on the relationship between facilities maintenance department cost and value of hospital room charges produces the following results:

Facilities maintenance department cost explained by value of hospital room charges	
Regression output	
Constant	£ 924
R^2	0.511
X coefficient(s)	0.012

While the positive sign of the variable cost estimate (+.012) appears to satisfy plausibility (that is, as hospital room charges increase we would expect facilities maintenance costs to also increase), the R^2 value, 0.511, indicates that the cost function using value of hospital room charges does not fit facilities maintenance department cost as well as the cost function using number of patient-days.

To use the information generated by regression analysis fully, an analyst must understand the meaning of the statistics and must be able to determine whether the statistical assumptions of regression are satisfied by the cost data. Indeed, one of the major reasons why cost analysts study statistics is to understand the assumptions of regression analysis better. With this understanding, analysts can provide their organisations with the best estimates of cost behaviour.

Summary problem for your review

PROBLEM

Comtell makes computer peripherals (disk drives, tape drives and printers). Until recently, managers predicted production scheduling and control (PSC) costs to vary in proportion to labour costs according to the following cost function:

$$\text{PSC costs} = 200\% \text{ of labour cost}$$

or

$$Y = 2 \times \text{labour cost}$$

Because PSC costs have been growing at the same time that labour cost has been shrinking, Comtell is concerned that its cost estimates are neither plausible nor reliable. Comtell's controller has just completed regression analysis to determine the most appropriate drivers of PSC costs. She obtained two cost functions using different cost drivers:

$$Y = 2 \times \text{labour cost}$$
$$R^2 = 0.233$$

and

$$Y = €10,000 \text{ per month} + (11 \times \text{number of components used})$$
$$R^2 = 0.782$$

1 How should the accountant determine which cost function better predicts PSC costs?

2 During a subsequent month, Comtell's labour costs were €12,000 and it used 2,000 product components. Actual PSC costs were €31,460. Using each of the preceding cost functions, prepare reports that show predicted and actual PSC costs and the difference or variance between the two.

3 What is the meaning and importance of each cost variance?

SOLUTION

1 The accountant should examine both the plausibility and the reliability of each cost function. Both costs seem plausible with positive signs on their respective variable cost estimates as we would expect. Regarding reliability, a statistical test of which function better explains past PSC costs compares the R^2 of each function. The second function, based on the number of components used, has a considerably higher R^2, so it better explains the past PSC costs. If the environment is essentially unchanged in the future, the second function probably will predict future PSC costs better than the first.

   A useful predictive test would be to compare the cost predictions of each cost function with actual costs for several months that were not used to measure the cost functions. The function that more closely predicted actual costs is probably the more reliable function.

2 Note that more actual cost data would be desirable for a better test, but the procedure would be the same. PSC cost predicted on a labour-cost basis follows:

Predicted cost	Actual cost	Variance
2 × €12,000 = €24,000	€31,460	€7,460 underestimate

PSC cost predicted on a component basis follows:

Predicted cost	Actual cost	Variance
€10,000 + (€11 × 2,000) = €32,000	€31,460	€540 overestimate

3 The cost function that relies on labour cost underestimated PSC cost by €7,460. The cost function that uses the number of components closely predicted actual PSC costs (off by €540). Planning and control decisions would have been based on more accurate information using this prediction than using the labour-cost-based prediction. An issue is whether the benefits of collecting data on the number of components used exceeded the added cost of the data collection.

Accounting vocabulary

account analysis, p. 88
activity analysis, p. 86
capacity costs, p. 81
coefficient of determination
   (R²), p. 94
committed fixed costs, p. 81
cost function, p. 84

cost measurement, p. 84
discretionary fixed costs,
   p. 82
engineering analysis, p. 87
high-low method, p. 91
least-squares regression, p. 94
linear-cost behaviour, p. 78

measurement of cost
   behaviour, p. 78
mixed costs, p. 79
regression analysis, p. 94
step costs, p. 79
visual-fit method, p. 93

Fundamental assignment material   MyAccountingLab

3.A1 Types of cost behaviour

Identify the following planned costs as (a) purely variable costs, (b) discretionary fixed costs, (c) committed fixed costs, (d) mixed costs, or (e) step costs. For purely variable costs and mixed costs, indicate the most likely cost driver.

1   Public relations employee compensation to be paid by Intel.
2   Crew supervisor in a John Lewis mail-order house; a new supervisor is added for every 12 workers employed.
3   Sales commissions based on revenue pounds sterling; payments to be made to advertising salespersons employed by Capital Radio, London.
4   Jet fuel costs of Ryanair.
5   Total costs of renting Lorries by the city of Birmingham; charge is a lump sum of £300 per month plus £.20 per mile.
6   Straight-line depreciation on desks in the office of an attorney.
7   Advertising costs, a lump sum, planned by Danone.
8   Rental payment by Royal Mail on a five-year lease for office space in a private office building.
9   Advertising allowance granted to wholesalers by 7-Up Bottling on a per-case basis.
10   Compensation of lawyers employed internally by Microsoft.
11   Total repairs and maintenance of a university classroom building.

3.A2 Activity analysis

Evergreen Signs makes customised wooden signs for businesses and residences. These signs are made of wood, which the owner glues and carves by hand or with power tools. After carving the signs, she paints them or applies a natural finish. She has a good sense of her labour and materials cost behaviour, but she is concerned that she does not have good measures of other support costs. Currently, she predicts support costs to be 60 per cent of the cost of materials. Close investigation of the business reveals that €50 times the number of power tool operations is a more plausible and reliable support cost relationship.

Consider estimated support costs of the following two signs that Evergreen Signs is making:

	Sign A	Sign B
Materials cost	€400	€200
Number of power tool operations	3	6
Support cost	?	?

1 Prepare a report showing the support costs of both signs using each cost driver and showing the differences between the two.

2 What advice would you give Evergreen Signs about predicting support costs?

3.A3 Division of mixed costs into variable and fixed components

Martina Fernandez, Managing Director of Evert Tool Co. Ltd, has asked for information about the cost behaviour of manufacturing support costs. Specifically, she wants to know how much support cost is fixed and how much is variable. The following data are the only records available:

Month	Machine hours	Support costs
May	850	£ 9,000
June	1,300	12,500
July	1,000	7,900
August	1,250	11,400
September	1,750	13,500

1 Find monthly fixed support cost and the variable support cost per machine-hour by the high-low method.

2 Explain how your analysis for requirement 1 would change if new October data were received and machine-hours were 1,700 and support costs were £15,800.

3 A least-squares regression analysis gave the following output:

$$\text{Regression equation: } Y = £3,355 + £6.10X$$

What recommendations would you give the Managing Director based on these analyses?

3.B1 Identifying cost behaviour patterns

At a seminar, a cost accountant spoke on identification of different kinds of cost behaviour. Tammy Li, a hospital administrator who heard the lecture, identified several hospital costs of concern to her. After her classification, Li presented you with the following list of costs and asked you to (1) classify their behaviour as one of the following: variable, step, mixed, discretionary fixed or committed fixed; and (2) to identify a likely cost driver for each variable or mixed cost.

1 Operating costs of X-ray equipment (€95,000 a year plus €3 per film).

2 Health insurance for all full-time employees.

3 Costs incurred by Dr Rath in cancer research.

4 Repairs made on hospital furniture.

5 Training costs of an administrative resident.

6 Straight-line depreciation of operating room equipment.

7 Costs of services of King Hospital Consulting.

8 Nursing supervisors' salaries (a supervisor is needed for each 45 nursing personnel).

3.B2 Activity analysis

Nampa Technology, a Portuguese manufacturer of printed circuit boards, has always estimated the support cost of its circuit boards with a 100 per cent 'markup' over its material costs.

An activity analysis suggests that support costs are driven primarily by the number of manual operations performed on each board, estimated at €4 per manual operation. Compute the estimated support costs of the following two typical circuit boards using the traditional markup and the activity analysis results:

	Board Z15	Board Q52
Material cost	€40.00	€60.00
Manual operations	15	7

Why are the cost estimates different?

Additional assignment material   MyAccountingLab

QUESTIONS

3.1 What is a cost driver? Give three examples of costs and their possible cost drivers.

3.2 Explain linear-cost behaviour.

3.3 'Step costs can be fixed or variable, depending on your perspective.' Explain.

3.4 Explain how mixed costs are related to both fixed and variable costs.

3.5 How do management's product and service choices affect cost behaviour?

3.6 Why are fixed costs also called capacity costs?

3.7 How do committed fixed costs differ from discretionary fixed costs?

3.8 Why are committed fixed costs the most difficult of the fixed costs to change?

3.9 What are the primary determinants of the level of committed costs? Discretionary costs?

3.10 'Planning is far more important than day-to-day control of discretionary costs.' Do you agree? Explain.

3.11 How can a company's choice of technology affect its costs?

3.12 Explain the use of incentives to control cost.

3.13 Why is it important for managers and accountants to measure cost functions?

3.14 Explain plausibility and reliability of cost functions. Which is preferred? Explain.

3.15 What is activity analysis?

3.16 What is engineering analysis? Account analysis?

3.17 Describe the methods for measuring cost functions using past cost data.

3.18 How could account analysis be combined with engineering analysis?

3.19 Explain the strengths and weaknesses of the high-low and visual-fit methods.

3.20 In the high-low method, does the high and low refer to cost-driver levels or to total cost levels? Explain.

3.21 Why is regression analysis usually preferred to the high-low method?

3.22 'You never know how good your fixed- and variable-cost measures are if you use account analysis or if you visually fit a line on a data plot. That's why I like least-squares regression analysis.' Explain.

3.23 (Appendix 3) Why should an analyst always plot cost data in addition to applying least-squares regression analysis?

3.24 (Appendix 3) What can we learn from R^2, the coefficient of determination?

3.25 At a conference, a consultant stated, 'Before you can control, you must measure.' An executive complained, 'Why bother to measure when work rules and guaranteed employment provisions in labour contracts prevent discharging workers, using part-time employees and using overtime?' Evaluate these comments.

CRITICAL THINKING EXERCISES

3.26 Mixed costs and the sales force

Wysocki Company pays its sales force a fixed salary plus a 5 per cent commission on all sales. Explain why sales force costs would be considered a mixed cost.

3.27 Committed and discretionary fixed costs in manufacturing

Among the fixed costs of Howarth Company are depreciation and research and development (R&D). Using these two costs as examples, explain the difference between committed and discretionary fixed costs.

3.28 Cost functions and decision making

Why is it important that decision makers in a corporation know the cost function for producing the company's products?

3.29 Statistical analysis and cost functions

What advantages does using regression analysis have over the visual-fit method for determining cost functions?

EXERCISES

3.30 Step costs

Which of the following are step costs? Why?

(a) Rent on a warehouse that is large enough for all anticipated orders.
(b) Teachers for a private elementary school; one teacher is needed for every 15 students.
(c) Sheet steel for a producer of machine parts; steel is purchased in carload shipments, where each carload contains enough steel for 1,000 parts.

3.31 Mixed Costs

The following cost function is a mixed cost. Explain why it is a mixed cost and not a fixed, variable, or step cost.

$$\text{Total cost} = €8,000 + €52 \times \text{units produced}$$

3.32 Various cost-behaviour patterns

In practice, there is often a tendency to simplify approximations of cost-behaviour patterns, even though the 'true' underlying behaviour is not simple. Choose from the following graphs A – H the one that matches the numbered items. Indicate by letter which graph best fits each of the situations described. Next to each number-letter pair, identify a likely cost driver for that cost.

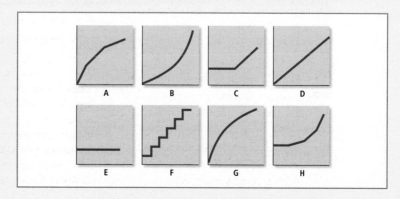

The vertical axes of the graphs represent total pounds sterling of costs incurred and the horizontal axes represent levels of cost driver activity during a particular time period. The graphs may be used more than once.

1 Cost of machining labour that tends to decrease as workers gain experience.

2 Price of an increasingly scarce raw material as the quantity used increases.

3 Guaranteed annual wage plan, whereby workers get paid for 40 hours of work per week even at zero or low levels of production that require working only a few hours weekly.

4 Water bill, which entails a flat fee for the first 10,000 gallons used and then an increasing unit cost for every additional 10,000 gallons used.

5 Availability of quantity discounts, where the cost per unit falls as each price break is reached.

6 Depreciation of office equipment.

7 Cost of sheet steel for a manufacturer of farm implements.

8 Salaries of supervisors, where one supervisor is added for every 12 phone solicitors.

9 Natural gas bill consisting of a fixed component, plus a constant variable cost per thousand cubic feet after a specified number of cubic feet are used.

3.33 Identifying discretionary and committed fixed costs

Identify and compute total discretionary fixed costs and total committed fixed costs from the following list prepared by the accounting supervisor for Huang Building Supply:

Advertising	€22,000
Depreciation	47,000
Health insurance for the company's employees	21,000
Management salaries	85,000
Payment on long-term debt	50,000
Property tax	32,000
Grounds maintenance	9,000
Office remodelling	21,000
Research and development	46,000

3.34 Cost effects of technology

Recreational Sports, an outdoor sports retailer, is planning to add a website for online sales. The estimated costs of two alternative approaches are as follows:

	Alternative 1	Alternative 2
Annual fixed cost	€200,000	€400,000
Variable cost per order	€ 8	€ 4
Expected number of orders	70,000	70,000

At the expected level of orders, which online approach has the lower cost? What is the indifference level of orders, or the 'break-even' level of orders? What is the meaning of this level of orders?

3.35 Account analysis

Custom Computers is a company started by two engineering students to assemble and market personal computers to faculty and students. The company operates out of the garage of one of the students' homes. From the following costs of a recent month, compute the total cost function and total cost for the month:

Telephone	€ 50, fixed
Utilities	260, fixed: 25% attributable to the garage, 75% to the house
Advertising	75, fixed
Insurance	80, fixed
Materials	7,500, variable, for five computers
Labour	1,800: €1,300 fixed plus €500 for hourly help for assembling five computers

3.36 High-low method

North Manchester Foundry produced 55,000 tons of steel in March at a cost of £1,150,000. In April, the foundry produced 35,000 tons at a cost of £950,000. Using only these two data points, determine the cost function for North Manchester.

3.37 Economic plausibility of regression analysis results

The head of the Warehousing Division of Lachton Co. Ltd, was concerned about some cost behaviour information given to him by the new assistant accountant, who was hired because of his recent training in cost analysis. His first assignment was to apply regression analysis to various costs in the department. One of the results was presented as follows:

> A regression on monthly data was run to explain building maintenance cost as a function of direct labour hours as the cost driver. The results are

$$Y = £7,810 - £.47X$$

> I suggest that we use the building as intensively as possible to keep the maintenance costs down.

The department head was puzzled. How could increased use cause decreased maintenance cost? Explain this counterintuitive result to the department head. What step(s) did the assistant accountant probably omit in applying and interpreting the regression analysis?

PROBLEMS

3.38 Controlling risk, capacity decisions, technology decisions

Consider the following hypothetical situation in the computer industry. HP had been outsourcing production to Acer and using overtime for as much as 20 per cent of production – HP's plants and assembly lines were running at 100 per cent of capacity and demand was sufficient for an additional 20 per cent. HP had considered increasing its capacity by building new, highly automated assembly lines and plants. However, the investment in high technology and capacity expansion was rejected.

Assume that all material and labour costs are variable with respect to the level of production and that all other costs are fixed. Consider one of HP's plants that makes the Pavillion model. The increase in annual fixed costs to convert the plant to use fully automated assembly lines is $20 million. The resulting labour costs would be significantly reduced and there would be no need for overtime or outsourced production. The annual costs, in millions of dollars, of the build option and the existing costs that include outsourcing and overtime are given in the following tables:

	Build option		
Per cent of current capacity	60	100	120
Material costs	$18	$30	$36
Labour costs	6	10	12
Other costs	40	40	40
Total costs	$64	$80	$88

	HP's existing costs using outsourcing/overtime		
Per cent of current capacity	60	100	120
Material costs	$18	$30	$ 36
Labour costs	18	30	44
Other costs	20	20	20
Total costs	$56	$80	$100

1 Prepare a line graph showing total costs for the two options: (a) build new assembly lines, and (b) continue to use overtime and outsource production of Pavillions. Give an explanation of the cost behaviour of the two options.

2 Which option enables HP's management to control risk better? Explain. Assess the cost-benefit trade-offs associated with each option.

3 A solid understanding of cost behaviour is an important prerequisite to effective managerial control of costs. Suppose you are an executive at HP. Currently the production (and sales) level is approaching the 100 per cent level of capacity, and the economy is expected to remain strong for at least one year. While sales and profits are good now, you are aware of the variability inherent in the computer business. Would you recommend committing HP to building automated assembly lines in order to service potential near-term increases in demand, or would you recommend against building, looking to the possible future downturn in business? Discuss your reasoning.

3.39 Separation of drug testing laboratory mixed costs into variable and fixed components

A staff meeting has been called at SportsLab, a drug-testing facility retained by several professional and sports leagues and associations. The chief of testing, Dr Hyde, has demanded an across-the-board increase in prices for a particular test because of the increased testing and precision that are now required.

The administrator of the laboratory has asked you to measure the mixed-cost behaviour of this particular testing department and to prepare a short report she can present to Dr Hyde. Consider the following limited data:

	Average test procedures per month	Average monthly cost of test procedures
Monthly averages, 20×7	400	£ 60,000
Monthly averages, 20×8	500	80,000
Monthly averages, 20×9	600	140,000

3.40 Interpretation of regression analysis

Study Appendix 3. The Tent Division of The Great Outdoor Equipment Company has had difficulty controlling its use of supplies. The company has traditionally regarded supplies as a purely variable cost. Nearly every time production was above average, however, the division spent less than predicted for supplies; when production was below average, the division spent more than predicted. This pattern suggested to Yuki Li, the new accountant, that part of the supplies cost was probably not related to production volume, or was fixed.

She decided to use regression analysis to explore this issue. After consulting with production personnel, she considered two cost drivers for supplies cost: (1) number of tents produced, and (2) square feet of material used. She obtained the following results based on monthly data.

	Cost driver	
	Number of tents	Square feet of material used
Constant	2,300	1,900
Variable coefficient	0.033	0.072
R^2	0.220	0.686

1 Which is the preferred cost function? Explain.

2 What percentage of the fluctuation of supplies cost depends on square feet of materials? Do fluctuations in supplies cost depend on anything other than square feet of materials? What proportion of the fluctuations is not explained by square feet of materials?

3.41 Regression analysis

Study Appendix 3. Mr Liao, CEO of a manufacturer of fine china and stoneware, is troubled by fluctuations in productivity and wants to compute how manufacturing support costs are related to the various sizes of batches of output. The following data show the results of a random sample of 10 batches of one pattern of stoneware:

Sample	Batch size, X	Support costs, Y
1	15	$180
2	12	140
3	20	230
4	17	190
5	12	160
6	25	300
7	22	270
8	9	110
9	18	240
10	30	320

1 Plot support costs, Y, versus batch size, X.

2 Using regression analysis, measure the cost function of support costs and batch size.

3 Predict the support costs for a batch size of 25.

4 Using the high-low method, repeat requirements 2 and 3. Should the manager use the high-low or regression method? Explain.

3.42 Review of Chapters 2 and 3

Manchester Musical Education Company (MME) provides instrumental music education to children of all ages. Payment for services comes from two sources: (1) a contract with Country Day School to provide private music lessons for up to 150 band students a year (where a year is 9 months of education) for a fixed fee of £150,000, and (2) payment from individuals at a rate of £100 per month for 9 months of education each year. In the Last school year, MME made a profit of £5,000 on revenues of £295,000:

Revenues:		
Country Day School contract	£150,000	
Private students	145,000	
Total revenues		£295,000
Expenses:		
Administrative staff	£ 75,000	
Teaching staff	81,000	
Facilities	93,500	
Supplies	40,500	
Total expenses		290,000
Profit		£ 5,000

MME conducted an activity analysis and found that teaching staff wages and supplies costs are variable with respect to student-months. (A student-month is one student educated for one month.) Administrative staff and facilities costs are fixed within the range of 2,000–3,000 student-months. At volumes between 3,000 and 3,500 student-months, an additional facilities charge of £8,000 would be incurred. During the last year, a total of 2,700 student-months of education were provided, 1,450 of which were for private students and 1,250 of which were offered under the contract with Country Day School.

1 Compute the following using cost information from last year's operations:

Fixed cost per year

Variable cost per student-month

2 Suppose that in the current year Country Day School decreased its use of MME to 120 students (that is, 1,080 student-months). The fixed contract price of £150,000 was still paid. If everything else stayed as it was Last year, what profit or loss would be made in the current year?

3 Suppose that at the beginning of the current year Country Day School decided not to renew its contract with MME, and the management of MME decided to try to maintain business as usual with only private students. How many students (each signing up for 9 months) would MME require to continue to make a profit of £5,000 per year?

CASES

3.43 Government health cost behaviour

Dr Stephanie White, the chief administrator of Dublin Clinic, a community mental health agency, is concerned about the dilemma of coping with reduced budgets in the next year and into the foreseeable future, despite increasing demand for services. In order to plan for reduced budgets, she first must identify where costs can be cut or reduced and still keep the agency functioning. The following are some data from the past year:

Programme area	Costs
Administration	
Salaries	
Administrator	€60,000
Assistant	35,000
Two secretaries	42,000
Supplies	35,000
Advertising and promotion	9,000
Professional meetings, dues and literature	14,000
Purchased services	
Accounting and billing	15,000
Custodial and maintenance	13,000
Security	12,000
Consulting	10,000
Community mental health services	
Salaries (two social workers)	46,000
Transportation	10,000
Outpatient mental health treatment	
Salaries	
Psychiatrist	86,000
Two social workers	70,000

1 Identify which costs you think are likely to be discretionary or committed costs.

2 One possibility is to eliminate all discretionary costs. How much would be saved? What do you think of this recommendation?

3 How would you advise Dr White to prepare for reduced budgets?

3.44 Identifying relevant data

eComp.com manufactures personal digital assistants (PDAs). Because these very small computers compete with laptops that have more functions and flexibility, understanding and using cost behaviour is very critical to eComp.com's profitability. eComp.com's controller, Kelly Hudson, has kept meticulous files on various cost categories and possible cost drivers for most of the important functions and activities of eComp.com. Because most of the manufacturing at eComp.com is automated, labour cost is relatively fixed. Other support costs comprise most of eComp.com's costs. Partial data that Hudson has collected over the past 25 weeks on one of these support costs, logistics operations (materials purchasing, receiving, warehousing and shipping), follow:

Week	Logistics costs, Y	Number of orders, X
1	€23,907	1,357
2	18,265	1,077
3	24,208	1,383
4	23,578	1,486
5	22,211	1,292
6	22,862	1,425

Week	Logistics costs, Y	Number of orders, X
7	23,303	1,306
8	24,507	1,373
9	17,878	1,031
10	18,306	1,020
11	20,807	1,097
12	19,707	1,069
13	23,020	1,444
14	20,407	733
15	20,370	413
16	20,678	633
17	21,145	711
18	20,775	228
19	20,532	488
20	20,659	655
21	20,430	722
22	20,713	373
23	20,256	391
24	21,196	734
25	20,406	256

1 Plot logistics costs, Y, versus number of orders, X. What cost behaviour is evident? What do you think happened in week 14?

2 What is your recommendation to Kelly Hudson regarding the relevance of the past 25 weeks of logistics costs and number of orders for measuring logistics cost behaviour?

3 Hudson remarks that one of the improvements that eComp.com has made in the past several months was to negotiate JIT deliveries from its suppliers. This was made possible by substituting an automated ordering system for the previous manual (labour-intensive) system. Although fixed costs increased, the variable cost of placing an order was expected to drop greatly. Do the data support this expectation? Do you believe that the change to the automated ordering system was justified? Why or why not?

CASE STUDY

Permaclean Products plc

David Otley, University of Lancaster

The central issue in this case concerns product pricing. The analysis requires the estimation of appropriate costs and assessing price-demand information using past sales data.

Permaclean Products is an old-established firm, located in Dunstable, manufacturing a comprehensive range of domestic cleaning materials. It has a sound reputation and a well-known brand name which has made it a market leader in a wide range of products designed for home use. Although Permaclean has several competitors, the total sales of each are small in comparison with those of Permaclean, mainly because none offers such a complete product range.

In 2009 the price of one of Permaclean's major products, Permashine, was raised from 75p per bottle to 99p when the product was repackaged in a newly designed bottle; however, the contents were identical to the previous pack, both in formulation and quantity. During the following two years sales fell by 27 per cent. At 75p per bottle Permashine had been competitively priced but when its price was increased manufacturers of similar products had not followed. In the period from 2007 to 2010 the price of competing products had been raised by only 5p.

Prices were fixed once a year, to come into force on 1 February, before the annual peak demand which occurred in the spring. In January 2011, John Williams, the marketing manager, met with Andrew Dutton, the chief accountant, to review the company's pricing policy for the coming year.

Permashine

Permashine is a proprietary cleaning product for bathrooms and in 2008 had accounted for over 10 per cent of the company's sales. Although there are a variety of competing products on the market, Permashine has special properties which make it especially suitable for cleaning baths made of acrylic materials. Such baths are becoming increasingly common, but great care has to be taken to avoid scratching them when they are being cleaned. Permashine contains no abrasive materials yet is able to clean acrylic surfaces with great efficiency, giving a surface shine that is very durable. No competing product appears to have this combination of advantages.

The process used in the manufacture of Permashine involves a hazardous chemical reaction that has to be precisely controlled. Production therefore takes place in a separate building on the same site as the main factory where the other products are made, but some distance from it. This production unit, which was constructed in 2003 for safety reasons, is not capable of being adapted for the manufacture of other Permaclean products without substantial expenditure. Although the manufacture of Permashine is potentially hazardous, no serious accidents have occurred during the 15 years in which it has been produced and the final product is itself completely harmless.

In early 2010, Andrew Dutton had installed an improved cost accounting system which allowed product costs to be determined and product profitability to be reviewed. With regard to Permashine, this took into account the new packaging costs, as well as the overhead costs that were separately attributable to the production unit. His analysis, shown in Table 1, indicated that the total cost of Permashine was greater than the current selling price of 75p. As a result, at the annual pricing review in 2009 the selling price was increased to 99p.

Although total industry sales continued to rise during 2009 and 2010, Permashine suffered a reduction in both its market share and its total sales, as shown in Table 2.

The 2011 pricing review

Both Mr Williams and Mr Dutton were concerned to improve the profitability of Permashine, as it was one of the company's major products. Mr Williams had joined the company in 2003 and had introduced a number of changes in the firm's marketing methods. One of his major successes had been his decision to replace wholesalers with a team of salaried sales representatives who sold the company's full product range direct to retailers. Mr Dutton had been appointed in 2007, following the retirement of the previous chief accountant and had been responsible for installing a modern computer-based accounting system.

Source: Otley, D. (1988) 'Permaclean Products plc', in D. Otley, D. Brownand C. Wilkinson (eds) *Case Studies in Management Accounting* (Hemel Hempstead, UK: Philip Allan Publishers). Reproduced with permission.

Table 1 Estimated costs of Permashine at various production volumes

Cost (p/bottle)	Annual production ('000 bottles)						
	250	300	400	500	600	700	800
Direct labour	17.5	17.5	17.0	17.0	17.0	17.5	18.0
Materials	8.0	8.0	8.0	8.0	8.0	8.0	8.0
Dept. overhead							
Variable	9.0	9.0	9.0	9.0	9.0	9.0	9.0
Fixed	14.4	12.0	9.0	7.2	6.0	5.1	4.5
Factory overhead							
(20% of direct labour)	3.5	3.5	3.4	3.4	3.4	3.5	3.6
Factory cost	52.4	50.0	46.4	44.6	43.4	43.1	43.1
Selling and							
administration cost							
at 80% of factory cost	41.9	40.0	36.3	35.7	34.7	34.5	34.5
Total cost	94.3	90.0	82.7	80.3	78.1	77.6	77.6

Table 2 Permashine: sales and price

	2004	2005	2006	2007	2008	2009	2010
Permashine sales ('000 bottles)	400	429	486	525	536	462	391
Total industry sales ('000 bottles)	2000	2050	2250	2200	2300	2650	2900
Permashine % of market	20	21	22	24	23	17.5	13.5
Permashine price (p)	60	70	70	75	75	99	99
Competitors' price range (p)	56–62	65–70	65–70	69–75	69–75	70–80	75–80

Mr Williams pressed for a return to the previous price of 75p for Permashine; at this price he was confident that the market share of the product could be increased to 20 per cent in 2011. He thought that total industry sales would continue to increase to at least 3 million bottles in 2011, and that Permashine was capable of regaining its previous position, provided that it was competitively priced. Because Permaclean had a modern production facility and a manufacturing output greater than any competitor, he was confident that factory production costs were the lowest in the industry. He therefore supported a policy of reducing the price so that other firms would find it uneconomic to continue to compete.

Mr Williams was convinced that sales would continue to fall if the price were to be maintained at 99p, although he believed that there would always be a premium market for Permashine because of its unique qualities. He thought that annual sales were unlikely to fall below 250 000 bottles even at the current price.

Mr Dutton replied that he was well aware of the problems being experienced in selling the higher-priced product. Nevertheless, his analysis showed that the 99p price covered the costs of the product, even at the lowest volume envisaged. If the price were reduced to 75p costs would fail to be covered, even if sales volume rose to the 800 000 bottles which represented the maximum practical capacity of the plant. He referred to his detailed costings (Table 1) to support his argument. These figures, he stated, were based on actual data from past years; where data were not available, he had made what he regarded as realistic assumptions.

Question

What price would you recommend for Permashine? Support your recommendation with detailed calculations, making the underlying assumptions on which your analysis is based as clear as possible.

Need more practice? Instant feedback?
Visit www.myaccountinglab.com

MyAccountingLab

Featuring unlimited practice questions, a personalised study plan that identifies the areas where you need to focus for better marks, and interactive material designed to help all kinds of learners, *MyAccountingLab* is a vital tool for maximising your understanding, confidence and success.

Log in at **www.myaccountinglab.com** to see why 92 per cent of students recently surveyed recommend *MyAccountingLab*.

Cost management systems and activity-based costing

Learning objectives

When you have finished studying this chapter, you should be able to:

1 Describe the purposes of cost management systems.

2 Explain the relationship among cost, cost object, cost accumulation and cost assignment.

3 Distinguish between direct and indirect costs.

4 Explain the major reasons for allocating costs.

5 Identify the main types of manufacturing costs: direct materials, direct labour and indirect production costs.

6 Explain how the financial statements of merchandisers and manufacturers differ because of the types of goods they sell.

7 Understand the main differences between traditional and activity-based costing (ABC) systems and why ABC systems provide value to managers.

8 Use activity-based management (ABM) to make strategic and operational control decisions.

9 Describe the steps in designing an activity-based costing system (Appendix 4).

Dell computers sit on desktops throughout the world.

Dell

Michael Dell founded Dell Inc. in 1984 while still a student at the University of Texas. He originally called the company PC's Limited. He changed the name to Dell Computer Corporation in 1988, the same year the company issued its first shares to the public, and to Dell Inc. in 2003. It made *Fortune* magazine's list of the world's 500 largest companies for the first time in 1992. By 1999 it had become the largest seller of personal computers in the United States. In 2004 Michael Dell stepped down as CEO.

In early 2005 Dell topped the list of *Fortune* magazine's 'Most admired companies'. However, by the end of the year Dell was experiencing difficulties – quality problems and declining sales. Between 2005 and 2007 Dell's market share fell from 19 per cent to 14 per cent, and it lost its market-share lead to Hewlett Packard. Michael Dell stepped back in as CEO in early 2007. In January 2011, IDC's *Worldwide Quarterly PC Tracker* reported HP's market share at 20.2 per cent, with Acer's at 12.8 per cent and Dell's at 11.9 per cent.

Dell pioneered the selling of personal computers directly to end users by selling them over the web. By waiting to produce a computer until it received an order and applying just-in-time manufacturing (see p. 14), Dell achieved a cost structure that gave it an advantage over its competitors. In the 10 years leading up to 2010, revenues increased from $12 billion to $53 billion. Michael Dell earlier summarised Dell's problems: 'As we evolved we lost focus and allowed our cost structure to become non-competitive.'

How does Dell face up to competitive challenges? Dell's 2010 Annual Report sheds light on this: 'We are committed to balancing our mix of products and services to optimise profitability, liquidity and growth. We believe this strategy will help us achieve higher margins, but may put pressure on our industry unit share position for personal computers and servers at certain times.' ■

Cost management systems

Objective 1
Describe the purposes of cost management systems.

To support managers' decisions, accountants develop **cost management systems (CMS)** – collections of tools and techniques that identify how management's decisions affect costs. A cost management system provides:

1 cost information for strategic management decisions;

2 cost information for operational control; and

3 measures of inventory value and cost of goods sold for financial reporting to investors, creditors and other external stakeholders.

External parties, such as investors and creditors, and internal managers use cost information. Financial statements for external users need *aggregate* measures of inventory value and the cost of goods sold. In contrast, managers need more detailed cost information on individual products or services for strategic and operational decisions. The management uses of information drive the need for sophisticated cost management systems.

Managers seek accurate and timely cost information for strategic reasons, such as deciding on the optimal product and customer mix, choosing the value-chain functions to receive special focus or to outsource, and making investment decisions. For these decisions, managers want to obtain the costs of individual products, services, customers and processes associated with value-chain functions. For example, Dell made a strategic decision in 2007 to begin selling PCs through retail outlets, in addition to selling computers via the internet and its telephone network. Such decisions rely both on specific cost information and wider strategic intent.

Managers also strive for efficiency by controlling costs. To assess process improvement efforts and other operational cost control programs, managers need accurate and timely feedback on costs. Consider the technical support services provided by Dell. To control costs and still provide needed services, Dell revamped its technical services operation, tailoring its services to fit the specific needs of different customers. For example, it now offers different support for IT staff and for non-IT professionals, and it outsourced some technical support to India. The accounting system reported the costs of various technical support activities and helped managers decide how best to minimise the cost of providing needed technical support.

Throughout this text, we describe many CMS tools and techniques that help managers make decisions. Examples include the contribution margin technique and cost–volume–profit analysis you read about in Chapter 2. All of these tools and techniques have one thing in common – the managers' desire to obtain accurate information about costs. This chapter focuses on **cost accounting**, the part of a cost management system that measures costs for the purposes of management decision making and financial reporting.

Cost accounting systems

Objective 2
Explain the
relationship among
cost, cost object,
cost accumulation
and cost assignment.

We define **cost** as a sacrifice or giving up of resources for a particular purpose. Consider the cost of labour resources. An organisation pays (gives up) cash or its equivalent to employees in exchange for their work. We measure the cost of labour resources by the dollars (or other monetary units such as yen or euros) paid to obtain the labour resources. However, managers generally want more from their accountants than simply the cost of the resources used. They often want to know the cost of something in particular, such as a product or a service. Anything for which decision makers desire a separate measurement of costs is a **cost object** (or **cost objective**). Although managers most often want to know the cost of a product or service, there are many other possible cost objects. Examples include customers, departments, territories and activities such as processing orders or moving materials. For example, one large manufacturer of pet food products recently changed its cost management system to report both the cost of products it makes and the cost to serve the company's major retail customers. It discovered that all its products were profitable, but the cost to sell to and service some customers was greater than the profit margin on the products sold to these customers. Knowing this, the company was able to develop a strategy to improve the profitability of these customers.

The cost data that managers use for decision making come from the **cost accounting system** – the techniques used to determine the cost of a product, service, customer or other cost object. The cost accounting system is the most fundamental component of a cost management system. It supports all other cost management system tools and techniques.

Cost accounting systems need to provide accurate and timely cost information to help managers make decisions. Without accurate and timely cost information, many decisions can be downright harmful.

All kinds of organisations – manufacturing firms, service companies and nonprofit organisations – need some form of cost accounting. Consider the following on the modern role of management accountants and cost accounting systems:

> *Because the [cost accounting] system now mirrors the manufacturing process, the engineers and production staff believe the cost data produced by the cost accounting system. Engineering and production regularly ask accounting to help find the product design combination that will optimize costs . . . The accountants now participate in product design decisions. They help engineering and production understand how costs behave . . . The system makes the professional lives of the accountants more rewarding.*
>
> Hewlett-Packard Company

A cost accounting system typically includes two processes:

1 **Cost accumulation.** Collecting costs by some 'natural' classification, such as materials or labour, or by activities performed such as order processing or machine processing.

2 **Cost assignment.** Attaching costs to one or more cost objects, such as activities, processes, departments, customers or products.

Exhibit 4.1 is a simple illustration of these two basic processes for materials costs. First, the system collects the costs of all materials. Then, it assigns these costs to the departments that use the materials and further to the specific activities performed in these departments.

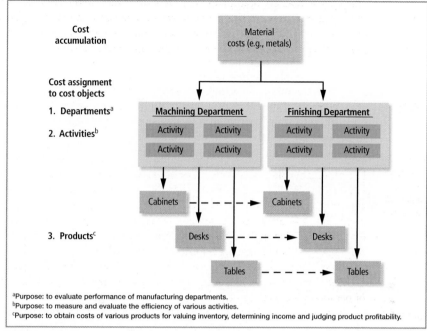

^aPurpose: to evaluate performance of manufacturing departments.
^bPurpose: to measure and evaluate the efficiency of various activities.
^cPurpose: to obtain costs of various products for valuing inventory, determining income and judging product profitability.

Exhibit 4.1 Cost accumulation and assignment

Last, the system assigns the accumulated costs to the products made – cabinets, tables and desks. The total materials cost of a particular product is the sum of the materials costs assigned to it in the various departments. For example, the cost of a finished desk would include the following materials costs:

● metal top, sides and legs produced by the various activities in the machining department;

● bolts, brackets, screws, drawers, handles and knobs pieced together by finishing department activities.

A company's cost accounting system can have a great influence on managers' decisions. Any manager who makes a decision based on financial data relies on the accuracy of the cost accounting system. In today's business environment, characterised by highly competitive global markets and complex production processes, designing cost accounting systems that provide accurate and useful information is a key success factor for all types of organisations. The financial director of a major manufacturing firm recently reported that the company's main competitive advantage was its financial information system, not its manufacturing or distribution capabilities.

This chapter describes some major types of cost accounting systems. However, before describing the systems, we need to develop an understanding of the various cost terms that managers and accountants commonly use.

Cost terms used for strategic decision making and operational control purposes

Accountants have their own language laced with jargon. As a manager, you will need to understand the basics of this language. This section focuses on three key terms: direct costs, indirect costs and cost allocation.

■ Direct costs, indirect costs and cost Allocation

Costs may be direct or indirect with respect to a particular cost object. Accountants can identify **direct costs** specifically and exclusively with a given cost object in an economically feasible way. Parts and materials included in a product are the most common types of direct cost. For example, to determine the cost of parts assembled into a Dell laptop computer, Dell's accountants simply look at the purchase orders for the specific parts used. A key characteristic of direct costs is that accountants can physically identify the amount of the cost that relates exclusively to a particular cost object. We call this **tracing** the direct cost to the cost object. In contrast, accountants cannot specifically and exclusively identify the amount of **indirect costs** related to a given cost object in an economically feasible way. Examples of indirect costs include facilities rental costs, depreciation on equipment and many staff salaries.

Consider whether the cost of labour is direct or indirect to the products being made. Some employees work specifically on particular products. Their costs are direct to those products because accountants can trace the costs to the products. Others, such as supervisors, general managers, accountants and legal staff, do not work on individual products. Because accountants cannot trace such labour costs to the products, they are indirect costs. A century ago, a large proportion of labour costs were direct. Why? Because most companies had a labour-intensive production process where a majority of the workers had hands-on involvement with producing their company's products. To produce 10 per cent more units of a particular product, a company typically needed about 10 per cent more workers. Today the situation is different. Automated production processes have eliminated many hands-on jobs and more employees just oversee automated processes that make many different products. The costs of such labour are indirect. Why? Because it is not economically feasible to trace their costs to the individual products.

Just because a cost is indirect does not mean it is unimportant. Companies cannot continue to make products without facilities, equipment, supervisors and even accountants. One of the most challenging tasks of a cost accounting system is to assign indirect costs to cost objects. Because indirect costs in many companies today exceed 50 per cent of total costs, accurate assignment of indirect costs is crucial. Decision makers who ignore indirect costs or receive inaccurate measures of indirect costs often make poor decisions.

In addition to knowing that a cost is indirect, managers also want to know whether it is fixed or variable – that is, whether it varies in proportion to production volume – as discussed in Chapter 2. Some indirect costs are variable. Examples are supplies such as tacks and glue in a furniture-making company and the cost of ink in a printing company. Others, such as most depreciation and supervisors' salaries, are fixed. Managers must distinguish between variable and fixed indirect costs to make informed decisions.

To assign indirect costs to cost objects, we use **cost allocation**, which assigns indirect costs to cost objects in proportion to the cost object's use of a particular **cost-allocation base**. A cost-allocation base is some measure of input or output that determines the amount of cost to be allocated to a particular cost object. An ideal cost-allocation base measures how much of the particular cost is *caused by* the cost object. Note the similarity of this definition to that of a cost driver – an output measure that causes costs. Therefore, *most cost-allocation bases are cost drivers*. Consider how much assembly-equipment depreciation, an indirect cost, Dell's accountants should assign to a particular model of laptop. They might allocate this indirect cost to various models based on the allocation base 'machine hours', a measure of the amount of assembly equipment time used to make a particular computer. If making a Latitude laptop uses two machine hours while making an Inspiron laptop uses only one, then Dell would allocate twice as much machine depreciation cost to the Latitude. Whenever an accountant uses the term *allocated*, we know the related cost is an indirect cost assigned to a cost object using a cost-allocation base.

Decision makers should be careful in using allocated indirect costs. When the allocation base measures how much cost is *caused by* the cost objects, allocated costs will be relevant for many decisions. When the allocation is not related to the cause of the costs, managers have reason to suspect the accuracy of the resulting costs.

Because cost allocations are so important to cost measurement in today's companies, let's look more deeply into why and how companies allocate their indirect costs.

Purposes of cost allocation

Objective 4
Explain the major reasons for allocating costs.

What logic should we use for allocating costs? The answer depends on the purpose(s) of the cost allocation. In short, there are no firm rules that we can rely on – there is no universally best cost-allocation system. Instead of cost allocation rules, we focus on general concepts that provide guidance when managers design these systems.

Recall that cost allocations support a company's CMS – the system providing cost measurements for strategic decision making, operational control and external reporting. Following are four purposes of cost allocation. The first two support strategic decision making and operational control, the third supports external reporting and the last one supports elements of all three:

1 *To predict the economic effects of strategic and operational control decisions.* Major strategic decisions include setting the optimal product and customer mix, establishing pricing policy and setting policy about which value-chain functions to develop as core competencies. Managers also need to predict the economic effects – both benefits and costs – of process improvement efforts. Managers within an organisational unit should be aware of all the consequences of their decisions, even consequences outside of their unit. Examples are the addition of a new course in a university that causes additional work in the registrar's office, the addition of a new flight or an additional passenger on an airline that requires reservation and booking services or the addition of a new specialty in a medical clinic that produces more work for the medical records department.

2 *To provide desired motivation and to give feedback for performance evaluation.* Companies often hold managers responsible for total costs that include allocated costs. Therefore, cost allocations influence management behaviour and can help motivate managers to make decisions that are in the company's best interests. For example, some organisations allocate the costs of legal services or internal management consulting services to spur managers to make sure the benefits of the services exceed the costs. Other organisations do not allocate such costs because top management wants to encourage their use.

3 *To compute income and asset valuations for financial reporting.* Companies allocate costs to products to measure inventory costs for their balance sheets and cost of goods sold for their income statements.

4 *To justify costs or obtain reimbursement.* Sometimes organisations base prices directly on costs. For example, government contracts often specify a price that includes reimbursement for costs plus some profit margin. In these instances, cost allocations directly determine the revenue received from a product or service.

Ideally, a single cost allocation would serve all four purposes simultaneously. However, thousands of managers and accountants will testify that most systems fail to achieve this ideal. Instead, cost allocations are often a major source of discontent and confusion to the affected parties. Allocating fixed costs usually causes the greatest problems. Why? Because it is often hard to find a cost-allocation base that accurately measures the amount of a fixed cost resource used by a cost object. When a system cannot meet all purposes simultaneously, managers and accountants need to identify which of the purposes are most important in a particular situation.

Often external reporting rules for measuring inventory and cost of goods sold dominate by default because they are externally imposed. Financial reporting standards in most contexts generally require a company to assign all production-related costs and only production-related costs to its products. Often these are not the costs managers want assigned to products for their decision-making purposes. For example, managers may prefer not to allocate all production-related indirect fixed costs. If a particular management decision does not affect such fixed costs, it can be misleading to include them as part of the cost of the product. In addition, managers may want to allocate costs from nonproduction parts of the value chain, such as R&D, marketing or administrative expenses. Management decisions might have a major effect on such costs and allocating them can make managers more aware of this effect. Thus, when managers need individual product or customer costs for decision making and performance evaluation, they often have to adjust the financial reporting standards' required. Generally, using allocations for planning and control that differ from those used for inventory-costing purposes creates benefits that exceed the added cost.

Methods of cost allocation

Now let's turn to the question of how companies allocate costs. Because final products or services are important cost objects to nearly all organisations, we focus on how companies trace direct costs and allocate indirect costs to these cost objects. Examine Exhibit 4.2 to see the difference between assigning direct costs (tracing) and indirect costs (allocation) to final products.

Physically tracing the direct costs is usually straightforward. For example, the cost accounting system can measure the amount and cost of each material added to a product. Workers can record the time spent on each product and the system can value each hour at the worker's appropriate wage rate. Systems to accurately measure direct costs have been available for decades, even centuries.

Allocating indirect costs is more complex and accountants have more chance to influence the resulting costs by the allocation choices they make. Because of the growth in indirect costs for most companies, allocating indirect costs is especially important. Allocation is a five-step process:

1   Accumulate indirect costs for a period of time, for example one month, into one or more cost pools. A **cost pool** is a group of individual costs that a company allocates to cost

Exhibit 4.2 Assignment of direct and indirect costs to products, services, customers or activities

objects using a single cost-allocation base. Many simple cost accounting systems place all indirect production costs in a single cost pool.

2 Select an allocation base for each cost pool. If possible, choose a cost driver – a measure that causes the costs in the cost pool. Companies that have a single cost pool for indirect costs often use direct-labour hours or direct-labour cost as the cost-allocation base.

3 Measure the units of the cost-allocation base used for each cost object (for example, the number of direct-labour hours used on a particular product) and compute the total units used for all cost objects.

4 Determine the percentage of total cost-allocation base units used for each cost object.

5 Multiply the percentage in step 4 by the total costs in the cost pool to determine the cost allocated to each cost object.

Consider the depreciation on Dell's assembly equipment mentioned on p. 118. How would Dell's accountants allocate July's $400,000 depreciation cost to Inspiron and Latitude laptop computers? Let's apply the five steps:

1 In July accountants measured the depreciation cost, the only cost in this cost pool, at $400,000.

2 The cost-allocation base selected is machine hours.

3 Dell used 2,000 machine hours in July to make Inspiron laptops and 3,000 machine hours to make Latitude laptops, for a total of 5,000 machine hours.

4 This means that Dell used 2,000 ÷ 5,000 = 40% of the machine hours for Inspiron and 3,000 ÷ 5,000 = 60% of the machine hours for Latitude.

5 The depreciation cost allocated to Inspiron is 40% × $400,000 = $160,000, and that allocated to Latitude is 60% × 400,000 = $240,000.

Another way of calculating this allocation is to compute the depreciation cost per machine hour or $400,000 ÷ (3,000 + 2,000) = $80. Then the allocation to Inspiron is $80 × 2,000 = $160,000 and the allocation to Latitude is $80 × 3,000 = $240,000. The allocation can be depicted using symbols as follows:

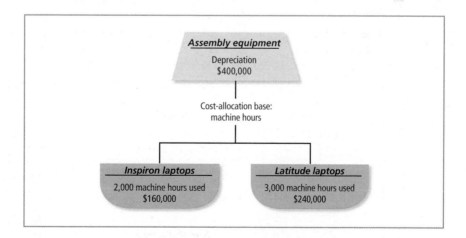

Companies also use cost allocation to assign indirect costs to cost objects other than products or services. Suppose we are allocating costs to departments. A logical cost-allocation base for allocating rent costs to departments is the square feet that each department occupies. Other logical cost-allocation bases include cubic feet for allocating depreciation of heating and air conditioning equipment and total direct cost for allocating general administrative expense.

Also note the varying terminology you will see in practice. Accountants use many different terms to describe cost allocation. You may encounter terms such as *allocate, apply, absorb, attribute, reallocate, assign, distribute, redistribute, load, burden, apportion* and *reapportion* being used interchangeably to describe the allocation of indirect costs to cost objects.

▣ Unallocated costs

There are some costs that lack an identifiable relationship to a cost object. Often it is best to leave such costs unallocated. **Unallocated costs** are costs that an accounting system records but does not allocate to any cost object. They might include research and development (R&D), process design, legal expenses, accounting, information services and executive salaries. Keep in mind, though, that an unallocated cost for one company may be an allocated cost or even a direct cost for another. Why? Because businesses vary considerably in their value chains and operating processes. For example, product design is a critical success factor for some businesses and, therefore, managers in such companies are willing to spend the time and effort to deploy sophisticated accounting systems to allocate or even directly trace product design costs. For other companies, this cost is not important enough to warrant special treatment.

Consider the statement of operating income for Li Company in panel A of Exhibit 4.3. Li Company makes cabinets, tables and chairs. Each item in panel A represents accumulated totals for all products sold for an entire reporting period. To help make a strategic decision regarding which of the three products to emphasise, it would be useful to 'unbundle' these totals to find the profitability of each product. How can we do this?

Consider cost of goods sold, which includes all manufacturing costs. Like most companies, Li Company finds that it is easy to trace direct-material costs to individual products. However,

Panel A Statement of operating income [external reporting purpose]		Panel B Contribution to corporate costs and profit [internal strategic decision-making purpose]			
		Cabinets	Tables	Chairs	Cost type, assignment method
Sales	$470,000	$280,000	$100,000	$90,000	
Cost of goods sold:					
Direct material	120,000	50,000	30,000	40,000	Direct, direct trace
Indirect manufacturing	110,000	45,000	30,000	35,000	Indirect, allocation based on machine hours
Total cost of goods sold	230,000	95,000	60,000	75,000	
Gross profit	240,000	185,000	40,000	15,000	
Selling expenses:					
Sales salaries	47,000	28,000	10,000	9,000	Direct, direct trace
Distribution	30,000	12,000	8,000	10,000	Indirect, allocation based on
Total selling expenses	77,000	40,000	18,000	19,000	weight
Contribution to corporate expenses and profit	163,000	$145,000	$22,000	$(4,000)	
Corporate expenses (unallocated):					
Administrative salaries	40,000				
Other administrative	60,000				
Total unallocated expenses	100,000				
Operating income	$63,000				

Exhibit 4.3 Direct, indirect and unallocated costs for Li Company

all other manufacturing costs are difficult to trace directly, so Li Company treats them as indirect and allocates them to products.

Let's assume that Li Company uses machine hours to allocate all indirect manufacturing costs. If the use of machine hours is closely related to the amount of indirect costs incurred, managers responsible for each of the products would be satisfied that the cost of goods sold and gross profit amounts in Exhibit 4.3 are accurately measured. Last year Li Company used 9,000, 6,000 and 7,000 machine hours to make cabinets, tables and chairs, respectively, a total of 22,000 machine hours. Therefore, the allocation of the $110,000 indirect manufacturing costs to cabinets is $110,000 \times (9,000 \div 22,000) = \$45,000$, to tables is $\$110,000 \times (6,000 \div 22,000) = \$30,000$ and to chairs is $\$110,000 \times (7,000 \div 22,000) = \$35,000$, as shown in Panel B of Exhibit 4.3.

Li Company also has both direct and indirect selling expenses. It can directly trace sales salaries to individual products because the company pays its sales force on a strictly commission basis. In addition, it allocates the expenses for the distribution of products to warehouses in a fair manner based on weight. Last year, shipments of cabinets, tables and chairs weighed 6,000, 4,000 and 5,000 pounds, respectively, for a total of 15,000 pounds. Consequently, the allocation of the $30,000 total distribution costs to cabinets is $\$30,000 \times (6,000 \div 15,000) = \$12,000$, to tables is $\$30,000 \times (4,000 \div 15,000) = \$8,000$ and to chairs is $\$30,000 \times (5,000 \div 15,000) = \$10,000$.

Because Li Company's allocation bases are good measures of what causes the indirect costs, managers are likely to view the allocated costs as fair. While the managers in charge of chairs may not be happy with the reported loss of $4,000, they would feel that it is a reasonable measure of profitability.

Li Company could find no reasonable means to allocate administrative salaries or other administrative expenses. Therefore, these corporate-level expenses remain unallocated. Why not allocate the administrative salaries and other administrative expenses to the products by using some simple measure, such as 'per cent of total revenue generated' or 'number of units sold'? Because managers generally want allocations to be a fair measure of the costs incurred on their behalf. If allocations are arbitrary, managers will not trust them and may make decisions based on other less relevant information. In Li Company, the work performed by the administrative personnel was not a simple function of the volume of units sold or revenue generated. Companies that cannot find such a causal measure often choose not to allocate the costs.

Assigning a cost as direct, indirect or unallocated requires judgement. Such judgements are based on the type of cost, its magnitude and how expensive it is to implement a system to trace or allocate the cost. If it is not too expensive, managers prefer costs to be direct rather than indirect. This gives them greater confidence in the reported costs of products, services or other cost objects. However, the cost of a system for tracing costs to cost objects should not be greater than its expected benefits. For example, a system for tracing the exact cost of steel and fabric (direct cost) to desk chairs may be worth its cost. However, it may be too expensive to trace the exact cost of rivets or thread (indirect costs) to the chairs, even though such a tracing is technically possible.

Frequently, managers want to know the costs of more than one cost object, such as departments, products, services, activities or resources. In these cases, companies allocate costs to more than one cost object. For example, suppose the manager of a local telephone company is faced with two decisions: (1) what price to charge for installing new phone service and (2) what costs to include in the installation department's budget. Among the various costs relevant to both decisions is the salary of a supervisor in the installation department who oversees both phone installations and routine service calls. For the pricing decision, the supervisor's salary is an indirect cost. Why? Because accountants cannot physically trace this cost to the phone installations or service calls and therefore must allocate the cost. However, for the department budget, the supervisor's salary is a direct cost. Why? Because accountants can physically identify 100 per cent of the cost as belonging to the department. This is an example of a cost that is both direct (to the department) and indirect (to the product or service). In general, many more costs are direct when the cost object is a department than when it is a product or service.

Cost terms used for external reporting purposes

While this text focuses mostly on costs used by managers, it is important to recognise that cost accounting systems also support the financial reporting process. One of the four purposes of cost management systems is to provide aggregate measures of inventory value and cost of goods manufactured for external reporting to investors, creditors and other external stakeholders. We will discuss four attributes of these costs: manufacturing costs, product versus period costs, costs on the balance sheet and costs on the income statement.

■ Categories of manufacturing costs

Objective 5
Identify the main types of manufacturing costs: direct materials, direct labour and indirect production costs.

Manufacturing companies differ from merchandising companies in the way they accumulate and report the cost of inventories. In manufacturing operations, which transform materials into other goods through the use of labour and factory facilities, products are frequently the cost object. Manufacturing companies classify production costs as either (1) direct material, (2) direct labour or (3) indirect production costs:

1 **Direct-material costs** include the acquisition costs of all materials that a company identifies as a part of the manufactured products and that it can trace to the products in an economically feasible way. Examples are iron castings, lumber, aluminium sheets and subassemblies. Direct materials often do not include minor items, such as tacks or glue, because the cost of tracing these items is greater than the possible benefit of having more precise product costs. Such items, often called supplies or indirect materials, are a part of indirect production costs.

2 **Direct-labour costs** include the wages (and, in some companies, related benefits) paid to employees that a company can trace specifically and exclusively to the manufactured goods in an economically feasible way. Examples are the wages of machine operators and assemblers. In highly automated factories with a flexible workforce, there may be no direct labour costs. Why? Because all workers may spend time overseeing numerous products, making it economically infeasible to physically trace any labour cost directly to specific products.

3 **Indirect production costs** (also called **indirect manufacturing costs, factory overhead, factory burden** or **manufacturing overhead**) include all costs associated with the production process that a company cannot trace to products or services in an economically feasible way. Accountants consider many labour costs, such as that of janitors, forklift truck operators, plant guards and storeroom clerks, to be indirect labour because it is impossible or economically infeasible to trace such activity to specific products. Other examples of factory overhead costs are power, supplies, supervisory salaries, property taxes, rent, insurance and depreciation.

Regardless of the type of cost accounting system a company uses for internal decision-making purposes, its production costs must appear in its financial statements for external financial reporting purposes. The costs appear both on the income statement, as cost of goods sold, and on the balance sheet, as inventory amounts.

■ Product costs and period costs

When preparing income statements and balance sheets, accountants frequently distinguish between product costs and period costs. **Product costs** are costs identified with products manufactured or purchased for resale. In a manufacturing company, product costs include direct materials, direct labour and indirect production costs. These costs first become part of the inventory; thus, we sometimes call them **inventoriable costs**. These inventoriable costs become expenses in the form of cost of goods sold when the company sells the inventory.

In contrast, **period costs** become expenses during the current period without becoming part of inventory. Period costs are associated with nonproduction value-chain functions (research and development, design, marketing, distribution and customer service). Accounting information systems accumulate these costs by departments, such as R&D, advertising and sales. Most firms' financial statements report these costs as selling and administrative expenses. In short, these costs do not become a part of the reported inventory cost of the manufactured products for financial reporting purposes.

Exhibit 4.4 illustrates product and period costs. The top half shows a merchandising company, such as a retailer or wholesaler, that acquires goods for resale without changing their basic form. The only product cost is the purchase cost of the merchandise. The company holds unsold goods as merchandise inventory and shows their costs as an asset on a balance sheet. As the company sells the goods, their costs become expenses in the form of 'cost of goods sold'. A merchandising company also has a variety of selling and administrative expenses. These costs are period costs because the company deducts them from revenue as expenses without ever being regarded as a part of inventory.

The bottom half of Exhibit 4.4 shows product and period costs in a manufacturing company. Note that the company transforms direct materials into salable items with the help of direct-labour and indirect production costs. You can see that the balance sheets of manufacturers and merchandisers differ with respect to inventories. Instead of one inventory account, a manufacturing concern has three inventory accounts that help managers trace all product costs through the production process to the time of sales. These accounts are as follows:

- **Direct-material inventory**: material on hand and awaiting use in the production process.

- **Work-in-process inventory**: goods undergoing the production process but not yet fully completed. Costs include appropriate amounts of the three major manufacturing costs: direct material, direct labour and indirect production costs.

- **Finished-goods inventory**: goods fully completed but not yet sold.

The only accounting difference between manufacturing and merchandising companies is in the composition of product costs. A merchandising company includes in product cost only the amount paid for the merchandise it sells. In contrast, a manufacturing company includes in product cost such items as insurance, depreciation and wages that are incurred in the production process in addition to the cost of materials. Although merchandising and manufacturing companies differ in how they account for product costs, they account for period costs the same. Regardless of the type of company, selling and administrative costs never become part of inventory – they are period costs.

Objective 6
Explain how the financial statements of merchandisers and manufacturers differ because of the types of goods they sell.

■ Balance sheet and income statement presentation of costs

How do published financial statements of merchandising and manufacturing companies differ in presenting costs? Let's first examine balance sheets and notice the extra detail provided by a manufacturer:

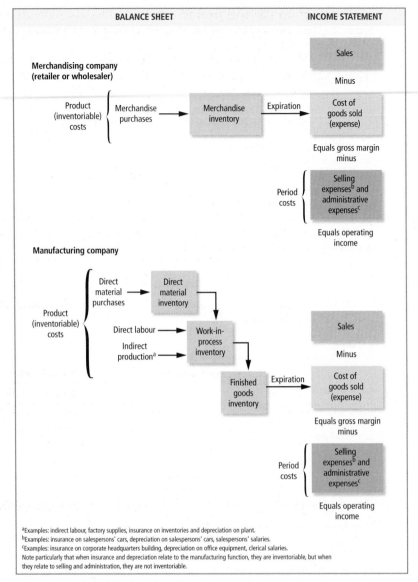

Exhibit 4.4 Relationship of product costs and period costs

Current asset sections of balance sheets

Manufacturer			Retailer or wholesaler	
Cash		$ 4,000	Cash	$ 4,000
Receivables		25,000	Receivables	25,000
Finished goods	$32,000			
Work in process	22,000			
Direct material	23,000			
Total inventories		77,000	Merchandise inventories	77,000
Other current assets		1,000	Other current assets	1,000
Total current assets		$107,000	Total current assets	$107,000

A manufacturer's balance sheet will show values for raw materials, work in process and finished goods, whereas that of a merchandiser (retailer or wholesaler) will show the value of the merchandise inventories.

Now consider income statements. We have already mentioned that the reporting of selling and administrative expenses is typically the same for manufacturing and merchandising organisations. What about the cost of goods sold? In published financial statements you will generally see one line for cost of goods sold regardless of the type of company. Only the way the companies calculate the cost of goods sold differs, as follows:

Manufacturer	Retailer or wholesaler
Manufacturing cost of goods produced and then sold, usually composed of the three major categories of cost: direct material, direct labour and indirect production costs	Merchandise cost of goods sold, usually composed of the purchase cost of items, including freight in, that are acquired and then resold

The following shows how manufacturers and retailers or wholesalers calculate their cost of goods sold (numbers assumed):

Cost of goods sold section of the income statement

Manufacturer			Retailer or wholesaler	
Beginning finished goods inventory		€ 4,000	Beginning merchandise inventory	€ 4,000
Cost of goods manufactured:			Purchases	40,000
Direct materials used	€20,000			
Direct labour	12,000			
Indirect production	8,000	40,000		
Cost of goods available for sale		44,000	Cost of goods available for sale	44,000
Ending finished goods inventory		8,000	Ending merchandise inventory	8,000
Cost of goods sold		€36,000	Cost of goods sold	€36,000

Sometimes confusion arises because accountants and managers use the terms *costs* and *expenses* loosely. *Cost* is a broad term that describes the amount paid for an activity, product or service. *Expenses* specifically denote all costs deducted from revenue on an income statement in a given period. All costs eventually become expenses, but they are not expenses until accountants deduct them from revenue in the income statement. Thus, manufacturing costs become an expense on an income statement (called cost of goods sold) via the multistep inventory procedure shown earlier in Exhibit 4.4. In contrast, selling and administrative costs become expenses immediately in all types of companies.

Now that we understand cost classifications, let's examine the types of cost accounting systems that accumulate and report costs. There are many different types of cost accounting systems, but we can describe most of the important features of these systems by looking at two general types – traditional and activity-based cost accounting systems.

Traditional and activity-based cost accounting systems

Objective 7
Understand the main differences between traditional and activity-based costing (ABC) systems and why ABC systems provide value to managers.

Companies adopt cost accounting systems that are consistent with their management philosophies and their production and operating technologies. Changes in philosophies or technologies often prompt corresponding changes in cost accounting systems. For example, when BorgWarner's Automotive Chain Systems Operation transformed its manufacturing operation to a just-in-time manufacturing system with work cells, it also changed its cost accounting system. This change in the way BorgWarner operated made the existing cost accounting system obsolete. According to management, the new cost accounting system, coupled with the new production systems, 'improved the overall reporting, controls and efficiency dramatically'.

Until the 1990s, most companies across the globe used **traditional costing systems** – those that do not accumulate or report costs of activities or processes. Traditional costing systems often use a single cost pool for all indirect production costs with labour cost or labour hours as a cost-allocation base. Such systems work well with simple production processes. Consider a company that makes only a few products for which direct-material and direct-labour costs are a high percentage of total costs. Indirect production costs are a small percentage of total costs so the system combines them into one cost pool and allocates them to products using only one cost allocation base, direct-labour hours. Such a company can achieve a high level of accuracy of product costs with a traditional costing system.

As companies grow, as they face increasing global competition and as their operations become more complex, they often refine their traditional costing systems to increase the accuracy of product or service costs. They do this by accumulating indirect costs into multiple cost pools, often one for each department. Consider a company that has two operating departments, assembly and finishing. The resources in the assembly department are mainly large, expensive machines. The finishing department has only a few machines but many employees. Because operations within each department are relatively simple, the company might choose a traditional costing system that allocates manufacturing overhead using machine hours as an allocation base in the assembly department and labour hours as an allocation base in the finishing department.

But what about a more complex situation where a company makes hundreds or thousands of different products and indirect production costs are a large percentage of total costs? What if the many different products consume resources at widely varying rates? Achieving a high level of cost accuracy in such an operating environment requires a more elabourate cost accounting system such as an **activity-based costing (ABC) system** – a system that first accumulates indirect resource costs for each of the *activities* of a particular plant, department, value-chain function or organisation and then assigns the cost of each activity to the products, services or other cost objects that require that activity. Most ABC systems provide highly accurate product or customer costs that a company can use for strategic decisions. Further, accumulating and reporting costs by activities helps managers to understand the cause–effect relationships between day-to-day activities and product or customer costs and thereby aids the operational control purpose of cost management systems. Many managers believe that ABC systems help them better manage their organisations. The 'Business first' box on p. 129 explains why some companies use ABC.

Comparing activity-based and traditional costing

Let's take a closer look at how ABC differs from traditional costing. One of the most important differences between traditional and ABC systems is the extent of allocation across the value chain. Traditional systems generally assign only production costs – and not the costs of other value-chain functions – to the products. Why? Because traditional systems often focus on simply measuring inventory values for financial reporting purposes.

ABC systems, in contrast, focus on the costs that are important to decision makers. They often allocate the costs of processes such as design, marketing, order processing and customer service in addition to production costs. As a result, ABC systems are more complex but promise more accurate costs to aid managerial decision making.

Activity-based costing also causes managers to look closely at the relationships among resources, activities and cost objects – essentially analysing the unit's production process. Many ABC teams find it useful to develop a **process map** – a schematic diagram that captures the interrelationships among cost objects, activities and resources. These maps can help accountants and managers to better understand the company's operations.

Let's see how to draw process maps by examining the two examples in Exhibit 4.5. We depict resources by the ▨ symbol. When a product, service or customer is the cost object, we will use the symbol ▬ for the cost object. When the cost object is an activity we use a ▨ .

BUSINESS FIRST
Use of activity-based costing

Republic Hospital, a 900-bed public hospital in Singapore, admits 55,000 patients, treats over 100,000 patients in its Accident and Emergency Department and sees 500,000 patients in its specialist outpatient clinics. A substantial portion of its revenue is derived from the government's subsidy to the patients. Even with the subsidies, the hospital requires a robust number of non-subsidised patients to maintain a healthy financial position. Republic faces keen competition with 20 other public and private hospitals for the non-subsidised patients. She needs to get a reasonable estimate of the cost of the medical services offered to be able to price them competitively and for proper control purposes. The current flat rates for each broad category of services hinder the process of competitive and efficient pricing by hiding cross-subsidisation in the system.

Dr Murthy, head of the medical intensive care unit (MICU) in the Republic Hospital, conducted a study to determine the feasibility of using activity-based costing (ABC) to provide a reasonably accurate estimate of the actual costs. His unit provides kidney dialysis that replaces the blood purification and water and electrolyte balance functions of the kidney. The typical patient comes into the MICU with multiple organ dysfunction, which contributes to the high variability in treatment time.

Amy undertook the study as a consultant. She observed the process and took notes on the timing of the activities in the process. She decides to focus on the use of nursing resources as the dialysis appears to be a nurse intensive activity. Once the dialysis starts, the nurse will monitor the patient's condition and the dialysis machine parameters hourly. Periodic blood tests are taken to evaluate the condition of the patient. She may be required to troubleshoot the machine to prevent the blood in the lines from clotting. The nurse, sometimes with the help of the doctor, has to make adjustments to the lines or even restart the dialysis.

Amy divides the dialysis processes into three phases, namely, the set-up phase, the monitoring phase and the completion phase. She finds that the start-up and the completion phases are quite straight-forward with almost a standard number of activities. The bulk of variability of the activity intensity and resource utilisation comes from the middle phase, where monitoring, periodic blood test, fluid change and trouble-shooting occur.

Dr Murthy was surprised when Amy reported that the patient who stays for 72 hours has contact with nurses for only about 25 per cent of the time. Furthermore, he finds that 67 per cent of the nursing cost varies with the length of the dialysis. This made him realise that cross-subsidisation had been occurring among the patients and the longer stay patients had been underpaying.

This case is based on a study of activity-based costing carried out by the case authors in a local hospital in Singapore.

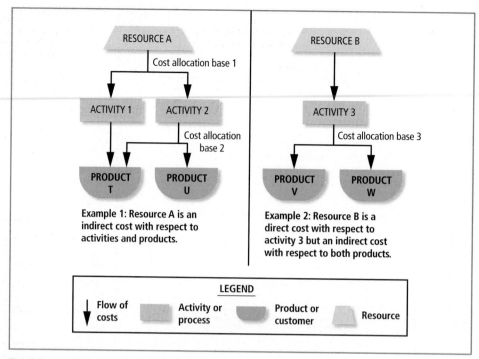

Exhibit 4.5 Basic concepts for process maps

When a resource supports only one activity or an activity applies to only one product, the cost of the resource or activity is direct. In Exhibit 4.5, the costs of Resource B and Activity 1 are direct to Activity 3 and Product T, respectively. When a resource supports two or more activities or an activity applies to two or more products, we must divide the cost among the activities or products. If we can physically trace the costs, they are direct. Otherwise we need to allocate them. In Exhibit 4.5 we assume that we allocate the costs of Resource A, Activity 2 and Activity 3, each to two cost objects. The process map identifies the cost-allocation base on the arrow between the resource or activity cost and the cost object.

An illustration of traditional and ABC systems

Now let's look at a simple example that demonstrates the main differences between traditional and ABC systems and shows the reasons why many managers prefer ABC systems. Lopez Plastics Company makes just two product lines, plastic casings for pens and plastic casings for mobile phones. The company had an operating loss last quarter of €64,500. Management needs to take immediate actions to improve profitability.

You are the vice president of operations. You have to decide which of the two product lines to emphasise to improve profitability. You also wish to reduce costs – especially in the production function of the value chain. Lopez Plastics currently uses a traditional cost accounting system, but you are considering deploying an ABC system to support strategic decision making and operational control.

Exhibit 4.6 shows the company's traditional cost accounting system in panel A and the related two financial reports for the most recent quarter in panel B. Notice the three types of costs: direct, indirect and unallocated. The traditional costing system traces the direct materials and direct labour costs to the products. Note that we depict these direct materials and direct labour costs with a product or customer symbol. It allocates the indirect production costs (€220,000) to each product in proportion to the direct-labour hours consumed

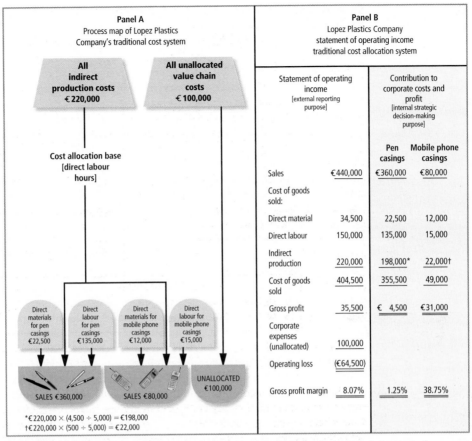

Exhibit 4.6 Lopez Plastics Company's traditional costing system and statement of operating income

in making the product. Last period, the company used 4,500 and 500 direct-labour hours to make pen casings and mobile phone casings, respectively, for a total of 5,000 hours. So it allocated $(4,500 \div 5,000) = 90\%$ of the indirect costs to pen casings and $(500 \div 5,000) = 10\%$ to mobile phone casings. Finally, the system does not assign the unallocated value-chain costs (€100,000) to either product. The gross profit and gross profit margin lines for both products, shown at the bottom of the two right-hand columns of panel B, indicate that mobile phone casings is the more profitable product line.

Many traditional systems, such as that of Lopez Plastics, use only one cost driver as a basis for allocating indirect production costs. When does a traditional costing system provide accurate product costs? When there is a plausible and reliable relationship between the single cost driver and all the indirect resource costs being allocated. In today's complex business environments, this is rare. Let's take a careful look at Lopez Plastics' production requirements to see if the traditional cost accounting system is providing the costing accuracy required for strategic decision making and operational control.

Pen casings have a simple design and a simple production process. The company produces them in high volumes, using 90 per cent of its direct-labour time. Pen casings rarely require special customer support or engineering work. This means that indirect production-support costs, such as design engineering of the pen casings, will be small.

Mobile phone casings, in contrast, have a more complex design and the company produces them in small volumes, accounting for only 10 per cent of its direct labour time.

Customers who buy mobile phone casings have specific design requirements that cause much production engineering work. Most of the engineering work performed at Lopez Plastics supports the production of mobile phones. So, common sense tells us that we should allocate most of the costs of engineering to the phone casings. How significant is the cost of engineering-related work? Of the €220,000 total indirect cost, engineering-related costs are €40,000.

But Lopez Plastics uses a traditional cost system. It does not separately identify or report the indirect costs of the engineering activity. Instead, the €40,000 of resources used for engineering activity – such as engineer salaries and depreciation of computer-aided design (CAD) equipment – is part of the single indirect resource cost pool. The company allocates all €40,000 of these indirect costs using the cost driver direct-labour time as the cost-allocation base. Thus, it allocates only 10 per cent of the engineering costs to the mobile phone casings. This simply does not make sense. We conclude that the traditional system probably does not provide the level of costing accuracy needed. How can we improve Lopez Plastics' costing accuracy? How can we change the design of the company's cost accounting system to better support strategic decision making and operational control?

We could use an ABC system to (1) identify a cost pool for each significant production activity – including engineering activity as one cost pool, (2) assign each indirect resource cost to the appropriate cost pool, and (3) allocate the costs in each activity-cost pool to products using plausible and reliable cost drivers as allocation bases. Exhibit 4.7 depicts a **two-stage ABC system**, which uses two stages of allocation to get from the original indirect resource cost to the final product or service cost. (At this point, Lopez Plastics uses the ABC system only for production costs, so the €100,000 of nonproduction value-chain costs remains unallocated.) The first stage allocates indirect resource costs to activity-cost pools, in this case two activities, processing activity and production-support activity. The second stage allocates activity costs to the products or services. In essence, the cost objects in the first stage are the activities and the cost objects in the second stage are the products. You will find a more detailed example of a two-stage ABC system in Appendix 4 on pp. 140–9.

In two-stage ABC systems, the first-stage allocation often uses estimated percentages as the allocation base. In our example, Lopez Plastics has only two indirect resources, (1) plant and machinery and (2) engineers and CAD equipment and only two activities, (1) processing and (2) production support, as shown in Exhibit 4.7. The cost of engineers and CAD equipment depends mainly on the amount of time engineers spend on a product. Engineers spend, on average, about 48 minutes each hour performing production-support activities, such as designing casings. They spend the other 12 minutes supervising the processing activity. Thus, we allocate $(48 \div 60) = 80\%$ and $(12 \div 60) = 20\%$ of the cost of engineers and CAD equipment to the production-support and processing activities, respectively.

The cost of plant and machinery depends mostly on the square feet of space used. Processing uses 75 per cent of the space and production support uses 25 per cent, so processing gets 75 per cent of the plant and machinery cost and production support gets 25 per cent. This gives us a total cost of the processing activity of €143,000 and a total cost of the production-support activity of €77,000.

Now consider the second-stage allocation. It allocates the costs of the two activities, processing and production support, to the two products, pen casings and mobile-phone casings. There are several possible cost-allocation bases for the production-support activity costs, including 'number of customer-generated engineering changes' and 'number of distinct parts'. The cost-allocation base should be a good measure of the consumption of production-support activity. Let's assume this is 'number of distinct parts'. Suppose pen casings have only 5 distinct parts compared to 20 for mobile phone casings. We would allocate $20 \div (20 + 5) \times €77,000 = €61,600$ of the production-support activity costs to mobile phone casings and the remaining €15,400 to pen casings. This allocation better measures the use of engineering services than does the allocation based on the traditional system. Why? Because mobile phone casings cause $(20 \div 25) = 80\%$ of the production-support activity costs, but the traditional system allocates

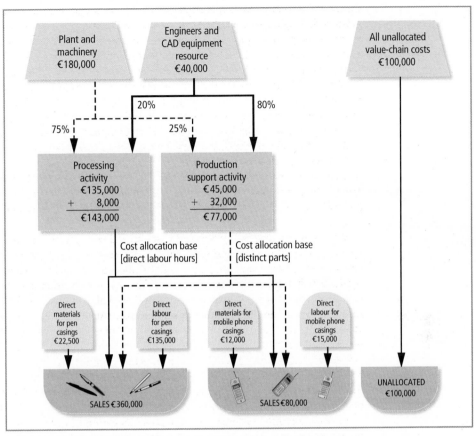

Exhibit 4.7 Lopez Plastics Company's ABC system

only 10 per cent of such costs to mobile phone casings. In contrast, the ABC system allocates the appropriate 80 per cent of the production-support activity costs to mobile phone casings.

We will continue this example in the 'Summary problem for your review' below, but first let's consider one more advantage of ABC systems. In many companies, managers try to gain cost savings by efficiently managing activities. If Lopez Plastics wants its managers to reduce the cost of producing mobile phone casings, the managers will probably focus on possible cost savings in either processing or production support. They may also redesign the product to reduce direct materials costs or reengineer the production process to reduce direct labour costs. But often the largest potential savings are in the indirect costs. By carrying out activities more efficiently, managers reduce the costs of the products that use those activities.

What information do managers need to examine the efficiency of activities? At a minimum, they need to know the cost of each activity. Traditional systems do not generate this cost information, while ABC systems do. Therefore, in addition to providing better costing activity, ABC systems can also promote better operating efficiency.

Traditional costing systems may fulfil initial cost information requirements within a firm but become obsolescent over a period of time. What are some signals that a cost system needs to be redesigned? Cooper (2007) identifies the following:

- functional managers want to drop seemingly profitable lines;
- profit margins are hard to explain;
- it is hard to make products show large profits;

Summary problem for your review

PROBLEM

Refer to the Lopez Plastics illustration, starting with the financial reports based on the traditional cost accounting system in panel B of Exhibit 4.6, p. 131. Based on these reports, a marketing manager has proposed a plan that emphasises mobile phone casings due to their large gross profit margin (38.75 per cent) compared to that of pen casings (1.25 per cent).

Now, management implements the ABC system shown in Exhibit 4.7, p. 133. The first stage of the two-stage ABC system has been completed and the results are the activity-cost-pool figures given in Exhibit 4.7 – processing activity costs of €143,000 and production-support activity costs of €77,000. You need to perform the second-stage allocations to determine the profitability of each product line. The cost-allocation base for processing activity is direct-labour hours and the cost-allocation base for production-support activity is number of distinct parts. Data on the use of these cost-allocation bases for the last quarter are as follows:

	Pen casings	Mobile phone casings
Direct labour hours	4,500	500
Distinct parts	5	20

Calculate the gross profit and gross profit margin for each product based on ABC. Do your results differ significantly from those based on the traditional cost accounting system in Exhibit 4.6? Explain. Evaluate marketing's plan. Propose a product-mix strategy for the company.

SOLUTION

The table that follows shows the gross profit for each product using ABC costs.

Financial reports for Lopez Plastics Company activity-based cost allocation system

	Panel A Statement of operating income [external reporting purpose]	Panel B Contribution to corporate costs and profit [internal strategic decision-making and operational-control purposes]	
		Pen casings	Mobile phone casings
Sales	€ 440,000	€ 360,000	€ 80,000
Cost of goods sold:			
Direct material	34,500	22,500	12,000
Direct labour	150,000	135,000	15,000
Processing activity	143,000	128,700*	14,300
Production-support activity	77,000	15,400†	61,600
Cost of goods sold	404,500	301,600	102,900
Gross profit	35,500	€ 58,400	€(22,900)

(*continues*)

	Panel A Statement of operating income [external reporting purpose]	Panel B Contribution to corporate costs and profit [internal strategic decision-making and operational-control purposes]	
		Pen casings	**Mobile phone casings**
Corporate expenses (unallocated):	100,000		
Operating loss	€(64,500)		
Gross profit margin	8.07%	16.22%	(28.63%)

* The cost driver is direct-labour hours. The company used $4,500 \div (4,500 + 500) = 90\%$ of direct-labour hours to produce pen casings. Thus, the allocation is €143,000 × .90 = €128,700.

† The cost driver is distinct parts. The company used $5 \div (20 + 5) = 20\%$ of distinct parts to make pen casings. Thus, the allocation is €77,000 × .20 = €15,400.

The ABC system gives results that are dramatically different from those of the traditional cost allocation system. Pen casings are generating substantial profits for the company, while mobile phone casings are losing money. Why is there such a dramatic difference between the two cost accounting systems? It's because the traditional cost-accounting system doesn't recognise differences in the production process for each of the two products. Only the mobile phone casings require large amounts of the production-support activity. The ABC system correctly allocates most of this cost to the mobile phone casings, while the traditional system allocates most of it to the pen casings. The ABC system first separates the processing-related costs from the production-support costs. Then, it allocates each activity cost to the products based on the proportion of the activity used by each product.

Marketing's plan most likely will result in significantly lower profitability. The company's top management should make the strategic decision to emphasise pen casings because of its large gross profit margin when accurately measured. The mobile phone casings are losing money, so that product line needs to be carefully evaluated. Possible actions include raising prices, changing the design by reducing the number of distinct parts, working with suppliers to reduce the cost of direct materials, improving the efficiency of direct labour or dropping the product line.

- departments have their own cost systems;
- the accountancy department spends a lot of time on special projects;
- you have a high margin niche all to yourself;
- competitors' prices are unrealistically low;
- customers do not mind price increases;
- the results of bids are hard to explain;
- vendor bids are lower than expected.[1]

Understanding these signals will enable organisations to swiftly redesign their costing system in support of corporate operations strategy.

We now are in a position to complete our ABC analysis and answer our strategic issue regarding our product mix strategy. We do this in the following 'Summary problem for your review'. It is important for you to work this problem carefully to gain a clear understanding of the basic concepts and value of an ABC system.

---

[1] R. Cooper 'Does your company need a new cost system?', *Journal of Cost Management* (Spring), 45 – 49.

MAKING MANAGERIAL DECISIONS

Suppose you have been asked to attend a meeting of top management of your company. When the meeting begins, you are asked to explain in general terms the main differences and similarities in traditional and ABC systems and why managers might prefer ABC costs for decision-making purposes. You have only Exhibits 4.6 and 4.7 as a guide, so you quickly display these side-by-side on a PowerPoint slide, and, after taking a deep breath, you begin to talk. What similarities and differences would you point out? What advantages do ABC costs have?

Answer

1 Traditional costing systems are much simpler than ABC systems and are usually less costly to maintain.
2 Traditional systems and ABC systems both have all three types of costs: direct, indirect and unallocated.
3 ABC systems identify multiple cost pools, each representing a particular production activity. Traditional systems use only one cost pool that

includes all indirect resource costs. This allows ABC systems to better match costs with the causes of those costs.
4 ABC systems assign indirect resource costs to cost objects in two stages of allocation, where the first stage allocates costs to activities and the second stage allocates activity costs to final cost objects such as products, services or customers. Traditional systems assign indirect resource costs to final cost objects in just one stage.
5 ABC systems require many more cost-allocation bases than do traditional systems. When these cost-allocation bases are both plausible and reliable cost drivers, the overall accuracy of product, service or customer cost is improved.
6 ABC systems provide more operational information on the costs of activities, which managers can use to reduce costs by improving operating efficiencies for each activity.

Activity-based management: a cost management system tool

Objective 8
Use activity-based management (ABM) to make strategic and operational control decisions.

As we mentioned previously, ABC systems not only develop more accurate costs, they also aid in the control of costs. Recall that managers' day-to-day focus is on managing activities, not costs. Because ABC systems also focus on activities, they are a very useful tool in cost management systems. **Activity-based management (ABM)** is using the output of an activity-based cost accounting system to aid strategic decision making and to improve operational control of an organisation. The strategic decision to emphasise pen casings at Lopez Plastics is an example of ABM. In the broadest terms, ABM aims to improve the value received by customers and to improve profits by identifying opportunities for improvements in strategy and operations.

One of the most useful applications of ABM is distinguishing between value-added and **non-value-added costs**. A **value-added cost** is the cost of an activity that a company cannot eliminate without affecting a product's value to the customer. Value-added costs are necessary (as long as the activity that drives such costs is performed efficiently). In contrast, companies try to minimise non-value-added costs, costs that a company can eliminate without affecting a product's value to the customer. Activities such as handling and storing inventories, transporting partly finished products from one part of the plant to another and changing the setup of production-line operations to produce a different model of the product are all non-value-adding activities. A company can often reduce, if not eliminate, them by careful redesign of the plant layout and the production process.

Another ABC-related technique is **benchmarking**, the continuous process of comparing products, services and activities to the best industry standards. Benchmarking is a tool to help an organisation measure its competitive posture. Benchmarks can come from within the organisation, from competing organisations or from other organisations having similar processes.

Consider the production of laptops at Dell. Unit costs for key activities provides the basis for benchmarking the work groups in one production facility with those at others and possibly with industry standards. In addition, Dell can use the cost-allocation bases for key activities – for example, the time to assemble a motherboard – as operational benchmarks. The most efficient work groups and centres can share their ideas for process improvements with other groups and centres.

Companies must exercise caution when benchmarking, especially when using financial benchmarks. Compare a Norwegian bank's branches in Hammerfest and Oslo. The bank's benchmarking system uses the financial benchmark *cost per deposit* to measure deposit-processing efficiency. The Oslo branch managers pointed out at least two problems that put them at a disadvantage. First, costs, especially labour costs, differ between Hammerfest and Oslo. Employees in metropolitan areas generally receive higher salaries because of their higher cost of living. Therefore, higher bank cashier salaries in Oslo increase the cost per deposit. Second, different branches can implement an ABC system in different ways. In this case, Hammerfest's ABC system does not allocate equipment depreciation to the deposit-processing activity; these costs remain unallocated. In contrast, the Oslo branch allocates this cost to the processing activity. This will also cause the cost per deposit to be higher at the Oslo branches. As a result, even if the cashiers process deposits faster and more accurately at the Oslo branch, their performance will not appear to be as good as the cashiers at the Hammerfest branch. Perhaps a better measure of the deposit process would be the *time to process a deposit*, a strictly nonfinancial benchmark.

■ Benefits of activity-based costing and activity-based management

Activity-based costing systems are more complex and costly than traditional systems. Thus, companies that have relatively simple operating systems may not realise sufficient benefits to warrant using ABC systems. But more organisations in both manufacturing and nonmanufacturing industries are adopting activity-based costing systems for a variety of reasons:

- Fierce competitive pressure has resulted in shrinking profit margins. Companies may know their overall margin, but they often do not have confidence in the accuracy of the margins for individual products or services. Some are winners and some are losers – but which ones are which? Accurate costs are essential for answering this question. Managers can use ABC information to set an optimal product mix and to estimate the profit margins of new products.

- Greater diversity in the types of products and services as well as customer classes results in greater operating complexity. Often in such situations the consumption of a company's shared resources also varies substantially across products and customers – a condition that adds to the value of ABC systems.

- Indirect costs are far more important in today's automated world-class manufacturing environment than they have been in the past. In many industries, automated equipment is replacing direct labour. Indirect costs are sometimes more than 50 per cent of total cost. Because ABC systems focus on indirect costs, they are more common in companies with automated production processes.

- The rapid pace of technological change has shortened product life cycles. Hence, companies do not have time to make price or cost adjustments once they discover costing errors. The accurate costs produced by ABC systems are essential.

- The costs associated with bad decisions that result from inaccurate cost estimates are substantial. Examples include bids lost due to overcosted products hidden losses from undercosted products and failure to detect activities that are not cost effective. Companies with accurate ABC product costs have a competitive advantage over those with inaccurate costs.

- Computer technology has reduced the costs of developing and operating ABC systems. Most ERP systems (see p. 14) routinely include ABC modules.

While many companies throughout the world are adopting ABC systems, some German companies, including Deutsche Telekom and Henkel, have gone a step further. They use a cost accounting system called **Grenzplankostenrechnung (GPK)**. Most GPK systems use between 400 and 2,000 cost pools to allocate indirect manufacturing costs. The 'Business first' box below summarises some of the characteristics of GPK.

BUSINESS FIRST
GPK and ABC: support for short-term and long-term decisions

Many companies throughout the world have developed sophisticated cost accounting systems. While many companies have adopted ABC, many northern European companies, especially in France, Norway, Sweden, the Netherlands and Germany are increasingly using GPK, a system first developed 50 years ago in Germany. Among the GPK companies are Porsche, STIHL, Deutsche Telekom and DaimlerChrysler.

Advances in computer technology have made widespread use of these cost accounting systems more practical. When companies adopt Enterprise Resource Planning (ERP) systems that include software for ABC and GPK, they can upgrade their cost accounting systems without a huge additional investment. The ERP system of SAP, a German software company that helped pioneer such systems, offers the framework for GPK as part of its management accounting module, a main factor in the expanding use of GPK. Because STIHL uses SAP worldwide, it was able to more easily roll out the use of GPK in its US subsidiary.

ABC and GPK embody both similarities and differences. Both allocate costs to products, services or customers using multiple cost pools with various cost-allocation bases. A main difference is that GPK separates fixed and variable costs and applies only variable costs to products or services. Although the ABC approach could do the same, most ABC systems focus on applying all production-related costs (and, often, some nonproduction value-chain costs). Thus, GPK systems measure profitability on a contribution-margin basis, while ABC systems generally produce full-cost margins. Another difference between ABC and GPK is how they define cost pools for allocation. ABC companies focus on activities, with only a few major identified activities. In contrast, GPK companies focus on cost centres and may have thousands of them.

Deutsche Telekom has about 20,000, although Porsche has only 450, and most companies have between 400 and 2,000. Most cost centres are work units of only a few people, often 10 workers or fewer. In both systems, the cost centre or activity is the focus of day-to-day cost control. The GPK systems bring this focus down to a much lower level than do most ABC systems.

Which is best, ABC or GPK? Like many management accounting issues, the answer is 'it depends'. Because GPK focuses on contribution margins, it provides information that is more relevant for short-term decisions. In contrast, ABC starts with a long-term perspective and produces information more suited to strategic decisions. However, GPK systems can add a full-cost calculation for long-term decision purposes and many ABC systems can separate fixed and variable costs for short-term decisions. Further, the difference between cost-centre and activity-based cost pools may not be especially significant because underlying cost pools and cost drivers can be similar in both systems. Although there remain basic philosophical differences related to allocation of fixed costs and definitions of cost pools, in practice companies that use a combination of GPK and ABC principles may find the best of both worlds. For example, the Hospital for Sick Children in Toronto merged GPK with its ABC system to produce financial information that was more useful to management.

Sources: G. Frield, H. Kupper and B. Pedell, 'Relevance added: combining ABC with German cost accounting', *Strategic Finance*, June 2005, pp. 56–61; K. Krumwiede, 'Rewards and realities of German cost accounting', *Strategic Finance*, April 2005, pp. 27–34; Carl S. Smith, 'Going for GPK,' *Strategic Finance*, April 2005, pp. 36–39; Brian Mackie, 'Merging GPK and ABC on the road to RCA', *Strategic Finance*, November 2006, pp. 33–39; P. Sharman and B. Mackie, 'Grenzplankostenrechnung (GPK): German cost accounting, flexible planning and control', IMA website, http://www.imanet.org/pdf/3202.pdf.

Highlights to remember

1 **Describe the purposes of cost management systems.** Cost management systems provide cost information for external financial reporting, for strategic decision making and for operational cost control.

2 **Explain the relationship between cost, cost object, cost accumulation and cost assignment.** Cost accounting systems provide cost information about various types of objects – products, customers, activities and so on. To do this, a system first accumulates resource costs by natural classifications, such as materials, labour and energy. Then, it assigns these costs to cost objects, either tracing them directly or assigning them indirectly through allocation.

3 **Distinguish between direct and indirect costs.** Accountants can specifically and exclusively identify direct costs with a cost object in an economically feasible way. When this is not possible, accountants may allocate costs to cost objects using a cost driver. Such costs are called indirect costs. The greater the proportion of direct costs, the greater the accuracy of the cost system. When the proportion of indirect costs is significant, accountants must take care to find the most appropriate cost drivers.

4 **Explain the major reasons for allocating costs.** The four main purposes of cost allocation are to predict the economic effects of planning and control decisions, to motivate managers and employees, to measure the costs of inventory and cost of goods sold and to justify costs for pricing or reimbursement. Some costs are unallocated because the accountants can determine no plausible and reliable relationship between resource costs and cost objects.

5 **Identify the main types of manufacturing costs: direct materials, direct labour and indirect production costs.** The main types of manufacturing costs are direct materials, direct labour and indirect production costs. Accountants can trace direct materials and direct labour to most cost objects and they allocate the indirect production costs using a cost allocation base.

6 **Explain how the financial statements of merchandisers and manufacturers differ because of the types of goods they sell.** The primary difference between the financial statements of a merchandiser and a manufacturer is the reporting of inventories. A merchandiser has only one type of inventory, whereas a manufacturer has three types of inventory – raw materials, work-in-process and finished goods.

7 **Understand the main differences between traditional and activity-based costing (ABC) systems and why ABC systems provide value to managers.** Traditional systems usually allocate only the indirect costs of the production function. ABC systems often allocate many of the costs of the value-chain functions. Traditional costing accumulates costs using categories such as direct material, direct labour and production overhead. ABC systems accumulate costs by activities required to produce a product or service. The key value of ABC systems is in their increased costing accuracy and better information provided that can lead to process improvements.

8 **Use activity-based management (ABM) to make strategic and operational control decisions.** Activity-based management is using ABC information to improve operations. a key advantage of an activity-based costing system is its ability to aid managers in decision making. ABC improves the accuracy of cost estimates, including product and customer costs and the costs of value-added versus non-value-added activities. ABC also improves managers' understanding of operations. managers can focus their attention on making strategic decisions, such as product mix, pricing and process improvements.

Appendix 4: Detailed illustration of traditional and activity-based cost accounting systems

As we mentioned in the chapter, ABC systems are more complex than traditional systems. In this appendix, we go more in depth than in the Lopez Plastics Company example. You will notice, however, that the main concepts are exactly the same – only the details will change.

Suppose the billing department of one of British Telecom (BT)'s smaller customer care centres requires accurate and useful information about the cost of providing account inquiry and bill printing services for its 120,000 residential and 20,000 commercial customer accounts. A local service bureau has offered to provide all the services currently performed by the billing department at £4.30 per residential account and £8.00 per commercial account. To make informed decisions, BT's managers need accurate estimates of the department's own cost per residential account and cost per commercial account. They also need to know the costs of the key activities performed in the department to determine whether they can achieve cost savings through better control of their activities.

Exhibit 4.8 depicts the residential and commercial customer classes (cost objects) and the resources used to support the billing department. All the costs incurred in the billing department are indirect. There are no direct costs or unallocated costs. The billing department currently uses a traditional costing system that allocates all indirect production costs based on the number of account inquiries.

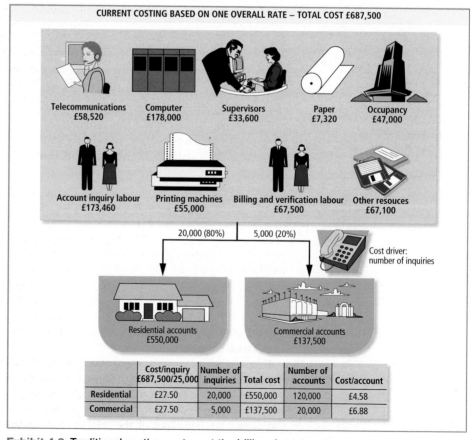

	Cost/inquiry £687,500/25,000	Number of inquiries	Total cost	Number of accounts	Cost/account
Residential	£27.50	20,000	£550,000	120,000	£4.58
Commercial	£27.50	5,000	£137,500	20,000	£6.88

Exhibit 4.8 Traditional costing system at the billing department

Exhibit 4.8 shows that the resources used in the billing department last month cost £687,500. The traditional cost accounting system simply adds together all indirect costs and then allocates them based on the number of inquiries the department receives from each customer class. The billing department received 25,000 account inquiries during the month, so the cost per inquiry was £687,500 ÷ 25,000 = £27.50. There were 20,000 residential account inquiries, 80 per cent of the total. Thus, we assign 80 per cent of the indirect production cost to residential accounts and 20 per cent to commercial accounts. The resulting cost per account is (£687,500 × .8) ÷ 120,000 = £4.58 and (£687,500 × .2) ÷ 20,000 = £6.88 for residential and commercial accounts, respectively. Does this traditional cost accounting system provide managers with accurate estimates of the cost to serve residential and commercial customers? If the answer is yes, the billing department management would accept the service bureau's proposal to service residential accounts because of the apparent savings of £4.58 – £4.30 = £.28 per account. The billing department would continue to service its commercial accounts because its costs are £8.00 – £6.88 = £1.12 less than the service bureau's bid.

MAKING MANAGERIAL DECISIONS

Suppose BT's management retains its traditional cost accounting system but believes that a more plausible and reliable cost driver is 'number of printed lines'. Each residential bill averages 12 lines and each commercial bill averages 50 lines. What would be the new cost per account for residential and commercial customers based on number of lines per bill? How would this new cost accounting information affect the outsourcing decision?

Answer

The total costs would be the same, but the allocation of the total cost to each customer class would change. Instead of allocating 80 per cent of total costs to residential customers, we would allocate only (12 × 120,000) ÷ [(12 × 120,000) + (50 × 20,000)] = 59% of total costs to residential customers and the other 41 per cent to commercial accounts. The cost per account for residential customers would then be (59% × £687,500) ÷ 120,000 = £3.38, and the cost per commercial account would be (41% × £687,500) ÷ 20,000 = £14.09. The outsourcing decision would likely change. We would outsource commercial accounts but not residential accounts. A key issue is how much confidence management has in the costs it uses for decision making. Poor cost data can lead to poor decisions.

Now suppose you are the billing department manager and you know that billing employees spend much of their time verifying the accuracy of commercial bills and very little time verifying residential bills. Yet the traditional cost accounting system allocates 80 per cent of the costs of this work to residential customers. Does this make sense to you? Do you have some doubt about the accuracy of the cost-per-account data? You also know that commercial accounts average 50 lines or two pages per bill, compared with only 12 lines or one page for residential accounts. This means that the billing department uses much more paper, computer time and printing machine time for each commercial account. Again, this does not agree with the percentage of allocations based on number of inquiries. In addition, you believe that the actual consumption of support resources for commercial accounts is much greater than 20 per cent because of their complexity.

As the billing department manager, you are also concerned about activities such as verification of commercial bills, inquiries from customers and correspondence resulting from customer inquiries. These activities consume costly resources but do not add value to BT's services from the customer's perspective. To reduce these costs, management needs a more thorough understanding of the relationships among key activities and resource costs.

In summary, you would probably conclude that BT needs to improve the billing department's traditional cost accounting system because it is not providing managers with useful information for strategic decisions or operational control. This is exactly what BT's management concluded. So, let's see how we might design an activity-based costing system for the billing department.

■ Design of an activity-based cost accounting system

How do managers actually design ABC systems? At the billing department of BT's customer-care centre, a team of managers from the billing department and BT's regional accountant used the following four-step procedure to design their new cost accounting system.

Step 1: Determine the key components of the activity-based cost accounting system

Objective 9

Describe the steps in designing an activity-based costing system.

The key components of an activity-based cost accounting system are cost objects, key activities, resources and related cost drivers. These components, together with the purpose of the new system, determine the scope of the ABC system. Management at BT wanted the system to (1) determine the billing department cost per account for each customer class to better support the strategic decision regarding outsourcing accounts to the local service bureau and (2) enhance the managers' understanding of key billing department activities to support operational cost control. Because the bid from the local service bureau includes performing all the activities of the department, the ABC system must include all department costs. Further, because management wants to understand the key activities and related costs, the team designed an activity-based system.

Through interviews with the department supervisors, management identified the following activities and related cost drivers to use as cost-allocation bases for the billing department.

Activity	Cost-allocation base
Account billing	Number of printed pages
Bill verification	Number of accounts verified
Account inquiry	Number of inquiries
Correspondence	Number of letters
Other activities	Number of printed pages

The four key billing department activities are account billing, bill verification, account inquiry and correspondence. These activities require the vast majority of the work done in the billing department. There are other activities performed in the billing department, such as routine printer and computer maintenance, training and preparing monthly reports. Management did not identify these as individual activities. Instead, the team lumped them together and labelled them 'other activities'. Why? Because the cost of the resources used for each of these individual activities was relatively small, the team could not find plausible and reliable cost drivers for them or the cost of collecting data was too high. The cost-allocation base selected for the 'other activities' cost pool is number of printed pages because most of the other activities, such as maintenance and training, are associated in some way with the printing function. Exhibit 4.8 shows the resources used by the billing department.

Step 2: Determine the relationships among cost objects, activities and resources

An important phase of any activity-based analysis is identifying the relationships among key activities and the resources consumed. The management team does this by interviewing personnel and analysing various internal data. BT interviewed all employees as part of its ABC study. For example, the company asked supervisors how they spend their time. Based on time records, the supervisors estimated that they spend most of their time (40 per cent) supervising account inquiry activity. They also estimated that they spend about 30 per cent of their time supervising billing activity and about 10 per cent of their time reviewing and signing correspondence. They spend the remaining 20 per cent of their time on all other department activities. Exhibit 4.9 shows the results of the interviews.

Implementing an ABC system requires a careful study of operations. As a result, managers often discover that they can trace directly to cost objects some previously indirect or even unallocated costs, thus improving the accuracy of product or service costs. During interviews with the billing department supervisors, the ABC team learned that several of the billing employees work exclusively on verification of commercial bills. Thus, the team could trace their salaries – £11,250 – directly to the verification activity. Further, because the billing department performs verification activity for only commercial accounts, they could also trace this cost pool directly to the commercial customer cost object.

Look at the computer resource row in Exhibit 4.9. The supervisor indicated that 45 per cent of this resource supports account inquiry, 5 per cent supports correspondence and so on. How did the supervisor determine these percentages? Initially, he or she might simply estimate them. Later, the supervisor might gather data to support the estimates. Now consider the occupancy resource row. The percentages used to allocate this resource might be based on the square feet used by the various employees for each activity compared to the total square feet in the department.

Next, the team determined which activities were needed by each cost object. The supervisors indicated that residential customers needed account inquiry, correspondence and billing activities. Commercial customers needed account inquiry, correspondence, billing and verification activities. Both also need other activities.

The process map in Exhibit 4.10 depicts the same information that was gathered from interviews. We allocate the costs of the 10 resources to the 5 activities. For example, account

Resource used to perform activity	Activity performed					
	Account inquiry activity	Correspondence activity	Billing activity	Verification activity	All other activities	Total
Supervisor	40%	10%	30%		20%	100%
Account inquiry labour	90	10				100%
Billing labour			30	70		100%
Verification labour				100		100%
Paper			100			100%
Computer	45	5	35	10	5	100%
Telecommunications	90				10	100%
Occupancy	65		15		20	100%
Printing machines		5	90		5	100%
All other department resources					100	100%

Exhibit 4.9 Analysis of interviews with supervisors from the billing department

inquiry activity consumes 40 per cent of supervisor resources, 90 per cent of account inquiry labour, 45 per cent of computer resources, 90 per cent of telecommunication resources and 65 per cent of occupancy costs. Then, we allocate the costs of the five activities to the two customer cost objects – residential and commercial. For example, commercial accounts require account inquiry, correspondence, billing, verification and other activities. We allocate the activity costs based on a measure of the amount of activity that each customer uses. For example, we allocate the account inquiry activity cost pool based on the number of inquiries received from residential and commercial accounts.

Process maps can be a key tool for managers to gain an understanding of operations. For example, BT's managers considered this process map critical because it revealed how BT conducted business. Managers were able to see how operating activities consume costly resources.

Exhibit 4.10 Two-stage cost allocation for billing department operations

Activity	Cost driver units	Number of cost driver units		
		Residential	Commercial	Total
Account inquiry	Inquiries	20,000	5,000	25,000
Correspondence	Letters	1,800	1,000	2,800
Billing	Printed pages	120,000	40,000	160,000
Verification	Accounts verified		20,000	20,000
Other activities	Printed pages	120,000	40,000	160,000

Exhibit 4.11 Number of cost driver units for the billing department

Normally, we do not collect the cost data and the cost driver data shown in Exhibit 4.10 until we have drawn the process map and identified the resources and cost drivers. The ABC team uses the process map as a guide for the next step in designing the ABC system – data collection.

Step 3: Collect relevant data concerning costs and the physical flow of the cost-driver units among resources and activities

Using the process map as a guide, billing department managers collected the required cost and operational data by further interviews with relevant personnel. Sources of data include the accounting records, special studies and sometimes 'best estimates of managers'. The managers collected resource cost information from the general ledger (Exhibit 4.8) and data on the flow of cost drivers from various operational reports (Exhibits 4.9 and 4.11). Exhibit 4.10 shows the data collected.

Management can now use the completed process map to determine costs for the strategic and operational decisions that they must make.

Step 4: Calculate and interpret the new activity-based cost information

After collecting all required financial and operational data, we can calculate the new activity-based information. Exhibit 4.12 summarises stage 1 allocations. It shows the total

Resource	Cost (from Exhibit 4.8)	Activity cost pool				
		Account Inquiry	Correspondence	Billing	Verification	Other
Supervisors	£ 33,600	£ 13,440[a]	£ 3,360[b]	£10,080[c]		£ 6,720[d]
Account inquiry labour	173,460	156,114	17,346			
Billing labour	56,250			16,875	£39,375	
Verification labour	11,250				11,250	
Paper	7,320			7,320		
Computer	178,000	80,100	8,900	62,300	17,800	8,900
Telecommunication	58,520	52,668				5,852
Occupancy	47,000	30,550		7,050		9,400
Printers	55,000		2,750	49,500		2,750
Other resources	67,100					67,100
Total cost	£687,500	£332,872	£32,356	£153,125	£68,425	£100,722

[a]From Exhibits 4.9 and 4.10, account inquiry activity uses 40 per cent of the supervisor resource. So the allocation is 40% × £33,600 = £13,440.
[b]10% × £33,600
[c]30% × £33,600
[d]20% × £33,600

Exhibit 4.12 Total cost of each activity in the billing department

Activity (driver units)		Driver costs		
		Total costs (from Exhibit 4.12) (1)	Total number of driver units (from Exhibit 4.11) (2)	Cost per driver unit (1) ÷ (2)
Account inquiry (inquiries)		£332,872	25,000 inquiries	£13.314880
Correspondence (letters)		£ 32,356	2,800 letters	£11.555714
Account billing (printed pages)		£153,125	160,000 printed pages	£ 0.957031
Bill verification (accounts verified)		£ 68,425	20,000 accounts verified	£ 3.421250
Other activities (printed pages)		£100,722	160,000 printed pages	£ 0.629513

		Cost per customer class			
		Residential		Commerical	
	Cost per driver unit	Number of driver units	Cost	Number of driver units	Cost
Account inquiry	£13.314880	20,000 inquiries	£266,298	5,000 inquiries	£ 66,574
Correspondence	£11.555714	1,800 letters	20,800	1,000 letters	11,556
Account billing	£ 0.957031	120,000 pages	114,844	40,000 pages	38,281
Bill verification	£ 3.421250			20,000 accts.	68,425
Other activities	£ 0.629513	120,000 pages	75,541	40,000 pages	25,181
Total cost			£477,483		£210,017
Number of accounts			120,000		20,000
Cost per account			£ 3.98		£ 10.50
Cost per account, traditional system from Exhibit 4.8			£ 4.58		£ 6.88

Exhibit 4.13 Key results of activity-based costing study

costs for each of the five activity cost pools. Notice that the total costs of £332,872 + £32,356 + £153,125 + £68,425 + £100,722 = £687,500 in Exhibit 4.12 equals the total indirect costs in Exhibit 4.8. Now we can determine the activity-based cost per account for each customer class (stage 2 allocations) from the data in step 3. Exhibit 4.13 shows the computations.

Examine the last two rows in Exhibit 4.13. Notice that traditional costing overcosted the high-volume residential accounts and substantially undercosted the low-volume, complex commercial accounts. The cost per account for residential accounts using ABC is £3.98, which is £0.60 (or 13 per cent) less than the £4.58 cost generated by the traditional costing system. The cost per account for commercial accounts is £10.50, which is £3.62 (or 53 per cent) more than the £6.88 cost from the traditional costing system. The analysis confirms management's belief that the traditional system undercosted commercial accounts. BT's management now has more accurate cost information for strategic decision-making and cost-control purposes.

Results like these are common when companies perform activity-based costing studies. Traditional systems generally overcost high-volume cost objects with simple processes. Which system makes more sense – the traditional allocation system that 'spreads' all support costs to customer classes based solely on the number of inquiries, or the ABC system that identifies key activities and assigns costs based on the consumption of units of cost drivers for each key activity? For BT, the probable benefits of the new ABC system appear to outweigh the costs of implementing and maintaining the new cost system.

■ Strategic decisions, operational cost control and ABM

Now let's see how billing department managers can use the ABC system to improve their strategic decisions and operational cost control. Suppose that the billing department needed to find a way to increase its capacity to handle more accounts due to an expected large increase in demand from a new housing development and a business centre. Managers proposed a strategic action – outsource certain customer accounts to a local service bureau. Billing department managers were also interested in reducing the operating costs of the department while not impairing the quality of the service it provided to its customers. To address both of these issues, they used the ABC information from Exhibit 4.13 to identify non-value-added activities that had significant costs. Account inquiry and bill verification activities are non-value-added and costly so management asked for ideas for cost reductions. The new information provided by the ABC system generated the following ideas:

Summary problem for your review

PROBLEM

Refer to the billing department illustration. Suppose that management at BT's York area customer care centre is implementing an ABC system. The centre has 98,000 residential customers and 25,000 commercial customers. An ABC team has collected the data shown in Exhibit 4.14. Management has decided not to allocate the other resource costs.

1 Using the same format as Exhibits 4.12 and 4.13, prepare schedules to determine the cost per driver unit for each activity and the activity-based cost per account for each customer type.

2 Consider the verification activity. Suppose the cost per account verified is £0.45. The centre verifies 50 per cent of residential and commercial bills. Given that there are, on average, 50 lines on each commercial bill and only 12 lines on each residential bill, criticise the use of accounts verified as a cost driver and suggest a more plausible and reliable cost driver.

SOLUTION

1 Exhibit 4.15 is a schedule showing the total cost of each activity of the billing department. From this we can determine the cost per driver unit and the activity-based cost per account for each customer class, as shown in Exhibit 4.16.

2 The ABC system allocates $49,000 \div (49,000 + 12,500) = 79.7\%$ of verification costs to residential accounts based on the number of accounts verified. However, the work performed to verify a bill is probably closely related to the number of lines on the bill. Using accounts verified assumes that employees expend the same amount of effort verifying residential accounts and commercial accounts, even though there are many fewer lines on residential bills. Thus, the cost driver 'lines verified' is more plausible and reliable. The number of lines verified for commercial accounts are 50 lines per account × 12,500 accounts = 625,000 lines and for residential accounts are 12 lines per account × 49,000 accounts = 588,000 lines. Thus, we would allocate $588,000 \div (588,000 + 625,000) = 48.5\%$ of verification costs to residential accounts based on lines verified. ABC teams should always exercise care when choosing cost drivers to use as allocation bases. The York team might also want to investigate the plausibility and reliability of the 'number of inquiries' cost driver because this assumes that residential and commercial customer inquiries require the same amount of work.

- Use the service bureau for commercial accounts because of the significant cost savings. From Exhibit 4.13, the service bureau's bid is £8.00 per account, compared to the billing department's activity-based cost of £10.50, a potential savings of £2.50 per account! In addition, department managers would try to eliminate or reduce bill verification, commercial account inquiry and commercial account correspondence activities, all non-value-adding activities.

    Suppose BT outsourced commercial customers to the service bureau. Would actual costs immediately decrease by £50,000 (£2.50 for each of 20,000 commercial accounts)? No. Only the variable portion of resource costs, such as paper, variable telecommunication charges, variable computer charges and overtime or part time labour, would decrease immediately. The fixed cost portion of all these resources would not change without some specific management actions. For example, suppose billing labour used for verification is a fixed-cost resource. Then, the time formerly required for verification is idle time, but the company must still pay wages. Management would have to decide whether to lay off billing employees or to keep them in anticipation of the increase in printing activity due to the expected increase in residential customers.

- Exhibit 4.13 indicates that account inquiry activity is very costly, accounting for a significant portion of total billing department costs. A benchmarking analysis showed the cost per inquiry of £13.31 was unusually high compared to similar measures at other customer care centres. By meeting with managers from centres that had significantly lower activity cost rates, the billing department managers developed ideas for process improvements. One idea that resulted from these meetings was to implement a web-based inquiry system to handle routine questions about bills.

The billing department, like so many companies that have adopted ABC and ABM, improved both strategic and operating decisions.

Resource	Monthly cost	Percentage of resource used in activity				
		Billing	Account inquiry	Correspondence	Verification	Other
Supervisors	£30,500	40%	35%	8%		17%
Account inquiry labour	102,000		85	15		
Billing labour	45,000	70			30	
Paper	5,800	100				
Computers	143,000	30	48	7	10	5
Telecommunications	49,620		85			15
Occupancy	56,000	15	70			15
Printers	75,000		80	5		15
Other	59,000					100
Total	£565,920					

Activity	Cost driver	Monthly number of cost driver Units		
		Residential	Commercial	Total
Billing	Lines	1,176,000	1,250,000	2,426,000
Account inquiry	Inquiries	9,800	7,500	17,300
Correspondence	Letters	1,960	2,500	4,460
Verification	Accounts verified	49,000	12,500	61,500

Exhibit 4.14 First stage percentage allocations and monthly number of cost driver units

Resource	Cost (from Exhibit 4.14)	Activity				
		Billing	Account inquiry	Correspondence	Verification	Other
Supervisors	£30,500	£12,200ᵃ	£10,675ᵇ	£ 2,440ᶜ		£5,185ᵈ
Account inquiry labour	102,000		86,700	15,300		
Billing labour	45,000	31,500			£13,500	
Paper	5,800	5,800				
Computer	143,000	42,900	68,640	10,010	14,300	7,150
Telecommunication	49,620		42,177			7,443
Occupancy	56,000	8,400	39,200			8,400
Printers	75,000	60,000		3,750		11,250
Other resources	59,000					59,000
Total cost	£565,920	£160,800	£247,392	£31,500	£27,800	£98,428

ᵃ40% × £30,500
ᵇ35% × £30,500
ᶜ8% × £30,500
ᵈ17% × £30,500

Exhibit 4.15 Total cost of each activity in the billing department

	Driver costs		
	Total costs (from Exhibit 4.15)	Total number of driver units (from Exhibit 4.14)	Cost per driver unit
Activity (driver units)	(1)	(2)	(1) ÷ (2)
Account inquiry (inquiries)	£247,392	17,300 inquiries	£14.300116
Correspondence (letters)	£ 31,500	4,460 letters	£ 7.062780
Account billing (lines)	£160,800	2,426,000 lines	£ 0.066282
Bill verification (accounts verified)	£ 27,800	61,500 accounts verified	£ 0.452033

		Cost per customer class			
		Residential		Commercial	
	Cost per driver unit	Number of driver units	Cost	Number of driver units	Cost
Account inquiry	£14.300116	9,800 inquiries	£140,141	7,500 inquiries	£107,251
Correspondence	£ 7.062780	1,960 letters	13,843	2,500 letters	17,657
Account billing	£ 0.066282	1,176,000 lines	77,947	1,250,000 lines	82,853
Bill verification	£ 0.452033	49,00018 accounts	22,149	12,500 accounts	5,650
Total cost			£254,081		£213,411
Number of accounts			98,000		25,000
Cost per account			£ 2.59		£ 8.54

Exhibit 4.16 Cost per driver unit and activity-based cost per account

Accounting vocabulary

activity-based costing (ABC) systems, p. 128

activity-based management (ABM), p. 136

benchmarking, p. 136

cost, p. 116

cost accounting, p. 116

cost accounting systems, p. 116

cost accumulation, p. 116

cost allocation, p. 118

cost assignment, p. 116

Fundamental assignment material   MyAccountingLab

4.A1 Direct, indirect and unallocated costs, process map

Lockyear Window Company makes and sells three product lines – custom detailed windows, large standard windows and small standard windows. The statement of operating income for the most recent period is shown next.

Lockyear Window Company statement of operating income		
		Total
Sales		£155,000
Cost of goods sold:		
Direct material	£40,000	
Indirect production costs	41,000	81,000
Gross profit		74,000
Selling and administrative expenses:		
Commissions	15,000	
Distribution to warehouses	10,400	25,400
Income before unallocated expenses		48,600
Unallocated expenses		
Administrative salaries	8,000	
Other administrative expenses	4,000	12,000
Operating income before taxes		
		£ 36,600

Lockyear uses a traditional cost accounting system. A process map developed to describe this system is shown in Exhibit 4.17. To aid in the company's analysis of its product mix strategy, you have been asked to determine operating income (loss) for each product line. Use a format similar to Exhibit 4.3 on p. 122 in the text.

4.A2 Financial statements for manufacturing and merchandising companies

Orinoco, SA, produces and sells wireless reading devices. A competitor, Nile Electronic Products (NEP) sells similar wireless reading devices that it purchases at wholesale from

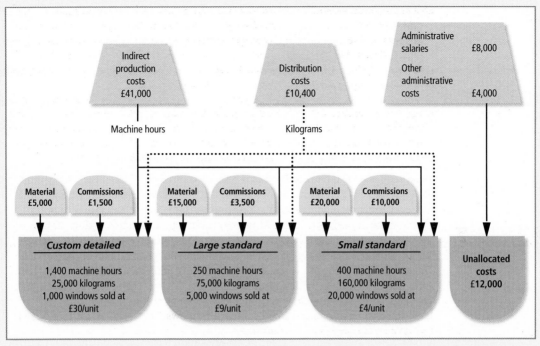

Exhibit 4.17 Process map for LockYear Window Company's traditional cost allocation system

Sonex for €97 each. Both sell the devices for €170. In 20X9 Orinoco produced 10,000 devices at the following costs:

Direct materials purchased		€570,000
Direct materials used		€530,000
Direct labour		290,000
Indirect production:		
Depreciation	€50,000	
Indirect labour	60,000	
Other	40,000	150,000
Total cost of production		€970,000

Assume that Orinoco had no beginning inventory of direct materials. Neither company had any beginning inventory of finished devices, but both had ending inventory of 1,000 finished devices. Ending work-in-process inventory for Orinoco was negligible.

Each company sold 9,000 devices for €1,530,000 in 20X9 and incurred the following selling and administrative costs:

Sales salaries and commissions	€105,000
Depreciation on retail store	40,000
Advertising	25,000
Other	15,000
Total selling and administrative cost	€185,000

1 Prepare the inventories section of the balance sheet for December 31, 20X9, for Nile.
2 Prepare the inventories section of the balance sheet for December 31, 20X9, for Orinoco.

3 Using the cost of goods sold format on p. 127 as a model, prepare an income statement for the year 20X9 for Nile.

4 Using the cost of goods sold format on p. 127 as a model, prepare an income statement for the year 20X9 for Orinoco.

5 Summarise the differences between the financial statements of Nile, a merchandiser and Orinoco, a manufacturer.

6 What purpose of a cost management system is being served by reporting the items in requirements 1–4?

4.A3 Activities, resources, cost drivers and the banking industry

Reto Bank is a local bank located in a residential area and it services mostly individuals and local businesses. Reto's four main services are transaction processing (withdrawals, cheques, currency exchange), loans, simple investments (individual clients) and complex investments (portfolios of large businesses). To support these activities, Reto employs 10 front-office staff, 12 back-office staff dealing with loan applications and investments and 2 people to consult with customers and manage complex portfolio investments. A team of 3 supervisors manages the overall operations of the bank. As part of Reto's implementation of activity-based costing, it needed to identify activities, resources and cost drivers. The following table summarises the cost-allocation bases Reto has chosen for its activities and resources:

Cost-allocation base
number of investments
number of applications
number of loans
number of person hours
number of minutes
number of computer transactions
number of square metres
number of loan inquiries
number of transactions
number of schedules
number of securities

For each of the brief descriptions that follows, indicate whether it is an activity (A) or a resource (R). For each activity or resource, choose the most appropriate cost-allocation base from the preceding list and indicate for each resource whether it is a fixed-cost (F) or variable-cost (V) resource. The first item is completed as a guide.

(a) Contract maintenance of building (R; number of square metres; F).

(b) Staff for front-line customer service.

(c) External computing services.

(d) Development of repayment schedules.

(e) Staff for consulting with customers and arranging the portfolios.

(f) External service bureau providing customer credit checks for loan applications.

(g) Preparing investment documents for customers.

(h) Research to evaluate a loan application.

(i) Overtime by back-office staff.

(j) Telephones/facsimile.

(k) Staff for service and background research.

(l) Establish customer collateral for approved loans.

4.A4 Activity-based costing in an electronics company

The wireless phone manufacturing division of a Spanish consumer electronics company uses activity-based costing. For simplicity, assume that its accountants have identified only the following three activities and related cost drivers for indirect production costs:

Activity	Cost driver
Materials handling	Direct-materials cost
Engineering	Engineering change notices
Power	Kilowatt hours

Three types of mobile phone are produced: Senior, Basic and Deluxe. Direct costs and cost-driver activity for each product for a recent month are as follows:

	Senior	Basic	Deluxe
Direct-materials cost	€25,000	€50,000	€125,000
Direct-labour cost	€ 4,000	€ 1,000	€ 3,000
Kilowatt hours	50,000	200,000	150,000
Engineering change notices	13	5	2

Indirect production costs for the month were as follows:

Materials handling	€12,000
Engineering	20,000
Power	16,000
Total indirect production cost	€48,000

1 Compute the indirect production costs allocated to each product with the ABC system.
2 Suppose all indirect production costs had been allocated to products in proportion to their direct-labour costs. Compute the indirect production costs allocated to each product.
3 In which product costs, those in requirement 1 or those in requirement 2, do you have the most confidence? Why?

4.B1 Direct, indirect and unallocated costs

Athens Tool Company (ATC) is a supplier that assembles purchased parts into components for three distinct markets – scooter parts, lawn mower parts and hand tool parts. Following is the statement of operating income for the most recent period:

ATC: statement of operating income

		Total
Sales		€990,000
Cost of goods sold:		
Direct material	€400,000	
Indirect production (allocated based on machine hours)	94,000	494,000
Gross profit		496,000

ATC: statement of operating income

		Total
Selling and administrative expenses:		
Commissions	55,000	
Distribution to warehouses (allocated based on weight in kilograms)	150,000	205,000
Income before unallocated expenses		291,000
Unallocated expenses:		
Corporate salaries	11,000	
Other general expenses	17,000	28,000
Operating income before taxes		€263,000

ATC uses a traditional cost accounting system. Operating data used in the cost accounting system are as follows:

	Scooter parts	Lawn mower parts	Hand tool part
Purchase cost of parts assembled	€175,000	€125,000	€100,000
Machine hours	8,500	1,750	1,500
Weight of parts shipped to distributors (kilograms)	100,000	400,000	250,000
Sales commissions per unit	€ 5.00	€ 0.8	€ 0.20
Units assembled and sold	5,000	25,000	50,000
Sales price per unit	€ 70.00	€ 15.20	€ 5.20

You have been asked to determine operating income (loss) for each product line. Use a format similar to Exhibit 4.3 on p. 122.

4.B2 Allocation, department rates and direct-labour hours versus machine hours

The Garcia Manufacturing Company has two producing departments, machining and assembly. Mr Garcia recently automated the machining department. The installation of a CAM system, together with robotic workstations, drastically reduced the amount of direct labour required. Meanwhile, the assembly department remained labour intensive. The company had always used one firm-wide rate based on direct-labour hours as the cost-allocation base for applying all costs (except direct materials) to the final products. Mr Garcia was considering two alternatives: (1) continue using direct-labour hours as the only cost-allocation base, but use different rates in machining and assembly, and (2) using machine hours as the cost-allocation base in the machining department while continuing with direct-labour hours in assembly. Budgeted data for 20X0 are as follows:

	Machining	Assembly	Total
Total cost (except direct materials)	€585,000	€495,000	€1,080,000
Machine hours	97,500	*	105,000
Direct-labour hours	15,000	30,000	45,000

* Not applicable.

1 Suppose Garcia continued to use one firm-wide rate based on direct-labour hours to apply all manufacturing costs (except direct materials) to the final products. Compute the cost-application rate that would be used.
2 Suppose Garcia continued to use direct-labour hours as the only cost-allocation base but used different rates in machining and assembly.
  (a) Compute the cost-application rate for machining.
  (b) Compute the cost-application rate for assembly.

3 Suppose Garcia changed the cost accounting system to use machine hours as the cost-allocation base in machining and direct-labour hours in assembly.
  (a) Compute the cost-application rate for machining.
  (b) Compute the cost-application rate for assembly.
4 Three products use the following machine hours and direct-labour hours:

	Machine hours in machining	Direct-labour hours in machining	Direct-labour hours in assembly
Product A	12.0	1.0	14.0
Product B	17.0	1.5	3.0
Product C	14.0	1.3	8.0

(a) Compute the manufacturing cost of each product (excluding direct materials) using one firm-wide rate based on direct-labour hours.
(b) Compute the manufacturing cost of each product (excluding direct materials) using direct-labour hours as the cost-allocation base, but with different cost-allocation rates in machining and assembly.
(c) Compute the manufacturing cost of each product (excluding direct materials) using a cost-allocation rate based on direct-labour hours in assembly and machine hours in machining.
(d) Compare and explain the results in requirements 4a, 4b and 4c.

4.B3 Traditional versus ABC costing systems

Kiku Yamamoto is the controller of Watanabe, Inc., an electronic controls company located in Osaka. She recently attended a seminar on activity-based costing (ABC) in Tokyo. Watanabe's traditional cost accounting system has three cost categories: direct materials, direct labour and indirect production costs. The company allocates indirect production costs on the basis of direct labour cost. The following is the 20X0 budget for the automotive controls department (in thousands of Japanese yen):

Direct materials	¥ 60,000
Direct labour	35,000
Indirect production costs	24,500
Total cost	¥119,500

After Ms Yamamoto attended the seminar, she suggested that Watanabe experiment with an ABC system in the Automotive Controls Department. She identified four main activities that cause indirect production costs in the department and selected a cost driver to use as a cost-allocation base for each activity as follows:

Activity	Cost-allocation base	Predicted 20X0 cost (¥000)
Receiving	Direct materials cost	¥ 4,800
Assembly	Number of control units	13,800
Quality control	QC hours	1,800
Shipping	Number of boxes shipped	4,100
Total		¥24,500

In 20X0 the Automotive Controls Department expects to produce 92,000 control units, use 600 quality control hours and ship 8,200 boxes.

1   Explain how Watanabe, Inc., allocates its indirect production costs using its traditional cost system. Include a computation of the allocation rate used.

2   Explain how Watanabe, Inc., would allocate indirect production costs under Ms Yamamoto's proposed ABC system. Include a computation of all the allocation rates used.

3   Suppose Watanabe prices its products at 30 per cent above total production cost. An order came in from Nissan for 5,000 control units. Yamamoto estimates that filling the order will require ¥8,000,000 of direct materials cost and ¥2,000,000 of direct labour. It will require 50 hours of QC inspection time and will be shipped in 600 boxes.

   (a) Compute the price charged for the 5,000 control units if Watanabe uses its traditional cost accounting system.

   (b) Compute the price charged for the 5,000 control units if Watanabe uses the ABC system proposed by Ms Yamamoto.

4   Explain why costs are different in the two costing systems. Include an indication of which costs you think are most accurate and why.

4.B4 Traditional costing and ABC, activity-based management

Refer to the text discussion of Lopez Plastics Company on pp. 130–5. Assume that the company has the traditional cost accounting system described in Exhibit 4.6. The top management team wants to reverse the pattern of quarterly losses. The company president, Angie Oaks, has emphasised the importance of profit improvement by linking future pay raises of the two product-line managers to their respective gross profit margins. She is concerned about the profitability of the pen casing product line, while pleased with the profitability of the mobile phone casing line. She also believes that the unallocated costs of the company are too high compared to competitors. The office of controller, whose costs are included in the unallocated costs, is responsible for vendor relations and purchasing of direct materials. The controller and head of the engineering department present the following idea:

> We should use more standard parts in mobile phone casings, which will dramatically reduce the purchasing department's work required for purchasing. I believe this should cut our office's costs by as much as €20,000 per quarter. Product engineering agrees that this idea is not only feasible but, if implemented, would substantially reduce the design work required for mobile phone casings. Quality would also improve.

The controller, marketing manager and head of the engineering department provided the following summary of actions and related effects.

Action	Related effects
Reduce prices of mobile phone casings 25%	The vice president of sales estimates that the improved quality of mobile phone casings combined with the price reduction will yield a 100% increase in demand for mobile phone casings per quarter.
Use standard parts wherever possible in mobile phone casings	The use of fewer suppliers will reduce vendor-relations work by the purchasing department. This will result in unallocated costs decreasing by €20,000.
	One of the two engineers can be let go at an annual cost savings of €80,000.
	Less of the plant and machinery will be used by production support so the allocation percentages will change from 75% and 25% to 80% and 20%. Much less engineer and CAD equipment costs will be needed for production support so these percentages will change from 80% and 20% to 50% and 50%.
	Processing time, measured in direct-labour hours, will increase by 500 hours due to expected 100% increase in sales and production of mobile phone casings, but there is adequate capacity of labour and machine time. Direct-labour costs are fixed as are all of the indirect production costs.
	Quality of mobile phone casings will improve due to reduced complexity of processing.

1 Evaluate this idea using the traditional cost allocation system shown in Exhibit 4.6 on page 131. What would be the predicted profitability for each product line and the company as a whole? What would be the most likely level of support for the controller's idea by the product managers of the pen casing product line and the cell phone casing product line? What would be the level of support by the president?

2 Assume that you have the ABC system described in Exhibit 4.7 on page 133 with the gross margin percentages as shown in the table on pp. 134–5. Often, managers with ABC systems can anticipate more effects of improvement ideas because of their increased understanding of the operating system. In this case, although the total number of parts used would not change, the idea would reduce the number of distinct parts for mobile phone casings from 20 to 11. Evaluate the controller's idea using the ABC system described in Exhibit 4.7. What would be the predicted profitability for each product line and the company as a whole? What would be the most likely level of support for the controller's idea by the product managers of the pen casing product line and the mobile phone casing product line? What would be the level of support by the president?

3 As vice president, you have expressed concern about the traditional cost-allocation system's product-cost accuracy and its ability to provide relevant information for operational control. Does the new ABC system satisfy your concerns? Explain.

Additional assignment material   MyAccountingLab

QUESTIONS

4.1 Define a cost management system and give its three purposes.

4.2 Cost management systems have three primary purposes. For each of the decisions listed next, indicate the purpose of the CMS being applied.
  (a) A production manager wants to know the cost of performing a setup for a production run in order to compare it to a target cost established as part of a process improvement programme.
  (b) Top management wants to identify the profitability of several product lines to establish the optimum product mix.
  (c) Financial managers want to know the manufactured cost of inventory to appear on the balance sheet of the annual report.

4.3 Name four cost objects.

4.4 'Products are the main cost objects. Departments are seldom cost objects.' Do you agree? Explain.

4.5 What is the major purpose of detailed cost accounting systems?

4.6 What are the two major processes performed by a cost accounting system? Describe both of them.

4.7 Why are cost accounting systems critically important to managers?

4.8 Distinguish between direct, indirect and unallocated costs.

4.9 'The same cost can be direct and indirect.' Do you agree? Explain.

4.10 How does the idea of economic feasibility relate to the distinction between direct and indirect costs?

4.11 What are four purposes for cost allocation?

4.12 Why do companies assign all production costs and only production costs to products for external reporting purposes?

4.13 'A cost pool is a group of costs that accounting systems physically trace to the appropriate cost objective.' Do you agree? Explain.

4.14 List five terms that are sometimes used as substitutes for the word *allocate*.

4.15 'The typical traditional accounting system does not allocate costs associated with value-chain functions other than production to units produced.' Do you agree? Explain.

4.16 'It is better not to allocate some costs than to use a cost-allocation base that does not make any sense.' Do you agree? Explain.

4.17 Production equipment maintenance, sales commissions and process design costs are part of a company's costs. Identify which of these costs are most likely direct, indirect and unallocated with respect to the products manufactured.

4.18 'For a furniture manufacturer, glue or tacks become an integral part of the finished product, so they would be direct material.' Do you agree? Explain.

4.19 'Depreciation is a period expense for financial statement purposes.' Do you agree? Explain.

4.20 Distinguish between costs and expenses.

4.21 Distinguish between manufacturing and merchandising companies. How do their accounting systems differ?

4.22 Why is there a direct-materials inventory account but no direct-labour inventory account on a manufacturing company's balance sheet?

4.23 'ABC systems are always more accurate than traditional costing systems.' Do you agree? Explain.

4.24 Contrast activity-based costing (ABC) with activity-based management (ABM).

4.25 Explain how the layout of a plant's production equipment can reduce non-value-added costs.

4.26 Why do managers want to distinguish between value-added activities and non-value-added activities?

4.27 What is benchmarking? What do companies use it for? How do they determine benchmarks?

4.28 Why should caution be exercised when comparing company performance to benchmarks?

4.29 Why are more organisations adopting ABC systems?

4.30 (Appendix 4) Name four steps in the design and implementation of an ABC system.

CRITICAL THINKING EXERCISES

4.31 Marketing and capacity planning

A company has just completed its marketing plan for the coming year. When the company's management accountant entered the projected increases in sales volume into a process map (which relates activities and resources), the accountant discovered that the company will exceed several key resource capacities. What are the three alternative courses of action to solve this dilemma?

4.32 ABC and ABM compared

During seminars on ABM, participants often ask about the difference between ABC and ABM. Explain briefly. Why is this important to managers?

4.33 ABC for product costing and operational control

When companies implement an ABC system they often use it first for product costing. Some managers think that is the only use for an ABC system. A typical comment is, 'Activity-based allocation is useful for product costing, but not for operational control.' Do you agree? Explain.

4.34 ABC and cost management systems

Cost management systems have three primary purposes. Two of these are providing information for strategic and operational purposes. Companies often adopt ABC systems to increase the accuracy of cost information used by managers for strategic and operational decisions. Suppose a company produces only one product. This means that 100 per cent of its costs are direct with respect to the product cost object. The accurate product unit cost is simply all costs incurred divided by the total units produced. Might this company be interested in an ABC system? Why or why not?

4.35 ABC and benchmarking

Suppose that BT used benchmarking to compare the activity-based costs among its various divisions. As part of its benchmarking efforts, BT compared the activity cost per driver unit for similar activities and cost per customer for its billing departments in various geographic regions. For example, BT compared the costs at the York area billing department with the similar costs in the London area. Are these meaningful comparisons? Why or why not?

EXERCISES

4.36 Classification of manufacturing costs

Costs are either direct or indirect depending on whether they can be traced to a cost object and either variable or fixed depending on whether they vary with changes in volume. Classify each of the following as direct (D) or indirect (I) and as variable (V) or fixed (F). For each of the 10 items you will have two answers, D or I and V or F.

1 Factory rent.
2 Salary of a factory storeroom clerk.
3 Cement for a road builder.
4 Supervisor training programme.
5 Abrasives (e.g., sandpaper).
6 Cutting bits in a machinery department.
7 Food for a factory cafeteria.
8 Workers' compensation insurance in a factory.
9 Steel scrap for a blast furnace.
10 Paper towels for a factory washroom.

4.37 Confirm your understanding of the classification of manufacturing costs

Classify each of the following as direct or indirect with respect to traceability to product and as variable or fixed with respect to whether the costs fluctuate in total as volume of production changes over wide ranges. Explain your classifications.

1 The cost of components that are assembled into a final product.
2 The cost of supplies consumed when maintenance is performed on machines.
3 The wages of machine operators who work on only one product.
4 The cost of training mechanics who service processing machinery.

4.38 Variable costs and fixed costs; manufacturing and other costs

For each of the numbered items, choose the appropriate classifications from the lettered items for a manufacturing company. If in doubt about whether the cost behaviour is basically variable or fixed, decide on the basis of whether the total cost will fluctuate substantially over a wide range of volume. Most items have two answers among the following possibilities:

(a) Manufacturing costs, direct.
(b) Manufacturing costs, indirect.
(c) General and administrative cost.
(d) Selling cost.
(e) Fixed cost.
(f) Variable cost.
(g) Other (specify).

Examples:

Direct material	a, f
President's salary	c, e
Bond interest expense	e, g (financial expense)

Items for your consideration:

1 Welding supplies.
2 Salespersons' commissions.
3 Salespersons' salaries.

4 Supervisory salaries, production control.
5 Supervisory salaries, assembly department.
6 Supervisory salaries, factory storeroom.
7 Factory power for machines.
8 Fire loss.
9 Sandpaper.
10 Company picnic costs.
11 Overtime premium, punch press.
12 Idle time, assembly.
13 Freight out.
14 Property taxes.
15 Paint for finished products.
16 Heat and air conditioning, factory.
17 Materials-handling labour, punch press.
18 Straight-line depreciation, salespersons' automobiles.

4.39 Direct, indirect and unallocated costs

Refer to the Lopez Plastics Company example on pp. 130–5 and to Exhibit 4.7. The following list gives various resources used by Lopez Plastics Company. Use the letters D, I and U to indicate how the cost of each resource cost would be classified with respect to products manufactured: D = direct, I = indirect and U = unallocated.

1 Depreciation of the plant.
2 Resin used to make pen casings.
3 Salary of plant manager.
4 Salaries of cost accountants.
5 Depreciation on computers used by engineers to design mobile phone casings.
6 Salaries of engineers.
7 Salaries of operating labour processing pen casings.
8 Travel costs of purchasing agent while investigating potential new suppliers of resin.

4.40 Cost Allocation in ABC

Refer to the Lopez Plastics Company illustration on pp. 130–5 and to Exhibit 4.7. Also see the table on pp. 134–5. Based on new information, management has adjusted the percentages that apply to the first stage of the ABC system as shown in the following table. Prepare a schedule that shows the gross margins for both products.

	Indirect resource	
	Plant and machinery	Engineers and CAD equipment
Per cent of resource used in		
Processing activity	90	30
Production support activity	10	70

4.41 Activity-based costing

The Deutsche Toy Company makes a variety of alpine dolls at its operation in Munich.
Its manufacturing process is highly automated. A recently installed ABC system has four activity centres:

Activity centre	Cost driver	Cost per driver unit
Materials receiving and handling	Kilograms of materials	€1.20 per kg
Production setup	Number of setups	€60 per setup
Cutting, sewing and assembly	Number of units	€.40 per unit
Packing and shipping	Number of orders	€10 per order

Two dolls are called 'Hansel' and 'Gretel'. They require .20 and .40 kg of materials, respectively, at a materials cost of €1.50 for Hansel and €2.20 for Gretel. One computer-controlled assembly line makes all dolls. When a production run of a different doll is started, a setup procedure is required to reprogram the computers and make other changes in the process. Normally, 600 Hansel dolls are produced per setup, but only 240 Gretel dolls. Products are packed and shipped separately so a request from a customer for, say, three different products is considered three different orders.

Suppose the gift shop at the Munich Toy Museum (*Spielzeugmuseum*) just placed an order for 100 Hansel dolls and 50 Gretel dolls.

1 Compute the cost of the products shipped to the Munich Toy Museum gift shop.
2 Suppose the products made for the Munich Toy Museum gift shop required 'Spielzeugmuseum' to be printed on each doll. Because of the automated process, printing the letters takes no extra time or materials, but it requires a special production setup for each product. Compute the cost of the products shipped to the Munich Toy Museum gift shop.
3 Explain how the activity-based-costing system helps Deutsche Toy Company to measure costs of individual products or orders better than a traditional system that allocates all non-materials costs based on direct labour.

PROBLEMS

4.42 Cost accumulation and allocation

The Kyoto Manufacturing Company has two departments, machining and finishing. For a given period, the following costs were incurred by the company as a whole: direct material, ¥200,000; direct labour, ¥75,000; and indirect production, ¥80,000. The grand total was ¥355,000.

The machining department incurred 70 per cent of the direct-material costs, but only 33⅓ per cent of the direct-labour costs. As is commonplace, indirect production costs incurred by each department were allocated to products in proportion to the direct-labour costs of products within the departments. Three products were produced.

Product	Direct material	Direct labour
Sigma	40%	30%
Chi	30%	30%
Delta	30%	40%
Total for the machining department	100%	100%
Sigma	33⅓%	40%
Chi	33⅓%	40%
Delta	33⅓%	20%
Total added by finishing department	100%	100%

The indirect production costs incurred by the machining and finishing departments and allocated to all products therein amounted to machining, ¥38,000 and finishing, ¥42,000.

1 Compute the total costs incurred by the machining department and added by the finishing department.
2 Compute the total costs of each product that would be shown as finished-goods inventory if all the products were transferred to finished stock on completion. (There were no beginning inventories.)

4.43 Hospital allocation base

Emilio Moreno, the administrator of Turin Community Hospital, has become interested in obtaining more accurate cost allocations on the basis of cause and effect. The €210,000 of laundry costs had been allocated on the basis of 600,000 kgs processed for all departments, or €.35 per kg.

Moreno is concerned that government healthcare officials will require weighted statistics to be used for cost allocation. He asks you, 'Please develop a revised base for allocating laundry costs. It should be better than our present base, but not be overly complex either.'

You study the situation and find that the laundry processes a large volume of uniforms for student nurses and physicians and for dietary, housekeeping and other personnel. In particular, the coats or jackets worn by personnel in the radiology department take an unusual amount of handwork.

A special study of laundry for radiology revealed that 7,500 of the 15,000 kgs were jackets and coats that were five times as expensive to process as regular laundry items. Several reasons explained the difference, but it was principally because of handwork involved.

Assume that no special requirements were needed in departments other than radiology. Revise the cost-allocation base and compute the new cost-allocation rate. Compute the total cost charged to radiology using kilograms and using the new base.

4.44 Traditional and ABC cost accounting, activity-based management

Refer to the text discussion of Lopez Plastics Company on pp. 130–5. Assume that the company has the traditional cost accounting system described in Exhibit 4.6. The top management team wants to reverse the pattern of quarterly losses. The company president, Angie Oaks, has emphasised the importance of profit improvement by linking future pay raises of the two product-line managers to their respective gross profit margins. She is concerned about the profitability of the pen casing product line while pleased with the profitability of the mobile phone casing line. She also believes that the unallocated costs of the company are too high compared to those of competitors. The office of controller, whose costs are included in the unallocated costs, is responsible for vendor relations and purchasing of direct materials. The controller presents the following idea:

> *We should use more standard parts in mobile phone casings, which will dramatically reduce the purchasing department's work required for purchasing. I believe this should cut our office's costs by as much as €25,000 per quarter. In addition, using standard parts eliminates the need to purchase several expensive resins. The larger volume of purchases of less costly resin from fewer vendors will cut the mobile phone casing direct material cost by 10 per cent. Product engineering agrees that this idea is not only feasible but, if implemented, would improve the overall quality of mobile phone casings.*

The controller and marketing manager provided the following summary of actions and related effects:

Action	Expected effects
Reduce prices of mobile phone casings 25 per cent.	The vice president of sales estimates that the improved quality of mobile phone casings combined with the price reduction will yield a 100 per cent increase in demand for mobile phone casings per quarter.
Use standard parts wherever possible in mobile phone casings.	Total number of parts for each mobile phone casing will not change, but the direct material cost per casing will be reduced by 10 per cent due to volume discounts from preferred vendors. The use of fewer suppliers will reduce vendor-relations work by the purchasing department. This will result in unallocated costs decreasing by €25,000.
	Processing time, measured in direct-labour hours, will increase by 500 hours due to expected 100 per cent increase in sales and production of mobile phone casings, but there is adequate capacity of labour and machine time. Direct-labour costs are fixed as are all of the indirect manufacturing costs.
	Quality of mobile phone casings will improve due to reduced complexity of processing.

1 Evaluate this idea using the traditional cost allocation system shown in Exhibit 4.6 on p. 131. What would be the predicted profitability for each product line and the company as a whole? What would be the most likely level of support for the controller's idea by the product managers of the pen casing product line and the mobile phone casing product line? What would be the level of support by the president?

2 Assume that you have the ABC system described in Exhibit 4.7 on p. 133 with the gross profit margins shown in the table on pp. 134–5. Often, managers with ABC systems can anticipate more effects of improvement ideas because of their increased understanding of the operating system. In this case, although the total number of parts would not change, the idea would reduce the number of distinct parts for mobile phone casings from 20 to 9. Evaluate the controller's idea using the ABC system described in Exhibit 4.7. What would be the predicted profitability for each product line and the company as a whole? What would be the most likely level of support for the controller's idea by the product managers of the pen casing product line and the mobile phone casing product line? What would be the level of support by the president?

3 As vice president, you have expressed concern about the traditional cost-allocation system's product-cost accuracy and its ability to provide relevant information for operational control. Does the new ABC system satisfy your concerns? Explain.

4.45 Activity-based costing and product line profitability

Hipercor is a grocery company with stores throughout Spain. Suppose the company is planning an expansion of its store in central Madrid. A preliminary analysis has shown the packaged food department to be the most profitable, so the company plans to increase its space the most.

Assume that the Madrid store has just three departments: produce, packaged food and meat. The most recent annual report for the store showed sales of €3,283,200, which generated a gross margin of €883,200. Sales and gross margins of the three departments were as follows:

	Produce	Packaged food	Meat	Total
Revenues	€634,800	€1,680,480	€967,920	€3,283,200
Cost of products sold	480,000	1,200,000	720,000	2,400,000
Gross margin	€154,800	€ 480,480	€247,920	€ 883,200

In addition to cost of products sold, the store has €720,000 of support costs, so operating income is €883,200 – €720,000 = €163,200. Hipercor currently uses an accounting system that uses cost of products sold as a cost-allocation base for allocating support costs.

Ramon Flores, controller of Hipercor, recently attended a seminar on activity-based costing. He suggests that Hipercor management should undertake further analysis before deciding which product gets the largest increase in space in the expansion. He has asked you, his assistant, to lead this analysis.

1 The starting point of your analysis is to determine product profitability under the existing cost accounting system. Compute the operating income and the operating income as a percent of sales for each department using Hipercor's existing system. Use this information to assess the relative profitability per euro of sales of each of the three departments.

2 Flores asks you next to develop product costs using an activity-based accounting system. You determine that there are five major activities, each with a different cost driver to be used as a cost-allocation base:

 (a) Ordering – Placing of orders for purchases
 (b) Delivery – Physical delivery and receipt of merchandise
 (c) Shelf-stocking – Stocking of merchandise on store shelves, including ongoing restocking
 (d) Customer support – Assistance to customers, including check out and bagging
 (e) Produce monitoring – Constantly checking on the stacking and freshness of produce.

The cost drivers for each activity are as follows:

Ordering	Number of purchase orders
Delivery	Number of deliveries
Shelf-stocking	Hours of stocking time
Customer support	Number of items sold
Produce monitoring	Direct trace to the Produce Department

You have determined the following information about the cost drivers:

	Produce	Packaged food	Meat	Total
Number of purchase orders	1,440	3,360	1,440	6,240
Number of deliveries	1,200	8,760	2,640	12,600
Hours of shelf-stocking	216	2,160	1,080	3,456
Items sold	50,400	441,600	122,400	614,400

The total cost of each activity was as follows:

Ordering	€124,800
Delivery	201,600
Shelf-stocking	138,240
Customer support	245,760
Product monitoring	9,600
Total	€720,000

Using these data and activity-based costing, calculate the operating income and operating income as a per cent of sales for each product. (For example, note that each purchase order costs €124,800 ÷ 6,240 = €20 to process.)

3 Propose a strategy for expansion. Which information, that based on the current costing system or that based on the activity-based costing system, is most useful? Why? What additional information would you like to have before making a more definitive recommendation on an expansion strategy?

4.46 Activity-based costing and activity-based management, automotive supplier

O'Sullivan Company is an automotive component supplier. O'Sullivan has been approached by Honda of Ireland's Cork plant to consider expanding its production of part 24Z2 to a total annual quantity of 2,000 units. This part is a low-volume, complex product with a high gross margin that is based on a proposed (quoted) unit sales price of €7.50. O'Sullivan uses a traditional costing system that allocates indirect manufacturing costs based on direct-labour costs. The rate currently used to allocate indirect manufacturing costs is 400% of direct-labour cost. This rate is based on the €3,200,000 annual factory overhead cost divided by €800,000 annual direct-labour cost. To produce 2,000 units of 24Z2 requires €5,000 of direct materials and €1,000 of direct labour. The unit cost and gross margin percentage for part 24Z2 based on the traditional cost system are computed as follows:

	Total	Per unit (÷2,000)
Direct material	€ 5,000	€2.50
Direct labour	1,000	.50
Indirect production:(400% × direct labour)	4,000	2.00
Total cost	€10,000	€5.00
Sales price quoted		7.50
Gross margin		€2.50
Gross margin percentage		33.3%

The management of O'Sullivan decided to examine the effectiveness of their traditional costing system versus an activity-based costing system. The following data have been collected by a team consisting of accounting and engineering analysts:

Activity Centre	Factory overhead costs (annual)
Quality	€ 500,000
Production scheduling	50,000
Setup	700,000
Shipping	300,000
Shipping administration	50,000
Production	1,600,000
Total indirect production cost	€3,200,000

Activity centre: cost drivers	Annual cost-driver quantity
Quality: Number of pieces scrapped	10,000
Production scheduling and set up: Number of setups	500
Shipping: Number of containers shipped	60,000
Shipping administration: Number of shipments	1,000
Production: Number of machine hours	10,000

The accounting and engineering team has performed activity analysis and provides the following estimates for the total quantity of cost drivers to be used to produce 2,000 units of part 24Z2:

Cost driver	Cost-driver consumption
Pieces scrapped	120
Setups	4
Containers shipped	10
Shipments	5
Machine hours	15

1 Prepare a schedule calculating the unit cost and gross margin of part 24Z2 using the activity-based costing approach. Use the cost drivers given as cost-allocation bases.
2 Based on the ABC results, which course of action would you recommend regarding the proposal by Honda of Ireland? List the benefits and costs associated with implementing an ABC system at O'Sullivan.

4.47 Review of Chapters 2, 3 and 4

The Sharma Company provides you with the following miscellaneous data regarding operations in 20X9:

Gross profit	£ 40,000
Net profit	15,000
Sales	120,000
Direct material used	35,000
Direct labour	25,000
Fixed manufacturing overhead	15,000
Fixed selling and administrative expenses	12,000

There are no beginning or ending inventories.

Compute (a) variable selling and administrative expenses, (b) contribution margin in pounds sterling, (c) variable manufacturing overhead, (d) break-even point in sales pounds sterling, and (e) manufacturing cost of goods sold.

4.48 Review of Chapters 2, 3 and 4

Kyu Lee Corporation provides you with the following miscellaneous data regarding operations for 20X0 (in thousands of South Korean won, ₩):

Break-even point in sales	₩84,000
Direct material used	29,000
Gross profit	20,000
Contribution margin	25,000
Direct labour	30,000
Sales	100,000
Variable manufacturing overhead	5,000

There are no beginning or ending inventories.

Compute (a) the fixed manufacturing overhead, (b) variable selling and administrative expenses, and (c) fixed selling and administrative expenses.

CASES

4.49 Multiple allocation bases

The Liverpool Company produces three types of circuit boards; call them Alpha, Beta and Gamma. The cost accounting system used by Liverpool until 2009 applied all costs except direct materials to the products using direct-labour hours as the only cost driver. In 2009, the company undertook a cost study. The study determined that there were six main factors that incurred costs. A new system was designed with a separate cost pool for each of the six factors. The factors and the costs associated with each are as follows:

1 Direct-labour hours – direct-labour cost and related fringe benefits and payroll taxes.
2 Machine hours – depreciation and repairs and maintenance costs.
3 Pounds of materials – materials receiving, handling and storage costs.
4 Number of production setups – labour used to change machinery and computer configurations for a new production batch.
5 Number of production orders – costs of production scheduling and order processing.
6 Number of orders shipped – all packaging and shipping expenses.

The company is now preparing a budget for 2010. The budget includes the following predictions:

	Alpha	Beta	Gamma
Units to be produced	10,000	800	5,000
Direct-materials cost	£70/unit	£88/unit	£45/unit
Direct-labour hours	4/unit	18/unit	9/unit
Machine hours	7/unit	15/unit	7/unit
Pounds of materials	3/unit	4/unit	2/unit
Number of production setups	100	50	50
Number of production orders	300	200	70
Number of orders shipped	1,000	800	2,000

The total budgeted cost for 2010 is £3,866,250, of which £995,400 was direct-materials cost and the amount in each of the six cost pools defined above is as follow:

Cost pool*	Cost
1	£1,391,600
2	936,000
3	129,600
4	160,000
5	25,650
6	228,000
Total	£2,870,850

*Identified by the cost driver used.

1 Prepare a budget that shows the total budgeted cost and the unit cost for each circuit board. Use the new system with six cost pools (plus a separate direct application of direct-materials cost).
2 Compute the budgeted total and unit costs of each circuit board if the old direct-labour-hour system had been used.
3 How would you judge whether the new system is better than the old one?

4.50 Identifying activities, resources and cost drivers in manufacturing

International Plastics is a multinational, diversified organisation. One of its manufacturing divisions, Northeast Plastics, has become less profitable due to increased competition. The division produces three major lines of plastic products within its single plant. Product line A is high-volume, simple pieces produced in large batches. Product line B is medium-volume, more complex pieces. Product line C is low-volume, small-order, highly complex pieces.

Currently, the division allocates indirect production costs based on direct labour cost. The director of manufacturing is uncomfortable using the traditional cost figures. He thinks the company is underpricing the more complex products. He decides to conduct an ABC analysis of the business.

Interviews were conducted with the key managers in order to identify activities, resources, cost drivers and their interrelationships.

INTERVIEWEE: PRODUCTION MANAGER

Q1 *What activities are carried out in your area?*
A1 All products are manufactured using three similar, complex and expensive moulding machines. Each moulding machine can be used in the production of the three product lines. Each setup takes about the same time irrespective of the product.
Q2 *Who works in your area?*
A2 Last year, we employed 30 machine operators, 2 maintenance mechanics and 2 supervisors.
Q3 *How are the operators used in the moulding process?*
A3 It requires nine operators to support a machine during the actual production process.
Q4 *What do the maintenance mechanics do?*
A4 Their primary function is to perform machine setups. However, they are also required to provide machine maintenance during the moulding process.
Q5 *Where do the supervisors spend their time?*
A5 They provide supervision for the machine operators and the maintenance mechanics. For the most part, the supervisors appear to spend the same amount of time with each of the employees that they supervise.
Q6 *What other resources are used to support manufacturing?*
A6 The moulding machines use energy during the moulding process and during the setups. We put meters on the moulding machines to get a better understanding of their energy consumption. We discovered that for each hour that a machine ran, it used 6.3 kilowatts of energy. The machines also require consumable shop supplies (e.g., lubricants, hoses and so on). We have found a direct correlation between the amount of supplies used and the actual processing time.

Q7 *How is the building used, and what costs are associated with it?*

A7 We have a 100,000-square-metre building. The total rent and insurance costs for the year were €675,000. These costs are allocated to production, sales and administration based on area.

1 Identify the activities and resources for the division. For each activity, suggest an appropriate cost driver.
2 For each resource identified in requirement 1, indicate its cost behaviour with respect to the activities it supports (assume a planning period of 1 month).

CASE STUDY 1

Tankmaster Manufacturing Company

This case requires students to consider the merits of activity-based costing in an altered production environment. It also deals with behavioural and organisational culture issues.

The Tankmaster Manufacturing Company, a large manufacturer of domestic oil tanks, is located in Amersham, Buckinghamshire. Since it came into existence in 1970, the company has enjoyed steady growth in both sales and profits.

Davina Tankmaster, the founder's daughter, joined the company in 2005 after graduating with a degree in Accounting and Finance from Manchester University. One of her first tasks was to revise the costing system, as there was a need for more accurate product cost information to support the company's strategy of offering keen prices in a highly competitive market dominated by a few large firms.

Davina had faced considerable opposition to the changes she had suggested, with several managers being willing to accept the shortcomings of the old system because they had 'learned to live with it'. Davina won the day largely because of her father's support as the latter was convinced that 'learned to live with' was a euphemism for 'learned to manipulate to our own advantage'.

Davina's father has now retired so that Davina is now conscious of the need to prove herself. Accordingly, the last thing she wants at present is the upset of another major change in the costing system. However, profits are below budget and the accountant is critical of the current costing system, saying that it is hopelessly out of line with the company's updated manufacturing methods and also with current theories on product costing. He says, 'We are still absorbing overheads on labour-hours and we have an absurdly high overhead absorption rate of £150 per labour-hour. We are pricing ourselves out of the market on our old established products. Product costs would be more meaningful if we absorbed overheads on machine-hours.'

Davina decides she must investigate. Over the past five years, overhead costs had risen to £599,300 per month, a 46 per cent increase, while direct labour-hours have risen from £168,200 to £170,000, a negligible amount. The product processes are now largely mechanised with a relatively high level of automation. Direct labour-hours are 4,000 compared with machine-hours of 6,500 (it is possible that some labour is still being classed as direct when in fact changes in technology have altered its nature to indirect).

Davina asks the production manager about the rise in overhead costs, causing him to virtually explode: 'How can I keep costs down when marketing ignore our standard specifications and insist on 23 different versions of every product? I need more specialist engineers to monitor the changes, and they don't come cheap. Also there are completely new parts coming through from design with huge material costs; materials handling is a real headache. And the number of specials going through on small production runs continues to increase. I need many more set-ups per shift and that is skilled work, but you can't pick up that sort of skilled labour easily, so overtime is through the roof.'

Davina talks to the marketing manager next: 'We are facing fierce competition for our bread-and-butter, high-volume lines and we just can't match the low prices in the market. However, we have successfully increased our sales of the more specialised tanks despite an increase in prices forced on us by production. So we are meeting our overall sales targets and as we encourage this trend towards the higher margin specialist products, our profits will rise. I don't see any problem here at present, but there will be if you don't make production get control of the cost increases.'

Davina starts to pull the information together and gets frustrated at the inconsistencies: 'We are meeting our sales targets but production costs are rising because of the switch to specialist products. However, as these are sold at higher margins, we should be improving profits. I don't understand why profits are falling.'

As Davina designed the costing system, she is reluctant to admit that it is at fault and she remembers clearly the opposition she had when she last recommended changes. She no longer has her father to support her so that she decides to bring in a consultant (you) to help identify the problem and to advise on the necessary changes and on a suitable implementation policy. Davina supplies you with the following information:

Budgeted overhead costs per month

	£
Machines	279 500
Set-up and engineering support	200 200
Materials handling	119 600
Total overhead	599 300
Direct labour	170 000
Total manufacturing cost excluding direct materials	769 300
Further details:	
Budgeted labour rate*	£42.500/labour-hour
Budgeted overhead burden*	£149.825/labour-hour
Total cost per labour-hour	£192.325

*Based on budgeted direct labour-hours of 4000.

	Labour-hours	Machine-hours	No. of set-ups	No. of stores orders
Standard products (high volume)	2500	3500	80	160
Specialised products (low volume)	1500	3000	200	300
Total	4000	6500	280	460

Questions

1 Analyse the problem and give advice as to the advantages of switching to machine-hours as the overhead recovery base.

2 Show how an ABC system would change the analysis of the costs between the standard and specialist products.

3 Advise on the implementation of an ABC system. How can Davina's fears be allayed?

Source: Based on a case written by Ken Bates, Victoria University of Wellington.

CASE STUDY 2

Siemens Electric Motor Works (A) (abridged)

Ten years ago our electric motor business was in real trouble. Low labour rates allowed the Eastern Bloc countries to sell standard motors at prices were unable to match. We had become the high cost producer in the industry. Consequently, we decided to change our strategy and become a specialty motor producer. Once we adopted our new strategy, we discovered that while our existing cost system was adequate for costing standard motors, it gave us inaccurate information when we used it to cost specialty motors.

Mr Karl-Heinz Lotte, director of Business Operations, EMW

Siemens Corporation

Headquartered in Munich, Siemens AG, a producer of electrical and electronic products, was one of the world's largest corporations. Revenues totalled 51 billion deutschmarks in 1987, with roughly half this amount representing sales outside the Federal Republic of Germany. The Siemens organisation was split into seven major groups and five corporate divisions. The largest group, Energy and Automation accounted for 24% of total revenues. Low wattage alternating current (A/C) motors were produced at the Electric Motor Works (EMW), which was part of the Manufacturing Industries Division of the Engery and Automation Group. High wattage motors were produced at another facility.

The Electric Motor Works

Located in the small town of Bad Neustadt, the original Siemens EMW plant was built in 1937 to manufacture refrigerator motors for 'Volkskuhlschraenke' (people's refrigerators). Less than a year later, Mr Siemens halted the production of refrigerator motors and began to produce electric motors for other applications. At the end of World War II, the Bad Neustadt plant was the only Siemans factory in West Germany capable of producing electric motors. All the other Siemens production facilities had been completely destroyed or seized by Eastern Bloc countries. After an aggressive rebuilding programme, Bad Neustadt emerged as the firm's primary producer of electric motors.

Through the 1970s, EMW produced about 200 different types of standard motors, at a total annual volume around 230,000 motors. Standard motors accounted for 80 per cent of sales volumes – the remaining 20 per cent was customised motors. The production process was characterised by relatively long runs of a single type of motor. Because identical motors were used by a wide range of customers, standard motors were inventoried and shipped as orders were received. The market for standard A/C motors was extremely competitive. The firm was under constant pressure to reduce costs so that it could price aggressively and still make a profit. Despite a major expansion and automation programme begun in 1974, by the early 1980s EMW found it could not lower its costs sufficiently to offset the lower labour rates of its Eastern Bloc competitors.

Change in strategy

An extensive study revealed that EMW could become a profitable producer of low volume, customised A/C motors. To help implement this strategy, the Bad Neustadt plant was enlarged and dedicated to the manufacture A/C motors with power ratings ranging from 0.06 to 18.5 kilowatts. These motors supported a number of applications including automation engineering,

---

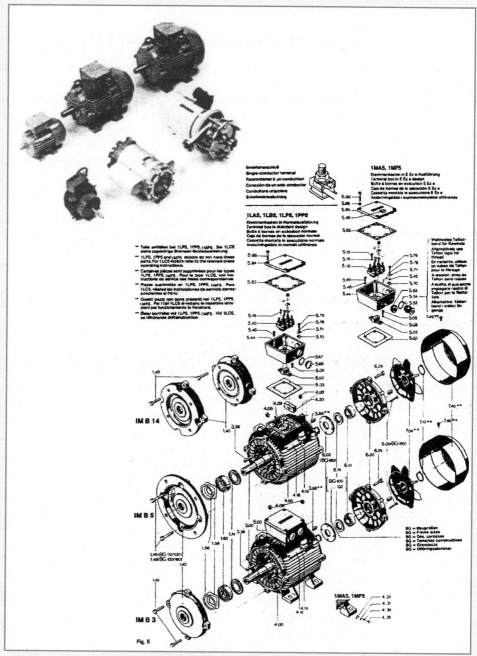

Figure 1 A small part of our large supply programme. Photo, top left: Three examples of three-phase standard motors; Diagram, right: Three custom-built variants.

machine tools, plastic processing and paper and printing machines. Figure 1 presents a detailed diagram of an A/C motor and shows one standard and one customised version of three motors.

For the new strategy to succeed, EMW needed to be able to manufacture efficiently a large variety of motors in small production runs. Between 1985 and 1988 EMW spent DM50 million a year to replace almost every machine on the shopfloor and thereby create a production environment that could support its new strategy.

By 1987 the production process was highly automated with numerically controlled machines, flexible machining centres and robotically fed production processes used throughout the factory. Large volume common components were manufactured using dedicated automated equipment, while very low volume components might be made in manual production processes. Where possible flexible manufacturing was used to produce small volume specialty components. While a normal annual production volume for common components might be 100,000 units, a single component could have up to 10,000 custom variations that might have to be produced one at a time.

To design a custom motor, modifications were made to a standard motor design. The process involved determining where standard components could not be used. These standard components were replaced by custom components that provided the functionality required by the customer.

By 1987, the EMW strategy seemed to be successful (see Figure 2). Of a total of 65,625 orders accepted, 90 per cent were for custom motors; 48 per cent for only one motor and 74 per cent for fewer than five motors. But EMW high-volume standard motors still accounted for almost half the total annual output of 630,000 motors.

Change in the calculation of product costs

EMW's product cost system assigned materials and labour costs directly to the products. Overhead costs were divided into three categories: materials related, production related and support related. **Materials related overhead,** containing costs associated with material acquisition, was allocated to products based on their direct materials costs. **Production related overhead** was directly traced to the 600 production cost centres. A production cost centre had been created for each type of machine. Cost centres with high labour intensity used direct labour hours to allocate costs to products. For centres with automated machines whose operation required few direct labour hours, machine hours was used as the allocation base. **Support related overhead,** was allocated to products based on manufacturing costs to date: the sum of direct materials and direct labour costs, materials overhead and production overhead. The breakdown of each cost category as a percent of total costs was as follows:

	Per cent of total costs	Burden rate
Direct materials	29%	
Direct labour	10	
Materials overhead	2	6% of materials cost
Production overhead	33	DSM/DLhour or DM/Mhr (600 rates)
Support related overhead	26	35% of other manufacturing costs
Total	100%	

Two years after the change in strategy, problems with the traditional cost system became apparent. The traditional cost system seemed unable to capture the relation between the increased support costs and the change in product mix. Management felt that most support costs related more closely to the number of orders received or the number of customised components in a motor rather than to materials expense or to the quantity of labour and machine hours required to build the motor.

An extensive study was undertaken to identify the support costs that management believed were driven by the processing of orders and the processing of special components. The following departments' costs were most affected by the large increases in number of orders and number of special components.

Costs related to order processing	Costs related to special components
Billing	Inventory handling
Order receiving	Product costing and bidding
Product costing and bidding	Product development
Shipping and handling	Purchasing
	Receiving
	Scheduling and production control
	Technical examination of incoming orders

An analysis of the Order processing costs revealed that the same resources were required to process an order of one custom motor as for an order of 200 standard motors. A similar analysis indicated that the number of different types of special components in each motor design determined the work load for the departments affected by Special components. The demand for work in these departments was not strongly affected by the total number of special components produced. For example, an order of five custom motors requiring ten special components per unit generated the same amount of work as an order of one custom motor with a design requiring ten special components. In 1987, the factory used 30,000 different special components to customise their motors. The special components were processed 325,000 different times for customised orders.

The costs in each support department associated with these two activities were removed from the support related cost pool and assigned to two new cost pools. Table 1 illustrates, for 1987, the formation of the two new cost pools. The first column presents total costs grouped by traditional costing system definitions. The new cost system removes 6.3 million from engineering support costs and 27.0 million from administrative support costs. These expenses are then assigned to the new cost pools. 13.8 million to order processing costs and 19.5 million to special components costs.

Table 2 shows the cost buildup for five typical motor orders. The base motor cost includes direct materials and labour costs, materials and production overhead and the portion of support overhead not assigned to the two new cost pools. To this base motor cost must be added the cost of processing the order and the materials, labour, production overhead and support overhead required for the special components.

Effect of the new cost system

In 1987 EMW received close to DM1 billion in orders, accepted only DM450 million and ran the factory at 115 per cent of rated capacity. Mr Karl-Heinz Lottes, director of Business Operations, EMW commented on the role of redesigned cost system with the new strategy:

Without the new cost system, our new strategy would have failed. The information it generated helped us to identify those orders we want to accept. While some orders we lose to competitors, most we turn down because they are not profitable. Anyone who wants to understand the importance of the system, can simply compare some typical orders costed with the traditional system with the costs produced by our new system.

Figure 2

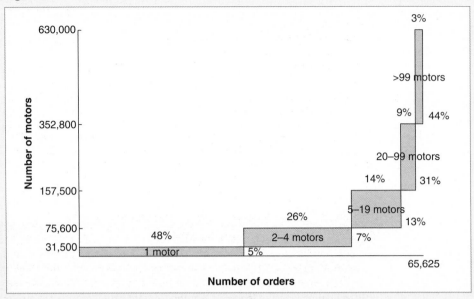

Table 1 1987 Reconciliation transforming the traditional cost system (000 DM)

	Traditional		Transferred	New	
Materials	105,000			105,000	
Materials overhead	6,000			6,000	
Labour	36,000			36,000	
Labour or machine overhead	120,000			120,000	
Manufacturing cost	267,000	(74%)[a]		267,700	(74%)
Engineering costs	12,000		6,300	5,700	
Tooling costs	22,500		0	22,500	
Administrative costs	60,00		27,000	33,000	
Support related costs	94,500	(26%)[b]	33,300 (9%)	61,200	(17%)
Order processing cost			13,800	13,800	
Special components cost			19,500	19,500	
Total cost	361,500		0	361,500	

[a] Percentage of total cost
[b] This figure corresponds to the 26% of support-related overhead on page 172.

Table 2 Manufacturing costs for five motor orders

	A	B	C	D	E
Cost of base motor (without assignment from new cost pools	304.0	304.0	304.0	304.0	304.0
Cost of all special components[a] (without assignment from new cost pools)	39.6	79.2	118.8	198.0	396.0
Number of different types of special components per motor	1	2	3	5	10
Number of motors ordered	1	1	1	1	1

(continued)

	Base motor cost	Special components cost
Materials	90	12.0
Materials overhead	5	0.7
Direct labour	35	4.5
Manufacturing overhead	117	15.0
	247	32.2
Support related overhead[b]	57	7.4
Unit manufacturing costs	304	39.6

[a] For illustrative purposes, all different types of special components are assumed to cost 39.6 a piece.

[b] Support related overhead excludes the expenses associated with processing individual customer orders and handling special components.

Relevant information for decision making with a focus on pricing decisions

Learning objectives

When you have finished studying this chapter, you should be able to:

1 Discriminate between relevant and irrelevant information for making decisions.

2 Apply the decision process to make business decisions.

3 Construct absorption and contribution-margin income statements, and identify their relevance for decision making.

4 Decide to accept or reject a special order using the contribution-margin technique.

5 Explain why pricing decisions depend on the characteristics of the market.

6 Identify the factors that influence pricing decisions in practice.

7 Compute a sales price by various approaches, and compare the advantages and disadvantages of these approaches.

8 Use target costing to decide whether to add a new product.

Mercadona

Low prices can be key to the survival of some companies. For Mercadona it is a unique strength. Spain's largest supermarket has over 1,300 stores, annual sales exceeding €16 billion and surging profits

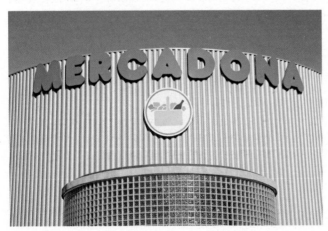

following extensive cost cutting. The company eliminated over 1,000 products from its shelves in 2009. It increased its own-label brands and made simple product adjustments such as reduced packaging. This led to €2.2 billion in shaved costs. Mercadona refers to its customers as 'bosses'. Its products are ranked number one in terms of value for money. (*The Economist* 4 June 2011, p. 85.)

Mercadona's managers can use the contribution-margin technique introduced in Chapter 2. Among the influences on pricing discussed in this chapter, costs and customer demands are the most important to the supermarket. The prices charged must not only ensure a reasonable profit, they must also appeal to the customer.

Costs are important in the pricing decisions of many types of companies. What price should a Safeway store charge for a pound of hamburger? What should Boeing charge for a 787 airplane? Should a clothing manufacturer accept a special order from Primark? Managers rely on accounting information to answer these questions and to make important decisions on a daily basis. However, not all accounting information applies to each type of decision. In this chapter, we'll focus on identifying relevant information for decision making and apply what we learn to pricing decisions. The ability to separate relevant from irrelevant information is often the difference between success and failure in modern business.[1] ■

The concept of relevance

What information is relevant? That depends on the decision being made. Decision making is essentially choosing among several alternative courses of action. Decision makers identify the available alternatives by an often time-consuming search and screening process, perhaps carried out by a company team that includes engineers, accountants and operating executives. The accountant's role is primarily that of a technical expert on financial analysis who provides information that may be useful to the decision maker. However, the decision maker, who has the best understanding of the decision and the available alternatives, must understand what information is relevant.

■ What is relevance?

Objective 1
Discriminate between relevant and irrelevant information for making decisions.

Making business decisions requires managers to compare two or more alternative courses of action. Two criteria determine whether information is relevant: (1) Information must be an expected future revenue or cost, and (2) it must have an element of difference among the alternatives. That is, **relevant information** is the predicted future costs and revenues that will differ among the alternatives.

Note that relevant information is a prediction of the future, not a summary of the past. Historical (past) information has no direct bearing on a decision. Such information can have an indirect bearing on a decision because it may help in predicting the future. But past figures, in themselves, are irrelevant to the decision itself. Why? Because the decision cannot change the past. Decisions affect the future. Nothing can alter what has already happened.

Of the expected future information, only data that will differ across alternatives are relevant to the decision. Any item that will remain the same regardless of the alternative selected is irrelevant. For instance, if a department manager's salary will be the same regardless of the products produced, the salary is irrelevant to the selection of products. Here are some examples to help you clarify the sharp distinctions between relevant and irrelevant information.

Suppose you always buy fuel from either of two nearby petrol stations. Yesterday you noticed that one station was selling fuel at €2 per litre. The other was selling it at €1.90. Your car needs fuel today and in making your choice of stations, you assume that these prices have not changed. The relevant costs are €2.00 and €1.90, the expected future costs that will differ between the alternatives. You use your past experience (that is, what you observed yesterday) for predicting today's price. Note that the relevant cost is not what you paid in the past, or what you observed yesterday, but what you expect to pay when you drive in to get fuel. This cost meets our two criteria: (1) it is the expected future cost and (2) it differs between the alternatives.

---

[1] Throughout this and the next chapter, to concentrate on the fundamental ideas, we shall ignore the time value of money and income taxes (discussed in Chapter 11).

You may also plan to buy a bag of potato crisps when you stop for fuel. Suppose you expect the price of a bag of crisps to be the same at either station. This expected future cost is irrelevant to your decision about which station to stop at because it will be the same under either alternative. It does not meet our second criterion.

On a business level, consider the following decision. A food container manufacturer is thinking of using aluminium instead of tin in making a line of large cans. The cost of direct material is expected to decrease from €.30 per can if tin is used to €.20 per can if the manufacturer uses aluminium. The direct-labour cost will continue to be €.70 per unit regardless of the material used. Direct-labour cost is irrelevant because our second criterion – an element of difference between the alternatives – is not met.

	Aluminium	Tin	Difference
Direct material	€.20	€.30	€.10
Direct labour	.70	.70	–

In this example, the relevant costs are the costs of direct materials. We can safely exclude direct labour from the comparison of alternatives because it does not differ between the alternatives.

A decision model

Objective 2
Apply the decision process to make business decisions.

Exhibit 5.1 illustrates this simple decision process and it serves to show the appropriate framework for more complex decisions. Box 1(A) represents historical data from the accounting system. Box 1(B) represents other data, such as price indices or industry statistics, gathered from outside the accounting system. Regardless of their source, the data in step 1 help the formulation of predictions in step 2. (Remember that historical data are only relevant as a guide to predicting future costs and revenues. In the large can manufacturing example, the historical costs of tin and aluminium are only relevant as predictors of future prices.)

In step 3, these predictions become inputs to the decision model. A **decision model** is any method used for making a choice. Such models sometimes require elaborate quantitative procedures, such as a petroleum refinery's mathematical method for choosing what products to manufacture for any given day or week. A decision model, however, may also be simple. It may be confined to a single comparison of costs for choosing between two materials, as in the previous example of the tin versus aluminium cans. In this example, our decision model is to compare the predicted unit costs and, assuming that everything else is equal, select the alternative with the lower cost.

The decision process in Exhibit 5.1 applies to all business decisions, no matter how simple or complicated they may be. By using this process, you will be able to focus squarely on the relevant information – the predicted future differences between alternatives – in any decision. In the rest of this chapter, we will use this decision process to apply the concept of relevance to several specific pricing decisions.

Accuracy and relevance

In the best of all possible worlds, decision-making information would always be both perfectly relevant and precisely accurate. However, in reality, such information is often too difficult or too costly to obtain. Accountants are sometimes forced to choose between more relevance or more accuracy.

Precise but irrelevant information is worthless for decision making. For example, a university vice-chancellor's salary may be £340,000 per year, to the penny, but may have no bearing on

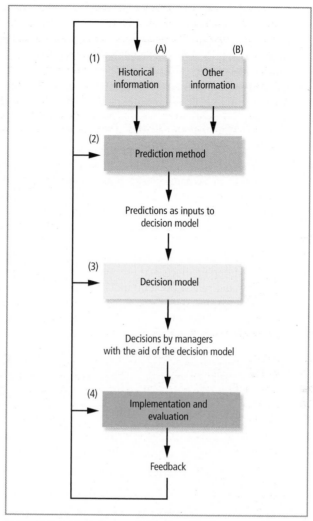

Exhibit 5.1 Decision process and role of information

the question of whether to buy or rent data-processing equipment. In contrast, imprecise but relevant information can be useful. For example, sales predictions for a new product may be subject to error, but they still are helpful in deciding whether to manufacture the product. Relevant information must be reasonably accurate but not precisely so.

The degree to which information is relevant or precise often depends on the degree to which it is qualitative or quantitative. Qualitative aspects are those for which measurement in money terms is difficult and imprecise; quantitative aspects are those for which measurement is easy and precise. Accountants, statisticians and mathematicians try to express as many decision factors as feasible in quantitative terms. Why? Because this approach reduces the number of qualitative (subjective) factors they need to consider. Just as we noted that relevance is more crucial than precision in decision making, so qualitative aspects may dominate quantitative (financial) impacts in many decisions. For example, the extreme opposition of a militant labour union to new labour-saving machinery may cause a manager to forgo installation of such machinery even if it would reduce manufacturing costs. In a similar way, a company may pass up the opportunity to purchase a component from a supplier at a price below the cost of producing it themselves to avoid a long-range dependence on that particular supplier.

Likewise, managers sometimes introduce new technology (for example, advanced computer systems or automated equipment) even though the expected quantitative results seem unattractive. Managers defend such decisions on the grounds that failure to keep abreast of new technology will surely bring unfavourable financial results in the long run.

▓ The relevance of alternative income statements

Objective 3
Construct absorption and contribution-margin income statements and identify their relevance for decision making.

In many cases, income statement information is relevant to decision making because it specifies how alternative choices impact income. Additionally, since executives use income statements to evaluate performance, managers need to know how their decisions will affect income as reported on the statements. There are different ways to organise income statement information. Some income statements track fixed and variable costs using the contribution approach, whereas others adopt the absorption approach used in reporting to external parties.

Let's examine the relevance of contribution and absorption income statements. To highlight the different effects of these approaches, consider the Cordell Company. Suppose Cordell produces and sells 1,000,000 units of seat covers for seats on airplanes, buses and railway carriages. Cordell sells these to companies such as Cathay Pacific and Eurostar. The total manufacturing cost of making 1,000,000 seat covers is €30,000,000. The unit manufacturing cost of the product is €30,000,000 ÷ 1,000,000, or €30 per unit. We will assume that in 20X1 the Cordell Company has direct-materials costs of €14 million and direct-labour costs of €6 million. Assume also that the company incurs the indirect manufacturing costs illustrated in Exhibit 5.2 and the selling and administrative expenses illustrated in Exhibit 5.3. Finally, assume there are no beginning or ending inventories and total sales are predicted at €40 million.

Note that Exhibits 5.2 and 5.3 subdivide costs as variable or fixed. As explained next, most companies do not make such subdivisions in their absorption income statements for external reporting. However, many companies use these subdivisions in contribution income statements to align with the information managers should use in decision making. Note also that it is sometimes difficult to classify a given cost as variable, fixed or partially fixed (for example, repairs).

Schedule 1: Variable costs		
Supplies (lubricants, expendable tools, coolants, sandpaper)	€ 600	
Materials-handling labour (forklift operators)	2,800	
Repairs on manufacturing equipment	400	
Power for factory	200	€ 4,000
Schedule 2: Fixed costs		
Managers' salaries in factory	€ 400	
Factory employee training	180	
Factory picnic and holiday party	20	
Factory supervisory salaries	1,400	
Depreciation, plant and equipment	3,600	
Property taxes on plant	300	
Insurance on plant	100	6,000
Total indirect manufacturing costs		€10,000

Exhibit 5.2 Cordell Company – schedules of predicted indirect manufacturing costs for the year ended 31 December 20X1 (thousands of euros)

Schedule 3: Selling expenses

Variable		
Sales commissions	€1,400	
Shipping expenses for products sold	600	€2,000
Fixed		
Advertising	€1,400	
Sales salaries	2,000	
Other	600	4,000
Total selling expenses		€6,000
Schedule 4: Administrative expenses		
Variable		
Some clerical wages	€ 160	
Computer time rented	40	€ 200
Fixed		
Office salaries	€ 200	
Other salaries	400	
Depreciation on office facilities	200	
Public-accounting fees	80	
Legal fees	200	
Other	720	1,800
Total administrative expenses		€2,000

Exhibit 5.3 Cordell Company – schedules of predicted selling and administrative expenses for the year ended 31 December 20X1 (thousands of euros)

Absorption approach

Exhibit 5.4 presents Cordell's income statement using the **absorption approach** (or **absorption costing**), the approach used by companies for external financial reporting. Firms that take this approach consider all direct and indirect manufacturing costs (both variable and fixed) to be product (inventoriable) costs that become an expense in the form of manufacturing cost of goods sold only as sales occur.

Note that gross profit or gross margin is the difference between sales and the manufacturing cost of goods sold. Note too that the primary classifications of costs on the income statement are by three major management functions: manufacturing, selling and administrative.

Contribution approach

In contrast, Exhibit 5.5 presents Cordell's income statement using the **contribution approach** (also called variable costing or direct costing). International accounting standards do not allow the contribution approach for external financial reporting. However, many companies use the contribution approach for internal decision-making purposes and an absorption format for external purposes. Why? Because they expect the benefits of making better decisions using the contribution approach to exceed the extra costs of using two different reporting systems simultaneously.

For decision purposes, the major difference between the contribution approach and the absorption approach is that the former emphasises the distinction between variable and fixed costs. Its primary classifications of costs is by variable- and fixed-cost behaviour patterns, not by business functions.

The contribution income statement provides a contribution margin – revenue less all variable costs, including variable selling and administrative costs. This approach makes it easier to

Sales		€40,000
Less: Manufacturing costs of goods sold		
Direct materials	€14,000	
Direct labour	6,000	
Indirect manufacturing (Schedules 1 plus 2)*	10,000	30,000
Gross margin or gross profit		€10,000
Selling expenses (Schedule 3)	€ 6,000	
Administrative expenses (Schedule 4)	2,000	
Total selling and administrative expenses		8,000
Operating income		€ 2,000
* Schedules 1 and 2 are in Exhibit 5.2. Schedules 3 and 4 are in Exhibit 5.3.		

Exhibit 5.4 Cordell Company – predicted absorption income statement for the year ended 31 December 20X1 (thousands of euros)

Sales		€40,000
Less: Variable expenses		
Direct materials	€14,000	
Direct labour	6,000	
Variable indirect manufacturing costs (Schedule 1)*	4,000	
Total variable manufacturing cost of goods sold	€24,000	
Variable selling expenses (Schedule 3)	2,000	
Variable administrative expenses (Schedule 4)	200	
Total variable expenses		26,200
Contribution margin		€13,800
Less: Fixed expenses		
Manufacturing (Schedule 2)	€ 6,000	
Selling (Schedule 3)	4,000	
Administrative (Schedule 4)	1,800	11,800
Operating income		€ 2,000
*Note: Schedules 1 and 2 are in Exhibit 5.2. Schedules 3 and 4 are in Exhibit 5.3.		

Exhibit 5.5 Cordell Company – predicted contribution income statement for the year ended 31 December 20X1 (thousands of euros)

understand the impact of changes in sales demand on operating income. It also dovetails nicely with the cost–volume–profit (CVP) analysis illustrated in Chapter 2 and the decision analyses in this chapter and Chapter 6.

Another major benefit of the contribution approach is that it stresses the role of fixed costs in operating income. Before a company can earn income, its total contribution margin must exceed the fixed costs it has incurred for manufacturing and other value-chain functions. This highlighting of contribution margin and total fixed costs focuses management attention on cost behaviour and control in making both short-run and long-run decisions. Remember that advocates of the contribution approach do not maintain that fixed costs are unimportant or irrelevant. They do stress, however, that the distinctions between behaviours of variable and fixed costs are crucial for certain decisions. Decisions usually affect fixed costs in a different way than they affect variable costs.

The distinction between the gross margin (from the absorption approach) and the contribution margin (from the contribution approach) is important for manufacturing companies. Why? Because absorption-costing systems regard fixed manufacturing costs as a part of cost of goods sold and these fixed costs reduce the gross margin accordingly. However, fixed manufacturing costs do not reduce the contribution margin, which is simply the difference between revenues and variable costs. On the other hand, the contribution approach regards variable selling and administrative costs as part of total variable expenses and these reduce contribution margin accordingly. However, variable selling and administrative costs do not reduce gross margin.

◼ Comparing contribution and absorption approaches

In essence, the contribution approach separates fixed costs from variable costs. It deducts variable costs from sales to compute a contribution margin and then deducts fixed costs to measure profit. In contrast, the absorption approach separates manufacturing costs from nonmanufacturing costs. It deducts manufacturing costs from sales to compute a gross margin and then deducts nonmanufacturing costs to measure profit. Both formats can be relevant for decision making, depending on the type of decision being contemplated. In situations where decisions affect variable costs differently than they affect fixed costs, such as the short-run pricing decisions we will discuss in this chapter, the contribution approach will yield great value. In contrast, the absorption approach is well suited for long-run pricing decisions, where it is important that the prices over a product's life cover all manufacturing costs, including fixed costs.

Pricing special sales orders

Before considering more general approaches to pricing, it is helpful to examine how a manager might approach a specific pricing decision – whether to accept a proposed price for a special sales order. We will highlight the value of the contribution approach in such a decision.

◼ Illustrative example

In our illustration, we'll focus again on the Cordell Company. Suppose Branson Gray Line Tours offered Cordell €26 per unit for a 100,000-unit special order of seat covers that (1) would not affect Cordell's regular business in any way, (2) would not affect total fixed costs, (3) would not require any additional variable selling and administrative expenses, (4) would use some otherwise idle manufacturing capacity and (5) would not raise any monopoly issues concerning price discrimination. Should Cordell sell the 100,000 seat covers for the price of €26 each?

Perhaps we should state the question more succinctly: What is the difference in the short-run financial results between not accepting and accepting the order? As usual, the key question is as follows: What are the differences between alternatives? Exhibit 5.5 presents the income statement of the Cordell Company without the special order, using the contribution approach. Let's see how Cordell's operating income would change if it accepts the special order.

◼ Correct analysis – focus on relevant information and cost behaviour

Objective 4
Decide to accept or reject a special order using the contribution-margin technique.

The correct analysis focuses on determining relevant information and cost behaviour. It employs the contribution-margin technique. As Exhibit 5.6 shows, this particular order affects only variable manufacturing costs, at a rate of €24 per unit. All other variable costs and all fixed costs are unaffected and, thus, irrelevant. Therefore, a manager may safely

	Without special order 1,000,000 units	Effect of special order, 100,000 units		With special order, 1,100,000 units
		Total	Per unit	
Sales	€40,000,000	€2,600,000	€26	€42,600,000
Less: Variable expenses				
Manufacturing	€24,000,000	€2,400,000	€24	€26,400,000
Selling and administrative	2,200,000	–	–	2,200,000
Total variable expenses	€26,200,000	€2,400,000	€24	€28,600,000
Contribution margin	€13,800,000	€ 200,000	€ 2	€14,000,000
Less: Fixed expenses				
Manufacturing	€ 6,000,000	–	–	€ 6,000,000
Selling and administrative	5,800,000	–	–	5,800,000
Total fixed expenses	€11,800,000	–	–	€11,800,000
Operating income	€ 2,000,000	€ 200,000	€ 2	€ 2,200,000

Exhibit 5.6 Cordell Company – comparative predicted income statements, contribution-margin technique for year ended 31 December 20X1

ignore them in making this special-order decision. Note how the contribution-margin technique's distinction between variable- and fixed-cost behaviour patterns aids the necessary cost analysis. Total short-run income will increase by €200,000 if Cordell accepts the order – despite the fact that the unit selling price of €26 is less than the total unit manufacturing cost of €30.

Why did we include fixed costs in Exhibit 5.6? After all, they are irrelevant because they do not differ across the alternatives considered in this decision. We included them because management often focuses on the bottom line – operating income. Both the contribution margin and the operating income increase by €200,000 so we could ignore the fixed costs and come to the same conclusion. However, management may prefer to see the effect of its decisions on operating income, so we include the irrelevant fixed costs in the presentation.

Analysis – misuse of unit cost

Faulty cost analysis sometimes occurs because of misinterpreting unit fixed costs, especially with an absorption approach. For instance, Cordell's managers might erroneously use the €30 per-unit total manufacturing cost under the absorption approach (€30,000,000 ÷ 1,000,000 units per Exhibit 5.4) to make the following prediction for the year:

Incorrect analysis	Without special order 1,000,000 units	Incorrect effect of special order 100,000 units	With special order 1,100,000 units
Sales	€40,000,000	€ 2,600,000	€42,600,000
Less: Manufacturing cost of goods sold at €30	30,000,000	3,000,000	33,000,000
Gross margin	10,000,000	(400,000)	9,600,000
Selling and administrative expenses	8,000,000	–	8,000,000
Operating income	€ 2,000,000	€ (400,000)	€ 1,600,000

MAKING MANAGERIAL DECISIONS

Suppose you are at a meeting of Cordell Company managers and someone asked the following questions. Some of the answers given by your colleagues follow:

Q   *What will be the change in the contribution margin if we accept this order?*

A   The contribution margin will increase to €14,000,000.

Q   *In your analysis (Exhibit 5.6), you show that fixed costs do not change if we accept the order. Are these costs relevant?*

A   No. Fixed costs are not relevant.

Q   *OK. But do fixed costs that we incur have an effect on the bottom line of our company?*

A   Certainly. That is why we deduct fixed costs from the contribution margin to get operating income.

Q   *Well, if fixed costs affect the bottom line, how can you say they are not relevant?*

Comment on your colleague's answers and answer the last question.

Answer

Your colleague's answer to the first question is technically incorrect. The question asks for change, not the new total contribution margin. The correct answer to this question is that contribution margin will increase by €200,000 (and therefore become €14,000,000 in total). Be careful to differentiate between terms that imply totals and terms that imply changes. In this case, €14,000,000 is the answer to 'What is the new total contribution margin if we accept the order?'

Your colleague's responses to the second and third questions are correct. The fixed costs of Cordell are not relevant for this particular special order situation. Nevertheless, the bottom line – operating income – includes all costs or total costs and revenues. Do not confuse this with the relevant costs – a term we associated with this specific decision. In a decision situation, relevant costs include only those future costs that will differ if we accept the order. If a manager wants to know the 'bottom line' after accepting the order, we would need to include the fixed cost. However, the fixed costs do not affect the difference between the preorder bottom line and the bottom line after accepting the order. The difference is the same €200,000 amount by which the contribution margin increases.

The incorrect prediction of a €3 million increase in costs results from multiplying 100,000 units by €30. The fallacy in this approach is that it treats a fixed cost (fixed manufacturing cost) as if it were variable. Avoid the temptation to use total unit costs as a basis for predicting how total costs will behave. Unit costs are useful for predicting variable costs, but unit costs can be misleading when used to predict fixed costs.

Confusion of variable and fixed costs

Consider the relationship between total fixed manufacturing costs and a fixed manufacturing cost per unit of product (per Exhibit 5.5):

$$\frac{\text{fixed manufacturing cost}}{\text{per unit of product}} = \frac{\text{total fixed manufacturing costs}}{\text{some selected volume level as the denominator}}$$

$$= \frac{€6,000,000}{1,000,000 \text{ units}} = €6 \text{ per unit}$$

As we noted in Chapter 1, the typical cost accounting system serves two purposes simultaneously: (1) planning and control and (2) product costing. We can graph the total fixed cost for planning and control purposes as a lump sum:

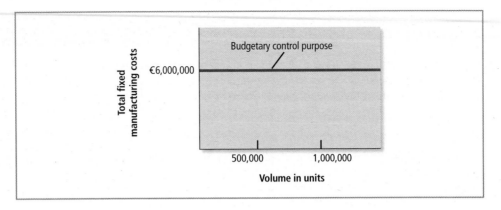

For product-costing purposes, however, using the total unit manufacturing cost implies that these fixed costs behave as if they are variable costs, which is contrary to fixed-cost behaviour:

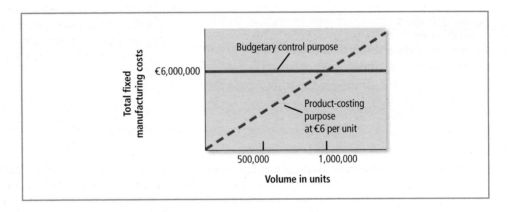

The addition of 100,000 units will not add any fixed costs as long as total output is within the relevant range. The incorrect analysis, however, includes 100,000 × €6 = €600,000 of additional fixed cost in the predictions of increases in total costs.

In short, we should compute the increase in manufacturing costs by multiplying 1,000,000 units by €24, not by €30. The €30 includes a €6 component that will not affect the total manufacturing costs as volume changes within the relevant range. Alternatively, one could entirely avoid this pitfall of unitising fixed costs by using the contribution approach as in Exhibit 5.6.

■ Activity-based costing, special orders and relevant costs

To identify relevant costs affected by a special order (or by other special decisions), more firms are going a step beyond simply identifying fixed and variable costs. As we pointed out in Chapters 3 and 4, a company's operations include many different activities. Businesses that have identified all their significant activities and related cost drivers can produce more detailed relevant information to predict the effects of special orders more accurately.

Suppose the Cordell Company examined its €24 million of variable manufacturing costs very closely and identified two significant activities and related cost drivers: €21 million of processing activity that varies directly with units produced (€14 million in direct materials, €6 million in direct labour and €1 million of variable manufacturing overhead) at a rate of €21 per unit and €3 million of setup activity (the remainder of variable manufacturing overhead)

MAKING MANAGERIAL DECISIONS

We have presented two key lessons so far in this chapter: relevant information and misuse of unit costs. We cannot stress enough how important it is to clearly understand the definition and concept of relevant information. It is also important to understand why the use of unit fixed costs can lead to an incorrect analysis.

Suppose you are a manager in a company that makes small appliances. You are deciding whether to accept or reject a special order for 1,000 units. (Assume there is sufficient excess capacity available for the order.)

1 Which of the following costs are relevant: (a) parts for the order, (b) supervisor's salary, (c) assembly equipment depreciation, (d) power to operate the assembly equipment?

2 Suppose the total unit manufacturing cost for the 1,000 units is €100 per unit. We determined this amount by dividing the total cost by 1,000 units. If the customer decided to double the order to 2,000 units, which costs listed in number 1 would change? Which costs per unit would change? Would the total cost of the order double?

Answers

1 Relevant costs and revenues are predicted future costs and revenues that differ among alternative courses of action. In this case, the cost of parts and power would increase if management accepts the order and, thus, they are relevant. The other costs are fixed costs that would not change because excess capacity is available.

2 Only the relevant costs, in this case the variable costs, would change: parts and power. Fixed costs would be unaffected. In contrast, the fixed cost per unit will change, whereas the variable cost per unit will stay the same. For example, fixed supervisory salaries will be divided by 2,000 units instead of by only 1,000 units and hence per-unit supervisory cost will decrease. The parts cost per unit would stay the same, as would the power cost per unit. So, the total unit cost would fall and the total cost of the order would not double.

that varies with the number of production setups. Normally, Cordell produces 2,000 units per setup. Therefore, for processing 1,000,000 units, Cordell has 500 setups at a cost of €6,000 per setup. Additional sales generally require a proportional increase in the number of setups.

Now suppose the special order is for 100,000 units that vary only slightly in production specifications. Instead of the normal 50 setups, Cordell will need only 5 setups. So processing 100,000 units will take only €2,130,000 of additional variable manufacturing cost:

Additional unit-based variable manufacturing cost, 100,000 × €21	€2,100,000
Additional setup-based variable manufacturing cost, 5 × €6,000	30,000
Total additional variable manufacturing cost	€2,130,000

Instead of the original estimate of 100,000 × €24 = €2,400,000 additional variable manufacturing cost, the special order will cost only €2,130,000, or €270,000 less than the original estimate. Therefore, activity-based costing (ABC) allows managers to realise that the special order is €270,000 more profitable than predicted from the simple unit-based assessment of variable manufacturing cost.

A special order may also be more costly than predicted by a simple fixed- and variable-cost analysis. Suppose the 100,000-unit special order called for a variety of models and colours delivered at various times so that it requires 100 setups. The variable cost of the special order would be €2.7 million, €300,000 more than the original estimate of €2.4 million:

Additional unit-based variable manufacturing cost, 100,000 × €21	€2,100,000
Additional setup-based variable manufacturing cost, 100 × €6,000	600,000
Total additional variable manufacturing cost	€2,700,000

ABC systems provide useful operating information for special-order decisions, but the fundamental concepts remain the same – focus your attention on future costs and revenues that differ because of the special order. Also, be careful to recognise and properly use terms such as *impact, change* and *total*. The summary problem for your review that follows gives you more practice at analysing a special order.

Summary problem for your review

PROBLEM

1 Suppose Nike produces and sells 500,000 units of the LeBron James 'Six Chalk Edition' shirt. The selling price is €35 and there is excess capacity to produce an additional 300,000 shirts. The absorption cost of the shirts is €10,000,000 ÷ 500,000, or €20 per shirt, consisting of variable manufacturing costs of €7,000,000 (€7,000,000 ÷ 500,000 or €14 per shirt) and fixed manufacturing costs of €3,000,000 (€3,000,000 ÷ 500,000 or €6 per shirt). Variable selling and administrative costs are €3 per shirt and fixed selling and administrative costs are €2,000,000. Assume Nike receives an offer from Eurosport to buy 100,000 shirts at a price of €18.00 per shirt. If Nike accepts the order it would not incur any additional variable selling and administrative costs, but it would have to pay a flat fee of €80,000 to the manufacturer's agent who had obtained the potential order. Should Nike accept the special order?

2 What if the order was for 250,000 units at a selling price of €13.00 and there was no €80,000 agent's fee? One manager argued for acceptance of such an order as follows: 'Of course, we will lose €1.00 each on the variable manufacturing costs (€13 − €14), but we will gain €2.00 per unit by spreading our fixed manufacturing costs over 750,000 shirts instead of 500,000 shirts. Consequently, we should take the offer because it represents an advantage of €1.00 per shirt.' The manager's analysis follows:

Old fixed manufacturing cost per unit, €3,000,000 ÷ 500,000	€6.00
New fixed manufacturing cost per unit, €3,000,000 ÷ 750,000	4.00
'Savings' in fixed manufacturing cost per unit	€2.00
Loss on variable manufacturing cost per unit, €13.00 − €14.00	1.00
Net savings per unit in manufacturing cost	€1.00

Explain why this is faulty thinking.

SOLUTION

1 Focus on relevant information – the differences in revenues and costs. In this problem, in addition to the difference in variable costs, there is a difference in fixed costs between the two alternatives.

Additional revenue, 100,000 units at €18.00 per shirt	€1,800,000
Less: Additional costs	
Variable costs, 100,000 units at €14 per unit	1,400,000
Fixed costs, agent's fee	80,000
Increase in operating income from special order	€ 320,000

So, from a strictly financial perspective, Nike should accept the special order.

2 The faulty thinking comes from attributing a 'savings' to the decrease in unit fixed costs. Regardless of how we 'unitise' the fixed manufacturing costs or 'spread' them over the units produced, the special order will not change the total of €3 million. Remember that we have a negative contribution margin of €1.00 per unit on this special order. Thus, there is no way we can cover any amount of fixed costs! Fixed costs are not relevant to this decision.

Basic principles for pricing decisions

One of the major decisions managers face is pricing. Actually, pricing can take many forms. In addition to pricing special orders, managers make the following pricing decisions:

1 Setting the price of a new or refined product
2 Setting the price of products sold under private labels
3 Responding to a new price of a competitor
4 Pricing bids in both sealed and open bidding situations.

Pricing decisions are so important that we will spend the rest of the chapter discussing the many aspects of pricing. Let us now take a look at some of the basic concepts behind pricing.

■ The concept of pricing

Objective 5
Explain why pricing decisions depend on the characteristics of the market.

Pricing decisions depend on the market characteristics in which a firm operates. In **perfect competition** all competing firms sell the same type of product at the same price. Thus, a firm can sell as much of a product as it can produce, all at a single market price. If it charges more, no customer will buy. If it charges less, it sacrifices profits. Therefore, every firm in such a market will charge the market price and the only decision for managers is how much to produce.

Although costs do not directly influence prices in perfect competition, they do affect the production decision. Consider the marginal cost curve in Exhibit 5.7. The **marginal cost** is the additional cost resulting from producing and selling one additional unit – for the Cathay Pacific, it's one additional passenger; for Fiat, it's one additional car. With a fixed set of production facilities, the marginal cost often decreases as production increases up to a point because of efficiencies created by larger volumes. At some point, however, marginal costs begin to rise with increases in production because facilities become overcrowded or overused, resulting in inefficiencies.

Exhibit 5.7 also includes a marginal revenue curve. The **marginal revenue** is the additional revenue resulting from the sale of an additional unit. In perfect competition, the marginal revenue curve is a horizontal line equal to the price per unit at all volumes of sales.

As long as the marginal cost is less than the marginal revenue (price), additional production and sales are profitable. When marginal cost exceeds price, however, the firm loses money on each additional unit. Therefore, the profit-maximising volume is the quantity at which marginal cost equals price. In Exhibit 5.7, the firm should produce V_0 units. Producing fewer units passes up profitable opportunities and producing more units reduces profit because each additional unit costs more to produce than it generates in revenue.

In **imperfect competition**, the price a firm charges for a unit influences the quantity of units it sells. At some point, the firm must reduce prices to generate additional sales. Exhibit 5.8 contains a *demand curve* (also called the *average revenue curve*) for imperfect competition that shows the volume of sales at each possible price. To sell additional units, the firm must reduce the price of all units sold. Therefore, the *marginal revenue curve*, also shown in Exhibit 5.8, is

Exhibit 5.7 Marginal revenue and cost in perfect competition

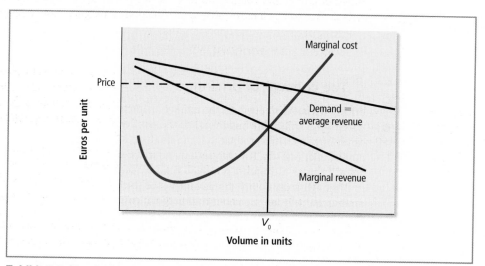

Exhibit 5.8 Marginal revenue and cost in imperfect competition

below the demand curve. That is, the marginal revenue for selling one additional unit is less than the price at which the company sells it because the price of all other units falls as well. For example, suppose a firm can sell 10 units for €50 per unit. However, the firm must drop the price to €49 per unit to sell 11 units, to €48 to sell 12 units and to €47 to sell 13 units. The fourth column of Exhibit 5.9 shows the marginal revenue for units 11–13. Notice that the marginal revenue decreases as volume increases.

To estimate marginal revenue, managers must predict the **price elasticity** – the effect of price changes on sales volume. If small price increases cause large volume declines, demand is highly elastic. If prices have little or no effect on volume, demand is highly inelastic.

For the marginal costs shown in the fifth column of Exhibit 5.9, the optimal production and sales level is 12 units. The last column of that exhibit illustrates that the eleventh unit adds €4 to profit and the twelfth adds €1, but production and sale of the thirteenth unit would decrease profit by €2. In general, firms should produce and sell units until the marginal

Units sold	Price per unit	Total revenue	Marginal revenue	Marginal cost	Profit from production and sale of additional unit
10	€50	10 × €50 = €500			
11	49	11 × 49 = 539	€539 − €500 = €39	€35	€39 − €35 = €4
12	48	12 × 48 = 576	576 − 539 = 37	36	37 − 36 = 1
13	47	13 × 47 = 611	611 − 576 = 35	37	35 − 37 = (2)

Exhibit 5.9 Profit maximisation in imperfect competition

revenue equals the marginal cost, represented by volume V_0 in Exhibit 5.8. The optimal price charged will be the amount that creates a demand for V_0 units.

Notice that the marginal cost is relevant for pricing decisions. In managerial accounting, marginal cost is essentially the variable cost. What is the major difference between marginal cost and variable cost? Accountants assume that variable cost is constant within a relevant range of volume, whereas marginal cost may change with each unit produced. Within large ranges of production volume, however, changes in marginal cost are often small. Therefore, variable cost can be a reasonable approximation of marginal cost in many situations.

Pricing and accounting

Accountants seldom compute marginal revenue and marginal cost curves. Instead, they use estimates based on judgement to predict the effects of additional production and sales on profits. In addition, they examine selected volumes, not the whole range of possible volumes. Such simplifications are justified because the cost of a more sophisticated analysis would exceed the benefits.

Consider a division of Bosch that makes microwave ovens. Suppose market researchers estimate that Bosch can sell 700,000 ovens at €200 per unit and 1,000,000 ovens at €180. The variable cost of production is €130 per unit at production levels of both 700,000 and 1,000,000. Both volumes are also within the relevant range so that changes in volume do not affect fixed costs. Which price should Bosch charge?

Bosch's accountant would determine the relevant revenues and costs. The additional revenue and additional costs of the 300,000 additional units of sales at the €180 prices are as follows:

Additional revenue: (1,000,000 × €180) − (700,000 × €200) =	€40,000,000
Additional costs: 300,000 × €130 =	39,000,000
Additional profit	€ 1,000,000

So the €180 price is optimal since it generates €1,000,000 more profit. On the other hand, the accountant could compare the total contribution for each alternative:

Contribution at €180: (€180 − €130) × 1,000,000 =	€50,000,000
Contribution at €200: (€200 − €130) × 700,000 =	49,000,000
Difference	€ 1,000,000

Notice that comparing the total contributions is essentially the same as computing the additional revenues and costs − both use the same relevant information. Further, both approaches correctly ignore fixed costs, which are unaffected by this pricing decision.

General influences on pricing in practice

Several factors interact to shape the market in which managers make pricing decisions. Legal requirements, competitors' actions and customer demands all influence pricing.

Legal requirements

Objective 6
Identify the factors
that influence pricing
decisions in practice.

Managers must consider constraints imposed by international laws when making pricing decisions. These laws often protect consumers, but they also help protect competing companies from predatory and discriminatory pricing.

Predatory pricing means setting prices so low that they drive competitors out of the market. The predatory pricer then has no significant competition and can raise prices dramatically. For example, Aberdeen Journals has been fined £1.3 million for abusing a dominant market position. The Office of Fair Trading found that the company deliberately incurred losses when selling advertising in the *Aberdeen Herald and Post* in an attempt to expel the *Aberdeen and District Independent*, its only direct rival, from the market. The predatory pricing started in response to the launch of the latter paper. Generally, it is illegal for a company to lose money as a tactic to drive competitors out of business.

Discriminatory pricing is charging different prices to different customers for the same product or service. For example, a large group of retail druggists and big drugstore chains sued several large drug companies. The drugstores alleged that the drug companies' practice of allowing discounts, some as large as 40 per cent, to mail-order drug companies, health maintenance organisations and other managed-care entities constitutes discriminatory pricing. However, pricing is not discriminatory if it reflects a cost differential incurred in providing the good or service.

Both predatory and discriminatory pricing practices are not only illegal but unethical business practices. Management accountants have an ethical obligation to perform their duties in accordance with relevant laws and to refrain from engaging in or supporting any activity or practice that would discredit the profession.

Competitors' actions

Competitors usually react to the price changes of their rivals. Many companies gather information regarding a rival's capacity, technology and operating policies. In this way, managers make more informed predictions of competitors' reactions to a company's prices. The study of game theory focuses on predicting and reacting to competitors' actions.

A manager's expectations of competitors' reactions and of the overall effects of price changes on the total industry demand for the good or service in question heavily influence pricing policies. For example, an airline might cut prices even if it expects matching price cuts from its rivals, hoping that total customer demand for the tickets of all airlines will increase sufficiently to offset the reduction in the price per ticket.

Competition is becoming increasingly global in its scope. Overcapacity in some countries often causes aggressive pricing policies for a company's exported goods. For example, companies might 'dump' products by selling them at a low price in a foreign market that is isolated from its other markets. As you can imagine, when companies' markets expand globally, their pricing policies become more complex.

Customer demands

More than ever before, managers are recognising the needs of customers. Pricing is no exception. If customers believe a price is too high, they may turn to other sources for the product or service, substitute a different product, or decide to produce the item themselves. Eurostar travellers often choose to fly when train journey prices prove too high.

Cost-plus pricing

Accounting influences pricing by providing costs. The exact role costs play in pricing decisions depends on both the market conditions and the company's approach to pricing. This section discusses cost-plus pricing, the most common use of costs in pricing decisions.

What is cost-plus pricing?

Many managers set prices by 'cost-plus' pricing. For example, Eurostar sets its prices by computing an average cost and then adding a desired **markup** – the amount by which price exceeds cost – that will generate a desired level of income. The key, however, is the 'plus' in cost plus. Instead of being a fixed markup, the 'plus' will usually depend on both costs and the demands of customers. For example, the railway has a standard (rack rate) price that does not change during the year, but it often offers discounts during non-peak times.

Prices are most directly related to costs in industries where revenue is based on cost reimbursement. Cost-reimbursement contracts generally specify how to measure costs and what costs are allowable. For example, the government reimburses only economy-class (not first-class) airfares for business travel.

Ultimately, though, the market sets prices. Why? Because companies inevitably adjust the price as set by a cost-plus formula 'in light of market conditions'. The maximum price a company can charge is the one that does not drive the customer away. The minimum price might be considered to be zero (for example, companies may give out free samples to gain entry into a market).

A more practical guide is that, in the short run, the minimum price sales personnel should quote on an order is the marginal cost that the company incurs if it gets the order (in effect its relevant costs of filling the order) – often all variable costs of producing, selling and distributing the good or service. However, in the long run, the price must be high enough to cover all costs, including fixed costs. Therefore, many companies add allocated fixed unit costs to the variable costs to get a minimum price they want to achieve in the long run. They acknowledge that market conditions sometimes dictate sales at a price lower than this long-run minimum price. Yet, to continue to produce and sell such a product, there must be a prospect of eventually achieving a price at or above the long-run minimum.

Cost bases for cost-plus pricing

Objective 7
Compute a sales price by various approaches and compare the advantages and disadvantages of these approaches.

To set a desired price for products or services, managers often add a markup to some measure of costs – thus, the term *cost plus*. The size of the 'plus' depends on the definition of cost and the desired operating income. Prices can be based on a host of different markups that are in turn based on a host of different definitions of cost. Thus, there are many ways to arrive at the same price.

Exhibit 5.10 displays the relationships of costs to selling prices, assuming a desired operating income of €1 million on a volume of 1 million units. The exhibited percentages represent four popular markup formulas for pricing: (1) as a percentage of variable manufacturing costs, (2) as a percentage of total variable costs, (3) as a percentage of total manufacturing cost and (4) as a percentage of full costs. Notice that the first two formulas are consistent with the contribution approach and the latter two are based on absorption costing numbers. Note also that **full cost** means the total of all manufacturing costs plus the total of all selling and administrative costs. As noted in earlier chapters, we use 'selling and administrative' to include all value-chain functions other than production.

To achieve the same prices, the percentages in Exhibit 5.10 differ for each definition of cost. For instance, the markup on variable manufacturing costs is 66.67 per cent and on full

			Alternative markup percentages to achieve same sales price
	Sales price	€20.00	
	Variable cost:		
(1)	Manufacturing	€12.00	(€20.00 − €12.00) ÷ €12.00 = 66.67%
	Selling and administrative*	1.10	
(2)	Unit variable costs	€13.10	(€20.00 − €13.10) ÷ €13.10 = 52.67%
	Fixed costs:		
	Manufacturing†	€ 3.00	
	Selling and administrative	2.90	
	Unit fixed costs	€ 5.90	
(3)	Full costs	€19.00	(€20.00 − €19.00) ÷ €19.00 = 5.26%
	Desired operating income	€ 1.00	

* Selling and administrative costs include costs of all value chain functions other than production.
† (4) A frequently used formula is based on total manufacturing costs: [€20.00 − (€12.00 + €3.00)] ÷ €15.00 = 33.33%.

Exhibit 5.10 Relationships of costs to same target selling price

costs it is only 5.26 per cent. Regardless of the formula used, the pricing decision maker will be led toward the same €20 price. If the decision maker is unable to obtain such a price consistently, the company will not achieve its €1 million operating income objective.

We have seen that managers can base prices on various types of cost information, from variable manufacturing costs to full costs. Each of these costs can be relevant to the pricing decision. Each approach has advantages and disadvantages.

■ Advantages of the contribution approach in cost-plus pricing

Prices based on variable costs represent a contribution approach to pricing. When used intelligently, the contribution approach has some advantages over the total-manufacturing-cost and full-cost approaches because the latter two often fail to highlight different cost behaviour patterns.

The contribution approach offers more detailed information because it displays variable- and fixed-cost behaviour patterns separately. Because the contribution approach is sensitive to cost-volume-profit relationships, it is a helpful basis for developing pricing formulas. As a result, this approach allows managers to prepare price schedules at different volume levels. The correct analysis in Exhibit 5.11 shows how changes in volume affect operating income. The contribution approach helps managers with pricing decisions by readily displaying the interrelationships among variable costs, fixed costs and potential changes in selling prices.

In contrast, pricing with full costing presumes a given volume level. When the volume changes, the unit cost used at the original planned volume may mislead managers. Managers sometimes erroneously assume that they can compute the change in total costs by multiplying any change in volume by the full unit cost.

The incorrect analysis in Exhibit 5.11 shows how using the €19 full cost per unit (based on a volume of 1,000,000 units from Exhibit 5.10) to predict effects of volume changes on operating income can mislead managers. Suppose a manager uses the €19 figure to predict an operating income of €900,000 if the company sells 900,000 instead of 1,000,000 units. If actual operating income is €310,000 instead, as the correct analysis predicts, that manager may be stunned – and possibly looking for a new job. Notice the only volume where the incorrect analysis is actually correct is at the 1 million unit volume level, which is also the only volume where the €19 full cost per unit is valid.

The contribution approach also offers insight into the short-run versus long-run effects of cutting prices on special orders. For example, recall the 100,000 unit special order at a lower

	Correct analysis			Incorrect analysis		
Volume in units	900,000	1,000,000	1,100,000	900,000	1,000,000	1,100,000
Sales at €20.00	€18,000,000	€20,000,000	€22,000,000	€18,000,000	€20,000,000	€22,000,000
Unit variable costs at €13.10*	11,790,000	13,100,000	14,410,000			
Contribution margin	6,210,000	6,900,000	7,590,000			
Fixed costs†	5,900,000	5,900,000	5,900,000			
Full costs at €19.00*				17,100,000	19,000,000	20,900,000
Operating income	€ 310,000	€ 1,000,000	€ 1,690,000	€ 900,000	€ 1,000,000	€ 1,100,000

* From Exhibit 5.10.	
† Fixed manufacturing costs	€3,000,000
Fixed selling and administrative costs	2,900,000
Total fixed costs	€5,900,000

Exhibit 5.11 Analyses of effects of changes in volume on operating income

than normal selling price (€26 versus €40) for Cordell Company displayed in Exhibit 5.6 (p. 184). As you saw earlier, the contribution approach generated the most relevant information, showing that accepting this special order yielded a short-run advantage of €200,000.

However, the manager should also consider long-run effects. Will acceptance of the offer undermine the long-run price structure? In other words, is the short-run advantage of €200,000 more than offset by highly probable long-run financial disadvantages? The manager may think so and, thus, reject the offer. But – and this is important – by doing so the manager is, in effect, forgoing €200,000 now to protect certain long-run market advantages. Generally, the manager can assess problems of this sort by asking whether the probability of long-run benefits is worth an 'investment' equal to the forgone contribution margin (€200,000, in this case). Under full-cost approaches, the manager must ordinarily conduct a special study to find the immediate effects. Under the contribution approach, the manager has a system that will routinely provide such information.

■ Advantages of absorption-cost approaches in cost-plus pricing

Frequently, companies do not employ a contribution approach because they fear that managers will indiscriminately substitute variable costs for full costs and will, therefore, lead to suicidal price cutting. This problem should not arise if managers use the data wisely. However, if top managers perceive a pronounced danger of underpricing when they reveal variable-cost data, they may justifiably prefer an absorption-cost approach (either total manufacturing costs or full costs) for guiding pricing decisions.

Actually, absorption costs are far more widely used in practice than is the contribution approach. Why? In addition to the reasons we have already mentioned, managers have cited the following:

1 In the long run, a firm must recover all costs to stay in business. Sooner or later, fixed costs do indeed fluctuate as volume changes. Therefore, it is prudent to assume that all costs are variable (even if some are fixed in the short run).

2 Computing prices based on absorption cost may indicate what competitors might charge, especially if they have approximately the same level of efficiency as you and also aim to recover all costs in the long run.

3 Absorption-cost formula pricing meets the cost-benefit test. It is too expensive to conduct individual cost-volume tests for the many products (sometimes thousands) that a company offers.

4   There is much uncertainty about the shape of the demand curves and the correct price-output decisions. Absorption-cost pricing copes with this uncertainty by not encouraging managers to take too much marginal business.

5   Absorption-cost pricing tends to promote price stability. Managers prefer price stability, primarily because it makes planning more dependable.

6   Absorption-cost pricing provides the most defensible basis for justifying prices to all interested parties, including government antitrust investigators.

7   Absorption-cost pricing provides convenient reference points to simplify hundreds or thousands of pricing decisions.

Using multiple approaches

To say that either a contribution approach or an absorption-cost approach provides the 'best' guide to pricing decisions is a dangerous oversimplification of one of the most perplexing issues in business. Lack of understanding and judgement can lead to unprofitable pricing regardless of the kind of cost data available or cost accounting system used.

Basically, no single method of pricing is always best. Many companies use both full-cost and variable-cost information in pricing decisions. Modern accounting systems, such as ERP systems, often identify variable and fixed costs, producing both full-cost and variable-cost information. This allows assessment of both short-run and long-run effects. In contrast, most older systems focus on absorption-cost and do not organise their data collection to distinguish between variable and fixed costs. When using such older systems, managers must use special studies or educated guesses to designate costs as variable or fixed.

Managers are especially reluctant to focus on variable costs and ignore allocated fixed costs when their performance evaluations and possibly their bonuses, are based on income shown in published financial statements. Why? Because companies base such statements on full costing and thus allocations of fixed costs affect reported income.

Formats for pricing

Exhibit 5.10 showed how to compute alternative general markup percentages that would produce the same selling prices if used day after day. In practice, the format and arithmetic of quote sheets, job proposals or similar records vary considerably.

Exhibit 5.12 is from an actual quote sheet used by the manager of a small job shop that bids on welding machinery orders in a highly competitive industry. The approach in Exhibit 5.12 is a tool for informed pricing decisions. Notice that the maximum price is not a matter of cost at all. It is what you think you can obtain. The minimum price is the total variable cost.

The manager will rarely bid the minimum price. Businesses do need to make a profit. Still, the manager wants to know the effect of a job on the company's total variable costs. Occasionally, a company will bid near or even below that minimum price to establish a presence in new markets or with a new customer, especially when cost reductions can be achieved in the future or when the new product is tied to other products that generate profits for the firm, as in the 'Business first' box on page 198 regarding Microsoft's Xbox.

Note that Exhibit 5.12 classifies costs specifically for the pricing task. More than one person may make pricing decisions in a particular company. The accountant's responsibility is to prepare an understandable format that requires a minimum of computations. Exhibit 5.12 combines direct labour and variable manufacturing overhead. It lumps together all fixed costs, whether manufacturing, selling or administrative, and applies them to the job using a single fixed-overhead rate per direct labour hour. If the company wants more accuracy, it could formulate many more detailed cost items and overhead rates. To obtain the desired accuracy, many companies are turning to activity-based costing.

Direct materials, at cost	€25,000
Direct labour and variable manufacturing overhead, 600 direct labour hours × €30 per hour	18,000
Sales commission (varies with job)	2,000
Total variable costs – minimum price*	45,000
Add fixed costs allocated to job, 600 direct labour hours × €20 per hour	12,000
Total costs	57,000
Add desired markup	30,000
Selling price – maximum price that you think you can obtain*	€87,000

*This sheet shows two prices, maximum and minimum. Any amount you can get above the minimum price provides contribution margin.

Exhibit 5.12 Quote sheet for pricing

Some managers, particularly in construction and in service industries (such as auto repair), compile separate categories of costs of (1) direct materials, parts and supplies and (2) direct labour. These managers then use different markup rates for each category. They use these rates to provide enough revenue to cover both indirect and unallocated costs and operating profit. For example, a car repair shop might have the following format for each job:

	Billed to customers
Car parts (€200 cost plus 40% markup)	€280
Direct labour (Cost is €20 per hour. Bill at 300% to recover indirect and unallocated costs and provide for operating profit. Billing rate is €20 × 300% = €60 per hour. Total billed for 10 hours is €60 × 10 = €600.)	600
Total billed to customer	€880

Another example is an Italian printing company in Milan that wants to price its jobs so that each one generates a margin of 28 per cent of revenues – 14 per cent to cover selling and administrative expenses and 14 per cent for profit. To achieve this margin, the manager uses a pricing formula of 140 per cent times predicted materials cost plus €25 per hour of production time. The latter covers labour and overhead costs of €18 per hour. For a product with €400 of materials cost and 30 hours of production time, the price would be €1,310:

	Cost	Price	Margin
Materials	€400	€ 560	€160
Labour and overhead	540	750	210
Total	€940	€1,310	€370

The profit of €370 is approximately 40 per cent of the cost of €940 and 28 per cent of the price of €1,310.

You can see there are numerous ways to compute selling prices. However, some general words of caution are appropriate here. Managers are better able to understand their options and the effects of their decisions on profits if they know their costs. That is, it is more informative to pinpoint costs first, before adding markups, than to have a variety of markups already embedded in the 'costs' used as guides for setting selling prices. For example, if materials cost €1,000, a price quotation guide should show them at €1,000, not at, for example, a marked-up €1,400 because that is what the seller hopes to get.

BUSINESS FIRST
Xbox pricing

Despite all the hype surrounding the Xbox 360 video game console in May of 2005, Microsoft didn't initially make any money on the machine itself. A tear-down analysis by market researcher iSuppli of the high-end Xbox 360 found that the materials (e.g., hard drive, computer chip, cables, etc.) cost Microsoft $525 before assembly. The console initially sold at retail for $399, for a loss of $126 per unit. iSuppli analyst Chris Crotty said efficiency gains would shave $50 off chip costs, which, with other reductions over time, would get Microsoft closer to breakeven. Microsoft expected that, including sales of its own game software, the Xbox line would start out 'gross margin neutral' – breakeven – and would eventually turn a profit.

Microsoft continued this low-price strategy by reducing the price of its Xbox 360 Arcade system to less than $200 in 2008. As a result, Asian shipments of the Xbox in October 2008 grew by 53 per cent compared to the prior month. Microsoft officials claim '. . . what is really driving our growth momentum right now is how we are broadening our consumer base to include not only hardcore gamers but also individuals who would have previously not thought about buying

a game console.' Microsoft also commented that '. . . current shipment volumes had reached such high levels that the company could afford to depend on volume to rake in a profit despite the lower prices.' This pricing strategy is also sure to boost company profits from related software-game sales for the Xbox, which is consistent with its fundamental claim that 'Microsoft is a software company by heart, and we will continue to work with our partners and by ourselves to develop new software for the market.'

In November 2006, the manufacturing cost of a 20 GB Playstation 3 by Sony was $805.85 according to electronics specialist firm iSuppli. Sony was said to be losing $306.85 per unit, which it sold for $499. It lost $241.35 on its 60 GB model being sold at $599. By 2010, Playstation was bringing in $435 million in profits for Sony following growth in sales and reduced manufacturing costs.

Sources: ArikKesseldahl, 'For every Xbox, a big fat loss', *Business Week*, 5 December 2005; Reuters, 'Microsoft eyes '09 market-beating Xbox sales', 17 December 2008; www.destructoid. com 'Playstation brand makes €435m in profit', 5 June 2011.

Summary problem for your review

PROBLEM

Custom Graphics is a London printing company that bids on a wide variety of design and printing jobs. The owner of the company, Janet Solomon, prepares the bids for most jobs. Her cost budget for 20X1 follows:

Materials		£ 350,000
Labour		250,000
Overhead		
Variable	£300,000	
Fixed	150,000	450,000
Total production cost of jobs		£1,050,000
Selling and administrative expenses[*]		
Variable	£ 75,000	
Fixed	125,000	200,000
Total costs		£1,250,000

[*]These expenses include costs of all value chain functions other than production.

Solomon has a target profit of £250,000 for 20X1.

Compute the average target markup percentage for setting prices as a percentage of the following:

1 Materials plus labour.

2 Variable production cost of jobs (assume labour is a variable-cost resource).

3 Total production cost of jobs.

4 All variable costs.

5 All costs.

SOLUTION

The purpose of this problem is to emphasise that many different approaches to pricing might be used that would achieve the same selling price. To achieve £250,000 of profit, the desired revenue for 20X1 is £1,250,000 + £250,000 = £1,500,000. The required markup percentages are as follows:

1 Per cent of materials and labour $= \dfrac{(£1,500,000 - £600,000)}{£600,000} = 150\%$

2 Per cent of variable production cost of jobs $= \dfrac{(£1,500,000 - £900,000)}{£900,000} = 66.7\%$

3 Per cent of total production cost of jobs $= \dfrac{£1,500,000 - £1,050,000)}{£1,050,000} = 42.9\%$

4 Per cent of all variable costs $= \dfrac{(£1,500,000 - £975,000)}{£975,000} = 53.8\%$

5 Per cent of all costs $= \dfrac{(£1,500,000 - £1,250,000)}{£1,250,000} = 20\%$

Target costing

Objective 8
Use target costing to decide whether to add a new product.

The pricing approaches so far have all developed a price based on measures of costs. Another approach to the relationship between costs and prices is to take a product's market price as given and determine the maximum cost the company can spend to make the product and still achieve the desired profitability. We call this **target costing**.

Consider a company that is deciding whether to develop and market a new product. In evaluating the feasibility of the new product, management must predict both the cost to produce the product and the price at which it will sell. The degree to which management actions can affect price and cost determines the most effective approach to use for pricing and cost management purposes. Companies use cost-plus pricing for products where management actions (for example, advertising) can influence the market price. Although cost management is important in this case, there is a strong focus on marketing and the revenue side of the profit equation.

But what if the market conditions are such that management cannot influence prices? If a company is to achieve management's desired profit, it must focus on the product's cost. What management needs is an effective tool to reduce costs without reducing value to the customer. A growing number of companies faced with this situation are adopting target costing. Based on the product's predicted price and the company's desired profit, managers set a desired, or target, cost before creating or even designing the product. Managers must then design the product and manufacturing process so that the product's cost does not exceed its target cost. Why focus on the product design phase? Because the design affects a vast majority of costs. For example, the design of the product and the associated production process largely determines the costs of resources, such as new machinery, materials, parts and even future refinements. It is not easy to reduce these costs once production begins. So, the emphasis of target costing is on proactive, up-front planning throughout every activity of the new-product development process.

■ Target costing and new product development

Exhibit 5.13 shows a real company's target costing process for a new product. Based on the existing technology and related cost structure, the new product has three parts, requires direct labour and has four types of indirect costs. The first step in the target-costing process is to determine the market price. The market sets this price. So why does management have to determine it? Remember that the product is new and has not actually been on the market. So, management has to estimate what the market will pay for the product. There are several tools, such as market focus group studies and surveys, that a firm can use to determine this price. Management also sets a desired gross margin for the new product. The market price less the gross margin is the target cost for the new product. The company determines the existing cost structure for the product by building up costs on an individual component level. This product has two components. Component 1 consists of parts A and B. Component 2 is part C. Both components and the final assembly use direct labour. Finally, the activities necessary to plan and process the product create indirect costs.

Marketing plays a large role in target costing. Market research in the early planning stages guides the whole product development process by supplying information about customer demands and requirements. One of the key characteristics of successful target costing is a

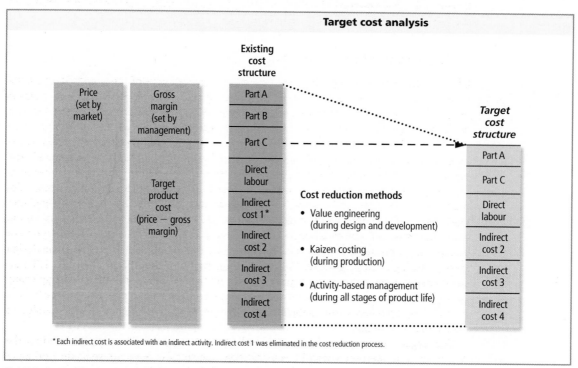

* Each indirect cost is associated with an indirect activity. Indirect cost 1 was eliminated in the cost reduction process.

Exhibit 5.13 The target costing process

strong emphasis on understanding customer demands. Many companies actively seek customer input on the design of product features. Then, they compare the cost of each feature to its value to determine whether to add it to the product. For example, one of Boeing's customers wanted heated floors in its airplanes. However, the cost of the heated floors was too high and the customer reconsidered.

In the example in Exhibit 5.13, the existing cost is too large to generate the desired profit. Does this mean that the new product is not feasible? Not necessarily. A cross-functional team consisting of engineers, sales personnel, key suppliers and accountants now must determine if the company can implement cost reductions large enough to meet the target cost. In the example in Exhibit 5.13, the company reduced the cost of parts by changing the design of the product so that it could use part C in place of part B. The company also asked suppliers of parts A and C to reduce their costs. Design and process engineers were also able to eliminate the activity that generated the first type of indirect cost. These cost reductions resulted from **value engineering** – a cost-reduction technique, used primarily during the design stage, that uses information about all value-chain functions to satisfy customer needs while reducing costs. In total, the planned cost reductions were adequate to reduce costs to the target.

Not all the reductions in cost have to take place before production begins. For example, **kaizen costing** is the Japanese term for continuous improvement during manufacturing. How do companies apply kaizen costing? They establish kaizen goals each year as part of the planning process. Examples include the continual reduction in setup and processing times due to increased employee familiarity with the procedure. In total, target costing during design and kaizen costing during manufacturing may allow the firm to achieve the target cost over the product's life, even if initial cost predictions look too high.

Underlying these cost-reduction methods is the need for accurate cost information. Activity-based costing often provides this information. Companies can then use activity-based management (ABM) to identify and eliminate non-value-added activities, waste and their related costs. ABM is applied throughout both the design and manufacturing stages of the product's life. For examples of how accountants are using ABC and ABM in target costing, see the 'Business first' box on p. 202.

▧ Illustration of target costing

Consider the target-costing system used by ITT Automotive – one of the world's largest automotive suppliers. The company designs, develops and manufactures a broad range of products including brake systems, electric motors and lamps. Also, the company is the worldwide market leader in antilock braking systems (ABS), producing 20,000 such systems per day.

What pricing approach does ITT Automotive use for the ABS? The pricing process starts when one of ITT's customers, for example Mercedes-Benz, sends an invitation to bid. The market for brake systems is so competitive that very little variance exists in the prices companies can ask (bid). ITT then forms a target-costing group and charges it with determining whether the price and costs allow for enough of a profit margin. This group includes engineers, management accountants and sales personnel. Factors the group considers in determining the feasibility of earning the desired target profit margin include competitor pricing, inflation rates, interest rates and potential cost reductions during both the design (target costing) and production (kaizen costing) stages of the ABS product life. ITT purchases many of the component parts that make up the ABS. Thus, the target-costing group works closely with suppliers. After making product and process design improvements and receiving commitments from suppliers, the company has the cost information needed to decide the price to bid.

The target-costing system has worked well at ITT Automotive. The company's bid for the ABS resulted in Mercedes-Benz US International selecting ITT Automotive as the developer and supplier of ABS for the automaker's M-Class All-Activity Vehicle.

■ Target costing and cost-plus pricing compared

Successful companies understand the market in which they operate and use the most appropriate pricing approach. To see how target costing and cost-plus pricing can lead to different decisions, suppose that ITT Automotive receives an invitation from Ford to bid on the ABS to be used in a new model car.

Assume the following data apply:

● The specifications contained in Ford's invitation lead to an estimated current manufacturing cost (component parts, direct labour and manufacturing overhead) of $154.

BUSINESS FIRST
Target costing, ABC and the role of management accounting

Many companies use target costing together with an ABC system. Target costing requires a company to first determine what a customer will pay for a product and then work backward to design the product and production process that will generate a desired level of profit. ABC provides data on the costs of the various activities needed to produce the product. Knowing the costs of activities allows product and production process designers to predict the effects of their designs on the product's cost. Target costing essentially takes activity-based costs and uses them for strategic product decisions.

For example, Culp, a North Carolina manufacturer of furniture upholstery fabrics and mattress fabrics, uses target costing and ABC to elevate cost management into one of the most strategically important areas of the firm. Culp found that 80 per cent of its product costs are predetermined at the design stage, but earlier cost control efforts had focused only on the other 20 per cent. By shifting cost management efforts to the design stage and getting accurate costs of the various activities involved in production, cost management at Culp evolved into a process of cutting costs when engineers design a product, not identifying costs that are out of line after the production is complete.

A basic goal of target costing is to reduce costs before they occur. After all, once a company has incurred costs, it cannot change them. Such a strategy is especially important when product life cycles are short. Because most product life cycles are shrinking, use of target costing is expanding. Target costing focuses on reducing costs in the product design and development stages – when costs can

really be affected. For example, target costing heavily influenced Siemens' pricing of specialised design features in its fibre optic products and Procter & Gamble's CEO credits target costing for helping eliminate costs that could cause managers to price products too high for the market to bear. According to Ron Gallaway, CFO of Micrus Semiconductors (now part of Phillips Semiconductors), 'The design process is where you can truly leverage [reduce] your costs.'

What role does management accounting play in target costing? At Micrus, management accountants are responsible for setting final target costs for all components and processes. One survey reports that 86 per cent of companies using target costing take data directly from their cost systems to estimate product costs during product design. At Eastman Kodak, management accountants are a vital part of the cross-functional team that implements target costing. This team includes design and manufacturing engineers, procurement and marketing, as well as management accounting. Peter Zampino, director of research at the Consortium for Advanced Manufacturing – International, agrees: 'It's like anything else; if finance doesn't bless the numbers, they won't have the credibility throughout the organisation.'

Sources: Adapted from R. Banham, 'Off target', *CFO*, May 2000; D. Swensen, S. Anasri, J. Bell and I. Kim, 'Best practices in target costing', *Management Accounting Quarterly*, Winter, 2003, pp. 12–17; G. Boer and J. Ettlie, 'Target costing can boost your bottom line', *Strategic Finance*, July 1999, pp. 49–52; J. Brausch, 'Target costing for profit enhancement', *Management Accounting*, November 1994, pp. 45–49; G. Hoffman, 'Future vision', *Grocery Marketing*, March 1994, p. 6.

- ITT Automotive had a desired gross margin rate of 30 per cent on sales, which means that actual cost should make up 70 per cent of the price.
- Highly competitive market conditions exist and have established a sales price of $200 per unit.

If ITT had used cost-plus pricing to bid on the ABS, the bid price would be $154 ÷ .7 = $220. Ford would most likely reject this bid because others are likely to bid $200. ITT Automotive's pricing approach would lead to a lost opportunity.

Suppose that managers at ITT Automotive recognise that market conditions dictate a set price of $200. If ITT used a target-costing system, what would be its pricing decision? The target cost is $140 (that is, $200 × .7) so a required cost reduction of $14 per unit is necessary. The target-costing group would work with product and process engineers and suppliers to determine if they could reduce the average unit cost by $14 over the product's life. Note that it is not necessary to get costs down to the $140 target cost before production begins. The initial unit cost will likely be higher, for example, $145. Continuous improvement over the product's life will result in the final $5 of cost reductions. If the managers receive commitments for cost reductions, they will decide to bid $200 per unit. Note that if ITT Automotive wins the bid, it must carry through with its focus on cost management throughout the life of the product.

Target costing originated in Japan and is a common practice there. However, a growing number of companies now use it worldwide, including Boeing, Eastman Kodak, Mercedes-Benz, Procter & Gamble and Caterpillar, as well as ITT Automotive. Even some hospitals use target costing.

Why the increasing popularity of target costing? With increased global competition in many industries, companies are increasingly limited in influencing market prices. Cost management then becomes the key to profitability. Target costing forces managers to focus on costs to achieve the desired profits.

Highlights to remember

1 **Discriminate between relevant and irrelevant information for making decisions.** To be relevant to a particular decision, a cost (or revenue) must meet two criteria: (1) It must be an expected future cost (or revenue) and (2) it must have an element of difference among the alternative courses of action.

2 **Apply the decision process to make business decisions.** All managers make business decisions based on some decision process. The best processes help decision making by focusing the manager's attention on relevant information.

3 **Construct absorption and contribution-margin income statements and identify their relevance for decision making.** The major difference between the absorption and contribution approaches for the income statement is that the contribution approach focuses on cost behaviour (fixed and variable), whereas the absorption approach reports costs by business functions (manufacturing versus nonmanufacturing). The contribution approach makes it easier for managers to evaluate the effects of changes in volume on income and thus is well suited for shorter-run decision making.

4 **Decide to accept or reject a special order using the contribution-margin technique.** Decisions to accept or reject a special sales order should use the contribution-margin technique and focus on the additional revenues and additional costs of the order.

5 **Explain why pricing decisions depend on the characteristics of the market.** Market demand and supply, the degree of competition and marginal revenue and marginal cost concepts impact market price and must be incorporated into any pricing decision.

6 **Identify the factors that influence pricing decisions in practice.** Market conditions, the law, customers, competitors and costs influence pricing decisions. The degree that management actions can affect price and cost determines the most effective approach to use for pricing and cost- management purposes.

7 **Compute a sales price by various approaches and compare the advantages and disadvantages of these approaches.** Companies use cost-plus pricing for products when management actions can influence the market price. They can add profit markups to a variety of cost bases including variable manufacturing costs, all variable costs, full manufacturing costs, or all costs. The contribution approach to pricing has the advantage of providing detailed cost behaviour information that is consistent with cost – volume – profit analysis.

8 **Use target costing to decide whether to add a new product.** When market conditions are such that management cannot significantly influence prices, companies must focus on cost control and reduction. They use target costing primarily for new products, especially during the design phase of the value chain. They deduct a desired target margin from the market-established price to determine the target cost. Cost management then focuses on controlling and reducing costs over the product's life cycle to achieve that target cost. ∎

Accounting vocabulary

absorption approach, p. 181	imperfect competition, p. 189	predatory pricing, p. 192
absorption costing, p. 181	kaizen costing, p. 201	price elasticity, p. 190
contribution approach, p. 181	marginal cost, p. 189	relevant information, p. 177
decision model, p. 178	marginal revenue, p. 189	target costing, p. 199
discriminatory pricing, p. 192	markup, p. 193	value engineering, p. 201
full cost, p. 193	perfect competition, p. 189	

Fundamental assignment material   MyAccountingLab

5.A1 Straightforward income statements

The Irish-based Independence Company had the following manufacturing data for the year 20X1 (in thousands of euros):

Beginning and ending inventories	None
Direct material used	€400
Direct labour	330
Supplies	20
Utilities – variable portion	40
Utilities – fixed portion	15
Indirect labour – variable portion	90
Indirect labour – fixed portion	50
Depreciation	200
Property taxes	20
Supervisory salaries	60

Selling expenses were €300,000 (including €80,000 that were variable) and general administrative expenses were €144,000 (including €25,000 that were variable). Sales were €2.2 million.

Direct labour and supplies are regarded as variable costs.

1 Prepare two income statements, one using the contribution approach and one using the absorption approach.
2 Suppose that all variable costs fluctuate directly in proportion to sales and that fixed costs are unaffected over a very wide range of sales. What would operating income have been if sales had been €2.0 million instead of €2.2 million? Which income statement did you use to help obtain your answer? Why?

5.A2 Special order

Consider the following details of the income statement of the Manteray Pen Company (MPC) for the year ended 31 December 20X0:

Sales	€ 11,000,000
Less cost of goods sold	6,500,000
Gross margin or gross profit	€ 4,500,000
Less selling and administrative expenses	3,000,000
Operating income	€ 1,500,000

MPC's fixed manufacturing costs were €3.0 million and its fixed selling and administrative costs were €2.2 million. Sales commissions of 3 per cent of sales are included in selling and administrative expenses.

The division had produced and sold 2 million pens. Near the end of the year, Pizza Hut offered to buy 150,000 pens on a special order. To fill the order, a special Pizza Hut logo would have to be added to each pen. Pizza Hut intended to use the pens for special promotions in an eastern city during early 20X1.

Even though MPC had some idle plant capacity, the president rejected the Pizza Hut offer of €660,000 for the 150,000 pens. He said,

> The Pizza Hut offer is too low. We'd avoid paying sales commissions, but we'd have to incur an extra cost of €.40 per pen to add the logo. If MPC sells below its regular selling prices, it will begin a chain reaction of competitors' price cutting and of customers wanting special deals. I believe in pricing at no lower than 8% above our full costs of €9,500,000 ÷ 2,000,000 units = €4.75 per unit plus the extra €.40 per pen less the savings in commissions.

1 Using the contribution-margin technique, prepare an analysis similar to that in Exhibit 5.6 on p. 184. Use four columns: without the special order, the effect of the special order (one column total and one column per unit) and totals with the special order.
2 By what percentage would operating income increase or decrease if the order had been accepted? Do you agree with the president's decision? Why?

5.A3 Formulas for pricing

Randy Azarski, a building contractor, builds houses in tracts, often building as many as 20 homes simultaneously. Azarski has budgeted costs for an expected number of houses in 20X0 as follows:

Direct materials	€3,500,000
Direct labour	1,000,000
Job construction overhead	1,500,000
Cost of jobs	€6,000,000
Selling and administrative costs	1,500,000
Total costs	€7,500,000

The job construction overhead includes approximately €800,000 of fixed costs, such as the salaries of supervisors and depreciation on equipment. The selling and administrative costs include €500,000 of variable costs, such as sales commissions and bonuses that depend fundamentally on overall profitability.

Azarski wants an operating income of €1.5 million for 20X0.

Compute the average target markup percentage for setting prices as a percentage of the following:

1 Direct materials plus direct labour.
2 The full 'cost of jobs'.
3 The variable 'cost of jobs'.
4 The full 'cost of jobs' plus selling and administrative costs.
5 The variable 'cost of jobs' plus variable selling and administrative costs.

5.A4 Target costing

Lowest Cost Corporation uses target costing to aid in the final decision to release new products to production. A new product is being evaluated. Market research has surveyed the potential market for this product and believes that its unique features will generate a total demand over the product's life of 70,000 units at an average price of €360. The target costing team has members from market research, design, accounting and production engineering departments. The team has worked closely with key customers and suppliers. A value analysis of the product has determined that the total cost for the various value-chain functions using the existing process technology are as follows:

Value-chain function	Total cost over product life
Research and development	€ 2,300,000
Design	750,000
Manufacturing (70% outsourced to suppliers)	8,000,000
Marketing	1,800,000
Distribution	2,200,000
Customer service	950,000
Total cost over product life	€16,000,000

Management has a target contribution to profit percentage of 40 per cent of sales. This contribution provides sufficient funds to cover corporate support costs, taxes and a reasonable profit.

1 Should the new product be released to production? Explain.
2 Approximately 70 per cent of manufacturing costs for this product consists of materials and parts that are purchased from suppliers. Key suppliers on the target-costing team have suggested process improvements that will reduce supplier cost by 20 per cent. Should the new product be released to production? Explain.
3 New process technology can be purchased at a cost of €220,000 that will reduce non-outsourced manufacturing costs by 25 per cent. Assuming the supplier's process improvements and new process technology are implemented, should the new product be released to production? Explain.

5.B1 Contribution and absorption income statements

The following information is taken from the records of the Kingland Manufacturing Company for the year ending 31 December 20X1. There were no beginning or ending inventories.

Sales	€13,000,000	Long-term rent, factory	€ 100,000
Sales commissions	500,000		
Advertising	400,000	Factory superintendent's salary	30,000
Shipping expenses	300,000	Factory supervisors' salaries	100,000
		Direct materials used	4,000,000
Administrative executive salaries	100,000	Direct labour	2,000,000
		Cutting bits used	60,000
Administrative clerical salaries (variable)	400,000	Factory methods research	40,000
		Abrasives for machining	100,000
Fire insurance on factory equipment	2,000	Indirect labour	800,000
Property taxes on factory equipment	30,000	Depreciation on factory equipment	400,000

1 Prepare a contribution income statement and an absorption income statement. If you are in doubt about any cost behaviour pattern, decide on the basis of whether the total cost in question will fluctuate substantially over a wide range of volume. Prepare a separate supporting schedule of indirect manufacturing costs subdivided between variable and fixed costs.

2 Suppose that all variable costs fluctuate directly in proportion to sales and that fixed costs are unaffected over a wide range of sales. What would operating income have been if sales had been €12 million instead of €13 million? Which income statement did you use to help get your answer? Why?

5.B2 Special order, terminology and unit costs

Following is the income statement of Danube Company, a manufacturer of men's blue jeans:

Danube Company
Income statement for the year ended 31 December 20X0

	Total	Per unit
Sales	€40,000,000	€20.00
Less: Cost of goods sold	22,000,000	11.00
Gross margin	€18,000,000	€ 9.00
Less selling and administrative expenses	15,000,000	7.50
Operating income	€ 3,000,000	€ 1.50

Danube had manufactured 2 million pairs of jeans, which had been sold to various clothing wholesalers and department stores. At the start of 20X0, the president, Rosie Valenzuela, died unexpectedly. Her son, Ricardo, became the new president. Ricardo had worked for 15 years in the marketing phases of the business. He knew very little about accounting and manufacturing, which were his mother's strengths. Ricardo has several questions, including inquiries regarding the pricing of special orders.

1 To prepare better answers, you decide to recast the income statement in contribution form. Variable manufacturing cost was €18 million. Variable selling and administrative expenses, which were mostly sales commissions, shipping expenses and advertising

allowances paid to customers based on units sold, were €9 million. Prepare the revised income statement.

2 Ricardo asks, 'I can't understand financial statements until I know the meaning of various terms. In scanning my mother's assorted notes, I found the following pertaining to both total and unit costs: full manufacturing cost, variable cost, full cost, fully allocated cost, gross margin and contribution margin. Using our data for 20X0, please give me a list of these costs, their total amounts and their per-unit amounts.'

3 He also says, 'Near the end of 20X0, I brought in a special order from Costco for 100,000 jeans at €16 each. I said I'd accept a flat €20,000 sales commission instead of the usual 6 per cent of selling price, but my mother refused the order. She usually upheld a relatively rigid pricing policy, saying that it was bad business to accept orders that did not at least generate full manufacturing cost plus 80% of full manufacturing cost.

   That policy bothered me. We had idle capacity. The way I figured, our manufacturing costs would go up by 100,000 × €11 = €1,100,000, but our selling and administrative expenses would go up by only €20,000. That would mean additional operating income of 100,000 × (€16 − €11) minus €20,000, or €500,000 minus €20,000 or €480,000. That's too much money to give up just to maintain a general pricing policy. Was my analysis of the impact on operating income correct? If not, please show me the correct additional operating income.'

4 After receiving the explanations offered in number 2 and 3, Ricardo said, 'Forget that I had the Costco order. I had an even bigger order from Next. It was for 500,000 units and would have filled the plant completely. I told my mother I'd settle for no commission. There would have been no selling and administrative costs whatsoever because Lands' End would pay for the shipping and would not get any advertising allowances.

   Next offered €8.70 per unit. Our fixed manufacturing costs would have been spread over 2.5 million instead of 2 million units. Wouldn't it have been advantageous to accept the offer? Our old fixed manufacturing costs were €2.00 per unit. The added volume would reduce that cost more than our loss on our variable costs per unit.

   Am I correct? What would have been the impact on total operating income if we had accepted the order?'

Additional assignment material　　　　　MyAccountingLab

QUESTIONS

5.1 'The distinction between precision and relevance should be kept in mind.' Explain.

5.2 Distinguish between the quantitative and qualitative aspects of decisions.

5.3 Describe the accountnt's role in decision making.

5.4 'Any future cost is relevant.' Do you agree? Explain.

5.5 Why are historical or past data irrelevant to special decisions?

5.6 Describe the role of past or historical costs in the decision process. That is, how do these costs relate to the prediction method and the decision model?

5.7 What is the advanage of the contribution approach as compared with the absorption approach?

5.8 'The primary classifications of costs are by variable and fixed-cost behaviour patterns, not by business functions.' Name three commonly used terms that describe this type of income statement.

5.9 'There is a commonality of approach to various special decisions.' Explain.

5.10 'Fixed costs are not relevant costs.' Do you agree? Explain.

5.11 Why are customers one of the factors influencing pricing decisions?

5.12 What is target cost per unit?

5.13 What is value engineering?

5.14 What is kaizen costing?

5.15 'In target costing, prices determine costs rather than vice versa.' Explain.

5.16 Many companies that use target costing involve both customers and suppliers in product and process design. Explain why.

5.17 If a target-costing system is used and the existing cost cannot be reduced to the target cost through cost reductions, management should discontinue producing and selling the product. Do you agree? Explain.

5.18 'Basing pricing on only the variable costs of a job results in suicidal underpricing.' Do you agree? Why?

5.19 Provide three examples of pricing decisions other than the special order.

5.20 List three popular markup formulas for pricing.

5.21 Describe two long-run effects that may lead to managers' rejecting opportunities to cut prices and obtain increases in short-run profits.

5.22 Give two reasons why full costs are more widely used than variable costs for guiding pricing.

CRITICAL THINKING EXERCISES

5.23 Fixed costs and the sales function

Many sales managers have a good intuitive understanding of costs, but they often are imprecise in how they describe the costs. For example, one manager said the following: 'Increasing sales will decrease fixed costs because it spreads them over more units.' Do you agree? Explain.

5.24 Income statements and sales managers

Suppose Chee Wong is in charge of selling Nantucket Nectars' Juice Cocktails. What type of income statement, absorption or contribution, would Wong find most useful for his decisions? Why?

5.25 The economics of the pricing decision

Economic theory states that managers should set price equal to marginal cost in perfect competition. Accountants use variable cost to approximate marginal costs. Compare and contrast marginal cost and variable cost, and explain whether using variable costs as an approximation for marginal cost is appropriate for making pricing decisions.

5.26 Pricing decisions, ethics and the law

Managers should base pricing decisions on both cost and market factors. In addition, they must also consider ethical and legal issues. Describe the influence that ethics and the law have on pricing decisions.

5.27 Target costing and the value chain

According to Keith Hallin, programme affordability manager (target costing) for Boeing's MMA Programme in Integrated Defense Systems, reaching target costs is a challenge for the company's entire value chain. Explain how managers of the various value-chain functions at Boeing might be involved in the target costing process.

EXERCISES

5.28 Pinpointing relevant costs

Today you are planning to see a film and you can attend either of two cinemas. You have only a small budget for entertainment so prices are important. You have attended both cinemas recently. One charged €5 for admission; the other charged €7. You habitually buy popcorn in the cinema – each cinema charges €3. The films now being shown are equally attractive to you, but you are virtually certain that you will never see the film that you reject today.

Identify the relevant costs. Explain your answer.

5.29 Identification of relevant costs

Paul and Paula Petroceli were trying to decide whether to go to the symphony or to the football game. They already have two nonrefundable tickets to 'Pops Night at the Symphony' that cost €40 each. This is the only concert of the season they considered attending because it is the only one with the type of music they enjoy. The football game is the last one of the season and it will decide the league championship. They can purchase tickets to the game for €20 each.

The Petrocelis will drive 50 kilometres round-trip to either event. Variable costs for operating their automobile are €.18 per kilometre and fixed costs average €.13 per kilometre for the 15,000 kilometres they drive annually. Parking at the symphony is free, but it costs €6 at the baseball game.

To attend either event, Paul and Paula will hire a babysitter at €7 per hour. They expect to be gone 5 hours to attend the football game but only 4 hours to attend the symphony.

Compare the cost of attending the football game with the cost of attending the symphony. Focus on relevant costs. Compute the difference in cost and indicate which alternative is more costly to the Petrocelis.

5.30 Straightforward absorption statement

The Pierce Company had the following data (in thousands) for a given period:

Sales	€800
Direct materials	200
Direct labour	200
Indirect manufacturing costs	170
Selling and administrative expenses	150

There were no beginning or ending inventories. Compute the (1) manufacturing cost of goods sold, (2) gross profit, (3) operating income and (4) conversion cost (total manufacturing cost less materials cost).

5.31 Straightforward contribution income statement

Yoko Ltd, had the following data (in millions of yen) for a given period:

Sales	€950
Direct materials	290
Direct labour	160
Variable factory overhead	60
Variable selling and administrative expenses	100
Fixed factory overhead	120
Fixed selling and administrative expenses	45

There were no beginning or ending inventories. Compute the (a) variable manufacturing cost of goods sold, (b) contribution margin and (c) operating income.

5.32 Straightforward absorption and contribution statement

Anzola Company had the following data (in millions) for a recent period. Fill in the blanks. There were no beginning or ending inventories.

(a)	Sales	€920
(b)	Direct materials used	350
(c)	Direct labour	210
	Indirect manufacturing costs:	
(d)	Variable	100
(e)	Fixed	50
(f)	Variable manufacturing cost of goods sold	–
(g)	Manufacturing cost of goods sold	–
	Selling and administrative expenses:	
(h)	Variable	90
(i)	Fixed	80
(j)	Gross profit	–
(k)	Contribution margin	–

5.33 Absorption statement

Stein Jewellery had the following data (in thousands of South African rands, ZAR) for a given period. Assume there are no inventories. Fill in the blanks.

Sales	ZAR ___
Direct materials	370
Direct labour	___
Indirect manufacturing	___
Manufacturing cost of goods sold	780
Gross margin	120
Selling and administrative expenses	___
Operating income	20
Prime cost (direct materials + direct labour)	600

5.34 Contribution income statement

Jackson Company had the following data (in thousands) for a given period. Assume there are no inventories.

Direct labour	€170
Direct materials	150
Variable indirect manufacturing	110
Contribution margin	200
Fixed selling and administrative expenses	100
Operating income	10
Sales	890

Compute the (a) variable manufacturing cost of goods sold, (b) variable selling and administrative expenses and (c) fixed indirect manufacturing costs.

5.35 Special-order decision

Belltown Athletic Supply (BAS) makes game jerseys for athletic teams. The F. C. Kitsap soccer club has offered to buy 100 jerseys for the teams in its league for €15 per jersey. The team price for such jerseys normally is €18, an 80 per cent markup over BAS's purchase price of €10 per jersey. BAS adds a name and number to each jersey at a variable cost of €2 per jersey. The annual fixed cost of equipment used in the printing process is €6,000 and other fixed costs allocated to jerseys are €2,000. BAS makes about 2,000 jerseys per year, so the fixed cost is €4 per jersey. The equipment is used only for printing jerseys and stands idle 75 per cent of the usable time.

The manager of BAS turned down the offer, saying, 'If we sell at €15 and our cost is €16, we lose money on each jersey we sell. We would like to help your league, but we can't afford to lose money on the sale.'

1 Compute the amount by which the operating income of BAS would change if it accepted F. C. Kitsap's offer.
2 Suppose you were the manager of BAS. Would you accept the offer? In addition to considering the quantitative impact computed in requirement 1, list two qualitative considerations that would influence your decision – one qualitative factor supporting acceptance of the offer and one supporting rejection.

5.36 Unit costs and total costs

You are a chartered accountant who belongs to a downtown business club. Annual dues are £150. You use the club solely for lunches, which cost £9 each. You have not used the club much in recent years and you are wondering whether to continue your membership.

1 You are confronted with a variable-cost plus a fixed-cost behaviour pattern. Plot each on a graph, where the vertical axis is total cost and the horizontal axis is annual volume in number of lunches. Also plot a third graph that combines the previous two graphs.
2 What is the cost per lunch if you pay for your own lunch once a year? Twelve times a year? Two hundred times a year?
3 Suppose the average price of lunches elsewhere is £10. (a) How many lunches must you have at the luncheon club so that the total costs of the lunches would be the same, regardless of where you ate for that number of lunches? (b) Suppose you ate 200 lunches a year at the club. How much would you save in relation to the total costs of eating elsewhere?

5.37 Advertising expenditures and nonprofit organisations

Suppose Wilton College, a private sixth form college with excellent International Baccalaureate results, charges a comprehensive annual fee of £14,500 for tuition, room and board, and it has capacity for 2,500 students. The admissions department predicts enrollment of 2,000 students for 20X1. Costs per student for the 20X1 academic year are as follows:

	Variable	Fixed	Total
Educational programmes	£4,000	£ 4,200	£ 8,200
Room	1,300	2,200	3,500
Board	2,600	600	3,200
	£7,900	£7,000*	£14,900

*Based on 2,000–2,500 students for the year.

The assistant director of admissions has proposed a 2-month advertising campaign using radio and television advertisements, together with an extensive direct mailing of brochures.

1 Suppose the advertising campaign will cost £1.65 million. What is the minimum number of additional students the campaign must attract to make the campaign break even?
2 Suppose the admissions department predicts that the campaign will attract 350 additional students. What is the most Wilton should pay for the campaign and still break even?
3 Suppose a 3-month (instead of 2-month) campaign will attract 450 instead of 350 additional students. What is the most Wilton should pay for the 1-month extension of the campaign and still break even?

5.38 Variety of cost terms

Consider the following data:

Variable selling and administrative costs per unit	€ 4.00
Total fixed selling and administrative costs	€2,900,000
Total fixed manufacturing costs	€3,000,000
Variable manufacturing costs per unit	€ 10.00
Units produced and sold	500,000

Compute the following per unit of product: (a) total variable costs, (b) full manufacturing cost (c) full cost.

5.39 Acceptance of low bid

The Velasquez Company, a maker of a variety of metal and plastic products, is in the midst of a business downturn and is saddled with many idle facilities. Columbia Health Care has approached Velasquez to produce 300,000 nonslide serving trays. Columbia will pay €1.50 each.

Velasquez predicts that its variable costs will be €1.60 each. Its fixed costs, which had been averaging €1 per unit on a variety of other products, will now be spread over twice as much volume. The president commented, 'Sure we'll lose €.10 each on the variable costs, but we'll gain €.50 per unit by spreading our fixed costs. Therefore, we should take the offer because it represents an advantage of €.40 per unit.'

Suppose the regular business had a current volume of 300,000 units, sales of €600,000, variable costs of €480,000 and fixed costs of €300,000. Do you agree with the president? Why?

5.40 Pricing to maximise contribution

Reynolds Company produces and sells picture frames. One particular frame for 8 × 10 photos was an instant success in the market, but recently competitors have come out with comparable frames. Reynolds has been charging €12.50 wholesale for the frames and sales have fallen from 10,000 units last year to 7,000 units this year. The product manager in charge of this frame is considering lowering the price to €10 per frame. He believes sales will rebound to 10,000 units at the lower price, but they will fall to 6,000 units at the €12.50 price. The unit variable cost of producing and selling the frames is €6 and €60,000 of fixed cost is assigned to the frames.

1 Assuming that the only prices under consideration are €10 and €12.50 per frame, which price will lead to the largest profit for Reynolds? Explain why.
2 What subjective considerations might affect your pricing decision?

5.41 Target selling prices

Consider the following data from Blackmar Company's budgeted income statement (in thousands of euros):

Target sales	€90,000
Variable costs	
Manufacturing	30,000
Selling and administrative	6,000
Total variable costs	36,000
Fixed costs	
Manufacturing	8,000
Selling and administrative	6,000
Total fixed costs	14,000
Total of all costs	50,000
Operating income	€40,000

Compute the following markup percentages that would be used for obtaining the same target sales as a percentage of (1) total variable costs (2) full costs and (3) variable manufacturing costs.

5.42 Competitive bids

Griffy, Rodriguez and Martinez, an accounting firm, is preparing to bid for a consulting job. Although Alicia Martinez will use her judgement about the market in finalising the bid, she has asked you to prepare a cost analysis to help in the bidding. You have estimated the costs for the consulting job to be as follows:

Materials and supplies, at cost	€ 30,000
Hourly pay for consultants, 2,000 hours at €35 per hour	70,000
Fringe benefits for consultants, 2,000 hours at €12 per hour	24,000
Total variable costs	€124,000
Fixed costs allocated to the job	
Based on labour, 2,000 hours at €10 per hour	20,000
Based on materials and supplies, 80% of 30,000	24,000
Total cost	€168,000

Of the €44,000 allocated fixed costs, €35,000 will be incurred even if the job is not undertaken. Alicia normally bids jobs at the sum of (1) 150 per cent of the estimated materials and supplies cost and (2) €75 per estimated labour hour.

1 Prepare a bid using the normal formula.
2 Prepare a minimum bid equal to the additional costs expected to be incurred to complete the job.
3 Prepare a bid that will cover full costs plus a markup for profit equal to 20 per cent of full cost.

5.43 Target costing

Quality Corporation believes that there is a market for a portable electronic toothbrush that can be easily carried by business travelers. Quality's market research department has surveyed the features and prices of electronic brushes currently on the market. Based on this research, Quality believes that €70 would be about the right price. At this price, marketing believes that about 80,000 new portable brushes can be sold over the product's life cycle. It will cost about €1,000,000 to design and develop the portable brush. Quality has a target profit of 20 per cent of sales.

Determine the total and unit target cost to manufacture, sell, distribute and service the portable brushes.

5.44 Target costing

Best Cost Corporation has an aggressive research and development (R&D) programme and uses target costing to aid in the final decision to release new products to production. A new product is being evaluated. Market research has surveyed the potential market for this product and believes that its unique features will generate a total demand of 50,000 units at an average price of €230. Design and production engineering departments have performed a value analysis of the product and have determined that the total cost for the various value-chain functions using the existing process technology are as follows:

Value-chain function	Total cost over product life
Research and development	€ 1,500,000
Design	750,000
Manufacturing	5,000,000
Marketing	800,000
Distribution	1,200,000
Customer service	750,000
Total cost over product life	€10,000,000

Management has a target profit percentage of 20 per cent of sales. Production engineering indicates that a new process technology can reduce the manufacturing cost by 40 per cent, but it will cost €1,100,000.

1 Assuming the existing process technology is used, should the new product be released to production? Explain.
2 Assuming the new process technology is purchased, should the new product be released to production? Explain.

PROBLEMS

5.45 Pricing, ethics and the law

Great Lakes Pharmaceuticals Innovations (GLPI), produces both prescription and over-the-counter medications. In January, GLPI introduced a new prescription drug, Capestan, to relieve the pain of arthritis. The company spent more than €50 million over the last 5 years developing the drug, and advertising alone during the first year of introduction will exceed €10 million. Production cost for a bottle of 100 tablets is approximately €12. Sales in the first 3 years are predicted to be 500,000, 750,000 and 1,000,000 bottles, respectively. To achieve these sales, GLPI plans to distribute the medicine through three sources: directly to physicians, through hospital pharmacies and through retail pharmacies. Initially, the bottles will be given free to physicians to give to patients, hospital pharmacies will pay €25 per bottle and retail pharmacies will pay €40 per bottle. In the second and third year, the company plans to phase out the free distributions to physicians and move all other customers toward a €50-per-bottle sales price.

Comment on the pricing and promotion policies of GLPI. Pay particular attention to the legal and ethical issues involved.

5.46 Analysis with contribution income statement

The following data have been condensed from LaGrande Corporation's report of its operations during the year (in millions of euros):

	Variable	Fixed	Total
Manufacturing cost of goods sold	€300	€280	€580
Selling and administrative expenses	140	60	200
Sales			900

1 Prepare the year's income statement in contribution form, ignoring income taxes.
2 LaGrande's operations have been fairly stable from year to year. In planning for the future, top management is considering several options for changing the annual pattern of operations. You are asked to perform an analysis of their estimated effects. Use your contribution income statement as a framework to compute the estimated operating income (in millions) under each of the following separate and unrelated assumptions:
   (a) Assume that a 10 per cent reduction in selling prices would cause a 30 per cent increase in the physical volume of goods manufactured and sold.
   (b) Assume that an annual expenditure of €30 million for a special sales promotion campaign would enable the company to increase its physical volume by 10 per cent with no change in selling prices.
   (c) Assume that a basic redesign of manufacturing operations would increase annual fixed manufacturing costs by €80 million and decrease variable manufacturing costs by 15 per cent per product unit, but with no effect on physical volume or selling prices.
   (d) Assume that a basic redesign of selling and administrative operations would double the annual fixed expenses for selling and administration and increase the variable expenses for selling and administration by 25 per cent per product unit; it would also increase physical volume by 20 per cent. Selling prices would be increased by 5 per cent.
   (e) Would you prefer to use the absorption form of income statement for the preceding analyses? Explain.
3 Discuss the desirability of alternatives a–d in number 2. If only one alternative could be selected, which would you choose? Explain.

5.47 Cost analysis and pricing

The budget for the Oxford University Printing Company for 20X1 follows:

Sales		£1,100,000
Direct material	£280,000	
Direct labour	320,000	
Overhead	400,000	1,000,000
Net income		£ 100,000

The company typically uses a so-called cost-plus pricing system. Direct-material and direct-labour costs are computed, overhead is added at a rate of 125 per cent of direct labour costs, and 10 per cent of the total cost is added to obtain the selling price.

Edith Smythe, the sales manager, has placed a £22,000 bid on a particularly large order with a cost of £5,600 direct material and £6,400 direct labour. The customer informs her that she can have the business for £18,000, take it or leave it. If Smythe accepts the order, total sales for 20X1 will be £1,118,000.

Smythe refuses the order, saying, 'I sell on a cost-plus basis. It is bad policy to accept orders at below cost. I would lose £2,000 on the job.'

The company's annual fixed overhead is £160,000.

1 What would operating income have been with the order? Without the order? Show your computations.
2 Give a short description of a contribution-margin technique to pricing that Smythe might follow to achieve a price of £22,000 on the order.

5.48 Pricing of education

You are the director of continuing education programs for the European Business School, which is a subunit of European University. Courses for executives are especially popular and you have developed an extensive menu of one-day and two-day courses that are presented in various locations throughout the state. The performance of these courses for the current fiscal year, excluding the final course, which is scheduled for the next Saturday, is as follows:

Tuition revenue	€2,000,000
Costs of courses	800,000
Contribution margin	1,200,000
General administrative expenses	400,000
Operating income	€ 800,000

The costs of the courses include fees for instructors, rentals of classrooms, advertising and any other items, such as travel, that can be easily and exclusively identified as being caused by a particular course.

The general administrative expenses include your salary, your secretary's compensation and related expenses, such as a lump-sum payment to the university's central offices as a share of university overhead.

The enrolment for your final course of the year is 30 students, who have paid €200 each. Two days before the course is to begin, a city manager telephones your office. 'Do you offer discounts to nonprofit institutions?' he asks. 'If so, we'll send 10 managers. But our budget will not justify our spending more than €100 per person.' The extra cost of including these 10 managers would entail lunches at €20 each and course materials at €30 each.

1 Prepare a tabulation of the performance for the full year including the final course. Assume that the costs of the final course for the 30 enrollees' instruction, travel, advertising, rental of hotel classroom, lunches and course materials would be €3,000. Show a tabulation in four columns: before final course, final course with 30 registrants, effect of 10 more registrants and grand totals.
2 What major considerations would probably influence the pricing policies for these courses? For setting regular university tuition in private universities?

5.49 Effects of volume on operating income

The Wittred Division of Melbourne Sports Company in Australia manufactures boomerangs, which are sold to wholesalers and retailers. The division manager has set a target of 250,000 boomerangs for next month's production and sales has developed an accurate budget for that level of sales. The manager has also prepared an analysis of the effects on operating income of deviations from the target:

Volume in units	200,000	250,000	300,000
Sales at $3.00	$600,000	$750,000	$900,000
Full costs at $2.00	400,000	500,000	600,000
Operating income	$200,000	$250,000	$300,000

The costs have the following characteristics: Variable manufacturing costs are $.80 per boomerang; variable selling costs are $.60 per boomerang; fixed manufacturing costs per month are $125,000; and fixed selling and administrative costs per month are $25,000.

1 Prepare a correct analysis of the changes in volume on operating income. Prepare a tabulated set of income statements at levels of 200,000, 250,000 and 300,000 boomerangs. Also show percentages of operating income in relation to sales.
2 Compare your tabulation with the manager's tabulation. Why is the manager's tabulation incorrect?

5.50 Pricing of special order

The Drosselmeier Corporation, located in Munich, makes Christmas nutcrackers and has an annual plant capacity of 2,400 product units. Suppose its predicted operating results (in euros) for the year are as follows:

Production and sales of 2,000 units, total sales	€180,000
Manufacturing costs	
Fixed (total)	70,000
Variable (per unit)	25
Selling and administrative expenses	
Fixed (total)	30,000
Variable (per unit)	10

Compute the following, ignoring income taxes:

1 If the company accepts a special order for 300 units at a selling price of €40 each, how would the total predicted net income for the year be affected, assuming no effect on regular sales at regular prices?
2 Without decreasing its total net income, what is the lowest unit price for which the Drosselmeier Corporation could sell an additional 100 units not subject to any variable selling and administrative expenses, assuming no effect on regular sales at regular prices?
3 List the numbers given in the problem that are irrelevant (not relevant) in solving number 2.
4 Compute the expected annual net income (with no special orders) if plant capacity can be doubled by adding additional facilities at a cost of €500,000. Assume that these facilities have an estimated life of 4 years with no residual scrap value and that the current unit selling price can be maintained for all sales. Total sales are expected to equal the new total plant capacity each year. No changes are expected in variable costs per unit or in total fixed costs except for depreciation.

5.51 Pricing and confusing variable and fixed costs

Goldwyn Electronics had a fixed factory overhead budget for 20X0 of £10 million. The company planned to make and sell 2 million units of a particular communications device. All variable manufacturing costs per unit were £10. The budgeted income statement contained the following:

Sales	£40,000,000
Manufacturing cost of goods sold	30,000,000
Gross margin	10,000,000
Deduct selling and administrative expenses	4,000,000
Operating income	£ 6,000,000

For simplicity, assume that the actual variable costs per unit and the total fixed costs were exactly as budgeted.

1 Compute Goldwyn's budgeted fixed factory overhead per unit.
2 Near the end of 20X0, a large computer manufacturer offered to buy 100,000 units for £1.3 million on a one-time special order. The president of Goldwyn stated, 'The offer is a bad deal. It's foolish to sell below full manufacturing costs per unit. I realise that this order will have only a modest effect on selling and administrative costs. They will increase by a £20,000 fee paid to our sales agent.' Compute the effect on operating income if the offer is accepted.
3 What factors should the president of Goldwyn consider before finally deciding whether to accept the offer?
4 Suppose the original budget for fixed manufacturing costs was £10 million, but budgeted units of product were 1 million. How would your answers to numbers 1 and 2 change? Be specific.

5.52 Demand analysis

Zimmerman Manufacturing Limited produces and sells one product, a three-foot Austrian flag. During 20X0, the company manufactured and sold 50,000 flags at €26 each. Existing production capacity is 60,000 flags per year.

In formulating the 20X1 budget, management is faced with several decisions concerning product pricing and output. The following information is available:

1 A market survey shows that the sales volume depends on the selling price. For each €1 drop in selling price, sales volume would increase by 10,000 flags.
2 The company's expected cost structure for 20wX1 is as follows:
    (a) Fixed cost (regardless of production or sales activities), €360,000
    (b) Variable costs per flag (including production, selling and administrative expenses), €15.
3 To increase annual capacity from the present 60,000 flags to 90,000 flags, additional investment for plant, building, equipment and the like of €500,000 would be necessary. The estimated average life of the additional investment would be 10 years, so the fixed costs would increase by an average of €50,000 per year. (Expansion of less than 30,000 additional units of capacity would cost only slightly less than €500,000.)

Indicate, with reasons, what the level of production and the selling price should be for the coming year. Also indicate whether the company should approve the plant expansion. Show your calculations. Ignore income tax considerations and the time value of money.

5.53 Target costing

Lisboa Electrical makes small electric motors for a variety of home appliances. Lisboa sells the motors to appliance makers, who assemble and sell the appliances to retail outlets. Although Lisboa makes dozens of different motors, it does not currently make one to be used in garage-door openers. The company's market research department has discovered a market for such a motor.

The market research department has indicated that a motor for garage-door openers would likely sell for €26. A similar motor currently being produced has the following manufacturing costs:

Direct materials	€13.00
Direct labour	6.00
Overhead	8.00
Total	€27.00

Lisboa desires a gross margin of 20 per cent of the manufacturing cost.

1 Suppose Lisboa used cost-plus pricing, setting the price 20 per cent above the manufacturing cost. What price would be charged for the motor? Would you produce such a motor if you were a manager at Lisboa? Explain.

2 Suppose Lisboa uses target costing. What price would the company charge for a garage-door-opener motor? What is the highest acceptable manufacturing cost for which Lisboa would be willing to produce the motor?
3 As a user of target costing, what steps would Lisboa managers take to try to make production of this product feasible?

5.54 Target costing over product life cycle

Southeast Equipment makes a variety of motor-driven products for homes and small businesses. The market research department recently identified power lawn mowers as a potentially lucrative market. As a first entry into this market, Southeast is considering a riding lawn mower that is smaller and less expensive than those of most of the competition. Market research indicates that such a lawn mower would sell for about €995 at retail and €800 wholesale. At that price, Southeast expects life-cycle sales as follows:

Year	Sales
20X1	1,000
20X2	5,000
20X3	10,000
20X4	10,000
20X5	8,000
20X6	6,000
20X7	4,000

The production department has estimated that the variable cost of production will be €475 per lawn mower and annual fixed costs will be €900,000 per year for each of the 7 years. Variable selling costs will be €25 per lawn mower and fixed selling costs will be €50,000 per year. In addition, the product development department estimates that €5 million of development costs will be necessary to design the lawn mower and the production process for it.

1 Compute the expected profit over the entire product life cycle of the proposed riding lawn mower.
2 Suppose Southeast expects pretax profits equal to 10 per cent of sales on new products. Would the company undertake production and selling of the riding lawn mower?
3 Southeast Equipment uses a target costing approach to new products. What steps would management take to try to make a profitable product of the riding lawn mower?

CASES

5.55 Use of capacity

St Tropez S.A. manufactures several different styles of jewellery cases in southern France. Management estimates that during the second quarter of 20X1 the company will be operating at 80 per cent of normal capacity. Because the company desires a higher utilisation of plant capacity, it will consider a special order.

St Tropez has received special-order inquiries from two companies. The first is from Lyon, which would like to market a jewellery case similar to one of St Tropez's cases. The Lyon jewellery case would be marketed under Lyon's own label. Lyon has offered St Tropez €67.5 per jewellery case for 20,000 cases to be shipped by July 1, 20X1. The cost data for the

St Tropez jewellery case, which would be similar to the specifications of the Lyon special order, are as follows:

Regular selling price per unit	€100
Costs per unit:	
Raw materials	€ 35
Direct labour, .5 hour at €60	30
Overhead, .25 machine hour at €40	10
Total cost per unit	€ 75

According to the specifications provided by Lyon, the special-order case requires less expensive raw materials, which will cost only €32.5 per case. Management has estimated that the remaining costs, labour time and machine time will be the same as those for the St Tropez jewellery case.

The second special order was submitted by the Avignon Co., for 7,500 jewellery cases at €85 per case. These cases would be marketed under the Avignon label and would have to be shipped by 1 July 20X1. The Avignon jewellery case is different from any jewellery case in the St Tropez line. Its estimated per-unit costs are as follows:

Raw materials	€43
Direct labour, .5 hour at €60	30
Overhead, .5 machine hour at €40	20
Total costs	€93

In addition, St Tropez will incur €15,000 in additional setup costs and will have to purchase a €20,000 special device to manufacture these cases; this device will be discarded once the special order is completed.

The St Tropez manufacturing capabilities are limited by the total machine hours available. The plant capacity under normal operations is 90,000 machine hours per year or 7,500 machine hours per month. The budgeted fixed overhead for 20X1 amounts to €2.16 million or €24 per hour. All manufacturing overhead costs are applied to production on the basis of machine hours at €40 per hour.

St Tropez will have the entire second quarter to work on the special orders. Management does not expect any repeat sales to be generated from either special order. Company practice precludes St Tropez from subcontracting any portion of an order when special orders are not expected to generate repeat sales.

Should St Tropez accept either special order? Justify your answer and show your calculations. (Hint: Distinguish between variable and fixed overhead.)

CASE STUDY

La Grande Alliance: Restaurant Français

In April 1976, one week before La Grande Alliance was opened to the public, M. Pierre Jacquard, maitre d'hotel and manager of the new restaurant faced the problem of determining final prices for the menu. M. Jacquard did not believe he could relinquish the task of setting prices to a subordinate or an accountant, for it required the delicate balancing of factors of profitability, volume and restaurant image. Because the prices were printed on a large, artistic menu which was both difficult and expensive to reprint, the prices M. Jacquard determined in April would have to stand, except for extremely minor alterations, for at least six months. The initial six months of a restaurant's operation were known to be crucial in determining its reputation and the size of its clientele for months and years to come.

La Grande Alliance was the major 'showpiece' restaurant of the Hotel Lafayette, a brand-new luxury hotel in downtown Boston, which opened its doors in April 1976. The Lafayette was owned by a consortium of European investors, mainly French, and was managed by L'Union des Grands Hotels a highly respected French hotel chain which had a substantial equity investment in the enterprise.

In honor of the United States Bicentennial celebration (perceived by most hoteliers as a major stimulus to tourism within the United States), the hotel was named after the Marquis de Lafayette, renowned French hero of the American Revolution. Names within the hotel were also chosen to commemorate the United States' revolution against Great Britain and the assistance rendered the early Republic by the French. The restaurants name 'La Grande Alliance' referred to the first Franco-American treaty of friendship and alliance concluded in 1778. The restaurants two dining rooms (salles) were named 'Vergennes' and 'Franklin' respectively after the French and American diplomats responsible for the success of the pact.

M. Pierre Jacquard, 33, was a long-time employee of UGH with 10 years of experience in European restaurants of the first rank. He was generally recognised as having a bright future in restaurant and hotel management with a flair for atmosphere and presentation as well as the ability to work within a budget and make profits. La Grande Alliance was M. Jacquard's second experience of restaurant management and his first assignment outside the continent. He had made one previous journey to the United States in the fall of 1974 when he had been enrolled (for UGH) in the PMD program at a well known eastern business school. M. Jacquard wondered if he would be able to apply the accounting and marketing techniques learned at school to the management of La Grande Alliance.

To facilitate the pricing of individual items on the menu, M. Jacquard prepared (with the cooperation of M. Florentine Lestrade, the chef, as well as Gilles and Roger, the sous-chefs) the menu fact sheet* shown in Table 1. The fact sheet held for each dish on the menu an estimate of: (1) cost of raw materials, (2) preparation time (time for a moderately experienced chef to prepare a 'batch' of the dish in question) (3) minimum number of servings per preparation (the nature of some dishes made it impossible to prepare a single serving although there was usually no problem in stretching the number of servings per batch) and (4) difficulty – rated from least difficult to most different on a scale from 1 to 5.

In conversation with M. Jacquard, on the subject of the fact sheet, Chef Lestrade emphasised two points. First, the cost of raw materials shown was a *normalised estimate* of the *target cost* of an individual dish, as of April 1976. In general, the cost of food varies greatly from week to week and month to month. Some fluctuations are seasonally determined and predictable, others are random: Lestrade's estimates took into account foreseeable fluctuations from April to November, i.e., they were *normalised* over the six months starting April 1976.

This case was prepared by Research Assistant Carliss Y. Baldwin under the direction of Assistant Professor Claudine B. Malone as a basis for class discussion rather than to illustrate either effective or ineffective handling of an administrative situation. (Malone, C. and Baldwin, C. 1988).

*Detailed recipes for the LaGrande Alliance menu are found in the supplement, on pp. 226–230.

Table 1 Selected menu costs – dinner

	Cost of raw materials (1 serving)	Recipe preparation time (minutes)	Recipe # servings per. prep.	Difficulty 1 – 5
Appetisers				
Artichoke Hearts Biarritz	$1.35	30	10	3
**Quiche Lorraine	.75	20	10	2
Escargots à la Bourguignonne (6)	1.75	5	1	1
Oyster Cocktail (6)	1.50	10	1	2
**Pâté de Foie en Brioche	1.25	45	15	4
Soups				
Consommé à la Royale (hot)	$ .25	10	20*	2
Soupe à l'Oignon, Gratinée (hot)	.25	35	20*	3
Créme Vichyssoise Glacée (cold)	.30	30	20*	2
Entrées				
Filet of Sole Dugléré	$2.00	40	6	2
**Crab Créole en Casserole	2.55	20	1*	2
**Coquilles St Jacques Florentine	2.35	30	1*	2
Poulet Poché a l'Estragon	1.65	40	10	4
**Duckling, Sauce Bigarde	2.05	40	2*	4
Escalope de Veau Parisien	2.80	10	1*	3
**Lamb Ragout Printanière	2.55	60	10*	4
Tournedos Rossini	3.50	10	1*	2
**Roast Filet de Boeuf, Béarnaise	3.15	20	10*	2
All entrees include:				
Salad	$ .20	15	10*	1
Potato	.20	15	10*	3
Vegetable	.25	10	10*	2
Desserts				
Strawberries Parisienne	$ .75			
Crème Bavaroise	.65	Purchased from outside supplier		
Pastry assortment	.80			
Bananes Flambées	.60	5	2	1

* Up to three or four mutiple recipes of these items may be prepared with no additional preparation time.
** These items require prior preparation.

Lestrade's normalised estimates were further idealised in that they reflected the theoretical cost of the food content of an individual serving. In practice, raw food usage, and therefore cost, would be increased by waste in preparation, imperfections in measurement, 'fix-ups' (usually necessitating the addition of butter or cream to a recipe) and simple mistakes. Even after adjustment for such considerations, the total cost of food served would understate the restaurant's total expenditure on food, since provision would have to be made for feeding the kitchen and dining staffs, spoilage and pilfering. Chef Lestrade had indicated with extreme vehemence that management of food, including forecasts, purchasing, utilisation of leftovers and food control, was a major responsibility of the chef and an extremely important dimension of his skill.

Chef Lestrade's second point with regard to the fact sheet was that preparation time as shown represented time spent on an individual dish and did not take into account time spent on prior preparations. In any well-managed restaurant, in order to minimise final preparation time, the kitchen keeps on hand many intermedicate preparations - stocks, sauces, dough, etc. These preparations are made in large quantities at times when the kitchen is relatively free and are used in numerous dishes. Chef Lestrade felt it almost impossible to include time spent on prior preparations in the estimates of preparation time for individual dishes. When pressed by M. Jacquard, the chef indicated that as much as 30% of his staffs time would be spent on prior preparations.

La Grande Alliance could seat 100 people at one time in the Salle Franklin and Salle Vergennes combined. Given its location near the centre of the shopping and financial districts of downtown Boston, M. Jacquard and executives of the Hotel Lafayette felt they could expect to serve 1½ seatings (150 people) at lunch on every working day. For dinner (including Sunday dinner at noon) they expected to accommodate, on average 700 people per week, but expected that the pattern of weekly usage would on average be as follows:

Day	Number of meals served
Sunday (noon)	60
Monday	85
Tuesday	85
Wednesday	85
Thursday	85
Friday	150
Saturday	150
	700

Thus plans and budgets for La Grande Alliance were based on volume projections of 750 lunches and 700 dinners served per week, 4.3 weeks per month. A rough rule of thumb which M. Jacquard felt could be applied in Boston, said that in the customers' eyes, lunch is half of dinner, in other words, that people generally spend one-half as much on lunch as they would in the same restaurant on a full course dinner. M. Jacquard was of the opinion, that, as a fine restaurant in a sophisticated urban setting, La Grande Alliance could aim for an 'average check' of €15.00 for dinner and €7.50 for lunch (not including liquor). (N.B. Lunch and dinner menus were separate and substantially different at La Grande Alliance; the dinner menu alone is the subject of this case.)

When making the menu price decision in April 1976, M. Jacquard had already received from the hotel's accounting department, the restaurants projected expense budget for May 1976 Table 2. The budget which had been drawn up by the accounting department in consultation with M. Jacquard reflected the restaurant's present staffing (as of the day it opened) and projected raw foods costs based on forecast number of meals served. The budget also included charges for breakage and supply replacement, depreciation of kitchen equipment (brand-new) and an assessment for advertising and for general overhead. As part of a large hotel establishment La Grande Alliance did not pay directly for a number of services shared with other hotel areas (e.g., laundry, cleaning), thus the overhead assessment was naturally quite large.

The budget did not provide for the cost of sommeliers (wine waiters), nor for the cost of wine and liquor served in the restaurant. It was standard UGH practice for the wine cellar to be managed by the beverage department, which also managed all liquor inventories and the hotel bars. Although La Grande Alliance would receive a partial credit for wine and whiskey sold through the restaurant, it was not within M. Jacquard's power (except as a consultant) to determine either the wine list or wine prices. It was Jacquard's goal, therefore, that La Grande Alliance be sustained (financially, that is) by food alone – that the restaurant would not use food as a loss leader in the purveyance of liquor.

Table 2 Monthly expense budget

Sales		
700 Dinners[1]	$45,150	
750 Lunches[2]	24,187	$ 69,337
Cost of Food		
700 dinners[3]	$13,545	
750 lunches[3]	7,256	$ 20,801
Salaries		
1 Chef $2,500	$ 2,500	
2 Sous-chefs $1,500	3,000	
2 Apprentice chefs $833	1,666	
1 Maitre d'Hotel $2,333	2,333	
2 Captains $1,250	2,500	
8 Waiters $667[4]	5,336	
2.5 Busboys $582[5]	1,455	
2 Dishwashers $500	1,000	19,790
Materials, Breakage and Supplies		$ 1,500
Depreciation Kitchen Equipment		1,000
Advertising and Promotion (1st 6 months)[6]		5,000
Allocation for General Overhead:		
Includes charges for laundry, cleaning, heat,		
electricity, maintenance, depreciation		
(on building) & general administration		10,571
Total Expenses		$ 58,625
Profit Before Taxes		$ 10,712
Net Investment in Restaurant		$500,000

Notes:

(1) Assumes 4.3 weeks per month, average dinner check $15.00.

(2) Assumes 4.3 weeks per month, average lunch check $7.50.

(3) Assumes raw food cost to average 30% of sales.

(4) Fine restaurants average 1 waiter to every 10 or 15 customers.

(5) Busboys are hired on a part-time basis. Their schedules may be made to coincide with the restaurant's busiest hours.

(6) For the first 6 months of its operation, The Lafayette Hotel was committed to a nationwide advertising and promotion campaign, a portion of which expense was allocated to LaGrande Alliance. The restaurant had also been given discretionary funds for local advertising.

As the hotel became well established, both national and local advertising would decrease (M. Jacquard believed) to an average $2,000 per month.

Although La Grande Alliance was a new restaurant in a new hotel, the internal accounting staff of UGH had considerable experience in budgeting for restaurants within hotels. M. Jacquard had been consulted in detail on the preparation of the budget and believed it to be fair. Jacquard was willing that the profitability of La Grande Alliance as well as his own success as maitre d'hotel and manager of the restaurant be measured according to the budgeted format.

In reviewing his pricing strategy, M. Jacquard was aware of two not-mutually-exclusive goals. First, he was ambitious to run a profitable centre within the UGH establishment. Second, he was eager that La Grande Alliance be known as the finest restaurant in the city of Boston.

SUPPLEMENT

Appetisers

Artichoke Hearts Biarritz

MOISTEN 1 cup flaked cooked crab meat with a little mayonnaise. Arrange large artichoke hearts on slices of ripe tomato, top with the crab meat mixture and garnish with equal parts of mayonnaise and whipped cream (to which a little caviar may be added) forced through a pastry bag fitted with a star-shaped tube. Sprinkle with capers and serve the artichokes very cold on crisp lettuce.

Quiche Lorraine

LINE a 9-inch pie plate with unsweetened tart pastry rolled out 1/8 inch thick. Prick the dough with the tines of a fork and chill it for 30 minutes. Cover the inside of the shell with wax paper and fill it with dry rice or beans. Bake the shell in a hot oven (400° F) for 10 minutes, or until the pastry is set but not browned. Remove the paper and rice and cool the shell.

Broil 6 rather thick slices of bacon and drain them on absorbent paper. Cut 12 thin slices of Swiss cheese about the same size as the bacon slices. Cut the bacon slices in half and cover the piecrust with overlapping layers of cheese and bacon. Beat 4 eggs with ½ teaspoon salt, a generous grating of nutmeg and a few grains of cayenne. Add 2 cups heavy cream and stir in 1½ tablespoons melted butter. Strain the custard over the bacon and cheese and bake the *quiche* in a moderately hot oven (375° F) for 30 to 35 minutes, or until the custard is set and the top is nicely browned. Serve warm.

Escargots à la Bourguignonne

FOR 36 snails prepare butter as follows: Cream 1¼ cups butter and blendin thoroughly 2 teaspoons finely chopped shallot, 2 garlic cloves, crushed, 1 teaspoon each of finely chopped parsley and chives, and salt and pepper to taste. Put a little of the butter in each of 36 shells, put a snail in each shell and cover the snails with the remaining butter. Pour 2 tablespoons white wine into a flat baking dish or individual snail plates. Arrange the shells in the dish and sprinkle them with fine bread crumbs. Bake the snailsin a very hot oven (450° F) or put the dish under the broiler until the crumbs are golden brown. Serve the snails immediately with French bread.

Reprinted by permission from the *Gourmet Cookbook*, Vols I & II.

Oyster Cocktail

OPEN oysters by forcing an oyster knife between the shells and cutting the large muscle close to the flat upper shell. Cut the lower muscle attached to the deep bottom half of the shell and leave the oyster loose in the bottom half. Serve 6 opened oysters on each chilled plate. Sprinkle with freshly ground black pepper and garnish with a lemon wedge. Put a small dish of horseradish or cocktail sauce in the middle of the plate, if desired.

Pâté de Foie en Brioche

LINE a loaf pan with pate dough and bake it in a hot oven (400° F) for 10 minutes.

Grind coarsely 2 pounds each of pork liver and lean fresh pork. Add salt and freshly ground black pepper to taste, 2 garlic cloves, minced, 1 tablespoon chopped parsley and 1 egg, lightly beaten. Mix thoroughly. Line the bottom and sides of the prepared shell with tiny slices of fresh larding pork. Divide the liver pâté into 4 parts and fill the mould with alternate layers of the pâté and thin slices of fresh larding pork, finishing with a layer of the larding pork and 1 bay leaf. Cover the pâté with the remaining dough and bake it in a very hot oven (450° F) for 10 minutes. Reduce the temperature to slow (300° F) and bake the pâté for 1 hour and 20 minutes longer. Just before the end of the baking time, pour through the pastry-tube funnel ½ cup hot consommé and 1 tablespoon brandy. May be served hot or cold.

Soups

Consommé à la Royale

COMBINE 3 quarts beef stock with 1½ pounds lean beef, coarsely chopped, 3 leeks, 2 medium-sized onions, and 1 stalk of celery, all chopped, 1 medium-sized carrot, sliced, 6 peppercorns, and, for clarifying, the whites and shells of 2 eggs. Bring the stock slowly to a boil, lower the heat, and simmer it for 1 hour. Strain the consommé through several thicknesses of cheesecloth. Chill it and remove the layer of fat. Pour the consommé carefully into quart jars to prevent any sediment at the bottom from mixing with the clear liquid. This will make about 3 quarts clear consommé, Add 2 tablespoons quick-cooking tapioca to 1 quart consommé and bring the consommé to a boil, stirring constantly. Combine 2 tablespoons chopped string beans, 2 tablespoons green peas, and 8 large asparagus tips, all cooked, with 2 tablespoons spinach purée. Put a little of the vegetable mixture into each cup and pour in the hot consommé.

Soupe à L'oignon, Gratinée

PEEL and thinly slice 4 large onions, separating the rings. In a large saucepan in ¼ cup butter sauté the onion rings very, very gently over low heat, stirring almost constantly with a wooden spoon, until they are an even golden brown. Sprinkle them with 1 tablespoon flour, stirring until the flour is blended, and gradually pour in 1½ quarts beef consommé, or a mixture of consommé and water, stirring constantly until the soup begins to boil. Lower the heat and simmer the soup gently for about 20 minutes.

Adjust the seasoning and serve the soup in individual tureens, each one containing a toasted round of French bread heaped with grated Gruyère cheese. Serve toasted rounds of French bread and a bowl of grated cheese on the side.

French onion soup may also be served gratinée. When it is ready to serve, half fill a flameproof soup casserole with thin rounds of toasted French bread covered with grated Gruyère and pour the onion soup over the toast. Sprinkle the top with grated cheese and put the casserole under the broiler or in a hot oven (400° F) until the cheese browns.

Créme Vichyssoise Glacée

SLICE very finely 1 medium-sized onion and the white parts of 4 leeks and sauté the vegetables in 2 tablespoons butter until they just begin to turn golden. Add 5 medium-sized potatoes, peeled and sliced, 1 quart chicken broth or water, or a combination of both, and 1 tablespoon salt. Bring the liquid to a boil and simmer it gently for 35 to 40 minutes. Rub the mixture through a fine sieve, return it to the heat and add 2 cups milk and 2 cups medium cream. Season to taste and bring the soup to a boil. Cool the soup and rub it through a very fine sieve. When it is cold, add 1 cup heavy cream and chill the soup thoroughly. Serve in cups and sprinkle with finely chopped chives. Serves eight.

Entreés

Filet of Sole Dugléré

MELT 2 tablespoons butter in a large shallow pan and sprinkle with 1 tablespoon finely chopped shallot or onion. Season 6 filets of sole with salt and arrange them side by side in the pan. Peel, seed and chop coarsely 4 tomatoes and spread them over the fish. Add ½ cup tomato juice, 1 garlic clove and 1 tablespoon chopped parsley. Cover the fish with a circle of buttered paper with a tiny hole in the centre, bring the liquid to a boil, cover the pan and simmer the fish for 10 to 12 minutes, depending upon the thickness of the filets. Discard the garlic and transfer the filets to a heated serving dish. Reduce the sauce rapidly over high heat by one-third. Thicken it with *beurre manié* made by kneading together 2 tablespoons butter and 1 teaspoon flour. Stir the sauce until it is well blended, correct the seasoning with salt and pepper and finish by swirling in 1 tablespoon sweet butter. Pour the sauce over the filets and sprinkle the fish with chopped parsley. Other filets may also be prepared by this recipe.

Crab Créole in Casserole

CHOP finely 1 medium-sized onion and sauté it in 1 tablespoon butter for 2 minutes, stirring constantly. Stir in 2 tablespoons flour and brown it lightly. Add 4 medium-sized tomatoes, peeled and cut in small pieces, 1 cup fish stock, ¼ cup green olives, 1 small green pepper and 2 tablespoons parsley, all finely chopped. Combine the mixture thoroughly, season to taste with salt, pepper and a tiny pinch each of thyme leaves and mace and simmer it gently for 10 minutes. Stir in 2 teaspoons Worcestershire sauce and 2 cups flaked cooked crab meat. Turn the mixture into an oiled earthenware casserole and sprinkle the top with buttered bread crumbs. Bake the casserole in a moderate oven (350° F) for 15 to 20 minutes, or until the crumbs are delicately browned. Serve in the casserole.

Coquilles St Jacques Florentine

WASH and drain 2 pounds scallops and put them in a saucepan with 1 cup white wine, ½ cup fish stock or water, 1 onion, sliced, 4 peppercorns, ½ bay leaf, 2 sprigs of parsley and salt to taste. Bring the mixture to a boil and simmer it gently for 3 minutes. Strain it, reserving the broth and slice the scallops. Keep the broth hot.

In a skillet in ¼ cup butter sauté ½ pound mushrooms, cleaned and sliced, and 3 ripe tomatoes, peeled, seeded and chopped for 10 minutes, stirring frequently, and add the scallops.

Melt 3 tablespoons butter in a saucepan, add 4 tablespoons flour and stir the *roux* until it is well blended. Stir in gradually the reserved broth. Cook the sauce, stirring constantly, until it is smooth and thickened. Stir in 2 tablespoons heavy cream and mix the sauce with the scallops, mushrooms and tomatoes. Fill scallop shells or ramekins with the mixture, sprinkle with bread crumbs and dot with butter. Brown the filling in a hot oven (400° F) or under the broiler and sprinkle with a little paprika and chopped parsley.

Poulet Poché a L'estragon

PUT 3 prepared chicken breasts in a saucepan with 1 small carrot and 1 onion, both thinly sliced, 3 sprigs of tarragon and ½ cup white wine. Add enough water or chicken stock barely to cover, bring the liquid to a boil and simmer the breasts, covered, for 25 minutes. Arrange them on a warm serving platter. Strain the liquid and reduce it over high heat to 2 cups. In a saucepan melt 3 tablespoons butter, stir in 3 tablespoons flour and add gradually the hot reduced liquid. Cook the sauce, stirring, until it is smooth and thickened. Season to taste with salt and pepper, stir in bit by bit 2 tablespoons butter and simmer the sauce for 6 minutes. Add 1 tablespoon chopped tarragon leaves and stir in 1 egg yolk lightly beaten with 3 tablespoons heavy cream and a little of the hot sauce. Pour the sauce over the chicken and garnish with blanched tarragon leaves.

Duckling, Sauce Bigarde

TRIM the wing tips and cut off the neck of a 4- to 5-pound duckling. Wash it thoroughly, inside and out, with cold water and dry it carefully. Rub the cavity with lemon juice and in it put a few celery leaves and 1 onion, sliced. Place the duckling, breast side up, on a rack in a shallow baking pan. Cook the bird in a moderately slow oven (325° F) for 30 minutes. Drain the fat from the pan and add 1½ cups dry white wine. Baste the duckling and continue cooking it for 1½ hours, basting it with the pan juices every 20 minutes. If a very crisp skin is desired, brush the duckling with 1 tablespoon honey about 15 minutes before taking it from the oven and do not baste it again.

DRAIN the liquid from a large can of pitted cherries into a saucepan. Add the unstrained juice of 1 lemon, ½ cup sugar and 1 tablespoon maraschino. Cook the mixture until it begins to thicken, stirring constantly. Add the cherries.

Escalope de Veau Parisien

IN a skillet sauté 6 prepared veal cutlets cut ¼ inch thick from the top sirloin over high heat until they are golden, turning them several times.

Arrange the meat on a warm serving dish and place on each piece 5 cooked asparagus tips. On top of the asparagus place 5 or 6 crabs' legs, cooked in butter.

To the juices remaining in the skillet add 3 tablespoons water, reduce this a little and pour it over the meat. Put the platter in the oven to keep warm and, when ready to serve, pour béarnaise sauce over the meat, asparagus and crabs' legs.

Lamb Ragout Printanière

IN a large skillet in ¼ cup clarified butter cook 1 onion, thinly sliced, until it is lightly browned, stirring constantly. Sprinkle with 1 teaspoon paprika and blend well. Add 2 pounds neck or shoulder of lamb, cut into small serving pieces and cook the meat over low heat, stirring constantly, until itbegins to brown. Transfer the meat to a large pot and mix into the fat remaining in the skillet 1 cup each of tomato purée and meat stock. Pour the mixture over the meat and add 5 medium-sized potatoes, quartered, 1 cup mushrooms, a *bouquet garni*, 1 whole clove and salt and pepper to taste. Bring the liquid to a boil and boil it for 2 minutes. Lower the heat and simmer the meat very gently, covered, for 1 hour. Taste for seasoning, thicken the sauce, if necessary, with a little flour mixed with cold water and stir in ¾ cup cooked peas Add 1 cup sour cream and heat the sauce without letting it boil. Serve very hot, sprinkled with chopped parsley.

Tournedos Rossini

ARRANGE 6 tournedos on croutons on a platter and garnish each one with a slice of *pâté de foie gras* and 3 slices of truffle heated in the skillet in which the tournedos were cooked. Deglaze the skillet with ½ cup *demiglace* sauce or brown sauce and a little Madeira, stirring in all the brown bits. Taste for seasoning and pour the sauce around the tournedos. Garnish with small bunches of watercress and serve with château potatoes.

Brown Sauce

MELT ½ cup fat in a heavy saucepan, using fresh, unsalted beef, veal or pork drippings but not chicken fat. Add 1 small carrot and 2 onions, coarsely chopped and cook them until they just start to turn golden, shaking the pan to insure even cooking. Add ½ cup flour and cook the vegetables, stirring, until they are a rich brown. Add 3 cups boiling brown stock, 3 sprigs of parsley, 1 stalk of celery, 1 small bay leaf, 1 garlic clove and a pinch of thyme and cook the mixture, stirring frequently, until it thickens. Add 3 more cups stock and simmer the sauce slowly, stirring occasionally, for 1 to 1½ hours, or until it is reduced to about 3 cups. Skim off the fat as it accumulates on the surface. Add ¼ cup tomato sauce or ½ cup tomato purée, cook the sauce for a few minutes longer and strain it through a fine sieve. Add 2 more cups stock and continue to cook the sauce slowly for about 1 hour, skimming from time to time, until it is reduced to about 4 cups. Cool the sauce, stirring occasionally, seal it with a layer of melted fat and store it, covered, in the refrigerator. If the sauce is not used within a week, bring it again to a boil, cool it and reseal it. Return the jar to the refrigerator.

For a richer sauce, cook ½ cup diced fat salt pork with the carrot and onion and add before the final reduction ½ cup beef gravy or juice from roast beef.

Roast Filet of Beef

SIRLOIN or rib roast, like all large pieces of meat, should stand for at least an hour at room temperature before roasting. Time schedules for roasting can be only approximate, since the size and shape of the roast, the amount of bone and the proportions of lean and fat all affect cooking time. A meat thermometer, inserted in the fleshy part of the roast, insures accuracy. The thermometer must never rest in fat or on bone. A temperature of 140° F indicates arare roast, 160° F a medium roast and 170° F a well-done roast. Since largeroasts continue cooking for some time after they are removed from the oven, they should be removed when the thermometer is several degrees below the desired finished temperature. All roasts should rest for 20 minutes out of the oven to allow the juices to settle.

RUB a trimmed filet of beef with butter and with pepper to taste. Roast it in a moderately hot oven (375° F) for 25 to 35 minutes, depending on the size of the filet. Baste frequently with hot beef stock for the first 15 minutes, then with the juices from the pan for the remaining roasting time, being careful not to let the juices burn.

Béarnaise Sauce

COMBINE 1 cup white wine with 1 tablespoon each of tarragon vinegar and finely chopped shallots, 2 small stalks of tarragon, coarsely chopped, 1 small sprig of parsley, 1 small sprig of chervil, finely chopped and 2 bruised peppercorns. Cook the mixture over high heat until it is reduced by one third and strain it. Cool it slightly. Stirring constantly and vigorously, add 3 egg yolks, lightly beaten, alternately with 1 cup butter, melted, or enough butter to make the sauce the consistency of heavy cream. Blend the sauce thoroughly over low heat, strain it through a fine sieve and finish with a dash of cayenne and 1 teaspoon each of finely chopped tarragon and chervil. For meats or fish.

Desserts

Strawberries Parisienne

Wash and hull sound ripe strawberries. Sprinkle them with sugar to taste. Mix strawberries with whipped cream and add enough sweetened puree of wild strawberries to give a delicate pink color and a wild strawberry flavour.

Crème Bavaroise

Crème a l'Anglaise Collée:

Scald 1 cup milk with a 1-inch piece of vanilla bean and let it stand for 10 minutes to absorb the vanilla flavour. Beat 4 egg yolks with ½ cup sugar until the mixture is smooth and creamy. Pour the scalded milk gradually into the egg mixture, stirring constantly. Cook the mixture over low heat or in the top of a double boiler over simmering water, stirring constantly, until it is smooth and thick. If the cream is cooked over direct heat, remove it from the heat the moment it reaches the boiling point. Remove the vanilla bean, strain the cream into a chilled bowl and add 1 tablespoon gelatin softened in 2 tablespoons cold water and dissolved over hot water. Stir the cream briskly, cool it and chill it until it just begins to thicken and hold its shape.

Prepare crème a l'anglaise collée, adding 2 ounces bitter chocolate, melted, along with the gelatin.

Whip 1 cup heavy cream until it stands in soft peaks and fold it into creme a l'anglaise collee when the creme just begins to thicken and hold its shape. Pour the Bavarian cream into a 1-quart mould rinsed out in cold water. Chill the cream for about 30 minutes. Turn the mould out on a platter and decorate with whipped cream forced through a pastry bag fitted with a fancy tube.

Bananes Flambées

Peel and quarter 6 red or yellow bananas, not quite ripe, sprinkle them with lime or lemon juice and saute them lightly in butter. Sprinkle them with salt to taste. Make a syrup of 1 cup each of any sweet red wine except Port and brown sugar, 1½ teaspoons grated orange rind, ½ teaspoon each of nutmeg and cinnamon and ¼ teaspoon ground cloves. Put the bananas in a buttered casserole, pour over them the spiced syrup and cover them with a ¼-inch-thick layer of crushed macaroons and very finely chopped almonds. Brown the topping in a moderate over (350° F) and just before serving, add ¼ cup heated dark rum. Ignite the spirit and serve flaming.

Relevant information for decision making with a focus on operational decisions

Learning objectives

When you have finished studying this chapter, you should be able to:

1 Use a differential analysis to examine income effects across alternatives and show that an opportunity–cost analysis yields identical results.

2 Decide whether to make or to buy certain parts or products.

3 Choose whether to add or delete a product line using relevant information.

4 Compute the optimal product mix when production is constrained by a scarce resource.

5 Decide whether to process a joint product beyond the split-off point.

6 Decide whether to keep or replace equipment.

7 Identify irrelevant and misspecified costs.

8 Discuss how performance measures can affect decision making.

Maersk Line

Container shipping management entails a complex maze of decisions. In February 2011, Maersk Line, a Danish shipper, ordered ten colossal vessels for €1.3 billion from South Korea's Daewoo Shipbuilding, with an option to order 20 more. Not only will they be the largest vessels of any kind afloat when launched in 2013; each ship will carry 18,000 boxes – 2,500 more than the largest container ships currently in service and also operated by Maersk – and the vessels will use 50 per cent less fuel per container than presently attainable. Maersk announced profits of

€1.7 billion in 2010 and expects global trade to grow by 6–8 per cent per year in the immediate future. The company deals with complex decisions relating to shipping, fuel, personnel, maintenance and capacity utilisation costs.

As with Maersk Line, managers in other companies must make similar operational decisions. Should Toyota make the tyres it mounts on its cars, or should it buy them from suppliers? Should General Mills sell the flour it mills, or should it use the flour to make more breakfast cereal? Should Air France add routes to use idle airplanes, or should it sell the planes? These decisions all require a good deal of accounting information. But what information will be relevant to each decision? In Chapter 5, we identified relevant information for pricing decisions. We now need to determine relevance in the operational area. The basic framework for identifying relevant information remains the same for operations as it was for pricing. We are still looking only for future costs that differ among alternatives. However, we now expand our analysis by introducing the concepts of opportunity costs and differential costs. ■

Analysing relevant information: focusing on the future and differential attributes

■ Opportunity, outlay and differential costs and analysis

Objective 1
Use a differential analysis to examine income effects across alternatives and show that an opportunity–cost analysis yields identical results.

Management decision making is a matter of comparing two or more alternative courses of action. Suppose a manager has only two alternatives to compare. The key to determining the financial difference between the alternatives is to identify the differential costs and revenues. **Differential cost (differential revenue)** is the difference in total cost (revenue) between two alternatives. For example, consider the decision about which of two machines to purchase. Both machines perform the same function. The differential cost is the difference in the price paid for the machines plus the difference in the costs of operating the machines. We call a decision process that compares the differential revenues and costs of alternatives a **differential analysis**.

When managers analyse the differential costs between the existing situation and a proposed alternative, they often refer to this as **incremental analysis**. They examine the incremental (additional) costs and benefits of the proposed alternative compared with the current situation. The **incremental costs** are additional costs or reduced revenues generated by the proposed alternative. **Incremental benefits** are the additional revenues or reduced costs generated by the proposed alternative. For instance, suppose Nantucket Nectars a producer of fruit juices, juice cocktails, teas, lemonades and other carbonated drinks, proposes to increase production of its NectarFizz juice drink from 1,000 bottles to 1,200 bottles per week. The incremental costs of the proposed alternative are the costs of producing the additional 200 bottles each week. The incremental benefits are the additional revenues generated by selling the extra 200 bottles.

When there are multiple alternative courses of action, managers often compare one particular action against the entire set of alternatives. For example, Nantucket Nectars might consider introducing a new 100 per cent juice drink, Papaya Mango. There are many alternatives to introducing Papaya Mango, including introducing other new 100 per cent juice drinks, expanding production of existing drinks such as juice cocktails or blended nectars, or producing non-juice products. Computing the differential costs and revenues between producing Papaya Mango and every alternative could be cumbersome. Thus, Nantucket Nectars managers might use another approach.

Introducing Papaya Mango would entail two types of costs, outlay costs and opportunity costs. An **outlay cost** requires a future cash disbursement. Outlay costs include costs for items such as materials and labour. **Opportunity cost** applies to a resource that a company already owns or that it has already committed to purchase. It is the maximum available benefit forgone (or passed up) by using such a resource for a particular purpose instead of the best alternative use. Suppose Nantucket Nectars has a machine for which it paid €100,000 several years ago and it is sitting idle. It can use the machine to produce Papaya Mango or to increase the production of the Original Peach 100% Juice. The contribution margin from the additional sales of the Original Peach would be €60,000. A third alternative is selling the machine for €50,000 cash. What is the opportunity cost of the machine when we analyse the Papaya Mango alternative? It is €60,000, the larger of the €50,000 or €60,000, the two possible gains that the company could achieve using the machine in its alternative uses. The €100,000 paid for the machine is not relevant because, as we learned from our discussion of relevant costs in Chapter 5, it is not a future cost.

Now suppose that Nantucket Nectars will have total sales over the life cycle of Papaya Mango 100% Juice of €500,000. The production and marketing costs (outlay costs), excluding the cost of the machine, are €400,000. The net financial benefit from the Papaya Mango is €40,000:

Revenues	€500,000
Costs:	
Outlay costs	400,000
Financial benefit before opportunity costs	€100,000
Opportunity cost of machine	60,000
Net financial benefit	€ 40,000

Nantucket Nectars will gain €40,000 more financial benefit using the machine to make Papaya Mango than it would make using it for the next most profitable alternative.

An alternative to the opportunity-cost analysis is to conduct an incremental analysis. In an incremental analysis, we compare the revenues and outlay costs of the proposed alternative to those of the next best alternative use of the machine. In this case, the revenue less outlay costs for Papaya Mango of €100,000 is €40,000 higher than the predicted contribution margin on the Original Peach. The result of the incremental analysis is equivalent to that of the opportunity-cost approach.

To further illustrate this equivalence, consider Maria Morales, an accountant employed by a large accounting firm for a salary of €60,000 per year. She is considering an alternative use of her time, her most valuable resource. The alternative is to start an independent accounting practice. Maria's practice would have revenues of €200,000. This is €140,000 more than she would make as an employee of the large firm. However, she would also have to pay €120,000 to rent office space, lease equipment, buy advertising and cover other out-of-pocket expenses.

An incremental analysis follows:

Assume Maria opens her own independent practice	
Incremental benefits, €200,000 – €60,000 of increased revenues	€140,000
Incremental costs, €120,000 – €0 of additional costs	120,000
Incremental income effects per year	€ 20,000

If Maria opens her own practice, her income will be €20,000 higher than it is as an employee of the large firm.

Now let's take an opportunity-cost approach. We will look at the alternative of operating an independent practice, essentially comparing it to the alternative uses of Maria's time (which in this case is simply the alternative of working for the large firm). To do this we must consider another cost. Had Maria remained an employee, she would have made €60,000. By starting her own company, Maria will forgo this profit. Thus, the €60,000 is an opportunity cost of starting her own business:

		Alternative chosen: independent practice
Revenue		€200,000
Expenses		
Outlay costs (operating expenses)	€120,000	
Opportunity cost of employee salary	60,000	180,000
Income effects per year		€ 20,000

Consider the two preceding tabulations. Each produces the correct key difference between alternatives, €20,000. The first tabulation does not mention opportunity cost because we measured the differential economic impacts – differential revenues and differential costs – compared to the alternative. The second tabulation mentions opportunity cost because we included the €60,000 annual net economic impact of the excluded alternative as a cost of the chosen alternative. If we had failed to recognise opportunity cost in the second tabulation, we would have misstated the difference between the alternatives.

Why do we use opportunity costs when an incremental analysis produces the same result? When there is only one resource and one alternative opportunity to use that resource, the incremental analysis is more straightforward. However, suppose you were analysing a project that uses five existing machines each with 10 alternative uses. An incremental analysis would require comparing the project with $10^5 = 100,000$ alternatives – every combination of alternative uses of the five machines. Using opportunity costs allows you to simplify the analysis. You just assess the 10 alternatives for each machine, pick the best one to use in determining each machine's opportunity cost, and add the five opportunity costs to the outlay costs of the project. The opportunity-cost approach is simpler than the incremental approach in such a situation.

MAKING MANAGERIAL DECISIONS

Suppose you are a warehouse manager at Lego, the toy company. Ace Hardware approaches you asking to rent warehouse space for January–April for storage of garden tools for the spring sales season. What is the likely opportunity cost to Lego of the warehouse space? What if the request were for September–November?

Answer

At a toy company, excess warehouse space is a seasonal phenomenon. There is unlikely to be excess space late in the year as the holiday season approaches, but in January–April Lego may have little use for the space. You might look for other temporary alternatives, ones that use the space for only a few months. If there are no such alternatives, the opportunity cost would be close to zero. If other alternatives exist, the opportunity cost would be the benefit received from the next best alternative use. If the request came in September, the opportunity cost would likely be high because Lego needs the space to accommodate its own toy inventory for holiday sales.

This does not mean that estimating opportunity costs is easy. They depend on estimated revenues and costs for hypothetical alternatives – alternatives not taken. Furthermore, they depend on the alternatives that are available at a particular point in time. The same alternatives may not be available at a different time. For example, excess capacity in September does not mean that there will also be excess capacity in October. Finally, there is little historical information – sale or purchase prices – to help predict benefits for hypothetical alternatives.

We will next use the concepts in this section to analyse a variety of operational decisions. Just as we focused on relevant costs for pricing decisions in Chapter 5, we will focus on relevant costs for operational decisions in this chapter.

Make-or-buy decisions

Objective 2
Decide whether to make or to buy certain parts or products.

Managers often must decide whether to produce a product or service within the firm or purchase it from an outside supplier. If they purchase products or services from an outside supplier, we often call it **outsourcing**. They apply relevant cost analysis to a variety of outsourcing decisions such as the following:

- Boeing must decide whether to buy or make many of the tools used in assembling 787 airplanes.

- Apple must decide whether to develop its own internet search software for a new computer or to buy it from a software vendor.

The 'Business first' box on p. 237 describes outsourcing and its growing popularity.

Basic make-or-buy decisions and idle facilities

A basic make-or-buy question is whether a company should make its own parts that it will use in its final products or buy the parts from vendors. Sometimes the answer to this question is based on qualitative factors. For example, some manufacturers always make parts because they want to control quality. Alternatively, some companies always purchase parts to protect long-run relationships with their suppliers. These companies may deliberately buy from vendors even during slack times to avoid difficulties in obtaining needed parts during boom times, when there may well be shortages of materials and workers, but no shortage of sales orders.

What quantitative factors are relevant to the decision of whether to make or buy? The answer, again, depends on the situation. A key factor is whether there are idle facilities. Many companies make parts only when they cannot use their facilities to better advantage.

Assume that Nantucket Nectars reports the following costs:

Nantucket Nectars Company – cost of making
12-ounce glass bottles

	Total cost for 1,000,000 bottles	Cost per bottle
Direct materials	€ 60,000	€.06
Direct labour	20,000	.02
Variable factory overhead	40,000	.04
Fixed factory overhead	80,000	.08
Total costs	€200,000	€.20

BUSINESS FIRST
An example of make or buy: outsourcing

Make-or-buy decisions (or outsourcing decisions) apply to services as well as to products. Companies are increasingly deciding to hire service firms to handle some of their internal operations. According to the Outsourcing Institute, outsourcing is 'the strategic use of outside resources to perform activities traditionally handled by internal staff and resources.'

Companies use outsourcing for many business processes within various value-chain functions. The most common business functions outsourced fall within the value-chain functions of corporate support (e.g., administration, human resources, finance and IT) and marketing (e.g., sales and call centres). Additionally, some companies outsource production processes and even research and development activities. For example, Eli Lilly has moved some of its chemistry lab work to China and is conducting more clinical trial activities overseas, primarily to reduce costs.

Although companies can outsource many processes, the internet has driven much of the recent growth in outsourcing of computer applications. By the beginning of the twenty-first century, many companies realised that the huge investments necessitated by ERP systems may be unnecessary. They could purchase the required services over the internet without investing in the systems' purchase and development costs. The formerly expensive process of communication using service providers had become essentially free via the internet. A new group of computing service providers – called application service providers (ASPs) – arose to provide outsourcing opportunities for a variety of computing applications.

What are the key reasons for outsourcing? Over half of the companies in Outsourcing Institute's annual survey said they wanted to improve the company's focus and reduce operating costs. According to Todd Kertley,

who manages IBM's outsourcing services, 'Corporations increasingly want to focus on their core businesses, not technology.' As the complexity of data processing and especially networking has grown, companies have found it harder and harder to keep current with the technology. Instead of investing huge sums in personnel and equipment and diverting attention from the value-added activities of their own businesses, many firms have found outsourcing financially attractive. Additionally, many companies are discovering that outsourcing aids corporate growth, making better use of skilled labour, and even job creation. Such 'transformational outsourcing' exploits the enormous gains in efficiency, productivity, and revenues that accrue to firms from leveraging offshore talent.

The big stumbling block to outsourcing has been subjective factors, such as control. To make outsourcing attractive, the services must be reliable, be available when needed, and be flexible enough to adapt to changing conditions. Companies that have successful outsourcing arrangements have been careful to include the subjective factors in their decisions.

Outsourcing has become so profitable that more than 75 per cent of *Fortune* 500 companies outsource some aspect of their business support services. The McKinsey Global Institute estimates that companies have shifted abroad more than $18 billion in global IT work and over $11 billion in business process services.

Sources: Adapted from T. Kearney, 'Why outsourcing is in', *Strategic Finance*, January 2000, pp. 34–38; J. Hechinger, 'IBM to take over operations of auto-parts maker Visteon', *Wall Street Journal*, 12 February 2003; P. Engardio, M. Arndt and D. Foust, 'The future of outsourcing', *Business Week*, 30 January 2006; and the Outsourcing Institute (www.outsourcing.com).

Another manufacturer offers to sell Nantucket Nectars the bottles for €.18. Should Nantucket Nectars make or buy the bottles?

Although the €.20 unit cost seemingly indicates that the company should buy, the answer is rarely so obvious. The essential question is 'What is the difference in expected future costs between the alternatives?' If the €.08 fixed overhead per bottle consists of costs that will continue regardless of the decision, the entire €.08 becomes irrelevant. Examples of such fixed factory costs include depreciation, property taxes, insurance and foreman salaries for the plant.

Are only the variable costs relevant? No. Perhaps Nantucket Nectars will eliminate €50,000 of the fixed costs if the company buys the bottles instead of making them. For example, the company may be able to release a supervisor with a €50,000 salary. In that case, the fixed costs that the company will be able to avoid in the future are relevant.

For the moment, suppose the capacity now used to make bottles will become idle if the company purchases the bottles. Further, the €50,000 supervisor's salary is the only fixed cost that the company would eliminate. The relevant computations follow:

	Make		Buy	
	Total	Per bottle	Total	Per bottle
Purchase cost			€180,000	€.18
Direct materials	€ 60,000	€.06		
Direct labour	20,000	.02		
Variable factory overhead	40,000	.04		
Fixed factory overhead that can be avoided by not making (supervisor's salary)	50,000*	.05*		
Total relevant costs	€170,000	€.17	€180,000	€.18
Difference in favour of making	€ 10,000	€.01		

*Note that unavoidable fixed costs of €80,000 − €50,000 = €30,000 are irrelevant. Thus, the irrelevant costs per unit are €.08 − €.05 = €.03.

The key to wise make-or-buy decisions is identifying and accurately measuring the additional costs for making (or the costs avoided by buying) a part or component. Companies with accurate cost accounting systems, such as ABC systems discussed in Chapter 4, are in a better position to perform make-or-buy analysis.

Make or buy and the use of facilities

Make-or-buy decisions are rarely as simple as the one in our Nantucket Nectars example. As we said earlier, the use of facilities is a key to the make-or-buy decision. For simplicity, we assumed that the Nantucket Nectars facilities would remain idle if the company chose to buy the bottles. This means that the opportunity cost of the facilities is zero. In most cases, companies will not leave their facilities idle. Instead, they will often put idle facilities to some other use, and we must consider the financial outcomes of these uses when choosing to make or buy. The value received from the best of these alternative uses is an opportunity cost for the internal production of the parts or components.

Suppose Nantucket Nectars can use the released facilities in our example in some other manufacturing activity to produce a contribution to profits of €55,000 or can rent them out for €25,000. We now have four alternatives to consider. The following table is an incremental analysis that summarises all the costs and revenues that differ among the four alternatives (amounts are in thousands):

	Make	Buy and leave facilities idle	Buy and rent out facilities	Buy and use facilities for other products
Rent revenue	€ —	—	€ 25	€ —
Contribution from other products	—	—	—	55
Relevant cost of bottles	(170)	(180)	(180)	(180)
Net relevant costs	€(170)	€(180)	€(155)	€(125)

MAKING MANAGERIAL DECISIONS

Suppose a company uses its facilities, on average, 80 per cent of the time. However, because of seasonal changes in the demand for its product, the actual demand for the facilities varies from 60 per cent in the off season to over 100 per cent in the peak season when it must outsource production of some parts. Under what circumstances would the company choose to take on work for other companies during the off season? Why might it continue to outsource production of parts during the peak season – that is, why would the company choose not to expand its capacity?

Answer

During the off season, the company would decide to take on work for other manufacturers (on a subcontract) if it is profitable. Such work may not be profitable enough to cover the cost of expanding the capacity of the facilities. The company will use facilities for these orders only when the opportunity cost of using the facilities is close to zero, that is, when there are no other more profitable uses for them. In contrast, during the peak season, the company meets the high volume by outsourcing the production of some parts. Again, the cost of purchased parts may be higher than the cost to make them in the company's own facilities if there were idle capacity, but purchasing the parts is less costly than expanding the facilities to produce them. Additionally, a company may increase production above demand (but below capacity) in the off-season in order to build inventory for the busy season.

The final column indicates that buying the bottles and using the vacated facilities for the production of other products would yield the lowest net costs in this case, €170,000 − €125,000 = €45,000 less than the cost of making the bottles.

We can also analyse this choice using opportunity costs. The opportunity cost of the facilities is €55,000 because that is the maximum benefit Nantucket Nectars could get if it did not use the facilities to make bottles. Add that to the outlay cost, and the total cost of making the bottles is €225,000. This is €45,000 higher than the €180,000 cost of purchasing them.

Summary problem for your review

PROBLEM

Exhibit 6.1 contains data for the Block Company for the year just ended. The company makes industrial power drills. Exhibit 6.1 shows the costs of the plastic housing separately from the costs of the electrical and mechanical components. Answer each of the following questions independently. (Requirement 1 reviews Chapter 5.)

1 During the year, a prospective customer in an unrelated market offered €82,000 for 1,000 drills. The drills would be manufactured in addition to the 100,000 units sold. Block Company would pay the regular sales commission rate on the 1,000 drills. The president rejected the order because 'it was below our costs of €97 per unit.' What would operating income have been if Block Company had accepted the order?

2 A supplier offered to manufacture the year's supply of 100,000 plastic housings for €12.00 each. What would be the effect on operating income if the Block Company purchased rather than made the housings? Assume that Block Company would avoid €350,000 of the fixed costs assigned to housings if it purchases the housings.

3 Suppose that Block Company could purchase the housings for €13.00 each and use the vacated space for the manufacture of a deluxe version of its drill. Assume that it could make 20,000 deluxe units (and sell them for €130 each in addition to the sales of the 100,000 regular units) at a unit variable cost of €90, exclusive of housings and exclusive of the 10 per cent sales commission. The company could also purchase the 20,000 extra plastic housings for €13.00 each. All the fixed costs pertaining to the plastic housings would continue because these costs relate primarily to the manufacturing facilities used. What would operating income have been if Block had bought the housings and made and sold the deluxe units?

	(A) Electrical and Mechanical Components*	(B) Plastic housing	(A) + (B) Industrial drills
Sales: 100,000 units, at €100			€10,000,000
Variable costs			
Direct materials	€4,400,000	€ 500,000	€ 4,900,000
Direct labour	400,000	300,000	700,000
Variable factory overhead	100,000	200,000	300,000
Other variable costs	100,000	—	100,000
Sales commissions, at 10% of sales	1,000,000	—	1,000,000
Total variable costs	€6,000,000	€1,000,000	€ 7,000,000
Contribution margin			€ 3,000,000
Total fixed costs	€2,220,000	€ 480,000	2,700,000
Operating income			€ 300,000

*Not including the costs of plastic housing (column B).

Exhibit 6.1 Block company cost of industrial drills

SOLUTION

1 The costs of filling the special order follow:

Direct materials	€49,000
Direct labour	7,000
Variable factory overhead	3,000
Other variable costs	1,000
Sales commission at 10% of €82,000	8,200
Total variable costs	€68,200
Selling price	82,000
Contribution margin	€13,800

Operating income would have been €300,000 + €13,800 = €313,800 if Block Company had accepted the order. In a sense, the decision to reject the offer implies that the Block Company is willing to forgo €13,800 in immediate gains (an opportunity cost) in order to preserve the long-run selling price structure.

2 Assuming that Block Company could have avoided €350,000 of the fixed costs by not making the housings and that the other fixed costs would have continued, we can summarise the incremental costs and benefits of buying the housings compared with making them as follows:

Incremental cost (purchase cost of 100,000 × €12)	€1,200,000
Incremental benefits:	
Variable costs	€1,000,000
Avoidable fixed costs	350,000
Net incremental benefit	€ 150,000

If the facilities used for plastic housings became idle, the Block Company would prefer to buy the housings. Operating income would increase by €150,000.

3 The effect of purchasing the plastic housings and using the vacated facilities for the manufacture of a deluxe version of its drill follows:

Incremental benefit:		
Sales increase, 20,000 units, at €130		€2,600,000
Variable costs exclusive of housings increase, 20,000 units, at €90	€1,800,000	
Plus: sales commission, 10% of €2,600,000	260,000	€2,060,000
Contribution margin on 20,000 units		€ 540,000
Incremental cost:		
Housings: 120,000 rather than 100,000 would be needed; Buy 120,000 at €13	€1,560,000	
Versus make 100,000 at €10 (only the variable costs are relevant)	1,000,000	
Incremental cost of outside purchase		560,000
Fixed costs, unchanged		—
Net incremental cost to buying		€ 20,000

Operating income would decline to €300,000 − €20,000 = €280,000. The deluxe units bring in a contribution margin of €540,000, but the additional costs of buying rather than making housings is €560,000, leading to a net disadvantage of €20,000.

Deletion or addition of products, services or departments

Objective 3
Choose whether
to add or delete a
product line using
relevant information.

Relevant information also plays an important role in decisions about adding or deleting products, services or departments.

■ Avoidable and unavoidable costs

Often, existing businesses will want to expand or contract their operations to improve profitability. Decisions about whether to add or to drop products or whether to add or to drop departments will use the same analysis: examining all the relevant costs and revenues. For example, consider a store that has three major departments: groceries, general merchandise and drugs. Management is considering dropping the grocery department, which has consistently shown an operating loss. The following table reports the store's present annual operating income (in thousands of euros):

| | Total | Departments | | |
		Groceries	General merchandise	Drugs
Sales	€1,900	€1,000	€800	€100
Variable cost of goods sold and expenses*	1,420	800	560	60
Contribution margin	€ 480 (25%)	€ 200 (20%)	€240 (30%)	€ 40 (40%)
Fixed expenses (salaries, depreciation, insurance, property taxes, and so on):				
Avoidable	€ 265	€ 150	€100	€ 15
Unavoidable	180	60	100	20
Total fixed expenses	€ 445	€ 210	€200	€ 35
Operating income (loss)	€ 35	€ (10)	€ 40	€ 5

*Examples of variable expenses include product, paper shopping bags and sales commissions.

Notice that we have divided the fixed expenses into two categories, avoidable and unavoidable. **Avoidable costs** – costs that will not continue if an ongoing operation is changed or deleted – are relevant. In our example, avoidable costs include department salaries and other costs that the store could eliminate by not operating the specific department. **Unavoidable costs** – costs that continue even if a company discontinues an operation – are not relevant in our example because a decision to delete the department does not affect them. Unavoidable costs include many **common costs**, which are those costs of facilities and services that are shared by users. For example, store depreciation, heating, air conditioning, and general management expenses are costs of shared resources used by all departments. For our example, assume first that we will consider only two alternatives, dropping or continuing the grocery department, which shows a loss of €10,000. Assume further that the decision will not affect the total assets invested in the store. The vacated space would be idle, and the unavoidable costs would continue. Which alternative would you recommend? An analysis (in thousands of euros) follows:

	Store as a whole		
Income statements	**Total before change** (a)	**Effect of drop-ping groceries** (b)	**Total after change** (a) – (b)
Sales	€1,900	€1,000	€900
Variable expenses	1,420	800	620
Contribution margin	€ 480	€ 200	€280
Avoidable fixed expenses	265	150	115
Profit contribution to common space and other unavoidable costs	€ 215	€ 50	€165
Common space and other unavoidable costs	180	—	180
Operating income (loss)	€ 35	€ 50	€ (15)

The preceding analysis shows that matters would be worse, rather than better, if the store drops the groceries department and leaves the vacated facilities idle. In short, as the income statement shows, groceries bring in a contribution margin of €200,000, which is €50,000 more than the €150,000 fixed expenses the store would save by closing the grocery depart-ment. The grocery department showed a loss in the first income statement because of the unavoidable fixed costs charged (allocated) to it.

Most companies do not like having space left idle, so perhaps the preceding example was a bit too basic. Assume now that the store could use the space made available by the dropping of groceries to expand the general merchandise department. The space would be occupied by merchandise that would increase sales by €500,000, generate a 30 per cent contribution-margin percentage, and have additional (avoidable) fixed costs of €70,000. The €80,000 increase in operating income of general merchandise more than offsets the €50,000 decline from eliminating groceries, providing an overall increase in operating income of €65,000 – €35,000 = €30,000. The analysis is as follows:

	Effects of changes			
(in thousands of euros)	**Total before change** (a)	**Drop groceries** (b)	**Expand general merchandise** (c)	**Total after changes** (a) – (b) + (c)
Sales	€1,900	€1,000	€500	€1,400
Variable expenses	1,420	800	350	970
Contribution margin	€ 480	€ 200	€150	€ 430
Avoidable fixed expenses	265	150	70	185
Contribution to common space and other unavoidable costs	€ 215	€ 50	€ 80	€ 245
Common space and other unavoidable costs*	180	—	—	180
Operating income	€ 35	€ 50	€ 80	€ 65

*Includes the €60,000 of former grocery fixed costs, which were allocations of unavoidable common costs that will continue regardless of how the space is occupied.

This example illustrates that relevant costs are not always variable. The key to decision making is not relying on a hard and fast rule about what to include and what to ignore. Rather, you need to analyse all pertinent costs and revenues to determine what is and what is not relevant. In this case, the relevant costs included the avoidable fixed costs.

It is also important to remember that nonfinancial information can influence decisions to add or delete products or departments. For example, when deciding to delete a product or to close a plant, there are ethical considerations. What happens to the employees in the area being discontinued? What about customers who might be relying on customer support in the future? What about the community in which a discontinued operation is located? While the nonfinancial impacts of such considerations are hard to determine, they are still factors a company should consider. In addition, a stable, committed workforce and a supportive community can be important assets to a company. This may be a situation where good ethics is good business. Any negative impacts on employees, customers or communities could create future financial problems for the company that are much larger than short-term cost savings from discontinuing a product or plant.

MAKING MANAGERIAL DECISIONS

When managers face a decision about whether to add or delete a product, service or department, it is useful to classify the associated fixed costs as avoidable or unavoidable. Indicate whether the following fixed costs are typically avoidable or unavoidable if a company deletes a product. Assume that the company produces many products in a single plant.

1 Advertising costs for the product. The company places specific ads just for this product.

2 Salary of the plant manager.

3 Rent for the plant building.

4 Insurance costs on equipment used to produce the product. The company will sell the equipment if it discontinues the product.

Answer

Numbers 1 and 4 are avoidable fixed costs. The company is unlikely to change the salary of the plant manager if it discontinues only one product. Thus, it is unavoidable. The same is true for the plant rent. Hence, it is also an unavoidable cost.

Optimal use of limited resources: product-mix decisions

Objective 4
Compute the optimal product mix when production is constrained by a scarce resource.

Suppose a plant makes more than one product and is operating at capacity. If demand for its products exceeds the amount the company can produce, managers must decide which product mix to produce. The product-mix decision requires a focus on each product's contribution margin and its use of capacity. Managers should emphasise the product that makes the largest contribution per unit of the limiting factor. A limiting factor or scarce resource restricts or constrains the production or sale of a product or service. Limiting factors include labour hours and machine hours that limit production (and hence sales) in manufacturing firms, and square feet of floor space or cubic metres of display space that limit sales in department stores.

Managers must use the contribution margin technique wisely. They sometimes mistakenly favour those products with the biggest contribution margin or gross margin per unit or per sales euro, without regard to scarce resources. This could lead to incorrect decisions.

Consider two different athletic shoes produced by Nike, the Air Court tennis shoe and the Air Max running shoe. Assume that one factory is the only facility that produces these shoes, and Nike managers must decide how many shoes of each type to produce. Suppose machine time is the measure of capacity in this factory, and there is a maximum of 10,000 hours of machine time. The factory can produce 10 pairs of Air Court shoes or 5 pairs of Air Max shoes in 1 hour of machine time. Unit data follow:

	Air Court	Air Max
Selling price per pair	€80	€120
Variable costs per pair	60	84
Contribution margin per pair	€20	€ 36
Contribution margin ratio	25%	30%

Which is more profitable, the Air Court or Air Max? On which should Nike spend its resources? The correct answer is 'It depends.' Suppose the factory has excess capacity of 1,000 hours of machine time. Now a sports retailer approaches Nike and wants it to fill a special order for 1,000 pairs of shoes of either type. Which shoe would be most profitable to fill this order, the Air Court or the Air Max? It would be better to produce and sell an Air Max pair contributing €36 than an Air Court pair contributing €20. In this case, Air Max shoes generate more profit per pair. Thus, if the limiting factor is demand, that is, pairs of shoes, the more profitable product is the one with the higher contribution per unit.

Now suppose the demand for either shoe would exceed the factory's capacity. Capacity is now the limiting factor because there is only one factory in which to make either the Air Max or the Air Court. In this case, the Air Court shoe is more profitable. Why? Because it generates €2,000,000 of contribution margin from the capacity that is available compared to €1,800,000 for Air Max:

	Air Court	Air Max
1 Pairs of shoes from 10,000 hours	100,000	50,000
2 Contribution margin per pair	€ 20	€ 36
3 Contribution margin from 10,000 hours of capacity, (1) × (2)	€2,000,000	€1,800,000
Contribution margin per machine-hour, (3) ÷ 10,000	€ 200	€ 180

Each machine-hour used to produce Air Court shoes generates €200 of contribution, while an hour used to produce Air Max shoes generates only €180.

Now suppose that neither shoe alone has enough demand to fill the entire capacity, but the combined demand will more than fill the capacity. What our analysis tells us is the Air Court shoe is a better use of the production capacity than the Air Max shoe. Nike would want to make sure there are as many pairs of Air Court shoes available as customers demand, and only after satisfying this demand is it worth producing Air Max shoes.

This analysis depends on the relative use of capacity by the two products. Suppose the factory can produce seven instead of five Air Max shoes per hour of machine time. Then, the Air Max would be the most profitable use of the capacity. It would have a €252 contribution for each machine-hour compared with Air Court's €200.

	Air Court	Air Max
Contribution from 10,000 machine-hours	10,000 × 10 × €20 = €2,000,000	10,000 × 7 × €36 = €2,520,000
Contribution per machine-hour	€2,000,000 ÷ 10,000 = €200	€2,520,000 ÷ 10,000 = €252

Any way we express it, Air Max shoes will have more contribution per unit of capacity – per hour or per 10,000 hours. Note that each of these financial measures shows that Air Max shoes are 26 per cent more profitable than the Air Court. That is, (€252 – €200) ÷ €200 = 26%, and (€2,520,000 – €2,000,000) ÷ €2,000,000 = 26%.

This issue of optimising the use of scarce resources is important in non-manufacturing companies as well. In retail stores, the limiting resource is often floor space. Thus, they often focus either on products taking up less space or on using the space for shorter periods of time – greater **inventory turnover** (number of times the average inventory is sold per year). However, the product that is most profitable when one particular factor limits sales may be the least profitable if a different factor restricts sales. Consider an example of two department stores. The conventional gross profit percentage (gross profit ÷ selling price) is an insufficient clue to profitability because, as we said, profits depend on the space occupied and the inventory turnover. Discount department stores, have succeeded in using lower markups than traditional department stores because they have been able to increase turnover and, thus, increase the contribution to profit per unit of space. Exhibit 6.2 illustrates the same product, taking up the same amount of space, in each of two stores. The contribution margins per unit and per sales euro are less in the discount store, but faster turnover makes the same product a more profitable use of space in the discount store. In general, retail companies seek faster inventory turnover. A survey of retail shoe stores showed that those with above-average financial performance had an inventory turnover of 2.6 times per year compared to an industry average of 2.0.

	Regular department store	Discount department store
Retail price	€ 4.00	€ 3.50
Cost of merchandise and other variable costs	3.00	3.00
Contribution to profit per unit	€ 1.00 (25%)	€ .50 (14%)
Units sold per year	10,000	22,000
Total contribution to profit, assuming the same space allotment in both stores	€10,000	€11,000

Exhibit 6.2 Effect of inventory turnover on profit

Joint product costs: sell or process further decisions

Objective 5
Decide whether to process a joint product beyond the split-off point.

We now examine another operating decision for which relevant costs are important – decisions about whether to sell a product as it is or to further process it. In this section, we will examine how joint product costs affect such decisions.

Consider ConAgra, which produces meat products with brand names such as Swift, Armour and Butterball. ConAgra cannot kill a sirloin steak; it has to purchase and slaughter a steer, which supplies various cuts of dressed meat, hides and trimmings. So how does ConAgra determine the proper allocation of the purchase cost paid for the steer to the various manufactured meat products? When two or more manufactured products (1) have relatively significant sales values and (2) are not separately identifiable as individual products until their split-off point, we call them **joint products**. The **split-off point** is that juncture of manufacturing where the joint products become individually identifiable. Any costs beyond that stage are **separable costs** because they are not part of the joint process and the accounting system can exclusively identify them with individual products. We call the costs of manufacturing joint products prior to the split-off point **joint costs**. Further examples of joint products include chemicals, lumber, flour and the products of petroleum refining.

To illustrate joint costs, suppose Saint Cobain produces two chemical products, X and Y, as a result of a particular joint process. The joint processing cost is €100,000. This includes raw material costs and the cost of processing before the joint products X and Y reach the split-off point. At the split-off point, Saint Cobain either sells X and Y or processes them further before selling them to the petroleum industry, which uses them as ingredients of gasoline. The relationships follow:

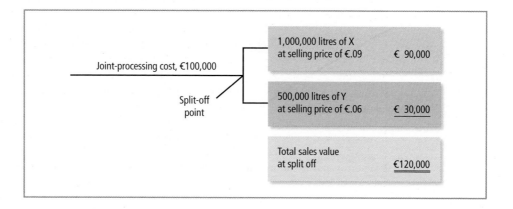

Let's see how Saint Cobain's managers develop relevant information to help them decide whether to sell joint products X and Y at the split-off point or to further process one or both of them.

Sell or process further

Suppose Saint Cobain can further process the 500,000 litres of Y and sell it to the plastics industry as product YA, an ingredient for plastic sheeting. The additional processing cost would be €.08 per litre for manufacturing and distribution, a total of €40,000 for 500,000 litres. The net sales price of YA would be €.16 per litre, a total of €80,000.

Saint Cobain cannot process product X further and will sell it at the split-off point, but management is undecided about product Y. Should the company sell Y at the split-off point or should it process Y into YA? To answer this question, we need to find the relevant costs involved. Consider first the joint costs – those before the split-off point. They cannot affect anything beyond the split-off point. They violate both attributes of relevancy; they are neither future costs nor differential across alternatives. Therefore they are irrelevant to the question of whether to sell or process further. The only approach that will yield valid results is to concentrate on the separable costs and revenues beyond split-off, as shown in Exhibit 6.3.

This analysis shows that it would be €10,000 more profitable to process Y beyond split-off than to sell Y at split-off. The rule is to extend processing on a joint product if the additional revenue exceeds the additional expenses.

Exhibit 6.4 illustrates another way to compare the alternatives of (1) selling Y at the split-off point and (2) processing Y beyond split-off. It includes the joint costs, which are the same for each alternative and, therefore, do not affect the difference.

Because joint costs would not affect the decision (as Exhibit 6.4 demonstrates), we have not allocated the joint costs to products. However, no matter how we might allocate them, the total income effects for the firm would not change. We provide additional coverage of the allocation of joint costs and inventory valuation in Chapter 12.

	Sell at split-off as Y	Process further and sell as YA	Difference
Revenues	€30,000	€80,000	€50,000
Separable costs beyond split-off at €.08	—	40,000	40,000
Income effects	€30,000	€40,000	€10,000

Exhibit 6.3 Illustration of sell or process further

	(1) Alternative one			(2) Alternative two			(3) Differential effects
	X	Y	Total	X	YA	Total	
Revenues	€90,000	€30,000	€120,000	€90,000	€80,000	€170,000	€50,000
Joint costs			€100,000			€100,000	—
Separable costs			—		40,000	40,000	40,000
Total costs			€100,000			€140,000	€40,000
Income effects			€ 20,000			€ 30,000	€10,000

Exhibit 6.4 Sell or process further analysis – firm as a whole

Keeping or replacing equipment

Objective 6
Decide whether to keep or replace equipment.

We next examine a common decision in business, the replacement of old equipment. One important aspect of such a situation is that the book value of the old equipment is not a relevant consideration in deciding whether to purchase a replacement. Why? Because it is a past cost, not a future cost. When a company purchases equipment, it spreads the cost via a **depreciation** expense over the future periods in which it will use the equipment. The equipment's **book value**, or **net book value**, is the original cost less accumulated depreciation. **Accumulated depreciation** is the sum of all depreciation charged to past periods. For example, suppose a €10,000 machine with a 10-year life span has depreciation of €1,000 per year. At the end of 6 years, accumulated depreciation is 6 × €1,000 = €6,000, and the book value is €10,000 − €6,000 = €4,000.

Consider the following data for a decision about whether to replace an old machine:

	Old machine	Replacement machine
Original cost	€10,000	€8,000
Useful life in years	10	4
Current age in years	6	0
Useful life remaining in years	4	4
Accumulated depreciation	€ 6,000	0
Book value	€ 4,000	Not acquired yet
Disposal value (in cash) now	€ 2,500	Not acquired yet
Disposal value in 4 years	0	0
Annual cash operating costs (maintenance, power, repairs, coolants, and so on)	€ 5,000	€3,000

Let's prepare a comparative analysis of the two alternatives. Before proceeding, consider some important concepts. The most widely misunderstood facet of replacement decision making is the role of the book value of the old equipment in the decision. We often call the book value a **sunk cost**, which is really just another term for historical or past cost, a cost that the company has already incurred and, therefore, is irrelevant to the decision-making process. Nothing can change what has already happened.

The irrelevance of past costs for decisions does not mean that knowledge of past costs is useless. Often managers use past costs to help predict future costs. In addition, past costs affect future payments for income taxes (as explained in Chapter 11). However, the past cost itself is not relevant. The only relevant cost is the predicted future cost.

In deciding whether to replace or keep existing equipment, we must consider the relevance of four commonly encountered items:

1 Book value of old equipment: irrelevant because it is a past (historical) cost. Therefore, depreciation on old equipment is also irrelevant.

2 Disposal value of old equipment: relevant because it is an expected future inflow that usually differs across alternatives.

3 Gain or loss on disposal: This is the difference between book value and disposal value. It is therefore a meaningless combination of irrelevant and relevant items. The combination form, loss (or gain) on disposal, blurs the distinction between the irrelevant book value and the relevant disposal value. Consequently, it is best to think of each separately.

4 Cost of new equipment: relevant because it is an expected future outflow that will differ across alternatives. Therefore, the initial cost of new equipment (or its allocation in subsequent depreciation charges) is relevant.

Exhibit 6.5 shows the relevance of these items in our example. Book value of old equipment is irrelevant regardless of the decision-making technique we use. The 'difference' column in Exhibit 6.5 shows that the €4,000 book value of the old equipment does not differ between alternatives. We should completely ignore it for decision-making purposes. The difference is merely one of timing. The amount written off is still €4,000, regardless of any available alternative. The €4,000 appears on the income statement either as a €4,000 deduction from the €2,500 cash proceeds received to obtain a €1,500 loss on disposal in the first year or as €1,000 of depreciation in each of 4 years. But how it appears is irrelevant to the

	Four years together		
	Keep	Replace	Difference
Cash operating costs	€20,000	€12,000	€8,000
Old equipment (book value)			
Periodic write-off as depreciation	4,000	—	—
or			
Lump-sum write-off		4,000*	
Disposal value	—	−2,500*	2,500
New machine			
Acquisition cost	—	8,000†	−8,000
Total costs	€24,000	€21,500	€2,500

The advantage of replacement is €2,500 for the 4 years together.
*In a formal income statement, these two items would be combined as 'loss on disposal' of €4,000 − €2,500 = €1,500.
†In a formal income statement, written off as straight-line depreciation of €8,000 ÷ 4 = €2,000 for each of 4 years.

Exhibit 6.5 Cost comparison – replacement of equipment including relevant and irrelevant items replacement decision. In contrast, the €2,000 annual depreciation on the new equipment is relevant because the total €8,000 depreciation is a future cost that we can avoid by not replacing. The three relevant items – operating costs, disposal value, and acquisition cost – give replacement a net advantage of €2,500.

MAKING MANAGERIAL DECISIONS

It is sometimes difficult to accept the proposition that past or sunk costs are irrelevant to decisions. Consider the ticket you have to a major football game in December. After getting the ticket, you learn that the game will be on TV, and you really prefer to watch the game in the comfort of your warm home. Does your decision about attending the game or watching it on TV depend on whether you were given the ticket for free or you paid €80 for it? What does this tell you about a manager's decision to replace a piece of equipment?

Answer

The amount paid, whether it be €0, €80 or €1,000, should make no difference to the decision. You have the ticket, and you have paid for it. That cannot be changed. If you really prefer to watch the game on television, it

may have been a bad decision to pay €80 for a ticket. But you cannot erase that bad decision. All you can do is choose the future action that has the most value to you. You should not suffer through a less pleasant experience just because you paid €80 for the ticket.

A manager must make the same analysis regarding the replacement of a piece of equipment. What the company spent for the old equipment is irrelevant. Keeping equipment that is no longer economical is just like using a ticket for an event that you would rather not attend. Additionally, keeping the equipment creates an opportunity cost because the company forgoes the disposal value of the old equipment, in the same way that keeping the ticket prevents you from reselling it to another fan (which is a relevant item in this scenario).

Summary problem for your review

PROBLEM

Exhibit 6.5 looks beyond 1 year. Examining the alternatives over the equipment's entire life ensures that peculiar nonrecurring items, such as loss on disposal, will not obstruct the long-run view vital to many managerial decisions. However, Exhibit 6.5 presents both relevant and irrelevant items. Prepare an analysis that concentrates on relevant items only.

SOLUTION

Exhibit 6.6 presents the analysis with relevant items only – the cash operating costs, the disposal value of the old equipment, and the acquisition cost of the new equipment. To demonstrate that the amount of the old equipment's book value will not affect the answer, suppose the book value of the old equipment is €500,000 rather than €4,000. Your final answer will not change. The cumulative advantage of replacement is still €2,500. (If you are in doubt, rework this example, using €500,000 as the book value.)

	Four years together		
	Keep	Replace	Difference
Cash operating costs	€20,000	€12,000	€8,000
Disposal value of old machine	—	−2,500	2,500
New machine, acquisition cost	—	8,000	−8,000
Total relevant costs	€20,000	€17,500	€2,500

Exhibit 6.6 Cost comparison – replacement of equipment, relevant items only

Identify irrelevant or misspecified costs

Objective 7
Identify irrelevant and misspecified costs.

The ability to recognise irrelevant or misspecified costs is sometimes just as important to decision makers as identifying relevant costs. How do we know that past costs, although sometimes good predictors of future costs, are irrelevant in decision making? Let's consider such past costs as obsolete inventory and see why they are irrelevant to decisions.

Suppose Rolls Royce has 100 obsolete aircraft turbine parts in its inventory. The original manufacturing cost of these parts was €100,000. Rolls Royce can (1) re-machine the parts for €30,000 and then sell them for €50,000 or (2) sell them as scrap for €5,000. Which should it do? This is an unfortunate situation, yet the €100,000 past cost is irrelevant to the decision to re-machine or scrap. The only relevant factors are the expected future revenues and costs:

	Remachine	Scrap	Difference
Expected future revenue	€ 50,000	€ 5,000	€45,000
Expected future costs	30,000	—	30,000
Relevant excess of revenue over costs	€ 20,000	€ 5,000	€15,000
Accumulated historical inventory cost*	100,000	100,000	—
Net overall loss on project	€ (80,000)	€ (95,000)	€15,000

*Irrelevant because it is unaffected by the decision.

As you can see from the fourth line of the preceding table, we can completely ignore the €100,000 historical cost and still arrive at the €15,000 difference, the key figure in the analysis that yields re-machining as the optimal decision.

In addition to past costs, some future costs may be irrelevant because they will be the same under all feasible alternatives. These, too, we may safely ignore for a particular decision. Top management salaries are examples of expected future costs that may be unaffected by the decision at hand.

Other irrelevant future costs include fixed costs that will be the same whether a company selects machine X or machine Y. However, it is not merely a case of saying that fixed costs are irrelevant and variable costs are relevant. Variable costs can be irrelevant, and fixed costs can be relevant. For instance, sales commissions are a variable cost that is irrelevant to a decision on whether to produce a product in plant G or plant H. The rental cost of a warehouse is a fixed cost that is relevant if one alternative requires the warehouse while the other does not. In sum, future costs (both variable and fixed) are irrelevant whenever they do not differ among the alternatives at hand and are relevant whenever they do differ between the alternatives.

Finally, it is also critical in decision making to identify misspecified costs. The pricing illustration in Chapter 5 showed that managers should analyse unit costs with care in decision making. There are two major ways to go wrong: (1) including irrelevant costs, such as the €.03 allocation of unavoidable fixed costs in the Nantucket Nectars make-or-buy example (pp. 236–8) that would result in a unit cost of €.20 instead of the relevant unit cost of €.17 and (2) comparing unit costs not computed on the same volume basis, as the following example demonstrates. Machinery sales personnel often brag about the low unit costs of using the new machines. Sometimes they neglect to point out that the unit costs are based on outputs far in excess of the volume of activity of their prospective customer. Assume that a new €100,000 machine with a 5-year life span can produce 100,000 units a year at a variable cost of €1 per unit, as opposed to a variable cost per unit of €1.50 with an old machine. A sales representative claims that the new machine will reduce total cost by €.30 per unit after allowing €.20 per unit for depreciation on the new machine. Is the new machine a worthwhile acquisition?

The new machine is attractive at first glance. If the customer's expected volume is 100,000 units, unit-cost comparisons are valid, provided that new depreciation is also considered. Assume that the disposal value of the old equipment is zero. Because depreciation is an allocation of historical cost, the depreciation on the old machine is irrelevant. In contrast, the depreciation on the new machine is relevant because the new machine entails a future cost that the customer can avoid by not acquiring it.

	Old machine	New machine
Units	100,000	100,000
Variable costs	€150,000	€ 100,000
Straight-line depreciation	—	20,000
Total relevant costs	€150,000	€ 120,000
Unit relevant costs	€ 1.50	€ 1.20

Apparently, the sales representative is correct. However, if the customer's expected volume is only 30,000 units per year, the unit costs change in favour of the old machine.

	Old machine	New machine
Units	30,000	30,000
Variable costs	€45,000	€30,000
Straight-line depreciation	—	20,000
Total relevant costs	€45,000	€50,000
Unit relevant costs	€ 1.50	€1.6667

Generally, be wary of unit fixed costs. When feasible, use total fixed cost in your analysis, not fixed cost per unit. Why? Because you need to calculate a new fixed cost per unit for every different volume of production – often a cumbersome task – and if you don't recalculate it, your costs will be misspecified.

Conflicts between decision making and performance evaluation

Objective 8
Discuss how
performance
measures can affect
decision making.

You should now know how to make good decisions based on relevant data. However, knowing how to make these decisions and actually making them are two different things. Managers might be tempted to make decisions they know are poor – not in the best interests of the company – if the performance measures in place will reward them for those decisions. To motivate managers to make optimal decisions, methods of evaluating managers' performance should be consistent with their appropriate decision model.

Let's look at an example of a conflict between the analysis for decision making and the method used to evaluate performance. Consider the replacement decision shown in Exhibit 6.6 on p. 251, where replacing the machine had a €2,500 advantage over keeping it. To motivate managers to make the right choice, the method used to evaluate performance should be consistent with the decision model – that is, it should show better performance when managers replace the machine than when they keep it. Assume that top management uses accounting income to measure a manager's performance. The effect on accounting income in the first year after replacement compared with that in years 2, 3 and 4 follows:

	Year 1		Years 2, 3 and 4	
	Keep	**Replace**	**Keep**	**Replace**
Cash operating costs	€5,000	€3,000	€5,000	€3,000
Depreciation	1,000	2,000	1,000	2,000
Loss on disposal (€4,000 – €2,500)	—	1,500	—	—
Total cost	€6,000	€6,500	€6,000	€5,000

First-year costs will be €6,500 − €6,000 = €500 lower, making first-year income €500 higher, if the manager keeps the machine rather than replacing it. Because managers naturally want to make decisions that maximise the measure of their performance, the manager may be inclined to keep the machine.

The conflict is especially severe if a company often transfers managers from one position to another. Why? Because the €500 first-year increase in income for keeping the machine will be offset by a €1,000 annual decrease in income in years 2 to 4. (Note that the net difference of €2,500 in favour of replacement over the 4 years together is the same as in Exhibit 6.6.) A manager who moves to a new position after the first year, however, bears the entire loss on disposal without reaping the benefits of lower operating costs in years 2 to 4.

The decision to replace a machine earlier than planned also reveals a possible error in the original decision to purchase the machine. The company bought the old machine 6 years ago for €10,000. Its expected life span was 10 years. However, if a better machine is now available, then the useful life of the old machine was really 6 years, not 10. This feedback on the actual life of the old machine has two possible effects, the first good and the second bad. First, managers might learn from the earlier mistake. If the manager overestimated the useful life of the old machine, how believable is the prediction that the new machine will have a 4-year life span? Feedback can help avoid repeating past mistakes. Second, another mistake might be made to cover up the earlier one. A 'loss on disposal' could alert superiors to the incorrect economic-life prediction used in the earlier decision. By avoiding replacement, the manager can spread the €4,000 remaining book value over the future as 'depreciation', a more appealing term than 'loss on disposal'. The superiors may never find out about the incorrect prediction of economic life. Using accounting income for performance evaluation mixes the financial effects of various decisions, hiding both the earlier misestimation of useful life and the current failure to replace.

The conflict between decision making and performance evaluation is a widespread problem in practice. Unfortunately, there are no easy solutions. In theory, accountants could evaluate performance in a manner consistent with decision making. In our equipment example, this would mean predicting year-by-year income effects over the planning horizon of 4 years, noting that the first year would be poor, and evaluating actual performance against the predictions.

The trouble is that evaluating performance decision by decision is a costly procedure. Therefore, we generally use aggregate measures. For example, an income statement shows the results of many decisions, not just the single decision of buying a machine. Consequently, in many cases like our equipment example, the first-year effects on the income statement may be the major influence on managers' decisions. Thus, managers refrain from taking the longer view that would benefit the company.

Chapters 5 and 6 introduced the important topics of relevant information and decision making. Our major focus was on how to determine and use relevant information when faced with various managerial decisions such as pricing, special orders, make or buy, adding or deleting a product line and equipment replacement. We have emphasised the importance of understanding cost behaviour in each of these decision situations. Now, we shift our emphasis from decision-making techniques to planning and control techniques. One of the most important planning techniques you will use as a manager is budgeting – the major topic in Chapters 7 and 8.

Highlights to remember

1 **Use a differential analysis to examine income effects across alternatives, and show that an opportunity-cost analysis yields identical results.** A differential analysis is a valuable tool for analysing decisions; it focuses on the relevant items in the situation – differential revenues and differential costs. One should always consider opportunity costs when deciding on the use of limited resources. The opportunity cost of a course of action is the maximum profit forgone from other alternative actions. Decision makers may fail to consider opportunity costs because accountants do not report them in the financial accounting system.

2 **Decide whether to make or to buy certain parts or products.** One of the most important production decisions is the make-or-buy decision. Should a company make its own parts or products or should it buy them from outside sources? Both qualitative and quantitative factors affect this decision. In applying relevant cost analysis to a make-or-buy situation, a key factor to consider is often the opportunity cost of facilities.

3 **Choose whether to add or delete a product line using relevant information.** Relevant information also plays an important role in decisions about adding or deleting products, services or departments. Decisions on whether to delete a department or product line require analysis of the revenues forgone and the costs saved from the deletion.

4 **Compute the optimal product mix when production is constrained by a scarce resource.** When production is constrained by a limiting resource, the key to obtaining the maximum profit from a given capacity is to obtain the greatest possible contribution to profit per unit of the limiting or scarce resource.

5 **Decide whether to process a joint product beyond the split-off point.** Another typical production situation is deciding whether to process further a joint product or sell it at the

split-off point. The relevant information for this decision includes the costs that differ beyond the split-off point. Joint costs that occur before split-off are irrelevant.

6   **Decide whether to keep or replace equipment.** In the decision to keep or replace equipment, the book value of old equipment is irrelevant. This sunk cost is a past or historical cost that a company has already incurred. Relevant costs normally include the disposal value of old equipment, the cost of new equipment, and the difference in the annual operating costs.

7   **Identify irrelevant and misspecified costs.** In certain production decisions, it is important to recognise and identify irrelevant costs. In the decision to dispose of obsolete inventory, the original cost of the inventory is irrelevant. Unit fixed costs can be misleading because of the differences in the assumed level of volume on which they are based. The more units a company makes, the lower the unit fixed cost will be. You can avoid being misled by unit costs by always using total fixed costs.

8   **Discuss how performance measures can affect decision making.** If companies evaluate managers using performance measures that are not in line with relevant decision criteria, there could be a conflict of interest. Managers often make decisions based on how the decision affects their performance measures. Thus, performance measures work best when they are consistent with the long-term good of the company.

Accounting vocabulary

accumulated depreciation, p. 248
avoidable costs, p. 242
book value, p. 248
common costs, p. 242
depreciation, p. 248
differential analysis, p. 233
differential cost, p. 233
differential revenue, p. 233

incremental analysis, p. 233
incremental benefits, p. 233
incremental costs, p. 233
inventory turnover, p. 246
joint costs, p. 247
joint products, p. 246
limiting factor, p. 244
net book value, p. 248

opportunity cost, p. 233
outlay cost, p. 233
outsourcing, p. 236
scarce resource, p. 244
separable costs, p. 246
split-off point, p. 246
sunk cost, p. 249
unavoidable costs, p. 242

Fundamental assignment material   MyAccountingLab

6.A1 Make or buy

Sunshine Fruit Company sells premium-quality oranges and other citrus fruits by mail order. Protecting the fruit during shipping is important so the company has designed and produces shipping boxes. The annual cost to make 80,000 boxes is:

Materials	€112,000
Labour	20,000
Indirect manufacturing costs	
Variable	16,000
Fixed	60,000
Total	€208,000

Therefore, the cost per box averages €2.60.

Suppose Weyerhaeuser submits a bid to supply Sunshine with boxes for €2.10 per box. Sunshine must give Weyerhaeuser the box design specifications, and the boxes will be made according to those specs.

1 How much, if any, would Sunshine save by buying the boxes from Weyerhaeuser?
2 What subjective factors should affect Sunshine decision about whether to make or buy the boxes?
3 Suppose all the fixed costs represent depreciation on equipment that was purchased for €600,000 and is just about at the end of its 10-year life. New replacement equipment will cost €800,000 and is also expected to last 10 years. In this case, how much, if any, would Sunshine save by buying the boxes from Weyerhaeuser?

6.A2 Choice of products

The Ibunez Tool Company has two products: a plain circular saw and a professional circular saw. The plain saw sells for €70 and has a variable cost of €55. The professional saw sells for €100 and has a variable cost of €75.

1 Compute contribution margins and contribution-margin ratios for plain and professional saws.
2 The demand is for more units than the company can produce. There are only 20,000 machine-hours of manufacturing capacity available. Two plain saws can be produced in the same average time (1 hour) needed to produce one professional saw. Compute the total contribution margin for 20,000 hours for plain saws only and for professional saws only. Which product is the best use of machine hours?
3 Use two or three sentences to state the major lesson of this problem.

6.A3 Joint products: sell or process further

The Mussina Chemical Company produced three joint products at a joint cost of €117,000. These products were processed further and sold as follows:

Chemical Product	Sales	Additional processing costs
A	€230,000	€190,000
B	330,000	300,000
C	175,000	100,000

The company has had an opportunity to sell at split-off directly to other processors. If that alternative had been selected, sales would have been A, €54,000; B, €32,000; and C, €54,000.

The company expects to operate at the same level of production and sales in the forthcoming year.

Consider all the available information, and assume that all costs incurred after split-off are variable.

1 Could the company increase operating income by altering its processing decisions? If so, what would be the expected overall operating income?
2 Which products should be processed further and which should be sold at split-off?

6.A4 Role of old equipment replacement

On 2 January, the S. H. Park Company installed a brand new €90,000 special moulding machine for producing a new product. The product and the machine have an expected life of 3 years. The machine's expected disposal value at the end of 3 years is zero.

On 3 January of that year, Kimiyo Lee, a star salesperson for a machine tool manufacturer, tells Mr Park, 'I wish I had known earlier of your purchase plans. I can supply you with a technically superior machine for €99,000. The machine you just purchased can be sold for €15,000. I guarantee that our machine will save €38,000 per year in cash operating costs, although it too will have no disposal value at the end of 3 years.'

Park examines some technical data. Although he has confidence in Lee's claims, Park contends, 'I'm locked in now. My alternatives are clear: (a) Disposal will result in a loss, (b) keeping and using the 'old' equipment avoids such a loss. I have brains enough to avoid a loss when my other alternative is recognising a loss. We've got to use that equipment until we get our money out of it.'

The annual operating costs of the old machine are expected to be €60,000, exclusive of depreciation. Sales, all in cash, will be €910,000 per year. Other annual cash expenses will be €810,000 regardless of this decision. Assume that the equipment in question is the company's only fixed asset.

Ignore income taxes and the time value of money.

1 Prepare statements of cash receipts and disbursements as they would appear in each of the next 3 years under both alternatives. What is the total cumulative increase or decrease in cash for the 3 years?
2 Prepare income statements as they would appear in each of the next 3 years under both alternatives. Assume straight-line depreciation. What is the cumulative increase or decrease in net income for the 3 years?
3 Assume that the cost of the 'old' equipment was €1 million rather than €90,000. Would the net difference computed in numbers 1 and 2 change? Explain.
4 As Kimiyo Lee, reply to Mr Park's contentions.
5 What are the irrelevant items in each of your presentations for numbers 1 and 2? Why are they irrelevant?

6.B1 Make or buy

Suppose a BMW executive in Germany is trying to decide whether the company should continue to manufacture an engine component or purchase it from Frankfurt Corporation for €50 each. Demand for the coming year is expected to be the same as for the current year, 200,000 units. Data for the current year follow:

Direct material	€ 5,000,000
Direct labour	1,900,000
Factory overhead, variable	1,100,000
Factory overhead, fixed	3,000,000
Total costs	€ 11,000,000

If BMW makes the components, the unit costs of direct material will increase by 10 per cent.

If BMW buys the components, 30 per cent of the fixed costs will be avoided. The other 70 per cent will continue regardless of whether the components are manufactured or purchased. Assume that variable overhead varies with output volume.

1 Prepare a schedule that compares the make-or-buy alternatives. Show totals and amounts per unit. Compute the numerical difference between making and buying. Assume that the capacity now used to make the components will become idle if the components are purchased.
2 Assume also that the BMW capacity in question can be rented to a local electronics firm for €1,150,000 for the coming year. Prepare a schedule that compares the net relevant costs of the three alternatives: make, buy and leave capacity idle, buy and rent. Which is the most favourable alternative? By how much in total?

6.B2 Unit costs and capacity

Fargo Manufacturing Company produces two industrial solvents for which the following data have been tabulated. Fixed manufacturing cost is applied to products at a rate of €1.00 per machine-hour.

Per unit	XY-7	BD-4
Selling price	€6.00	€4.00
Variable manufacturing costs	3.00	1.50
Fixed manufacturing cost	.75	.25
Variable selling cost	2.00	2.00

The sales manager has had a €150,000 increase in her budget allotment for advertising and wants to apply the money on the most profitable product. The solvents are not substitutes for one another in the eyes of the company's customers.

1　How many machine-hours does it take to produce one XY-7? To produce one BD-4? (Hint: Focus on applied fixed manufacturing cost.)
2　Suppose Fargo has only 100,000 machine-hours that can be made available to produce XY-7 and BD-4. If the potential increase in sales units for either product resulting from advertising is far in excess of these production capabilities, which product should be produced and advertised, and what is the estimated increase in contribution margin earned?

6.B3 Dropping a product line

Hamleys Toy Store is on Regent Street in London. It has a magic department near the main door. Suppose that management is considering dropping the magic department, which has consistently shown an operating loss. The predicted income statements, in thousands of pounds (£), are shown below (for ease of analysis, only three product lines are shown).

The £300,000 of magic department fixed expenses include the compensation of employees of £120,000. These employees will be released if the magic department is abandoned. All of the magic department's equipment is fully depreciated, so none of the £300,000 pertains to such items. Furthermore, disposal values of equipment will be exactly offset by the costs of removal and remodelling.

If the magic department is dropped, the manager will use the vacated space for either more general merchandise or more electronic products. The expansion of general merchandise would not entail hiring any additional salaried help, but more electronic products would require an additional person at an annual cost of £30,000. The manager thinks that sales of general merchandise would increase by £250,000; electronic products, by £200,000. The manager's modest predictions are partially based on the fact that she thinks the magic department has helped lure customers to the store and, thus, improved overall sales. If the magic department is closed, that lure would be gone.

	Total	General merchandise	Electronic products	Magic department
Sales	£6,000	£5,000	£400	£ 600
Variable expenses	4,090	3,500	200	390
Contribution margin	£1,910 (32%)	£1,500 (30%)	£200 (50%)	£ 210 (35%)
Fixed expenses (compensation, depreciation, property taxes, insurance, etc.)	1,100	750	50	300
Operating income (loss)	£ 810	£ 750	£150	£(90)

Should the magic department be closed? Explain, showing computations.

6.B4 Sell or process further

ConAgra produces meat products with brand names such as Healthy Choice, Armour and Butterball. Suppose one of the company's plants processes beef cattle into various products. For simplicity, assume that there are only three products: steak, hamburger and hides, and that the average steer costs €700. The three products emerge from a process that costs €100 per steer to run, and output from one steer can be sold for the following net amounts:

Steak (100 pounds)	€ 400
Hamburger (500 pounds)	600
Hide (120 pounds)	100
Total	€1,100

Assume that each of these three products can be sold immediately or processed further in another ConAgra plant. The steak can be the main course in frozen dinners sold under the Healthy Choice label. The vegetables and desserts in the 400 dinners produced from the 100 pounds of steak would cost €110, and production, sales and other costs for the 400 meals would total €330. Each meal would be sold wholesale for €2.10.

The hamburger could be made into frozen Salisbury steak patties sold under the Armour label. The only additional cost would be a €200 processing cost for the 500 pounds of hamburger. Frozen Salisbury steaks sell wholesale for €1.70 per pound.

The hide can be sold before or after tanning. The cost of tanning one hide is €80 and a tanned hide can be sold for €170.

1 Compute the total profit if all three products are sold at the split-off point.
2 Compute the total profit if all three products are processed further before being sold.
3 Which products should be sold at the split-off point? Which should be processed further?
4 Compute the total profit if your plan in number 3 is followed.

6.B5 Replacing old equipment

Consider the data regarding Douglas County's photocopying requirements below.

The county administrator is trying to decide whether to replace the old equipment. Because of rapid changes in technology, she expects the replacement equipment to have only a 3-year useful life. Ignore the effects of taxes.

1 Prepare a schedule that compares both relevant and irrelevant items for the next 3 years. (Hint: See Exhibit 6.5, p. 249.)
2 Prepare a schedule that compares all relevant items for the next 3 years. Which tabulation is clearer, this one or the one in requirement 1? (Hint: See Exhibit 6.6, p. 251.)
3 Prepare a simple 'shortcut' or direct analysis to support your choice of alternatives.

	Old equipment	Proposed replacement equipment
Useful life, in years	5	3
Current age, in years	2	0
Useful life remaining, in years	3	3
Original cost	€25,000	€15,000
Accumulated depreciation	10,000	0
Book value	15,000	Not acquired yet
Disposal value (in cash) now	6,000	Not acquired yet
Disposal value in 3 years	0	0
Annual cash operating costs for power, maintenance, toner and supplies	14,000	9,000

6.B6 Decision and performance models

Refer to the preceding problem.

1 Suppose the 'decision model' favoured by top management consisted of a comparison of a 3-year accumulation of cash under each alternative. As the manager of office operations, which alternative would you choose? Why?

2 Suppose the 'performance evaluation model' emphasised the minimisation of overall costs of photocopying operations for the first year. Which alternative would you choose?

Additional assignment material   MyAccountingLab

QUESTIONS

6.1 Distinguish between an opportunity cost and an outlay cost.

6.2 'I had a chance to rent my summer home for 2 weeks for €800. But I chose to have it idle. I didn't want strangers living in my summer house.' What term in this chapter describes the €800? Why?

6.3 'Accountants do not ordinarily record opportunity costs in the formal accounting records.' Why?

6.4 Distinguish between an incremental cost and a differential cost.

6.5 'Incremental cost is the addition to costs from the manufacture of one unit.' Do you agree? Explain.

6.6 'The differential costs or incremental costs of increasing production from 1,000 automobiles to 1,200 automobiles per week would be the additional costs of producing the additional 200 automobiles.' If production were reduced from 1,200 to 1,000 automobiles per week, what would the decline in costs be called?

6.7 'Qualitative factors generally favour making over buying a component.' Do you agree? Explain.

6.8 'Choices are often mislabelled as simply make or buy.' Do you agree? Explain.

6.9 'The key to decisions to delete a product or department is identifying avoidable costs.' Do you agree? Explain.

6.10 Give four examples of limiting or scarce factors.

6.11 What are joint products? Name several examples of joint products.

6.12 What is the split-off point, and why is it important in analysing joint costs?

6.13 'No technique used to assign the joint cost to individual products should be used for management decisions regarding whether a product should be sold at the split-off point or processed further.' Do you agree? Explain.

6.14 'Inventory that was purchased for €5,000 should not be sold for less than €5,000 because such a sale would result in a loss.' Do you agree? Explain.

6.15 'Recovering sunk costs is a major objective when replacing equipment.' Do you agree? Explain.

6.16 'Past costs are indeed relevant in most instances because they provide the point of departure for the entire decision process.' Do you agree? Why?

6.17 Which of the following items are relevant to replacement decisions? Explain.

(a) Book value of old equipment.
(b) Disposal value of old equipment.
(c) Cost of new equipment.

6.18 'Some expected future costs may be irrelevant.' Do you agree? Explain.

6.19 'Variable costs are irrelevant whenever they do not differ among the alternatives at hand.' Do you agree? Explain.

6.20 There are two major reasons why unit costs should be analysed with care in decision making. What are they?

6.21 'Machinery sales personnel sometimes erroneously brag about the low unit costs of using their machines.' Identify one source of an error concerning the estimation of unit costs.

6.22 Give an example of a situation in which the performance evaluation model is not consistent with the decision model.
6.23 'Evaluating performance, decision by decision, is costly. Aggregate measures, such as the income statement, are frequently used.' How might the wide use of income statements affect managers' decisions about buying equipment?

CRITICAL THINKING EXERCISES

6.24 Measurement of opportunity cost

'Accountants cannot measure opportunity cost. Only managers have the knowledge to measure it.' Do you agree with this statement? Why or why not?

6.25 Outsourcing decisions

Decisions on whether to outsource services such as payroll accounting and systems development are much like make-or-buy decisions. What cost factors should influence the decision on whether to outsource payroll functions?

6.26 Unitised costs

Suppose you are a manager in a manufacturing company. Your accountant has just presented you with a very detailed cost analysis for a decision about whether to outsource or make a component of a product. You have to use this analysis in a meeting with other managers. Since the analysis is shown in totals and your colleagues prefer simple reports and unit costs, you divide the bottom-line amounts by the total units to be made or bought (outsourced) and present just these in a simple report. Your colleagues are pleased that your report is so easy to understand and simple to use. Then they begin to predict the total cost differences for several other possible numbers of units to be made or outsourced by simply multiplying the unit costs by the volume to be outsourced. Why should you feel uncomfortable?

6.27 Historical costs and inventory decisions

Explain why it is sometimes best to sell inventory for less than the amount paid for it.

EXERCISES

6.28 Opportunity costs

Martina Bridgeman is a lawyer employed by a large legal firm at a salary of €110,000 per year. She is considering whether to become a sole practitioner, which would probably generate annually €350,000 in operating revenues and €220,000 in operating expenses.

1 Present two tabulations of the annual income effects of these alternatives. The second tabulation should include the opportunity cost of Bridgeman's compensation as an employee.
2 Suppose Bridgeman prefers less risk and chooses to stay an employee. Show a tabulation of the income effects of rejecting the opportunity of independent practice.

6.29 Opportunity cost of home ownership

Oliver Kamp has just made the final payment on his mortgage. He could continue to live in the home; cash expenses for repairs and maintenance (after any tax effects) would be €500 monthly. Alternatively, he could sell the home for €200,000 (net of taxes), invest the proceeds in 5 per cent municipal tax-free bonds and rent an apartment for €12,000 annually. The landlord would then pay for repairs and maintenance.

Prepare two analyses of Kamp's alternatives, one showing no explicit opportunity cost and the second showing the explicit opportunity cost of the decision to hold the present home.

6.30 Hospital opportunity cost

An administrator at Saint Jude Hospital is considering how to use some space made available when the outpatient clinic moved to a new building. She has narrowed her choices, as follows:

(a) Use the space to expand laboratory testing. Expected future annual revenue would be €330,000; future costs, €290,000.

(b) Use the space to expand the eye clinic. Expected future annual revenue would be €500,000; future costs, €480,000.

(c) The gift shop is rented by an independent retailer who wants to expand into the vacated space. The retailer has offered €11,000 for the yearly rental of the space. All operating expenses will be borne by the retailer.

The administrator's planning horizon is unsettled. However, she has decided that the yearly data given will suffice for guiding her decision.

Tabulate the total relevant data regarding the decision alternatives. Omit the concept of opportunity cost in one tabulation, but use the concept in a second tabulation. As the administrator, which tabulation would you prefer if you could receive only one?

6.31 Make or buy

Assume that a division of Bose makes an electronic component for its speakers. Its manufacturing process for the component is a highly automated part of a just-in-time production system. All labour is considered to be an overhead cost and all overhead is regarded as fixed with respect to output volume. Production costs for 100,000 units of the component are as follows:

Direct materials		€400,000
Factory overhead		
Indirect labour	€80,000	
Supplies	30,000	
Allocated occupancy cost	40,000	150,000
Total cost		€550,000

A small, local company has offered to supply the components at a price of €4.20 each. If the division discontinued its production of the component, it would save two-thirds of the supplies cost and €30,000 of indirect-labour cost. All other overhead costs would continue.

The division manager recently attended a seminar on cost behaviour and learned about fixed and variable costs. He wants to continue to make the component because the variable cost of €4.00 is below the €4.20 bid.

1 Compute the relevant cost of (a) making and (b) purchasing the component. Which alternative is less costly and by how much?

2 What qualitative factors might influence the decision about whether to make or to buy the component?

6.32 Deletion of product line

Zurich American School is an international private elementary school. In addition to regular classes, after-school care is provided between 3:00 PM and 6:00 PM at CHF 12 per child per hour. Financial results for the after-school care for a representative month are:

Revenue, 600 hours at CHF 12 per hour		CHF 7,200
Less		
Teacher salaries	CHF 6,000	
Supplies	800	
Depreciation	1,300	
Sanitary engineering	100	
Other fixed costs	200	8,400
Operating income (loss)		CHF (1,200)

The director of Zurich American School is considering discontinuing the after-school care services because it is not fair to the other students to subsidise the after-school care programme. He thinks that eliminating the programme will free up CHF 1,200 a month to support regular classes.

1 Compute the financial impact on Zurich American School from discontinuing the after-school care programme.

2 List three qualitative factors that would influence your decision.

6.33 Sell or process further

An Exxon petrochemical factory produces two products, L and M, as a result of a particular joint process. Both products are sold to manufacturers as ingredients for assorted chemical products.

Product L sells at split off for €.25 per litre; M, for €.30 per litre. Data for April follow:

Joint processing cost	€1,600,000
Gallons produced and sold	
L	4,000,000
M	2,500,000

Suppose that in April the 2,500,000 litres of M could have been processed further into Super M at an additional cost of €165,000. The Super M output would be sold for €.36 per litre. Product L would be sold at split off in any event.

Should M have been processed further in April and sold as Super M? Show your computations.

6.34 Obsolete inventory

The ROCG bookstore bought more 'Buckeye Champs' calendars than it could sell. It was nearly June and 200 calendars remained in stock. The store paid €4.50 each for the calendars and normally sold them for €8.95. Since February they had been on sale for €6.00 and 2 weeks ago the price was dropped to €5.00. Still, few calendars were being sold. The bookstore manager thought it was no longer worthwhile using shelf space for the calendars.

The proprietor of Hurricane Collectibles offered to buy all 200 calendars for €100. He intended to sell them as novelty items.

The bookstore manager was not sure she wanted to sell for €.50 calendars that cost €4.50. The only alternative, however, was to scrap them because the publisher would not take them back.

1 Compute the difference in profit between accepting the €100 offer and scrapping the calendars.

2 Describe how the €4.50 × 200 = €900 paid for the calendars affects your decision.

6.35 Weak division

Lake Forest Electronics Company paid €7 million in cash 4 years ago to acquire a company that manufactures CD-ROM drives. This company has been operated as a division of Lake Forest and has lost €500,000 each year since its acquisition.

The minimum desired return for this division is that, when a new product is fully developed, it should return a net profit of €500,000 per year for the foreseeable future.

Recently, the IBM Corporation offered to purchase the division from Lake Forest for €5 million. The president of Lake Forest commented, 'I've got an investment of €9 million to recoup (€7 million plus losses of €500,000 for each of 4 years). I have finally got this situation turned around, so I oppose selling the division now.'

Prepare a response to the president's remarks. Indicate how to make this decision. Be as specific as possible.

6.36 Opportunity cost

Renee Behr is a psychiatrist who is in heavy demand. Even though she has raised her fees considerably during the past 5 years, Dr Behr still cannot accommodate all the patients who wish to see her.

Behr has conducted 6 hours of appointments a day, 6 days a week, for 48 weeks a year. Her fee averages €150 per hour.

Her variable costs are negligible and may be ignored for decision purposes. Ignore income taxes.

1 Behr is weary of working a 6-day week. She is considering taking every other Saturday off. What would be her annual income (a) if she worked every Saturday and (b) if she worked every other Saturday?
2 What would be her opportunity cost for the year of not working every other Saturday?
3 Assume that Dr Behr has definitely decided to take every other Saturday off. She loves to repair her sports car by doing the work herself. If she works on her car during half a Saturday when she otherwise would not see patients, what is her opportunity cost?

PROBLEMS

6.37 Hotel rooms and opportunity costs

The Marriott Corporation operates many hotels throughout the world. Suppose one of its Chicago hotels is facing difficult times because of the opening of several new competing hotels.

To accommodate its flight personnel, American Airlines has offered Marriott a contract for the coming year that provides a rate of €70 per night per room for a minimum of 50 rooms for 365 nights. This contract would assure Marriott of selling 50 rooms of space nightly, even if some of the rooms are vacant on some nights. Assume zero variable costs.

The Marriott manager has mixed feelings about the contract. On several peak nights during the year, the hotel could sell the same space for €150 per room.

1 Suppose the Marriott manager signs the contract. What is the opportunity cost of the 50 rooms on October 20, the night of a big convention of retailers when every nearby hotel room is occupied? What is the opportunity cost on December 28, when only 10 of these rooms would be expected to be rented at an average rate of €100?
2 If the year-round rate per room averaged €110, what percentage of occupancy of the 50 rooms in question would have to be rented to make Marriott indifferent about accepting the offer?

6.38 Extension of preceding problem

Assume the same facts as in the preceding problem. However, also assume that the variable costs per room, per day are €10.

1 Suppose the best estimate is a 62 per cent general occupancy rate for the 50 rooms at an average €110 room rate for the next year. Should Marriott accept the contract?
2 What percentage of occupancy of the 50 rooms in question would make Marriott indifferent about accepting the offer?

6.39 Make or buy

Lehr is a global manufacturer of highly engineered products that serve industrial, vehicle, construction, commercial, aerospace and semiconductor markets. Lehr's sales last year were €10.3 billion. It frequently subcontracts work to other manufacturers, depending on whether Lehr's facilities are fully occupied. Suppose Lehr is about to make some final decisions regarding the use of its manufacturing facilities for the coming year.

The following are the costs of making part EC113, a key component of an emissions control system:

	Total cost for 50,000 units	Cost per unit
Direct materials	€ 400,000	€ 8
Direct labour	250,000	5
Variable factory overhead	150,000	3
Fixed factory overhead	300,000	6
Total manufacturing costs	€1,100,000	€22

Another manufacturer has offered to sell the same part to Lehr for €20 each. The fixed overhead consists of depreciation, property taxes, insurance and supervisory salaries. All the fixed overhead would continue if Lehr bought the component except that the cost of €150,000 pertaining to some supervisory and custodial personnel could be avoided.

1 Assume that the capacity now used to make parts will become idle if the parts are purchased. Should Lehr buy or make the parts? Show computations.
2 Assume that the capacity now used to make parts will either (a) be rented to a nearby manufacturer for €75,000 for the year or (b) be used to make oil filters that will yield a profit contribution of €100,000. Should Lehr buy or make part EC113? Show your computations.

6.40 Relevant-cost analysis

Following are the unit costs of making and selling a single product at a normal level of 5,000 units per month and a current unit selling price of €90:

Manufacturing costs	
Direct materials	€35
Direct labour	12
Variable overhead	8
Fixed overhead (total for the year, €300,000)	5
Selling and administrative expenses	
Variable	15
Fixed (total for the year, €480,000)	8

Consider each requirement separately. Label all computations and present your solutions in a form that will be comprehensible to the company president.

1 This product is usually sold at a rate of 60,000 units per year. It is predicted that a rise in price to €98 will decrease volume by 10 per cent. How much may advertising be increased under this plan without having annual operating income fall below the current level?

2 The company has received a proposal from an outside supplier to make and ship this item directly to the company's customers as sales orders are forwarded. Variable selling and administrative costs would fall 40 per cent. If the supplier's proposal is accepted, the company will use its own plant to produce a new product. The new product would be sold through manufacturer's agents at a 10 per cent commission based on a selling price of €40 each. The cost characteristics of this product, based on predicted yearly normal volume, are shown below.

What is the maximum price per unit that the company afford to pay to the supplier for subcontracting production of the entire old product? Assume the following:

- Total fixed factory overhead and total fixed selling expenses will not change if the new product line is added.

	Per unit
Direct matterials	€ 6
Direct labour	12
Variable overhead	8
Fixed overhead	6
Manufacturing costs	€32
Selling and administrative expenses	
Variable (commission)	10% of selling price
Fixed	€ 2

- The supplier's proposal will not be considered unless the present annual net income can be maintained.
- Selling price of the old product will remain unchanged.
- All €300,000 of fixed manufacturing overhead will be assigned to the new product.

6.41 Hotel pricing and use of capacity

A growing firm in a large city has offered a 200-room Holiday Inn a 1-year contract to rent 40 rooms at reduced rates of €50 per room instead of the regular rate of €86 per room. The corporation will sign the contract for 365-day occupancy because its visiting manufacturing and marketing personnel are virtually certain to use all the space each night.

Each room occupied has a variable cost of €12 per night (for cleaning, laundry, lost linens and extra electricity).

The hotel manager expects an 85 per cent occupancy rate for the year so she is reluctant to sign the contract. If the contract is signed, the occupancy rate on the remaining 160 rooms will be 95 per cent.

1 Compute the total contribution margin for the year with and without the contract. Is the contract profitable to Holiday Inn?

2 Compute the lowest room rate that the hotel should accept on the contract so that the total contribution margin would be the same with or without the contract.

6.42 Analysis of unit costs

Home Appliances Company manufactures small appliances, such as electric can openers, toasters, food mixers and irons. The peak manufacturing season is at hand and the president is trying to decide whether to produce more of the company's standard line of can openers or its premium line that includes a built-in knife sharpener, a better finish and a higher-quality motor. The unit data follow:

	Product	
	Standard	**Premium**
Selling price	€29	€39
Direct material	€ 8	€13
Direct labour	2	1
Variable factory overhead	4	6
Fixed factory overhead	6	9
Total cost of goods sold	€20	€29
Gross profit per unit	€ 9	€10

The sales outlook is very encouraging. The plant could operate at full capacity by producing either product or both products. Both the standard and the premium products are processed through the same departments. Selling and administrative costs will not be affected by this decision so they may be ignored.

Many of the parts are produced on automatic machinery. The factory overhead is allocated to products by developing separate rates per machine-hour for variable and fixed overhead. For example, the total fixed overhead is divided by the total machine-hours to get a rate per hour. Thus, the amount of overhead allocated to products is dependent on the number of machine-hours used by the product. It takes 1 hour of machine time to produce one unit of the standard product.

Direct labour may not be proportionate with overhead because many workers operate two or more machines simultaneously.

Which product should be produced? If more than one should be produced, indicate the proportions of each. Show computations. Explain your answers briefly.

6.43 Use of available facilities

The Oahu Audio Company manufactures electronic subcomponents that can be sold as is or can be processed further into 'plug-in' assemblies for a variety of intricate electronic equipment. The entire output of subcomponents can be sold at a market price of KSh 2.20 per unit. The plug-in assemblies have been generating a sales price of KSh 5.70 for 3 years, but the price has recently fallen to KSh 5.30 on assorted orders.

Janet Okondo, the vice president of marketing, has analysed the markets and the costs. She thinks that production of plug-in assemblies should be dropped whenever the price falls below KSh 4.70 per unit. However, at the current price of KSh 5.30, the total available capacity should currently be devoted to producing plug-in assemblies. She has cited the data in Exhibit 6.7.

Direct-materials and direct-labour costs are variable. The total overhead is fixed; it is allocated to units produced by predicting the total overhead for the coming year and dividing this total by the total hours of capacity available.

The total hours of capacity available are 600,000. It takes 1 hour to make 60 subcomponents and 2 hours of additional processing and testing to make 60 plug-in assemblies.

1 If the price of plug-in assemblies for the coming year is to be KSh 5.30, should sales of subcomponents be dropped and all facilities devoted to the production of plug-in assemblies? Show your computations.
2 Prepare a report for the vice president of marketing to show the lowest possible price for plug-in assemblies that would be acceptable.

3 Suppose 40 per cent of the manufacturing overhead is variable with respect to processing and testing time. Repeat numbers 1 and 2. Do your answers change? If so, how?

		Subcomponents
Selling price, after deducting relevant selling costs		KSh 2.20
Direct materials	KSh 1.10	
Direct labour	.30	
Manufacturing overhead	.60	
Cost per unit		2.00
Operating profit		KSh .20
		Plug-in assemblies
Selling price, after deducting relevant selling costs		KSh 5.30
Transferred-in variable cost for subcomponents	KSh 1.40	
Additional direct materials	1.45	
Direct labour	.45	
Manufacturing overhead	1.20*	
Cost per unit		4.50
Operating profit		KSh .80

*For additional processing to make and test plug-in assemblies.

Exhibit 6.7 Oahu Audio Company product profitability data

6.44 Joint costs and incremental analysis

Jacque de Paris, a high-fashion women's dress manufacturer, is planning to market a new cocktail dress for the coming season. Jacque de Paris supplies retailers in Europe and the United States.

Four yards of material are required to lay out the dress pattern. Some material remains after cutting, which can be sold as remnants. The leftover material could also be used to manufacture a matching cape and handbag. However, if the leftover material is to be used for the cape and handbag, more care will be required in the cutting, which will increase the cutting costs.

The company expects to sell 1,250 dresses if no matching cape or handbag is available. Market research reveals that dress sales will be 20 per cent higher if a matching cape and handbag are available. The market research indicates that the cape and handbag will not be sold individually, but only as accessories with the dress. The various combinations of dresses, capes and handbags that are expected to be sold by retailers are as follows:

	Per cent of total
Complete sets of dress, cape and handbag	70
Dress and cape	6
Dress and handbag	15
Dress only	9
Total	100

The material used in the dress costs €80 a yard, or €320 for each dress. The cost of cutting the dress if the cape and handbag are not manufactured is estimated at €100 a dress and the resulting remnants can be sold for €28 for each dress cut out. If the cape and handbag are to be manufactured, the cutting costs will be increased by €30 per dress. There will be no salable remnants if the capes and handbags are manufactured in the quantities estimated. The selling prices and the costs to complete the three items once they are cut are as follows:

	Selling price per unit	Unit cost to complete (excludes cost of material and cutting operation)
Dress	€1,050	€400
Cape	140	100
Handbag	50	30

1 Calculate the incremental profit or loss to Jacque de Paris from manufacturing the capes and handbags in conjunction with the dresses.
2 Identify any non-quantitative factors that could influence the company's management in its decision to manufacture the capes and handbags that match the dress.

6.45 Relevant cost

Debraceny Company's unit costs of manufacturing and selling a given item at the planned activity level of 10,000 units per month are:

Manufacturing costs	
Direct materials	€4.20
Direct labour	.60
Variable overhead	.90
Fixed overhead	.80
Selling expenses	
Variable	3.20
Fixed	1.15

Ignore income taxes in all requirements. These four parts have no connection with each other.

1 Compute the planned annual operating income at a selling price of €13 per unit.
2 Compute the expected annual operating income if the volume can be increased by 20 per cent when the selling price is reduced to €12. Assume that the implied cost behaviour patterns are correct.
3 The company desires to seek an order for 5,000 units from a foreign customer. The variable selling expenses for the order will be 40 per cent less than usual, but the fixed costs for obtaining the order will be €6,000. Domestic sales will not be affected. Compute the minimum break-even price per unit to be considered.
4 The company has an inventory of 3,000 units of this item left over from last year's model. These must be sold through regular channels at reduced prices. The inventory will be valueless unless sold this way. What unit cost is relevant for establishing the minimum selling price of these 3,000 units?

6.46 New machine

A new €300,000 machine is expected to have a 5-year life and a terminal value of zero. It can produce 40,000 units a year at a variable cost of €4 per unit. The variable cost is €6.50 per unit with an old machine, which has a book value of €100,000. It is being depreciated on a straight-line basis at €20,000 per year. It too is expected to have a terminal value of zero. Its current disposal value is also zero because it is highly specialised equipment.

The salesperson of the new machine prepared the following comparison:

	New machine	Old machine
Units	40,000	40,000
Variable costs	€160,000	€260,000
Straight-line depreciation	60,000	20,000
Total cost	€220,000	€280,000
Unit cost	€ 5.50	€ 7.00

He said, 'The new machine is obviously a worthwhile acquisition. You will save €1.50 for every unit you produce.'

1 Do you agree with the salesperson's analysis? If not, how would you change it? Be specific. Ignore taxes.
2 Prepare an analysis of total and unit differential costs if the annual volume is 20,000 units.
3 At what annual volume would both the old and new machines have the same total relevant costs?

6.47 Book value of old equipment

Consider the following data:

	Old equipment	Proposed new equipment
Original cost	€24,000	€12,000
Useful life in years	8	3
Current age in years	5	0
Useful life remaining in years	3	3
Accumulated depreciation	€15,000	0
Book value	9,000	*
Disposal value (in cash) now	3,000	*
Annual cash operating costs		
(maintenance, power, repairs, lubricants, etc.)	€11,000	€ 6,000

*Not acquired yet.

1 Prepare a cost comparison of all relevant items for the next 3 years together. Ignore taxes.
2 Prepare a cost comparison that includes both relevant and irrelevant items. (See Exhibit 6.5, p. 249.)
3 Prepare a comparative statement of the total charges against revenue for the first year. Would the manager be inclined to buy the new equipment? Explain.

6.48 Review of relevant costs

Since the early 1960s, Neil Simon has been one of Broadway's most successful playwrights. The *New York Times* reported that Neil Simon planned to open his play, *London Suite*, off Broadway. Why? For financial reasons. Producer Emanuel Azenberg predicted the following costs before the play even opened:

	On Broadway	Off Broadway
Sets, costumes, lights	€ 357,000	€ 87,000
Loading in (building set, etc.)	175,000	8,000
Rehearsal salaries	102,000	63,000
Director and designer fees	126,000	61,000
Advertising	300,000	121,000
Administration	235,000	100,000
Total	€1,295,000	€440,000

Broadway ticket prices average €60 and theatres can seat about 1,000 persons per show. Off-Broadway prices average only €40 and the theatres seat only 500. Normally, plays run eight times a week, both on and off Broadway. Weekly operating expenses off Broadway average €102,000; they average an extra €150,000 on Broadway for a weekly total of €252,000.

1 Suppose 400 persons attended each show, whether on or off Broadway. Compare the weekly financial results from a Broadway production to one produced off Broadway.
2 Suppose attendance averaged 75 per cent of capacity, whether on or off Broadway. Compare the weekly financial results from a Broadway production to one produced off Broadway.
3 Compute the attendance per show required just to cover weekly expenses (a) on Broadway and (b) off Broadway.
4 Suppose average attendance on Broadway was 600 per show and off Broadway was 400. Compute the total net profit for a 26-week run (a) on Broadway and (b) off Broadway. Be sure to include the pre-opening costs.
5 Repeat requirement 4 for a 100-week run.
6 Using attendance figures from numbers 4 and 5, compute (a) the number of weeks a Broadway production must run before it breaks even and (b) the number of weeks an off-Broadway production must run before it breaks even.
7 Using attendance figures from numbers 4 and 5, determine how long a play must run before the profit from a Broadway production exceeds that from an off-Broadway production.
8 If you were Neil Simon, would you prefer *London Suite* to play on Broadway or off Broadway? Explain.

6.49 Make or buy

Tempor, SA, estimates it will produce 30,000 units of a part that goes into its final product. It currently produces this part internally, but is considering outsourcing this activity. Current internal capacity permits for a maximum of 60,000 units of the part. The production manager has prepared the following information concerning the internal manufacture of 60,000 units of the part:

	Per unit
Direct materials	€ 3.00
Direct labour	4.00
Variable overhead	5.00
Fixed overhead	6.00
Total cost	€18.00

The fixed overhead of €6 per unit includes a €1.50 per unit allocation for salary paid to a supervisor to oversee production of the part. The fixed costs would not be reduced by outsourcing, except the supervisor would be terminated. Assume that if Tempor outsources, its purchase price from the outsourcer is €12 per unit.

1 Should Tempor outsource?
2 Assume Tempor has received a special order for 10,000 units of the part from Adigen, SA. Adigen will pay Tempor €23 per part, but will take the parts only if they have been manufactured by Tempor. Thus, Adigen will engage in the special order only if Tempor does not outsource any of its production. Should Tempor accept the special order?

6.50 Irrelevance of past costs at Starbucks

Starbucks purchases and roasts high-quality, whole-bean coffees, its hallmark and sells them along with other coffee-related products primarily through its company-operated retail stores.

Suppose that the quality-control manager at Starbucks in Paris discovered a 1,000-kilo batch of roasted beans that did not meet the company's quality standards. Company policy would not allow such beans to be sold with the Starbucks name on them. However, they could be reprocessed, at which time they could be sold by Starbucks' retail stores, or they could be sold as is on the wholesale coffee bean market.

Assume that the beans were initially purchased for €3,000, and the total cost of roasting the batch was €2,500, including €500 of variable costs and €2,000 of fixed costs (primarily depreciation on the equipment).

The wholesale price at which Starbucks could sell the beans was €3.65 per kilo. Purchasers would pay the shipping costs from the Starbucks plant to their individual warehouses.

If the beans were reprocessed, the processing cost would be €800 because the beans would not require as much processing as new beans. All €800 would be additional costs, that is, costs that would not be incurred without the reprocessing. The beans would be sold to the retail stores for €5.00 per kilo, and Starbucks would have to pay an average of €.20 per kilo to ship the beans to the stores.

1 Should Starbucks sell the beans on the market as is for €3.65 per kilo, or should the company reprocess the beans and sell them through its own retail stores? Why?
2 Compute the amount of extra profit Starbucks earns from the alternative you selected in number 1 compared to what it would earn from the other alternative.
3 What cost numbers in the problem were irrelevant to your analysis? Explain why they were irrelevant.

CASES

6.51 Make or buy

The Minnetonka Company, which produces and sells to wholesalers a highly successful line of water skis, has decided to diversify to stabilise sales throughout the year. The company is considering the production of cross-country skis.

After considerable research, a cross-country ski line has been developed. Because of the conservative nature of the company management, however, Minnetonka's president has decided to introduce only one type of the new skis for this coming winter. If the product is a success, further expansion in future years will be initiated.

The ski selected is a mass-market ski with a special binding. It will be sold to wholesalers for €80 per pair. Because of available capacity, no additional fixed charges will be incurred to produce the skis. A €125,000 fixed charge will be absorbed by the skis, however, to allocate a fair share of the company's present fixed costs to the new product.

Using the estimated sales and production of 10,000 pairs of skis as the expected volume, the accounting department has developed the following costs per pair of skis and bindings:

Direct labour	€35
Direct materials	30
Total overhead	15
Total cost	€80

Minnetonka has approached a subcontractor to discuss the possibility of purchasing the bindings. The purchase price of the bindings from the subcontractor would be €5.25 per binding or €10.50 per pair. If the Minnetonka Company accepts the purchase proposal, it is predicted that direct-labour and variable-overhead costs would be reduced by 10 per cent and direct-materials costs would be reduced by 20 per cent.

1 Should the Minnetonka Company make or buy the bindings? Show calculations to support your answer.
2 What would be the maximum purchase price acceptable to the Minnetonka Company for the bindings? Support your answer with an appropriate explanation.
3 Instead of sales of 10,000 pairs of skis, revised estimates show sales volume at 12,500 pairs. At this new volume, additional equipment, at an annual rental of €10,000, must be acquired to manufacture the bindings. This incremental cost would be the only additional fixed cost required, even if sales increased to 30,000 pairs. (The 30,000 level is the goal for the third year of production.) Under these circumstances, should the Minnetonka Company make or buy the bindings? Show calculations to support your answer.
4 The company has the option of making and buying at the same time. What would be your answer to number 3 if this alternative were considered? Show calculations to support your answer.
5 What nonquantifiable factors should the Minnetonka Company consider in determining whether they should make or buy the bindings?

6.52 Make or buy

The Rohr Company's old equipment for making subassemblies is worn out. The company is considering two courses of action: (a) completely replacing the old equipment with new equipment or (b) buying subassemblies from a reliable outside supplier, who has quoted a unit price of €1 on a 7-year contract for a minimum of 50,000 units per year.

Production was 60,000 units in each of the past 2 years. Future needs for the next 7 years are not expected to fluctuate beyond 50,000 to 70,000 units per year. Cost records for the past 2 years reveal the following unit costs of manufacturing the subassembly:

Direct materials	€ .30
Direct labour	.35
Variable overhead	.10
Fixed overhead (including €.10 depreciation and €.10 for direct departmental fixed overhead)	.25
	€1.00

The new equipment will cost €188,000 cash, will last 7 years and will have a disposal value of €20,000. The current disposal value of the old equipment is €10,000.

The sales representative for the new equipment has summarised her position as follows: the increase in machine speeds will reduce direct labour and variable overhead by

€.35 per unit. Consider last year's experience of one of your major competitors with identical equipment. It produced 100,000 units under operating conditions very comparable to yours and showed the following unit costs.

Direct materials	€.30
Direct labour	.05
Variable overhead	.05
Fixed overhead, including depreciation of €.24	.40
Total	€.80

For purposes of this case, assume that any idle facilities cannot be put to alternative use. Also assume that €.05 of the old Rohr unit cost is allocated fixed overhead that will be unaffected by the decision.

1 The president asks you to compare the alternatives on a total-annual-cost basis and on a per-unit basis for annual needs of 60,000 units. Which alternative seems more attractive?
2 Would your answer to number 1 change if the needs were 50,000 units? 70,000 units? At what volume level would Rohr be indifferent between making and buying subassemblies? Show your computations.
3 What factors, other than the preceding ones, should the accountant bring to the attention of management to assist them in making their decision? Include the considerations that might be applied to the outside supplier.

6.53 Make or buy

Levoy Company, estimates it will produce 25,000 units of an electronic sensor part that goes into one of its final products, called a Fluctotron. It currently produces this sensor internally but is considering outsourcing this activity. Current internal capacity permits the production of a maximum of 40,000 sensors. The production manager has prepared the following information concerning the internal manufacture of 40,000 sensors:

	Per sensor
Direct materials	€15.00
Direct labour	8.00
Variable overhead	10.00
Fixed overhead	11.00
Total cost	€44.00

The fixed overhead of €11 per unit includes a €2 per unit allocation for salary paid to a supervisor to oversee production of sensors. The fixed costs would not be reduced by outsourcing, except the supervisor would be fired (the company would terminate his contract). Assume that if Levoy outsources, its purchase price from the outsourcer is €38 per unit.

1 Should Levoy outsource? Why or why not?
2 Assume that if Levoy outsourced, it would create sufficient excess capacity such that it would retain the supervisor and have him oversee production of a new optical reading product, called a Scanmeister. If each Scanmeister generates a contribution margin of €15 and the company produces 10,000 Scanmeisters, what is the maximum price Levoy would accept for outsourcing the sensors?

CASE STUDY

Hereford Steak Houses

Thomas Ahrens, United Arab Emirates University and Christopher Chapman, Imperial College London

I'd love to know where I am as an area manager. I don't know what to do with food margin. Shall I say to my restaurant managers, well done? Thank you? You're fired?

Hereford Steak Houses operated a chain of more than 200 wholly owned, full-service restaurants across the UK. Over the past 10 years the division had achieved substantial growth in revenues and earnings through the addition of new restaurants. More recently, however, with increasing numbers of new entrants to the UK eating-out market and the growing saturation of Hereford Steak Houses' own outlets, senior managers were increasingly turning their attention to internal financial controls as a means to sustain earnings growth.

National branding and marketing for the chain was managed centrally by Hereford Steak Houses' head office. Most significant to this was the nationwide menu that defined the food specifications, cost and price of all dishes for sale in all outlets. Menus were designed to deliver a target food gross profit margin that was agreed between the boards of Hereford Steak Houses and the corporate leisure group of which it was part and applied to all of Hereford Steak Houses' outlets. While food cost was a primary element of restaurant controllable costs, as the above quotation from an area manager indicates, there was a lack of agreement on how the food margin reports should be used to evaluate a restaurant manager. Restaurant managers emphasised that they wanted leeway to meet the demand of their local clientele.

The gross profit margin was defined as sales minus cost of food used and was generally referred to as the 'food margin'. For each new menu a selection of dishes was iteratively developed in order to achieve the target food margin (in terms of percentage and cash). This was a complicated process since the menu needed to contain dishes at a range of price points to appeal to different customers. Depending on the selling price, different levels of margin were realistic. For example, a very high margin on high-cost dishes resulted in unrealistic sales prices, but could be sustainable on low-cost dishes. High-volume dishes offered scope for the centralised purchasing department on negotiate substantial price discounts. Hereford Steak Houses' position as a buyer of large quantities of food also allowed them to enforce strict quality standards for raw materials.

The process of developing individual restaurant budgets started with an estimation of the achievable level of sales growth based on expected number of dishes and prices from the central menu. Budgets were painstakingly built up. They drew on the database of standard ingredient costs, which included a standard allowance for wastage (Table 1). Then dish specifications, prices and expected sales mix were decided Table 2). For weekly management reporting this data was used to generate a target food margin based on each restaurant's actual dish-mix that could be compared with the actual cost of food used (Table 3). The actual cost of food was calculated by adding the opening inventory to deliveries received minus closing inventory (see Table 4).

In order to take advantage of centralised purchasing and also to ensure tight control over quality standards, restaurants sourced all their food purchases through the centralised supply chain. Especially for seasonal produce it was normal for Hereford Steak Houses to agree price bands with their food suppliers. Fluctuations in the price of food purchased were accounted for by the central purchasing department. The weekly budget reports for the restaurants were based on the standard costs that had been defined during the design of the menu.

Source: Thomas Ahrens, United Arab Emirates University and Christopher Chapman, Imperial College London.

Table 1 Menu design ingredients database report

	Standard wastage percentage: 1%			
Ingredient no.	Description	Input cost	Wastage	Standard cost
100	1 pat butter	0.05	0.001	0.05
101	1 standard garnish	0.20	0.002	0.20
102	1 sachet ketchup	0.05	0.001	0.05
151	1 bread roll	0.15	0.002	0.15
297	1 portion of fries	0.60	0.006	0.61
314	1 carton vegetable soup	2.40	0.024	2.42
601	9 oz rump steak	6.00	0.060	6.06
907	6 oz frozen cod fillet	3.60	0.036	3.64
915	1 fish finger	0.25	0.003	0.25

Table 2 Dish specification and costing report @ standard cost

Dish no.	Description	% sales	Ingredients	Cost (£)	Sales price (£)	Gross profit margin (%)	(£)
1	Soup	10.0%					
			1 pat butter	0.05			
			1 bread roll	0.15			
			1 carton vege-table soup	2.42			
			Total	£2.63	£5.50	52.3%	£2.87
11	Steak and chips	45.0%					
			1 standard garnish	0.20			
			1 portion of fries	0.61			
			9 oz rump steak	6.06			
			Total	£6.87	£11.95	42.5%	£5.08
12	Fish and chips	25.0%					
			1 standard garnish	0.20			
			1 portion of fries	0.61			
			6 oz frozen cod fillet	3.64			
			Total	£4.44	£8.50	47.7%	£4.06
21	Fish fingers	20.0%					
			1 sachet ketchup	0.05			
			1 portion of fries	0.61			
			3 fish fingers	0.75			
			Total	£1.41	£4.95	71.4%	£3.54

Table 3 Restaurant no. 219 budget report – week 48

	Budget	Actual
Dishes	1 500	1 600
Revenue	13 563.75	13 116.00
Cost	7120.50	6 805.50
Gross profit margin (£)	6433.25	6 310.50
Gross profit margin (%)	47.5%	48.1%

	Actual dishes sold
Soup	240
Steak and chips	480
Fish and chips	480
Fish fingers	400

Table 4 Restaurant no. 219 stock-keeping report – week 48

Ingredient no.	Description	Opening stock count	Purchases during week	Closing stock count
100	1 pat butter	200	120	30
101	1 standard garnish	200	1300	300
102	1 sachet ketchup	300	400	300
151	1 bread roll	300	100	60
297	1 portion of fries	2000	900	1840
314	1 carton vegetable soup	100	180	40
601	9 oz rump steak	300	400	160
907	6 oz frozen cod fillet	250	300	70
915	1 fish finger	200	1200	200

Questions

1 Calculate the following variances for restaurant no. 219: static budget variance, sales volume variance, sales mix variance, sales quantity variance and the flexible budget variance.
2 Calculate usage variances for all ingredients for restaurant no. 219.
3 If you were the manager of restaurant no. 219, what would you do?
4 Recently the central purchasing department managed to secure a 5 per cent reduction on the input cost for steaks and a 15 per cent reduction in the input costs of portions of fries compared with those shown in Table 1. Calculate the resulting price variances for restaurant no. 219 for week 48.

Introduction to budgets and preparing the master budget

Learning objectives

When you have finished studying this chapter, you should be able to:

1 Explain how budgets facilitate planning and coordination.

2 Anticipate possible human relations problems caused by budgets.

3 Explain potentially dysfunctional incentives in the budget process.

4 Explain the difficulties of sales forecasting.

5 Explain the major features and advantages of a master budget.

6 Follow the principal steps in preparing a master budget.

7 Prepare the operating budget and the supporting schedules.

8 Prepare the financial budget.

9 Use a spreadsheet to develop a budget (Appendix 7).

A Ritz-Carlton hotel projects an image of quality. High quality is expensive, so during the master budgeting process Ritz-Carlton managers must assess the planned expenditures for quality-enhancing features versus the added revenues these features bring.

Ritz-Carlton

If you have ever travelled, you know that there is a big difference between staying in a cheap hotel and staying in a five-star, world-class hotel. The cheap hotel takes care of your basic needs, but the five-star hotel surrounds you in comfort and luxury, catering to your every whim. No one understands the difference better than the managers of the Ritz-Carlton chain of hotels. After all, the word *ritzy*, which means glamorous and luxurious, is actually derived from the name of the Ritz Hotel. Thanks to fierce competition in the industry, though, Ritz-Carlton managers have their share of challenges in maintaining standards that keep their hotels successful.

What does it take to run a world-class hotel successfully? Good location, exquisite food, luxury, personalised service and quality are all essential ingredients. But you might be surprised to learn that the budgeting process is also a key to success. According to Ralph Vick, former general manager of the Phoenix Ritz-Carlton, 'Budgets are crucial to the ultimate financial success of our hotels.' Why are budgets so important? Mainly because they serve as a road map toward achieving goals. Budgets are a manager's tool to understand, plan and control operations, and Ritz-Carlton wants to give its managers the best tools possible. As a result, the company takes the budgeting process very seriously.

At the Ritz-Carlton hotels, all employees, from the hotel manager, to the Chief Accountant, to the newest housekeeper, are involved in the budgeting process. Working in teams, managers set budget targets for the expenses they can control. These target figures help not only in planning, but also in controlling and evaluating employee performance. Managers compare actual results with previously budgeted target figures, and they evaluate performance based on the differences. In addition to financial reports, Ritz-Carlton managers also use nonfinancial measures, such as quality and customer satisfaction, to evaluate and reward employees.

Another famous hotel is The Savoy, in London, which opened over 120 years ago. It was the first luxury hotel in Britain, introducing electric lights, electric lifts and bathrooms inside most of the rooms. In 2007, the hotel closed for extensive renovations and re-opened in late 2010. The cost of renovations were originally budgeted at £100 million, but following structural and systems problems the restoration costs grew to £220 million.

Planning is the key to good management. This statement is certainly true for the Ritz-Carlton and The Savoy, and it is also true for other types of organisations – small, family-owned companies, large corporations, government agencies and nonprofit organisations. All organisations need budgets to make the best and most profitable use of their resources.

Budgeting can cover such diverse issues as how much time to spend inspecting a product and how much money the company will allot to research and development in the coming year. Naturally, budgets can be revised as operations and changed circumstances dictate. In this chapter, we look at the benefits (and costs) of budgets and illustrate the construction of a comprehensive, detailed budget. ■

Budgets and the organisation

Many people associate the word *budget* primarily with limitations on spending. For example, management often gives individual units within an organisation a spending budget and then expects them to maintain expenditures within the limits prescribed by the budget. However, well-managed organisations use budgets for more than simple limits on spending. Budgets formalise the planning process, allowing managers to take steps to avoid problems or take advantage of opportunities. Budgets provide a comprehensive financial overview that helps coordinate financial and operational activities. Budgets provide an important two-way communication channel. They convey information about strategies and expectations downward from the upper levels of the organisation and communicate information about capabilities and opportunities upward from the lower levels of the organisation. Managers also use budgets for performance evaluation. Budgets act as a benchmark – a measure of expected or desired performance – against which they compare actual performance.

Budgeting moves planning to the forefront of the manager's mind. There are numerous examples of seemingly healthy businesses that failed because managers did not bother to construct budgets that would have identified problems in advance or they failed to monitor and adjust budgets to changing conditions. While there will always be debate about the costs and benefits of budgeting, as indicated in the 'Business first' box on p. 281, the vast majority of managers continue to use budgeting as an effective cost-management tool. One study of more than 150 organisations listed budgeting as the most frequently used cost-management tool.

Advantages of budgets

Objective 1
Explain how budgets facilitate planning and coordination.

In Chapter 1, we defined a budget as a quantitative expression of a plan of action. Sometimes plans are informal, perhaps even unwritten, and informal plans sometimes work in a small organisation. However, as an organisation grows, seat-of-the-pants planning is not enough. Budgets impose the formal structure – a budgetary system – that is needed for all but the smallest organisations.

Budgeting is the process of formulating an organisation's plans. Four major benefits of effective budgeting are as follows:

1 Budgeting compels managers to think ahead by formalising their responsibilities for planning.

2 Budgeting provides an opportunity for managers to reevaluate existing activities and evaluate possible new activities.

3 Budgeting aids managers in communicating objectives and coordinating actions across the organisation.

4 Budgeting provides benchmarks to evaluate subsequent performance.

Let's look more closely at each of these benefits.

Formalisation of planning

Budgeting forces managers to devote time to planning. On a day-to-day basis, managers often move from extinguishing one business brush fire to another, leaving no time for thinking beyond the next day's problems. Planning takes a backseat to, or is actually obliterated by, daily pressures.

To prepare a budget, a manager should set goals and objectives and establish policies to aid their achievement. The objectives are the destination points, and budgets are the road maps guiding us to those destinations. In the absence of goals and objectives, results are difficult to interpret, managers do not foresee problems, and company operations lack direction. The budgeting process formalises the need to anticipate and prepare for changing conditions.

Evaluation of activities

Budgeting typically uses the current activities of the organisation as a starting point for planning, but how managers use this starting point varies widely. At one extreme, in some organisations the budget process automatically assumes that activities for the new budget period will be the same as the activities for the previous period. At the other extreme, some organisations use a form of **zero-base budget**, which starts with the assumption that current activities will not automatically be continued. The term zero-base comes from the fundamental assumption that the budget for every activity starts at zero, and managers must justify all activities (including continuation of existing activities) in each new budget.

In practice, budgeting for most organisations falls somewhere between these two extremes. An effective budget process will encourage managers to think carefully about whether to continue current activities and methods, whether there are opportunities to modify activities, and whether to add new activities to help the organisation better achieve its goals in response to changing conditions. Used in this way, budgeting encourages managers to review whether a particular plan allocates resources optimally among the firm's various activities.

Communication and coordination

The most effective budget processes facilitate communication both from the top down and from the bottom up. Top management communicates the broad goals and objectives of the organisation in its budgetary directives. Lower-level managers and employees contribute their own ideas and provide feedback on the goals and objectives. The result is two-way communication about opportunities and challenges that lie ahead.

BUSINESS FIRST
Budgeting: value driver or value buster?

There is an ongoing debate about the costs and benefits of budgeting, focusing on four issues: (1) The budgeting process is time-consuming and expensive; (2) budgets are not accurate because marketplace change is frequent and unpredictable; (3) evaluating performance against a budget causes managers to bias their budgets, resulting in inaccurate planning; and (4) budget targets create incentives for individuals to take actions to meet targets even when the actions make the firm as a whole worse off.

Some studies suggest that the annual budgeting process can take up to 30 per cent of management's time. For example, estimates place Ford Motor Company's cost of budgeting at €1.2 billion a year. Companies can justify such large budgeting costs only when there are corresponding large benefits. Companies that fail to incorporate budgeting in their planning activities and those that react to changing economic conditions by ignoring the budget rather than learning and then adapting the budget will find it hard to justify large budgeting costs.

Skeptical managers sometimes claim, 'I face too many uncertainties and complications to make budgeting worthwhile for me.' While it is true that budgeting is more difficult in uncertain or complicated environments, it is also true that the potential benefits are largest in these environments. When conditions are changing rapidly, a budget provides a framework for systematic response rather than chaotic reaction.

When managers anticipate that budget information will be used to set targets used in their subsequent performance evaluations, they may provide budget information that is biased to make it easier to meet the targets. Biases severely limit the usefulness of budget

information for planning and coordination. Moreover, widespread understanding and acceptance of built-in biases can create a pernicious 'culture of lying' within the organisation.

When managers realise that meeting budget targets affects their rewards, either explicitly through bonus plans or implicitly through promotion and recognition, they have incentives to take actions to meet the targets. This can be a positive motivation, but it can also lead to unethical behaviour, such as 'cooking the books' or putting pressure on employees to meet targets using whatever means possible.

Most companies that have experienced problems with their budgeting process are not abandoning traditional budgeting but instead are modifying their approach to budgeting. For example, some companies now separate planning budgets from control budgets, comparing actual performance to benchmarks based on actual performance of peers and best-in-class operations rather than to budgets. Further, most managers still agree that budgeting, when correctly used, has significant value to management. More than 92 per cent of the companies in a recent survey use budgets, and they rank budgeting among their top three cost-management tools.

Sources: Adapted from R. Banham, 'Better budgets', *Journal of Accountancy*, February 2000, pp. 37–40; J. Hope and R. Fraser, 'Who needs budgets?' *Harvard Business Review*, February 2003, pp. 108–115; T. Hatch and W. Stratton, 'Scorecarding in North America: who is doing what?' Paper presented at the CAM-I/CMS 3rd quarter meeting, Portland, Oregon, 10 September 2002; M. Jensen, 'Corporate budgeting is broken, let's fix it,' *Harvard Business Review*, November 2001, pp. 94–101; M. Jensen, 'Paying people to lie: the truth about the budgeting process', *European Financial Management*, Vol. 9 No. 3, (2003), pp. 379–406.

Budgets also help managers coordinate activities across the organisation. For example, a budget allows purchasing personnel to integrate their plans with production requirements, while production managers use the sales budget and delivery schedule to help them anticipate and plan for the employees and physical facilities they will need. Similarly, financial officers use the sales budget, purchasing requirements, and other planned expenditures to anticipate the company's need for cash. Thus, budgeting forces managers to visualise and quantify the relationship of their department's activities to those of other departments and the company as a whole.

Performance evaluation

Budgeted performance goals generally provide a better basis for evaluating actual results than would a simple comparison with past performance. The news that a company had sales of €100 million this year, as compared with €80 million the previous year, may or may not indicate that company objectives have been met – perhaps the sales goal for this year was €110 million. The major drawback of relying only on historical results for judging current performance is that inefficiencies may be concealed in past performance. Changes in economic conditions, technology, personnel, competition and other factors also limit the usefulness of comparisons with the past. And for start-up companies and firms with new products or services, there is no prior performance to compare against current results.

MAKING MANAGERIAL DECISIONS

Consider L3C Company, which provides a range of integrated communications services. The company has had losses for a number of years, which it attributes to a difficult competitive environment. The 20X8 annual report states 'We believe that . . . these factors created an unsustainable level of competition in the market. We believe that this was evidenced by both the number of competitors vying for similar business and by the amount of inventory or capacity each brought to the market for many services. The result of these actions was an oversupply of capacity and an intensely competitive environment.' The net loss has steadily increased from €458 million in 20X4 to €638 million in 20X5 to €744 million in 20X6 to €1,114 million in 20X7.

The company's actual loss for 20X8 was €290 million. Suppose the company budgeted to break even for 20X8. Evaluate operating performance for 20X8.

Answer

L3C's performance in 20X8 is substantially better than would be projected by looking at past results and the trend of steadily increasing losses over the past 4 years. However, if the company budgeted for break even in 20X8, then performance is much worse than budgeted. This situation illustrates that comparisons to past results can provide a very different conclusion than comparisons to the budget.

■ Potential problems in implementing budgets

In this section, we discuss three problems that can limit, in some cases severely, the advantages of budgeting:

1 Low levels of participation in the budget process and lack of acceptance of responsibility for the final budget.

2 Incentives to lie and cheat in the budget process.

3 Difficulties in obtaining accurate sales forecasts.

Budget participation and acceptance of the budget

Objective 2
Anticipate possible human relations problems caused by budgets.

The advantages of budgeting are fully realised only when employees throughout the organisation fully accept and take responsibility for the final budget. The main factors affecting budget acceptance are the perceived attitude of top management, the level of participation in the budget process and the degree of alignment between the budget and other performance goals.

The attitude of top management will heavily influence lower-level managers' and employees' attitudes toward budgets. If top management does not use budgets effectively in controlling operations and adapting to change, others in the organisation may come to view budgeting as irrelevant. Even with the support of top management, however, budgets – and the managers who implement them – can run into opposition.

Lower-level managers sometimes have negative attitudes toward budgets because they believe the primary purpose of the budget is to limit spending. These negative attitudes are reinforced when companies evaluate managerial performance by comparing actual expenditures against amounts budgeted without substantive input from the managers. Ensuring that managers at all levels participate in setting budgets is one way to reduce negative attitudes and improve the quality of planning decisions. Budgets created with the active participation of all affected employees – called **participative budgeting** – are generally more effective than budgets imposed on subordinates. For example, Ritz-Carlton's budgeting system involves all hotel employees and is thus a participative system. Employee 'buy-in' to the budget is so important at Ritz-Carlton that self-directed employee teams at all levels of the company have the authority to change operations based on budgets as they see fit.

Misalignment between the performance goals stressed in budgets versus the performance measures the company uses to reward employees and managers can also limit the advantages of budgeting. For example, suppose a company rewards managers based on actual profit compared to budgeted profit and also on quality (defect rate) and timely delivery to customers (per cent on time). Increased quality and more timely deliveries typically require higher costs so the message conveyed by the budget system (minimise cost) may be misaligned with the incentives provided by the compensation system (maximise quality and timely delivery). Companies can manage the apparent misalignment by clearly specifying and communicating the tradeoff between costs and quality measures. This is particularly important for performance goals where the short-term impact on current performance relative to budget is negative but the long-term impact due to improved customer satisfaction is positive. We explore these issues in more detail in Chapter 9.

There is often too much concern with the mechanics of budgets and too little attention paid to the fact that the effectiveness of any budgeting system depends directly on whether the affected managers and employees understand and accept the budget. Management should seek to create an environment where there is a true two-way flow of information in the budget process where lower level managers and employees perceive that their input has a real effect on budget outcomes. Top management must emphasise the importance of budgets in planning and communication and demonstrate how budgets can help each manager and employee achieve better results. Only then will the budgets become a positive aid in motivating employees at all levels to work toward goals, set objectives, measure results accurately and direct attention to the areas that need investigation.

Incentives to lie and cheat

Objective 3
Explain potentially dysfunctional incentives in the budget process.

Effective budgets provide targets for managers and motivate them to achieve the organisation's objectives. However, misuse of budgets can lead to undesirable incentives – incentives to lie and cheat. Not only do such incentives lead managers to make poor decisions, they undercut attempts to maintain high ethical standards in the organisation.

Let's first consider lying. Lying can arise if the budget process creates incentives for managers to bias the information that goes into their budgets. What might cause managers to create biased budgets – essentially to lie about their plans? Managers may want to increase the resources allocated to their department – resources such as space, equipment and personnel – and larger budgets may justify such allocations. Why do managers want more resources? Day-to-day managing is easier when the department has more resources to achieve its output targets. Further, it is common for managers of larger units with more resources to receive higher pay, higher status and greater prospects for promotion. Recognising the incentives for bias allows organisations to implement budgets in a way that minimises bias. For example, when employees understand, accept and participate in the budget process, they are less likely to introduce biased information. Also, decision makers can be aware of expected bias when they make decisions based on budget information.

Additional lying incentives arise when organisations use budgets as a target for performance evaluations. This may prompt managers to create **budgetary slack** or **budget padding** – that is, managers may overstate their budgeted costs or understate their budgeted revenues to create a budget target that is easier to achieve. Budgetary slack also helps buffer managers from budget cuts imposed by higher-level management and provides protection

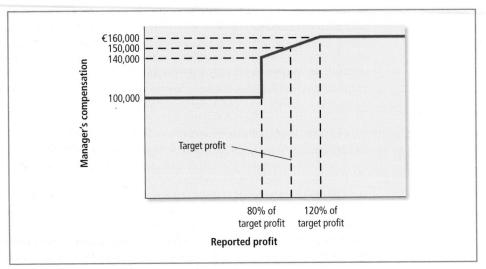

Exhibit 7.1 Bonus payments tied to profit levels

against cost increases or revenue shortfalls due to unforeseen events. But these incentives can lead to the following deleterious cycle: lower-level managers bias budgets to create budgetary slack, so upper-level managers attempt to correct for this bias in their inputs to the budget process. Lower-level managers, recognising that upper-level managers are making this correction, then incorporate additional bias to compensate. Upper-level managers then introduce larger corrections to compensate for the increased bias and the cycle of increasing distortion continues. This cycle of increasing bias and increasing bias corrections can cause the budget process to spiral out of control as inputs from both upper-level and lower-level managers become increasingly meaningless.

Now let's add one more complication – managerial bonuses based on making budget. Suppose a manager with a €100,000 annual salary will receive a bonus ranging from 80 per cent to 120 per cent of a target bonus of €50,000 if her division achieves between 80 per cent and 120 per cent of its budgeted profit target, as shown in Exhibit 7.1. In this example, representative of bonus plans commonly encountered in practice, there is a minimum level of division profit below which no bonus is paid (the bonus drops from a €40,000 bonus at 80 per cent of budgeted profit to zero bonus at any profit level below 80 per cent of budgeted profit) and a maximum level of division profit above which the maximum bonus is capped (above 120 per cent of budgeted profit, the bonus is capped at €60,000).

We should first recognise that within the relevant range of 80–120 per cent of profits this system creates appropriate incentives to work harder, more efficiently and more effectively to achieve desired results. But suppose, despite a manager's best efforts, it appears that reported profit will fall below 80 per cent of the target profit in Exhibit 7.1. What inappropriate incentives does this bonus system provide for the manager? There are incentives to 'cheat', to make results appear better or worse than they actually are. The incentive to cheat is particularly strong when the division is in danger of falling just short of 80 per cent of the profit target, so that a small increase in reported profit would lead to a large jump in the amount of the bonus.

An extreme form of cheating is to 'cook the books', that is, report false profit numbers. The division manager may accomplish this by recording fictitious sales or omitting costs. For example, a few years ago Enron and other energy companies recorded questionable sales of energy contracts and WorldCom increased reported income by treating expenses as capital investments. Such actions have serious ethical and legal consequences, but sometimes the pressure to meet profit targets has been great enough to motivate managers to go to such extremes.

Managers may instead choose less extreme actions to increase reported profits. They may increase current sales by offering customers discounts that cause them to accelerate purchases from future periods to the current period, or offer better credit terms that are costly to the company through increased financing costs or increased credit risk. Managers may cut discretionary expenditures, such as research and development (R&D) and advertising, trading future sales for current profits. These short-term actions allow managers to achieve their current bonus, but cheat the company and its shareholders whenever the actions are not in the company's best long-run interests.

There are also incentives to *decrease* profits when the manager sees actual profits exceeding 120 per cent of the profit target in Exhibit 7.1 or when profits fall so far short of the 80 per cent profit target that there is no hope of achieving a bonus. Why would managers take actions to decrease current reported profit? First, moving this year's sales into next year or moving next year's expenses into this year increases next year's income, ensuring a higher level of reported profit (and probably a higher bonus) next year. Second, by decreasing this year's income, the manager may avoid increasing performance expectations for the next year – and thus may avoid a higher budgeted profit target for next year. Managers may move current sales into the next year by encouraging customers to defer purchases until the next year, thus effectively transferring current income to the future. They might also speed up actual expenditures (for example, moving maintenance planned for future years into the current year) or accelerate recognition of expenses (for example, writing off costs of equipment that remains in use), taking as current period expenses some costs that rightly belong to future periods.

Perhaps the most serious concern raised by these inappropriate incentives for lying and cheating is that they foster cynicism about the budget process and create a culture of unethical behaviour in the organisation. When managers know that the budget and evaluation processes encourage employees to provide biased information and make questionable decisions, not only does information quality suffer, but a lack of trust begins to pervade the organisation.

How can organisations avoid unwanted incentives in budgetary systems? The main way to avoid lying in preparing the budget is to reward good budget forecasts as well as good performance against the budget. If managers take personal responsibility for their budgets and their superiors take the budgeting process seriously so that good planning is just as important as good performance for managers, accurate budgets will generally result. To minimise the incentives to cheat, performance-linked payment plans should avoid 'discontinuities' in payments. Note that in Exhibit 7.1 the manager's payment jumps up – that is, it is discontinuous – at 80 per cent of the target profit level and the payment levels off – is discontinuous – at the maximum bonus level. To minimise incentives to transfer income between periods, we can make bonuses and total payments increase continuously over the entire range of possible performance so that there is no point at which a small change in profit has a large effect on pay.

Difficulties of obtaining accurate sales forecasts

Objective 4
Explain the difficulties of sales forecasting.

The third problem that limits the advantages of budgets is the difficulty of obtaining accurate sales forecasts. The sales budget is the foundation of budgeting. Why? Because the accuracy of all components of the budget depends on the accuracy of budgeted sales, as illustrated later in the chapter in the discussion of the master budget. At the Ritz-Carlton hotels, the process of developing the sales budget involves forecasting levels of room occupancy, group events, banquets and other activities. Upper management initially sets the sales targets. Then, employee teams in each department provide their inputs. Once everyone agrees on a sales forecast, managers prepare monthly departmental budgets based on the sales forecast.

The sales budget and the sales forecasts are conceptually distinct. A **sales forecast** is a prediction of sales under a given set of conditions. The **sales budget** is the specific sales forecast that is the result of decisions to create the conditions that will generate a desired level of sales. For example, you may have various forecasts of sales corresponding to various levels of advertising. The sales forecast for the one level of advertising you decide to implement becomes the sales budget.

The top sales executive usually directs the preparation of sales forecasts. Important factors considered by sales forecasters include the following:

1 *Past patterns of sales*. Past experience combined with detailed past sales by product line, geographic region and type of customer can help predict future sales.

2 *Estimates made by the sales force*. A company's sales force is often the best source of information about the desires and plans of customers.

3 *General economic conditions*. The financial press regularly publishes predictions for many economic indicators, such as gross domestic product and industrial production indexes (local and foreign). Knowledge of how sales relate to these indicators can aid sales forecasting.

4 *Competitors' actions*. Sales depend on the strength and actions of competitors. To forecast sales, a company should consider the likely strategies and reactions of competitors, such as changes in their prices, product quality or services.

5 *Changes in the firm's prices*. A company should consider the effects of planned price changes on customer demand (see Chapter 5). Normally, lower prices increase unit sales while higher prices decrease unit sales.

6 *Changes in product mix*. Changing the mix of products often can affect not only sales levels but also overall contribution margin. Identifying the most profitable products and devising methods to increase their sales is a key part of successful management.

7 *Market research studies*. Some companies hire marketing experts to gather information about market conditions and customer preferences. Such information is useful to managers making sales forecasts and product-mix decisions.

8 *Advertising and sales promotion plans*. Advertising and other promotional costs affect sales levels. A sales forecast should be based on anticipated effects of promotional activities.

Sales forecasting usually combines various techniques. In addition to the opinions of the sales staff, statistical analysis of correlations between sales and economic indicators (prepared by economists and members of the market research staff) provide valuable help. The opinions of line management also heavily influence the final sales forecasts. No matter how many technical experts a company uses in forecasting, the sales budget should ultimately be the responsibility of line management. Line managers who participate fully in setting the sales budget will be more committed to achieving the budget goals.

Governments and other nonprofit organisations face a similar problem in forecasting revenues from taxes, contributions or other sources. For example, city revenues may depend on a variety of factors, such as property taxes, traffic fines, parking fees, licence fees and city income taxes. In turn, property taxes depend on the extent of new construction and general increases in real estate values. Thus, forecasting revenues for a government or nonprofit organisation may require just as much sophistication as sales forecasts of a for-profit firm.

Types of budgets

Businesses use several different types of budgets. The most forward-looking and least detailed budget is the **strategic plan**, which sets the overall goals and objectives of the organisation. While the strategic plan does not deal with a specific time frame and does not produce forecasted financial statements, it provides the overall framework for the **long-range plan**. Long-range plans typically produce forecasted financial statements for 5- to 10-year periods. Decisions made during long-range planning include addition or deletion of product lines, design and location of new plants, acquisitions of buildings and equipment, and other long-term commitments. Companies coordinate their long-range plans with **capital budgets**, which detail the planned expenditures for facilities, equipment, new products and other long-term investments. Short-term plans and budgets guide day-to-day operations.

Managers who pay attention only to short-term budgets will quickly lose sight of long-term goals. Similarly, managers who pay attention only to the long-term budget could wind up mismanaging day-to-day operations. Effective managers balance detailed attention to their short-term budgets with a broad awareness of long-term plans.

Objective 5
Explain the major features and advantages of a master budget.

The **master budget** is a detailed and comprehensive analysis of the first year of the long-range plan. It quantifies targets for sales, purchases, production, distribution and financing in the form of forecasted financial statements and supporting operating schedules. These schedules provide detailed information beyond what appears in the forecasted financial statements. Thus, the master budget includes forecasts of sales, expenses, balance sheets and cash receipts and disbursements.

Many companies break their annual budgets into 4 quarterly or even 12 monthly budgets. **Continuous budgets** or **rolling budgets** are master budgets that simply add a month (or quarter) in the future as they drop the month (or quarter) just ended. In this way, budgeting becomes an ongoing process instead of an annual exercise. Continuous budgets force managers to always think about the next full year, not just the remainder of the current fiscal year.

■ Components of the master budget

The two major parts of a master budget are the operating budget and the financial budget. The **operating budget** – sometimes called the **profit plan** – focuses on the income statement and its supporting schedules or, in an organisation with no sales revenues, on budgeted expenses and supporting schedules. In contrast, the **financial budget** focuses on the effects that the operating budget and other plans (such as capital budgets and repayments of debt) will have on cash balances. The distinction between the operating budget and the financial budget is important because of the distinction between profitability and financial position. There are many examples of firms with strong profits where a weak cash position placed them in bankruptcy. There are also many examples of firms whose strong financial position allowed them to survive periods of temporary unprofitability.

The terms used to describe specific budget schedules vary from organisation to organisation. However, most master budgets share common elements. The usual master budget for a merchandising company has the following components as shown in Exhibit 7.2:

A Operating budget

    1 Sales budget
    2 Purchases and cost-of-goods-sold budget
    3 Operating expense budget
    4 Budgeted statement of income

B Financial budget

    1 Capital budget
    2 Cash budget
    3 Budgeted balance sheet

Other companies add to or adapt these categories depending on the nature of their operations. For example, manufacturing companies add budgets for raw material, work-in-process, and finished good inventories and budgets for each type of resource activity, such as labour, materials and factory overhead. Similarly, a consulting company might adapt the operating expense budget to focus on its major cost, consultant salaries. In addition to the master

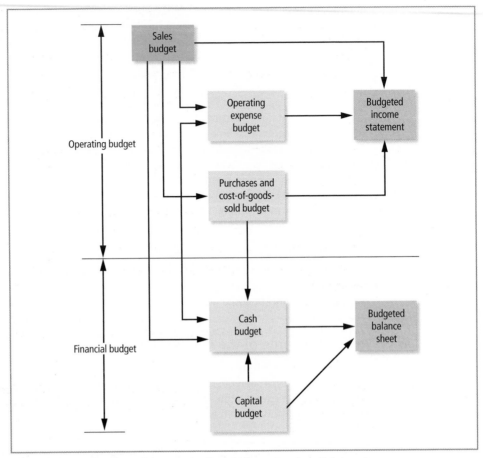

Exhibit 7.2 Preparation of the master budget for a merchandising company

budget, there are countless forms of special budgets and related reports. For example, a report might detail goals and objectives for improvements in quality or customer satisfaction during the budget period.

Preparing the master budget

Let's return to Exhibit 7.2 and trace the preparation of the master budget components. Although the process involves a large number of detailed calculations, always keep the big picture in mind. Remember that the master budgeting process provides an overview of company operations and an opportunity to review key decisions regarding all aspects of the company's value chain. Early drafts of the budget often lead to decisions that, in turn, lead to revisions in subsequent budget drafts. This cycle may be repeated several times before the budget is finalised.

■ The Cooking Hut

We illustrate the budgeting process using the Cooking Hut Company (CHC), a retailer of a wide variety of kitchen and dining room items, such as coffeemakers, silverware and table linens, based in Cork, Ireland. Although master budgets normally cover a full year, for the

Assets		
Current assets		
Cash	€10,000	
Accounts receivable, net (.4 × March sales of €40,000)	16,000	
Merchandise inventory, €20,000 + .7 (.8 x April sales of €50,000)	48,000	
Unexpired insurance (for April–December 20X1)	1,800	€ 75,800
Plant assets		
Equipment, fixtures and other	€37,000	
Accumulated depreciation	12,800	24,200
Total assets		€100,000
Liabilities and owners' equity		
Current liabilities		
Accounts payable (.5 × March purchases of €33,600)	€16,800	
Accrued wages and commissions payable (€1,250 + €3,000)	4,250	€ 21,050
Owners' equity		78,950
Total liabilities and owners' equity		€100,000

Exhibit 7.3 The Cooking Hut Company – Balance sheet 31 March 20X1

sake of brevity this illustration shows only the first 3 months of CHC's fiscal year, April–June. Exhibit 7.3 is the closing balance sheet for the previous fiscal year ending 31 March 20x1.

Sales budget

Preparation of the master budget for the first 3 months of the new fiscal year requires a sales budget for 1 month beyond the 3 months because CHC bases its budgeted inventory purchases on the following month's sales. The sales budget for the next 4 months is as follows:

April	€50,000
May	€80,000
June	€60,000
July	€50,000

The master budget also requires information about actual sales in the previous month because CHC collects cash for the credit sales in the month following the sale. On average, 60 per cent of sales are cash sales and the remaining 40 per cent are credit sales. Sales in March were €40,000 and the €16,000 of accounts receivable (debtors) on March 31 represents credit sales made in March (40 per cent of €40,000). Uncollectible accounts are negligible and thus ignored. For simplicity's sake, we also ignore all taxes for this illustration.

Planned inventory levels

Because deliveries from suppliers and customer demands are uncertain, at the end of each month CHC wants to have on hand a base inventory of €20,000 plus additional inventory equal to 80 per cent of the expected cost of goods sold for the following month. The cost of goods sold averages 70 per cent of sales. Therefore, the inventory on 31 March is €20,000 + .7(.8 × April sales of €50,000) = €20,000 + €28,000 = €48,000. The purchase terms available to CHC are net, 30 days. CHC pays for each month's purchases as follows: 50 per cent during the month of purchase and 50 per cent during the next month. Therefore, the accounts payable balance (creditors) on 31 March is 50 per cent of March purchases, or €33,600 × .5 = €16,800.

Wages and commissions

CHC pays wages and commissions twice each month, with payments lagged half a month after they are earned. Each payment consists of two components: (i) one-half of monthly fixed wages of €2,500, and (ii) commissions, equal to 15 per cent of sales, which we assume are uniform throughout each month. To illustrate the wage and commission payments, the 31 March balance of accrued wages and commissions payable is (.5 × €2,500) + .5(.15 × €40,000) = €1,250 + €3,000 = €4,250. Because of the half-month lag, CHC will pay this €4,250 balance on 15 April.

Capital expenditures and operating expenditures

CHC's only planned capital expenditure is the purchase of new fixtures for €3,000 cash in April. CHC has monthly operating expenses as follows:

Miscellaneous expenses	5% of sales, paid as incurred
Rent	€2,000, paid as incurred
Insurance	€200 expiration per month
Depreciation, including new fixtures	€500 per month

Cash balances

Because collections lag credit sales, CHC often struggles to come up with the cash to pay for purchases, employee wages and other outlays. To meet cash needs, CHC uses short-term loans from local banks, paying them back when excess cash is available. CHC maintains a minimum €10,000 cash balance at the end of each month for operating purposes and can borrow or repay loans only in multiples of €1,000. Assume that borrowing occurs at the beginning and repayments occur at the end of the month. Also assume that interest of 1 per cent per month is paid in cash at the end of each month.

■ Steps in preparing the master budget

The principal steps in preparing the master budget are as follows:

Supporting budgets and schedules

Objective 6
Follow the principal steps in preparing a master budget.

1 Using the data given, prepare the following budgets and schedules for each of the months of the planning horizon:

    Schedule a. Sales budget
    Schedule b. Cash collections from customers
    Schedule c. Purchases and cost-of-goods-sold budget
    Schedule d. Cash disbursements for purchases
    Schedule e. Operating expense budget
    Schedule f. Cash disbursements for operating expenses

Operating budget

2 Using the supporting budgets and schedules, prepare a budgeted income statement for the 3 months ending 30 June 20X1 (Exhibit 7.4).

Financial budget

3 Prepare the following budgets and forecasted financial statements:

(a) Capital budget.

(b) Cash budget, including details of borrowings, repayments and interest for each month of the planning horizon (Exhibit 7.5).

(c) Budgeted balance sheet as of 30 June 20X1 (Exhibit 7.6).

Organisations with effective budget systems have specific guidelines for the steps and timing of budget preparation. Although the details differ, the guidelines invariably include the preceding steps. As we follow these steps to prepare CHC's master budget, be sure that you understand the source of each figure in each schedule and budget.

■ Step 1: Preparing basic data

Step 1a: Sales budget

Objective 7
Prepare the
operating budget
and the supporting
schedules.

The sales budget is the starting point for budgeting because planned inventory levels, purchases and operating expenses all depend on the expected level of sales. Schedule a includes information about actual March sales because March credit sales affect cash collections in April.

Schedule a: Sales budget

	March	April	May	June	April–June total
Total sales	€40,000	€50,000	€80,000	€60,000	€19,000

Step 1b: Cash collections from customers

Schedule b uses the sales budget to plan when CHC will collect cash. In turn, we will use Schedule b to prepare the cash budget in Step 3. Cash collections from customers include the current month's cash sales plus collection of the previous month's credit sales.

Schedule b: Cash collections from customers

	April	May	June
Cash sales (60% of current month sales)	€30,000	€48,000	€36,000
Collection of last month's credit sales (40% of previous month sales)	16,000	20,000	32,000
Total collections	€46,000	€68,000	€68,000

Step 1c: Purchases budget

The elements of the purchases budget are tied together by a simple intuitive identity that ignores minor complications such as returns and defects but relates the fundamental uses of inventory to the sources: inventory is either sold or else carried over to the next period as ending inventory. Inventory comes from either beginning inventory or purchases. Therefore, cost of goods sold plus ending inventory equals beginning inventory plus purchases.

We budget cost of goods sold by multiplying the cost of merchandise sold percentage (70 per cent) by budgeted sales. The total merchandise needed is the sum of budgeted cost of goods sold plus the desired ending inventory. Finally, we compute required purchases by subtracting beginning inventory from the total merchandise needed:

Schedule c: Purchases budget

	March	April	May	June	April–June total
Budgeted cost of goods sold[†]		€35,000	€ 56,000	€42,000	€133,000
Plus: Desired ending inventory		64,800	53,600	48,000	
Total merchandise needed		€99,800	€109,600	€90,000	
Less: Beginning inventory		48,000‡	64,800	53,600	
Purchases	€33,600*	€51,800	€ 44,800	€36,400	

* Purchases for March were ending inventory (€48,000 as shown in Exhibit 7.3) plus cost of goods sold (.7 × March sales of €40,000) less beginning inventory (€42,400 = €20,000 + [.8 × March cost of goods sold of €28,000]).

† .7 × April sales of €50,000 = €35,000; .7 × May sales of €80,000 = €56,000; .7 × June sales of €60,000 = €42,000.

‡ Ending inventory from March was €48,000 as shown in Exhibit 7.3.

Step 1d: Disbursements for Purchases

We use the purchases budget to develop Schedule d. In our example, disbursements are 50 per cent of the current month's purchases and 50 per cent of the previous month's purchases.

Schedule d: Cash disbursements for purchases

	April	May	June
50 per cent of last month's purchases	€16,800	€25,900	€22,400
Plus 50 per cent of this month's purchases	25,900	22,400	18,200
Disbursements for purchases	€42,700	€48,300	€40,600

Step 1e: Operating expense budget

Month-to-month changes in sales volume and other cost-driver activities directly influence many operating expenses. Examples of expenses driven by sales volume include sales commissions and delivery expenses – these are included in miscellaneous expenses for CHC. Other expenses, such as rent, insurance, depreciation and wages, are not influenced by sales (within appropriate relevant ranges) and we regard them as fixed. Schedule e summarises operating expenses for CHC.

Schedule e: Operating expense budget

	March	April	May	June	April–June total
Wages (fixed)	€2,500	€ 2,500	€ 2,500	€ 2,500	
Commissions (15 per cent of current month's sales)	6,000	7,500	12,000	9,000	
Total wages and commissions	€8,500	€10,000	€14,500	€11,500	€36,000
Miscellaneous expenses (5 per cent of current sales)		2,500	4,000	3,000	9,500
Rent (fixed)		2,000	2,000	2,000	6,000
Insurance (fixed)		200	200	200	600
Depreciation (fixed)		500	500	500	1,500
Total operating expenses		€15,200	€21,200	€17,200	€53,600

Step 1f: Disbursements for operating expenses

Disbursements for operating expenses are based on the operating expense budget. Disbursements include 50 per cent of last month's wages and commissions, 50 per cent of this month's wages and commissions, and miscellaneous and rent expenses. There is no monthly cash disbursement for Insurance (which is paid annually at the beginning of the year) nor for depreciation (which does not involve any periodic cash disbursement). We use the total of these disbursements for each month in preparing the cash budget, Exhibit 7.5.

Schedule f: Disbursements for operating expenses

	April	May	June
Wages and commissions			
50 per cent of last month's expenses	€ 4,250	€ 5,000	€ 7,250
50 per cent of this month's expenses	5,000	7,250	5,750
Total wages and commissions	€ 9,250	€12,250	€13,000
Miscellaneous expenses	2,500	4,000	3,000
Rent	2,000	2,000	2,000
Total disbursements	€13,750	€18,250	€18,000

Step 2: Preparing the Operating Budget

Steps 1a, 1c and 1e, along with interest expense from Exhibit 7.5, provide information to construct the budgeted income statement in Exhibit 7.4. Budgeted income from operations is often a benchmark for judging management performance.

Step 3: Preparation of Financial Budget

The second major part of the master budget is the financial budget, which consists of the capital budget cash budget and ending balance sheet.

Step 3A: Capital budget

In our illustration, the €3,000 planned purchase of new fixtures in April is the only item in the capital budget. More complex capital budgets are illustrated in Chapter 11.

	Data	Source of data
Sales	€190,000	Schedule a
Cost of good sold	133,000	Schedule c
Gross margin	€ 57,000	
Operating expenses:		
Wages and commissions €36,000		Schedule e
Rent 6,000		Schedule e
Miscellaneous 9,500		Schedule e
Insurance 600		Schedule e
Depreciation 1,500	53,600	Schedule e
Income from operations	€ 3,400	
Interest expense	410	
Net income	€ 2,990	

Exhibit 7.4 The Cooking Hut Company – Budgeted income statement for three months ending 30 June 20X1

Step 3b: Cash budget

Objective 8
Prepare the financial budget.

The **cash budget** is a statement of planned cash receipts and disbursements. Cash budgets help management avoid having unnecessary idle cash, on the one hand, or unnecessary cash deficiencies, on the other. The cash budget is heavily affected by the level of operations summarised in the budgeted income statement.

The cash budget has the following major sections, where the letters x, y and z refer to the lines in Exhibit 7.5 that summarise the effects of that section:

- The available cash balance (x) is the amount by which the beginning cash balance exceeds CHC's €10,000 minimum cash balance. Companies maintain a minimum cash balance to allow for fluctuations in the level of cash during the month – daily balances during the month typically fluctuate relative to the beginning and ending cash balances – and also to provide for unexpected cash needs.

- Net cash receipts and disbursements (y):
  1 Cash receipts depend on collections from customers' accounts receivable, cash sales and on other operating cash income sources, such as interest received on notes receivable or bank deposits. Trace total collections from Schedule b to Exhibit 7.5.
  2 Disbursements for purchases depend on the credit terms extended by suppliers and the bill-paying habits of the buyer. Trace disbursements for merchandise from Schedule d to Exhibit 7.5.
  3 Payroll depends on wages and commission terms and on payroll dates. Some costs and expenses depend on contractual terms for installment payments, mortgage payments, rents, leases and miscellaneous items. Trace disbursements for operating expenses from Schedule f to Exhibit 7.5.
  4 Other disbursements include outlays for fixed assets, long-term investments, dividends and the like. An example is the €3,000 expenditure for new fixtures.

	April	May	June
Beginning cash balance	€ 10,000	€10,410	€10,720
Minimum cash balance desired	10,000	10,000	10,000
Available cash balance (x)	€ 0	€ 410	€ 720
Cash receipts and disbursements			
Collections from customers (Schedule b*)	€ 46,000	€68,000	€68,000
Payments for merchandise (Schedule d)	(42,700)	(48,300)	(40,600)
Payments for operating expenses (Schedule f)	(13,750)	(18,250)	(18,000)
Purchase of new fixtures (Step 3a)	(3,000)		
Net cash receipts and disbursements (y)	€ (13,450)	€ 1,450	€ 9,400
Excess (deficiency) of cash before financing ($x + y$)	(13,450)	€ 1,860	€10,120
Borrowing (at beginning of month)	€ 14,000†		
Repayments (at end of month)		€ (1,000)	€(9,000)
Interest payments (1% per month, end of month‡)	(140)	(140)	(130)
Total cash increase (decrease) from financing (z)	€ 13,860	€ (1,140)	€ (9,130)
Ending cash balance (beginning + y + z)	€ 10,410	€10,720	€10,990

* Letters x, y and z are keyed to the explanation in the text.
† Borrowing and repayment of principal are made in multiples of €1,000, at an interest rate of 1 per cent per month.
‡ Interest computations: €14,000 × .01 = €140; €14,000 × .01 = €140; €13,000 × .01 = €130.

Exhibit 7.5 The Cooking Hut Company – Cash budget for three months ending 30 June 20X1

- The total cash increase (decrease) from financing (z) depends on the total available cash balance (x) and the net cash receipts and disbursements (y). If cash available plus net cash receipts less disbursements is negative, borrowing is necessary – Exhibit 7.5 shows that CHC will borrow €14,000 in April to cover the planned deficiency. If cash available plus net cash receipts less disbursements is sufficiently positive, CHC can repay loans – it repays €1,000 and €9,000 in May and June, respectively. This section of the cash budget also generally contains the outlays for interest expense. Trace the calculated interest expense, which in our example is the same as the cash interest payments for the 3 months, to Exhibit 7.4, which then will be complete.

- The ending cash balance is the beginning cash balance $+ y + z$. Financing, z, has either a positive (borrowing) or a negative (repayment) effect on the cash balance. The illustrative cash budget shows the pattern of short-term, 'self-liquidating' financing. Seasonal peaks often result in heavy drains on cash – for merchandise purchases and operating expenses – before the company makes sales and collects cash from customers. The resulting loan is 'self-liquidating' – that is, the company uses borrowed money to acquire merchandise for sale and uses the proceeds from sales to repay the loan. This 'working capital cycle' moves from cash to inventory to receivables and back to cash.

Step 3c: Budgeted balance sheet

The final step in preparing the master budget is to construct the budgeted balance sheet (Exhibit 7.6) that projects each balance sheet item in accordance with the business plan as expressed in the previous schedules. Specifically, the beginning balances at 31 March would be increased or decreased in light of the expected cash receipts and cash disbursements in Exhibit 7.5 and in light of the effects of noncash items appearing on the income statement in

Assets		
Current assets		
Cash (Exhibit 7.5)	€10,990	
Accounts receivable, net (.4 × June sales of €60,000)	24,000	
Inventory (Schedule c)	48,000	
Unexpired insurance (for July–December)	1,200	€ 84,190
Plant assets		
Equipment, fixtures and other (€37,000 + €3,000)	€40,000	
Accumulated depreciation (€12,800 + €1,500)	(14,300)	25,700
Total assets		€109,890
Liabilities and owners' equity		
Current liabilities		
Accounts payable (.5 × June purchase of €36,400)	€18,200	
Short-term bank loan	4,000	
Accrued wages and commissions payable (.5 × 11,500)	5,750	€ 27,950
Owners' equity (78,950 + 2,990 net income)		81,940
Total liabilities and owners' equity		€109,890

Note: 31 March 20X1 beginning balances are used for computations of unexpired insurance, plant assets and owners' equity.

Exhibit 7.6 The Cooking Hut Company – Budgeted balance sheet 30 June 20X1

BUSINESS FIRST
Business plans and budgets

Start-up companies in a variety of industries have mushroomed into multibillion-dollar companies. How do these companies get started? An essential component in securing initial funding for a start-up is the development of a business plan. A business plan could be structured as follows:

1 The business – includes a description of the business, a marketing plan, an assessment of the competition, a list of operating procedures and a roster of personnel.

2 Financial data – includes the following items:
   - Loan applications
   - Capital equipment and supply list
   - Pro forma balance sheet
   - Break-even analysis
   - Pro forma income projections (income statements):
   - Three-year summary
   - Detail by month, first year
   - Detail by quarters, second and third years
   - Assumptions upon which projections were based
   - Pro forma cash flow statements.

3 Supporting documents – includes a variety of legal documents and information about the principals involved, suppliers, customers, etc.

Financial data are an important part of a business plan, the centrepiece of which is the master budget. The budgeted income statement and budgeted cash flow statement are essential to predicting the future prospects of any business. They are especially critical to assessing the prospects of a new company that has little history to analyse.

Budgeting is often not the most exciting task for entrepreneurs. However, lack of a credible budget is one of the main reasons venture capitalists cite when they refuse funding for a start-up. Further, a cash shortage is one of the main causes of failure among start-up companies. Anyone wanting to be an entrepreneur would be well-advised to study budgeting and learn how it can be a powerful tool both for managing the company and for promoting the company to potential investors.

Sources: Adapted from Small Business Administration, *The Business Plan: Roadmap to Success* (www.sba.gov/starting/indexbusplans.html).

Exhibit 7.4. For example, unexpired insurance is a noncash item that would decrease from its balance of €1,800 on 31 March to €1,200 on 30 June.

The master budget is an important management tool for evaluating and revising strategy. For example, the initial formulation of the financial statements may prompt management to consider new sales strategies to generate more demand. Alternatively, management may explore the effects of various adjustments in the timing of cash receipts and disbursements. The large cash deficiency in April, for example, may lead to an emphasis on cash sales or an attempt to speed up collection of accounts receivable. In any event, the first draft of the master budget is rarely the final draft. As managers revise strategy, the budgeting process becomes an integral part of the management process itself–budgeting is planning and communicating. The 'Business first' box above describes the important role of budgets in start-up companies.

■ Activity-based master budgets

The budget process we have described thus far in this chapter can be called **functional budgeting** because the focus is on preparing budgets by function, such as production, selling and administrative support. Organisations that have implemented activity-based cost accounting systems often use these systems as a vehicle to prepare **activity-based budgets (ABB)** – budgets that focus on the budgeted cost of activities required to produce and sell products and services.

MAKING MANAGERIAL DECISIONS

Some managers focus on the operating budget, while others are more concerned with the financial budget. How does the operating budget differ from the financial budget?

Answer

The operating budget focuses on the income statement, which uses accrual accounting. It measures revenues and expenses. Line operating managers usually prepare and use the operating budget. In contrast, the financial budget focuses primarily on cash flow. It measures the receipts and disbursements of cash. Financial managers, such as controllers and treasurers, focus on the financial budget. The operating budget is a better measure of long-run performance, but the financial budget is essential to plan for short-term cash needs and manage cash balances. A shortage of cash can get a company into financial trouble even when operating performance appears to be okay. Thus, both operating and financial budgets are important to an organisation.

Summary problem for your review

Be sure you understand every step of the CHC example before you tackle this review problem.

PROBLEM

The Country Store is a retail outlet for a variety of hardware and housewares. The owner is eager to prepare a budget and is especially concerned with her cash position. The company will have to borrow in order to finance purchases made in preparation for high expected sales during the busy last quarter of the year. When the company needs cash, borrowing occurs at the end of a month. When cash is available for repayments, the repayment occurs at the end of a month. The company pays interest in cash at the end of every month at a monthly rate of 1 per cent on the amount outstanding during that month.

Review the structure of the example in the chapter and then prepare the Country Store's master budget for the months of October, November and December. The owner has gathered the data shown in Exhibit 7.7 to prepare the simplified budget. In addition, she will purchase equipment in October for €19,750 cash and pay dividends of €4,000 in December.

Balance sheet as of 30 September 20X1		Budgeted expenses (per month):	
Assets		Wages and salaries	€ 7,500
Cash	€ 9,000	Freight out as a percentage of sales	6%
Accounts receivable	48,000	Advertising	€ 6,000
Inventory	12,600	Depreciation	€ 2,000
Plant and equipment (net)	200,000	Other expense as a percentage of sales	4%
Total assets	€269,600	Minimum inventory policy as a percentage of	
		next month's cost of goods sold	30%
Liabilities and stockholders' equity		Budgeted sales:	
Interest payable	0		
Note payable	0	September (actual)	€ 60,000
Accounts payable	18,300	October	70,000
Capital stock	180,000	November	85,000
Retained earnings	71,300	December	90,000
Total liabilities and stockholders' equity	€269,600	January 20X2	50,000

Exhibit 7.7 The Country Store – Budget data

(continued overleaf)

(continued from p. 297)

Other data:			Inventory paid for in	
Required minimum cash balance	€ 8,000		Month purchased	50%
Sales mix, cash/credit			Month after purchase	50%
Cash sales	20%		Wages and salaries, freight-out advertising	
Credit sales (collected the following month)	80%		and other expenses are paid in cash in the	
Gross profit rate	40%		month incurred.	
Loan interest rate (interest paid in cash monthly)	12%			

SOLUTION

Schedule a: Sales budget

	October	November	December	Total
Credit sales, 80%	€56,000	€68,000	€72,000	€196,000
Cash sales, 20%	14,000	17,000	18,000	49,000
Total sales	€70,000	€85,000	€90,000	€245,000

Schedule b: Cash collections from customers

	October	November	December	Total
Cash sales	€14,000	€17,000	€18,000	€ 49,000
Collections from prior month	48,000	56,000	68,000	172,000
Total collections	€62,000	€73,000	€86,000	€221,000

Schedule c: Purchases budget

	October	November	December	Total
Desired ending inventory	€15,300	€16,200	€ 9,000	€ 40,500
Plus cost of goods sold	42,000	51,000	54,000	147,000
Total needed	€57,300	€67,200	€63,000	€187,500
Less: Beginning inventory	12,600	15,300	16,200	44,100
Total purchases	€44,700	€51,900	€46,800	€143,400

Schedule d: Cash disbursements for purchases

	October	November	December	Total
For September*	€18,300			€ 18,300
For October	22,350	€22,350		44,700
For November		25,950	€25,950	51,900
For December			23,400	23,400
Total disbursements	€40,650	€48,300	€49,350	€138,300

*The amount payable on the 30 September 20X1, balance sheet.

Schedules e and f: Operating expenses and disbursements for expenses (except interest)

	October	November	December	Total
Cash expenses:				
Salaries and wages	€ 7,500	€ 7,500	€ 7,500	€22,500
Freight-out	4,200	5,100	5,400	14,700
Advertising	6,000	6,000	6,000	18,000
Other expenses	2,800	3,400	3,600	9,800
Total disbursements for expenses	€20,500	€22,000	€22,500	€65,000
Noncash expenses:				
Depreciation	2,000	2,000	2,000	6,000
Total expenses	€22,500	€24,000	€24,500	€71,000

The Country Store.
Cash budget for the months of October–December 20X1

	October	November	December
Beginning cash balance	€ 9,000	€ 8,000	€ 8,000
Minimum cash balance desired	8,000	8,000	8,000
Available cash balance	1,000	0	0
Cash receipts and disbursements:			
Collections from customers	62,000	73,000	86,000
Payments for merchandise	(40,650)	(48,300)	(49,350)
Operating expenses	(20,500)	(22,000)	(22,500)
Equipment purchases	(19,750)	0	0
Dividends	0	0	(4,000)
Interest*	0	(179)	(154)
Net cash receipts and disbursements	(18,900)	2,521	9,996
Excess (deficiency) of cash before financing	€(17,900)	€ 2,521	€ 9,996
Financing:			
Borrowing†	€ 17,900	€ 0	€ 0
Repayments	0	(2,521)	(9,996)
Total cash from financing	17,900	(2,521)	(9,996)
Ending cash balance	€ 8,000	€ 8,000	€ 8,000

* Interest is paid on the loan amounts outstanding during the month. November: $(.01) \times$ (€17,900) = €179; December: $(.01) \times$ (€17,900 − €2,521) = €154.
† Borrowings are at the end of the month in the amounts needed. Repayments also are made at the end of the month in the amount that excess cash permits.

The Country Store
Budget income statement for October–December 20X1

	October	November	December	October–December total
Sales	€70,000	€85,000	€90,000	€245,000
Cost of goods sold	42,000	51,000	54,000	147,000
Gross margin	28,000	34,000	36,000	98,000

(continued)

The Country Store *(continued)*

	October	November	December	October–December total
Operating expenses				
Salaries and wages	7,500	7,500	7,500	22,500
Freight-out	4,200	5,100	5,400	14,700
Advertising	6,000	6,000	6,000	18,000
Other	2,800	3,400	3,600	9,800
Interest*		179	154	333
Depreciation	2,000	2,000	2,000	6,000
Total operating expense	€22,500	€24,179	€24,654	€ 71,333
Net operating income	€ 5,500	€ 9,821	€11,346	€ 26,667

* Interest expense is the monthly interest rate times the borrowed amount held for the month.
November: $(.01) \times €17,900 = €179$; December: $(.01) \times €15,379 = €154$.

The Country Store
Budgeted balance sheets as of the ends of October–December 20X1

	October	November	December*
Assets			
Current assets			
Cash	€ 8,000	€ 8,000	€ 8,000
Accounts receivable	56,000	68,000	72,000
Inventory	15,300	16,200	9,000
Total current assets	79,300	92,200	89,000
Plant, less accumulated depreciation†	217,750	215,750	213,750
Total assets	€297,050	€307,950	€302,750
Liabilities and Equities			
Liabilities			
Accounts payable	€ 22,350	€ 25,950	€ 23,400
Notes payable	17,900	15,379	5,383
Total liabilities	40,250	41,329	28,783
Stockholders' equity			
Capital stock	180,000	180,000	180,000
Retained earnings	76,800	86,621	93,967
Total equities	256,800	266,621	273,967
Total liabilities and equities	€297,050	€307,950	€302,750

* The 30 December 20X1 balance sheet is the ending balance sheet for the quarter.
† October ending balance in Plant = beginning balance + equipment purchases − depreciation =
€200,000 + €19,750 − €2,000 = €217,750.

An activity-based budgetary system emphasises the planning and control purpose of cost management. Our discussion of activity-based costing (ABC) in Chapter 4 focused on designing cost accounting and cost allocation systems that provided more accurate product and service costs. However, once a company has designed and implemented an ABC system, it can use the same framework for its budgetary system. Exhibit 7.8 highlights the main concepts and differences between ABC allocation of resource costs to activities and products, and ABB.

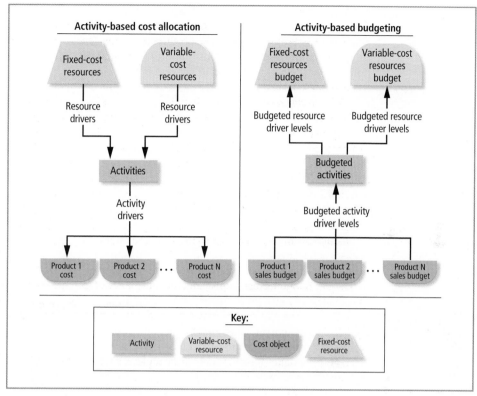

Exhibit 7.8 ABC and ABB compared

Just as in functional budgeting (see Exhibit 7.2), ABB begins with the forecasted demand for products or services – the sales budget. In functional budgeting, the next step is to determine the ending-inventory budget, then the material purchases and the cost-of-goods-sold budget. In ABB, the focus is on estimating the demand for each activity's output as measured by its cost driver. Then, we use the rate at which activities consume resources to estimate or budget the resources needed. As we can see from comparing Exhibits 7.2 and 7.8, functional budgeting determines the resources needed directly from the predicted sales of products or services, while ABB uses the sales predictions to estimate the required activities, which in turn determines the resources needed. Because of the emphasis on activities and their consumption of resources, some managers believe that ABB is more useful for controlling waste and improving efficiency – a primary objective of budgeting.

Budgets as financial planning models

A well-made master budget that considers all aspects of the company (the entire value chain) provides the basis for an effective **financial planning model**, a mathematical model that can incorporate the effects of alternative assumptions about sales, costs or product mix. Today, many large companies have developed large-scale financial planning models based on the master budget to predict how various decisions might affect the company. For example, a manager might want to predict the consequences of changing the mix of products offered for sale to emphasise several products with the highest prospects for growth. A financial planning model would provide operational and financial budgets under alternative assumptions about the product mix, sales levels, production constraints, quality levels, scheduling and so on. Most importantly, managers can get answers to what-if questions, such as 'What if sales are 10 per cent below forecasts? What if material prices increase 8 per cent instead of 4 per cent as expected? What if the new union contract grants a 6 per cent raise in consideration for productivity improvements?'

Using the master budget in this way is a step-by-step process in which managers revise their tentative plans as they exchange views on various aspects of expected activities. For instance, Dow Chemical's model uses 140 separate, constantly revised cost inputs that are based on several different cost drivers. By mathematically describing the relationships among all the operating and financial activities and among the other major internal and external factors that affect the results of management decisions, financial planning models allow managers to assess the predicted impacts of various alternatives before they make final decisions.

Financial planning models have shortened managers' reaction times dramatically. We can prepare in minutes (or even seconds) a revised plan for a large company that once took many accountants many days to prepare by hand.

The use of spreadsheet software has put financial planning models within reach of even the smallest organisations. Appendix 7 illustrates how to use a spreadsheet model for planning. Ready access to powerful modelling, however, does not guarantee plausible or reliable results. Financial planning models are only as good as the assumptions and the inputs used to build and manipulate them – what computer specialists call GIGO (garbage in, garbage out). Nearly every finance director or chief accountant has a horror story to tell about following the bad advice generated from a financial planning model with accurate calculations but faulty assumptions or inputs.

Highlights to remember

1 **Explain how budgets facilitate planning and coordination.** A budget expresses, in quantitative terms, an organisation's objectives and possible steps for achieving them. Thus, a budget is a tool that helps managers in both their planning and control functions. Budgets provide a mechanism for communication between units and across levels of the organisation. In an environment that encourages open communication of the opportunities and challenges facing the organisation, the budget process allows managers to coordinate ongoing activities and plan for the future.

2 **Anticipate possible human relations problems caused by budgets.** The success of a budget depends heavily on employee reaction to it. Negative attitudes toward budgets often prevent realisation of many of the potential benefits. Such attitudes are usually caused by managers who use budgets only to limit spending or to punish employees. Budgets generally are more useful when all affected parties participate in their preparation.

3 **Explain potentially dysfunctional incentives in the budget process.** When managers want to increase the resources allocated to their unit or when managers are evaluated based on performance relative to budgeted amounts, there are incentives to bias the information that goes into their budgets. When managers are compensated using typical bonus schemes, there may be pressure to report inflated results and incentives to make short-run decisions that are not in the best long-run interests of the organisation. Not only do such incentives lead managers to make poor decisions, they undercut efforts to maintain high ethical standards in the organisation.

4 **Explain the difficulties of sales forecasting.** Sales forecasting combines various techniques as well as opinions of sales staff and management. Sales forecasters must consider many factors, such as past patterns of sales, economic conditions and competitors' actions. Sales forecasting is difficult because of its complexity and the rapid changes in the business environment in which most companies operate.

5 **Explain the major features and advantages of a master budget.** The two major parts of a master budget are the operating budget and the financial budget. Advantages of budgets include formalisation of planning, providing a framework for judging performance and aiding managers in communicating and coordinating their efforts.

6 **Follow the principal steps in preparing a master budget.** Master budgets typically cover relatively short periods – usually 1 month to 1 year. The steps involved in preparing the master budget vary across organisations but follow the general outline given on pp. 290–6. Invariably, the first step is to forecast sales or service levels. The next step should be to forecast cost-driver activity levels, given expected sales and service. Using these forecasts and knowledge of cost behaviour, collection patterns and so on, managers can prepare the operating and financing budgets.

7 **Prepare the operating budget and the supporting schedules.** The operating budget includes the income statement for the budget period. Managers prepare it using the following supporting schedules: sales budget, purchases budget and operating expense budget.

8 **Prepare the financial budget.** The second major part of the master budget is the financial budget. The financial budget consists of a cash budget, capital budget and a budgeted balance sheet. Managers prepare the cash budget from the following supporting schedules: cash collections, disbursements for purchases, disbursements for operating expenses and other disbursements. ■

Appendix 7: Use of spreadsheet models for sensitivity analysis

Objective 9
Use a spreadsheet to develop a budget.

Spreadsheet software is an extremely powerful and flexible tool for budgeting. An obvious advantage of a spreadsheet is that arithmetic errors are virtually nonexistent. The real value of spreadsheets, however, is that they can be used to make a mathematical model (a financial planning model) of the organisation. At very low cost, this model can be applied with a variety of assumptions that reflect possible changes in expected sales, cost drivers, cost functions and so on. The objective of this appendix is to illustrate how to use a spreadsheet model for **sensitivity analysis**.

Recall the chapter's Cooking Hut Company (CHC) example. Suppose CHC has prepared its master budget using spreadsheet software. To simplify making changes to the budget, we have placed the relevant forecasts and other budgeting details in Exhibit 7.9. Note that for simplification, we have included only the data necessary for the purchases budget. The full master budget would require a larger table with all the data given in the chapter.

Each cell of the spreadsheet is referenced by its column (a letter) and its row (a number). For example, the beginning inventory for the budget period is in 'D4', which is shown as €48,000. By referencing the budget data's cell addresses, you can generate the purchases budget (Exhibit 7.11) within the same spreadsheet by entering formulas instead of numbers into the schedule. Consider Exhibit 7.10. Instead of typing €48,000 as April's beginning inventory in the purchases budget at cell D17, type a formula with the cell address for the beginning inventory from the preceding table, =D4 (the cell address preceded by an '=' sign – the common spreadsheet indicator for a formula). Likewise, all the cells of the purchases budget will contain formulas that include cell addresses instead of numbers. The total inventory needed in April (cell D16) is =D13 + D14, and budgeted purchases in April (cell D19) are =D16 − D17. We can compute the figures for May and June similarly within the respective columns. This approach gives the spreadsheet the most flexibility because you can change any number in the budget data in Exhibit 7.9 (for example, a sales forecast), and the software automatically recalculates the numbers in the entire purchases budget. Exhibit 7.10 shows the formulas used for the purchases budget. Exhibit 7.11 is the purchases budget displaying the numbers generated by the formulas in Exhibit 7.10 using the input data in Exhibit 7.9.

Now, what if you want to know the effect on budgeted purchases if the sales forecast is revised upward by 10 per cent? By changing the sales forecasts in spreadsheet Exhibit 7.9, you obtain a nearly instantaneous revision of the purchases budget. Exhibit 7.12 shows the revised budget based on these alternative sales forecasts. The revised sales forecasts are shown in red type and the revised purchases budget is shown in blue type. We could alter any piece of budget data in the table and easily view or print out the effects on purchases. This sort of analysis, assessing the effects of varying one of the budget inputs, up or down, is sensitivity analysis. **Sensitivity analysis** for budgeting is the systematic varying of budget data input to determine the effects of each variation on the budget. This type of what-if analysis is one of the most powerful uses of spreadsheets for financial planning models. Note that while you can vary more than one type of budget input at a time, it becomes more difficult to isolate the effects of each change.

We can prepare every schedule, operating budget and financial budget of the master budget on a spreadsheet. We link each schedule by the appropriate cell addresses just as we linked the budget input data (Exhibit 7.9) to the purchases budget (Exhibits 7.10 and 7.11). As in the purchases budget, ideally all cells in the master budget are formulas, not numbers. That way, every budget input can be the subject of sensitivity analysis by simply changing the budget data in Exhibit 7.9.

Preparing the master budget on a spreadsheet is time-consuming the first time. Once the spreadsheet is prepared, the time savings in subsequent periods and the benefits from increased planning and sensitivity analysis capabilities are enormous. In order to obtain these benefits, it is essential for the master budget model to be well documented. Any assumptions that are made should be described either within the spreadsheet or in a separate budget preparation document that is readily available to subsequent users.

	A	B	C	D	E	F
1	Budgeted data					
2	Sales forecasts		Other information			
3						
4	March (actual)	€40,000	Beginning inventory	€48,000		
5	April	50,000	Desired ending inventory: Base amount	€20,000		
6	May	80,000	Plus percentage of next			
7	June	60,000	month's cost of			
8	July	50,000	goods sold	80%		
9			Cost of goods sold			
10			as percentage of sales	70%		

Exhibit 7.9 The Cooking Hut Company – Budget data (column and row labels are given by the spreadsheet)

	A	B	C	D	E	F
11	Schedule c					
12	Purchases budget			April	May	June
13	Desired ending inventory			= D5 + D8* (D10*B6)	= D5 + D8* (D10*B7)	= D5 + D8* (D10*B8)
14	Plus cost of goods sold			= D10*B5	= D10*B6	= D10*B7
15						
16	Total needed			= D13 + D14	= E13 + E14	= F13 + F14
17	Less beginning inventory			= D4	= D13	= E13
18						
19	Purchases			= D16 D17	= E16 − E17	= F16 F17

Exhibit 7.10 The Cooking Hut Company – Purchases budget formulas

	A	B	C	D	E	F
11	Schedule c					
12	Purchases budget			April	May	June
13	Desired ending inventory			€64,800	€53,600	€48,000
14	Plus cost of goods sold			35,000	56,000	42,000
15						
16			Total needed	99,800	109,600	90,000
17	Less beginning inventory			48,000	64,800	53,600
18						
19	Purchases			€51,800	€44,800	€36,400

Exhibit 7.11 The Cooking Hut Company – Purchases budget

	A	B	C	D	E	F
1	Budgeted data					
2	Sales forecasts		Other information			
3						
4	March (actual)	€40,000	Beginning inventory	€48,000		
5	April	55,000	Desired ending inventory:			
			Base amount	€20,000		
6	May	88,000	Plus percentage of next			
7	June	66,000	month's cost of			
8	July	55,000	goods sold	80%		
9			Cost of goods sold			
10			as percentage of sales	70%		
11	Schedule c					
12	Purchases budget			April	May	June

Exhibit 7.12 The Cooking Hut Company – Purchases budget

	A	B	C	D	E	F
13	Desired ending inventory			€69,280	€56,960	€50,800
14	Plus cost of goods sold			38,500	61,600	46,200
15						
16	Total needed			107,780	118,560	97,000
17	Less beginning inventory			48,000	69,280	56,960
18						
19	Purchases			€59,780	€49,280	€40,040

Exhibit 7.12 (*continued*)

Accounting vocabulary

activity-based budgets (ABB),
   p. 296
budgetary slack, p. 283
budget padding, p. 283
capital budget, p. 287
cash budget, p. 294
continuous budget, p. 287

financial budget, p. 287
financial planning model, p. 301
functional budgeting, p. 296
long-range plan, p. 286
master budget, p. 287
operating budget, p. 287
participative budgeting, p. 283

profit plan, p. 287
rolling budget, p. 287
sales budget, p. 285
sales forecast, p. 285
sensitivity analysis, p. 303
strategic plan, p. 286
zero-base budget, p. 280

Fundamental assignment material   MyAccountingLab

Special note: Problems 7.A1 and 7.B1 provide single-problem reviews of most of the chapter topics. Those readers who prefer to concentrate on the fundamentals in smaller chunks should consider any of the other problems.

7.A1 Prepare master budget

You are the new manager of the Rapidbuy Electronics store. Top management of Rapidbuy Electronics is convinced that management training should include the active participation of store managers in the budgeting process. You have been asked to prepare a complete master budget for your store for June, July and August. All accounting is done centrally so you have no expert help on the premises. In addition, tomorrow the branch manager and the assistant accountant will be here to examine your work; at that time, they will assist you in formulating the final budget document. The idea is to have you prepare the initial budget on your own so that you gain more confidence about accounting matters. You want to make a favourable impression on your superiors, so you gather the data at the top of p. 307 as of 31 May 20 × 8:

Credit sales are 90 per cent of total sales. Eighty per cent of each credit account is collected in the month following the sale and 20 per cent is collected in the subsequent month. Assume that bad debts are negligible and can be ignored. The accounts receivable on 31 May are the result of the credit sales for April and May:

$$(.20 \times .90 \times €60,000) + (1.0 \times .90 \times €70,000) = €73,800.$$

Cash	€ 5,800	**Recent and projected sales**	
Inventory	86,800	April	€ 60,000
		May	70,000
Accounts receivable	73,800	June	140,000
Net furniture and fixtures	33,600	July	80,000
Total assets	€200,000	August	80,000
Accounts payable	€ 97,800	September	60,000
Owner's equity	102,200		
Total liabilities and owners' equities	€200,000		

The average gross profit on sales is 38 per cent.

The policy is to acquire enough inventory each month to equal the following month's projected cost of goods sold. All purchases are paid for in the month following purchase.

Salaries, wages and commissions average 20 per cent of sales; all other variable expenses are 4 per cent of sales. Fixed expenses for rent, property taxes and miscellaneous payroll and other items are €11,000 monthly. Assume that these variable and fixed expenses require cash disbursements each month. Depreciation is €500 monthly.

In June, €11,000 is going to be disbursed for fixtures acquired and recorded in furniture and fixtures in May. The 31 May balance of accounts payable includes this amount.

Assume that a minimum cash balance of €5,000 is to be maintained. Also assume that all borrowings are effective at the beginning of the month and all repayments are made at the end of the month of repayment. Interest is compounded and added to the outstanding balance each month, but interest is paid only at the ends of months when principal is repaid. The interest rate is 10 per cent per year; round interest computations and interest payments to the nearest euro. Interest payments may be any euro amount, but all borrowing and repayments of principal are made in multiples of €1,000.

1 Prepare a budgeted income statement for the coming June–August quarter, a cash budget (for each of the next 3 months) and a budgeted balance sheet for 31 August 20X8. All operations are evaluated on a before-income-tax basis, so income taxes may be ignored here.

2 Explain why there is a need for a bank loan and what operating sources supply cash for repaying the bank loan.

7.B1 Prepare master budget

Wallaby Kite Company, a small Melbourne firm that sells kites on the web, wants a master budget for the 3 months beginning 1 January 20X2. It desires an ending minimum cash balance of €20,000 each month. Sales are forecasted at an average wholesale selling price of €8 per kite. Merchandise costs average €4 per kite. All sales are on credit, payable within 30 days, but experience has shown that 60 per cent of current sales are collected in the current month, 30 per cent in the next month and 10 per cent in the month thereafter. Bad debts are negligible.

In January, Wallaby Kite is beginning just-in-time (JIT) deliveries from suppliers, which means that purchases will equal expected sales. On January 1, purchases will cease until inventory decreases to €24,000, after which time purchases will equal sales. Purchases during any given month are paid in full during the following month.

Monthly operating expenses are as follows:

Wages and salaries	€60,000
Insurance expired	500
Depreciation	1,000
Miscellaneous	10,000
Rent	€1,000/month + 10% of quarterly sales over €40,000

Cash dividends of €6,000 are to be paid quarterly, beginning 15 January and are declared on the fifteenth of the previous month. All operating expenses are paid as incurred, except insurance, depreciation and rent. Rent of €1,000 is paid at the beginning of each month and the additional 10 per cent of sales is settled quarterly on the tenth of the month following the end of the quarter. The next rent settlement date is 10 January.

The company plans to buy some new fixtures for €12,000 cash in March.

Money can be borrowed and repaid in multiples of €2,000. Management wants to minimise borrowing and repay rapidly. Simple interest of 10 per cent per annum is computed monthly but paid when the principal is repaid. Assume that borrowing occurs at the beginning and repayments at the end, of the months in question. Compute interest to the nearest euro.

Assets as of 31 December 20X1		Liabilities and equities as of 31 December 20X1	
Cash	€20,000	Accounts payable	€142,200
Accounts receivable	50,000	(merchandise)	
Inventory*	156,200	Dividends payable	6,000
Unexpired insurance	6,000	Rent payable	31,200
Fixed assets, net	50,000	Owners' Equity	102,800
	€282,200		€282,200

* November 30 inventory balance = €64,000.

Recent and forecasted sales:

October	€152,000	December	€100,000	February	€280,000	April	€180,000
November	100,000	January	248,000	March	152,000		

1 Prepare a master budget including a budgeted income statement, balance sheet, cash budget and supporting schedules for the months January–March 20X2.

2 Explain why there is a need for a bank loan and what operating sources provide the cash for the repayment of the bank loan.

Additional assignment material

MyAccountingLab

QUESTIONS

7.1 What are the major benefits of budgeting?

7.2 Is budgeting used primarily for scorekeeping, attention directing or problem solving?

7.3 How do strategic planning, long-range planning and budgeting differ?

7.4 'I oppose continuous budgets because they provide a moving target. Managers never know at what to aim.' Discuss.

7.5 Why is it important to align performance goals of the company and the system used to evaluate and reward employees?

7.6 Explain the cycle of bias by lower-level managers and bias-adjustment by upper-level managers that can spiral out of control and result in meaningless budgets.

7.7 What are the incentives for inappropriate behaviours to *increase* reported profit when it appears that profits are likely to fall just short of a manager's bonus target?

7.8 Why is there an incentive for a manager to inappropriately *reduce* reported profit when it appears that profits are likely to be above the upper limit of a manager's bonus range?

7.9 Why is budgeted performance better than past performance as a basis for judging actual results?

7.10 'Budgets are okay in relatively certain environments. But everything changes so quickly in the electronics industry that budgeting is a waste of time.' Comment on this statement.

7.11 'Budgeting is an unnecessary burden on many managers. It takes time away from important day-to-day problems.' Do you agree? Explain.

7.12 Why is the sales forecast the starting point for budgeting?

7.13 What factors influence the sales forecast?

7.14 Differentiate between an operating budget and a financial budget.

7.15 Distinguish between operating expenses and disbursements for operating expenses.

7.16 What is the principal objective of a cash budget?

7.17 'Education and salesmanship are key features of budgeting.' Explain.

7.18 What are the main differences between functional and activity-based budgets?

7.19 'Financial planning models guide managers through the budget process so that managers do not really need to understand budgeting.' Do you agree? Explain.

7.20 Study Appendix 7. 'I cannot be bothered with setting up my monthly budget on a spreadsheet. It just takes too long to be worth the effort.' Comment.

7.21 Study Appendix 7. How do spreadsheets aid the application of sensitivity analysis?

CRITICAL THINKING EXERCISES

7.22 Budgets as limitations on spending

Many nonprofit organisations use budgets primarily to limit spending. Why does this limit the effectiveness of budgets?

7.23 Sales personnel and budgeting

The sales budget is the foundation of the entire master budget. How do sales personnel help formulate the budget? Compare the role of sales personnel to that of a central staff function, such as market research.

7.24 Master budgets for research and development

The text focuses on budgets for organisations that have revenues and expenses. Suppose you were the manager of a research and development division of a biotech company that has no revenue. How would budgets be helpful to you?

7.25 Production budgets and performance evaluation

The African Tire Company prepares an annual master budget each November for the following year. At the end of each year, it compares the actual costs incurred to the budgeted costs. How can African Tire get employees to accept the budget and strive to meet or beat the budgeted costs?

EXERCISES

7.26 Fill in the blanks

Enter the word or phrase that best completes each sentence.

1 The financial budget process includes the following budgets:

    (a) ——

    (b) ——

    (c) ——

2 The master budget process usually begins with the _____ budget.
3 A _____ budget is a plan that is revised monthly or quarterly, dropping one period and adding another.
4 Strategic planning sets the _____.

7.27 Cash budgeting

Blake Henderson and Anna Kraft are preparing a plan to submit to venture capitalists to fund their business, Music Masters. The company plans to spend €380,000 on equipment in the first quarter of 20X8. Salaries and other operating expenses (paid as incurred) will be €35,000 per month beginning in January 20X8 and will continue at that level thereafter. The company will receive its first revenues in January 20X9, with cash collections averaging €30,000 per month for all of 20X9. In January 20X0, cash collections are expected to increase to €100,000 per month and continue at that level thereafter.

Assume that the company needs enough funding to cover all its cash needs until cash receipts start exceeding cash disbursements. How much venture capital funding should Blake and Anna seek?

7.28 Purchases and cost of goods sold

Ronco Products, a wholesaler of fishing equipment, budgeted the following sales for the indicated months:

	June 20X8	July 20X8	August 20X8
Sales on account	€1,820,000	€1,960,000	€2,100,000
Cash sales	280,000	240,000	260,000
Total sales	€2,100,000	€2,200,000	€2,360,000

All merchandise is marked up to sell at its invoice cost plus 25 per cent. Target merchandise inventories at the beginning of each month are 30 per cent of that month's projected cost of goods sold.

1 Compute the budgeted cost of goods sold for the month of June 20X8.
2 Compute the budgeted merchandise purchases for July 20X8.

7.29 Purchases and sales budgets

All sales of Jenny's Jeans and Uniforms (JJU) are made on credit. Sales are billed twice monthly, on the fifth of the month for the last half of the prior month's sales and on the twentieth of the month for the first half of the current month's sales. For accounts paid within the first 10 days after the billing date, JJU gives customers a 3 per cent discount; otherwise the full amount is due within 30 days of the billing date and customers that do not pay within the 10-day discount period generally wait the full 30 days before making payment. Based on past experience, the collection experience of accounts receivable is as follows:

Within the 10-day discount period	80%
At 30 days after billing	18%
Uncollectible	2%

Sales for May 20X8 were €700,000. The forecast sales for the next 4 months are as follows:

June	€800,000
July	950,000
August	900,000
September	600,000

JJU's average markup on its products is 40 per cent of the sales price.

JJU purchases merchandise for resale to meet the current month's sales demand and to maintain a desired monthly ending inventory of 25 per cent of the next month's cost of goods sold. All purchases are on credit. JJU pays for one-half of a month's purchases in the month of purchase and the other half in the month following the purchase.

All sales and purchases occur uniformly throughout the month.

1 How much cash can JJU plan to collect from accounts receivable collections during July 20X8?
2 Compute the budgeted euro value of JJU inventory on May 31, 20X8.
3 How much merchandise should JJU plan to purchase during June 20X8?
4 How much should JJU budget in August 20X8 for cash payments for merchandise purchased?

7.30 Sales budget

Suppose a lumber yard has the following data:
- Accounts receivable, 31 May: (.3 × May sales of €350,000) = €105,000
- Monthly forecasted sales: June, €430,000; July, €440,000; August, €500,000; September, €530,000

Sales consist of 70 per cent cash and 30 per cent credit. All credit accounts are collected in the month following the sales. Uncollectible accounts are negligible and may be ignored.

Prepare a sales budget schedule and a cash collections budget schedule for June, July and August.

7.31 Sales budget

A Kyoto clothing wholesaler was preparing its sales budget for the first quarter of 20X8. Forecast sales are as follows (in thousands of yen):

January	¥200,000
February	¥200,000
March	¥240,000

Sales are 20 per cent cash and 80 per cent on credit. Fifty per cent of the credit accounts are collected in the month of sale, 40 per cent in the month following the sale, and 10 per cent in the following month. No uncollectible accounts are anticipated. Accounts receivable at the beginning of 20X8 are ¥96 million (10 per cent of November credit sales of ¥180 million and 50 per cent of December credit sales of ¥156 million).

Prepare a schedule showing sales and cash collections for January, February and March 20X8.

7.32 Cash collection budget

Northwest Equipment offers a 2 per cent discount to customers who pay cash at the time of sale and a 1 per cent discount to customers who pay within the first 10 days of the month after sale. Past experience shows that cash collections from customers tend to occur in the following pattern:

Cash collected at time of sale	50%
Collected within cash discount period in first 10 days of month after sale	10
Collected after cash discount period in first month after month of sale	25
Collected after cash discount period in second month after month of sale	12
Never collected	3

Compute the total cash budgeted to be collected in March if sales forecasts are €360,000 for January, €400,000 for February and €450,000 for March.

7.33 Purchases budget

Renovation Lighting Supply plans inventory levels (at cost) at the end of each month as follows: May, €275,000; June, €220,000; July, €200,000; and August, €240,000.

Sales are expected to be June, €440,000; July, €350,000; and August, €300,000. Cost of goods sold is 60 per cent of sales.

Purchases in April were €250,000 and in May they were €180,000. Payments for each month's purchases are made as follows: 10 per cent during that month, 80 per cent the next month and the final 10 per cent the next month.

Prepare budget schedules for June July and August for purchases and for disbursements for purchases.

7.34 Purchases budget

Linkenheim GmbH has adopted the following policies regarding merchandise purchases and inventory. At the end of any month, the inventory should be €15,000 plus 90 per cent of the cost of goods to be sold during the following month. The cost of merchandise sold averages 60 per cent of sales. Purchase terms are generally net, 30 days. A given month's purchases are paid as follows: 20 per cent during that month and 80 per cent during the following month.

Purchases in May had been €150,000 and the inventory on May 31 was higher than planned at €210,000. The manager was upset because the inventory was too high. Sales are expected to be June, €300,000; July, €290,000; August, €340,000; and September, €400,000.

1 Compute the amount by which the inventory on May 31 exceeded the company's policies.
2 Prepare budget schedules for June, July and August for purchases and for disbursements for purchases.

Sales		€290
Inventory, 31 May	€ 50	
Purchases	192	
Available for sale	242	
Inventory, 30 June	40	
Cost of goods sold		202
Gross margin		€ 88
Operating expenses		
Wages	€ 36	
Utilities	5	
Advertising	10	
Depreciation	1	
Office expenses	4	
Insurance and property taxes	3	59
Operating income		€ 29

Exhibit 7.13 Carlson Company – Budgeted income statement for the month ended 30 June 20X4 (in thousands)

7.35 Cash budget

Consider the budgeted income statement for Carlson Company for June 20X4 in Exhibit 7.13.

The cash balance, 31 May 20X4, is €15,000.

Sales proceeds are collected as follows: 80 per cent the month of sale, 10 per cent the second month and 10 per cent the third month.

Accounts receivable are €44,000 on 31 May 20X4, consisting of €20,000 from April sales and €24,000 from May sales.

Accounts payable on 31 May 20X4 are €145,000.

Carlson Company pays 25 per cent of purchases during the month of purchase and the remainder during the following month.

All operating expenses requiring cash are paid during the month of recognition, except that insurance and property taxes are paid annually in December for the forthcoming year.

Prepare a cash budget for June. Confine your analysis to the given data. Ignore income taxes.

PROBLEMS

7.36 Cash budget

Daniel Merrill is the manager of an airport gift shop, Merrill News and Gifts. From the following data, Mr Merrill wants a cash budget showing expected cash receipts and disbursements for the month of April and the cash balance expected as of 30 April 20X7.

Planned cash balance, 31 March 20X7: €100,000

Customer receivables as of 31 March: €530,000 total, €80,000 from February sales, €450,000 from March sales

Accounts payable, 31 March: €460,000

Merchandise purchases for April: €450,000, 40 per cent paid in month of purchase, 60 per cent paid in next month

Payrolls due in April: €90,000

Other expenses for April, payable in April: €45,000

Accrued taxes for April, payable in June: €7,500

Bank note due April 10: €90,000 plus €7,200 interest

Depreciation for April: €2,100

Two-year insurance policy due 14 April for renewal: €1,500, to be paid in cash

Sales for April: €1,000,000, half collected in month of sale, 40 per cent in next month, 10 per cent in third month

Prepare the cash budget for the month ending 30 April 20X7.

7.37 Cash budget

Prepare a statement of estimated cash receipts and disbursements for October 20X7 for the Botanica Company, which sells one product, herbal soap, by the case. On 1 October 20X7, part of the trial balance showed the following:

	Dr	Cr
Cash	€ 4,800	
Accounts receivable	15,600	
Allowance for bad debts		€1,900
Merchandise inventory	9,000	
Accounts payable, merchandise		6,600

The company pays for its purchases within 10 days of purchase so assume that one-third of the purchases of any month are due and paid for in the following month.

The cost of the merchandise purchased is €12 per case. At the end of each month, it is desired to have an inventory equal in units to 50 per cent of the following month's sales in units.

Sales terms include a 1 per cent discount if payment is made by the end of the calendar month. Past experience indicates that 60 per cent of sales will be collected during the month of the sale, 30 per cent in the following calendar month, 6 per cent in the next following calendar month and the remaining 4 per cent will be uncollectable. The company's fiscal year begins 1 August.

Unit selling price	€	20
August actual sales	€	12,000
September actual sales		36,000
October estimated sales		30,000
November estimated sales		22,000
Total sales expected in the fiscal year		€360,000

Exclusive of bad debts, total budgeted selling and general administrative expenses for the fiscal year are estimated at €61,500, of which €24,000 is fixed expense (which includes a €13,200 annual depreciation charge). The Botanica Company incurs these fixed expenses uniformly throughout the year. The balance of the selling and general administrative expenses varies with sales. Expenses are paid as incurred.

7.38 Budgeting at Ritz-Carlton

The Ritz-Carlton has four hotels and resorts in the Caribbean and Mexico. For one of these hotels, management expects occupancy rates to be 95 per cent in December January and February; 85 per cent in November, March and April; and 70 per cent the rest of the year. This hotel has 300 rooms and the average room rental is €290 per night. Of this, on average 10 per cent is received as a deposit the month before the stay, 60 per cent is received in the month of the stay and 28 per cent is collected the month after. The remaining 2 per cent is never collected.

Most of the costs of running the hotel are fixed. The variable costs are only €30 per occupied room per night. Fixed salaries (including benefits) run €400,000 per month, depreciation is €350,000 a month, other fixed operating costs are €120,000 per month and interest expense is €600,000 per month. Variable costs and salaries are paid in the month they are incurred, depreciation is recorded at the end of each quarter, other fixed operating costs are paid as incurred and interest is paid semi-annually each June and December.

1 Prepare a monthly cash budget for this Ritz-Carlton hotel for the entire year. For simplicity, assume that there are 30 days in each month.

2 How much would the hotel's annual profit increase if occupancy rates increased by 5 per cent each month in the off-season (that is, from 70 per cent to 75 per cent in May–October)?

7.39 Activity-based budgeting

A recent directive from Sandy Jensen, Managing Director of Duluth Manufacturing, had instructed each department to cut its costs by 10 per cent. The traditional functional budget for the shipping and receiving department was as follows:

Salaries, four employees at €42,000	€168,000
Benefits at 20%	33,600
Depreciation, straight-line basis	76,000
Supplies	43,400
Overhead at 35% of direct costs	112,350
Total	€433,350

Therefore, the shipping and receiving department needed to find €43,335 to cut.

June Steele, a recent MBA graduate, was asked to pare €43,335 from the shipping and receiving department's budget. As a first step, she recast the traditional budget into an activity-based budget.

Receiving, 620,000 kgs	€ 93,000
Shipping, 404,000 boxes	202,000
Handling, 11,200 moves	112,000
Record keeping, 65,000 transactions	26,350
Total	€433,350

1 What actions might Steele suggest to attain a €43,335 budget cut? Why would these be the best actions to pursue?

2 Which budget helped you most in answering number 1? Explain.

7.40 Budgeting, behaviour and ethics

Mathew Philp, president of North Mining Ltd, has made budgets a major focus for managers. Making budget was such an important goal that the only two managers who had missed their budgets in 20X7 (by 2 per cent and 4 per cent, respectively) had been summarily fired. This caused all managers to be wary when setting their 20X8 budgets.

The Red Mountain Copper Division of North Mining had the following results for 20X7:

Sales, 1.6 million kgs at €.95/kg	€1,520,000
Variables costs	880,000
Fixed costs, primarily depreciation	450,000
Pretax profit	€ 190,000

Molly Stark, general manager of Red Mountain Copper, received a memo from Philp that contained the following:

We expect your profit for 20X8 to be at least €209,000. Prepare a budget showing how you plan to accomplish this.

Stark was concerned because the market for copper had recently softened. Her market research staff forecast that sales would be at or below the 20X7 level and prices would likely be between €.92 and €.94 per kg. Her manufacturing manager reported that most of the fixed costs were committed and there were few efficiencies to be gained in the variable costs. He indicated that perhaps a 2 per cent savings in variable costs might be achievable but certainly no more.

1 Prepare a budget for Stark to submit to headquarters. What dilemmas does Stark face in preparing this budget?

2 What problems do you see in the budgeting process at North Mining?

3 Suppose Stark submitted a budget showing a €209,000 profit. It is now late in 20X8 and she has had a good year. Despite an industry-wide decline in sales, Red Mountain Copper's sales matched last year's 1.6 million kgs and the average price per kg was €.945, nearly at last year's level and well above that forecast. Variable costs were cut by 2 per cent through extensive efforts. Still, profit projections were more than €9,000 below budget. Stark was concerned for her job so she approached the accountant and requested that depreciation schedules be changed. By extending the lives of some equipment for 2 years, depreciation in 20X8 would be reduced by €15,000. Estimating the economic lives of equipment is difficult, and it would be hard to prove that the old lives were better than the new proposed lives. What should the accountant do? What ethical issues does this proposal raise?

7.41 Spreadsheets and sensitivity analysis of income statement

Study Appendix 7. A Speedy-Mart Store in North Mall has the following budgeted sales, which are uniform throughout the month:

May	€450,000
June	375,000
July	330,000
August	420,000

Cost of goods sold averages 70 per cent of sales and merchandise is purchased and paid for essentially as needed. Employees earn fixed salaries of €22,000 monthly and commissions of 10 per cent of the current month's sales, paid as earned. Other expenses are rent, €6,000, paid on the first of each month for that month's occupancy; miscellaneous expenses, 6 per cent of sales, paid as incurred; insurance, €450 per month, from a 1-year policy that was paid for on January 2; and depreciation, €2,850 per month.

1 Using spreadsheet software, prepare a table of budget data for the Speedy-Mart Store.

2 Continue the spreadsheet in number 1 to prepare budget schedules for (a) disbursements for operating expenses and (b) operating income for June, July and August.

3 Adjust the budget data appropriately for each of the following scenarios independently and recompute operating income using the spreadsheet:

(a) A sales promotion that will cost €30,000 in May could increase sales in each of the following 3 months by 5 per cent.

(b) Eliminating the sales commissions and increasing employees' salaries to €52,500 per month could decrease sales thereafter by a net of 2 per cent.

7.42 Spreadsheets and sensitivity analysis of operating expenses

Study Appendix 7. The High Definition LCD Division (HDLD) of Fisher Displays produces displays for HD LCD televisions. The displays are assembled from purchased components. The costs (value) added by HDLD are indirect costs, which include assembly labour, packaging and shipping. HDLD produces two sizes of displays: 42" and 50". Cost behaviour of HDLD is as follows:

	Fixed cost/month	Variable cost
Purchased components		
50" Displays		£80 per component
42" Displays		55 per component
Assembly labour	£40,000	16 per component
Packaging	8,000	4 per display
Shipping	8,000	2 per display

Both displays require five components per display. Therefore, the total cost of components for 50" displays is £400 and for 42" displays is £275. HDLD uses a 6-month continuous budget that is revised monthly. Sales forecasts for the next 8 months are as follows:

	50" Displays	42" Displays
October	3,200 units	4,000 units
November	2,400	3,000
December	5,600	7,000
January	3,200	4,000
February	3,200	4,000
March	2,400	3,000
April	2,400	3,000
May	2,800	3,500

Treat each event in succession.

1 Use spreadsheet software to prepare a table of budgeting information and an operating expense budget for HDLD for October–March. Incorporate the expectation that sales of 42" displays will be 125 per cent of 50" displays. Prepare a spreadsheet that can be revised easily for succeeding months in parts 2 and 3.
2 October's actual sales were 2,800 50" displays and 3,600 42" displays. This outcome has caused HDLD to revise its sales forecasts downward by 10 per cent. Revise the operating expense budget for November–April.
3 At the end of November, HDLD decides that the proportion of 50" to 42" displays is changing. Sales of 42" displays are expected to be 150 per cent of 50" displays sales. Expected sales of 50" displays are unchanged from number 2. Revise the operating expense budget for December–May.

CASES

7.43 Comprehensive cash budgeting

Ms Morrissio, treasurer of Sardinia Lake Light Opera (SLLO), was preparing a loan request to the Sardinia National Bank in December 20X4. The loan was necessary to meet the cash needs of the SLLO for year 20X5. In a few short years, the SLLO had established itself as a premier opera company. In addition to its regular subscription series, it started a series for new composers and offered a very popular holiday production. The holiday production was the most financially successful of the SLLO's activities, providing a base to support innovative productions that were artistically important to the SLLO but did not usually succeed financially.

In total, the SLLO had done well financially, as shown in Exhibits 7.14 and 7.15. Its profitable operations had enabled it to build its own building and generally acquire a large number of assets. It had at least broken even every year since its incorporation and management anticipates continued profitable operations. The Corporate Community for the Arts in Sardinia Lake and several private foundations had made many grants to the SLLO and such grants are expected to continue. Most recently, the largest bank in town had agreed to sponsor the production of a new opera by a local composer. The SLLO's director of development, expected such corporate sponsorships to increase in the future.

To provide facilities for the Opera's anticipated growth, SLLO began work on an addition to its building 2 years ago. The new facilities are intended primarily to support the experimental

	20X2	20X3	20X4
Assets			
Cash	€2,688	€ 229	€ 208
Accounts receivable	2,942	3,372	4,440
Supplies inventory	700	700	500
Total current assets	€6,330	€4,301	€ 5,148
Plant and equipment	2,643	4,838	5,809
Total assets	€8,973	€9,193	€10,957
Liabilities and equities			
Bank loan	€ 0	€ 0	€ 1,620*
Accounts payable	420	720	780
Accrued payroll expenses	472	583	646
Mortgage, current	250	250	250
Total current liabilities	€1,142	€1,553	€ 3,296
Other payables	270		
Mortgage payable, long-term	3,750	3,500	3,250
Net assets†	3,811	4,086	4,411
Total liabilities and equities	€8,973	€9,139	€10,957

* Includes €32,000 of accrued interest.
† The 'Net assets' account for a nonprofit organisation is similar to 'Stockholders' equity' for a corporation.

Exhibit 7.14 Sardinia Lake Light Opera – Balance sheets as of 31 December (in thousands of euros)

	20X2	20X3	20X4
Tickets sales	€3,303	€4,060	€5,263
Contributions	1,041	1,412	1,702
Grants and other revenues	1,202	1,361	1,874
Total revenues	€5,546	€6,833	€8,839
Expenses*			
Production	€4,071	€4,805	€6,307
Operations	271	332	473
Public relations and community development	1,082	1,421	1,734
Total expenses	€5,424	€6,558	€8,514
Excess of revenues over expenses	€ 122	€ 275	€ 325

* Expenses include depreciation of €355, €370 and €470 and general and administrative expenses of €1,549, €1,688 and €2,142 in the years 20X2, 20X3 and 20X4, respectively.

Exhibit 7.15 Sardinia Lake Light Opera – Income statements for the year ended 31 December (in thousands of euros)

offerings that were becoming more numerous. The capital expansion was to be completed in 20X5; all that remained was acquisition and installation of lighting, sound equipment and other new equipment to be purchased in 20X5.

SLLO had borrowed working capital from Sardinia National Bank for the past several years. To qualify for the loans, the SLLO had to agree to the following:

1 Completely pay off the loan for 1 month during the course of the year.
2 Maintain cash and accounts receivable balances equal to (or greater than) 120 per cent of the loan.
3 Maintain a compensating cash balance of €200,000 at all times.

In the past, the SLLO has had no problem meeting these requirements. However, in 20X4 the SLLO had been unable to reduce the loan to zero for an entire month. Although the bank continued to extend the needed credit, the loan manager expressed concern over the situation. She asked for a quarterly cash budget to justify the financing needed for 20X5. Ms Morrissio began to assemble the data needed to prepare such a budget.

SLLO received revenue from three main sources: ticket sales, contributions and grants. Ms Morrissio formed Exhibit 7.16 to calculate the accounts receivable balance for each of these sources for 20X5. She assumed that SLLO would continue its normal practices for collecting pledges and grant revenues.

Most expenses were constant from month to month. An exception was supplies, which were purchased twice a year in December and June. In 20X5, SLLO expects to purchase €200,000 of supplies in June and €700,000 in December on terms of net, 30 days. The supplies inventory at the end of December was expected to be €600,000. Depreciation expense of €500,000 was planned for 20X5 and other expenses were expected to run at a steady rate of €710,000 a month throughout the year, of which €700,000 was payroll costs. Salaries and wages were paid on the Monday of the first week following the end of the month. The remaining €10,000 of other expenses were paid as incurred.

The major portion of the new equipment to be installed in 20X5 was to be delivered in September; payments totalling €400,000 would be made in four equal monthly installments beginning in September. In addition, small equipment purchases are expected to run €20,000 per month throughout the year. They will be paid for on delivery.

In late 20X2, SLLO had borrowed €4 million (classified as a mortgage payable) from Sardinia Life Insurance Company. The SLLO is repaying the loan over 16 years, in equal principal payments in June and December of each year. Interest at 8 per cent annually is also paid on the unpaid balance on each of these dates. Total interest payments for 20X5, according to Ms Morrissio's calculations, would be €275,000.

Interest on the working capital loan from Sardinia National Bank was at an annual rate of 10 per cent. Interest is accrued quarterly but paid annually; payment for 20X4's interest would be made on 10 January 20X5 and that for 20X5's interest would be made on 10 January 20X6. Working capital loans are taken out on the first day of the quarter that funds are needed and they are repaid on the last day of the quarter when extra funds are generated. SLLO has tried to keep a minimum cash balance of €200,000 at all times, even if loan requirements do not require it.

	Ticket sales		Contributions		Grants	
	Revenues	End of quarter receivables	Revenues	End of quarter receivables	Revenues	End of quarter receivables
First quarter	€ 852	€2,795	€ 75	€ 794	€ 132	€1,027
Second quarter	1,584	3,100	363	888	448	1,130
Third quarter	2,617	3,407	1,203	1,083	1,296	1,240
Fourth quarter	1,519	3,683	442	1,170	528	1,342

Exhibit 7.16 Sardinia Lake Light Opera – Estimated quarterly revenues and end of quarter receivables for the year ended 31 December 20X5 (in thousands of euros)

1 Compute the cash inflows and outflows for each quarter of 20X5. What are SLLO's loan requirements each quarter?
2 Prepare a projected income statement and balance sheet for SLLO for 20X5.
3 Prepare the projected statement of cash flows for 20X5.
4 What financing strategy would you recommend for SLLO?

7.44 Cash budgeting for a hospital

Evergreen Hospital provides a wide range of health services in its community. Evergreen's board of directors has authorised the following capital expenditures:

Intra-aortic balloon pump	€1,400,000
Computed tomographic scanner	850,000
X-ray equipment	550,000
Laboratory equipment	1,200,000
Total	€4,000,000

The expenditures are planned for 1 October 20X7, and the board wishes to know the amount of borrowing, if any, necessary on that date. Rebecca Singer, hospital accountant, has gathered the following information to be used in preparing an analysis of future cash flows.

Billings, made in the month of service, for 20X7 are shown next, with actual amounts for January–June and estimated amounts for July–December:

Month	Amount billed
January	€5,300,000
February	5,300,000
March	5,400,000
April	5,400,000
May	6,000,000
June	6,000,000
July (estimated)	5,800,000
August (estimated)	6,200,000
September (estimated)	6,600,000
October (estimated)	6,800,000
November (estimated)	7,000,000
December (estimated)	6,600,000

Ninety per cent of Evergreen billings are made to private insurance companies as third-party billings. The remaining 10 per cent of the billings are made directly to patients. Historical patterns of billing collections are as follows:

	Third-party billings	Direct-patient billings
Month of service	20%	10%
Month following service	50	40
Second month following service	20	40
Uncollectible	10	10

Singer expects the same billing and collection patterns that have been experienced during the first 6 months of 20X7 to continue during the last 6 months of the year. The following schedule presents the purchases that have been made during the past 3 months and the planned purchases for the last 6 months of 20X7.

Month	Amount
April	€1,300,000
May	1,450,000
June	1,450,000
July	1,500,000
August	1,800,000
September	2,200,000
October	2,350,000
November	2,700,000
December	2,100,000

All purchases are made on account and accounts payable are remitted in the month following the purchase.

- Salaries for each month during the remainder of 20X7 are expected to be €1,800,000 per month plus 20 per cent of that month's billings. Salaries are paid in the month of service.
- Evergreen's monthly depreciation charges are €150,000.
- Evergreen incurs interest expenses of €180,000 per month and makes interest payments of €540,000 on the last day of each calendar quarter.
- Endowment fund income is expected to continue to total €210,000 per month.
- Evergreen has a cash balance of €350,000 on 1 July 20X7 and has a policy of maintaining a minimum end-of-month cash balance of 10 per cent of the current month's purchases.
- Evergreen Hospital employs a calendar-year reporting period.

1 Prepare a schedule of budgeted cash receipts by month for the third quarter of 20X7.
2 Prepare a schedule of budgeted cash disbursements by month for the third quarter of 20X7.
3 Determine the amount of borrowing, if any, necessary on 1 October 20X7, to acquire the capital items totalling €4,000,000.

7.45 Comprehensive budgeting for a university

Suppose you are the accountant for Bristol Metro University which is a privately funded university. The university president, Lisa Larsson, is preparing for her annual fund-raising campaign for 20X7–20X8. To set an appropriate target, she has asked you to prepare a budget for the academic year. You have collected the following data for the current year (20X6–20X7):

	Undergraduate division	Graduate division
Average salary of faculty member	€58,000	€58,000
Average faculty teaching load in semester credit-hours per year (eight undergraduate or six graduate courses)	24	18
Average number of students per class	30	20
Total enrollment (full-time and part-time students)	3,600	1,800

	Undergraduate division	Graduate division
Average number of semester credit-hours carried each year per student	25	20
Full-time load, semester hours per year	30	24

For 20X7–20X8, all faculty and staff will receive a 6 per cent salary increase. Undergraduate enrollment is expected to decline by 2 per cent, but graduate enrollment is expected to increase by 5 per cent.

- The 20X6–20X7 budget for operation and maintenance of facilities was €500,000, which includes €240,000 for salaries and wages. Experience so far this year indicates that the budget is accurate. Salaries and wages will increase by 6 per cent and other operating costs will increase by €12,000 in 20X7–20X8.
- The 20X6–20X7 and 20X7–20X8 budgets for the remaining expenditures are as follows:

	20X6–20X7	20X7–20X8
General administrative Library	€500,000	€525,000
Acquisitions	150,000	155,000
Operations	190,000	200,0000
Health services	48,000	50,000
Intramural athletics	56,000	60,000
Intercollegiate athletics	240,000	245,000
Insurance and retirement	520,000	560,000
Interest	75,000	75,000

- Tuition is €92 per credit hour. In addition, the state provides €780 per full-time-equivalent student at private universities. (A full-time equivalent is 30 undergraduate hours or 24 graduate hours.) Full-tuition scholarships are given to 30 full-time undergraduates and 50 full-time graduate students.
- Revenues other than tuition and the legislative apportionment are as follows:

	20X6–20X7	20X7–20X8
Endowment income	€200,000	€210,000
Net income from auxiliary services	325,000	335,000
Intercollegiate athletic receipts	290,000	3,000

- The chemistry/physics classroom building needs remodelling during the 20X7–20X8 period. Projected cost is €575,000.

1 Prepare a schedule for 20X7–20X8 that shows, by division, (a) expected enrollment, (b) total credit hours, (c) full-time-equivalent enrollment and (d) number of faculty members needed.
2 Calculate the budget for faculty salaries for 20X7–20X8 by division.
3 Calculate the budget for tuition revenue and legislative apportionment for 20X7–20X8 by division.
4 Prepare a schedule for President Larsson showing the amount that must be raised by the annual fund-raising campaign.

CASE STUDY

Cresta Plating Company Ltd

This case focuses on the design of a management control system in a company where 'control by observation' is no longer deemed appropriate and where management by objectives is being implemented. It engages in a discussion of decentralisation and responsibility accounting issues.

Company background

Cresta Plating Company Ltd was purchased in 1990 by a group of companies to carry out the plating works of its many subsidiary companies. Cresta is one company within a division of the main group, the division being concerned predominantly with metal finishing in the widest sense. The company is located in the London area and this was a significant factor in the decision to purchase, since the majority of the companies in the group were also situated in the south east of England.

Apart from plating work for companies within the division and within the group generally, the company carries out a substantial amount of plating for companies outside the group. The proportions of work for group companies and non-group companies have recently been equal.

The company had its origins in the early 1970s and from tin-shed beginnings it expanded by the time of the purchase in 1990 to a reasonable size and had gained a sound technical reputation. All the remnants of private family business management have now disappeared. However, despite the efforts of the parent company and a number of recent executive appointments which have been group-inspired, the 'group image' is not well established.

Production and progress

The company is in the electro-plating jobbing industry and this presents problems not met in a plating shop in a factory handling work that is produced in that factory alone. This is an important factor, for it results in the company having limited knowledge of the orders that are coming into the factory premises. Production planning and control is extremely difficult, especially when linked to the quick delivery so vital to secure orders. The company aims at a 48-hour turnaround from the receipt of an order to its despatch.

Since 1990 the company has grown rapidly and now employs about 350 people at two factories in London, one in Newcastle and another in Sheffield, the last two factories being recent acquisitions of family businesses which, although technically sound, have not been satisfactory in the financial sense.

At Cresta, both barrel plating and vat plating are used. Most of the vats are hand-operated in order to achieve a flexibility necessary to cope with the different mixes of products. On the barrel-plating side, there are two large automatic plants to cope with the steady flow of work from group companies. There are also a few hand-operated barrels. The company handles a wide variety of work, ranging from small orders of a few kilograms weight, to huge orders where the total weight of the products involved could be as much as one tonne. A wide variety of finishes is catered for, such as zinc, cadmium, tin, chromium, nickel, copper, precious metals such as gold and silver and also plastics.

The company has been profitable for a number of years and the continuation of this trend can be seen in recent results. This success has been partly due to the fact that the company has an assured market within the group. Intra-group pricing is a touchy matter within the company and Cresta is under constant pressure to reduce transfer prices which, by the strength of its top management, it seems to withstand successfully.

Source: Adapted from 'Cresta Plating Company Ltd', *Management Accounting*, 1988.

Accounting methods

The accounting department has a staff of 12 who cover the duties of financial accounting, cost accounting and wages for all the factories. There are, however, two clerical workers on routine accounting and wages matters, both at Newcastle and Sheffield. Until a few months ago, the only costing work being done was the recalculation of cost rates for the purpose of estimating for price fixing. This recalculation was undertaken annually and was on an absorption costing basis. Overhead costs are categorised as fixed or variable on a basis specified by head office and this analysis is a requirement of the trading statement prepared and submitted to head office.

The appointment was made in 2009 of a new man to the post of company secretary/chief accountant. He has proved to be quite an innovator and one of the first tasks he undertook was to review the financial and cost accounting procedures. At one of the early board meetings he attended it was stressed that better financial controls were needed. This attitude was supported by the argument that, as the company was continuing to expand, control by observation became increasingly difficult. The new man formed the impression that a certain amount of lip-service was being paid to the idea of management accounting and information services. He found that monthly and quarterly interim trading statements were being prepared, but he was disappointed that these were only total trading statements for the company. He proceeded to give immediate thought to the departmentalisation of the figures. One of the factors which weighed heavily with him was the fact that during his four weeks 'acclimatisation' at head office, he had been introduced to a management by objectives programme which was in the process of being launched throughout the group. Two points that particularly impressed him about this programme were:

1 The overall financial objective which was to be built into the programme, namely a return on capital employed of 20 per cent before tax.
2 The desire to set objectives and key tasks for individual managers and executives.

This second point matched comments which had been made at the Cresta board meeting that production managers needed measures which they did not have at the moment.

Budgets

The accountant also had work to do on accounting returns for head office. The statements in Table 1 include a budget and actual trading statement return, prepared to the group uniform pattern. The budget is an annual affair and worries the accountant somewhat, since he believes that it should have its roots in departmental budgets. This is not so at the moment, because it is produced as an overall business budget.

Table 1 Budget and actual trading statements, September 2011

	September 2011		January to September 2011	
	Budget	Actual	Budget	Actual
Sales: to group companies	£22 000	£29 161	£220 000	£287 103
Sales: outside group	38 000	27 277	380 000	285 046
Total sales	60 000	56 438	600 000	572 149
Variable costs of sales	35 000	32 231	350 000	335 203
Gross margin	25 000	24 207	250 000	236 946
Other costs				
Depreciation	2 600	2 416	26 000	24 720
Fixed works expenses	5 200	6 637	52 000	58 634
Admin. expenses	2 800	3 029	28 000	29 327

Table 1 (Continued)

	September 2011		January to September 2011	
	Budget	Actual	Budget	Actual
Fixed sales expenses	2 400	1 448	24 000	20 772
	£13 000	£13 530	£130 000	£133 012
	£12 000	£10 677	£120 000	£103 934

Accounting developments

As far as Cresta was concerned, it seemed to the accountant that departmentalisation could logically be carried to profit centres. There was vat plating and barrel plating and there were some less significant sections; further, there were natural subsections in each of which were definite factory locations with directly identifiable sales. There was already in being a simple sales analysis to these profit centres. To develop the existing records into a departmental system of accounting was only a matter of arranging the necessary cost analysis procedures. These were partly in existence in a rough-and-ready fashion and were used to facilitate the task of recalculating cost rates annually. The extra work created by a full-scale cost allocation and apportionment exercise carried out each monthly accounting period was performed by two additional cost office staff especially appointed for the purpose.

There were, inevitably, some joint costs and much thought had to be given to them, particularly on the matter of how these should be apportioned between the profit centres. In addition, there were service department costs, administration expenses and some general fixed costs and for all of these bases of apportionment had to be determined. It was a hard slog, but it was finally done and it was possible to produce interim profit centre trading statements.

Profit centre trading statements

The first man to see the new statements was the managing director, who took some time to warm to them, but he eventually did. The other executives were brought into a meeting to study them and there was general agreement that they were very informative. This was the first information which top management had ever received on the profitability of different units, so that inevitably some surprise was registered about some of the figures. On this first set of departmental trading statements, the new accountant had gone no further than to analyse sales, costs and profits or losses. There was, however, a feeling at the meeting that the next statement should show an analysis of capital employed in profit centres in order that 'profitability' could be computed on a departmental basis. Interest was running high and the accountant was pleased.

The next step was the analysis of capital employed and the accountant and his staff found this analysis to profit centres was just as difficult as cost analysis. Some of the fixed capital could be identified directly with departments, but some was of a more general type. He was not at all sure about the working capital, which he felt was very much more a function of the product itself and of the customer than it was of any production department. There was also the problem of capital employed in the service departments of the company. But again, the interest in department profitability was something to be cultivated and he felt that the management accounting service had an opportunity here to justify itself. The net result of all these efforts is the type of trading statement which appears in Table 2.

'Can these assessments be right?'

The next phase in relationships between accounting and management generally at Cresta can best be described as a 'Can these assessments be right?' phase. Arguments raged about

Table 2 Profit centre analysis – Panel A

	Totals	Barrel	Vat	HD	Spec. fin.	Misc.
September 2011 Sales						
Group companies	£29 161	£21 625	£ 2 604	£ 1 445	£ 1 877	£ 1 610
Others	27 277	3 630	7 564	3 457	11 426	1 200
Total	56 438	25 255	10 168	4 902	13 303	2 810
Process materials	8 271	3 599	1 885	502	1 857	428
Direct labour	7 140	1 374	2 003	818	2 702	243
Indirect labour	1 501	497	474	28	455	47
Labour overheads	1 296	282	366	112	497	39
Consumables	2 308	127	470	195	857	659
Power	4 653	1 851	452	603	1 278	469
Maintenance	1 947	974	238	100	575	60
Jigs	576	–	133	203	240	–
Services	4 539	1 950	726	633	1 205	25
Variable costs	32 231	10 654	6 747	3 194	9 666	1 970
Gross margin	24 207	14 601	3 421	1 708	3 637	840
Fixed works expenses	9 053	3 589	1 487	1 352	2 303	322
Admin. and sales expenses	4 477	2 037	729	395	93	1 223
	13 530	5 626	2 216	1 747	2 396	1 545
Profit (loss)	£10 677	£ 8 975	£ 1 205	(£39)	£ 1 241	(£ 705)
January–September 2011						
Sales	572 149	260 093	105 623	61 078	120 467	24 888
Profit (loss)	103 934	77 909	8 101	4 568	9 356	4 000
% of sales	18.2	29.9	7.6	7.5	7.8	16.0
Annual rate of profit	138 578	103 879	10 801	6 091	12 475	5 333
Assets employed	350 000	130 000	58 000	43 000	109 000	10 000
ROI%	39.5	79.8	18.6	14.2	11.4	53.3

the allocation and apportionment of costs to profit centres. Time and again the accountant made the point that any allocation is arbitrary, no matter how detailed the process by which the allocation rule is determined. On the other hand, he never failed to add that each profit centre must bear its fair share of all expenses.

There is no doubt that many of the management team at Cresta had been shattered by the figures. Some profit centres were shown to be less profitable than they had been thought to be. Perhaps it was natural that there were recriminations. There were comments like 'We always felt that Bert was efficient, but look how much money he's losing us.' All this worried the accountant. Surely it was logical to have profit centre reporting? But where were the ties between profitability and efficiency, if any?

Transfer pricing

Discussions between the accountant, managers and parties aggrieved by his efforts brought out many points which he felt deserved attention. The overriding one seemed to be the subject of transfer pricing. The point was made that there were inconsistencies in pricing which stemmed from two main causes: firstly, insufficient work measurement had been done to enable the establishment of reasonable standards or estimating; and secondly, the managing director had involved himself extensively in pricing decisions. On the first point, everyone agreed that proper work measurement was difficult in this type

Table 2 Profit centre analysis – Panel B

	Total Barrel	A Automatic	B Automatic	Horizontal	Chrome	Small orders	Anodising	Spec.fin.
September 2011								
Sales								
Group companies	£ 21 625	£ 5 791	£ 3 191	£ 7 985	£ 3 923	£ 427	£ 150	£ 158
Others	3 630	247	1 926	1 177	63	217	–	–
Total	25 255	6 038	5 117	9 162	3 986	644	150	158
Process materials	5 599	516	533	2 105	137	213	18	77
Direct labour	1 374	282	226	474	165	112	40	75
Indirect labour	497	65	190	150	45	39	8	–
Labour overheads	282	50	67	94	30	25	6	10
Consumables	127	26	47	44	–	10	–	–
Power	1 851	520	568	570	118	40	15	20
Maintenance	974	65	261	375	209	64	–	–
Services	1 930	378	379	666	370	100	32	25
Variable costs	10 654	1 902	2 271	4 478	1 074	603	119	207
Gross margin	14 601	4 136	2 846	4 684	2 912	41	31	(49)
Fixed works expenses	3 589	754	1 095	1 065	465	170	20	20
Admin. and Sales expenses	2 037	486	412	738	324	52	12	13
	5 626	1 240	1 507	1 803	789	222	32	33
Profit (loss)	£ 8 975	£ 2 896	£ 1 339	£ 2 881	£ 2 123	(£181)	(£1)	(£82)
January–September 2011								
Sales	260 093	73 424	57 916	82 491	35 228	7 326	1 802	1 906
Profit (loss)	77 909	24 969	10 734	24 003	19 026	(700)	180	(303)
% of sales	29.9	34.0	14.6	23.1	54.0	(9.7)	10.0	(16.0)
Annual rate of profit	103 879	33 292	14 312	32 004	25 368	(933)	240	(404)
Assets employed	130 000	27 000	44 000	37 000	14 000	6 000	1 000	1 000
ROI%	79.8	123.3	32.5	86.5	181.2	(15.5)	24.0	(40.4)

of manufacture. Then, since it had never been seen in this company's history as providing much more than a basis for wages payment, no very clear need had been established. On the second point, the managing director had been very successful in price negotiations with group companies. Using the argument of quick turnround and quality, coupled with his prestige in the trade and his forcefulness of character, he had been able to extract advantageous prices from group companies. Clearly, this was a factor in the profitability of the various profit centres.

Question

Matters were brought to a head when the group management accountant called a meeting of executives at head office to consider a wide variety of matters, which included the profit centre reporting at Cresta. The managing director and the accountant were invited to this meeting.

As the accountant, you have been asked to prepare a short review of the management accounting system in use at Cresta. This should review the main problems with the present system, as you see them, and any possibilities which you see for improvement.

Flexible budgets and variance analysis

Learning objectives

When you have finished studying this chapter, you should be able to:

1 Distinguish between flexible budgets and static budgets.
2 Use flexible-budget formulas to construct a flexible budget based on the volume of sales.
3 Prepare an activity-based flexible budget.
4 Explain the performance evaluation relationship between static budgets, flexible budgets and actual results.
5 Compute activity-level variances and flexible-budget variances.
6 Compute and interpret price and quantity variances for materials and labour.
7 Compute variable-overhead spending and efficiency variances.
8 Compute the fixed-overhead spending variance.

McDonald's

McDonald's is consistently ranked among the world's best-known brands in *BusinessWeek*'s annual ranking of global brands. You can eat a Big Mac under the Golden Arches in more than 110 countries.

With more than 58 million customers daily and sales of more than $45 billion, the challenge is to ensure that the taste of each Big Mac is the same at each of the more than 30,000 company-owned, franchised or affiliated restaurants. How does McDonald's maintain cost and quality control? How does it ensure that each of the customers it serves daily receives the same value? It uses standards, budgets and variance analysis. For example, the standards for material are the same for hamburgers wherever they are sold – 1 bun, 1 hamburger patty, 1 pickle slice, 1/8 tablespoon of dehydrated onion, 1/4 tablespoon mustard and 1/2 ounce of ketchup. For each of these ingredients management determines variances – differences between the amount actually used and what should have been used given the number and types of sandwiches sold.

McDonald's managers budget sales for each hour during the day. Based on the sales budgeted, they construct a budget for each of the materials that make up their menu. They use the budget for planning (to make sure materials will be available when needed) and control (to evaluate the use of materials). McDonald's applies these planning and control concepts not just to material costs, but also to labour and overhead costs. Further, McDonald's uses budgets for planning and control of revenues, as well as costs. Understanding what went wrong and what went right helps managers plan and manage more effectively in future periods.

McDonald's also uses nonfinancial standards to meet its quality and service goals. Here are three examples: (1) The standard time for a drive-through customer is 310 seconds, from pulling up to the menu board to driving away; (2) employees must destroy cooked meat that is not used in a sandwich within 30 minutes; and (3) once employees make a sandwich and place it in the transfer bin, they must sell it within 10 minutes or throw it away.

This chapter focuses on flexible budgets and variances. Flexible budgets extend the budget developed in Chapter 7 for a single level of activity to multiple levels of activity. Variances are deviations of actual results from expected (or planned) results. Each variance should cause a manager to ask, 'Why did results differ from plan?' Variances are an important evaluation tool that directs management to areas that deserve attention and helps managers identify ways to improve future decisions and results. ■

Using budgets and variances to evaluate results

To illustrate how companies use budgets and variances, consider the Dominion Company, a firm in Thessaloniki that manufactures a wheeled, collapsible suitcase carrier popular with airline flight crews. Assume for simplicity that the company produces a single product. To further simplify the example, assume that sales are equal to production and inventory levels are zero. The results for the actual sales volume of 7,000 units in June 20X1 appear in column 1 of Exhibit 8.1.

	Actual (1)	Static budget (2)	Static budget variances (3)
Units	7,000	9,000	2,000 U
Sales	€217,000	€279,000	€62,000 U
Variable costs			
Variable manufacturing costs	€151,270	€189,000	€37,730 F
Shipping costs (selling)	5,000	5,400	400 F
Administrative costs	2,000	1,800	200 U
Total variable costs	€158,270	€196,200	€37,930 F
Contribution margin	€ 58,730	€ 82,800	€24,070 U
Fixed expenses			
Fixed manufacturing costs	€ 37,300	€ 37,000	€ 300 U
Fixed selling and administrative costs	33,000	33,000	–
Total fixed costs	€ 70,300	€ 70,000	€ 300 U
Operating income (loss)	€(11,570)	€ 12,800	€24,370 U

U = Unfavourable cost variances occur when actual costs are more than budgeted costs. Unfavourable revenue (or profit) variances occur when actual revenues (or profits) are less than budgeted.

F = Favourable cost variances occur when actual costs are less than budgeted costs. Favourable revenue (or profit) variances occur when actual revenues (or profits) are more than budgeted.

Exhibit 8.1 The Dominion Company – Performance report using a static budget for the month ended 30 June 20X1

Favourable and unfavourable variances

Recall from Chapter 1 that variances are deviations from plans. While we can compute variances for any type of deviation from plans, in this chapter we focus on deviations of profits, revenues and costs from budgeted amounts. We label profit, revenue and cost variances as favourable or unfavourable depending on the direction of the effect on profitability. **Favourable profit variances** arise when actual profits exceed budgeted profits. **Unfavourable profit variances** arise when actual profits fall below budgeted profits. Because increases in revenues increase profits, revenue variances work in exactly the same way: when actual revenues exceed budgeted revenues we have **favourable revenue variances** and actual revenues below budgeted revenues result in **unfavourable revenue variances**. However, cost variances work in the opposite way because increases in costs decrease profitability: When actual costs exceed budgeted costs we have **unfavourable cost variances** and actual costs less than budgeted costs result in **favourable cost variances**. The following chart summarises these relationships using the abbreviations that we will use for favourable (F) and unfavourable (U) variances.

Favourable (F) versus unfavourable (U) variances

	Profits	Revenues	Costs
Actual > Expected	F	F	U
Actual < Expected	U	U	F

Static budgets versus flexible budgets

Objective 1
Distinguish between flexible budgets and static budgets.

Let's consider two ways to prepare a budget. A budget prepared for only one expected level of activity is a **static budget**. A budget that adjusts to different levels of activity is a **flexible budget** (sometimes called a **variable budget**). To illustrate these concepts, suppose the Dominion Company expects to sell 9,000 units in 20X1. Its static budget consists of the revenues, costs and profits expected at a volume of 9,000 units. If the Dominion Company realises that there is uncertainty about the expected sales volume, it might prepare a flexible budget that predicts revenues, costs and profits at, say, any volume between 7,000 and 9,000 units.

How does the master budget introduced in Chapter 7 relate to static and flexible budgets? The modifier 'master' refers to the scope of the budget, not to whether it is static or flexible. The master budgets used in Chapter 7 were static master budgets. They presumed one fixed level of volume, the most common way to prepare master budgets. However, there is no reason that a company could not prepare a flexible master budget.

Static-budget variances versus flexible-budget variances

How should we evaluate the performance of the Dominion Company for June 20X1? The basic approach is to compare actual amounts with budgeted amounts. However, we now have two candidates for 'the' budgeted amount: the static budget for the original expected level of output or the flexible budget for the achieved level of output.

Static-budget variance

Let's begin by comparing the Dominion Company's actual results with the static budget for a projected sales volume of 9,000 units. Differences between actual results and the static budget for the original planned level of output are **static-budget variances**. Column 2 of Exhibit 8.1 shows the static budget for projected sales of 9,000 units. Column 3 shows the static-budget variances.

Exhibit 8.1 shows the €24,370 U static-budget operating income variance that results from an actual operating loss of €11,570 when budgeted operating income was €12,800.

Exhibit 8.1 also shows static-budget variances for the revenue and cost components of the €24,370 U static-budget income variance. First, the €62,000 unfavourable revenue variance shows that sales were €62,000 below the amount budgeted for sales of 9,000 units. The unfavourable revenue variance helps us understand part of the reason why actual results were worse than expected: lower sales normally lead to lower profit. Second, the €37,930 favourable total variable cost variance shows that total variable costs were less than projected in the static budget. Finally, the €300 unfavourable variance for fixed costs shows that we spent €300 more than the budget.

The static-budget variances show the differences between actual results and the original budgeted amounts for sales of 9,000 units, but they do not take into account that the actual level of sales was only 7,000 units. This is particularly a concern for variable cost variances. Considering the lower-than-projected level of sales activity, was cost control really satisfactory? When you produce only 7,000 units wouldn't you expect variable costs to be lower than the €196,200 amount shown in the static budget for production of 9,000 units? Of course! Therefore, the favourable static-budget variances for the variable costs provide an incomplete picture of how well the Dominion Company controlled variable costs.

Flexible-budget variance

Differences between actual results and the flexible budget for the actual level of output achieved are **flexible-budget variances**. Flexible budget variances are more useful for evaluating variable costs because deviations from the flexible budget better reflect how costs deviate from what was expected given the actual level of activity. The flexible-budget approach says, 'Give me any activity level you choose and I'll provide a budget tailored to that particular level.' For example, when Dominion's sales turn out to be 7,000 units instead of 9,000, the flexible budget shows what the total variable costs should be based on the achieved sales level of 7,000 units. Many companies routinely 'flex' their budgets to provide a better benchmark for evaluating performance.

Consider a McDonald's restaurant that expects to sell 1 million Big Macs and budgets $100,000 for buns at $.10 per bun. Suppose the restaurant sells only 900,000 Big Macs and pays $94,000 for buns. The static-budget variance is a $100,000 − $94,000 = $6,000 favourable variance. However, the static-budget variance does not adjust for the expected decrease in costs due to the decrease in volume relative to the static-budget sales level of 1 million Big Macs. In contrast, the flexible budget yields an expected cost of $90,000 for the actual sales of 900,000 Big Macs, so the flexible-budget variance is $94,000 − $90,000 = $4,000 unfavourable variance. The flexible-budget variance shows that the restaurant spent $4,000 more for buns than it should have given the lower actual sales level of 900,000 Big Macs.

■ Flexible-budget formulas

Objective 2
Use flexible-budget formulas to construct a flexible budget based on the volume of sales.

To develop a flexible budget, managers use flexible-budget formulas that describe revenue and cost behaviour with respect to appropriate cost drivers. The cost functions that we introduced in Chapter 2 and estimated in Chapter 3 are examples of flexible-budget formulas. The flexible budget incorporates effects of changes in activity on each revenue and cost.

Exhibit 8.2 shows the Dominion Company's flexible budget that uses flexible-budget formulas based on a single cost driver, units of output. The three columns of Exhibit 8.2 are flexible budgets for output levels of 7,000, 8,000 and 9,000 units, respectively. Exhibit 8.3 shows a graphical version of the flexible-budget formula. The solid line between 7,000 and 9,000 units indicates that the relevant range for these flexible-budget formulas is 7,000 to 9,000 units. Within this range, we expect fixed costs to be constant at €70,000 per month, the point where the line meets the vertical axis, and variable costs to be €21.80 per unit, the

	Flexible-budget formula	Flexible budgets for various levels of sales/production activity		
Units		7,000	8,000	9,000
Sales	€ 31.00	€217,000	€248,000	€279,000
Variable costs				
Variable manufacturing Costs	€ 21.00	€147,000	€168,000	€189,000
Shipping costs (selling)	.60	4,200	4,200	5,400
Administrative costs	.20	1,400	1,600	1,800
Total variable costs	€ 21.80	€152,600	€174,400	€196,200
Contribution margin	€ 9.20	€ 64,400	€ 73,600	€ 82,800
Fixed costs per month				
Fixed manufacturing costs	€37,000	€ 37,000	€ 37,000	€ 37,000
Fixed selling and administrative costs	33,000	33,000	33,000	33,000
Total fixed costs	€70,000	€ 70,000	€ 70,000	€ 70,000
Operating income (loss)		€ (5,600)	€ 3,600	€ 12,800

Exhibit 8.2 The Dominion Company – Flexible budgets

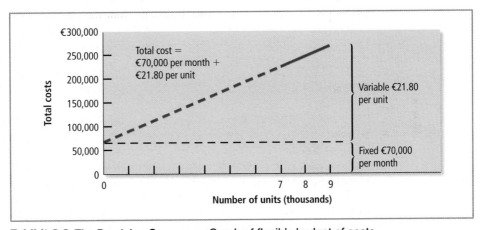

Exhibit 8.3 The Dominion Company – Graph of flexible budget of costs

slope of the line. The dashed line below 7,000 units indicates that this portion of the flexible-budget line is outside the relevant range.

Note that the static budget is just the flexible budget for the original planned level of activity. Thus, the amounts shown in the static budget column in Exhibit 8.1 for sales of 9,000 units are exactly the same as the amounts in the far right column of Exhibit 8.2, the flexible budget for sales of 9,000 units.

■ Activity-based flexible budgets

Objective 3
Prepare an activity-based flexible budget

The Dominion Company's flexible budget in Exhibit 8.2 is based on a single cost driver – units of output. This is an appropriate approach to flexible budgeting when 'units of output' is a plausible and reliable cost driver for all of a company's costs. But what if some of a company's costs are driven by activities such as order processing or setting up for production? A company that has an activity-based costing system with multiple cost drivers, such as the systems described in Chapter 4, will prepare an **activity-based flexible budget** by budgeting costs for each activity using the related cost driver.

Exhibit 8.4 shows an activity-based flexible budget for the Dominion Company. There are four activities: processing, setup, marketing and administration. For each activity, costs depend on a different cost driver. For example, in Exhibit 8.4 we assume that setup costs are variable with respect to the 'number of setups,' whereas in Exhibit 8.2 we assumed that the €12,000 of setup costs included in the manufacturing costs of €37,000 are fixed with respect to 'units of output'. To see why setup costs might be expected to vary with respect to the number of setups but not with respect to the number of units, consider the example of setup supplies. Each time employees set up a production run, they use a batch of setup supplies. However, once the run is set up, production of additional units uses no additional setup supplies. Thus, the cost of supplies varies directly with the number of setups (at a cost of €500 per setup) but does not vary directly with the number of units produced.

	Budget formula			
		Units		
Sales in units		7,000	8,000	9,000
Sales in euros	€ 31.00/unit	€217,000	€248,000	€279,000
ACTIVITY				
Processing		**Cost driver: number of machine hours (MH)**		
Cost-driver level		14,000	16,000	18,000
Variable costs	€ 10.50/MH	€147,000	€168,000	€189,000
Fixed costs	€ 13,000	€ 13,000	€ 13,000	€ 13,000
Total costs of processing activity		€160,000	€181,000	€202,000
Setup		**Cost driver: number of setups**		
Cost-driver level		20	22	24
Variable costs	€ 500/setup	€ 10,000	€ 11,000	€ 12,000
Fixed costs	€ 12,000	€ 12,000	€ 12,000	€ 12,000
Total costs of setup activity		€ 22,000	€ 23,000	€ 24,000
Marketing		**Cost driver: number of orders**		
Cost-driver level		350	400	450
Variable costs	€12.00/order	€ 4,200	€ 4,800	€ 5,400
Fixed costs	€ 15,000	€ 15,000	€ 15,000	€ 15,000
Total costs of marketing activity		€ 19,200	€ 19,800	€ 20,400
Administration		**Cost driver: number of units**		
Cost-driver level		7,000	8,000	9,000
Variable costs	€ 20/unit	€ 1,400	€ 1,600	€ 1,800
Fixed costs	€ 18,000	€ 18,000	€ 18,000	€ 18,000
Total costs of administration activity		€ 19,400	€ 19,600	€ 19,800
Total costs		€220,600	€243,400	€266,200
Operating income (loss)		€ (3,600)	€ 4,600	€ 12,800

Exhibit 8.4 The Dominion Company – Activity-based flexible budget for the month ended 30 June 20X1

Compare the traditional flexible budget (Exhibit 8.2) and the activity-based flexible budget (Exhibit 8.4). Note that assumptions about fixed and variable costs differ in the two exhibits. Because of differing assumptions about cost behaviour, the calculated cost using a single cost driver differs from the calculated cost using multiple activity-based cost drivers.

When should a company use a more sophisticated activity-based flexible budget with multiple cost drivers rather than a simple flexible budget with a single cost driver, such as units of output? When a significant portion of its costs vary with cost drivers other than units of output. For the remainder of this chapter, we return to using a flexible budget based on the assumption of a single cost driver, units of output.

■ Evaluation of financial performance using flexible budgets

Objective 4
Explain the performance evaluation relationship between static budgets, flexible budgets and actual results.

We saw earlier that two quite different factors combine to cause static-budget variances. Actual results might differ from the static budget because (1) actual output levels were not the same as in the static budget, or (2) actual revenues and costs differed from those in the flexible budget for the actual level of output achieved. The flexible budget allows us to separate these two effects by calculating one set of variances based on differences between the static budget and the flexible budget and a second set of variances based on differences between the flexible budget and actual results. The differences between the static budget amounts and the flexible budget amounts are **activity-level variances**. Differences between the flexible budget amounts and actual results are flexible-budget variances. Thus, the static-budget variance, the difference between actual results and the static budget, can be divided into two components, (1) the activity-level variance and (2) the flexible-budget variance:

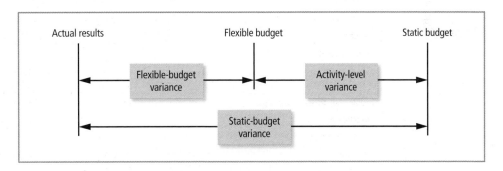

Accountants use flexible-budget variances to draw attention to unexpected results that managers can correct (if the effects are detrimental) or enhance (if the effects are beneficial). Because the flexible budget adjusts planned revenues and planned costs to reflect the actual level of output, only departures of actual costs or revenues from flexible-budget formula amounts cause any variances between the flexible budget and actual results. In contrast, changes in output (activity) levels, not cost control, cause the differences between the static budget and the flexible budget.

The division of static-budget variances into flexible-budget variances and activity-level variances is illustrated for the Dominion Company in Exhibit 8.5. The flexible budget (column 3) for sales of 7,000 units taken from Exhibit 8.2 (and simplified) provides an explanatory bridge between the static budget (column 5) for sales of 9,000 units and the actual results (column 1). The bottom lines of Exhibit 8.5 summarise the variances for income. Note that the sum of the

	Actual results at actual activity level* (1)	Flexible-budget variances† (2) = (1) − (3)	Flexible budget for actual sales activity‡ (3)	Sales-activity variances (4) = (3) − (5)	Static budget* (5)
Units	7,000	–	7,000	2,000 U	9,000
Sales	€217,000	–	€217,000	€62,000 U	€279,000
Variable costs	158,270	5,670 U	152,600	43,600 F	196,200
Contribution margin	€ 58,730	€5,670 U	€ 64,400	€18,400 U	€ 82,800
Fixed costs	70,300	300 U	70,000	–	70,000
Operating income	€(11,570)	€5,970 U	€ (5,600)	€18,400 U	€ 12,800

↑ Total flexible-budget variances   Total sales-activity variances ↑

€ 5,970 U   €18,400 U

Total static budget variances, €24,370 U

U = Unfavourable. F = Favourable.
*Figures are from Exhibit 8.1.
†Figures are shown in more detail in Exhibit 8.6.
‡Figures are from the 7,000-unit column in Exhibit 8.2.

Exhibit 8.5 The Dominion Company – Summary of performance for the month ended 30 June 20X1

activity-level variances (here **sales-activity variances** because sales is used as the cost driver) and the flexible-budget variances equals the total of the static-budget variances: €18,400 U + €5,970 U = €24,370 U.

Isolating the causes of variances

When evaluating performance, managers try to distinguish between **effectiveness** – the degree to which an organisation meets an objective – and **efficiency** – the degree to which an organisation minimises the resources used to achieve an objective. Performance may be effective, efficient, both or neither.

For example, the Dominion Company set a static-budget objective of manufacturing and selling 9,000 units. It actually made and sold only 7,000 units. Was Dominion's performance effective? No. Dominion failed to meet its sales objective and, therefore, performance (as measured by sales-activity variances) was ineffective. Was Dominion's performance efficient? Managers judge the degree of efficiency by comparing actual inputs used (such as the costs of direct materials and direct labour) to budgeted inputs for the level of output achieved (7,000 units). The less input used to produce a given output, the more efficient the operation. The unfavourable flexible-budget variances indicate that Dominion was inefficient because the actual cost of its inputs exceeded the cost expected for the actual level of output.

A McDonald's restaurant could use this same analysis. Effectiveness – the difference between the static budget and the flexible budget – depends on the degree to which the restaurant meets its sales objectives. Efficiency – the difference between the actual results and the flexible budget – is the difference between actual profit and the profit expected for the level of sales actually attained.

MAKING MANAGERIAL DECISIONS

Consider a company that plans to sell 1,000 units for €3 per unit. Budgeted variable costs are €2 per unit, budgeted fixed costs are €700 and the static-budget profit is €300. Suppose the company actually sells 800 units and income is €110. Compute and interpret the static-budget profit variance, the sales-activity profit variance and the flexible-budget profit variance.

Answer

There is a €190 unfavourable static-budget profit variance, the difference between static budgeted profit of €300 and the actual profit of €110. The static budget variance is the sum of two components:

the sales-activity variance and the flexible-budget variance. The sales-activity profit variance is the difference between the static-budgeted profit of €300 for planned production of 1,000 units versus the flexible-budgeted profit of €100 for production of 800 units, a €200 unfavourable variance. The flexible-budget profit variance is the difference between the flexible-budgeted profit of €100 versus the actual profit of €110, a favourable variance of €10. The €10 favourable flexible-budget variance indicates that the operation was efficient while the €200 unfavourable sales-activity variance indicates the company was not effective.

Flexible-budget variances

Objective 5
Compute activity-level variances and flexible-budget variances.

Recall that flexible-budget variances measure the efficiency of operations at the actual level of activity. The first three columns of Exhibit 8.5 provide comparisons of actual results with the flexible-budget amounts. The flexible-budget variances are the differences between columns 1 and 3. For income, the flexible-budget variance is €5,970 unfavourable:

$$\text{flexible-budget income variance} = \text{actual income} - \text{flexible-budget income}$$

$$(\text{at actual sales level})$$

$$= (-€11,570) - (-€5,600)$$

$$= €5,970 \text{ unfavourable}$$

Just as we can divide income into its component revenues minus costs, we can divide the flexible-budget income variance into revenue and cost variances. In the Dominion Company example, the flexible-budget revenue variance is zero because there is no difference between the actual sales price and the flexible-budgeted sales price. Therefore, for this example we focus on cost variances for variable and fixed costs, the differences between actual costs and flexible-budget costs.

Exhibit 8.6 gives a line-by-line computation of flexible-budget variances for all cost items at Dominion and provides new details about variable and fixed manufacturing costs. Note that most of the costs with favourable static-budget variances (see Exhibit 8.1) have unfavourable flexible-budget variances. Why is this so? Sales fell far short of the target and, therefore, budgeted costs in the flexible budget based on actual sales of 7,000 units were much lower than budgeted costs in the static budget based on target sales of 9,000 units, yielding favourable static-budget variances. However, in most instances where actual costs were lower than the static budget, the actual costs were higher than the flexible budget, yielding unfavourable flexible-budget variances.

It is tempting to assume that favourable flexible-budget variances are always good and unfavourable flexible-budget variances are always bad, but beware of this assumption. Favourable flexible-budget variances might at first seem to indicate that costs are well-managed. However, favourable variances, where actual costs are less than the flexible budget, might instead indicate that the company is spending too little. For example, actual

	Actual costs incurred	Flexible budget*	Flexible-budget variances†	Possible explanation
Units	7,000	7,000	–	
Variable costs				
Direct materials	€ 69,920	€ 70,000	€ 80 F	Lower prices but higher usage
Direct labour	61,500	56,000	5,500 U	Higher wage rates and higher usage
Indirect labour	9,100	11,900	2,800 F	Decreased setup time
Idle time	3,500	2,800	750 U	Excessive machine breakdowns
Cleanup time	2,500	2,100	400 U	Cleanup of spilled solvent
Supplies	4,700	4,200	500 U	Higher prices and higher usage
Variable manufacturing costs	€151,270	€147,000	€4,270 U	
Shipping	5,000	4,200	800 U	Use of air freight to meet delivery
Administration	2,000	1,400	600 U	Excessive copying and long-distance calls
Total variable costs	€158,270	€152,600	€5,670 U	
Fixed costs				
Factory supervision	€ 14,700	€ 14,400	€ 300 U	Salary increase
Factory rent	5,000	5,000	–	
Equipment depreciation	15,000	15,000	–	
Other fixed factory costs	2,600	2,600	–	
Fixed manufacturing costs	€ 37,300	€ 37,300	€ 300 U	
Fixed selling and administrative costs	33,000	33,000	–	
Total fixed costs	€ 70,300	€ 70,000	€ 300 U	
Total variable and fixed costs	€228,570	€222,600	€5,970 U	

*From 7,000-unit column of Exhibit 8.2.
†This is a line-by-line breakout of the variances in column 2 of Exhibit 8.5.

Exhibit 8.6 The Dominion Company – Cost-control performance report for the month ended 30 June 20X1

maintenance costs that are less than budgeted may indicate that the company is not keeping up with required maintenance. Similarly, shipping costs that are below budget because slow ground shipments are being used instead of air shipments may mean that customers will be alienated by the slower deliveries. On the other hand, significantly unfavourable variances, where costs exceed the flexible budget, may not mean that costs are out of control. For example, higher than budgeted direct-labour costs may be explained by a budget that did not reflect an increase in pay rates. Similarly, higher than budgeted material costs may be explained by a decision to switch to higher-quality, higher-cost materials that are expected to result in labour-cost savings that will more than offset the increase in material costs. In sum, do not assume that the 'favourable' and 'unfavourable' labels tell you everything you need to know. Instead, always look for underlying explanations for any significant deviation of actual cost from the flexible budget. The last column of Exhibit 8.6 provides examples of some possible explanations for the Dominion Company's variances.

Sales-activity variances

For the Dominion Company, we assume that the driver for variable costs in the flexible budget is unit sales volume, so the activity-level variances are sales-activity variances. The Dominion Company's sales activity fell 2,000 units short of the planned level. The sales-activity variances (totalling €18,400 U) in the final three columns of Exhibit 8.5 measure the budgeted effect of falling short of the original sales objective. Note that changes in unit prices or unit variable costs do not affect activity-level variances. Why? Only the unit sales volume affects the sales-activity variances because the flexible budget and the static budget differ only due to different assumed levels of activity, but use the same budgeted unit prices, unit variable costs and total fixed costs. Also note that there can never be a sales-activity variance for fixed costs. Why? Because the total budgeted fixed-costs are the same in the flexible budget and the static budget.

The sales-activity income variance informs the manager that falling short of the sales target by 2,000 units explains €18,400 of the shortfall of income relative to the amount initially budgeted (a €5,600 flexible-budget loss instead of a €12,800 static-budget profit). We can also express this €18,400 variance as the shortfall of 2,000 units multiplied by the budgeted contribution margin of €9.20 per unit (from the first column of Exhibit 8.2):

$$\begin{aligned} \text{Sales-activity income variance} &= (\text{actual units} - \text{static budget units}) \\ &\quad \times \text{ budgeted contribution per unit} \\ &= (9,000 - 7,000) \times €9.20 \\ &= €18,400 \text{ unfavourable} \end{aligned}$$

Who has responsibility for the sales-activity income variance? Marketing managers usually have the primary responsibility for reaching the sales level specified in the static budget. Many factors can cause variations in sales, including poor production quality and missed delivery schedules. Nevertheless, marketing managers are typically in the best position to explain why actual sales levels differed from plans.

Think about the situation for many companies at the end of 2008 as the effects of the economic crisis caused actual sales to fall far short of the original budgeted level of sales. Even if their operations were efficient (that is, no unfavourable flexible-budget variances), large unfavourable sales-activity variances explain why income often fell far below predicted (static-budget) income levels.

Setting standards

To establish flexible budgets, managers must determine standard costs. A **standard cost** is a carefully developed cost per unit. Standards are popular, used by more than 85 per cent of US companies. But standards mean different things to different companies. Many companies set standard cost equal to **expected cost**, the cost that is most likely to be attained. However, it is also common to intentionally set standards above or below expected costs to create desired incentives. What standard of performance should a company use in its flexible budgets? Should a standard be so strict that the company rarely, if ever, meets it? Should the company attain the standard about 50 per cent of the time? 90 per cent? 20 per cent? Individuals who have worked a lifetime setting and evaluating standards for performance disagree on this question, so there are no universal answers. As described in the 'Business first' box on p. 00, more companies are adapting standards to fit their particular needs.

Perfection standards (also called **ideal standards**) are expressions of the most efficient performance possible under the best conceivable conditions, using existing specifications and equipment. Perfection standards make no provision for waste, spoilage, machine breakdowns and the like. Those who favour using perfection standards maintain that the resulting unfavourable variances will constantly remind personnel of the need for continuous improvement in all phases of operations. Though concern for continuous improvement is widespread, perfection standards are not widely used because they often have an adverse effect on employee motivation. Employees tend to ignore goals that they know cannot be reached.

Currently attainable standards are levels of performance that managers can achieve by realistic levels of effort. They make allowances for normal defectives, spoilage, waste and nonproductive time. There are at least two popular approaches to setting currently attainable standards.

The first approach sets standards so that employees regard their attainment as highly probable if normal effort and diligence are exercised. Hence, the standards are predictions of what will likely occur, anticipating some normal level of inefficiencies. Under normal conditions this approach yields variances that are random and negligible. Managers accept the standards as being reasonable goals. The major advantages of this approach to setting currently attainable standards are as follows:

1 The resulting standards serve multiple purposes. Because the standards represent what is expected under normal conditions, companies can use the same standard costs for financial budgeting and inventory valuation. In contrast, they cannot use perfection standards for inventory valuation or financial budgeting because they know that the resulting standard costs are unrealistically low.

BUSINESS FIRST
The need to adapt standard cost approaches

Critics of standard costs and variance analysis maintain that predetermined standards do not work well in today's dynamic, fast-paced, just-in-time environment. None the less, companies continue to use standards and to measure performance against them. Surveys in nine different countries have shown that between 56 per cent and 92 per cent of manufacturing companies use standard costs. Companies have apparently adapted the approach to fit their modern environments.

To apply standards in a dynamic environment, how should managers measure and report variances? First, they should continually evaluate their standards. If a company is in a state of continuous improvement, it must continually revise its standards. Second, standards and variances should measure key strategic variables. The concept of setting a benchmark, comparing actual results to the benchmark and identifying causes for any differences is universal. We can apply it to many types of measures, such as production quantity or quality, as well as to costs. Finally, variances should not lead to affixing blame. Standards are plans and things do not always go according to plan – often with no one being at fault.

One company that has adapted standard costs to meet its particular needs is the Brass Products Division (BPD) at Parker Hannifin Corporation, a company that produces motion and control technologies and systems. BPD uses standard costs and variances to pinpoint

problem areas that need attention if the division is to meet its goal of continuous improvement. Among the changes that have increased the value of the standard cost information are more timely product cost information, variances computed at more detailed levels and regular meetings to help employees understand their impact on the variances.

Managers and accountants adapt the standard cost concept to fit the particular needs of a company. For example, BPD created three new variances: (1) The standard run quantity variance examines the effect of actual compared to optimal batch size for production runs; (2) the material substitution variance compares material costs to the costs of alternative materials; and (3) the method variance measures costs using actual machines compared to costs using alternative machines. All three variances use the concept of setting a standard and comparing actual results to the standard, but they do not apply the traditional standard cost-variance formulas.

Sources: Adapted from D. Johnsen and P. Sopariwala, 'Standard costing is alive and well at Parker Brass', *Management Accounting Quarterly*, Winter 2000, pp. 12–20; C. B. Cheatham and L. R. Cheatham, 'Redesigning cost systems: is standard costing obsolete?' *Accounting Horizons*, December 1996, pp. 23–31; C. Horngren, G. Foster and S. Datar, *Cost Accounting: A Managerial Emphasis*, 12th edn (Upper Saddle River, NJ: Prentice Hall, 2006), p. 229; and Parker Hannifin Corp., *Parker Hannifin 2008 Annual Report*.

2 Reasonable standards have a desirable motivational impact on employees, especially when combined with incentives for continuous improvement. The standard represents reasonable future performance, not unrealistic goals. Therefore, unfavourable variances direct attention to performance that is not meeting reasonable expectations.

A second approach to setting currently attainable standards falls somewhere between perfection standards and the first approach to setting currently attainable standards. This approach sets standards so that employees regard them as 'stretch goals', where meeting the standard is difficult but possible. Managers can achieve such standards only by very efficient operations. Variances tend to be unfavourable; nevertheless, employees accept the standards as being tough but not unreasonable goals.

Is it possible to achieve continuous improvement using currently attainable standards? Yes, but managers must continually update such standards to recognise improved productivity and management must also use incentive systems that reward continuous improvement.

Trade-offs among variances

Because the various activities of an organisation are interrelated, the level of performance in one area will often affect performance in other areas. Often there are trade-offs among costs. For example, McDonald's may generate favourable labour variances by hiring less-skilled and lower-paid employees, but this might also lead to more waste because substandard products need to be scrapped, resulting in unfavourable materials variances. As another example, Fiat may experience unfavourable materials variances by purchasing higher-quality materials at a higher than planned price, but this may be more than offset by other favourable variances due to lower waste, fewer inspections and higher-quality products.

Because of the many interdependencies among activities, an 'unfavourable' or 'favourable' label should not lead a manager to jump to conclusions. By themselves, variances merely raise questions and provide clues to the causes of performance. Variances are attention directors, not problem solvers. Furthermore, the cause of unfavourable variances might be unrealistically high standards rather than poor execution by managers. One of the first questions a manager should consider when investigating a large variance is whether expectations were valid.

When to investigate variances

When should management investigate a variance? For some critical items, any deviation may prompt a follow-up. However, for most items, managers recognise that, even if everything operates normally, variances are unlikely to be exactly zero. For these items, managers specify a range of 'acceptable' variances based on economic analysis of how big a variance must be before investigation would be worth the effort. While the acceptable range is sometimes stated in percentage terms, it is important to also consider the euro deviation from budget. For example, a 4 per cent variance in a €1 million material cost may deserve more attention than a 20 per cent variance in a €1,000 repair cost. Because knowing exactly when to investigate is difficult, many organisations have developed rules of thumb that incorporate both absolute and relative size measures such as 'Investigate all variances exceeding either €5,000 or 15 per cent of expected cost.'

Comparisons with prior period's results

Some organisations compare actual results with last year's results for the same period rather than using flexible-budget benchmarks. However, simplistic comparisons with prior period results should be used cautiously. In general, a carefully developed flexible budget provides a better benchmark than prior period results for evaluating performance. Why? First, using actual results from the prior year as a benchmark assumes that prior year values are what we aspire to achieve and do not contain any inefficiencies or substandard results. Second, many changes occur in the environment and in the organisation and these changes can make a comparison to the prior year invalid. Few organisations and environments are so stable that the only difference between now and a year ago is merely the passage of time. For example, the turmoil in the stock market in 2008 led many financial institutions to make sweeping changes in operations. Comparisons of operating results in 2008 to 2007 would not have been meaningful because the economic climate was so different in 2008. Further changes in the economic climate during 2009 implied that simple comparisons of operating results in 2009 to 2008 were also not meaningful. Even comparisons with the prior month's actual results may not be as useful as comparisons with an up-to-date flexible budget. Comparisons with previous years may be useful for analysing trends in such key variables as sales volume, market share and product mix, but they do not help answer questions such as the Dominion Company's 'Why did we have a loss of €11,570 in June, when we expected a profit of €12,800?'.

Summary problem for your review

PROBLEM

Refer to the data in Exhibits 8.1 and 8.2. Suppose actual production and sales were 8,500 units instead of 7,000 units; actual variable costs were €188,800; and actual fixed costs were €71,200. The selling price remained at €31 per unit.

1 Compute the static-budget variance for income. What does this tell you about the efficiency of operations? The effectiveness of operations?

2 Compute the sales-activity variance for income. Is the performance of the marketing function the sole explanation for this variance? Why?

3 Using a flexible budget at the actual activity level, compute the budgeted contribution margin, budgeted income and flexible-budget variance for income. What do you learn from this variance?

SOLUTION

1

$$\text{actual operating income} = (8{,}500 \times €31) - €188{,}800 - €71{,}200$$
$$= €3{,}500$$
$$\text{static-budget operating income} = €12{,}800 \text{ (from Exhibit 8.1)}$$
$$\text{static budget variance} = €12{,}800 - €3{,}500 = €9{,}300 \text{ U}$$

Three factors affect the static-budget variance: sales activity, efficiency and price changes. There is no way to tell from the static-budget variance alone how much of the €9,300 U was caused by each of these factors.

2 sales-activity variance = budgeted unit contribution margin × difference between the static budget unit sales and the actual unit sales
$$= €9.20 \text{ per unit CM} \times (8{,}500 - 9{,}000)$$
$$= €4{,}600 \text{ U}$$

The sales-activity variance for income quantifies the impact of the deviation from an original sales target while holding price and efficiency factors constant. This is a measure of the effectiveness of Dominion in meeting its sales objective. Management might attribute the failure to reach target sales to ineffectiveness of marketing personnel or to causes beyond the control of marketing personnel, such as material shortages, factory breakdowns, delivery problems and so on.

3 The budget formulas in Exhibit 8.2 are the basis for the following answers:

$$\text{flexible-budget contribution margin} = €9.20 \times 8,500 = €78,200$$
$$\text{flexible-budget operating income} = €78,200 - €70,000 \text{ fixed costs} = €8,200$$
$$\text{actual operating income} = €3,500 \text{ (from number 1)}$$
$$\text{flexible budget variance} = €8,200 - €3,500 = €4,700 \text{ U}$$

The flexible-budget variance shows that the company spent €4,700 more to produce and sell the 8,500 units than it should have spent if operations had been efficient and costs had not changed. Note that this €4,700 U flexible-budget variance plus the €4,600 U sales-activity variance total to the €9,300 U static-budget variance.

Flexible-budget variances in detail

The remainder of this chapter explains how to further analyse flexible-budget variances by dividing them into component variances. We begin with direct labour and direct material variances and then briefly discuss overhead variances.

Variances for direct material and direct labour

We can express the actual cost and flexible-budget cost for labour or materials as quantity multiplied by price. Actual cost is the actual quantity used multiplied by the actual price per unit. Flexible-budget cost is the standard quantity allowed for the actual level of activity multiplied by the standard price per unit. Therefore, the flexible-budget variance (the difference between actual cost incurred and the flexible-budget cost) can be divided into (1) a quantity variance, attributable to the difference between actual quantity used and standard quantity allowed, and (2) a price variance, attributable to the difference between actual price per unit and standard price per unit.

Let's consider the components of the direct-material and direct-labour flexible-budget variances for the Dominion Company. As shown in Exhibit 8.6, the flexible-budget variances for direct material and direct labour are €80 F and €5,500 U, respectively:

	(1) Actual costs	(2) Flexible budget	(3) Flexible-budget variance
Direct materials	€69,920	€70,000	€ 80 F
Direct labour	61,500	56,000	5,500 U

To divide the flexible-budget variances into quantity and price variances, we need further information about the underlying actual and budgeted quantities and prices of direct labour and materials.

We turn first to the flexible budget quantities and prices. The Dominion Company's flexible budget shows the amounts that Dominion expected to spend based on standard quantities and standard costs for direct materials and direct labour to produce the output achieved, computed as follows:

$$\frac{\text{flexible}}{\text{budget}} = \frac{\text{units of actual}}{\text{output achieved}} \times \frac{\text{input allowed}}{\text{per unit of output}} \times \frac{\text{standard unit}}{\text{price of input}}$$

Note that the flexible budget is constructed for the level of actual output achieved. We will refer to the flexible budget for the actual output achieved as 'standard cost allowed'.

Exhibit 8.6 presented flexible-budget amounts based on €10 per unit of output for direct materials and €8 per unit of output for direct labour. Let's assume the company derived these flexible budget amounts as the product of two components, a standard quantity of an input and a standard price for the input, as shown in the following table:

	Standards		
	Standard quantity of input allowed per unit of output	Standard price per unit of input	Flexible budget formula per unit of output
Direct materials	5 kgs	€2/kg	€10
Direct labour	½ hour	€16/hour	8

For the 7,000 units of output achieved by Dominion, these flexible-budget amounts for direct material and direct labour translate into the following standard costs allowed:

$$\text{direct-materials cost allowed} = 7{,}000 \text{ units} \times 5 \text{ kg} \times €2.00 \text{ per kg} = €70{,}000$$

$$\text{direct-labour cost allowed} = 7{,}000 \text{ units} \times \frac{1}{2} \text{ hour} \times €16.00 \text{ per hour} = €56{,}000$$

We next turn to additional information about actual costs. Let's assume the following actual prices and quantities explain the actual direct material and direct labour costs for Dominion:

- *Direct materials.* Dominion purchased and used 36,800 kg of material at an actual unit price of €1.90 for a total actual cost of $36{,}800 \times €1.90 = €69{,}920$.

- *Direct labour.* Dominion used 3,750 hours of labour at an actual hourly price (rate) of €16.40, for a total cost of $3{,}750 \times €16.40 = €61{,}500$.

▮ Computing price and quantity variances

Objective 6
Compute and interpret price and quantity variances for materials and labour.

The **price variance** indicates whether management paid more or less than the standard price for each input used:

$$\text{price variance} = (\text{actual price} - \text{standard price}) \times \text{actual quantity used}$$

The **quantity variance** indicates whether management used more or less than the standard quantity of input for the output achieved:

$$\text{quantity variance} = (\text{actual quantity used} - \text{standard quantity}$$
$$\text{allowed for actual output}) \times \text{standard price}$$

Let's examine the computation of price and quantity variances in more detail, as shown in Exhibit 8.7. Panel A shows the case where the actual price is equal to the standard price so there is solely a quantity variance, Panel B shows the case where the actual quantity is equal to the standard quantity so there is solely a price variance and Panel C shows the more common case with both quantity and price variances. In all three panels, the flexible budget is the standard quantity multiplied by the standard price – the rectangle shaded blue. However, the variances differ across the panels, depending on the difference between standard and actual price and the difference between standard and actual quantity.

In Panel A where there is solely a quantity variance, the variance is the quantity used in excess of the standard quantity times the standard price – the rectangle shaded green. In Panel B where there solely a price variance, the variance is the price paid in excess of the standard price times the standard quantity – the rectangle shaded purple.

Panel C illustrates the situation where both quantity and price variances exist. There is a joint effect of the two variances, represented by the cross-hatched purple region. In concept, this joint effect could be defined to be a separate, third variance. In practice, most companies

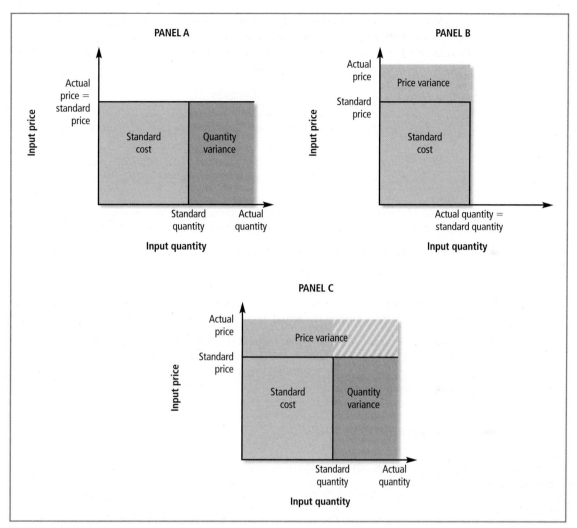

Exhibit 8.7 Graphical representation of quantity and price variances

include this joint effect as part of the price variance and this is the way the price variance was defined previously. This means we calculate the price variance by multiplying the difference between actual and standard price by the total actual quantity used. This definition includes the joint effect represented by the purple cross-hatched area as part of the price variance. The quantity variance is then the difference between actual and standard quantity multiplied by the standard price.

We use this approach to divide the Dominion Company's flexible-budget variances (column (3) in the table on p. 343) into price and quantity variances for material and labour. The price variances are as follows:

$$\text{Direct-materials price variance} = (\text{actual price} - \text{standard price}) \times \text{actual quantity}$$
$$= (€1.90 - €2.0) \text{ per kg} \times 36{,}800 \text{ kg}$$
$$= €3{,}680 \text{ favourable}$$

$$\text{Direct-labour price (rate) variance} = (\text{actual price} - \text{standard price}) \times \text{actual quantity}$$
$$= (€16.40 - €16.00) \text{ per hour} \times 3{,}750 \text{ hours}$$
$$= €1{,}500 \text{ unfavourable}$$

The quantity variances or **usage variances** are as follows:

$$\text{Direct-materials quantity variance} = (\text{actual quantity} - \text{standard quantity})$$
$$\times \text{ standard price}$$
$$= [36,800 - (7,000 \times 5)] \text{ kg} \times €2.00 \text{ per kg}$$
$$= [36,800 - 35,000] \text{ kg} \times €2.00 \text{ per kg}$$
$$= €3,600 \text{ unfavourable}$$

$$\text{Direct-labour quantity variance} = (\text{actual quantity} - \text{standard quantity}) \times \text{standard price}$$
$$= [3,750 - (7,000 \times 1/2)] \text{ hours} \times €16.00 \text{ per hour}$$
$$= [3,750 - 3,500] \text{ hours} \times €16.00 \text{ per hour}$$
$$= €4,000 \text{ unfavourable}$$

By definition, the sum of the direct-labour price and quantity variances equals the direct-labour flexible-budget variance. Similarly, the sum of the direct-materials price and quantity variances equals the total direct-materials flexible-budget variance.

$$\text{Direct-materials flexible-budget variance} = €3,680 \text{ favourable} + €3,600 \text{ unfavourable}$$
$$= €80 \text{ favourable}$$

$$\text{Direct-labour flexible-budget variance} = €1,500 \text{ unfavourable} + €4,000 \text{ unfavourable}$$
$$= €5,500 \text{ unfavourable}$$

You are likely to encounter a variety of terminology for price and quantity variances in practice. For example, many companies call a price variance applied to labour a **rate variance** and many refer to quantity variances as **usage** or **efficiency variances**. Moreover, you may encounter new variance definitions such as those created by the Brass Products Division in the 'Business first' box on p. 340 or in the 'Making managerial decisions' section on p. 348. Because there is so much variation in definitions and terminology, you should always ask whatever questions are necessary to be sure that you understand the exact definition of any variance that you encounter.

■ Framework for calculating materials and labour variances

Exhibit 8.8 summarises the framework used to divide direct-materials and direct-labour flexible-budget variances into price and quantity variances. Though the exhibit may seem complex at first, studying it will solidify your understanding of variance analysis.

Column A of Exhibit 8.8 contains the actual costs incurred based on the actual quantities used at actual prices. Column C is the flexible-budget amount based on standard input quantities allowed for the outputs achieved multiplied by standard prices. We insert column B, the actual input quantities used multiplied by standard prices, between A and C to separate price and quantity effects. The difference between columns A and B is due to different actual versus standard prices because we hold actual quantity constant across columns A and B. The difference between columns B and C is due to different actual versus standard quantities used because we hold price constant across columns B and C.

We measure activity in a flexible budget in terms of standard inputs allowed for actual outputs achieved (column C in Exhibit 8.8). For the Dominion Company, a single-product firm, standard inputs allowed is simply units of output multiplied by the standard quantity of input per unit. For companies that manufacture a variety of products, standard inputs allowed will be aggregated across multiple products, with different standard inputs for the output achieved for each product. For example, consider a furniture manufacturer that produced 12,000 chairs and 3,000 sofas. If each chair requires 1 standard labour hour and each sofa requires 2 standard labour hours, the manufacturer may express standard hours allowed for outputs achieved as $(12,000 \times 1) + (3,000 \times 2) = 18,000$. Standard hours allowed for output achieved is the result of translating disparate output units (chairs and sofas) into a common standard measure of activity (standard labour hours allowed for output achieved).

Exhibit 8.8 General approach to analysis of direct-labour and direct-material variances

▥ Interpreting price and quantity variances

By dividing flexible-budget variances into price and quantity variances, we can better evaluate managers on variances that they can control. Consider an operating manager who has control over the quantity of materials used in the production process but little control over the price. In that case, the quantity variance will be more relevant than the price variance in evaluating the operating manager. Who has control over the price variance? The manager in charge of purchasing materials likely has some control over the price and therefore is responsible for the price variance. However, even the purchasing manager may not have much control over price. Why? Because external market forces often are the primary influence on prices. Irrespective of whether any manager has control of price, it is useful to separate price and quantity variances whenever the quantity variance is important for evaluation. For example, the commodity prices of cane, cocoa and milk may be outside the control of Cadbury's managers. By separating price variances from quantity variances, the breakfast chocolate maker can focus on the quantity variance to assess whether managers used materials efficiently.

It is important to carefully consider the incentives created by price and quantity variances. Exclusive focus on material price variances can provide incentives that work against an organisation's JIT and total quality management goals. For example, a purchasing manager focused only on creating a favourable material price variance may achieve a lower price by buying in large quantities or buying lower-quality material. However, the result could be excessive inventory-handling and opportunity costs caused by large purchase quantities or increased manufacturing defects caused by faulty material. As another example, exclusive focus on labour price variances could motivate managers to use lower-cost (and lower-skilled) workers or to rush workers through critical tasks. In either case, the result could impair quality of products and services.

Companies that use variances primarily to fix blame often find that managers resort to heating and subversion to beat the system. Lower-level operations managers usually have more information about their operations than higher-level managers. If supervisors use that information against them, lower-level managers might withhold or misstate valuable information for their own protection. For example, one manufacturing firm actually followed a policy of reducing the next period's departmental budget by the amount of the department's unfavourable variances in the current period. If a division had a €50,000 expense budget for labour and €52,000 of actual labour costs resulting in a €2,000 unfavourable labour variance, the following period's budget would be set at €48,000. This system led managers to cheat and to falsify reports to avoid unfavourable variances and avoid reductions in their budgets. We can criticise departmental managers' ethics in this situation, but the system design was also at fault.

Variances by themselves cannot provide the complete picture of why the company achieved or failed to achieve the budgeted income. For instance, one possible explanation for Dominion's set of variances is that a manager made a trade-off. Perhaps the manager purchased substandard-quality materials at a favourable price, saving €3,680 (the favourable materials price variance) knowing that the substandard material would lead to extra waste of materials (the €3,600 unfavourable material quantity variance). In this case, the material price variance more than offset the material quantity variance, as indicated by the net materials flexible-budget variance of €80 favourable.

Of course, to fully understand the effect of the decision to purchase substandard materials, still more investigation and analysis might be required. For example, the material waste due to substandard materials might also have caused at least part of the excess use of direct labour. Why? Perhaps Dominion used direct labour time working on units that ended up being defective, thus wasting that time. Suppose the labour wasted on the defective units was more than the €80 favourable materials flexible budget variance described in the previous paragraph. Then, the decision to purchase substandard material was not successful because the labour cost inefficiencies caused by using substandard materials exceeded the materials cost savings from the favourable price. The important point here is that variances are useful tools that provide clues and direct attention to problems, but variances are only the starting point of the search for answers to the complex question of why actual results differ from expectations.

MAKING MANAGERIAL DECISIONS

Managers can apply the concepts of variance analysis to construct new variance definitions to fit new situations. For example, consider a production plant that plans to produce 50 units per hour and work 8 hours per day for a total planned production of 400 units each day. On 23 March, the plant produced just 276 units for a total unfavourable production variance of 124 units.

Because of machine breakdowns, the plant operated for only 6 hours that day. Using a three-column framework like that used in Exhibit 8.8, define variances that separate how much of the 124 unit shortfall in production was caused by operating only 6 hours versus how much was caused by low production efficiency during the 6 hours of actual operation.

MAKING MANAGERIAL DECISIONS (CONTINUED)

Answer

Column A shows actual production of 276 units over 6 actual operating hours equates to 46 units per hour. Column C shows standard production of 8 hours per day × 50 units per hour = 400 units per day. Column B shows standard production rates for actual operating hours, 6 hours of production × 50 units per hour = 300 units. The difference between columns B and C is the production shortfall caused by loss of 2 hours of operating time due to the machine breakdowns, 2 hours × 50 units per hour = 100 unit unfavourable variance. The difference between columns A and B is the shortfall caused by an actual rate of production (276 ÷ 6 × 46 units per hour) lower than the standard rate of 50 units per hour. This difference is the rate shortfall (4 units per hour) multiplied by the actual hours worked for the day (6 hours) = 24 unit unfavourable variance. The total variance, 100 units + 24 units = 124 units, is the difference between columns A and C.

Overhead variances

Objective 7
Compute variable overhead spending and efficiency variances.

The evaluation of overhead variances is different from the evaluation of direct materials and direct labour because overhead costs are generally indirect costs that companies allocate rather than trace to output. In this section, we outline the framework used to construct variable overhead variances and then briefly discuss variances for fixed overhead.

Variable overhead variances

Companies allocate variable overhead to output based on some cost driver. For example, the variable-overhead cost driver for the Dominion Company is direct-labour hours. The variable-overhead flexible-budget variance can be divided into two variances. When actual cost-driver activity differs from the standard amount allowed for the actual output achieved, we have a **variable-overhead efficiency variance**, calculated as follows:

$$\begin{array}{l} \text{variable-overhead} \\ \text{efficiency variance} \end{array} = \left(\begin{array}{l} \text{actual cost} \\ \text{driver activity} \end{array} - \begin{array}{l} \text{standard cost-driver} \\ \text{activity allowed} \end{array} \right) \times \begin{array}{l} \text{standard} \\ \text{variable-overhead} \\ \text{rate per cost-driver unit} \end{array}$$

The variable-overhead efficiency variance depends entirely on whether the quantity of the cost driver used is more or less than the quantity allowed for the actual output achieved. It measures how control of the cost driver activity affected variable overhead costs.

The **variable-overhead spending variance**, arises when actual variable overhead costs differ from the amount predicted for the actual cost-driver activity:

$$\begin{array}{c}\text{variable-overhead}\\\text{spending variance}\end{array} = \begin{array}{c}\text{actual variable}\\\text{overhead}\end{array} - \left(\begin{array}{c}\text{standard variable}\\\text{overhead rate per}\\\text{unit of cost-driver}\end{array} \times \begin{array}{c}\text{actual cost-driver}\\\text{activity used}\end{array}\right)$$

This variance combines price and quantity effects and tells us how the actual variable overhead cost compares to the predicted amount for the actual level of cost-driver activity.

Exhibit 8.9 illustrates the calculation of variable and fixed overhead variances for the Dominion Company. The exhibit breaks the €500 unfavourable flexible-budget variable overhead variance for supplies into spending and efficiency variances. We compute the efficiency variance by multiplying the standard variable overhead rate times the difference between the quantity of the cost driver used and the quantity of the cost driver allowed for the output achieved. For the Dominion Company, standards allow ½ hour of the cost driver direct labour for each unit of output, or 3,500 hours allowed for the 7,000 units of output achieved. Therefore, the flexible budget amount of €4,200 for supplies in Exhibit 8.6 translates to €4,200 ÷ 3,500 hours = €1.20 per direct-labour hour allowed for output achieved. Because the Dominion Company used 3,750 labour hours when the standard for production of 7,000 units is ½ hour/unit × 7,000 units = 3,500 standard hours allowed, it used an excess of 250 labour hours. Each labour hour drives €1.20 of variable overhead, so the excess labour hours drive 250 units × €1.20/unit = €300 of extra variable overhead costs.

$$\begin{array}{c}\text{variable-overhead}\\\text{efficiency variance}\\\text{for supplies}\end{array} = \left(\begin{array}{c}\text{actual direct-}\\\text{labour hours}\end{array} - \begin{array}{c}\text{standard direct-labour}\\\text{hours allowed}\end{array}\right) \times \begin{array}{c}\text{standard}\\\text{variable-overhead}\\\text{rate per hour}\end{array}$$

$$= \left(\begin{array}{c}3,750 \text{ actual}\\\text{hours}\end{array} - \begin{array}{c}3,500 \text{ standard}\\\text{hours allowed}\end{array}\right) \times €1.20 \text{ per hour}$$

$$= (250 \text{ excess hours}) \times €1.20 \text{ per hour}$$

$$= €300 \text{ unfavourable}$$

This example illustrates a general principle: When actual cost-driver activity exceeds the activity allowed for the actual output achieved, variable-overhead efficiency variances are unfavourable and vice versa. In essence, the variable-overhead efficiency variance tells management how much variable overhead cost it wastes if the variance is unfavourable (or saves, if the variance is favourable) due to cost-driver activity.

The other component of the flexible-budget variance measures control of overhead spending given actual cost-driver activity. The variable-overhead spending variance is the difference between the actual variable overhead and the amount of variable overhead predicted when using 3,750 actual direct-labour hours:

$$\begin{array}{c}\text{variable-overhead}\\\text{spending variance}\end{array} = \begin{array}{c}\text{actual variable}\\\text{overhead}\end{array} - \left(\begin{array}{c}\text{standard variable}\\\text{overhead rate}\end{array} \times \begin{array}{c}\text{actual direct-}\\\text{labour hours used}\end{array}\right)$$

$$= €4,700 \quad - (€1.20 \quad\quad\quad \times 3,750)$$

$$= €4,700 \quad - €4,500$$

$$= €200 \text{ unfavourable}$$

	A	B	C
	Actual overhead costs incurred	Predicted overhead based on actual driver use × standard prices	Flexible budget: standard driver use allowed for output achieved × standard prices
Variable overhead: supplies	€4,700 (given)	3,750 hr × €1.20/hr = €4,500	3,500 hr × €1.20/hr = €4,200

Spending variance (A − B)
€4,700 − €4,500 = €200 U

Efficiency variance (B − C)
€4,500 − €4,200 = €300 U

Flexible-budget variance (A − C)
€4,700 − €4,200 = €500 U

Fixed overhead: factory supervision	€14,700	€14,400	€14,400

Spending variance (A − B) =
€14,700 − €14,400 = €300 U

Never a variance (B − C) = 0
€14,400 − €14,400 = 0 by definition

Flexible-budget variance (A − C)
€14,700 − €14,400 = €300 U

Exhibit 8.9 General approach to analysis of overhead variances

Like other variances, a variable-overhead variance does not by itself identify the causes of results that differ from the static and flexible budgets. The distinction between efficiency and spending variances for variable overhead provides a springboard for more investigation, but the only way for management to discover why overhead performance did not agree with the budget is to investigate possible causes.

■ Fixed overhead variances

Objective 8
Compute the fixed-overhead spending variance.

The framework for analysis of fixed overhead variances differs from the framework for variable cost variances. Consider factory supervision, a fixed cost, shown at the bottom of Exhibit 8.9. The flexible budget in column B based on actual use of the cost driver and the flexible budget in column C based on standard use of the cost driver are always the same. Why? Because fixed overhead does not vary with the level of use of the cost driver. Because there is no difference between columns B and C, the entire fixed overhead flexible-budget variance in Exhibit 8.9 is due to the difference between columns A and B. This difference between the actual fixed-overhead cost in column A and the budgeted cost in columns B and C is the **fixed-overhead spending variance**. For example, the Dominion Company's factory supervision fixed-overhead spending variance is the flexible-budget variance of €14,700 − €14,400 = €300 unfavourable, the difference between the actual cost of factory supervision and the budgeted fixed amount.

In Chapter 13, you will encounter a second type of fixed-overhead variance, the production-volume variance. Because this second type of variance does not involve the control of costs, we consider only the fixed-overhead spending variance in this chapter.

Summary problem for your review

PROBLEM

The following questions are based on the data contained in the Dominion Company illustration used in this chapter.

- Direct materials: standard, 5 kg per unit at €2 per kg
- Direct labour: standard, $\frac{1}{2}$ hour at €16 per hour

Suppose the following were the actual results for production of 8,500 units:

- Direct materials: Dominion purchased and used 46,000 kg at an actual unit price of €1.85 per kg, for an actual total cost of €85,100.
- Direct labour: Dominion used 4,125 hours of labour at an actual hourly rate of €16.80, for a total actual cost of €69,300.

1. Compute the flexible-budget variance and the price and quantity variances for direct labour and direct material.
2. In requirement 1, you should have computed a direct-materials price variance of €6,900 favourable. Is this a good outcome? Explain.

SOLUTION

1. The variances are as follows:

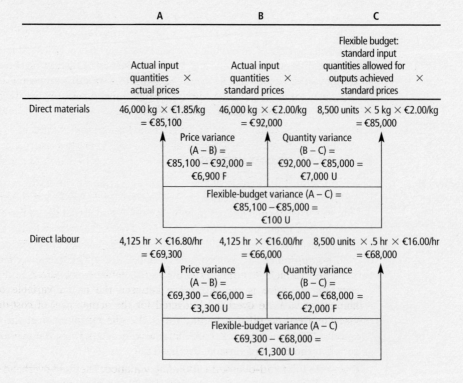

	A	B	C
	Actual input quantities × actual prices	Actual input quantities × standard prices	Flexible budget: standard input quantities allowed for outputs achieved × standard prices ×
Direct materials	46,000 kg × €1.85/kg = €85,100	46,000 kg × €2.00/kg = €92,000	8,500 units × 5 kg × €2.00/kg = €85,000

Price variance (A − B) = €85,100 − €92,000 = €6,900 F

Quantity variance (B − C) = €92,000 − €85,000 = €7,000 U

Flexible-budget variance (A − C) = €85,100 − €85,000 = €100 U

Direct labour	4,125 hr × €16.80/hr = €69,300	4,125 hr × €16.00/hr = €66,000	8,500 units × .5 hr × €16.00/hr = €68,000

Price variance (A − B) = €69,300 − €66,000 = €3,300 U

Quantity variance (B − C) = €66,000 − €68,000 = €2,000 F

Flexible-budget variance (A − C) = €69,300 − €68,000 = €1,300 U

2 The favourable price variance may not be a good outcome. When prices are low, it may motivate the Dominion Company managers to buy extra inventory in excess of its immediate needs, causing extra storage and handling costs. The favourable price variance may also mean that lower quality material has been purchased. The favourable materials price variance is a good outcome only if it exceeds any unfavourable material, labour and overhead variances caused by the volume and quality of materials purchased.

Highlights to Remember

1 **Distinguish between flexible budgets and static budgets.** Flexible budgets are geared to changing levels of cost-driver activity rather than to the single level of the static budget. Organisations tailor flexible budgets to particular levels of sales or cost-driver activity – before or after the fact. Flexible budgets tell how much revenue and cost to expect for any level of activity.

2 **Use flexible-budget formulas to construct a flexible budget based on the volume of sales.** Cost functions, or flexible-budget formulas, reflect fixed- and variable-cost behaviour and allow managers to compute budgets for any volume of output achieved. We compute the flexible-budget amounts for variable costs by multiplying the variable cost per unit of output times the level of output. The flexible-budgeted fixed cost is a lump sum, independent of the level of output (within the relevant range).

3 **Prepare an activity-based flexible budget.** When a significant portion of operating costs varies with cost drivers other than volume of production, a company benefits from using activity-based flexible budgets. These budgets are based on budgeted costs for each activity and related cost driver.

4 **Explain the performance evaluation relationship between static budgets, flexible budgets and actual results.** The differences or variances between the static budget and the flexible budget are due to activity levels, not cost control. The variances between the flexible budget and actual costs reflect cost control given the achieved level of activity.

5 **Compute activity-level variances and flexible-budget variances.** The flexible-budget variance is the difference between the actual result and the corresponding flexible-budget amount. The activity-level variance is the difference between the static budget and the corresponding flexible budget amount.

6 **Compute and interpret price and quantity variances for materials and labour.** Managers often find it useful to subdivide flexible-budget variances for variable inputs into price (or rate or spending) and quantity (or usage or efficiency) variances. Price variances reflect the effects of changing input prices, holding inputs constant at actual input use. Quantity variances reflect the effects of different levels of input usage, holding prices constant at standard prices.

7 **Compute variable-overhead spending and efficiency variances.** The variable-overhead spending variance is the difference between the actual variable overhead and the amount of variable overhead budgeted for the actual level of cost-driver activity. The variable-overhead efficiency variance is the difference between the actual cost-driver activity and the amount of cost-driver activity allowed for the actual output achieved, costed at the standard variable-overhead rate.

8 **Compute the fixed-overhead spending variance.** The fixed-overhead spending variance is the difference between the actual fixed overhead expenditures and the budgeted amount of fixed overhead. ■

Accounting vocabulary

activity-based flexible
   budget, p. 334
activity-level variances, p. 335
currently attainable
   standards, p. 340
effectiveness, p. 336
efficiency, p. 336
efficiency variance, p. 346
expected cost, p. 339
favourable cost variance, p. 331
favourable profit variance, p. 331
favourable revenue
   variance, p. 331

fixed-overhead spending
   variance, p. 351
flexible budget, p. 331
flexible-budget
   variance, p. 332
ideal standards, p. 339
perfection standards, p. 339
price variance, p. 344
quantity variance, p. 344
rate variance, p. 346
sales-activity variances, p. 336
standard cost, p. 339
static budget, p. 331

static-budget variance, p. 331
unfavourable cost
   variance, p. 331
unfavourable profit
   variance, p. 331
unfavourable revenue variance,
   p. 331
usage variance, p. 346
variable budget, p. 331
variable-overhead efficiency
   variance, p. 349
variable-overhead spending
   variance, p. 350

Fundamental assignment material   MyAccountingLab

8.A1 Flexible and static budgets

Burton Transportation Company's general manager reports quarterly to the company president on the firm's operating performance. The company uses a budget based on detailed expectations for the forthcoming quarter. The general manager has just received the condensed quarterly performance report shown in Exhibit 8.10.

Although the general manager was upset about not obtaining enough revenue, she was happy that her cost performance was favourable; otherwise, her net income would be even worse.

The president was not satisfied with the performance report and remarked, 'I can see some merit in comparing actual performance with budgeted performance because we can see whether actual revenue coincided with our best guess for budget purposes. But I can't see how this performance report helps me evaluate cost-control performance.'

1 Prepare a columnar flexible budget for Burton Transportation at revenue levels of €7,200,000, €8,000,000 and €8,800,000. Use the format of the last three columns of Exhibit 8.2, p. 333. Assume that the prices and mix of products sold are equal to the budgeted prices and mix.
2 Write out the flexible budget formula for costs as a function of revenue.
3 Prepare a condensed table showing the static budget variance, the sales-activity variance and the flexible-budget variance. Use the format of Exhibit 8.5, p. 336.

8.A2 Activity level variances

The systems consulting department of Bennett Products designs systems for data collection, encoding and reporting to fit the needs of other departments within the company. An overall cost driver is the number of requests made to the systems consulting department. The expected variable cost of handling a request was €500, and the number of requests expected for June 20X1 was 75. Bennett budgeted its monthly fixed costs for the department (salaries, equipment depreciation, space costs) at €65,000.

The actual number of requests serviced by systems consulting in June 20X1 was 90, and the total costs incurred by the department was €120,000. Of that amount, €76,000 was for fixed costs.

	Budget	Actual	Variance
Net revenue	€8,000,000	€7,600,000	€ 400,000 U
Variable costs			
Fuel	€ 160,000	€ 157,000	€ 3,000 F
Repairs and maintenance	80,000	85,000	5,000 U
Supplies and miscellaneous	800,000	788,000	12,000 F
Variable payroll	5,360,000	5,200,000	160,000 F
Total variable costs*	€6,400,000	€6,230,000	€ 170,000 F
Fixed costs			
Supervision	€ 180,000	€ 183,000	€ 3,000 U
Rent	160,000	160,000	—
Depreciation	480,000	480,000	—
Other fixed costs	160,000	158,000	2,000 F
Total fixed costs	980,000	981,000	€ 1,000 U
Total fixed and variable costs	€ 7,380,000	€7,211,000	€169,000 F
Operating income	€ 620,000	€389,000	€231,000 U

U = Unfavourable. F = Favourable.

* For purposes of this analysis, assume that all of these costs are totally variable with respect to sales revenue. In practice, many are mixed and would have to be subdivided into variable and fixed components before a meaningful analysis could be made. Also, assume that the prices and mix of services sold remain unchanged.

Exhibit 8.10 Burton Transportation operating performance report, second quarter, 20X1

Compute the static budget variances and the flexible-budget variances for variable and fixed costs for the systems consulting department for June 20X1.

8.A3 Direct-material and direct-labour variances

Barber Brass manufactures trumpets, trombones, tubas and other brass instruments. The following standards were developed for a line of trumpets:

	Standard inputs expected for each unit of output achieved	Standard price per unit of input
Direct materials	5 kg	€10 per kg
Direct labour	10 hours	€25 per hour

During April, Barber scheduled 550 trumpets for production. However, the company produced only 525.

Barber purchased and used 3,100 kg of direct materials at a unit price of €8.50 per kg. It used 5,500 hours of direct labour at an actual rate of €26.00 per hour.

1 Compute the standard cost per trumpet for direct materials and direct labour.
2 Compute the price variances and quantity variances for direct materials and direct labour.
3 Based on these sketchy data, what clues for investigation are provided by the variances?

8.B1 Summary performance reports

Consider the following data for David Skold Accounting Services:

● Static budget data: sales, 2,500 clients at €350 each; variable costs, €250 per client; fixed costs, €150,000.
● Actual results at actual prices: sales, 3,000 clients at €360 per client; variable costs, €800,000; fixed costs, €159,500.

1 Prepare a summary performance report similar to Exhibit 8.5, p. 336.
2 Fill in the blanks:

Static-budget income	€ __
Variances	
Sales-activity variances	€ __
Flexible-budget variances	__
Actual income	€ __

8.B2 Material and labour variances

Consider the following data for a manufacturing company:

	Direct material	Direct labour
Actual price per unit of input (kg and hr)	€7.80	€ 12.00
Standard price per unit of input	€7.00	€12.75
Standard inputs allowed per unit of output	10	2
Actual units of input	116,000	29,000
Actual units of output (product)	14,400	14,400

1 Compute the price, quantity and flexible-budget variances for direct materials and direct labour. Use U or F to indicate whether the variances are unfavourable or favourable.
2 Prepare a plausible explanation for the performance.

8.B3 Variable-overhead variances

You have been asked to prepare an analysis of the overhead costs in the order processing department of a mail-order company. As an initial step, you prepare a summary of some events that bear on overhead for the most recent period. Variable overhead is applied based on hours of processing-clerk labour. The standard variable-overhead rate per order was €.06. The rate of 10 orders per hour is regarded as standard productivity per clerk. The total overhead incurred was €203,600, of which €135,900 was fixed. The fixed-overhead spending variance was €400 unfavourable.

The variable-overhead flexible-budget variance was €5,600 unfavourable. The variable-overhead spending variance was €3,000 favourable.

Find the following:

1 Variable-overhead efficiency variance.
2 Actual hours of input.
3 Standard hours of input allowed for output achieved.
4 Budgeted-fixed overhead.

Additional assignment material

MyAccountingLab

QUESTIONS

8.1 Distinguish between favourable and unfavourable cost (and revenue) variances.

8.2 'The flex in the flexible budget relates solely to variable costs.' Do you agree? Explain.

8.3 'We want a flexible budget because costs are difficult to predict. We need the flexibility to change budgeted costs as input prices change.' Does a flexible budget serve this purpose? Explain.

8.4 Explain the role of understanding cost behaviour and cost-driver activities for flexible budgeting.

8.5 'An activity-based flexible budget has a 'flex' for every activity.' Do you agree? Explain.

8.6 'Effectiveness and efficiency go hand in hand. You can't have one without the other.' Do you agree? Explain.

8.7 Differentiate between a static-budget variance and a flexible-budget variance.

8.8 'Managers should be rewarded for favourable variances and punished for unfavourable variances.' Do you agree? Explain.

8.9 'A good control system places the blame for every unfavourable variance on someone in the organisation. Without affixing blame, no one will take responsibility for cost control.' Do you agree? Explain.

8.10 Who is usually responsible for sales-activity variances? Why?

8.11 Differentiate between perfection standards and currently attainable standards.

8.12 What are two possible approaches to setting 'currently attainable standards'?

8.13 'A standard is one point in a band or range of acceptable outcomes.' Evaluate this statement.

8.14 'Price variances should be computed even if prices are regarded as being outside of company control.' Do you agree? Explain.

8.15 What are some common causes of unfavourable quantity variances?

8.16 'Failure to meet price standards is the responsibility of the purchasing officer.' Do you agree? Explain.

8.17 'The variable-overhead efficiency variance is not really an overhead variance.' Evaluate this statement.

8.18 Why do the techniques for controlling overhead differ from those for controlling direct materials?

CRITICAL THINKING EXERCISES

8.19 Interpretation of favourable and unfavourable variances

A division budgeted an operating profit of €3,000 on sales of €8,000 and relevant costs of €5,000. However, at the beginning of the period one of the division's machines broke down and could not be fixed until the end of the period. When the machine broke, the division manager determined that there were two feasible alternatives: first, production and sales could be cut back by 25 per cent, reducing sales to €6,000 and relevant costs to €4,000. (Note that costs are not reduced by 25 per cent because some of the costs are fixed.) Second, a replacement machine could be obtained and installed, allowing sales to be maintained at €8,000 but increasing relevant costs to €6,500. The division manager analysed the alternatives and concluded that revenues less costs would be greater if sales were reduced (€6,000 less €4,000 = €2,000 operating profit) than if the replacement machine was obtained (€8,000 less €6,500 = €1,500 operating profit). The manager, therefore, chose not to replace the machine. However, because revenue was lower than planned by €2,000, there is an unfavourable revenue variance of €2,000. Comment on how the unfavourable revenue variance should be interpreted in evaluating the performance of the manager.

8.20 Marketing responsibility for sales-activity variances

Suppose a company budgeted an operating profit of €100 on sales of €1,000. Actual sales were €900. The marketing department claimed that because sales were down 10 per cent, it was responsible for only 10 per cent of €100 or €10 of any drop in profit. Any further shortfall must be someone else's responsibility. Comment on this claim.

8.21 Production responsibility for flexible-budget variances

Suppose a plant manager planned to produce 100 units of product at a total cost of €1,000. Instead, actual production was 10 per cent higher at 110 units. When costs came in at less than a 10 per cent increase in costs or €1,100, the plant manager claimed that she should get credit for a favourable variance equal to the amount by which the actual costs fell short of €1,100. Comment on this claim.

8.22 Responsibility of purchasing manager

A company's purchasing manager bought 5,000 kg of material for €5.50 per kg instead of the budgeted €6.00 per kg, resulting in a favourable variance of €2,500. The company has a policy of rewarding employees with 20 per cent of any cost savings they generate. Before awarding a €500 bonus to the purchasing manager, what other variances would you look at to determine the total effect of the purchasing decision? Explain.

8.23 Variable-overhead efficiency variance

Birmingham Company had a €1,000 U variable-overhead efficiency variance. Neither the plant manager, who was responsible primarily for labour scheduling, nor the administrative manager, who was responsible for most support services, felt responsible for the variance. Who should be held responsible? Why?

EXERCISES

8.24 Flexible budget

Stang Sports Equipment Company made 40,000 tennis balls in a given year. Its manufacturing costs were €256,000 variable and €95,000 fixed. Assume that no price changes will occur in the following year and that no changes in production methods are applicable. Compute the budgeted cost for producing 44,000 tennis balls in the following year.

8.25 Basic flexible budget

The superintendent of police of the city of Rollag is attempting to predict the costs of operating a fleet of police cars. Among the items of concern are fuel, €.24 per kilometre and depreciation, €6,000 per car per year.

The manager is preparing a flexible budget for the coming year. Prepare the flexible-budget amounts for fuel and depreciation for each car at a level of 30,000, 40,000 and 50,000 miles.

8.26 Flexible budget

Scottish Designs has a department that makes high-quality leather cases for iPods. Consider the following data for a recent month:

	Budget formula per unit	Various levels of output		
Units		6,000	7,000	8,000
Sales	£ 15	£ ?	£ ?	£ ?
Variable costs				
Direct materials	?	39,000	?	?
Hand labour	4	?	?	?
Fixed costs				
Depreciation		?	19,000	?
Salaries		?	?	34,000

Fill in the unknowns.

8.27 Basic fexible budget

The budgeted prices for materials and direct labour per unit of finished product are €11 and €5, respectively. The production manager is delighted about the following data:

	Static budget	Actual costs	Variance
Direct materials	€77,000	€72,000	€5,000 F
Direct labour	35,000	31,000	4,000 F

Is the manager's happiness justified? Prepare a report that might provide a more detailed explanation of why the static budget was not achieved. Good output was 5,800 units.

8.28 Direct-material variances

Bangkok Custom Shirt Company uses a special fabric in the production of dress shirts. During August, Bangkok Custom Shirt purchased and used 7,900 square yards in the production of 3,800 shirts at a total cost of B5,490,500. (B stands for the Thai baht. There are roughly 35 bahts to a US dollar.) The standard allows two yards at B700 per yard for each shirt.

Calculate the material price variance and the material quantity variance.

8.29 Labour variances

Elizabeth Chuk, the manager of the city of Reno road maintenance shop uses standards to judge performance. Because a clerk mistakenly discarded some labour records, however, Liz has only partial data for April. She knows that the total direct-labour flexible-budget variance was $1,855 favourable. Moreover, a recent pay raise produced an unfavourable labour price variance for April of $1,085. The actual hours of input were 1,750 and the standard labour price was $14 per hour.

1 Find the actual labour rate per hour.
2 Determine the standard hours allowed for the output achieved.

8.30 Quantity variances

Tanzania Toy Company produced 10,000 stuffed bears. The standard direct-material allowance is 1.75 kilograms per bear, at a cost per kilo of Sh3. Actually, 16,500 kilos of materials (input) were used to produce the 10,000 bears (output).

Similarly, the standard allowance for direct labour is 4.6 hours to produce one bear and the standard hourly labour cost is Sh6. But 48,000 hours (input) were used to produce the 10,000 bears.

Compute the quantity variances for direct materials and direct labour.

8.31 Labour and material variances

Standard direct-labour rate	€14.00
Actual direct-labour rate	€12.20
Standard direct-labour hours	12,000
Direct-labour quantity variance – unfavourable	€9,800
Standard unit price of materials	€ 4.50
Actual quantity purchased and used	1,800
Standard quantity allowed for actual production	1,650
Materials purchase price variance – favourable	€ 198

1 Compute the actual hours worked, rounded to the nearest hour.
2 Compute the actual purchase price per unit of materials, rounded to the nearest penny.

8.32 Material and labour variances

Consider the following data:

	Direct materials	Direct labour
Costs incurred: actual inputs × actual prices incurred	€154,000	€77,800
Actual inputs × expected prices	170,000	74,000
Standard inputs allowed for actual outputs achieved × expected prices	172,500	71,300

Compute the price, quantity and flexible-budget variances for direct materials and direct labour. Use U or F to indicate whether the variances are unfavourable or favourable.

8.33 Flexible and static budgets

London Business School's Entrepreneur Society recently held a dinner dance. The original (static) budget and actual results were as follows:

	Static budget	Actual	Variance
Attendees	75	90	
Revenue	£ 2,625	£3,255	£630 F
Chicken dinners at £19.00	1,425	1,767	342 U
Beverages, £6 per person	450	466	16 U
Club rental, at £81	81	81	0
Music, 3 hours at £250 per hour	750	875	125 U
Profit	£ (81)	£ 66	£147 F

1 Subdivide each variance into a sales-activity variance portion and a flexible-budget variance portion. Use the format of Exhibit 8.5, p. 336.
2 Provide possible explanations for the variances.

8.34 Summary explanation

Higgins Company produced 80,000 units, 8,000 more than budgeted. Production data are as follows. Except for physical units, all quantities are in dollars.

	Actual results at actual prices	Flexible-budget variances	Flexible budget	Sales-activity variances	Static budget
Physical units	80,000	–	?	?	72,000
Sales	?	6,400 F	?	?	720,000
Variable costs	492,000	?	480,000	?	?
Contribution margin	?	?	?	?	?
Fixed costs	?	30,000 U	?	?	150,000
Income	?	?	?	?	?

1 Fill in the unknowns.
2 Give a brief summary explanation of why the original target income was not attained.

8.35 Explanation of variance in income

Damerow Credit Services produces reports for consumers about their credit ratings. The company's standard contribution margins average 70 per cent of euro sales and average selling prices are €50 per report. Average productivity is four reports per hour. Some employees work for sales commissions and others for an hourly rate. The static budget for 20X1 had predicted processing 800,000 reports, but Damerow processed only 700,000 reports.

Fixed costs of rent, supervision, advertising and other items were budgeted at €22 million, but the budget was exceeded by €600,000 because of extra advertising in an attempt to boost revenue. There were no variances from the average selling prices, but the actual commissions paid to preparers and the actual productivity per hour resulted in flexible-budget variances (i.e., total price and quantity variances) for variable costs of €900,000 unfavourable.

The general manager of Damerow was unhappy because the budgeted income of €6 million was not achieved. He said, 'Sure, we had unfavourable variable-cost variances, but our income was down far more than that. Please explain why.'

Explain why the budgeted income was not attained. Use a presentation similar to Exhibit 8.5, p. 336. Enough data have been given to permit you to construct the complete exhibit by filling in the known items and then computing the unknowns. Complete your explanation by summarising what happened, using no more than three sentences.

8.36 Activity and flexible-budget variances at KFC

Suppose a chain of KFC franchises in Beijing had budgeted sales for 2009 of RMB 7.3 million (where RMB stands for the Chinese unit of currency, officially the renminbi, also called the yuan). Cost of goods sold and other variable costs were expected to be 60 per cent of sales. Budgeted annual fixed costs were RMB 1.8 million. A strong Chinese economy caused actual 2009 sales to rise to RMB 9.2 million and actual profits to increase to RMB 1,570,000. Fixed costs in 2009 were as budgeted. The franchisee was pleased with the increase in profit.

1 Compute the sales-activity variance and the flexible-budget variance for income for 2009. What can the franchisee learn from these variances?
2 Suppose that in 2010 the Chinese economy weakened and the franchise's sales fell back to the RMB 7.3 million level. Given what happened in 2009, what do you expect to happen to profits in 2010?

8.37 Summary of airline performance

The performance (in thousands of euros) of Kenmore Airlines for the most recent year is shown in the following table:

	Actual results at actual prices	Static budget	Variance
Revenue	€ ?	€300,000	€ ?
Variable expenses	200,000	195,000*	5,000 U
Contribution margin	?	105,000	?
Fixed expenses	87,000	80,000	7,000 U
Income	€ ?	€ 25,000	€ ?

*Includes jet fuel of €90,000.

The static budget had been based on a budget of €.20 revenue per passenger mile. A passenger mile is one paying passenger flown one mile. An average airfare decrease of 8 per cent had helped generate an increase in passenger miles flown that was 10 per cent in excess of the static budget for the year.

The price per gallon of jet fuel rose above the price used to formulate the static budget. The average jet fuel price increase for the year was 10%.

1 Prepare a summary report similar to Exhibit 8.5, p. 336, to help the president understand performance for the most recent year.
2 Assume that jet fuel costs are purely variable and the quantity of fuel used was at the same level of efficiency as predicted in the static budget. What part of the flexible-budget variance for variable expenses is attributable to jet fuel expenses? Explain.

8.38 Hospital costs and explanation of variances

The emergency room at Rochester General Hospital in Sydney, Australia, uses a flexible budget based on patients seen as the measure of activity. The hospital must maintain an adequate staff of attending and on-call physicians at all times so patient activity does not affect physician scheduling. Nurse scheduling varies as volume changes, however. A standard of .5 nurse-hours per patient visit was set. Hourly pay for nurses ranges from $9 to $18 per hour and the average pay rate is $15 per hour. The hospital considers all materials to be supplies, a part of overhead; there are no direct materials. A statistical study showed that the cost of supplies and other variable overhead is more closely associated with nurse-hours than with patient visits. The standard for supplies and other variable overhead is $10 per nurse-hour.

The head physician of the emergency room unit, Brad Narr, is responsible for control of costs. During October the emergency room unit treated 4,000 patients. The budget and actual costs were as follows:

	Budget	Actual	Variance
Patient visits	3,800	4,000	200
Nurse-hours	1,900	2,080	180
Nursing cost	$ 28,500	$ 33,180	$4,680
Supplies and other variable overhead	19,000	20,340	1,340
Fixed costs	92,600	92,600	0
Total cost	$140,100	$146,120	$6,020

1 Calculate price and quantity variances for nursing costs.
2 Calculate spending and efficiency variances for supplies and other variable overhead.
3 The hospital's chief administrator has asked Dr Narr to explain the variances. Provide possible explanations.

8.39 Flexible budgeting

For the convenience of its reporters and staff based in London, CNN operates a motor pool. The motor pool operated with 25 vehicles until February of this year, when it acquired an additional car. The motor pool furnishes petrol (gasoline), oil and other supplies for the cars and hires one mechanic who does routine maintenance and minor repairs. Major repairs are done at a nearby commercial garage. A supervisor manages the operations.

Each year the supervisor prepares an operating budget, informing CNN management of the funds needed to operate the pool. Depreciation on the cars is recorded in the budget in order to determine the cost per mile.

The following schedule presents the annual budget approved by the news division. The actual costs for March are compared with one-twelfth of the annual budget.

CNN London motor pool
Budget report for March 20X1

	Annual budget	One-month budget	March actual	Over (under)
Fuel	£ 82,500	£ 6,875	£ 8,200	£1,325
Oil, minor repairs, parts and supplies	30,000	2,500	2,540	40
Outside repairs	2,700	225	50	(175)
Insurance	4,800	400	416	16
Salaries and benefits	21,600	1,800	1,800	—
Depreciation	22,800	1,900	1,976	76
Total costs	£ 164,400	£13,700	£14,982	£1,282
Total kilometres	1,500,000	125,000	140,000	
Cost per kilometre	£ .1096	£ .1096	£ .1070	
Number of cars	25	25	26	

The annual budget was constructed based on the following assumptions:

1 25 cars in the pool.
2 60,000 kilometres per year per car.
3 8 kilometres per litre of petrol for each car.
4 £.44 per litre of petrol.
5 £.02 per kilometre for oil, minor repairs, parts and supplies.
6 £108 per car in outside repairs.

The supervisor is unhappy with the monthly report comparing budget and actual costs for March; she claims it presents her performance unfairly. Her previous employer used flexible budgeting to compare actual costs with budgeted amounts.

1 Employing flexible-budgeting techniques, prepare a report that shows budgeted amounts, actual costs and monthly variation for March.
2 Explain briefly the basis of your budget figure for outside repairs.

8.40 Activity-based flexible budget

Cost behaviour analysis for the four activity centres in the billing department of Fargo Power Company is given next.

	Traceable costs		
Activity centre	Variable	Fixed	Cost-driver activity
Account inquiry	€79,910	€156,380	3,300 labour hours
Correspondence	9,800	25,584	2,800 letters
Account billing	154,377	81,400	2,440,000 lines
Bill verification	10,797	78,050	20,000 accounts

The billing department constructs a flexible budget for each activity centre based on the following ranges of cost-driver activity.

Activity centre	Cost driver	Relevant range	
Account inquiry	Labour hours	3,000	5,000
Correspondence	Letters	2,500	3,500
Account billing	Lines	2,000,000	3,000,000
Bill verification	Accounts	15,000	25,000

1 Develop flexible-budget formulas for each of the four activity centres.
2 Compute the budgeted total cost in each activity centre for each of these levels of cost-driver activity: (a) the smallest activity in the relevant range, (b) the midpoint of the relevant range and (c) the highest activity in the relevant range.
3 Determine the total cost function for the billing department.
4 The following table gives the actual results for the billing department. Prepare a cost-control performance report comparing the flexible budget to actual results for each activity centre. Compute flexible-budget variances.

Activity centre	Actual cost-driver level	Actual cost
Account inquiry	4,300 labour hours	€235,400
Correspondence	3,200 letters	38,020
Account billing	2,950,000 lines	285,000
Bill verification	23,000 accounts	105,320

8.41 Variance analysis

The Zurich Chocolate Company uses standard costs and a flexible budget to control its manufacture of fine chocolates. The purchasing agent is responsible for material price variances and the production manager is responsible for all other variances. Operating data for the past week are summarised as follows:

1 Finished units produced: 4,000 boxes of chocolates.
2 Direct materials: Purchased and used, 4,300 pounds of chocolate at 15.5 Swiss francs (CHF) per pound; standard price is CHF 16 per pound. Standard allowed per box produced is 1 pound.
3 Direct labour: Actual costs, 6,400 hours at CHF 30.5 or CHF 195,200. Standard allowed per box produced is 1.5 hours. Standard price per direct-labour hour is CHF 30.
4 Variable manufacturing overhead: Actual costs, CHF 69,500. Budget formula is CHF 10 per standard direct-labour hour.

Compute the following:
  1 (a) Materials purchase-price variance.
    (b) Materials quantity variance.
    (c) Direct-labour price variance.
    (d) Direct-labour quantity variance.
    (e) Variable manufacturing-overhead spending variance.
    (f) Variable manufacturing-overhead efficiency variance.
    (Hint: For format, see the solution to the 'Summary problem for your review', p. 352.)
  2 (a) What is the budget allowance for direct labour?
    (b) Would it be any different if production were 5,000 boxes?

8.42 Similarity of direct-labour and variable-overhead variances

The Kevin Koh Company has had great difficulty controlling costs in Singapore during the past 3 years. Last month, the company installed a standard-cost and flexible-budget system. A condensation of results for a department follows:

	Expected cost per standard direct-labour hour	Flexible-budget variance
Lubricants	$ .60	$330 F
Other supplies	.30	225 U
Rework	.60	450 U
Other indirect labour	1.50	450 U
Total variable overhead	$3.00	$795 U

F = Favourable. U = Unfavourable.

The department had initially planned to manufacture 9,000 audio speaker assemblies in 6,000 standard direct-labour hours allowed. Material shortages and a heat wave resulted in the production of 8,100 units in 5,800 actual direct-labour hours. The standard wage rate is $5.25 per hour, which was $.15 higher than the actual average hourly rate.

1 Prepare a detailed performance report with two major sections: direct labour and variable overhead.
2 Prepare a summary analysis of price and quantity variances for direct labour and spending and efficiency variances for variable overhead.
3 Explain the similarities and differences between the direct-labour and variable-overhead variances. What are some of the likely causes of the overhead variances?

8.43 Material, labour and overhead variances

Poulsbo Kayak Company makes moulded plastic kayaks. Standard costs for an entry-level whitewater kayak are as follows:

Direct materials, 60 lb at $5.50/lb	$330
Direct labour, 1.5 hr at $16/hr	24
Overhead, at $12 per kayak	12
Total	$366

The overhead rate assumes production of 450 kayaks per month. The overhead cost function is €2,808 + (€5.76 × number of kayaks).

During March, Poulsbo produced 430 kayaks and had the following actual results:

Direct materials purchased and used	27,000 pounds at $5.30/lb
Direct labour	670 hours at $15.90/hr
Actual overhead	$5,335

1 Compute material, labour and overhead variances.
2 Interpret the variances.
3 Suppose the cost function for variable overhead was $3.84 per labour hour instead of $5.76 per kayak. Compute the variable-overhead efficiency variance and the total overhead spending variance. Would these variances lead you to a different interpretation of the overhead variances from the interpretation in requirement 2? Explain.

8.44 Automation and direct labour as overhead

Kilgore Precision Machining (KPM) has a highly automated manufacturing process for producing a variety of auto parts. Through the use of computer-aided manufacturing and robotics, the company has reduced its labour costs to only 5 per cent of total manufacturing costs. Consequently, the company does not account for labour as a separate item but instead accounts for labour as part of overhead.

Consider a part used in antilock braking systems. The static budget for producing 750 units in March 20X1 is as follows

Direct materials	€18,000*
Overhead	
Supplies	1,875
Power	1,310
Rent and other building services	2,815
Factory labour	1,500
Depreciation	4,500
Total manufacturing costs	€30,000

*3 kg/unit × €8/lb × 750 units.

Supplies and power are variable and the other overhead items are fixed costs.
Actual costs in March 20X1 for producing 900 units of the brake part were as follows:

Direct materials	€21,840*
Overhead	
Supplies	2,132
Power	1,612
Rent and other building services	2,775
Factory labour	1,618
Depreciation	4,500
Total manufacturing costs	€34,477

*KPM purchased and used 2,800 kg of materials at €7.80 per kg.

1 Compute (a) the direct-materials price and quantity variances and (b) the flexible-budget variance for each overhead item.
2 Comment on the way KPM accounts for and controls factory labour.

8.45 Standard material allowances

Chesapeake Chemical Company supplies primarily industrial users. Your superior has asked you to develop a standard product cost for a new solution the company plans to introduce.

The new chemical solution is made by combining altium and bollium, boiling the mixture, adding credix and bottling the resulting solution in 20-litre containers. The initial mix, which is 20 litres in volume, consists of 24 kilograms of altium and 19.2 litres of bollium. A 20 per cent reduction in volume occurs during the boiling process. The solution is then cooled slightly before adding 10 kilograms of credix to each 20-litre container; the addition of credix does not affect the total liquid volume.

The purchase prices of the raw materials used in the manufacture of this new chemical solution are as follows:

Altium	€2.20 per kilogram
Bollium	€4.60 per litre
Credix	€3.20 per kilogram

Determine the standard quantity for each of the raw materials needed to produce 20 litres of Chesapeake Chemical Company's new chemical solution and the total standard materials cost of 20 litres of the new product.

8.46 Review of major points in this chapter

The following questions are based on the Dominion Company data contained in Exhibit 8.1 (p. 330) and in the table near the top of p. 344.

1 Suppose actual production and sales were 8,000 units instead of 7,000 units. (a) Compute the sales-activity variance. Is the performance of the marketing function the sole explanation for this variance? Why? (b) Using a flexible budget, compute the budgeted contribution margin, the budgeted income, budgeted direct material and budgeted direct labour.

2 Suppose the following were the actual results for the production of 8,000 units.
   Direct materials: 42,000 pounds were used at an actual unit price of €1.86, for a total actual cost of €78,120.
   Direct labour: 4,140 hours were used at an actual hourly rate of €16.40, for a total actual cost of $67,896.
   Compute the flexible-budget variance and the price and quantity variances for direct materials and direct labour. Present your answers in the form shown in Exhibit 8.8, p. 347.

3 Evaluate the Dominion Company's performance based on the variances you calculated in numbers 1 and 2.

8.47 Review problem on standards and flexible budgets; answers are provided

The Des Moines Leather Company makes a variety of leather goods. It uses standard costs and a flexible budget to aid planning and control. Budgeted variable overhead at a 45,000-direct-labour-hour level is €81,000.

During April, the company had a favourable variable-overhead efficiency variance of €2,970. Material purchases were €241,900. Actual direct-labour costs incurred were €422,100. The direct-labour quantity variance was €15,300 unfavourable. The actual average wage rate was €.60 lower than the standard average wage rate.

The company uses a variable-overhead rate of 20 per cent of standard direct-labour cost for flexible-budgeting purposes. Actual variable overhead for the month was €92,250.

Compute the following amounts; use U or F to indicate whether variances are unfavourable or favourable.

1 Standard direct-labour cost per hour.
2 Actual direct-labour hours worked.
3 Total direct-labour price variance.
4 Total flexible budget for direct-labour costs.
5 Total direct-labour flexible-budget variance.
6 Variable-overhead spending variance in total.

Answers to Problem 8.47

1 €9. The variable-overhead rate is €1.80, obtained by dividing €81,000 by 45,000 hours. Therefore, the direct-labour rate must be €1.80 ÷ .20 = €9

2 50,250 hours. Actual costs, €422,100 ÷ ($9–$.60) = 50,250 hours.

3 €30,150 F. 50,250 actual hours × €.60 = €30,150.

4 €436,950. Quantity variance was €15,300 U. Therefore, excess hours must have been €15,300 ÷ €9 = 1,700. Consequently, standard hours allowed must be 50,250 − 1,700 = 48,550. Flexible budget = 48,550 × €9 = €436,950.

5　€14,850 F. €436,950 − €422,100 = €14,850 F; or €30,150 F − €15,300 U = €14,850 F.
6　€7,830 U. Flexible budget = 48,550 × 1.80 = €87,390. Total variance = €92,250 − €87,390 = €4,860 U. Spending variance = Total variance − Efficiency variance = €4,860 + €2,970 = €7,830 U. Check: €92,250 − .20 × €422,100 = €7,830.

CASES

8.48 Activity-based costing and flexible budgeting

A new printing department provides printing services to the other departments of Farmers & Mechanics Insurance Company (FMIC). Before the establishment of the in-house printing department, the departments contracted with external printers for their printing work. FMIC's printing policy is to charge departments for the variable printing costs on the basis of number of pages printed. The company recovers fixed costs in pricing of external jobs.

The first year's budget for the printing department was based on the department's expected total costs divided by the planned number of pages to be printed.

The projected annual number of pages to be printed was 420,000 and budgeted total variable costs were €420,000. Most government accounts and all internal jobs were expected to use only single-colour printing. Commercial accounts use primarily four-colour printing. FMIC estimated its variable costs based on the typical mix of single-colour versus four-colour printing and the average variable cost of printing a four-colour page that is one-fourth graphics and three-fourths text. The expected annual costs for each division were as follows:

Department	Planned pages printed	Variable cost per page	Budgeted charges
Government accounts	120,000	€1	€ 90,000
Commercial accounts	250,000	1	300,000
Central administration	50,000	1	30,000
Total	420,000		€420,000

After the first month of using the internal printing department, the printing department announced that its variable cost estimate of €1 per page was too low. The first month's actual costs were €51,000 to print 40,000 pages.

Government accounts	9,000 pages
Commercial accounts	27,500
Central administration	3,500

Three reasons were cited for higher-than-expected costs: All departments were using more printing services than planned and government and internal jobs were using more four-colour printing and more graphics than anticipated in the original variable cost projections. The printing department also argued that it would have to purchase additional four-colour printing equipment if demand for four-colour printing continued to grow.

1　Compare the printing department actual results, static budget and flexible budget for the month just completed.
2　Discuss possible reasons why the printing department static budget was inaccurate.

3 An ABC study completed by a consultant indicated that printing costs are driven by number of pages (at €.35 per page) and use of colours (at €1 extra per page for colour).

(a) Discuss the likely effects of using the ABC results for budgeting and control of printing department use.

(b) Discuss the assumptions regarding cost behaviour implied in the ABC study results.

(c) All commercial accounts during the first month (27,500 pages) used four colours per page. Compare the cost of commercial accounts under the old and the proposed ABC system.

8.49 Analysing performance

Hopkins Community Hospital operates an outpatient clinic in a town several miles from the main hospital. For several years the clinic has struggled just to break even. The clinic's financial budget for 20X7 is shown in Exhibit 8.12.

On the average, billings for each patient-visit are expected to be €180. Costs in 20X7 are expected to average €183 per patient-visit, as follows:

Physician time	€ 60
Nurse and technician time	45
Supplies	15
Overhead	63
Total	€183

The clinic is generally staffed by one physician who must be present whether or not there is a patient to see. Currently, about 10 per cent of the physician's time is idle. The clinic employs nurses and technicians to meet the actual workload necessitated by patient appointments. Their cost averages €30 per hour and usage varies proportionately with the number of patient-visits. Supplies cost is also variable with respect to patient-visits. Fixed overhead in 20X7 was expected to be €180,000; the remaining €72,000 of overhead varies with respect to patient visits. Included in the fixed overhead was €30,000 of hospital-wide administrative costs that the hospital allocates to the clinic and €37,500 of depreciation on the clinic's property and equipment.

Cindy Ryden, controller of Hopkins Community Hospital, reported the actual loss of €20,200 in 20X7 shown next. This represented the fifth straight year of losses. She does not feel it is right for patients in the main hospital to subsidise those using the clinic. Therefore, she suggested that unless the situation could be changed, the clinic should be closed. Brett Johnson, administrative vice president of the hospital, charged with oversight of the clinic, disagreed: 'We provide a valuable service to the community with the clinic. Even if we are losing money, it is worthwhile to keep it open.'

	Total		Per patient
Revenues (4,000 patients at €180 each)		€720,000	€180
Cost of services			
Physicians	€240,000		
Nurses and technicians	180,000		
Supplies	60,000		
Overhead	252,000	732,000	183
Net loss		€ (12,000)	€ (3)

Exhibit 8.12 Outpatient clinic – 20X7 budget

At the end of 20X7, the clinic's actual results for the year were as follows:

		Total
Revenues (3,800 patients at €180)		€684,000
Cost of services		
Physicians	€231,000	
Nurses and technicians (5,800 hours)	182,700	
Supplies	58,500	
Overhead	232,000	704,200
Net loss		€ (20,200)

1   Would Hopkins Community Hospital have saved money in 20X7 if the outpatient clinic was closed? Explain.
2   Explain the difference between the budgeted loss of €12,000 and the actual loss of €20,200 (that is, the static-budget variance of €8,200) in as much detail as possible. From the analysis of the 20X7 results, what actions would you suggest to avoid a loss in 20X8?

8.50 Complete variance analysis

Gates Video Games manufactures video game machines. Market saturation and technological innovations have caused pricing pressures that have resulted in declining profits. To stem the slide in profits until the company can introduce new products, top management has turned its attention to both manufacturing economies and increased production. To realise these objectives, management developed an incentive programme to reward production managers who contribute to an increase in the number of units produced and achieve cost reductions. In addition, the company instituted a JIT purchasing program so that it purchases raw materials on an as-needed basis.

The production managers have responded to the pressure to improve manufacturing performance in several ways that have resulted in an increase in the number of completed units over normal production levels. The video game machines put together by the assembly group require parts from both the printed circuit boards (PCB) and the reading heads (RH) departments. To attain increased production levels, the PCB and RH departments started rejecting parts from suppliers that previously would have been tested and modified to meet manufacturing standards. Preventive maintenance on machines used in the production of these parts has been postponed with only emergency repair work being performed to keep production lines moving. The maintenance staff is concerned that there will be serious breakdowns and unsafe operating conditions.

The more aggressive assembly group production supervisors have pressured maintenance personnel to attend to their machines at the expense of other groups. This has resulted in machine downtime in the PCB and RH departments which, when coupled with demands for accelerated parts delivery by the assembly department, has led to more frequent parts rejections and increased friction among departments. Gates Video Games operates under a standard-costing system. The standard costs at a production level of 24,000 units per year are in part A of Exhibit 8.13.

Gates Video Games prepares monthly income statements based on actual expenses. Part B of Exhibit 8.13 shows the statement for May, when production and sales both reached 2,200 units. The budgeted sales price was €200 per unit and budgeted (normal) production and sales were 24,000 units per year. Top management was surprised by the low profit in spite of increased sales for May. The original budget had called for income before taxes of €62,000 and with the added sales, the president had expected at least €68,200

		Standard cost per unit		
	Quantity	Cost		Total
A. Standard cost report				
Direct materials:				
Housing unit	1 unit	€	20	€ 20
Printed circuit boards (PCB)	2 boards		15	30
Reading heads (RH)	4 heads		10	40
Direct labour:				
Assembly department	2.0 hours		8	€ 16
PCB department	1.0 hour		9	9
RH department	1.5 hours		10	15
Overhead:				
Variable	4.5 hours	€	2	€ 9
Fixed	4.5 hours		4	18
Total manufacturing cost per unit				€ 157
Selling and administrative:				
Fixed		€	12	€ 12
Total standard cost per unit				€ 169

B. Income Statement for May

Revenues (2,200 units)		€440,000
Variable costs:		
Direct materials	220,400	
Direct labour	93,460	
Variable overhead	18,800	
Fixed costs:		
Overhead	37,600	
Selling and administrative	22,000	
Total costs		392,260
Income before taxes		€47,740

C. Usage report for May

Cost Item	Actual quantity	Actual cost
Direct materials:		
Housing units	2,200 units	€ 44,000
Printed circuit boards	4,700 boards	75,200
Reading heads	9,200 heads	101,200
Direct labour:		
Assembly department	3,900 hours	31,200
PCB department	2,400 hours	23,760
RH department	3,500 hours	38,500
Overhead:		
Variable		18,800
Fixed		37,600
Total manufacturing costs		€370,260

Exhibit 8.13 Gates video games

of income (€6,200 more income; 200 extra units × €31 per unit). The president called on Michelle Barber, director of cost management, to report on the reasons for the shortfall in income. After a thorough review of the data, Barber prepared the report in part C of Exhibit 8.13.

1 Prepare a budgeted income statement in contribution margin format for Gates Video Games showing why the company expected income before taxes to be €62,000.

2 Assume that you have been given Michelle Barber's task. Prepare a complete analysis explaining the reason for the difference between the original projected income before taxes of €62,000 and the actual of €47,740. Compute all the variances that are helpful in explaining this difference, and explain what you learn from the variances.

CASE STUDY

Zeros plc

Falconer Mitchell, University of Edinburgh

This case is concerned with the use of ROI to measure divisional performance. It also addresses the use of an integrated standard costing system to produce meaningful profit statements where standard setting is problematic.

The board of Zeros plc assesses divisional performance within the company primarily on the basis of a return on investment ratio. This is computed as follows:

$$\frac{\text{Operating profit}}{\text{Book value of total assets}} \times 100 = \text{ROI}$$

The figure of operating profit is obtained from a standard-costing-based profit statement (see Table 1 for the two recent such statements).

The Blank Division

In terms of turnover the Blank Division is the second largest division within the company. The divisional manager is Joe Cool who has worked in the division for over 30 years, initially as a management accountant and then as manager from 2001. He is 63 years old and will retire in 18 months' time. In accordance with a board policy introduced to improve motivation at divisional level, his current remuneration contains a substantial bonus element based on divisional operating profit. In addition, his retirement pension will be based upon his average total earnings in his last three working years.

The Blank Division was resituated in a town-centre freehold site which was purchased in 1995. A custom-built factory was erected on the site with considerable financial aid from the government and was equipped with what were, at the time, the most modern machines available. It is a matter of considerable pride to Joe that much of this equipment has been conscientiously maintained and is still in use today. In the accounting records the freehold site and factory building are still valued at historic cost.

The Blank Division produces a wide range of sizes of surgical needles, although all are sold at a standard price (see Table 2). Although the market is growing the competition is intense, being based on both price and, particularly, product quality.

Source: Mitchell, F. (1988) 'Zeros plc', in Otley, D. Brown and C. Wilkinson (eds) *Case Studies in Management Accounting* (Hemel Hempstead, UK: Philip Allan Publishers). Reproduced with permission.

Table 1 Annual profit statement

	2010 (£000)	2011(£000)
Budgeted sale	8000	10940
Selling price variance	–	–
Sales volume variance	(1600) U	(2735) U
Actual sales	6400	8205
Standard cost of sales	4800	6150
Standard operating profit	1600	2055
Cost variances		
Direct material price	(100) U	(80) U
Direct material usage	(220) U	(280) U
Labour rate	(150) U	(130) U
Labour efficiency	(200) U	(300) U
Variable overhead spending	(180) U	(300) U
Variable overhead efficiency	(250) U	(275) U
Fixed overhead spending	(120) U	(150) U
Fixed overhead volume	–	–
Operating profit	380	540

Table 2 Unit standard costs and selling price

	2010	2011
Unit standard cost		
Direct material	0.50	0.60
Direct labour	0.75	0.90
Variable overheads	0.50	0.60
Fixed overheads	1.25	2.00
	3.00	4.10
Actual unit selling prices	4.00	5.47

Standard costs are revised at the start of each financial year (see Table 2) and are based on the middle-range size of surgical needle produced in the division.

It is frequently pointed out at board meetings by Joe Cool that the Blank Division can still achieve a 33 per cent mark-up on its standard unit cost and that no competing firm can approach this level of margin.

In recent years the Blank Division has produced highly satisfactory return-on-investment figures and a reasonable profit growth. The board has, however, been concerned by the large unfavourable variances which have been consistently reported. The normal retort of the Blank Division manager to queries on the size of variances has been the state unequivocally that 'it is the bottom line that matters; if that's OK you can forget the rest'. He has also consistently promoted the performance of the division during 2010 and 2011 to the board as 'excellent' and rebuffed any judgements to the contrary. Results for the last two years are given in Table 1 and Table 3.

Table 3 Records of production and sales

	2010 ('000 units)	2011 ('000 units)
Opening stock	200	600
Production	2000	2000
Sales	(1600)	(1500)
Closing stock	600	1100

Questions

1 What criticism would you make of the approach to divisional-performance assessment employed by the board of Zeros plc?

2 Would you agree with Joe Cool's assessment that his division's performance was 'excellent' during 2010 and 2011?

3 What suggestions would you make for improving the divisional-performance measurement in Zeros plc?

Management control systems and responsibility accounting

Learning objectives

When you have finished studying this chapter, you should be able to:

1 Describe the relationship of management control systems to organisational goals.

2 Explain the importance of evaluating performance and describe how it impacts on motivation, goal congruence and employee effort.

3 Develop performance measures and use them to monitor the achievements of an organisation.

4 Use responsibility accounting to define an organisational subunit as a cost centre, a profit centre or an investment centre.

5 Prepare segment income statements for evaluating profit and investment centres using the contribution margin and controllable-cost concepts.

6 Measure performance against nonfinancial performance measures such as quality, cycle time and productivity.

7 Use a balanced scorecard to integrate financial and nonfinancial measures of performance.

8 Describe the difficulties of management control in service and nonprofit organisations.

Diesel

Fashionwear is an intensely competitive business. Renzo Rosso was passionate about clothes, but disappointed in the options available in his hometown, Molvena, in Italy. He decided to make the clothes he wanted to wear. He was drawn to denim and decided to create jeans that allowed him and others to express themselves in ways other clothing could not match. Renzo went from selling his handcrafted jeans from the back of his van around Italy to being the owner and CEO of Diesel. The company's sales exceeded $1.3 billion in 2009, selling its products across 5,000 retail outlets in 80 countries.

Diesel's mindset is to put sales and profits second to building something special – something 'cool'. Key to the company's promotion and marketing strategy is for Diesel to engage the customer with the lifestyle rather than sell to them. The concept of a brand for 'successful living' allows Diesel jeans to be sold at premium prices.

This chapter builds on concepts developed in previous chapters to explore how managers blend the individual tools of management accounting to help achieve organisational goals. Tools such as activity-based costing, relevant costing, budgeting and variance analysis are each useful by themselves. They are most useful, however, when they are parts of an integrated system – a comprehensive plan to coordinate and evaluate all the activities of the organisation's value chain. Just as in the case of Diesel, managers of most organisations today realise that long-run success requires a focus on cost, quality and service – the three components of the competitive edge. This chapter considers how the management control system helps managers achieve such a focus. As you will see, no single management control system is inherently superior to another. The 'best' system for any organisation is the one that most consistently leads to actions that meet the organisation's goals and objectives. ■

Management control systems

A **management control system** is a logical integration of techniques for gathering and using information to make planning and control decisions, for motivating employee behaviour and for evaluating performance. A well-designed management control system supports and coordinates the decision-making process and motivates individuals throughout the organisation to act in concert. It also facilitates forecasting and budgeting. An effective management control system should

- clearly define and communicate the organisation's goals;
- ensure that managers and employees understand the specific actions required to achieve organisational goals;
- communicate results of actions across the organisation; and
- motivate managers and employees to achieve the organisation's goals.

Based on the preceding criteria, Exhibit 9.1 describes elements of the planning and control processes and emphasises their interrelationships. As we pointed out in Chapter 1, planning and control are so strongly interrelated that it is somewhat artificial to separate them in practice. To the extent we can separate them, planning includes defining goals (A) and establishing and carrying out plans to achieve the goals (B). Control includes measuring and reporting results (C) and performance evaluation (D). The clockwise ordering of the elements represents the order that managers would naturally follow when designing and evaluating the management control system. However, once an organisation has implemented the control system, it continuously adapts all the interrelated elements and revises them through feedback and learning. For example, the organisation may revise the measures used to monitor and report in C to fit better with the goals in A. Similarly, it might realign the performance evaluation system in D to better fit with the specific plans and objectives in B. We will refer to Exhibit 9.1 often as we consider the design and operation of management control systems.

Management control systems and organisational goals

Objective 1
Describe the relationship of management control systems to organisational goals.

The first and most basic component in a management control system is the organisation's goals. Exhibit 9.2 illustrates how managers at all levels of the organisation set goals and objectives and develop related performance measures for their section of the organisation. Top managers set organisation-wide goals, performance measures and targets, which they generally review annually. These goals provide a long-term framework around which an organisation

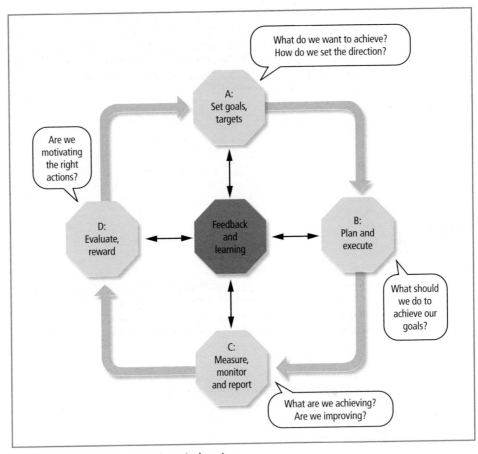

Exhibit 9.1 The management control system

will form its comprehensive plan for positioning itself in the market. Goals address the question in Exhibit 9.1, 'What do we want to achieve?' However, goals without performance measures do not motivate managers.

A basic adage of management control is that 'you get what you measure'. Because measures of performance set direction and motivate managers' decisions, every performance measure should be consistent with organisational goals. Otherwise, managers who achieve high performance measures may not create value for the company and its owners. An ideal management control system should include at least one performance measure related to every goal.

To illustrate the correspondence between organisational goals and performance measures, suppose a major luxury hotel chain, Scottsdale Luxury Suites, has the following goals and related measures:

Organisational goals	Performance measures
Exceed guest expectations	• Customer satisfaction index • Number of repeat stays
Maximise revenue yield	• Occupancy rate • Average room rate • Income before fixed costs
Focus on innovation	• New products/services implemented per year • Number of employee suggestions

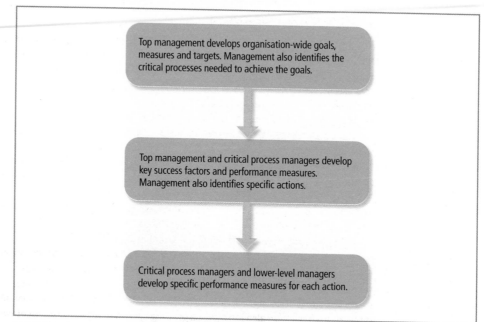

Exhibit 9.2 Translating goals and objectives into performance measures

The company sets quantifiable targets for each of the measures. For example, a target for the performance measure occupancy rate might be 'at least 70 per cent'. Note that every goal has at least one performance measure and every measure is related to at least one goal.

As shown in Exhibit 9.2, performance measures become more specific as we move to lower levels of the organisation. For example, higher-level managers work with subordinates within each business unit to select specific tangible short-term actions (or activities) that managers can carry out, along with observable performance measures. One approach to selecting these actions and measures is for top managers to identify **key success factors** – characteristics or attributes that managers must achieve in order to drive the organisation toward its goals. For a luxury hotel chain a key success factor for the goal to exceed guest expectations is timeliness. This key success factor suggests that the chain should consider specific actions, such as implementing an express check-in system. In addition, it should measure timeliness by using performance measures, such as time to check in, time to check out and response time to guest requests (for example, number of rings before someone at the front desk answers the telephone).

Balancing various goals is an important part of designing a management control system. Managers often face trade-offs. For example, a manager may meet a goal of increased customer satisfaction by establishing a more generous policy for accepting returned merchandise. However, this policy will also impose additional costs that decrease short-term profitability. Choosing the best trade-off between short-term profitability and long-term customer satisfaction is often difficult, especially when the long-term benefits of increased customer satisfaction are hard to predict.

Designing management control systems

To design a management control system that meets the organisation's needs, managers must identify what motivates employees, develop performance measures based on these motivations and establish a monitoring and reporting structure for these measures. Let's look at each of these.

Motivating employees

Objective 2
Explain the
importance
of evaluating
performance and
describe how
it impacts on
motivation, goal
congruence and
employee effort.

An important goal of the management control system is to motivate employees to work in the best interests of the organisation. A good management control system fosters both goal congruence and managerial effort. An organisation achieves **goal congruence** when employees, working in their own perceived best interests, make decisions that help meet the overall goals of the organisation. **Managerial effort** – exertion toward a goal or objective – must accompany goal congruence. Effort here includes not only working harder or faster but also working better. It includes all conscious actions (such as supervising, planning and thinking) that result in more efficiency and effectiveness.

As we saw in Exhibit 9.1, the challenge of management control system design is to induce (or at least not discourage) employee decisions that would achieve organisational goals. For example, an organisation may identify continuous improvement in employee efficiency and effectiveness as one of its goals. Employees, however, might perceive that continuous improvements will result in tighter standards, faster pace of work and loss of jobs. Even though they may agree with management that continuous improvements are competitively necessary, management should not expect them to exert effort for continuous improvements unless rewards are in place to make this effort in their own best interests.

As another example, students may enroll in a college course because their goal is to learn about management accounting. The faculty and the students share the same goal, but goal congruence is not enough. Faculty also introduce a grading system to reward student effort. Grading is a form of performance evaluation, similar to organisations using management control reports for raises, promotions and other forms of rewards. Performance evaluation improves effort because most individuals tend to perform better when performance reports lead directly to personal rewards. For instance, manufacturers that set quality improvements as critical organisational goals put quality targets into the bonus plans of top managers and factory workers.

Motivation – the drive toward some selected goal that creates effort and action toward that goal – is key to management control. Yet employees differ widely in their motivations. This makes the system designer's task complex and ill-structured. Each system must fit the specific organisational environment and behavioural characteristics of the employees. The system designer must align individuals' self-interest with the goals of the organisation. Thus, the designer must predict the motivational impact of a particular system – how it will cause people to respond – and compare it to the motivational impact of other potential systems. Designing performance measures is not a back-office accounting task.

Budgets, variances and the entire inventory of management control tools should constructively influence behaviour. These tools are most effective when managers use them positively to encourage employees to improve performance, rather than negatively to punish, place blame or find fault. Used negatively, these tools pose a threat to employees, who will resist and undermine the use of such techniques. Critics have pointed to Enron's management control system as a major cause of the company's problems. Employees were heavily rewarded for good performance. More importantly, the employees who were ranked lowest at each evaluation were fired. This created intense competition, which at first seemed to create exceptional performance levels for the company. Later, it became clear that the pressure for good performance caused some employees to use unethical methods to increase their performance measures, which eventually led to the demise of the company.

Developing performance measures

Objective 3
Develop performance
measures and use
them to monitor the
achievements of an
organisation.

For most organisations, effective performance measurement requires multiple performance measures, including both financial and nonfinancial measures. Effective performance measures have the following characteristics:

1 Reflect key actions and activities that relate to the goals of the organisation.

2 Affected by actions of managers and employees.

3 Readily understood by employees.

4 Reasonably objective and easily measured.

5 Used consistently and regularly in evaluating and rewarding managers and employees.

6 Balance long-term and short-term concerns.

Sometimes accountants and managers focus too much on financial measures, such as operating budgets, profit targets or required return on investment, because the accounting system readily produces such measures. Further, it is often difficult to construct performance measures for nonfinancial goals such as customer satisfaction, improvements in quality, environmental stewardship, social responsibility and organisational learning, which many companies list as key goals. However, well-designed management control systems develop and report both financial and nonfinancial measures of performance because 'You can't manage something you can't measure.'

Nonfinancial measures often motivate employees toward achieving important performance goals. Financial measures often are lagging indicators that arrive too late to help prevent

BUSINESS FIRST
Performance measures in practice

An organisation's performance measures depend on its goals and objectives. For example, a software company and an auto manufacturer have different goals and objectives and therefore have vastly different performance measures. The measures also must span a variety of key success factors for the organisation. Performance measures too focused on one aspect of performance may foster neglect of other important factors.

Let's look at a classic management control system, the one developed by General Electric in the 1950s. The system focused on eight 'key result areas', as GE called them:

Financial key result areas

1 Profitability
2 Productivity
3 Market position

Nonfinancial key result areas

4 Product leadership
5 Personnel development
6 Employee attitudes
7 Public responsibility
8 Balance between short-run and long-range goals

Measures in each of these eight areas are just as relevant today as in the 1950s. These are clearly

long-run strategic goals. Measures might change as an organisation adapts the means of achieving the goals, but the basic framework of a management control system does not need to change as management fads come and go.

Some companies shift their focus and invest in different ways to re-orient employee behaviour. For instance, during the 1990s, Hyundai, the Korean car manufacturer, was more interested in the number of cars it could make than in how good it could make them. In 1999, however, when the firm's founder's son, Mong-Koo Chung, took the helm, Hyundai's focus shifted from volume to quality. It made quality a cross-functional responsibility with involvement from procurement, finance, sales and marketing. It put outside suppliers with its designers and engineers to work out problems before they occurred. It held quality oversight meetings every fortnight with Chairman Chung attending. The company installed Six Sigma at its engineering centre to measure improvements. On J.D. Power's study of new vehicle quality after 90 days of ownership, Hyundai ranked 32nd in 2001, 7th in 2004 and 4th in 2009. It had displaced Toyota with only Lexus, Porsche and Cadillac ahead of it. Its two-part quality target called CQ 3-3-5-5 helps Hyundai meet its quality performance objectives.

Sources: David Solomons, *Divisional Performance: Measurement and Control* (Homewood, IL: Irwin, 1965); Alex Taylor, 'Hyundai smokes the competition', *Fortune* January 2010.

problems and ensure the organisation's health. The effects of poor nonfinancial performance (for example, lack of organisational learning and low customer satisfaction) may not show up in the financial measures until the company has lost considerable ground. Many companies now stress management of the activities that drive revenues and costs, rather than waiting to explain the revenues or costs themselves. Superior financial performance usually follows from superior nonfinancial performance. Examples of both financial and nonfinancial measures are in the 'Business first' box above.

Monitoring and reporting results

Notice that Exhibit 9.1 has feedback and learning at the centre of the management control system. Organisation-wide learning is a foundation for gaining and maintaining financial strength. Some management experts have said that the only sustainable competitive advantage is the rate at which a company's managers learn. Harley-Davidson, a company with 2010 sales of about €4.2 billion, emphasises learning for operational excellence – getting out waste, improving quality and helping drive customer satisfaction.

Once a company has superior intellectual capital, how can it best maintain its leadership? Exhibit 9.3 shows how organisational learning leads to financial strength. Measures such as training time, employee turnover and staff satisfaction scores on employee surveys monitor organisational learning. The result of learning is continuous process improvement. Measures such as cycle time, number of defects (quality) and activity costs can assess improvement. Customers will value improved response time (lower cycle time), higher quality and lower prices and will increase their demand for products and services. Increased demand, combined with lower costs to make and deliver products and services, results in improved product profitability and earnings. Successful organisations do not stop with one cycle of learning → process improvement → increased customer satisfaction → improved financial strength. Instead, they continue to reinvest financial resources to further support both continuous learning and continuous process improvement.

There are no guarantees that each of the components automatically follows from success at the previous component. If efforts are not coordinated throughout the value chain, the cause-effect links can be broken. For example, new and improved products or services may fail if marketing and distribution techniques do not place them at the location desired by the customer. As another example, development of a great e-commerce website does no good if customers never visit the website. The point is that improvement in business processes must be coordinated across all parts of the value chain.

Another message from Exhibit 9.3 is that a key driver of enterprise performance is the culture within the company that fosters continual learning and growth at all levels of management. It is not sufficient to use money to train managers without making sure that the resulting learning translates into improved processes, products and services. This requires a culture of learning that motivates managers to translate learning into growth.

Siemens provides a good example of the application of the enterprise learning culture. With sales in 2010 of about €76 billion, Siemens has demonstrated a remarkable ability to generate formidable profits with products spanning electrical engineering and electronics including air traffic, healthcare, railroads, telecom, power, lighting and finance. The company's ex-CEO, Dr Heinrich von Pierer, has noted that 'between 60 and 80 per cent of the value added which Siemens creates is directly linked to knowledge. Therefore the first priority is to network and manage internal knowledge efficiently.'[1] While the development of a corporate knowledge sharing culture is important for Siemens and indicators of its learning progress are tracked, so are

---

[1] This was cited in G. Fink and N. J. Holden (2005) 'The global transfer of management knowledge: introduction', *Academy of Management Executive*, Special Issue on *Global Transfer of Management Knowledge*, Vol. 19, No. 2, pp. 5–8.

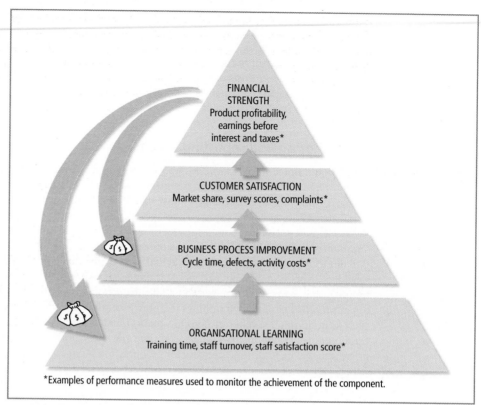

Exhibit 9.3 The components of a successful organisation and measures of achievement

financial targets. The company has a new 'One Siemens financial target system which defines metrics for revenue growth, capital efficiency, profitability and capital structure optimisation. As Peter Löscher, Siemens' President and CEO notes: 'With One Siemens we're entering new territory.' (Siemens 2010 Annual Report.) Siemens' approach provides a good example of the application of the enterprise learning culture.

As shown in Exhibit 9.1, monitoring and reporting the results of business activities are key components of a management control system. Exhibit 9.2 indicates that managers identify actions and related performance measures that are linked to the achievement of goals and objectives. The performance-reporting system provides periodic information on the achievement of desired outcomes. Effective performance reports align results with managers' goals and objectives, provide guidance to managers, communicate goals and their level of attainment throughout the organisation and enable organisations to anticipate and respond to change in a timely manner.

Weighing costs and benefits

The designer of a management control system must always weigh the costs and benefits of various alternatives. Benefits and costs of management control systems are often difficult to measure and both may become apparent only after experimentation or use. For example, the director of accounting policy of Citicorp stated that, after using a very detailed management control system for several years, the system proved to be too costly to administer relative to the perceived benefits. Accordingly, Citicorp returned to a simpler, less costly – though less detailed – management control system. While the economic benefits and costs of a system may be estimable, it is the case for all enterprises that the context will determine the form of management controls in use. The firm's pursued strategy, the style of management, the cultural and historically shaped preferences of customers and employees, the nature of technology used and the legal environment will all have a bearing on the specific management control system being deployed.

Summary problem for your review

PROBLEM

A luxury hotel chain called Luxhot is developing performance measures for each of its major goals. Top management established 'exceed guest expectations' as one organisation-wide goal. Among the key success factors are timeliness of customer service and quality of personalised service. Patty Bowen, manager of sales, is the manager responsible for the actions required to meet the goal of exceeding guest expectations. She has already identified one action (objective) for the coming year – upgrade customer service department capabilities.

1 Identify several possible performance measures for the quality-of-personalised-service key success factor.

2 Recommend several specific actions or activities associated with upgrading customer service department capabilities that would drive Luxhot toward its goal of exceeding customer expectations.

SOLUTION

1 Performance measures for the quality of personalised service might include the number of changes to registration, rating on the 'friendly, knowledgeable staff' question on the guest survey, number of complaints, percentage of return guests and percentage of customers with completed customer profile (profiles special needs of customers).

2 Specific actions or activities might include training employees, implementing a call checklist (list of services and options available to the guest) and monitoring compliance with the list, developing a customer satisfaction survey and reengineering the guest registration and reservation processes.

Controllability and measurement of financial performance

Management control systems often distinguish between controllable and uncontrollable events and between controllable and uncontrollable costs. These terms refer to relative rather than absolute controllability – no cost is completely under the control of a manager – and a controllable cost is one that a manager's decisions 'affect to a reasonable extent'. An **uncontrollable cost** is any cost that management cannot reasonably affect within a given time span. For example, the manager of a BASF factory may not be able to control the market price of the crude oil used to make various chemicals. In contrast, **controllable costs** include those costs that a manager's decisions and actions can influence to a reasonable extent. For example, BASF is likely to consider labour costs as controllable by the factory manager, even though the manager does not totally control labour costs because union contracts place constraints on both pay rates and labour usage. Similarly, the manager may be able to affect, though not completely control, the amount of crude oil used and most overhead costs in the factory. The distinction between controllable and uncontrollable costs is used in evaluating the performance of a manager. Costs that are completely uncontrollable tell nothing about a manager's decisions and actions because, by definition, nothing the manager does will affect the costs. In contrast, measuring and reporting controllable costs provides evidence about a manager's performance.

Identifying responsibility centres

Objective 4
Use responsibility accounting to define an organisational subunit as a cost centre, a profit centre or an investment centre.

Designers of management control systems identify the responsibilities of each manager in an organisation by establishing responsibility centres based on what a manager can control. A responsibility centre is a set of activities and resources assigned to a manager, a group of managers or other employees. A set of machines and machining activities, for example, may be a responsibility centre for a production supervisor. The full production department may be a responsibility centre for the department head. Finally, the entire organisation may be a responsibility centre for the president. In some organisations, groups of employees share management responsibility to create wide 'ownership' of management decisions, to allow creative decision making and to prevent one person's concern (or lack of concern) for risks of failure to dominate decisions.

An effective management control system gives each manager responsibility for a group of activities and actions and then, as Exhibit 9.1 shows, monitors and reports on (1) the results of the activities and (2) the manager's influence on those results. Such a system has intrinsic appeal for most top managers (because it helps them delegate decision making and frees them to focus on more strategic issues) and lower-level managers (who value the decision-making autonomy they inherit). Thus, system designers apply responsibility accounting to identify what parts of the organisation have primary responsibility for each action, develop performance measures and targets, and design reports of these measures by responsibility centre. Responsibility centres usually have multiple goals and actions that the management control system monitors. We classify responsibility centres as cost centres, profit centres or investment centres based on their managers' primary financial responsibilities.

Cost, profit and investment centres

In a cost centre, managers are responsible for costs only. A cost centre may encompass an entire department, or a department may contain several cost centres. For example, although one manager may supervise an assembly department, the department may contain several assembly lines and each assembly line may be considered a separate cost centre. Likewise, within each line, each separate machine may be its own cost centre. The determination of the number of cost centres depends on cost-benefit considerations – do the benefits (for planning, control and evaluation) of smaller, more numerous cost centres exceed the higher costs of reporting?

Unlike cost-centre managers, profit-centre managers are responsible for controlling revenues as well as costs – that is, profitability. Despite the name, a profit centre can exist in nonprofit organisations (though it might not be referred to as such) when a responsibility centre receives revenues for its services.

An investment centre adds responsibility for investment to profit-centre responsibilities. Investment-centre success depends on both income and invested capital, measured by relating income generated to the value of the capital employed.

Systems designers must understand operating processes and cost behaviour to help identify responsibility for controllable costs. For example, by isolating activities and related cost drivers, activity-based costing (see Chapter 4) can help to point out control-lable costs. Procter & Gamble credited its activity-based management control system with identifying controllable costs in one of its detergent divisions, which led to major strategic changes.

Responsibility centre managers are often able to explain their centre's uncontrollable costs, even in situations where they are not held responsible for these uncontrollable costs. For example, an exporter of cucumbers in Spain in mid-2011 suffered extreme losses in sales following an E. Coli outbreak which was later found not to be associated with Spanish cucumbers. The sales drop was beyond the import manager's control. The company held the manager responsible for efficiency (the flexible-budget variance [see Chapter 8]) but not the effects of activity volume (the sales-activity variance). Even though he was not held responsible for the sales-activity variance, the manager was in the best position to provide an explanation for the variance because he had the best information about the reasons for the decline in sales.

■ Contribution margin

Many organisations combine the contribution approach to measuring income with responsibility accounting – that is, they report by cost behaviour as well as by degrees of controllability. Exhibit 9.4 is an organisation chart showing selected units of a retail grocery company like Lidl or Uchumi. Exhibit 9.5 illustrates the contribution approach to measuring financial performance of the various units shown on the organisation chart. Segments are responsibility centres for which a company develops separate measures of revenues and costs. Exhibit 9.5 provides perspective on how a management-control system report can stress cost behaviour, controllability, manager performance and respon-sibility centre performance simultaneously.

Line (a) in Exhibit 9.5 shows the contribution margin, sales revenues less variable ex-penses. The contribution margin ratio, defined as the ratio of contribution margin to sales, is

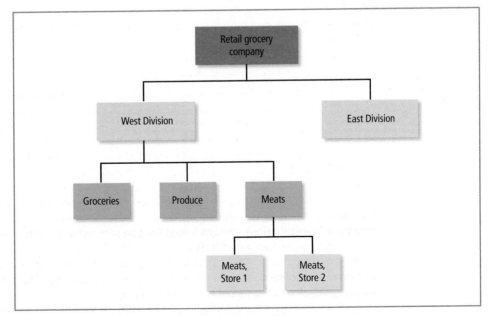

Exhibit 9.4 Retail grocery company organisation chart

	Company as a whole	Company breakdown into two divisions		Breakdown of West Division only				Breakdown of West Division, meats only		
		East Division	West Division	Not allocated[b]	Groceries	Produce	Meats	Not allocated[b]	Store 1	Store 2
Net sales	€4,000	€1,500	€2,500	—	€1,300	€300	€900	—	€600	€300
Variable costs										
Cost of merchandise sold	€3,000	€1,100	€1,900	—	€1,000	€230	€670	—	€450	€220
Variable operating costs[c]	260	100	160	—	100	10	50	—	35	15
Total variable costs	€3,260	€1,200	€2,060	—	€1,100	€240	€720	—	€485	€235
(a) Contribution margin	€740	€300	€440	—	€200	€60	€180	—	€115	€65
Less: fixed costs controllable by segment managers[d]	260	100	160	€20	40	10	90	€30	35	25
(b) Contribution controllable by segment managers	€480	€200	€280	€(20)	€160	€50	€90	€(30)	€80	€40
Less: fixed costs controllable by others[e]	200	90	110	20	40	10	40	10	22	8
(c) Contribution by segments	€280	€110	€170	€(40)	€120	€40	€50	€(40)	€58	€32
Less: unallocated costs[f]	100									
(d) Income before income taxes	€180									

[a] Three different types of segments are illustrated here: divisions, product lines and stores. As you read across, note that the focus becomes narrower; from East and West divisions to West Division only, to meats in West Division only.

[b] Only those costs clearly identifiable to a product line or store should be allocated.

[c] Principally wages and payroll-related costs.

[d] Examples are certain advertising, sales promotions, salespersons' salaries, management consulting, training and supervision costs.

[e] Examples are depreciation, property taxes, insurance and perhaps the segment manager's salary.

[f] These costs are not clearly or practically allocable to any segment except by some highly questionable allocation base.

Exhibit 9.5 Retail grocery store – Contribution approach: model income statement by segments[a] (thousands of euros) especially helpful for predicting the impact on income of short-run changes in sales volume. Managers may quickly calculate expected changes in income by multiplying the contribution margin ratio by the expected change in euro sales. For example, the contribution margin ratio for meats in the West Division is €180 ÷ €900 = .20. A €1,000 increase in sales of meats in the West Division should produce a €200 increase in contribution margin and income (.20 × €1,000 = €200) if there are no changes in selling prices, variable operating expenses per unit, fixed costs or mix of sales.

■ Contribution controllable by segment managers

Objective 5
Prepare segment income statements for evaluating profit and investment centres using the contribution margin and controllable-cost concepts.

Lines (b) and (c) in Exhibit 9.5 separate the contribution that segment managers control (b) from the overall segment contribution (c). Designers of management control systems distinguish between the segment as an economic investment and the manager as a decision maker. For instance, an extended period of drought coupled with an aging population may adversely affect the desirability of continued economic investment in a ski resort, but the resort manager may none the less be doing an excellent job under the circumstances.

Exhibit 9.5 separates costs by controllability. The manager of meats at Store 1 may have influence over some local advertising but not other advertising, some fixed salaries but not other salaries, and so forth. Moreover, the meat manager at both the division and store levels may have zero influence over store depreciation or the president's salary. Managers on all levels help explain the total segment contribution, but they are responsible only for the controllable contribution. Note that we deduct the fixed costs controllable by the segment managers from the contribution margin to obtain the contribution controllable by segment managers. These controllable costs are usually discretionary fixed costs such as local advertising and some salaries, but not the manager's own salary.

As we move to the right in Exhibit 9.5, we see allocations of only part of the fixed costs to lower levels in the organisation. For example, consider the line with fixed costs controllable by segment managers. Of the €160,000 fixed costs that the West Division manager controls, groceries, produce and meat departments control only €140,000. We do not allocate the remaining €20,000 of West Division fixed costs because they are not controllable this far down in the organisation. That is, the West Division manager controls all €160,000 of fixed costs, but subordinates (grocery, produce and meat managers) control only €140,000. Similarly, the meats manager controls €90,000 of fixed costs, but subordinates at Stores 1 and 2 control only €35,000 and €25,000, respectively.

■ Contribution by segments

The contribution by segments, line (c) in Exhibit 9.5, is an attempt to approximate the financial performance of the segment, as distinguished from the financial performance of its manager, which we measure in line (b). The 'fixed costs controllable by others' typically include committed costs (such as depreciation and property taxes) and discretionary costs (such as the segment manager's salary). Although the segment manager does not control these costs, they are necessary for the operation of the segment.

■ Unallocated costs

Exhibit 9.5 shows 'unallocated costs' immediately before line (d). These costs might include central corporate costs, such as the costs of top management and some corporate-level services (for example, legal and taxation). When an organisation cannot find a persuasive cause-and-effect or activity-based justification for allocating such costs, it generally does not allocate them to segments.

Summary

The correct classification of costs as illustrated in Exhibit 9.5 is sometimes ambiguous. Determining controllability is a problem when a company allocates service department costs to other departments. Should a store manager bear a part of the division headquarters' costs? If so, how much and on what basis? How much, if any, store depreciation or lease expenses should we deduct in computing the controllable contribution? There are no universally correct answers to these questions. Each organisation makes choices that balance costs and benefits. (This differs from the situation in external accounting systems, where tax or financial reporting regulations usually specify the required classification of costs.)

Because of the subjectivity involved in classification of costs, measures of financial performance like those illustrated in Exhibit 9.5 are subjective, especially at lower-level units. The calculation of the contribution margin near the top of the report tends to be the most objective, because managers can usually objectively identify and assign variable costs. As you read downward in the report, the allocations become increasingly subjective and the resulting measures of contributions become more subject to dispute. None the less, many organisations find that allocation of costs to units makes managers more aware of the costs of the entire organisation and leads to better organisational cost control.

MAKING MANAGERIAL DECISIONS

Managers should try to distinguish between controllable and uncontrollable costs when designing segment financial reports. For each of the following costs of a suburban Asda store, indicate whether it is a variable cost, fixed cost controllable by segment managers, fixed cost controllable by someone other than the segment manager, or a cost that a company normally does not allocate:

Property taxes

Supervision of local sales staff

Depreciation of store

Cost of goods sold

Local store advertising

Corporate-level advertising

Corporate-level public relations

Temporary sales labour

Answer

Variable costs are generally controllable by the store manager. Cost of goods sold and temporary sales labour are examples.

Fixed costs controllable by the segment (store) manager include local store advertising and supervision of the local sales staff. The store manager usually decides the appropriate level for these costs.

Fixed costs controllable by those other than the store manager include property taxes and depreciation of the store. These costs relate directly to the store, but the store manager cannot change them.

Unallocated costs include corporate-level advertising and public relations. These costs have a tenuous link to the store.

Summary problem for your review

PROBLEM

The Book & Game Company has two bookstores: Auntie's and Merlin's. Each store has managers who have a great deal of decision authority over their store. Advertising, market research, acquisition of books, legal services and other staff functions, however, are handled by a central office. The Book & Game Company's current accounting system allocates all costs to the stores. Results for 20X1 were as follows:

Item	Total company	Auntie's	Merlin's
Sales revenue	€700,000	€350,000	€350,000
Cost of merchandise sold	450,000	225,000	225,000
Gross margin	250,000	125,000	125,000
Salaries and wages	63,000	30,000	33,000
Supplies	45,000	22,500	22,500
Rent and utilities	60,000	40,000	20,000
Depreciation	15,000	7,000	8,000
Allocated staff costs	60,000	30,000	30,000
Total operating expenses	243,000	129,500	113,500
Operating income (loss)	€ 7,000	€ (4,500)	€ 11,500

Each bookstore manager makes decisions that affect salaries and wages, supplies and depreciation. In contrast, rent and utilities are beyond the managers' control because the managers did not choose the location or the size of the store.

Supplies are variable costs. Variable salaries and wages are equal to 8 per cent of the cost of merchandise sold; the remainder of salaries and wages is a fixed cost. Rent, utilities and depreciation also are fixed costs. Staff costs represent the cost of activities performed by the central office. Events at the individual bookstores do not affect staff costs; nevertheless, Book & Game Company allocates them as a proportion of sales revenue.

1 Using the contribution approach, prepare a performance report that distinguishes the performance of each bookstore from that of the bookstore manager.

2 Evaluate the financial performance of each bookstore.

3 Evaluate the financial performance of each manager.

SOLUTION

1 See Exhibit 9.6.

2 We can evaluate the financial performances of the bookstores (that is, segments of the company) using the line 'contribution by bookstore'. Merlin's has a substantially higher contribution, despite equal levels of sales revenues in the two stores. The major reason for this advantage is that Merlin's pays less for rent and utilities.

3 We can evaluate the financial performance of the managers using the line 'contribution controllable by managers'. By this measure, the performance of Auntie's manager is better than that of Merlin's. The contribution margin is the same for each store, but Merlin's manager paid €4,000 more in controllable fixed costs than did Auntie's manager. Note that the additional fixed costs could be beneficial in the long run. What is missing from each of these segment reports is the year's master budget and a flexible budget, which would be the best benchmark for evaluating both bookstores and bookstore managers.

Item	Total company	Auntie's	Merlin's
Sales revenue	€700,000	€350,000	€350,000
Variable costs			
Cost of merchandise sold	450,000	225,000	225,000
Salaries and wages – variable portion	36,000	18,000	18,000
Supplies	45,000	22,500	22,500
Total variable costs	531,000	265,500	265,500
Contribution margin by bookstore	169,000	84,500	84,500
Less: fixed costs controllable by bookstore managers			
Salaries and wages – fixed portion	27,000	12,000	15,000
Depreciation	15,000	7,000	8,000
Total controllable fixed costs	42,000	19,000	23,000
Contribution controllable by managers	127,000	65,500	61,500
Less: fixed costs controllable by others			
Rent and utilities	60,000	40,000	20,000
Contribution by bookstore	67,000	€ 25,500	€ 41,500
Unallocated costs	60,000		
Operating income	€ 7,000		

Exhibit 9.6 The Book & Game Company – Performance report

Measurement of nonfinancial performance

For many years, organisations have monitored their nonfinancial performance. For example, sales organisations have followed up on customers to ensure their satisfaction and manufacturers have tracked manufacturing defects and product performance. In recent years, many organisations have developed a new awareness of the importance of controlling nonfinancial performance areas. We first examine important examples of nonfinancial performance measures such as quality, cycle time and productivity. Then, we discuss the balanced scorecard, a popular approach to performance measurement that integrates financial and nonfinancial measures tied to the organisation's fundamental strategy.

■ Control of quality

Objective 6
Measure performance against nonfinancial performance measures such as quality, cycle time and productivity.

Most companies use performance metrics that measure the quality of their products or services. **Quality control** is the effort to ensure that products and services perform to customer requirements. In essence, customers or clients define quality by comparing their needs to the attributes of the product or service. For example, buyers judge the quality of a car based on reliability, performance, styling, safety and image relative to their needs, budget and the alternatives. Defining quality in terms of customer requirements is only half the battle. There remains the problem of reaching and maintaining the desired level of quality. There are many approaches to controlling quality.

The traditional approach was to inspect products after completing them and reject or rework those that failed the inspections. Because testing is expensive, companies often inspected only a sample of products. They judged the process to be in control as long as the number of defective products did not exceed an acceptable quality level. This meant that some defective products could still make their way to customers.

Many companies have moved away from the traditional approach to quality control. They have found that it is more cost effective to prevent defects than to detect and correct them. The resources consumed to detect defective products do not add value. If the company must scrap the defective product, it wastes the resources that were consumed to produce it. Even when the company can correct the product defects, it wastes the resources required for rework. When a company does not discover defects until the product reaches the customer, it is costly to repair products already in use by a customer or to win back a dissatisfied customer.

The high costs of achieving quality by the traditional approach of 'inspecting it in' are evident in a **cost of quality report**, which displays the financial impact of quality. The quality cost report shown in Exhibit 9.7 measures four categories of quality costs:

1 Prevention – costs incurred to prevent the production of defective products or delivery of substandard services including engineering analyses to improve product design for better manufacturing, improvements in production processes, increased quality of material inputs and programmes to train personnel.

2 Appraisal – costs incurred to identify defective products or services including inspection and testing.

3 Internal failure – costs of defective components and final products or services that are scrapped or reworked; also costs of delays caused by defective products or services.

4 External failure – costs caused by delivery of defective products or services to customers, such as field repairs, returns and warranty expenses.

Exhibit 9.7 shows that internal or external failures caused most of the costs incurred by Eastside Manufacturing Company. These costs almost certainly are understated, however, because they omit opportunity costs of internal delays and lost sales. For example, quality problems with Mercedes-Benz cars during 2000 and 2005 caused sales to drop for many years. The opportunity cost of these lost future sales were much more significant than the immediate tangible costs measured in any quality cost report. One analyst noted: 'There's no excuse for the quality collapse at Mercedes ... But once it slips, quality takes time to fix – sometimes a whole car generation.' (Gail Edmondson, *Bloomberg Business Week* 17 August 2007.) Another analyst commenting on the quality issues Toyota faced following the 'sudden acceleration' issues forcing extreme vehicle recalls by the company notes: 'The Toyota brand has been tarnished to the point that some will now view it as just another brand with respect to quality.' (David Aaher, www.prophet.com 8 December 2010.)

In recent years, more companies have been rethinking this approach to quality control. They have adopted an approach first espoused by an American, W. Edwards Deming and embraced by Japanese companies decades ago: **total quality management (TQM)**. Following the old adage 'an ounce of prevention is worth a pound of cure', it focuses on prevention of defects and on achievement of customer satisfaction. The TQM approach builds on the assumption that an organisation minimises the cost of quality when it achieves high quality levels. TQM is the application of quality principles to all of the organisation's endeavors to satisfy customers. TQM has significant implications for organisation goals, structure and management control systems. For TQM to work, though, employees must be well trained in the process, the product or service and the use of quality-control information.

Month			Quality cost area	Year to date		
Actual	Plan	Variance		Actual	Plan	Variance
			1. Prevention cost			
3	2	1	A. Quality – administration	5	4	1
16	18	(2)	B. Quality – engineering	37	38	(1)
7	6	1	C. Quality – planning by others	14	12	2
5	7	(2)	D. Supplier assurance	13	14	(1)
31	33	(2)	Total prevention cost	69	68	1
5.5%	6.1%		Percentage of total quality cost	6.2%	6.3%	
			2. Appraisal cost			
31	26	5	A. Inspection	55	52	3
12	14	(2)	B. Test	24	28	(4)
7	6	1	C. Inspection and test of purchased materials	15	12	3
11	11	0	D. Product quality audits	23	22	1
3	2	1	E. Maintenance of inspection and test equipment	4	4	0
2	2	0	F. Materials consumed in inspection and testing	5	4	1
66	61	5	Total appraisal cost	126	122	4
11.8%	11.3%		Percentage of total quality cost	11.4%	11.3%	
			3. Internal failure cost			
144	140	4	A. Scrap and rework-manufacturing	295	280	15
55	53	2	B. Scrap and rework-engineering	103	106	(3)
28	30	(2)	C. Scrap and rework-supplier	55	60	(5)
21	22	(1)	D. Failure investigation	44	44	0
248	245	3	Total internal failure cost	497	490	7
44.3%	45.4%		Percentage of total quality cost	44.9%	45.3%	
345	339	6	Total internal quality cost (1 + 2 + 3)	692	680	12
61.6%	62.8%		Percentage of total quality cost	62.6%	62.8%	
			4. External failure quality cost			
75	66	9	A. Warranty expense-manufacturing	141	132	9
41	40	1	B. Warranty expense-engineering	84	80	4
35	35	0	C. Warranty expense-sales	69	70	(1)
46	40	6	D. Field warranty cost	83	80	3
18	20	(2)	E. Failure investigation	37	40	(3)
215	201	14	Total external failure cost	414	402	12
38.4%	37.2%		Percentage of total quality cost	37.4%	37.2%	
560	540	20	Total quality cost	1,106	1,082	24
9,872	9,800		Total product cost	20,170	19,600	
5.7%	5.5%		Total quality cost as percentage of total production cost	5.5%	5.5%	

*Adapted from Allen H. Seed III, *Adapting Management Accounting Practice to an Advanced Manufacturing Environment* (Montvale, NJ: National Association of Accountants, 1988), Table 5-2, p. 76.

Exhibit 9.7 Eastside Manufacturing Company – Quality cost report* (thousands of dollars)

To implement TQM, an organisation trains employees to prepare, interpret and act on quality-control charts, such as that shown in Exhibit 9.8. The **quality-control chart** is a statistical plot of measures of various product quality dimensions or attributes. This plot helps detect process deviations and identify excessive variation in product dimensions or attributes that process or design engineers should address. The chart in Exhibit 9.8 shows that, except for a brief period near the end of April, the Eastside Manufacturing Company generally is not meeting its defects objective of .6 per cent defects. Managers looking at this chart would know that they should take corrective action.

The most recent trend in quality control is Six Sigma, defined in Chapter 1 as a continuous process improvement effort designed to reduce costs by improving quality. The name Six Sigma comes from the idea of an extremely low defect rate of fewer than 3.4 defects per million (far lower than the rate of 6 defects per thousand in the previous Eastside Manufacturing example). However, the Six Sigma approach has broadened into a general approach to defining, measuring, analysing and improving a production process to minimise errors. The focus is on measuring how many defects a company has in its process because, once a company measures the defects, it can take steps to eliminate them. Developed by Motorola, Six Sigma is making large impacts at companies such as HSBC, GSK, Korea Telecom, Wipro and Deutsche Telecom.

Control of cycle time

Reducing cycle time is a key to improving quality. **Cycle time**, or **throughput time**, is the time taken to complete a product or service. It is a summary measure of efficiency and effectiveness and is also an important cost driver. You may find it surprising that lower cycle times often lead to higher quality and lower defect rates. A lower cycle time requires smooth-running processes and high quality. It also creates increased flexibility and quicker reactions to customer needs. As a company decreases cycle time, quality problems become more apparent throughout the process. Decreasing cycle time also results in bringing products or services more quickly to customers, which makes for happy customers.

An effective means of measuring cycle time is to attach an identifier such as a bar code (similar to symbols on most grocery products) to each component or product and use a scanner to read the code at the end of each stage of completion. Cycle time for each stage is the time between readings of bar codes. Bar coding also permits effective tracking of materials and products for inventories, scheduling and delivery.

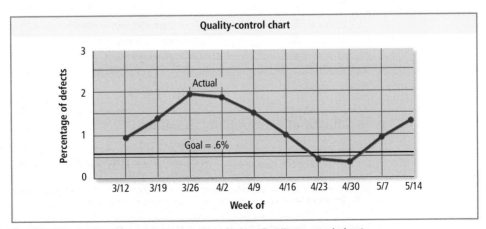

Exhibit 9.8 Eastside Manufacturing Company – Quality-control chart

Process stage	Actual cycle time*	Standard cycle time	Variance	Explanation
Materials processing	2.1	2.5	0.4 F	
Circuit board assembly	44.7	28.8	15.9 U	Poor-quality materials caused rework
Power unit assembly	59.6	36.2	23.4 U	Engineering change required rebuilding all power units
Product assembly	14.6	14.7	0.1 F	
Functional and environmental test	53.3	32.0	21.3 U	Software failure in test procedures required retesting

F = Favourable. U = Unfavourable.
*Average time per stage over the week.

Exhibit 9.9 Eastside Manufacturing Company – Cycle time report for the second week of May

Exhibit 9.9 is a sample cycle-time report showing that Eastside Manufacturing Company is meeting its cycle-time objectives at two of its five production process stages. This report is similar to the flexible budget reports of Chapter 8. Explanations of the variances indicate that poor-quality materials and poor design led to extensive rework and retesting.

Control of productivity

Many companies measure and manage productivity as part of the effort to improve their competitiveness. **Productivity** is a measure of outputs divided by inputs. The fewer inputs needed to produce a given output, the more productive the organisation. This simple definition, however, raises difficult measurement questions. How should the company measure outputs and inputs? Specific management control issues usually determine the most appropriate measures. Labour-intensive organisations, especially service organisations, focus on increasing the productivity of labour, so labour-based measures are appropriate. Highly automated companies focus on machine use and productivity of capital investments, so capacity-based measures, such as the percentage of time machines are available, may be most important to them. Manufacturing companies, in general, monitor the efficient use of materials. For them, measures of material yield (a ratio of material outputs over material inputs) may be useful indicators of productivity.

Exhibit 9.10 shows 12 examples of productivity measures. As you can see, they vary widely according to the type of resource that management wishes to use efficiently. In all cases, a measure of the resource that management wishes to control is in the denominator (the input) and a measure of the objective of using the resource is in the numerator (the output).

Choice of productivity measures

Which productivity measures should a company choose to manage? The choice depends on the behaviours desired. For example, if top management evaluates subordinates' performance based on direct-labour productivity, lower-level managers will focus on improving that specific measure.

The challenge in choosing productivity measures is to avoid motivating decisions that improve one measure of performance but hurt performance elsewhere in the organisation. For

Resource	Possible outputs (numerator)		Possible inputs (denominator)
Labour	Standard direct-labour hours allowed for good output	÷	Actual direct-labour hours used
	Sales revenue	÷	Number of employees
	Sales revenue	÷	Direct-labour costs
	Bank deposit/loan activity (by a bank)	÷	Number of employees
	Service calls	÷	Number of employees
	Customer orders	÷	Number of employees
Materials	Weight of output	÷	Weight of input
	Number of good units	÷	Total number of units
Equipment, capital, physical capacity	Time (e.g., hours) used	÷	Time available for use
	Time available for use	÷	Time (e.g., 24 hours per day)
	Expected machine hours for good output	÷	Actual machine hours
	Sales revenue	÷	Direct-labour cost

Exhibit 9.10 Measure of productivity

example, long production runs may improve productivity per machine but result in excessive inventory handling and holding costs. As another example, improved labour productivity achieved by motivating workers to spend less time on each unit produced may cause a high rate of product defects.

Use of a single measure of productivity is unlikely to result in overall improvements in performance. The choice of management controls requires anticipating the trade-offs that employees will make between performance measures. Many organisations focus management control on all of the most important activities, including nonfinancial measures such as control of quality and service and use multiple measures to monitor the actual benefits of improvements in these activities.

■ Productivity measures over time

Be careful when comparing productivity measures over time. Changes in the process or in the rate of inflation can make results misleading. For example, consider labour productivity at Adobe Systems. One measure of productivity is sales revenue per employee.

	2001	2008	Per cent change
Total revenue (millions)	$ 1,230	$ 3,579	191
Employees	÷ 3,043	÷ 7,544	148
Revenue per employee (unadjusted for inflation)	$404,206	$474,416	17

By this measure, Adobe appears to have achieved a 17 per cent increase in the productivity of labour because the number of employees grew more slowly than the total revenue.

However, total revenue has not been adjusted for the effects of inflation. Because of inflation, each 2001 dollar was equivalent to 1.19 dollars in 2008. Therefore, Adobe's 2001 sales revenue, expressed in 2008 dollars (so we can compare it with 2008 sales revenue), is $1,230 \times 1.19 = \$1,464$. The adjusted 2001 sales revenue per employee is as follows:

	2001 (adjusted)	2008	Per cent change
Total revenue (millions)	$ 1,464	$ 3,579	144
Employees	÷ 3,043	÷ 7,544	148
Revenue per employee (adjusted for inflation)	$481,104	$474,416	−1

Adjusting for the effects of inflation reveals that Adobe's labour productivity has actually decreased by 1 per cent rather than increased by 17 per cent.

The balanced scorecard

Objective 7
Use a balanced scorecard to integrate financial and nonfinancial measures of performance.

The best management control systems include both financial and nonfinancial measures. A **balanced scorecard (BSC)** is a system that strikes a balance between financial and nonfinancial measures in the performance measurement process, links performance to rewards and gives explicit recognition to the link between performance measurement and organisational goals and objectives. The balanced scorecard focuses management attention on measures that drive an organisation to achieve its goals. According to a study by Bain and Co., 44 per cent of North American firms use some version of the balanced scorecard, including Microsoft, American Express, ExxonMobil, Apple Computer and government nonprofit agencies, such as the US Department of Transportation and the United Way of America. In western Europe about 26 per cent of companies use this technique. BMW, Philips and Tata Motors all show positive results from its use. We describe some of the more successful in the 'Business first' box on p. 397.

The balanced scorecard helps line managers understand the relationship between nonfinancial measures and organisational goals. The balanced scorecard identifies performance measures from each of the four components of the successful organisation shown in Exhibit 9.3 on p. 382. Links between the measures and organisational objectives help managers throughout the organisation understand how their actions support the organisation's goals.

What does a balanced scorecard look like? The classic balanced scorecard developed by Robert Kaplan and David Norton includes **key performance indicators** – measures that drive the organisation to meet its goals – grouped into four categories: (1) financial, (2) customers, (3) internal business processes and (4) innovation and learning. Some companies use other terminology and some include additional categories – the most common additional categories are for employees or other stakeholders. However, all develop performance measures for each objective within each category. For example, Philips Electronics uses the categories and performance indicators in Exhibit 9.11. Most companies that use a balanced scorecard specify the categories that each business segment will use, but they allow the units to choose the relevant performance measures for each category. For example, every Microsoft division has measures for financial, customer, internal processes and learning perspectives, but the Latin American division has different measures in each category from those of the Seattle headquarters. The balanced scorecard should not be a straitjacket; rather it is a flexible framework for motivating and measuring performance.

BUSINESS FIRST
Balanced scorecard hall of fame

Robert Kaplan and David Norton created the BSC in 1992. In 2000, their company, Balanced Scorecard Collaborative, created a Balanced Scorecard Hall of Fame. To be selected for the Hall of Fame, a company must apply one or more of the following five principles to create a strategy-focused organisation: 'mobilise change through executive leadership; translate the strategy into operational terms; align the organisation around its strategy; make strategy everyone's job; and make strategy a continual process.' By the end of 2008, the Balanced Scorecard Collaborative had recognised a total of 120 Hall of Fame organisations. The inductees include the following: Army and Air Force Exchange Service [AAFES], St Mary's/Duluth Clinic Health System [SMDC], the City of Corpus Christi, BMW Financial Services and Wendy's International.

AAFES is a $9 billion global retailer with 50,000 employees serving 8.7 million customers in 3,100 stores in 30 countries. AAFES adopted the Balanced Scorecard to prepare the organisation to meet growing and diverse demands of its increasingly mobile customers. The BSC helps create alignment, drive accountability, optimise resource allocation and link strategy to operations. In 4 years revenue has increased by 11 per cent, dividends 19 per cent, employee satisfaction 16 per cent and customer satisfaction 17 per cent. Inventory has been reduced by about €108 million. Michael Howard, AAFES chief operating officer, observes the following: 'The BSC has given us the ability to look beyond traditional financial measures to drive long-term sustainability that focuses on employee optimization. The BSC aligns corporate resources and energies to drive performance that ensure AAFES continues to provide a valued benefit to the military market.'

SMDC operates 20 clinics, hospitals and specialty care facilities in northern Minnesota. It has gross revenue of about $700 million. CEO Peter Person comments 'our monthly scorecard review sessions are incredibly valuable to me as CEO. The scorecard enables us to easily scan and digest overall organizational performance and to identify any necessary course corrections.' SMDC has used the BSC to align its operations, link its budget to strategy and to spread strategic awareness to every employee.

The City of Corpus Christi is Texas's largest coastal city and the nation's sixth largest port. The city employs 3,300 serving a population of 295,000. The city adopted the BSC to clarify and communicate its strategy; align departments, divisions and employees; and make more timely and better informed decisions that impact citizens' lives. Constituent satisfaction has increased 16 per cent, workforce retention is up and citizen/customer wait time is down. The city's bond rating improved, fueled in part by the BSC management system. Angel R. Escobar, Interim City Manager says: 'Now, with the BSC, we know what we are great at and what we need to improve upon . . . our monthly BSC meetings unify departmental directors to collectively focus on and discuss solutions to real issues.'

BMW Financial Services was established in 1993 to support the sales and marketing efforts of BMW North America. The company has more than $15 billion in managed assets. It finances over half the new BMW vehicles sold in the United States. BMW Financial Services adopted the BSC in 1998 and has seen remarkable growth in annual sales and number of customer accounts. The company uses the scorecard to link objectives, initiatives and metrics to its strategy and communicate these links throughout the company.

Wendy's International is one of the world's largest restaurant operating and franchising companies, with more than 6,600 restaurants and 2008 revenue of $1.8 billion. The company implemented the BSC to get a better handle on intangible assets, such as intellectual capital and customer focus. CEO Jack Schuessler lauded the BSC's success in 'establishing targets and measuring our progress in key dimensions ranging from employee retention at the restaurant level, to restaurant evaluation scores, to business processes, to total revenue growth. They are all vitally important, not just the financial measures.' The BSC provides a framework for balancing financial and nonfinancial measures.

The BSC has helped these and other award-winning organisations in many different ways. It has gained wide acceptance and successful implementation in many companies since its introduction more than 15 years ago.

Sources: Balanced Scorecard Collaborative website (www.bscol.com); St Mary's/Duluth Clinic Health System website (www.smdc.org); BMW Financial Services website (www.fs.bmwusa.com); and Wendy's International, Inc., Wendy's International 2008 Annual Report; Palladium Group website 6 November 2008 press release(www.thepalladiumgroup.com).

Financial	Processes
Economic profit realised	Percentage reduction in process cycle time
Income from operations	Number of engineering changes
Working capital	Capacity utilisation
Operational cash flow	Order response time
Inventory turns	Process capability
Customers	**Competence**
Rank in customer survey	Leadership competence
Market share	Percentage of patent-protected turnover
Repeat order rate	Training days per employee
Complaints	Quality improvement team participation
Brand index	

Exhibit 9.11 Performance indicators for Philips Electronics' balanced scorecard

MAKING MANAGERIAL DECISIONS

The balanced scorecard emphasises the connections between performance measures and financial and nonfinancial goals. Indicate where each of the following goals of Whirlpool fits with the four components of a successful organisation shown in Exhibit 9.3 on p. 382, and explain how these components relate to one another:

People commitment

Total quality

Customer satisfaction

Financial performance

Growth and innovation

Answer

The components listed in Exhibit 9.3 depict the causal links from organisational learning to business process improvement, to customer satisfaction and finally to financial strength. The five goals set by top managers at Whirlpool suggest the following links among the goals:

If whirlpool makes a solid commitment to its people and invests in growth and innovation, the company will make progress in organisational learning. this will lead to business process improvements that decrease costs, increase efficiency and increase the total quality of its products, which will then lead to increased customer satisfaction. the ultimate result of satisfied customers is improved financial performance. sustainable financial strength should allow whirlpool to repeat the cycle and continue to invest in both organisational learning and internal business processes.

Management control systems in service, government and nonprofit organisations

Objective 8
Describe the difficulties of management control in service and nonprofit organisations.

Most service, government and nonprofit organisations face substantial difficulty implementing management control systems. Why? The main problem is that the outputs of service and nonprofit organisations are difficult to measure. For example, what is a good measure of output for a bank's call centre (where service representatives answer customers' questions)? Number of calls or total time spent on calls? The measure 'number of calls' might motivate many short calls that do not provide thorough answers to customers.

The measure 'total time spent on calls' might motivate long, time-wasting calls. It may be difficult to know the quality or sometimes even the quantity of the service provided until long after the organisation delivers the service. When quality and quantity of output are hard to measure, developing timely measures of input/output relationships is nearly impossible.

The keys to successful management control in any organisation are proper training and motivation of employees to achieve the organisation's strategic objectives, accompanied by consistent monitoring of measures chosen to fit with these objectives. These keys are equally important in service-oriented organisations. MBNA, a large issuer of bank credit cards, works hard to measure the amount and quality of its service. It identifies customer retention as its primary key success factor. MBNA trains its customer representatives carefully. Each day it measures and reports performance on various objectives consistent with customer retention and it rewards every employee based on those objectives. Measures include answering every call by the second ring, keeping the computer up 100 per cent of the time and processing credit-line requests within 1 hour. Employees have earned bonuses as high as 20 per cent of their annual salaries by meeting those objectives.

Nonprofit and government organisations have problems designing and implementing an objective that is similar to the financial 'bottom line' that often serves as the unifying goal in private industry. Furthermore, in nonprofit organisations, many people seek primarily non-monetary rewards. For example, volunteers in the Peace Corps receive little pay but derive much satisfaction from helping to improve conditions in underdeveloped countries. Thus, monetary incentives are generally less effective in nonprofit organisations. Management control systems in nonprofit organisations probably will never be as highly developed as are those in profit-seeking firms because of the following:

1 Organisational goals and objectives are less clear. Moreover, there are often multiple goals and objectives, requiring difficult trade-offs.

2 Professionals (for example, teachers, lawyers, physicians, scientists, economists) tend to dominate nonprofit organisations. Because of their perceived professional status, they are often less receptive to the installation of formal control systems.

3 Measurements are more difficult because

   (a) there is no profit measure; and
   (b) there are heavy amounts of discretionary fixed costs, which make the relationships of inputs to outputs difficult to specify and measure.

4 There is less competitive pressure from other organisations or 'owners' to improve management control systems. As a result, for example, many cities and constituencies in European countries are 'privatising' some essential services, such as sanitation, by contracting with private firms.

5 The role of budgeting, instead of being a rigorous planning process, is often more a matter of playing bargaining games with sources of funding to get the largest possible authorisation.

6 Motivations and incentives of employees may differ from those in for-profit organisations.

Future of management control systems

As organisations mature and as environments change, managers expand and refine their management control tools. The management control techniques that were satisfactory 10 or 20 years ago may not be adequate for many organisations today.

MAKING MANAGERIAL DECISIONS

Study Exhibit 9.3 again. Use the same four general components, but rearrange them a bit to reflect a framework that might help managers of a successful governmental or nonprofit organisation.

Answer

For governmental and nonprofit organisations, the ultimate objective is not to focus on financial results but to deliver the maximum benefits to customers (or citizens) based on an available pool of financial resources. Thus, the causal relationships might be as follows:

Organisational learning → process improvements in delivering programmes → fiscal or financial strength → greater programme benefits for citizens or clients

A changing environment often means that organisations adjust their goals or key success factors. New goals require different benchmarks for evaluating performance. The management control system must evolve, too, or the organisation may not manage its resources effectively or efficiently. A summary of management control principles that will always be important and that can guide the redesign of systems follows:

1 Always expect that individuals will be pulled in the direction of their own self-interest. You may be pleasantly surprised that some individuals will act selflessly, but management control systems should be designed to take advantage of more typical human behaviour. Be aware that managers in different cultures may perceive self-interest differently.

2 Design incentives so that individuals who pursue their own self-interest also achieve the organisation's objectives. Because there are usually multiple objectives, multiple incentives are appropriate. Do not underestimate the difficulty of balancing these incentives – some experimentation may be necessary to achieve multiple objectives.

3 Evaluate actual performance based on expected or planned performance. Where appropriate, revise planned performance to reflect actual output achieved. You can apply the concept of flexible budgeting to many goals and actions, both financial and nonfinancial.

4 Consider nonfinancial performance to be an important determinant of long-term success. In the short run, a manager may be able to generate good financial performance while neglecting nonfinancial performance, but it is not likely over a longer haul.

5 Array performance measures across the entire value chain of the company. This ensures that the management control system incorporates all activities that are critical to the long-run success of the company.

6 Periodically review the success of the management control system. Is the organisation achieving its overall goals? Do the actions motivated by the management control system lead to goal achievement? Do individuals understand the management control system and effectively use the information it provides?

7 Learn from the management control successes (and failures) of competitors around the world. Despite cultural differences, human behaviour is remarkably similar. Managers can learn from successful applications of new technology and management controls by reading books or attending courses that describe management control systems at other companies.

Highlights **to remember**

1 **Describe the relationship of management control systems to organisational goals.** The starting point for designing and evaluating a management control system is the identification of organisational goals as specified by top management.

2 **Explain the importance of evaluating performance and describe how it impacts on motivation, goal congruence and employee effort.** The way an organisation measures and evaluates performance affects individuals' behaviour. The more that it ties rewards to performance measures, the more incentive there is to improve the measures. Poorly designed measures may actually work against the organisation's goals.

3 **Develop performance measures and use them to monitor the achievements of an organisation.** A well-designed management control system measures both financial and nonfinancial performance. Superior nonfinancial performance usually leads to superior financial performance in time. The performance measures should tell managers how well they are meeting the organisation's goals.

4 **Use responsibility accounting to define an organisational subunit as a cost centre, a profit centre or an investment centre.** Responsibility accounting assigns revenue and cost objectives to the management of the subunit that has the greatest influence over them. Cost centres focus on costs only, profit centres on both revenues and costs and investment centres on profits relative to the amount invested.

5 **Prepare segment income statements for evaluating profit and investment centres using the contribution margin and controllable-cost concepts.** The contribution approach to measuring a segment's income aids performance evaluation by separating a segment's costs into those controllable by the segment management and those beyond management's control. It allows separate evaluation of a segment as an economic investment and the performance of the segment's manager.

6 **Measure performance against nonfinancial objectives such as quality, cycle time and productivity.** Measuring performance in areas such as quality, cycle time and productivity causes employees to direct attention to those areas. Achieving goals in these nonfinancial measures can help meet long-run financial objectives.

7 **Use a balanced scorecard to integrate financial and nonfinancial measures of performance.** The balanced scorecard helps managers monitor actions that are designed to meet the various goals of the organisation. It integrates key performance indicators that measure how well the organisation is meeting its goals.

8 **Describe the difficulties of management control in service and nonprofit organisations.** Management control in service and nonprofit organisations is difficult because of a number of factors, chief of which is a relative lack of clearly observable outcomes.

Accounting vocabulary

Fundamental assignment material   MyAccountingLab

9.A1 Responsibility of purchasing agent

Excel Electronics Company, a privately held enterprise, has a subcontract from a large aerospace company in Dundee. Although Excel was a low bidder, the aerospace company was reluctant to award the business to the company because it was a newcomer to this kind of activity. Consequently, Excel assured the aerospace company of its financial strength by submitting its audited financial statements. Moreover, Excel agreed to a pay a penalty of £5,000 per day for each day of late delivery for whatever cause.

Margie McMahon, the Excel purchasing agent, is responsible for acquiring materials and parts in time to meet production schedules. She placed an order with an Excel supplier for a critical manufactured component. The supplier, who had a reliable record for meeting schedules, gave McMahon an acceptable delivery date. McMahon checked up several times and was assured that the component would arrive at Excel on schedule.

On the date specified by the supplier for shipment to Excel, McMahon was informed that the component had been damaged during final inspection. It was delivered 10 days late. McMahon had allowed 4 extra days for possible delays, but Excel was 6 days late in delivering to the aerospace company and so had to pay a penalty of £30,000.

What department should bear the penalty? Why?

9.A2 Contribution approach to responsibility accounting

Dave Skold owns and operates a small chain of convenience stores in Waterloo and Poitiers. The company has five stores including a downtown store and a store in the Waterloo division; and a downtown store, a Solon store and an airport store in the Poitiers Division. There is also a separate administrative staff that provides market research, personnel and accounting and finance services.

The company had the following financial results for 20X1 (in thousands):

Sales revenue	**€8,000**
Cost of merchandise sold	3,500
Gross margin	4,500
Operating expenses	2,200
Income before income taxes	€2,300

The following data about 20X1 operations were also available:

1   All five stores used the same pricing formula; therefore, all had the same gross margin percentage.
2   Sales were largest in the two downtown stores, with 30 per cent of the total sales volume in each. The Solon and airport stores each provided 15 per cent of total sales volume and the store provided 10 per cent.
3   Variable operating costs at the stores were 10 per cent of revenue for the downtown stores. The other stores had lower variable and higher fixed costs. Their variable operating costs were only 5 per cent of sales revenue.
4   The fixed costs over which the store managers had control were €125,000 in each of the downtown stores, €160,000 at Solon and airport, and €80,000 at the store.
5   The remaining €910,000 of operating costs consisted of
     (a) €210,000 controllable by the Cedar Rapids division manager but not by individual stores,
     (b) €100,000 controllable by the Waterloo division manager but not by individual stores, and
     (c) €600,000 controllable by the administrative staff.

6 Of the €600,000 spent by the administrative staff, €350,000 directly supported the Poitiers division, with 20 per cent for the downtown store, 30 per cent for each of the Solon and airport stores, and 20 per cent for Poitiers operations in general. Another €140,000 supported the Waterloo division, 50 per cent for the downtown store, 25 per cent for the store and 25 per cent supporting Waterloo operations in general. The other €110,000 was for general corporate expenses.

Prepare an income statement by segments using the contribution approach to responsibility accounting. Use the format of Exhibit 9.4, p. 385. Column headings should be as follows:

Company as a whole	Breakdown into two divisions		Breakdown of Waterloo Division			Breakdown of Cedar Rapids Division			
	Waterloo	Poitiers	Not allocated	Downtown	Store	Not allocated	Downtown	Solon	Airport

9.A3 Comparison of productivity

Wells and Severson are manufacturing companies. Comparative data for 20X1 and 20X7 are as follows:

		Wells	Severson
Sales revenue	20X1	€5,660,000,000	€7,658,000,000
	20X7	€6,000,000,000	€9,667,000,000
Number of employees	20X1	56,600	75,900
	20X7	54,800	76,200

Assume that inflation has totalled 15 per cent during these 6 years so that each 20X1 euro is equivalent to 1.15 euros in 20X7, due to inflation.

1 Compute 20X1 and 20X7 productivity measures in terms of revenue per employee for Wells and Severson.
2 Compare the change in productivity between 20X1 and 20X7 for Wells with that for Severson.

9.B1 Responsibility accounting

The Kephart Company produces precision machine parts. Kephart uses a standard cost system, calculates standard cost variances for each department and reports them to department managers. Managers use the information to improve their operations. Superiors use the same information to evaluate managers' performance.

Liz Elder was recently appointed manager of the assembly department of the company. She has complained that the system as designed is disadvantageous to her department. Included among the variances charged to the departments is one for rejected units. The inspection occurs at the end of the assembly department. The inspectors attempt to identify the cause of the rejection so that the department where the error occurred can be charged with it. Not all errors can be easily identified with a department, however. The nonidentified units are totalled and apportioned to the departments according to the number of identified errors. The variance for rejected units in each department is a combination of the errors caused by the department plus a portion of the unidentified causes of rejects.

1 Is Elder's complaint valid? Explain the reason(s) for your answer.
2 What would you recommend that the company do to solve its problem with Elder and her complaint?

9.B2 Divisional contribution, performance and segment margins

The president of North Shore Railroad wants to obtain an overview of the company's operations, particularly with respect to comparing freight and passenger business. He has heard about 'contribution' approaches to cost allocations that emphasise cost behaviour patterns and contribution margins, contributions controllable by segment managers and contributions by segments. The president has hired you as a consultant to help him. He has given you the following information.

Total revenue in 20X3 was €80 million, of which €72 million was freight traffic and €8 million was passenger traffic. Fifty per cent of the passenger revenue was generated by division 1, 40 per cent by division 2 and 10 per cent by division 3.

Total variable costs were €40 million, of which €36 million was caused by freight traffic. Of the €4 million allocable to passenger traffic, €2.1, €1.6 and €.3 million could be allocated to divisions 1, 2 and 3, respectively.

Total separable discretionary fixed costs were €8 million, of which €7.6 million applied to freight traffic. For the remaining €400,000 applicable to passenger traffic, €80,000 could not be allocated to specific divisions, while €200,000, €100,000 and €20,000, were allocatable to divisions 1, 2 and 3, respectively.

Total separable committed costs, which were not regarded as being controllable by segment managers, were €25 million, of which 80 per cent was allocable to freight traffic. Of the 20 per cent traceable to passenger traffic, divisions 1, 2 and 3 should be allocated €3 million, €700,000, and €300,000, respectively; the balance was unallocable to a specific division.

The common fixed costs not clearly allocable to any part of the company amounted to €800,000.

1 The president asks you to prepare statements, dividing the data for the company as a whole between the freight and passenger traffic and then subdividing the passenger traffic into three divisions.

2 Some competing railroads actively promote a series of one-day sightseeing tours on summer weekends. Most often, these tours are timed so that the cars with the tourists are hitched on with regularly scheduled passenger trains. What costs are relevant for making decisions to run such tours? Other railroads, facing the same general cost structure, refuse to conduct such sightseeing tours. Why?

3 Suppose that the railroad has petitioned government authorities for permission to drop division 1. What would be the effect on overall company net income for 20X4, assuming that the figures are accurate and that 20X4 operations are expected to be in all respects a duplication of 20X3 operations?

9.B3 Balanced scorecard for a law firm

Young, Martinez and Cheung (YMC) is a firm of lawyers in Milan. The firm has had a very loose and relaxed management style that has served it well in the past. However, more aggressive law firms have been winning new clients faster than YMC has. Thus, the managing partner, Jerry Martinez, recently attended a Bocconi Business School seminar on performance measurement in law firms, where he learned about the balanced scorecard. He thought it might be a good tool for YMC, one that would allow the firm to keep its culture yet still more aggressively seek new clients.

Martinez identified the following strategic objectives that fit with the firm's core values and provide a framework for assessing progress toward the firm's goals:

Financial

(a) Steadily increase the firm's revenues and profits.

Customer

(a) Understand the firm's customers and their needs.
(b) Value customer service over self-interest.

Internal Business Process

(a) Encourage knowledge sharing among the legal staff.
(b) Communicate with each other openly, honestly and often.
(c) Empower staff to make decisions that benefit clients.

Organisational Learning

(a) Maintain an open and collaborative environment that attracts and retains the best legal staff.
(b) Seek staff diversity.

1 Develop at least one measure for each of the strategic objectives listed.
2 Explain how YMC can use this balanced scorecard to evaluate staff performance.
3 Should staff compensation be tied to the scorecard performance measures? Why or why not?

Additional assignment material   MyAccountingLab

QUESTIONS

9.1 What is a management control system?

9.2 What are the purposes of a management control system?

9.3 What are the major components of a management control system?

9.4 What is a key success factor?

9.5 'Goals are useless without performance measures.' Do you agree? Explain.

9.6 'There are corporate goals other than to improve profit.' Name three.

9.7 How does management determine its key success factors?

9.8 Give three examples of how managers may improve short-run performance to the detriment of long-run results.

9.9 Name three kinds of responsibility centres.

9.10 How do profit centres and investment centres differ?

9.11 List five characteristics of a good performance measure.

9.12 List four nonfinancial measures of performance that managers find useful.

9.13 'Performance evaluation seeks to achieve goal congruence and managerial effort.' Explain what is meant by this statement.

9.14 'Managers of profit centres should be held responsible for the centre's entire profit. They are responsible for profit even if they cannot control all factors affecting it.' Discuss.

9.15 'Variable costs are controllable and fixed costs are uncontrollable.' Do you agree? Explain.

9.16 'The contribution margin is the best measure of short-run performance.' Do you agree? Explain.

9.17 Give four examples of segments.

9.18 'Always try to distinguish between the performance of a segment and its manager.' Why?

9.19 'The contribution margin approach to performance evaluation is flawed because focusing on only the contribution margin ignores important aspects of performance.' Do you agree? Explain.

9.20 What is a balanced scorecard and why are more companies using one?

9.21 What are key performance indicators?

9.22 There are four categories of cost in the quality cost report; explain them.

9.23 Why are companies increasing their quality control emphasis on the prevention of defects?

9.24 'Nonfinancial measures of performance can be controlled just like financial measures.' Do you agree? Explain.

9.25 Identify three measures of labour productivity, one using all physical measures, one using all financial measures and one that mixes physical and financial measures.

9.26 Discuss the difficulties of comparing productivity measures over time.

9.27 'Control systems in nonprofit organisations will never be as highly developed as in profit-seeking organisations.' Do you agree? Explain.

CRITICAL THINKING EXERCISES

9.28 Management Control Systems and Innovation

The president of a fast-growing, high-technology firm remarked, 'Developing budgets and comparing performance with the budgets may be fine for some firms. But we want to encourage innovation and entrepreneurship. Budgets go with bureaucracy, not innovation.' Do you agree? How can a management control system encourage innovation and entrepreneurship?

9.29 Control systems and customer service function of the value chain

Companies increasingly use nonfinancial measures to supplement financial measures of performance. One of the most important areas of nonfinancial performance is customer service. The last decade has brought an increased focus on the customer and this focus is reflected in many companies' management control systems, where companies use 'customer-value metrics'. That is, they develop measures that monitor how well the company is meeting its customers' interests. What customer-value metrics might a company such as Volvo, the Swedish automobile company, use in its management control system?

9.30 Control systems and the production function of the value chain

In recent years, many organisations have focused on the value of controlling nonfinancial performance as a key to improved productivity. In particular, to gain and maintain a competitive edge, companies focus on quality and cycle time. Discuss how quality, cycle time and productivity are related.

EXERCISES

9.31 Responsibility for stable employment policy

The Mid-Atlantic Metal Fabricating Company has been manufacturing machine tools for a number of years and has had an industry-wide reputation for doing high-quality work. The company has been faced with fluctuations in demand over the years. It has been company policy to lay off welders as soon as there was insufficient work to keep them busy and to rehire them when demand warranted. Because of this lay-off policy, the company now has poor labour relations and finds it difficult to hire good welders. Consequently, the quality of the products has been declining steadily.

The plant manager has proposed that welders who earn £20 per hour be retained during slow periods to do menial plant maintenance work that is normally performed by workers earning £14 per hour in the plant maintenance department.

You, as accountant must decide the most appropriate accounting procedure to handle the wages of the welders doing plant maintenance work. What department(s) should be charged with this work and at what rate? Discuss the implications of your plan.

9.32 Salesclerk's compensation plan

You are the manager of a department store in Tokyo. Sales are subject to month-to-month variations, depending on the individual salesclerk's efforts and other factors. A new salary-plus-bonus plan has been in effect for 4 months and you are reviewing a sales performance report. The plan provides for a base salary of ¥50,000 per month, a ¥68,000 bonus each month if the salesclerk meets the monthly sales quota and an additional commission of 5 per cent of all sales over the monthly quota. Each month, the quota is reset at approximately 3 per cent above the previous month's sales to motivate clerks to continually increase sales. The monthly quotas and actual amounts for the first 4 months of the plan are shown in the sales report below (in thousands).

		Salesclerk A	Salesclerk B	Salesclerk C
January	Quota	¥4,500	¥1,500	¥7,500
	Actual	1,500	1,500	9,000
February	Quota	¥1,545	¥1,545	¥9,270
	Actual	3,000	1,545	3,000
March	Quota	¥3,090	¥1,590	¥3,090
	Actual	5,250	750	9,000
April	Quota	¥5,400	¥775	¥9,270
	Actual	1,500	780	4,050

1 Compute the compensation for each salesclerk for each month.
2 Evaluate the compensation plan. Be specific. What changes would you recommend?

9.33 Common measures on a balanced scorecard

Listed next are common performance measures appearing on balanced scorecards. Indicate whether the listed measure is primarily associated with the financial, customer, internal process or learning and growth perspective. (Note that some measures might reasonably be associated with more than one perspective.)

- Return on sales
- Retention of target customers
- Net cash flow
- Training hours
- Employee turnover rate
- Materials handling cost per unit

- Market share
- Product-development cycle time
- Revenue growth in segments
- Occupational injuries and illness
- Days sales in inventory
- Average cost per invoice

9.34 Goals and objectives at Health Net

Health Net provides health care to more than 6.7 million members. As a managed healthcare organisation, the company strives to provide high-quality healthcare at a reasonable cost. Many stakeholders have an interest in Health Net's operations, including doctors and other medical personnel, patients, insurance companies, government regulators and the general public.

Prepare a goal and one measure for assessing achievement of that goal for each of the following key areas:
- Customer satisfaction
- Efficient use of lab tests
- Usage of physician time
- Maintain state-of-the-art facilities
- Overall financial performance.

9.35 Performance evaluation

Daniel Merrill & Co. is a stock brokerage firm that evaluates its employees on sales activity generated. Recently, the firm also began evaluating its stockbrokers on the number of new accounts generated.

Discuss how these two performance measures are consistent and how they may conflict. Do you believe that these measures are appropriate for the long-term goal of profitability?

9.36 Quality theories compared

Examine the two graphs below. Compare the total quality management approach to the traditional theory of quality. Which theory do you believe represents the current realities of today's global competitive environment? Explain.

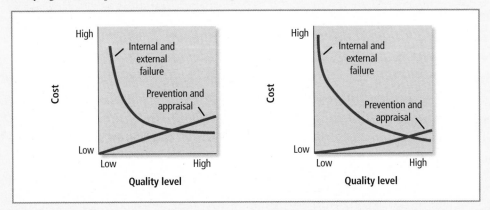

9.37 Quality-control chart

San Angelo Manufacturing Company was concerned about a growing number of defective units being produced. At one time, the company had the percentage of defective units down to less than 5 per thousand, but recently rates of defects have been near, or even above, 1 per cent. The company decided to graph its defects for the last 8 weeks (40 working days), beginning Monday, 1 September through Friday 24 October. The graph is shown in Exhibit 9.12.

Exhibit 9.12 San Angelo Manufacturing Company – Quality-control chart for 1 September through 24 October

1 Identify two important trends evident in the quality-control chart.
2 What might management of San Angelo do to deal with each trend?

9.38 Cycle-time reporting

The Pierre plant of Global Electronics produces computers. The plant monitors its cycle time closely to prevent schedule delays and excessive costs. The standard cycle time for the manufacture of printed circuit boards for one of its computers is 26 hours. Consider the following cycle-time data from the past 6 weeks of circuit board production:

Week	Units completed	Total cycle time
1	564	14,108 hours
2	544	14,592
3	553	15,152
4	571	16,598
5	547	17,104
6	552	16,673

Analyse circuit board cycle time performance in light of the 26-hour objective.

PROBLEMS

9.39 Multiple goals and profitability

The following multiple goals were identified by General Electric:

- Profitability
- Market position
- Productivity
- Product leadership
- Personnel development
- Employee attitudes
- Public responsibility
- Balance between short-range and long-range goals.

General Electric is a huge, highly decentralised corporation. At the time it developed these goals, GE had approximately 170 responsibility centres called departments, but that is a deceptive term. In most other companies, these departments would be called divisions. For example, some GE departments had sales of more than $500 million.

Each department manager's performance was evaluated annually in relation to the specified multiple goals. A special measurements group was set up to devise ways of quantifying accomplishments in each of the areas. In this way, the evaluation of performance would become more objective as the various measures were developed and improved.

1 How would you measure performance in each of these areas? Be specific.
2 Can the other goals be encompassed as ingredients of a formal measure of profitability? In other words, can profitability per se be defined to include the other goals?

9.40 Responsibility accounting, profit centres and contribution approach

Honda had the following data for the year's operations:

Sales of vehicles	€2,400,000
Sales of parts and service	600,000
Cost of vehicle sales	1,920,000
Parts and service materials	180,000
Parts and service labour	240,000
Parts and service overhead	60,000
General dealership overhead	200,000
Advertising of vehicles	120,000
Sales commissions, vehicles	48,000
Sales salaries, vehicles	60,000

The president of the dealership has long regarded the markup on material and labour for the parts and service activity as the amount that is supposed to cover all parts and service overhead plus some general overhead of the dealership. In other words, the parts and service department is viewed as a cost-recovery operation, while the sales of vehicles is viewed as the income-producing activity.

1 Prepare a departmentalised operating statement that harmonises with the views of the president.
2 Prepare an alternative operating statement that would reflect a different view of the dealership operations. Assume that €24,000 and €120,000 of the €200,000 general overhead can be allocated with confidence to the parts and service department and to sales of vehicles, respectively. The remaining €56,000 cannot be allocated except in some highly arbitrary manner.
3 Comment on the relative merits of numbers 1 and 2.

9.41 Incentives in planned economies

Often government-owned companies in planned economies reward managers based on nonfinancial measures. For example, the government might give managers a bonus for exceeding a 5-year-planned target for production quantities. A problem with this method is that managers tend to predict low volumes so that officials will set the targets low. This hinders planning because managers do not provide accurate information about production possibilities.

The former Soviet Union developed an alternative performance measurement and reward system. Suppose F is the forecast of production, A is actual production, and X, Y and Z are positive constants set by top officials, with $X, Y, Z > 0$. The following performance measure was designed to motivate both high production and accurate forecasts.

$$\text{performance measure} = (Y \times F) + [X \times (A - F)] \text{ if } F \le A$$
$$(Y \times F) + [Z \times (F - A)] \text{ if } F > A$$

Assume that Cuba adopted this measure at a time when Soviet influence was great. Consider the Havana Television Manufacturing Company (HTMC). During 19X3, the factory manager, Che Chavez, had to predict the number of televisions that HTMC could produce during the next year. He was confident that at least 700,000 televisions could be produced in 19X4, and most likely they could produce 800,000 televisions. With good luck, they might even produce 900,000. Government officials told him that the new performance evaluation measure would be used, and that $X = .50$, $Y = .80$, and $Z = 1.00$ for 19X4 and 19X5.

1 Suppose Chavez predicted production of 800,000 televisions and HTMC actually produced 800,000. Calculate the performance measure.

2 Suppose again that HTMC produced 800,000 televisions. Calculate the performance measure if Chavez had been conservative and predicted only 700,000 televisions. Also calculate the performance measure if he had predicted 900,000 televisions.

3 Now suppose it is November 19X4 and it is clear that HTMC cannot achieve the 800,000 target. Does the performance measure motivate continued efforts to increase production? Suppose it is clear that HTMC will easily meet the 800,000 target. Will the system motivate continued efforts to increase production?

9.42 Balanced scorecard

The Italian Pharmaceuticals Company (IPC) recently revised its performance evaluation system. The company identified four major goals and several objectives required to meet each goal. Andrea Dossi, accountant at IPC, suggested that a balanced scorecard be used to report on progress toward meeting the objectives. At a recent meeting, she told the managers of IPC that listing the objectives was only the first step in installing a new performance measurement system. Each objective has to be accompanied by one or more measures to monitor progress toward achieving the objectives. She asked the help of the managers in identifying appropriate measures.

The goals and objectives determined by the top management of IPC are as follows:

1 Maintain strong financial health.
   (a) Keep sufficient cash balances to assure financial survival.
   (b) Achieve consistent growth in sales and income.
   (c) Provide excellent returns to shareholders.
2 Provide excellent service to customers.
   (a) Provide products that meet the needs of customers.
   (b) Meet customer needs on a timely basis.
   (c) Meet customer quality requirements.
   (d) Be the preferred supplier to customers.
3 Be among the industry leaders in product and process innovations.
   (a) Bring new products to market before competition.
   (b) Lead competition in production process innovation.
4 Develop and maintain efficient, state-of-the-art production processes.
   (a) Excel in manufacturing efficiency.
   (b) Meet or beat product introduction schedules.

Propose at least one measure of performance for each of the objectives of IPC.

9.43 Six Sigma, mean and variance

A major objective of Six Sigma quality-control programmes is to better meet customers' needs. One place companies have applied Six Sigma is to order delivery times. They have directed efforts at reducing both the mean (average) time to delivery and the variance or standard deviation (dispersion) of the delivery times. Customers want to get their products sooner, as reflected in the mean. But they also want assurance that the product will arrive when promised. This requires delivery schedules to have little random variance.

Consider the following experience with the implementation of Six Sigma at a major manufacturing company:

Order delivery times (days)	
Before Six Sigma	After Six Sigma
30	22
12	20
11	5
13	8

(continued)

Order delivery times (days)	
Before Six Sigma	After Six Sigma
26	19
14	8
16	7
20	12
24	18
14	21

Compute the mean and standard deviation of order-delivery time before and after implementation of Six Sigma. From a customer's perspective, how would you view the results of this application of Six Sigma?

9.44 Productivity

In early 20X1, United Communications, a UK-based international telephone communications company, purchased the controlling interest in Bucharest Telecom Ltd (BTL) in Romania. A key productivity measure monitored by United is the number of customer telephone lines per employee. Consider the following data for United:

	20X1 without BTL	20X1 with BTL	20X0
Customer lines	15,054,000	19,994,000	14,615,000
Employees	74,520	114,590	72,350
Lines per employee	202	174	202

1 What are United's 20X0 productivity and 20X1 productivity without BTL?
2 What are BTL's 20X1 productivity and United's 20X1 productivity with BTL?
3 What difficulties do you foresee if United brings BTL's productivity in line?

CASES

9.45 Trade-offs among objectives

Computer Data Services (CDS) performs routine and custom information systems services for many companies in a large Spanish/metropolitan area. CDS has built a reputation for high-quality customer service and job security for its employees. Quality service and customer satisfaction have been CDS's primary subgoals – retaining a skilled and motivated workforce has been an important factor in achieving those goals. In the past, temporary downturns in business did not mean layoffs of employees, though some employees were required to perform other than their usual tasks. In anticipation of growth in business, CDS leased new equipment that, beginning in August, added €10,000 per month in operating costs. Three months ago, however, a new competitor began offering the same services to CDS customers at prices averaging 19 per cent lower than those of CDS. Rico Estrada, the company founder and president, believes that a significant price reduction is necessary to maintain the company's market share and avoid financial ruin, but he is puzzled about how to achieve it without compromising quality, service and the goodwill of his workforce.

CDS has a productivity objective of 20 accounts per employee. Estrada does not think that he can increase this productivity and still maintain both quality and flexibility to customer needs. CDS also monitors average cost per account and the number of customer satisfaction adjustments (resolutions of complaints). The average billing markup rate is 25 per cent of cost. Consider the following data from the past 6 months:

	June	July	August	September	October	November
Number of accounts	797	803	869	784	723	680
Number of employees	40	41	44	43	43	41
Average cost per account	€ 153	€ 153	€ 158	€ 173	€ 187	€ 191
Average salary per employee	€3,000	€3,000	€3,000	€3,000	€3,000	€3,000

1 Discuss the trade-offs facing Rico Estrada.
2 Can you suggest solutions to his trade-off dilemma?

9.46 Review of Chapters 1–9

William Whitebear, general manager of the Kamloops Division of Canada Enterprises, was preparing for a management meeting. His divisional controller gave him the following information:

1 The master budget for the fiscal year ended 30 June 20X4 follows:

Sales (50,000 units of A and 70,000 units of B)	$870,000
Manufacturing cost of goods sold	740,000
Manufacturing margin	$130,000
Selling and administrative expenses	120,000
Operating income	$ 10,000

2 The standard variable manufacturing cost per unit follows:

	Product A		Product B	
Direct materials	10 pieces at $.25	$2.50	5 pounds at $.30	$1.50
Direct labour	1 hour at $3.00	3.00	.3 hour at $2.50	.75
Variable overhead	1 hour at $2.00	2.00	.3 hour at $2.50	.75
Total		$7.50		$3.00

3 All budgeted selling and administrative expenses are common, fixed expenses; 60 per cent are discretionary expenses.
4 The actual income statement for the fiscal year ended 30 June 20X4 follows:

Sales (53,000 units of A and 64,000 units B)	$861,000
Manufacturing cost of goods sold	749,200
Manufacturing margin	$111,800
Selling and administrative expenses	116,000
Operating income	$ (4,200)

5 The budgeted sales prices for products A and B were $9 and $6, respectively. Actual sales prices equalled budgeted sales prices.

6 The schedule of the actual variable manufacturing cost of goods sold by product follows (actual quantities in parentheses):

Product A:	Materials	$134,500	(538,000 pieces)
	Labour	156,350	(53,000 hours)
	Overhead	108,650	(53,000 hours)
Product B:	Materials	102,400	(320,000 pounds)
	Labour	50,000	(20,000 hours)
	Overhead	50,000	(20,000 hours)
Total		$601,900	

7 Products A and B are manufactured in separate facilities. Of the budgeted fixed manufacturing cost, $130,000 is separable as follows: $45,000 to product A and $85,000 to product B. Ten per cent of these separate costs are discretionary. All other budgeted fixed manufacturing expenses, separable and common, are committed.
8 There are no beginning or ending inventories.

During the upcoming management meeting, it is quite likely that some of the information from your controller will be discussed. In anticipation you set out to prepare answers to possible questions.

1 Determine the firm's budgeted break-even point in dollars, overall contribution-margin ratio and contribution margins per unit by product.
2 Considering products A and B as segments of the firm, find the budgeted 'contribution by segments' for each.
3 It is decided to allocate the budgeted selling and administrative expenses to the segments (in number 2) as follows: committed costs on the basis of budgeted unit sales mix and discretionary costs on the basis of actual unit sales mix. What are the final expense allocations? Briefly appraise the allocation method.
4 How would you respond to a proposal to base commissions to salespersons on the sales (revenue) value of orders received? Assume all salespersons have the opportunity to sell both products.
5 Determine the firm's actual 'contribution margin' and 'contribution controllable by segment managers' for the fiscal year ended 30 June 20X4. Assume no variances in committed fixed costs.
6 Determine the 'sales-activity variance' for each product for the fiscal year ended 30 June 20X4.
7 Determine and identify all variances in variable manufacturing costs by product for the fiscal year ended 30 June 20X4.

COLLABORATIVE LEARNING EXERCISE

9.47 Goals, objectives and performance measures

There is increasing pressure on colleges and universities to develop measures of accountability. The objective is to specify goals and objectives and to develop performance measures to assess the achievement of those goals and objectives.

Form a group of four to six students to be a consulting team to the accounting department at your college or university. (If you are not using this book as part of a course in an accounting department, select any department at a local college or university.) Based on your collective knowledge of the department, its mission and its activities, formulate a statement of goals for the department. From that statement, develop several specific objectives, each of which can be measured. Then, develop one or more measure of performance for each objective.

An optional second step in this exercise is to meet with a faculty member from the department and ask them to critique your objectives and performance measures. To the department member, do the objectives make sense? Are the proposed measures feasible and will they correctly measure attainment of the objectives? Will they provide proper incentives to the faculty? If the department has created objectives and performance measures, compare them to those your group developed.

Management control in decentralised organisations

Learning objectives

When you have finished studying this chapter, you should be able to:

1 Define decentralisation and identify its expected benefits and costs.

2 Distinguish between responsibility centres and decentralisation.

3 Explain how the linking of rewards to responsibility-centre performance metrics affects incentives and risk.

4 Compute ROI, economic profit and economic value added (EVA) and contrast them as criteria for judging the performance of organisation segments.

5 Compare the advantages and disadvantages of various bases for measuring the invested capital used by organisation segments.

6 Define *transfer prices* and identify their purpose.

7 State the general rule for transfer pricing and use it to assess transfer prices based on total costs, variable costs and market prices.

8 Identify the factors affecting multinational transfer prices.

9 Explain how controllability and management by objectives (MBO) aid the implementation of management control systems.

Nike

In 30 years, Nike has become the largest sports and fitness company in the world. It has grown from a small Beaverton, Oregon, company into a global giant. Nike is the official sponsor and supplier for the US Olympic Committee for the London 2012 and Rio 2016 games. Ten years ago, Nike was only a minor factor in the world of football. Now Nike endorsement arrangements include the Italian and French national teams, as well as Arsenal, Manchester United, FC Barcelona, Inter Milan, Juventus, Aston Villa, Celtic and PSV Eindhoven. Nike has placed itself at the centre of attention for soccer fans worldwide.

From 1986 to 2011, Nike's revenues increased from $1 billion to more than $20 billion. During this same period, the percentage of revenues from outside the United States increased from 25 per cent to over 60 per cent. Nike now has more stores outside the United States than inside. While footwear still accounts for more than half of Nike's sales, apparel sales now account for nearly one-third. A sampling of endorsements (promotional contracts with famous sports teams, individuals and organisations) in addition to the football teams previously listed gives another perspective on the company's global presence: tennis stars Roger Federer, James Blake, Jim Courier, Andre Agassi, Rafael Nadal, Pete Sampras, Lindsay Davenport, Mary Pierce, Maria Sharapova, Serena Williams; seven-time Tour de France winner Lance Armstrong; basketball stars Kobe Bryant, Lebron James, Steve Nash and Michael Jordan; and golf's Trevor Immelman and Paul Casey. Watch almost any sports event on television and you are likely to see the Nike 'swoosh' logo.

Nike made a conscious decision to go global – a process that has generated substantial financial rewards. What are some of the keys to success when a company like Nike decides to significantly expand its operations abroad? To manage effectively in this decentralised environment, Nike needs information to help coordinate and evaluate widely dispersed operations. A well-designed management control system is essential.

One critical element is understanding the relevance of the brand to local markets. Nike has gained this understanding by delegating management decision making to the local market level. For example, local Nike managers in Germany made the decision to sign an endorsement contract with world-champion racecar driver Michael Schumacher. According to CEO Philip Knight, '[Previously] it would have taken a move from within the company headquarters to strike such a deal. . . . But this time it was a decision made in country.' The local German manager knew that Schumacher was extremely relevant to the German market and that this would be a 'profit driven, culturally significant, and brand enhancing move.' Knight credits this move toward decentralisation for Nike's rapid increase in international sales: 'It is a great example of what we are trying to do: Make decisions on the ground in faraway places.'

As organisations like Nike grow and undertake more diverse and complex activities, many elect to delegate decision-making authority to managers throughout the organisation. This delegation of the freedom to make decisions is called **decentralisation**. Decentralisation is a matter of degree. The lower in the organisation that this freedom exists, the greater the decentralisation. Increasing sophistication of communications – internet, e-mail and worldwide cellular phone coverage – aids decentralisation. Geographical separation no longer implies lack of access to information. More companies are locating sales and production divisions far from headquarters without sacrificing knowledge of what is happening in the units. While communications technology can help Nike and others get information quickly, the management control system determines what information they receive.

Objective 1
Define *decentralisation* and identify its expected benefits and costs.

This chapter focuses on the role of management control systems in decentralised organisations. After providing an overview of decentralisation, the chapter discusses how companies use performance metrics to motivate managers of decentralised units, including various ways of measuring unit profitability to encourage actions by managers that are in the company's best interests. Finally, we address the special problems created when one segment of an organisation charges another for providing goods or services. ■

Centralisation versus decentralisation

Centralisation is the process by which organisations concentrate decision making within a particular location or group. The best choice along the continuum between centralisation and decentralisation is seldom obvious. In fact, organisations and industries often seem to cycle from increasing decentralisation to increasing centralisation, and back again. For example, a decade or so ago most airlines, such as South China Airlines, Iberia Airlines and Air France, decentralised. In contrast, at the same time, Sabena, Belgium's state-owned airline until its bankruptcy in 2001, undertook a centralisation effort. In the insurance industry, Aetna decentralised at the same time AXA Equitable was centralising. Let's take a look at some of the factors companies consider as they choose their position along the centralisation/decentralisation continuum.

■ Costs and benefits

Most organisations realise benefits from some level of decentralisation. Managers of lower-level units (which we will refer to as 'local' managers), often have the best information concerning local conditions and, therefore, are able to make faster and better decisions on local issues than higher-level managers (which we will refer to as 'central' managers). By delegating decision-making authority to local managers, central managers free up time to deal with larger issues and fundamental strategy. In addition, decentralisation gives local managers an opportunity to develop their decision-making ability and other management skills that help them move upward in the organisation, ensuring that the organisation develops future leaders. Finally, local managers who are given more authority often have greater motivation and job satisfaction and enjoy higher status.

Decentralisation also has its costs. Local managers may make decisions that are not in the organisation's best interests. Why? Either because they act to improve their own segment's performance at the expense of the organisation or because they do not fully understand the effects of their decisions on other segments and the organisation as a whole. Innovative ideas to improve performance are less likely to be shared across units in a decentralised organisation. Local managers in decentralised organisations also tend to duplicate services that might be less expensive if centralised (e.g., accounting, advertising and personnel). Furthermore, costs of accumulating and processing information frequently rise under decentralisation because top management needs additional accounting reports to learn about and evaluate decentralised units and their managers. Finally, managers in decentralised units may waste time negotiating with other units about goods or services that are being transferred between units. You can see some of the costs and benefits of decentralisation in the 'Business first' box on p. 420.

Decentralisation is more popular in profit-seeking organisations (where accountants can more easily measure outputs and inputs) than in nonprofit organisations (where it is more difficult to find reliable performance measures, so granting managers freedom is more risky). Central management can give local managers more freedom when it can more easily measure the results of their decisions and thereby hold the local managers accountable for the results. Poor decisions in a profit-seeking firm quickly become apparent from the inadequate profit generated.

■ Middle ground

Organisations make many choices along the centralisation/decentralisation continuum and the optimal choice for one organisation is likely to differ from the optimal choice for another. For every Nike that finds the benefits of increased decentralisation exceeding the costs, another company finds the costs exceeding the benefits. In fact, the optimal choice for one part of the organisation may differ from the optimal choice for another part. For example, many companies decentralise much of the chief accountant's problem-solving and attention-directing functions and handle them at lower levels. In contrast, they generally centralise income tax planning and mass scorekeeping functions such as accounting for payroll. The degree of centralisation which exists in a firm is only to a degree the outcome of a conscious decision reflective of purposive and formal cost–benefit analysis. Context also plays a significant role. For instance, the corporate history of the company, its ownership structure, the social and political relationships between the various stakeholders, senior management predilection for centralised control and the corporate and national cultural characteristics may all play a part in influencing the level of centralisation in an enterprise.

Decentralisation is most successful when an organisation's segments are relatively independent of one another – that is, when the decisions of a manager in one segment will not affect other segments. When segments do much internal buying or selling, much buying from the same outside suppliers, or much selling to the same outside markets, they are candidates for more centralisation.

In Chapter 9, we stressed that managers should consider cost–benefit tests, goal congruence and managerial effort when designing a management control system. If management has decided in favour of heavy decentralisation, then **segment autonomy** – the delegation of decision-making power to managers of segments of an organisation – is also crucial. For decentralisation to work, however, this autonomy must be real, not just lip service. In most circumstances, top managers must be willing to abide by decisions made by segment managers.

◼ Responsibility centres and decentralisation

Objective 2
Distinguish between responsibility centres and decentralisation.

Design of a management control system should consider two separate dimensions of control: (1) the responsibilities of managers and (2) the amount of autonomy they have. Some managers confuse these two dimensions by assuming that profit-centre managers always have more decentralised decision-making authority than cost-centre managers. This does not need to be the case. Some profit centre managers, such as those at Siemens, possess vast freedom to make decisions concerning labour contracts, supplier choices, equipment purchases, personnel decisions and so on. In contrast, profit-centre managers at other companies may need top-management approval for almost all the decisions just mentioned. Similarly, cost centres may be more heavily decentralised than profit centres. The fundamental question in deciding between using a cost centre or a profit centre for a given segment is not whether heavy decentralisation exists. Instead, the fundamental question is, for whatever level of decentralisation that exists, 'Will a profit centre or a cost centre better solve the problems of goal congruence and management effort?'

The management control system should be designed to achieve the best possible alignment between local manager decisions and the actions central management seeks. For example, a plant may seem to be a 'natural' cost centre because the plant manager has no influence over decisions concerning the marketing of its products. Nevertheless, some companies insist on evaluating a plant manager by the plant's profitability. Why? Because they believe this broader evaluation base will positively affect the plant manager's behaviour. Instead of being concerned solely with running an efficient cost centre, the system motivates the plant manager to consider quality control more carefully and react to customers' special requests more sympathetically. A profit centre may thus provide more clear incentives for the desired plant-manager behaviour than does a cost centre. In designing accounting control systems, top managers must consider the system's impact on behaviour desired by the organisation.

BUSINESS FIRST
Benefits and costs of Decentralisation

Many companies believe that decentralisation is important to their success, including PepsiCo, Panasonic and Procter & Gamble. Consider Johnson & Johnson (with 2010 sales of $61.5 billion, more than 118,000 employees and more than 250 companies operating in 57 countries) is the maker of products such as Tylenol, Listerine, Johnson's Baby Powder, Neutrogena and Neosporin. The company has a long history of decentralisation, beginning in the 1930s. Its 2010 annual report states 'The company's structure is based upon the principle of decentralised management.' It adds, 'The company views its principles of decentralised management as an asset and fundamental to the success of a broadly based business.'

Under the company's management structure, each of its operating companies functions autonomously. One benefit is that decisions are made by executives who are closer to the marketplace. One disadvantage is the additional expense because many of the operating companies duplicate many overhead costs. Because of this, many companies use a combination of centralisation and decentralisation. For instance, the Forestry Commission in the UK cares for the country's woods and forests. In this organisation, policy making is centralised. This is to ensure Britain abides by international rules for sustainable forest management and different segments of the organisation do not produce different policies. However counties manage their own forest activities such as planting, recreation and education. This allows regional differences to be dealt with in different ways.

Some organisations make a conscious effort to decentralise. For instance, the National Health Service in the UK is due to undergo changes in the way it works. At present, Primary Care Trusts control a lot of the spending in the NHS. They buy in patient services such as clinics and hospital care. However, under the planned changes, General Practitioners will be given greater responsibility for spending the health budget. Some decisions will still be made at the national level, such as those relating to neurosurgery and dentistry, but greater responsibility for making spending decisions will be devolved to local, clinically led consortia made up of doctors, nurses and medical professionals.

As you can see, decentralisation has benefits and costs. Some companies have vacillated between decentralisation and centralisation, sometimes believing that the benefits of centralising common activities dominate the benefits of decentralisation, while at other times seeking the decision-making advantages of decentralisation. In contrast, Johnson & Johnson has continued its policy of decentralisation in good times and bad, through a long succession of top management leadership. The company has a long-term credo that mandates decentralisation. It would take a brave (or foolhardy) leader to change Johnson & Johnson's philosophy of decentralisation.

Sources: Adapted from *Johnson & Johnson 2010 Annual Report*; www.thetimes100.co.uk.

Performance metrics and management control

Objective 3
Explain how the linking of rewards to responsibility-centre performance metrics affects incentives and risk.

A major factor in designing decentralised management control systems is how the system's performance metrics affect managers' incentives. Incentives are the rewards, both implicit and explicit, for managerial effort and actions. A performance metric is a specific measure of management accomplishment. Organisations should choose performance metrics that improve the alignment of manager incentives with organisational objectives. The organisation wants managers to use decision-making autonomy to meet the company's objectives, not to pursue other goals. For example, Nike executives wanted the company's manager of German operations to sign F1 champion Michael Schumacher to a contract only if it would create additional profits for Nike, not to provide an entry for the manager into the inner circles of car racing.

■ Agency theory, performance and rewards

Agency theory provides a model to analyse relationships where one party (the principal) delegates decision-making authority to another party (the agent). Agency theory is useful to analyse situations where there is imperfect alignment between the principal's and agent's (1) information and (2) objectives. As discussed earlier, it is common for local managers to have better information about their units than do higher-level central managers. Because the local managers have different information than central managers, they make different decisions. Similarly, as discussed in Chapter 9, it is common for the objectives of local managers to differ in some ways from central manager and organisational objectives. Differences in objectives can again lead local managers to make different decisions. Agency theory provides a framework to analyse these differences in designing a management control system.

Exhibit 10.1 shows how the design of a management control system affects the actions of managers. Managers have beliefs about how alternative action choices will lead to outcomes for their unit, and the management control system specifies how outcomes translate into unit performance metrics and into both explicit and implicit rewards. Local managers choose the action that they believe will lead to the combination of outcomes, performance metrics and rewards with the highest value to the local manager. Managers' preferences motivate them to select actions that generate outcomes measured and rewarded by a company's management control system. The manager's understanding of how the control system links outcomes, performance metrics and rewards influences the manager's choice of actions. Thus, the right metrics and rewards motivate actions that are in the company's best interests. For example, if a company measures and explicitly rewards increases in divisional profit, managers have an incentive to expend effort to increase profits.

The links between outcomes and performance metrics and rewards are critical features of the management control system. While the importance of explicit links is clear, implicit links may be equally important. For example, the management control system might include an explicit link that specifies the amount of bonus that will be paid for different levels of profit, but there may be an important implicit link between performance and pay raises. Similarly, it is important to recognise that rewards may be monetary or nonmonetary. Examples of monetary rewards include pay raises and bonuses. Examples of nonmonetary rewards include promotions, praise, self-satisfaction, better offices and other perquisites. Thus, while we often focus on explicit monetary rewards, remember that implicit and nonmonetary rewards associated with outcomes and metrics play important roles in the management control system.

One important rule for performance measurement is clear: *You get what you measure!* Managers focus their efforts in areas where an organisation measures managerial performance, even when the management control system does not include explicit rewards tied to the measures. Therefore, it is important to choose accounting measures that provide objective and easy-to-understand evaluations of performance, where managers believe there is a clear connection between their action choices and the performance metric.

■ Agency theory and risk

Ideally, companies should reward managers based on their individual performance, but often an organisation cannot directly measure a manager's performance. For example, a company may not be able to separate the manager's effect on responsibility-centre results from the effect of other factors beyond a manager's control. The greater the influence of noncontrollable factors on responsibility-centre results, the more problems there are in using the results to measure and reward a manager's performance.

Consider a particular Niketown store. Suppose its profits increased dramatically. The following factors all contributed to the increase in profits:

Exhibit 10.1 Designing a management control system

- A lengthy strike by employees of a competitor resulted in many customers switching to Nike.

- The store implemented a new cost management system resulting in a significant reduction in the costs of handling merchandise.

- Overall population growth in the store's region has been much higher than that in other Niketown locations.

- Labour costs in the region have not increased as much as in most Niketown locations.

- Employee turnover is lower than the system average. Employees cite their excellent relationship with fellow employees and management as the reason for their high level of job satisfaction.

How should Nike evaluate the performance of the store manager? Should it measure the manager's performance by profit results compared to those of other Niketown stores? What other measures could Nike use? From the factors listed, it is likely that a significant portion of the store's profit increase was due to factors the store manager could not control (the competitor's strike, population growth and regional labour costs). However, it is also likely that the manager exerted a strong influence on other factors by improving the cost-management system and creating a productive working environment for all employees.

An ideal performance metric would measure and reward the manager for controllable factors and neither reward nor punish the manager for uncontrollable factors. Although this ideal is hard to achieve, agency theory can guide the design of a system to link performance metrics and rewards. When an organisation hires a manager, the employment contract details performance metrics and how they will affect rewards. For example, the contract might specify that a manager will receive a bonus of 15 per cent of their salary if their responsibility centre achieves its budgeted profit. However, not all rewards are explicitly specified in the contract. For example, a company can reward a manager with a promotion, but seldom are the requirements for promotion spelled out in detail.

According to agency theory, employment contracts will balance three factors:

1 *Incentive*. The more a manager's reward depends on a performance metric, the more incentive the manager has to take actions that maximise that measure. Top management should define the performance metric to promote goal congruence and base enough reward on it to achieve managerial effort.

2 *Risk*. The more uncontrollable factors affect a manager's reward, the more risk the manager bears. People generally avoid risk, so a company must pay managers more if it expects them to bear more risk. Creating incentive by linking rewards to responsibility-centre results, which is generally desirable, has the undesirable side effect of imposing risk on managers if noncontrollable factors affect some part of the centre's results.

3 *Cost of measuring performance.* The incentive versus risk trade-off is not necessary if a manager's performance can be perfectly measured. Why? Because managers completely control their own performance, perfect measurement of controllable performance would eliminate risk to the manager. With perfect performance measurement, a manager could be paid a fixed amount if they perform as agreed and nothing otherwise. But perfectly measuring controllable performance is usually inordinately expensive if not outright impossible. The cost–benefit criterion therefore leads companies to rely on imperfect but low-cost measures. Unfortunately, these more readily available measures frequently confound the manager's controllable performance with uncontrollable factors.

Consider the example of a promoter hired by a group of investors to promote and administer an outdoor concert. Suppose the investors offer the promoter a contract with part guaranteed pay and part bonus based on total attendance. A larger bonus portion compared with the guaranteed portion creates more incentive, but it also creates more risk for the promoter. For example, what happens if it rains? The promoter could do an outstanding job promoting the concert but the weather might keep fans away. To compensate the promoter for added risk, the expected total payment to the promoter will have to be higher for a contract where a higher portion of the total payment is based on attendance. The investors must decide on the optimal tradeoff between the benefit from the added incentive created by a larger bonus and the extra total payment necessary to compensate for the added risk. Note that these contracting issues would not arise if the investors could directly measure the promoter's effort and judgement, rather than basing the bonus on attendance at the concert, a low-cost and readily available measure that unfortunately is also influenced by factors outside the control of the promoter.

Regardless of how a company links rewards to performance metrics, one pervasive performance metric is profitability. While many organisations use performance measurement systems such as the balanced scorecard (discussed in Chapter 9) that incorporate goals and metrics beyond profitability, it is hard to imagine a company that does not include at least one measure of profitability among its performance metrics. We next look at how various measures of profitability affect managers' incentives.

Measures of profitability

Objective 4
Compute ROI, economic profit and economic value added (EVA) and contrast them as criteria for judging the performance of organisation segments.

Companies often evaluate segment managers in decentralised units based on their segment's profitability. The trouble is that there are many ways to measure profitability and it is not clear which is the best measure. Is it income? Is it income before or after interest and taxes? Is it an absolute amount? A percentage? If a percentage, is it a percentage of revenue or of investment? In this section, we consider the strengths and weaknesses of commonly used profitability measures.

Return on investment

Too often, managers stress net operating income and ignore the investment associated with generating that income. Suppose Puma has two divisions, A and B. To say that division A, with an operating income of €200,000, has better performance than division B, with an operating income of €150,000, ignores an important aspect of profitability. A more comprehensive measure of profitability is the rate of **return on investment (ROI)**, which is income divided by the investment required to obtain that income. For any given amount of investment required, the investor wants the maximum income (holding risk constant). If division A requires an investment of €500,000 and division B requires only €250,000, division B has the higher ROI:

$$ROI = \frac{income}{investment}$$

$$ROI\ division\ A = \frac{€200{,}000}{€500{,}000} = 40\%$$

$$ROI\ division\ B = \frac{€150{,}000}{€250{,}000} = 60\%$$

Every euro invested in division B is generating income of €.60, compared to the €.40 generated by every euro invested in division A.

In ROI calculations, we should measure invested capital as an average for the period under review. Why? Because income is a flow of resources over a period of time and we should measure the average investment that generates that flow. The most accurate measures of average investment take into account the amount invested month-by-month, or even day-by-day. However, a simple average of the beginning and ending balances often provides nearly the same result without going to the trouble required to produce greater accuracy. Suppose division A had €450,000 of investment at the beginning of the year and gradually increased it to €550,000 by the end of the year. The average of the beginning and ending investment amounts is (€450,000 + €550,000) ÷ 2 = €500,000.

ROI facilitates the comparison of a unit's performance with that of other segments within the company or with similar units outside the company. Why? Because, unlike income alone, ROI takes into account the investment required to generate the income. ROI is a return per unit of investment and does not depend on the size of the segments being compared.

As shown in the following equations, we can write ROI as the product of two items: **return on sales** (income divided by revenue) and **capital turnover** (revenue divided by invested capital).

$$return\ on\ investment = \frac{income}{invested\ capital}$$

$$= \frac{income}{revenue} \times \frac{revenue}{invested\ capital}$$

$$= return\ on\ sales \times capital\ turnover$$

ROI can be increased by increasing either return on sales or capital turnover without changing the other. Consider an example of these relationships (amounts are in thousands of euros):

	Rate of return on invested capital (%)	=	Income Revenue	×	Revenue Invested capital
Present outlook	20	=	$\frac{16}{100}$	×	$\frac{100}{80}$
Alternatives:					
1 Increase return on sales by reducing expenses relative to sales	25	=	$\frac{20}{100}$	×	$\frac{100}{80}$
2 Increase capital turnover by decreasing investment	25	=	$\frac{16}{100}$	×	$\frac{100}{64}$

Alternative 1 improves return on sales by decreasing expenses relative to sales without increasing investment. Alternative 2 increases capital turnover by decreasing investment without reducing sales. Either alternative will increase ROI. Increasing capital turnover by decreasing investment means using fewer assets, such as cash, receivables, inventories, or equipment, for each dollar of revenue generated.

Increasing turnover is one of the advantages of implementing the just-in-time (JIT) philosophy (see Chapter 1). Many companies implementing JIT purchasing and production systems have realised dramatic improvements in ROI because capital turnover increased due to lower inventory levels while the return on sales stayed the same.

Although evaluation based on ROI causes managers to consider both income and investment in their decisions, it may provide inappropriate incentives for managers to reject profitable investment opportunities or accept unprofitable investment opportunities, as explained in the following section. Alternative performance measures – metrics that focus more on economic profit – address this issue.

Economic profit or economic value added (EVA)

Performance measurement systems should motivate managers to make decisions that increase the value of the company. ROI includes both profit and investment, focusing on income as a percentage of investment. However, there are advantages to a metric that emphasises an absolute amount of income rather than a percentage. **Economic profit**, also called **residual income**, defined as net operating profit after-tax (NOPAT) less a capital charge, is such a metric. **Net operating profit after-tax (NOPAT)** is income before interest expense but after tax. The **capital charge** is the company's cost of capital multiplied by the amount of investment, where the **cost of capital** is the cost of long-term liabilities and stockholders' equity weighted by their relative size. In short, economic profit tells you how much a company's after-tax operating income exceeds what it is paying for capital. Consider division A in our earlier example. Suppose its after-tax operating income is €200,000, the average invested capital in the division for the year is €500,000, and the company's after-tax cost of capital is 10 per cent:

Divisional after-tax operating income	€200,000
Minus charge for average invested capital (.10 × €500,000)	50,000
Equals economic profit (or residual income)	€150,000

There are different ways to calculate measures of economic profit, depending on exactly how a company chooses to define the terms used. One popular variant developed and marketed by the consulting firm Stern Stewart & Co. is **economic value added (EVA)**. In formula form, Stern Stewart defines EVA as

$$\text{Eva} = \text{adjusted NOPAT} - (\text{after-tax cost of capital} \times \text{adjusted average invested capital})$$

Stern Stewart makes specific adjustments to financial-reporting measures of after-tax operating profit and invested capital. These adjustments are designed to convert after-tax operating income into a closer approximation of cash income and invested capital into a closer approximation of the cash invested in the economic resources the company uses to create value. Examples of these adjustments include the following:

- Use taxes paid rather than tax expense.
- Capitalise (rather than expense) research and development expenses.
- Use FIFO for inventory valuation (thus companies using LIFO must add back the LIFO reserve to invested capital and add the increase or deduct the decrease in the LIFO reserve to after-tax operating income).

- If a company deducts interest expense in computing operating income, it must add back after-tax interest expense to find NOPAT.

To illustrate, suppose a division of Puma spent €4 million at the beginning of year 1 for research and development of a new shoe. The shoe proved to be a success with a product life cycle of 4 years. Assume that before accounting for R&D, the division's operating income each year was €12 million, the division's capital is €50 million each year, and Puma's cost of capital is 10 per cent. For simplicity, we will ignore income taxes in our example, but remember that EVA uses after-tax numbers.

EVA companies look upon R&D as a capital investment. For purposes of calculating EVA, Puma's division capitalises these expenditures and expenses them over the product's life cycle. In addition, the division deducts from operating income a capital charge of 10 per cent of the average capital balance outstanding during the year, including the capitalised R&D.

Exhibit 10.2 shows a comparison of the income and capital effects between traditional economic profit and EVA. Total 4-year financial-reporting operating profit, the amount included on Puma's income statement, is €44 million. Traditional economic profit (without capitalising R&D) is €44 million less a capital charge of €20 million, or €24 million. EVA also deducts a capital charge but capital is adjusted upward by €4 milion at the beginning of the year to reflect the capitalised investment in R&D and then declines by €1 milion per year as R&D is amortised. After incorporating the effect of these adjustments on both income and investment, EVA = €44 million − €20.8 million = €23.2 million   That is, EVA deducts an additional €.8 million capital charge for the capital used for the R&D. Stern Stewart has identified more than 160 different adjustments such as the adjustment illustrated for R&D but usually recommends only a few for a specific client. Many companies using economic profit for performance evaluation develop their own set of adjustments to income and capital, but all companies use the basic concept of net operating profit after-tax less a capital charge.

Economic profit and EVA have received much attention recently as scores of companies are adopting them as financial performance metrics. Coca-Cola and Quaker Oats claim that using EVA motivated managers to make decisions that increased shareholder value. All these companies are successful. Why? Because they do a better job than many of their competitors at allocating, managing and redeploying scarce capital resources (fixed assets, such as heavy equipment, computers, real estate and working capital). Because EVA explicitly recognises the cost of the capital deployed, it may help managers in these companies make better capital allocation decisions. Further, some investment companies use economic profit to rate stocks for their investment clients.

Year	Accounting operating income	Adjusted operating income	Accounting capital	Adjusted average capital[a]	Economic profit capital charge at 10%[b]	EVA capital charge at 10%[c]	Economic profit	Economic value added
Year 1	€ 8	$8 + 4 - 1 = €11$[d]	€50	€53.5	€ 5	€ 5.35	€ 3	€ 5.65
Year 2	12	$12 - 1 = 11$	50	52.5	5	5.25	7	5.75
Year 3	12	$12 - 1 = 11$	50	51.5	5	5.15	7	5.85
Year 4	12	$12 - 1 = 11$	50	50.5	5	5.05	7	5.95
Total	€44	€44			€20	€20.80	€24	€23.20

[a]Adjusted average capital: Year 1, $\frac{1}{2} \times$ (€54 + €53); Year 2, $\frac{1}{2} \times$ (€53 + €52); Year 3, $\frac{1}{2} \times$ (€52 + €51); Year 4, $\frac{1}{2} \times$ (€51 + €50).
[b]10% × accounting capital.
[c]10% × adjusted average capital.
[d]Accounting operating income + R&D expense − R&D amortisation = €8 + €4 − €1 = €11.

Exhibit 10.2 Comparison of economic profit and EVA

MAKING MANAGERIAL DECISIONS

One company that improved its EVA performance dramatically during the 1990s is IBM. In 1993, its EVA was a negative $13 billion. By 2000, the company improved its EVA to $2.2 billion. Like most companies, the economic downturn in the early 2000s hurt its EVA, dropping it into the negative range by 2002. By 2005, IBM again had a positive EVA at just under $1 billion. Compute the EVA for IBM using the following data (in billions of dollars) without any of the specific adjustments recommended by Stern Stewart. As a manager, how would you explain the past history of EVA and the current EVA to investors?

Net operating profit after tax	$12.8
Invested capital	67
Cost of capital (assumed)	10%

Answer

Amounts are in billions as follows:

$$EVA = \text{Net operating profit after tax} - \text{cost-of-capital percentage} \times \text{capital invested}$$
$$= \$12.8 - .10 \times \$67$$
$$= \$12.8 - \$6.7 = \$6.1 \text{ billion}$$

The improvement from 1993 to 2000 was dramatic. The decline in EVA in 2002 was not unexpected since a majority of companies lost value in 2002. IBM had returned to positive EVA by 2005.

ROI or economic profit?

Why do some companies prefer economic profit (or EVA) to ROI? Because ROI can motivate divisional managers to make investment decisions that are not in the best interests of the company as a whole. Under ROI, the basic incentive is to maximise rate of return. This leads division managers to invest only in projects that will increase their division's ROI, that is, projects with an ROI greater than the division's current ROI. For example, if a company measures performance using only ROI, the manager of a division currently earning 20 per cent may be reluctant to invest in projects that earn 18 per cent, even if accepting such a project would be best for the company.

From the viewpoint of the company as a whole, division managers should accept projects that earn more than the cost of capital, rather than projects that earn more than the current ROI for the manager's division. Why? Suppose the company's cost of capital is 10 per cent. Investing in projects earning more than 10 per cent will increase the company's profitability. For every €100 of investment, the company gets more than €10 in operating income and pays only €10 for the capital, a net gain. When a company uses economic profit as a performance metric, managers have incentive to invest in any project earning more than the cost of capital because such an investment will increase the division's economic profit.

Consider two Puma divisions, division X with operating income of €200,000 and division Y with operating income of €40,000. Division X has average invested capital of €1 million and division Y has average invested capital of €800,000. Assume that Puma's cost of capital is 10 per cent, and, for simplicity, ignore taxes. Suppose each division is considering a new proposed project. Division X is considering Project A that will earn 15 per cent annually on a €500,000 investment, or €75,000 a year. Division Y is considering Project B that will earn 7 per cent annually on an €800,000 investment, or €56,000 a year. Exhibit 10.3 shows ROI and economic profit with and without the project for each division.

	Without project		With project	
	Division X	Division Y	Division X	Division Y
Net after-tax operating income	€ 200,000	€ 40,000	€ 275,000	€ 96,000
Invested capital	€1,000,000	€800,000	€1,500,000	€1,600,000
ROI (net operating income ÷ invested capital)	20%	5%	18.3%	6%
Capital charge (10% × invested capital)	€ 100,000	€ 80,000	€ 150,000	€ 160,000
Economic profit (net operating income − capital charge)	€ 100,000	€ (40,000)	€ 125,000	€ (64,000)

Exhibit 10.3 ROI and economic profit for Divisions X and Y

Suppose Puma bases performance evaluation on ROI. Would the manager of division X invest in Project A? No. Even though Project A earns a return of 15 per cent (which is above the 10 per cent cost of capital), it would decrease ROI for division X from 20 per cent to 18.3 per cent. Now suppose you are the manager of division Y. Would you invest in Project B? Yes. Even though Project B earns a return of 7 per cent (below the 10 per cent cost of capital), it would increase ROI for division Y from 5 per cent to 6 per cent. In general, the ROI profitability metric provides an incentive for divisions to invest in new projects that earn a return in excess of their current return, rather than an incentive to invest in new projects with a return in excess of the cost of capital. Thus, performance evaluation based on ROI leads division X to reject a project with a 15 per cent return and division Y to accept a project with a 7 per cent return.

Now suppose top management evaluates performance using economic profit. For division X, investing in Project A would increase economic profit by €25,000, from €100,000 to €125,000. This €25,000 increase in economic profit is the €75,000 annual return from the new project less the €50,000 annual cost of capital for the new project. In contrast to the decision under ROI, the division X manager would accept Project A. For division Y, investing in Project B would decrease economic profit by €24,000, from €–40,000 to €–64,000. This €24,000 decrease is the €56,000 annual return from the new project less the €80,000 annual cost of capital for the new project. Thus, the division Y manager would reject Project B, where ROI evaluation led to its acceptance. Evaluation based on economic profit motivates both managers to invest only in projects that earn a return in excess of the cost of capital, whereas evaluation based on ROI leads both managers to incorrect decisions – division A rejecting a desirable project and division B accepting an undesirable one. In general, use of economic profit or EVA will promote goal congruence and lead to better decisions than using ROI.

Many companies are convinced that EVA has played a large role in their success.

Siemens Corporation, Europe's largest electronics and electrical engineering firm and Stern Stewart's first EVA client in Europe, reported in its annual report that 'Siemens focuses on EVA as the yardstick by which we measure the success of our efforts. The EVA performance standard encourages our people to be efficient, productive and proactive in thinking about our customers and their customers. These attributes translate into profitable growth and higher returns.' Examples of actions taken by Siemens to improve EVA include the sale of Siecor, the fiberoptic cable business, to Corning, and the sale of its retail and banking business. As stated by Siemens, 'Divesting selected businesses has generated funds for more strategic investments.'

Despite the success of economic profit and EVA, many companies still use ROI. Why? Probably because it is easier for managers to understand and it facilitates comparison across divisions. Furthermore, combining ROI with appropriate growth and profit targets can minimise ROI's dysfunctional motivations.

Summary problem for your review

PROBLEM

Suppose a small division of Safaricom has assets of KSh2,000,000, invested capital of KSh1,800,000 and net operating income of KSh600,000. Ignore taxes.

1 What is the division's ROI?

2 If the weighted-average cost of capital is 14 per cent, what is the EVA?

3 Suppose management uses ROI as a performance metric. What effects on management behaviour do you expect?

4 Suppose management uses economic profit as a performance metric. What effects on management behaviour do you expect?

SOLUTION

1 ROI = KSh600,000 ÷ KSh1,800,000 = 33%.

2 EVA = KSh600,000 − .14(KSh1,800,000) = KSh600,000 − KSh252,000 = KSh348,000.

3 If the company uses ROI, the division manager has an incentive to reject new projects that do not earn an ROI of at least 33 per cent, the division's current ROI. From the viewpoint of the organisation as a whole, this is undesirable if the cost of capital is only 14 per cent. If a division is enjoying a high ROI, it is less likely to expand if top management evaluates performance using ROI than if it evaluates performance using EVA.

4 If the company uses EVA, the manager is inclined to accept all projects whose expected rate of return exceeds the weighted-average cost of capital. The manager is more likely to expand the division because their goal is to maximise a money amount rather than a rate.

A closer look at invested capital

Objective 5
Compare the advantages and disadvantages of various bases for measuring the invested capital used by organisation segments.

To apply either ROI or economic profit, we must measure both income and invested capital. However, there are many different interpretations of these concepts. To understand what ROI or economic profit figures really mean for a particular company, you must first determine how the company defines and measures invested capital and income. We discussed various definitions of income in Chapter 9, pp. 383–8, so we will not repeat them here. We will, however, explore various definitions of invested capital.

■ Definitions of invested capital

Consider the following balance sheet classifications:

Current assets	€ 400,000	Current liabilities		€ 200,000
Property, plant and		Long-term liabilities		400,000
equipment, net	900,000	Stockholders' equity		700,000
Total assets	€1,300,000	Total liabilities and stockholders' equity		€1,300,000

Possible definitions of invested capital and their values on the preceding balance sheet include the following:

1 Total assets: All assets are included, €1,300,000.

2 Total assets less short-term liabilities: All assets except that portion financed by short-term creditors, €1,300,000 − €200,000 = €1,100,000, the definition commonly used for EVA. This is sometimes expressed as long-term invested capital. Note that because of the identity assets = short-term liabilities + long-term liabilities + stockholders' equity, this can also be computed by adding the long-term liabilities and the stockholders' equity, €400,000 + €700,000 = €1,100,000.

3 Stockholders' equity: Focuses on the investment of the owners of the business, €700,000.

For measuring the performance of division managers, we recommend one of the first two definitions rather than the third, stockholders' equity. If the division manager's mission is to put all assets to their best use without regard to their financing, then total assets is best. If the manager has direct control over obtaining short-term credit, then total assets less current liabilities is best. To increase return or economic profit measures, managers will focus attention on reducing the measure of invested capital that a company adopts. In practice, most companies using ROI or economic profit include all assets in invested capital and about half (primarily companies using EVA) deduct some portion of current liabilities.

◼ Valuation of assets

Other issues in measuring invested capital are whether to value the assets contained in the investment base at **gross book value** (the original cost of an asset) or **net book value** (the original cost of an asset less any accumulated depreciation) and whether to base the values on historical cost or some version of current value. Practice is overwhelmingly in favour of using net book value based on historical cost. This means the numbers used for performance metrics are consistent with financial numbers reported to the public. However, the alternatives are attractive in certain circumstances. We first examine the historical cost versus current cost issue and then discuss gross versus net asset values.

Historical or current cost?

Most companies favour historical cost over any measure of current cost such as replacement cost or liquidation values. Yet, critics maintain that historical cost provides a faulty basis for decision making and performance evaluation. Historical costs may be far from what a company might pay to purchase the asset today or the amount it could get from selling it, the values relevant to decisions affecting the asset. Despite these criticisms, managers have been slow to depart from historical cost.

Why is historical cost so widely used? Some critics would say that sheer ignorance is the explanation. But a more persuasive answer comes from cost–benefit analysis. Accounting systems are costly. Companies must keep historical records for many legal purposes, so historical records are already in place. A company spends no additional money evaluating performance based on historical costs. Many top managers believe that a more sophisticated system would not improve collective operating decisions enough to warrant the added expense.

Plant and equipment: gross or net?

In valuing assets, we need to distinguish between net and gross book values. Most companies use net book value in calculating their investment base. However, a significant minority uses gross book value. The proponents of gross book value maintain that it facilitates comparisons between years and between plants or divisions. Under gross values, performance evaluations depend only on what assets are in use, not on the depreciation assumptions or how old the assets are.

Consider an example of a €600,000 piece of equipment with a 3-year life and no residual value.

Year	Operating income before depreciation	Depreciation	Operating income	Average net book value*	Net BV rate of return	Gross book value	Gross BV rate of return
1	€260,000	€200,000	€60,000	€500,000	12%	€600,000	10%
2	260,000	200,000	60,000	300,000	20	600,000	10
3	260,000	200,000	60,000	100,000	60	600,000	10

(€600,000 + €400,000) ÷2; (€400,000 + €200,000) ÷ 2; and so on.

Notice that the rate of return on net book value increases as the equipment ages. In contrast, the rate of return on gross book value is unchanged if operating income does not change. Proponents of using gross book value for performance evaluation maintain that a performance metric should not improve simply because assets are getting older. In contrast, advocates of using net book value maintain that it is less confusing because it is consistent with the assets shown on the conventional balance sheet and with net income computations.

Companies should focus on the effect on managers' incentives when choosing between net and gross book value. Managers evaluated using gross book value will tend to replace assets sooner than will managers in firms using net book value. Consider a division of Adidas that has a 4-year-old machine with an original cost of €1,000 and net book value of €200. The division can replace the machine with a new one that also costs €1,000. The choice of net or gross book value does not affect net income. However, if Adidas uses the net book value for measuring the investment base, replacement will increase the investment base from €200 to €1,000. In contrast, if Adidas uses gross book value, the base is €1,000 both before and after the replacement. In summary, to maximise ROI or economic profit, managers in firms using net book value have incentives to keep old assets with their low book value. Those in firms using gross book value will have less incentive to keep old assets. Therefore, using gross book value will motivate managers to use more state-of-the-art production technology. Net asset value will motivate a more conservative approach to asset replacement.

There are no universally correct answers with respect to such controversial issues as historical values versus current values or gross versus net asset values. Instead, each organisation must design its management control system to achieve the best possible decision making, taking into account the cost–benefit tradeoff. This approach is not concerned with 'truth' or 'perfection' by itself. Instead, the design should ask questions such as the following: Will improvements in the system be worth the added cost? Will a different system achieve better goal congruence and managerial effort? Or, will our existing imperfect system provide about the same set of decisions at lower cost?

Transfer pricing

Now that you understand some of the issues in measuring profitability, we will look at something that can further complicate the use of profitability as a performance metric. When all the segments of a decentralised organisation are independent of one another, managers' motivations that result from using profitability measures for performance evaluation are generally consistent with overall organisational goals. Segment managers can focus only on their own segments because what is best for their segment is generally best for the organisation as a whole. In contrast, when segments interact, there is a possibility that what helps one segment hurts another segment badly enough to have a negative net effect on the entire organisation. For example, two Bharti Airtel sales divisions may compete for the same customer by cutting prices and thereby reducing the company's overall margin on the business.

A major source of potential conflicts between segment and organisational interests occurs when one segment sells products or services to another segment of the same organisation for a price called the **transfer price**. For example, when one segment produces a subcomponent and sells it to another segment that then incorporates it in a final product, a transfer price is required. Transfer prices also apply to services, such as when a product manager buys advertising services from the marketing support segment. The transfer price for the subcomponent is revenue to the producing segment and a cost to the acquiring segment. Thus, a change in the transfer price increases the computed profit for one segment and decreases the profit for the other segment. However, it does not affect profit for the company as a whole.

Purposes of transfer pricing

Objective 6
Define *transfer prices* and identify their purpose.

What does a company want from its transfer pricing system? Ideally, it wants to ensure that managers who make decisions to improve their segment's performance also increase the performance of the organisation as a whole. When a company evaluates a segment based on profitability, it wants profitability metrics that reward the segment manager for decisions that increase both a segment's profitability and the profitability of the entire company. For example, transfer prices should guide managers to make the best possible decisions regarding whether to buy or sell products and services inside or outside the total organisation. Decisions by the buying and selling segment managers, acting without top management intervention, should be the best decisions for their segment and for the entire organisation. In other words, decisions that increase a segment's profit should also increase the profits of the entire company.

Another common goal of transfer-pricing systems is to preserve segment autonomy. Top management could dictate how much of any product or service one segment transfers to another. However, if an organisation has decided that decentralisation, with its focus on autonomy of segment managers, is desirable, then segment managers should be free to make their own decisions.

Organisations use a variety of transfer prices, cost-based prices for some transfers, market-based prices for other transfers and negotiated prices for others. Therefore, do not expect to obtain a single, universally applicable answer to the problem of transfer pricing. There is no perfect transfer-pricing system. Almost every manager in a decentralised organisation has had experience with transfer-pricing systems that seem less than ideal.

A general rule for transfer pricing

Objective 7
State the general rule for transfer pricing and use it to assess transfer prices based on total costs, variable costs and market prices.

Although no single rule always meets the goals of transfer pricing, a general rule can provide guidance:

$$\text{transfer price} = \text{outlay cost} + \text{opportunity cost}$$

As described on p. 233, outlay costs require a cash disbursement. They are essentially the additional amount the selling segment must pay to produce and transfer a product or service to another segment. In many cases, outlay costs are the variable costs for producing the item transferred. Opportunity cost is the contribution to profit that the selling segment forgoes by transferring the item internally. For example, if capacity constraints force a segment to either transfer an item internally or sell it externally – that is, it cannot produce enough to do both – the opportunity cost for internal transfer is the contribution margin the segment could have received from the external sale.

Why does this rule generally work? Consider the following example of two hypothetical divisions at Macron – an Italian sportswear designer. The fabric division (the selling division) is considering transferring the fabric required for a golf shirt to the sportswear division (the buying division):

Suppose the fabric division's €4 opportunity cost arises because it can get €10 by selling the fabric to a buyer outside the company. Thus, the foregone contribution by not selling to the outside buyer is €10 − €6 = €4. At any transfer price less than €10, the selling division is better off selling the fabrics to the outside buyer rather than transferring it. Thus, the minimum transfer price it would accept is €6 + €4 = €10.

Now consider how much the item is worth to the sportswear division. For the fabric to be profitable to the sportswear division, it must be able to sell the final product for more than the transfer price plus the other costs it must incur to finish and sell the product. Because it can sell the golf shirt for €25 and its other costs are €12, the maximum price the sportswear division would be willing to pay is €25 − €12 = €13. At any higher price, the sportswear division would choose not to produce the shirt at all. But there is a second constraint: The sportswear division will not pay more to the fabric division than it would have to pay to an outside supplier for an equivalent fabric. Thus, the largest transfer price acceptable to the sportswear division is the lesser of (1) €13 or (2) the cost charged by an outside supplier.

Now, from the company's point of view, transfer is desirable whenever (1) the total cost to the company for producing the fabric internally (€10, including opportunity cost, as determined by the fabric division) is less than its value to the company (€13 as determined by the sportswear division) and (2) the fabric division's costs (again including opportunity costs) are less than the price the sportswear division would have to pay to an outside supplier. The first criterion guarantees that the company does not decide to produce a product where the total cost to produce exceeds the final selling price to the end user. The second guarantees that it does not pay more to produce the fabric internally than it would have to pay to buy it in the marketplace. The only transfer price that will always meet these criteria is €10, the fabric division's outlay cost plus opportunity cost. Why? Any price between €10 and €13 meets the first criterion. However, only €10 meets the second because the sportswear division should purchase the fabric for €10 from the outside supplier for any transfer price above €10.

Exhibit 10.4 (overleaf) summarises the division's decision and the effect on Macron as a whole when an outside supplier offers the fabric at either greater than €10 or less than €10. At a €10 transfer price, regardless of what price outside suppliers offer, the division managers, acting independently, make the decision that is most profitable for the company as a whole. Any other transfer price creates a possibility of a manager making the decision that is best for their segment but not for the company as a whole. The fabric division would reject the transfer at less than €10 regardless of how much profit it creates for the sportswear division. The sportswear division would reject the transfer whenever the transfer price is greater than the price from alternative sources. Any transfer price greater than €10 runs the risk of the sportswear division purchasing outside the company even when the internal cost is lower. For example, with a transfer price of €12 and an outside bid of €11, the sportswear division would pay €11 to the outside supplier when the company could have spent only €10 (including opportunity cost) to produce the fabric in the fabric division.

This general rule does not always achieve all of the multiple goals of transfer-pricing systems; as we said earlier, there is no universally optimal transfer price. None the less, it

Outside supplier price	Decision by division managers	Decision best for company
Less than €10	Do not transfer – buying division rejects transfer because buying internally will reduce its profits	Buy from outside supplier because it is cheaper for the company as a whole
Greater than €10	If value to buying division is greater than €10: Transfer at €10 – both divisions benefit	Transfer because internal price is less than external price
	If value to buying division is less than €10: buying division rejects transfer	Do not transfer because the value of the fabric to the company is less than its cost

Exhibit 10.4 Summary effects of a €10 transfer price

provides a good benchmark by which to judge transfer-pricing systems. We will analyse the following transfer-pricing systems, the most popular systems in practice, by examining how close the transfer price comes to the benchmark of outlay cost plus opportunity cost:

1 Market-based transfer prices.

2 Cost-based transfer prices
   (a) Variable cost
   (b) Full cost (possibly plus profit).

3 Negotiated transfer prices.

In addressing these transfer-pricing systems, we will assume that a company has multiple divisions that transfer items to one another and that the company wants to preserve segment autonomy in a decentralised operation.

Market-based transfer prices

When there is a ready market for an item or service transferred from one segment to another, transfer pricing policies are straightforward. The common maxim is 'if a market price exists, use it'. The more competitive the market, the better the maxim applies.

If there is a competitive market for the product or service being transferred internally, using the market price as a transfer price will generally lead to goal congruence. Why? Because the market price equals the variable cost plus opportunity cost.

$$\text{transfer price} = \text{variable cost} + \text{opportunity cost}$$
$$= \text{variable cost} + (\text{market price} - \text{variable cost})$$
$$= \text{market price} + \text{variable cost} - \text{variable cost}$$
$$= \text{market price}$$

If the selling division avoids some marketing and delivery costs when selling internally, many companies will deduct these costs from the market price when computing the transfer price. That is, the opportunity cost in the preceding expression is the net amount the selling division would receive selling the item on the market after deducting variable cost and marketing and delivery costs.

To illustrate market-based transfer prices, reconsider the two hypothetical divisions of Macron. The fabric division makes fabrics it sells directly to external customers as well as to other Macron divisions, such as the sportswear division. The fabric division makes a particular fabric for an outlay cost of €6 and can sell it to external customers for €10. The sportswear division can buy that same fabric on the market for €10 and use it to make a golf shirt, spending an extra €12 in production costs. The golf shirt sells for €25. Should the sportswear division obtain the fabric from the fabric division of Macron or purchase it from an external supplier?

Assume for the moment that the fabric division can sell its entire production to external customers without incurring any marketing or shipping costs. The manager of the fabric division will not sell the fabric for less than €10. Why? Because he or she can sell it on the market for €10, so any price less than €10 will reduce the manager's division's profit. Furthermore, the sportswear division manager will refuse to pay a transfer price greater than €10 for the fabric for each golf shirt. Why? Because if the transfer price is greater than €10, he or she will purchase the fabric from the external supplier for the lower price of €10 in order to maximise their division's profit. The only transfer price that allows both managers to maximise their division's profit is €10, the market price. If the managers had autonomy to make decisions, at any transfer price other than €10 one of the managers would decline the internal transfer of the fabric.

Now suppose the fabric division incurs a €.75 per square yard marketing and shipping cost that it can avoid by transferring the fabric to the sportswear division instead of marketing it to outside customers. Most companies would then use a transfer price of €9.25, often called a 'market-price-minus' transfer price. The fabric division would get the same net amount from the transfer (€9.25 with no marketing or shipping costs) as from an external sale (€10 less €.75 marketing and shipping costs), whereas the sportswear division saves €.75 per shirt. Thus, Macron benefits overall.

This situation is similar to one where a noncompetitive market creates an external selling price for the fabric division of €9.25 and an external purchase price for the sportswear division of €10. A transfer price of €9.25 will motivate transfer of the fabric only when Macron as a whole will benefit from the transfer. The fabric division will produce and transfer the fabric only if the transfer price is at least €9.25, and the sportswear division will buy the fabric internally only if it costs less than €10 and is worth at least €9.25 to the division. These criteria drive a decision to transfer only if it is in Macron's overall best interests.

While market-based transfer prices generally provide the correct incentives, market prices are not always available. Therefore, we next discuss some other systems commonly used in the absence of market-based prices.

■ Transfers at cost

When market prices don't exist, most companies resort to cost-based transfer prices. In fact, about half the major companies in the world use a cost-based transfer-pricing system. However, there are many possible definitions of cost. Some companies use only variable cost, others use full cost, and still others use full cost plus a profit markup. Some use standard costs and some use actual costs. Cost-based transfer prices are easy to understand and use, but they can easily lead to **dysfunctional decisions** – decisions in conflict with the company's goals. The key to successful cost-based transfer prices is to minimise such dysfunctional decisions. Let's examine some of these cost-based transfer-pricing systems.

Transfers at variable cost

Companies that transfer items at variable cost implicitly assume that the selling division has no opportunity cost. Why? Because the outlay cost is generally about equal to variable cost: transfer price = outlay (variable) cost + €0. Therefore, a variable-cost transfer-pricing system is most appropriate when the selling division forgoes no opportunities when it transfers the item internally, for example when there is plenty of excess capacity in the selling division.

Variable-cost transfer prices cause dysfunctional decisions when the selling segment has significant opportunity costs. In our fabric division–sportswear division example, there are two ways this could happen. First, if there are positive opportunity costs, the fabric division manager would turn down any transfer, preferring to pursue the alternative opportunities, perhaps selling the fabric on the open market or using facilities to make a different, more profitable, fabric. This would be dysfunctional if the sportswear division could make more profit from its golf shirt than the fabric division makes from pursuing its alternative opportunities. Second, realising the lack of incentive for the fabric division to transfer the fabric, top management might insist that it produce and transfer the fabric. This would be against the company's interests if the fabric division passes up opportunities that yield more profit than the sportswear division's golf shirt. In addition, this policy violates segment autonomy.

BUSINESS FIRST
Activity-based costing and transfer pricing

Teva Pharmaceutical Industries Ltd is a global health-care company specialising in pharmaceuticals. It is headquartered in Israel and had 2010 sales of $16.1 billion. Teva entered the lucrative generic drug market in the mid-1980s. Each of the marketing divisions purchases generic drugs from the manufacturing division. As part of its strategy, the company decentralised its pharmaceutical business into cost and profit centres. Prior to decentralisation, each marketing division was a revenue centre. With the new organisational structure, management had to decide how to measure marketing division costs because profits were now the key financial performance metric.

A key cost to the marketing divisions is the transfer price paid for drugs purchased from the manufacturing division. Management considered several alternative bases for the company's transfer prices. Market price was not a feasible basis for transfer pricing because there was not a ready market. Negotiated prices were rejected because management believed that the resulting debates over the proper price would be lengthy and disruptive. Teva adopted variable cost (raw material and packaging costs) transfer pricing for a short time but eventually rejected it because it did not lead to congruent decisions – managers did not differentiate products using many scarce resources from those using few. Further, when a local source for the drug did exist, the market price was always above the variable-cost transfer price. Thus, managers in Teva's manufacturing division had little incentive to keep costs low.

Management also rejected traditional full cost that did not capture the actual cost structure of the manufacturing division. Specifically, the traditional full-cost system undercosted the low-volume products and

overcosted the large-volume products. The system traced only raw materials directly to products. It divided the remaining manufacturing costs into two cost pools and allocated them based on labour hours and machine hours. One problem with the traditional system was its inability to capture and correctly allocate the non-value-added cost of setup activity. Management did not know the size of the errors in product cost, but the lack of confidence in the traditional cost system led to rejection of full cost as the transfer-pricing base.

Then Teva's management adopted an activity-based-costing (ABC) system to improve the accuracy of its product costs. The ABC system has five activity centres and related cost pools: receiving, manufacturing, packaging, quality assurance and shipping. Because of the dramatic increase in costing accuracy, management was able to adopt full activity-based cost as the transfer price.

Teva's managers are pleased with their transfer-pricing system. The benefits include increased confidence that the costs being transferred are closely aligned with the actual short- and long-run costs being incurred, increased communication between divisions and an increased awareness of the costs of low-volume products and the costs of capacity required to support these products. They believe that their activity-based costs are the best approximation to outlay cost plus opportunity costs because the allocation of the fixed costs is a good measure of the value (opportunity cost) of the resources being consumed.

Sources: Adapted from Robert Kaplan, Dan Weiss and Eyal Desheh, 'Transfer pricing with ABC', *Management Accounting*, May, 1997, pp. 20–28; and Teva Pharmaceutical Industries Ltd 2010 *Annual Report*.

Transfers at full cost or full cost plus profit

Full-cost transfer prices include not only variable cost but also an allocation of fixed costs. In addition, some companies also add a markup for profit. This implicitly assumes that the allocation of fixed costs (and, if included, the profit markup) is a good approximation of the opportunity cost. In cases of constrained capacity, where the selling division cannot satisfy all internal and external demand for its products, the opportunity cost is positive. In such cases, variable-cost transfer prices are problematic. However, there is no guarantee that adding an allocation of fixed costs, with or without an additional profit component, is a good approximation of the opportunity cost. Yet, it may be a better approximation than assuming a zero opportunity cost. Some companies believe that using activity-based costing improves cost-based transfer prices, as described in the 'Business first' box on p. 436.

Dysfunctional decisions arise with full-cost transfer prices when the selling segment has opportunity costs that differ significantly from the allocation of fixed costs and profit. In our example, suppose the fabric division has excess capacity and thus nearly zero opportunity cost. Nevertheless, it has large fixed costs so that the full cost of the transferred fabric includes €8 of fixed cost in addition to the €6 variable cost. At a transfer price of €14, and assuming an external supplier either doesn't exist or would also charge at least €14, the sportswear division would refuse the transfer unless it could sell the golf shirt for at least €14 + €12 = €26. Therefore, because the shirt sells for €25, the sportswear division would decide not to produce it. But this decision costs Macron a contribution margin of €25 − (€6 + €12) = €7. The decision not to produce the shirt is dysfunctional – that is, it conflicts with Macron's goal of generating additional profit.

Cost-based transfer prices can create problems when a company uses actual cost rather than standard cost as a transfer price. Because the buying division will not know its actual cost in advance, it will not be able to accurately plan its costs. More importantly, a transfer price based on actual costs merely passes cost inefficiencies in the selling division along to the buying division. Therefore, the selling division lacks incentive to control its costs. Thus, we recommend using budgeted or standard costs instead of actual costs for cost-based transfer prices.

Finally, cost-based transfer prices can undercut segment autonomy and sometimes lead to conflicts between segment and organisational goals. Suppose managers believe that it's best for the company to transfer an item internally rather than purchasing it externally but also believe that the transfer price is unfair to their segment. They may either do what they think top management wants but resent its negative effect on their segment, or they may do what is best for their segment, ignoring its negative impact on the organisation as a whole. Neither alternative is desirable.

Supporters of cost-based transfer prices point out that they are easy to understand and inexpensive to implement. However, any cost-based transfer price can lead to dysfunctional decisions. Companies transferring goods or services in the absence of market prices must decide whether the effects of dysfunctional decisions are great enough to abandon cost-based transfer prices. One alternative is to give up decentralised decision making – essentially have top management dictate whether to transfer items internally or purchase them from external suppliers. However, suppose the benefits of decentralisation are large but so are the costs of dysfunctional decisions caused by cost-based transfer prices. In such a case, another alternative is negotiated transfer prices.

■ Negotiated transfer prices

Companies heavily committed to segment autonomy often allow managers to negotiate transfer prices. The managers may consider both costs and market prices in their negotiations, but no policy requires them to do so. Supporters of negotiated transfer prices maintain that the managers involved have the best knowledge of what the company will gain or lose by

MAKING MANAGERIAL DECISIONS

Consider the following data concerning a subassembly that Willamette Manufacturing Company produces in its fabricating division and uses in products assembled in its assembly division.

Fabricating division	
Variable cost of subassembly	€35
Excess capacity (in units)	1,000
Assembly division	
Market price for buying the subassembly from external sources	€50
Number of units needed	900

If you were the manager of the fabricating division, what is the lowest transfer price you would accept for the subassembly? If you were the manager of the assembly division, what is the most you would be willing to pay for the subassembly? Is there a transfer price that would motivate production and transfer of the subassembly? If so, what is the price?

Answer

The fabricating division has excess capacity, so its manager would be willing to accept any price above the variable cost of €35. The assembly division can buy the subassembly for €50 on the external market, so its manager would be willing to pay no more than €50 to buy it from the fabricating division. The transfer would take place at some price between €35 and €50.

producing and transferring the product or service, so open negotiation allows the managers to make optimal decisions. Critics of negotiated prices focus on the time and effort spent negotiating, an activity that adds nothing directly to the profits of the company.

Let's look at how our fabric division and sportswear division managers might approach a negotiation of a transfer price. The sportswear division manager might look at the selling price of the golf shirt, €25, less the additional cost the division incurs in making it, €12, and decide to purchase fabric at any transfer price less than €25 − €12 = €13. The sportswear division will add to its profit by making and selling the shirt if the transfer price is below €13. At a transfer price above €13, the sportswear division will choose to not make and sell the shirt, assuming there is no other supplier of fabric at a price below €13.

Similarly, the fabric division manager will look at what it costs to produce and transfer the fabric. If there is excess capacity and thus no opportunity cost, any transfer price above €6 will increase the fabric division's profit. Negotiation will result in a transfer if the maximum transfer price the sportswear division is willing to pay is greater than the minimum transfer price the fabric division is willing to accept. The fabric division manager is willing to accept any price above €6 and the sportswear division manager will pay up to €13. The exact transfer price will depend on the negotiating ability and power of the two division managers.

Now suppose there is no excess capacity in the fabric division and an outside customer is willing to pay €10 for the fabric. Transferring the fabric internally causes the division to give up a contribution of €4 as well as paying variable costs of €6, so the minimum transfer price acceptable to the fabric division is now €10. A transfer will take place at a price between €10 and €13. If the opportunity cost had been more than €7, a transfer would not occur. Why? Because the fabric division's minimum price of €6 variable costs plus opportunity cost would now be greater than €13 and the sportswear division's maximum price would be just €13. This decision is exactly what Macron would prefer. When the fabric division's opportunity cost is less than €7, the golf shirt is more profitable than the fabric division's other business, and the transfer should occur. When the fabric division's opportunity cost is greater than €7, the additional contribution from the fabric division's other business will be greater than the sportswear division's contribution on the shirt and the transfer should not occur. Therefore, the manager's decisions are congruent with the company's best interests.

What should top management of a decentralised organisation do if it sees segment managers making dysfunctional decisions through their negotiations? As usual, the answer is, 'It depends'. Top management can step in and force the 'correct' decision, but doing so undermines segment managers' autonomy and the overall notion of decentralisation. It also assumes that top management has the information necessary to determine the correct decision. Most important, frequent intervention results in recentralisation. Indeed, if more centralisation is desired, the organisation might want to reorganise by combining segments.

Top managers who wish to encourage decentralisation will often make sure that both producing and purchasing division managers understand all the facts and then allow the managers to negotiate a transfer price. Even when top managers suspect that the segments might make a dysfunctional decision, they may swallow hard and accept the segment manager's judgement as a cost of decentralisation. (Repeated dysfunctional decision making may be a reason to change the organisational design or to change managers.)

Well-trained and informed segment managers who understand opportunity costs and the behaviour of fixed and variable costs will often make better decisions than will top managers. The producing division manager knows best the various uses of its capacity and the purchasing division manager knows best what profit can be made on the items to be transferred. In addition, negotiation allows segments to respond flexibly to changing market conditions when setting transfer prices. One transfer price may be appropriate in a time of idle capacity and another when demand increases and operations approach full capacity.

■ Multinational transfer pricing

Objective 8
Identify the factors affecting multinational transfer prices.

So far, we have focused on how transfer-pricing policies affect the motivation of managers. However, in multinational companies, other factors may dominate. For example, multinational companies use transfer prices to minimise worldwide income taxes, import duties and tariffs. For example, Nike, Adidas and Puma may prefer to make profits in Singapore, where the marginal corporate tax rate is very low.

Suppose a division in a high-income-tax-rate country produces a subcomponent for another division in a low-income-tax-rate country. By setting a low transfer price, the company can recognise most of the profit from the production in the low-income-tax-rate country, thereby minimising taxes. Likewise, items produced by divisions in a low-income-tax-rate country and transferred to a division in a high-income-tax-rate country should have a high transfer price to minimise taxes.

Sometimes import duties offset income tax effects. Most countries base import duties on the price paid for an item, whether bought from an outside company or transferred from another division. Therefore, low transfer prices generally lead to low import duties.

Tax authorities also recognise the incentive to set transfer prices to minimise taxes and import duties. Therefore, most countries have restrictions on allowable transfer prices. Typically, multinationals must follow an rules specifying that transfers be priced at 'arm's-length' market values, or at the price one division would pay another if they were independent companies. Even with this rule, companies have some latitude in deciding an appropriate 'arm's-length' price.

Consider a high-end running shoe produced by an Irish Nike division with a 12 per cent income tax rate and transferred to a division in Germany with a 40 per cent rate. In addition, suppose Germany imposes an import duty equal to 20 per cent of the price of the item and that Nike cannot deduct this import duty for tax purposes. Suppose the full unit cost of a pair of the shoes is €100, and the variable cost is €60. If tax authorities allow either variable- or full-cost transfer prices, which should Nike choose? By transferring at €100 rather than at €60, the company gains €3.20 per unit:

Effect of transferring at €100 instead of at €60	
Income of the Irish division is €40 higher; (therefore, it pays 12% × €40 more income taxes	€(4.80)
Income of the German division is €40 lower; therefore, it pays 40% × €40 less income taxes	16.00
Import duty is paid by the German division on an additional €100 − €60 = €40; therefore, it pays 20% × €40 more duty	(8.00)
Net savings from transferring at €100 instead of €60	€ 3.20

Companies may also use transfer prices to avoid the financial restrictions imposed by some governments. For example, a country might restrict the amount of dividends paid to foreign owners. It may be easier for a company to get cash from a foreign division as payment for items transferred than as cash dividends.

In summary, transfer pricing is more complex in a multinational company than it is in a domestic company. Multinational companies try to achieve more objectives through transfer-pricing policies, and some of the objectives can conflict with one another.

Summary problem for your review

PROBLEM

Reconsider Macron's fabric division and sportswear division described on p. 433. In addition to the data there, suppose the fabric division has annual fixed manufacturing costs of €800,000 and expected annual production of enough fabric to make 100,000 golf shirts. The 'fully allocated cost' of the material for one golf shirt is as follows:

Variable costs	€ 6.00
Fixed costs, €800,000 ÷ 100,000 shirts	8.00
Fully allocated cost of the material for one golf shirt	€14.00

Assume that the fabric division has idle capacity. The sportswear division is considering whether to buy enough fabric for 10,000 golf shirts. It will sell each shirt for €25. The additional processing and selling costs in the sportswear division to produce and sell one shirt are €12. If Macron bases its transfer prices on fully-allocated cost, would the sportswear division manager buy? Explain. Would the company as a whole benefit if the sportswear division manager decided to buy? Explain.

SOLUTION

The sportswear division manager would not buy. The fully allocated cost-based transfer price of €14 would make the acquisition of the fabric unattractive to the sportswear division:

Sportswear division:		
Sales price of final product		€25
Deduct costs		
Transfer price paid to the fabric division (fully-allocated cost)	€14	
Additional processing and selling costs	12	
Total costs to the sportswear division		26
Contribution to profit of the sportswear division		€(1)
Company as a whole:		
Sales price of final product		€25
Deduct variable costs and opportunity costs		
Fabric department	€ 6	
Sportswear department	12	
Total variable and opportunity costs		18
Contribution to company as a whole		€7

The company as a whole would benefit by €70,000 (10,000 shirts × €7) if the fabric division produces and transfers the fabric.

The major lesson here is that when there is idle capacity in the supplier division transfer prices based on fully allocated costs may induce the wrong decisions. Working in their own best interests, the sportswear division manager has no incentive to buy from the fabric division.

Keys to successful management control systems

Like management in general, management control systems are more art than science. Companies such as Nike, Glaxo Smith Kline and Fiat will certainly include many subjective factors as well as more objective measures of profitability in their performance-evaluation system. Intelligent use of the available information is as important as generating the information itself. Next, we briefly explore three factors that help managers interpret and use management control information.

▪ Focus on controllability

Objective 9
Explain how controllability and management by objectives (MBO) aid the implementation of management control systems.

As Chapter 9 explained (see Exhibit 9.5, p. 386), companies should distinguish between the performance of the division manager and the performance of the division as an investment by the corporation. Top management should evaluate segment managers on the basis of their controllable performance. However, management should base decisions such as increasing or decreasing investment in a division on the economic viability of the division, not on the performance of its managers.

This distinction helps to clarify some vexing difficulties. For example, top management may use an investment base to gauge the economic performance of a retail store, but judge the store's manager by focusing on income and ignoring any investment allocations. The aim is to evaluate the manager on controllable factors, but controllability depends on what decisions managers can make. In a highly decentralised company such as Johnson & Johnson or Panasonic, for instance, managers can influence investments in assets and can exercise judgement regarding the appropriate amount of short-term credit and some long-term credit. Investment decisions that managers do not influence should not affect their performance evaluations.

Management by objectives and setting expectations

Management by objectives (MBO) describes the joint formulation by managers and their superiors of a set of goals and plans for achieving the goals for a forthcoming period. For our purposes here, the terms *goals* and *objectives* are synonymous. The plans often take the form of a responsibility accounting budget (together with supplementary goals, such as levels of management training and safety that managers may not incorporate into the accounting budget). The company then evaluates a manager's performance in relation to these agreed-on budgeted objectives. It is important that managers' expectations be consistent with those of their superiors.

An MBO approach tends to reduce complaints about lack of controllability because managers first agree on a reasonable budget. That is, a particular manager and their superior negotiate a budget for a particular period and a particular set of expected outside and inside influences. For example, by evaluating results compared to expectations, a manager may more readily accept an assignment to a less successful segment. Why? Because a manager can reasonably expect to meet goals that recognise that the segment is economically struggling. Thus, an MBO system is preferable to a system that emphasises absolute profitability for its own sake. Unless evaluation focuses on meeting reasonable expectations, able managers will be reluctant to accept responsibility for segments that are in economic trouble. Whether using MBO or not, skillful budgeting and intelligent performance evaluation will go a long way toward overcoming the common lament, 'I'm being held responsible for items beyond my control'.

MBO is also especially useful in nonprofit organisations where financial goals may be less important than nonfinancial goals. Managers can set objectives that fit well with overall organisational objectives. The 'Business first' box on p. 443 illustrates how an academic institution can use decentralisation to further the university's financial and nonfinancial objectives.

Budgets, performance targets and ethics

Organisations can minimise many of the troublesome motivational effects of performance evaluation systems by the astute use of budgets. We cannot overemphasise the desirability of tailoring budgets to a particular manager. For example, either an ROI or an economic profit system can promote goal congruence and managerial effort if top management gets everybody to focus on what is currently attainable in the forthcoming budget period.

Using budgets as performance targets also has its dangers. On pp. 283–5 of Chapter 7 we pointed out how misuse of budgets for performance evaluation can lead to lying and cheating. Companies that make meeting a budget too important when evaluating managers may motivate unethical behaviour. Top management at companies such as WorldCom gave 'making the numbers' such a high priority that, when it became clear that a segment would not meet its goals, managers fabricated the accounting reports. At Enron, the consequences of poor performance evaluations were so great that managers played bookkeeping games and allegedly manipulated electricity prices to make their performance look better. The lesson is that 'astute' use of budgets is good, but using budgets to put unreasonable pressure on managers can undermine the ethics of an organisation.

As we said earlier in the chapter, it is important to use measures that are consistent with organisational goals. Yet, measurement is only part of the management control system. Some accountants may be tempted to focus too much on the measurements. Managers should also think hard about how they use the measures to achieve the organisation's objectives. Even good measures can lead to dysfunctional decisions when managers misuse them. A management control system is only as good as the managers who use it.

BUSINESS FIRST
Decentralisation and teamwork across campuses

Alfred P. Sloan developed the concept of decentralisation; modern writers tout 'teamwork.' Many corporate models exist for the delegation of decision-making for charities, for non-profit organisations and for educational establishments like the Higher College of Technology (HCT) in the United Arab Emirates.

HCT decentralises decision making. Operating on 17 campuses located across the seven United Arab Emirates (UAE), this university has more than 20,000 students and over 2,000 faculty and staff. HCT provides 92 academic programmes for students; and 44,000 UAE nationals have graduated since the establishment of the first four campuses in 1987.

Consistency in the provision of educational services to students is essential. The dream is to contribute to national development through the education of its youth.

Something very special is happening in the UAE cities of Abu Dhabi, Madinat Zayed, Al Ain, Dubai, Ras Al Khaimah, Ruwais, Sharjah and Fujairah. HCT Colleges are providing a diversity of programmes in modern, technologically equipped campuses.

The chancellor of HCT appoints a director for each college. The director is responsible for finances and organisation. So each college operates like the national division of a multinational corporation. The colleges have a great deal of independence in addition to the highest quality in all programmes. HCT has put a rigorous programme quality assurance system (PQAS) in place for this purpose. HCT places a strong emphasis on international accreditation and benchmarking and each college also has its own separate budgets. Both nonfinancial and financial goals are consistent with the HCT philosophy of education, 'the lantern that lights your way in a dark alley', and the HCT commitment is to keep the lantern shining bright.

Since each college of HCT is responsible for its own revenues and expenses, the issues that arise day-to-day are similar to the issues faced by for-profit corporations. Like the corporate board of a multinational organisation, the board of HCT oversees the directors who are responsible for day-to-day operations. The board provides a vital resource, the opportunity for directors to share the issues that arise. This process is encouraged at every level so that the best solutions from the decentralised campuses are employed. Thus information from each of the campuses is generated to provide solution resources, but the board (quite intentionally) does not directly make decisions for each of the colleges – that is left to the directors.

In turn, the colleges share information within their organisations developing proprietary programmes and 'ownership' at each college location. So although independent of one another, the decentralised colleges work well together. As with multinational corporations difficulties can arise from time to time. interactions are inevitable among college faculties particularly, for example, when students admitted to one faculty take classes in another. As with multinational organisations a classic transfer-pricing problem arises. in this way HCT brings the advantages of local decision making and the accompanying superior motivation into HCT's overall philosophy of continuous improvement in higher education.

Highlights to remember

1 Define *decentralisation* and identify its expected benefits and costs. As companies grow, the ability of managers to effectively plan and control becomes more difficult because top managers are further removed from day-to-day operations. One approach to effective planning and control in large companies is to decentralise decision making. This means that top management gives mid- and lower-level managers the freedom to make decisions that impact the subunit's performance. The more that decision making is delegated, the greater the decentralisation. Often, the subunit manager is most knowledgeable of the factors that management should consider in the decision-making process.

2 Distinguish between responsibility centres and decentralisation. Top management must design the management control system so that it motivates managers to act in the

best interests of the company. This is done through the choice of responsibility centres and the appropriate performance metrics and rewards. The degree of decentralisation does not depend upon the type of responsibility centre chosen. For example, a cost-centre manager in one company may have more decision-making authority than does a profit-centre manager in a highly centralised company.

3 **Explain how the linking of rewards to responsibility-centre performance metrics affects incentives and risk.** It is generally a good idea to link managers' rewards to responsibility-centre results to promote goal congruence. However, linking rewards to results creates risk for the manager. The greater the influence of uncontrollable factors on a manager's reward, the more risk the manager bears.

4 **Compute ROI, economic profit and economic value added (EVA) and contrast them as criteria for judging the performance of organisation segments.** It is typical to measure the results of investment centres using a set of performance metrics that include financial measures, such as return on investment (ROI), economic profit, or economic value added (EVA). ROI is any income measure divided by the dollar amount invested and is expressed as a percentage. Economic profit, or economic value added, is operating income less a capital charge based on the capital invested (cost of capital). It is an absolute money amount.

5 **Compare the advantages and disadvantages of various bases for measuring the invested capital used by organisation segments.** The way an organisation measures invested capital determines the precise motivation provided by ROI, economic profit or EVA. Managers will try to reduce assets or increase liabilities that a company includes in their division's investment base. They will adopt more conservative asset replacement policies if the company uses net book value rather than gross book value in measuring the assets.

6 **Define *transfer prices* and identify their purpose.** In large companies with many different segments, one segment often provides products or services to another segment. Deciding on the amount the selling division should charge the buying division for these transfers (the transfer price) is difficult. Companies use various types of transfer pricing policies. The overall purpose of transfer prices is to motivate managers to act in the best interests of the company, not just their segment.

7 **State the general rule for transfer pricing and use it to assess transfer prices based on total costs, variable costs and market prices.** As a general rule, transfer prices should approximate the outlay cost plus opportunity cost of the producing segment. Each type of transfer price has its own advantages and disadvantages. Each has a situation where it works best and each can lead to dysfunctional decisions in some instances. When a competitive market exists for the product or service, using market-based transfer prices usually leads to goal congruence and optimal decisions. When idle capacity exists in the segment providing the product or service, the use of variable cost as the transfer price usually leads to goal congruence. Cost-based prices are readily available but should usually be based on planned, rather than actual, costs. If a company uses actual costs, there is little incentive for the selling segment manager to minimise costs and the receiving segment manager does not know the cost in advance, which makes cost planning difficult.

8 **Identify the factors affecting multinational transfer prices.** Multinational organisations often use transfer prices as a means of minimising worldwide income taxes, import duties and tariffs.

9 **Explain how controllability and management by objectives (MBO) aid the implementation of management control systems.** Regardless of what measures a management control system uses, measures used to evaluate managers should focus on only the controllable aspects of performance. MBO can focus attention on performance compared to expectations, which is better than evaluations based on absolute profitability. Misuse of budgets and performance metrics can motivate managers to violate ethical standards. ■

Accounting vocabulary

agency theory, p. 421
capital charge, p. 425
capital turnover, p. 424
centralisation, p. 418
cost of capital, p. 425
decentralisation, p. 417
dysfunctional decisions, p. 435
economic profit, p. 425

economic value added
(EVA), p. 425
gross book value, p. 430
incentives, p. 420
management by objectives
(MBO), p. 442
net book value, p. 430
net operating profit after-tax
(NOPAT), p. 425

performance metric, p. 420
residual income, p. 425
return on investment
(ROI), p. 423
return on sales, p. 424
segment autonomy, p. 419
transfer price, p. 432

Fundamental assignment material   MyAccountingLab

10.A1 ROI and economic profit calculations

Consider the following data (in thousands):

	Division		
	Tinker	Evers	Chance
Average invested capital	€2,000	€ 600	€1,800
Revenue	3,600	1,200	9,000
Income	180	126	360

1 For each division, compute the return on sales, the capital turnover and the return on investment (ROI).

2 Which division is the best performer if evaluation is based on ROI? Explain.

3 Suppose each division is assessed a cost of capital of 10 per cent on invested capital. Compute the economic profit for each division. Which division is the best performer based on economic profit? Explain.

10.A2 Transfer-pricing dispute

Bern Équipement, SA, a Swiss transportation equipment manufacturer, is heavily decentralised. Each division head has full authority on all decisions regarding sales to internal or external customers. The Graubunden division has always acquired a certain equipment component from the Ticino division. The Ticino division recently acquired specialised equipment that is used primarily to make this component. Because of the new depreciation charges on the equipment, the Ticino division has informed the Graubunden division that the unit price will be increased to CHF 325. However, the Graubunden division's management has now decided to purchase the component from outside suppliers at a price of CHF 300.

The Ticino division has supplied the following production cost data for this component:

Annual production of component (all for sale to Graubunden division)	3,000 units
Ticino's variable costs per unit	CHF 280
Ticino's fixed costs per unit	CHF 30

1 Suppose there are no alternative uses of the Ticino facilities and that fixed costs will continue if Ticino no longer produces the component for Graubunden. Will the company as a whole benefit if the Graubunden division buys from the outside suppliers for CHF 300 per unit? Show computations to support your answer.

2 Suppose there is an alternative use for the Ticino facilities. If the Ticino facilities are used to produce the component for the Graubunden division, the Ticino division will give up a contribution of CHF 75,000 from this alternative use. Should the Graubunden division purchase from outsiders at CHF 300 per unit?

3 Suppose that there are no alternative uses for Ticino's internal facilities and that the outsiders' selling price drops by CHF 30 to CHF 270. Should the Graubunden division purchase from outsiders?

4 As the president, how would you respond if the Ticino division manager's requests that you require the Graubunden division to purchase the component from Ticino? Would your response differ depending on the specific situations described in numbers 1–3 above? Why?

10.A3 Transfer pricing

Refer to problem 10.A2, number 1 only. Suppose the Ticino division could modify the component at an additional variable cost of CHF 17 per unit and sell the 3,000 units to other customers for CHF 325. Then, would the entire company benefit if the Graubunden division purchased the 3,000 components from outsiders at CHF 300 per unit?

10.A4 Rate of return and transfer pricing

Consider the following data regarding budgeted operations for 20X7 of the Portland division of Machine Products:

Average total assets	
Receivables	€220,000
Inventories	290,000
Plant and equipment, net	450,000
Total	€960,000
Fixed overhead	€300,000
Variable costs	€1 per unit
Desired rate of return on average total assets	25%
Expected volume	150,000 units

1 (a) What average unit sales price does the Portland division need to obtain its desired rate of return on average total assets?
 (b) What would be the expected capital turnover?
 (c) What would be the return on sales?
2 (a) If the selling price is as previously computed, what rate of return will the division earn on total assets if sales volume is 170,000 units?
 (b) If sales volume is 130,000 units?
3 Assume that the Portland division plans to sell 45,000 units to the Calgary division of Machine Products and that it can sell only 105,000 units to outside customers at the price computed in requirement 1a. The Calgary division manager has balked at a tentative transfer price of €4. She has offered €2.25, claiming that she can manufacture the units herself for that price. The Portland division manager has examined his own data. He had decided that he could eliminate €60,000 of inventories, €90,000 of plant and equipment, and

€22,500 of fixed overhead if he did not sell to the Calgary division and sold only 105,000 units to outside customers. Should he sell for €2.25? Show computations to support your answer.

10.B1 ROI or economic profit

Melbourne Co. is a large integrated Australian conglomerate with shipping, metals and mining operations throughout Asia. Melbourne is just starting a new manufacturing division and the newly-appointed general manager plans to submit a proposed capital budget for 20X8 for inclusion in the companywide budget.

The division manager has for consideration the following projects, all of which require an outlay of capital. All projects have equal risk.

Project	Investment required	Return
1	$4,800,000	$1,200,000
2	1,900,000	627,000
3	1,400,000	182,000
4	950,000	152,000
5	650,000	136,500
6	300,000	90,000

The division manager must decide which of the projects to take. The company has a cost of capital of 20 per cent. An amount of 12 million is available to the division for investment purposes.

1 What will be the total investment, total return, return on capital invested and economic profit of the rational division manager if
   (a) the company has a rule that managers should accept all projects promising a return on investment of at least 15 per cent?
   (b) the company evaluates division managers on their ability to maximise the return on capital invested (assume this is a new division so that invested capital will consist only of capital invested in new projects adopted by the manager)?
   (c) the division manager is expected to maximise economic profit computed using the 20 per cent cost of capital?
2 Which of the three approaches will induce the most effective investment policy for the company as a whole? Explain.

10.B2 Computing EVA

A company that uses EVA reported the following results for 20X4 and 20X5 (in millions):

	20X4	20X5
Pretax operating income	€5,698	5,700
Cash taxes	1,676	1,600

Average adjusted invested capital was €20,308 million in 20X4 and €18,091 million in 20X5, and the cost of capital was 9 per cent in both 20X4 and 20X5.

1 Compute the company's EVA for 20X4 and 20X5.
2 Compare the company's performance in creating value for its shareholders in 20X5 with that in 20X4.

10.B3 Transfer pricing

ISCTE Enterprises runs a chain of drive-in ice cream stands in Lisbon during the summer season. Managers of all stands are told to act as if they owned the stand and are judged on their profit performance. ISCTE Enterprises has rented an ice cream machine for the summer for €3,600 to supply its stands with ice cream. ISCTE is not allowed to sell ice cream to other dealers because it cannot obtain a dairy license. The manager of the ice cream machine charges the stands €4 per gallon. Operating figures for the machine for the summer are as follows:

Sales to the stands (16,000 gallons at €4)		€64,000
Variable costs, at €2.10 per gallon	€33,600	
Fixed costs		
Rental of machine	3,600	
Other fixed costs	10,000	47,200
Operating margin		€16,800

The manager of the Porto Drive-In, one of the ISCTE drive-ins, is seeking permission to sign a contract to buy ice cream from an outside supplier at €3.35 a gallon. The Porto Drive-In uses 4,000 gallons of ice cream during the summer. Victor Franco, chief accountant at ISCTE, refers this request to you. You determine that the other fixed costs of operating the machine will decrease by €900 if the Porto Drive-In purchases from an outside supplier. Franco wants an analysis of the request in terms of overall company objectives and an explanation of your conclusion. What is the appropriate transfer price?

10.B4 Rate of return and transfer pricing

The Tokyo division of Kaycee Toy Company manufactures units of the game Shogi and sells them in the Japanese market for ¥7,200 each. The following data are from the Tokyo division's 20X8 budget:

Variable cost	¥	5,000 per unit
Fixed overhead	¥	6,080,000
Total assets	¥	12,500,000

Kaycee has instructed the Tokyo division to budget a rate of return on total assets (before taxes) of 20 per cent.

1 Suppose the Tokyo division expects to sell 3,400 games during 20X8.
   (a) What rate of return will be earned on total assets?
   (b) What would be the expected capital turnover?
   (c) What would be the return on sales?
2 The Tokyo division is considering adjustments in the budget to reach the desired 20 per cent rate of return on total assets.
   (a) How many units must be sold to obtain the desired return if no other part of the budget is changed?
   (b) Suppose sales cannot be increased beyond 3,400 units. How much must total assets be reduced to obtain the desired return? Assume that for every ¥1,000 decrease in total assets, fixed costs decrease by ¥100.
3 Assume that only 2,400 units can be sold in the Japanese market. However, another 1,400 units can be sold to the European marketing division of Kaycee. The Tokyo manager has offered to sell the 1,400 units for ¥6,700 each. The European marketing division manager has countered with an offer to pay ¥6,200 per unit, claiming that she can subcontract

production to an Italian producer at a cost equivalent to ¥6,200. The Tokyo manager knows that if his production falls to 2,400 units, he could eliminate some assets, reducing total assets to ¥10 million and annual fixed overhead to ¥4.9 million. Should the Tokyo manager sell for ¥6,200 per unit? Support your answer with the relevant computations. Ignore the effects of income taxes and import duties.

Additional assignment material

MyAccountingLab

QUESTIONS

10.1 'Decentralisation has benefits and costs.' Name three of each.

10.2 Sophisticated accounting and communications systems aid decentralisation. Explain how they accomplish this.

10.3 Why is decentralisation more popular in profit-seeking organisations than in non-profit organisations?

10.4 'The essence of decentralisation is the use of profit centres.' Do you agree? Explain.

10.5 What kinds of organisations find decentralisation to be preferable to centralisation?

10.6 According to agency theory, employment contracts balance what three factors?

10.7 What is the major benefit of the ROI technique for measuring performance?

10.8 What two major items affect ROI?

10.9 How does economic profit differ from net income?

10.10 Define *economic value added (EVA)* and describe three ways a company can improve its EVA.

10.11 Division A's ROI is 20 per cent and B's is 10 per cent. The company pays each division manager a bonus based on his or her division's ROI. Discuss whether each division manager would accept or reject a proposed project with a rate of return of 15 per cent. Would either of them make a different decision if the company evaluated managers using economic profit with a capital charge of 11 per cent? Explain.

10.12 Give three possible definitions of invested capital that we can use in measuring ROI or economic profit.

10.13 'Managers who use a historical-cost accounting system look backward at what something cost yesterday, instead of forward to what it will cost tomorrow.' Do you agree? Why?

10.14 Ross Company uses net book value as a measure of invested capital when computing ROI. A division manager has suggested that the company change to using gross book value instead. What difference in motivation of division managers might result from such a change? Do you suppose most of the assets in the division of the manager proposing the change are relatively new or old? Why?

10.15 Why do companies need transfer-pricing systems?

10.16 Describe two problems that can arise when using actual full cost as a transfer price.

10.17 How does the presence or absence of idle capacity affect the optimal transfer-pricing policy?

10.18 'We use variable-cost transfer prices to ensure that we make no dysfunctional decisions.' Discuss.

10.19 What is the major advantage of negotiated transfer prices? What is the major disadvantage?

10.20 Discuss two factors that affect multinational transfer prices but have little effect on purely domestic transfers.

10.21 Describe management by objectives (MBO).

10.22 How can performance measurement lead to unethical behaviour by managers?

CRITICAL THINKING EXERCISES

10.23 Decentralisation

Many companies implement organisational changes to centralise or decentralise operations only to follow with later changes in the opposite direction. Why might a company that at one time decentralises decide later to centralise?

10.24 Comparing financial measures of performance

'Both ROI and economic profit use profit and invested capital to measure performance. Therefore it really doesn't matter which we use.' Do you agree? Explain.

10.25 Transfer pricing and organisational behaviour

The principal reason for transfer-pricing systems is to communicate data that will lead to goal-congruent decisions by managers of different business units. When managers take actions that conflict with organisational goals, dysfunctional behaviour exists. Why does top management sometimes accept a division manager's judgements, even if the division manager appears to behave in a dysfunctional manner?

EXERCISES

10.26 Simple ROI calculations

You are given the following data:

Sales	€120,000,000
Invested capital	€ 60,000,000
Net income	€ 6,000,000

Compute the following:

1 Turnover of capital
2 Return on sales
3 Return on investment (ROI).

10.27 Simple ROI calculation

Fill in the blanks:

	Division		
	A	B	C
Return on sales	7%	3%	__%
Capital turnover	3	—	4
Rate of return on invested capital	__%	18%	20%

10.28 Simple ROI and economic profit calculations

Consider the following data:

	Division		
	X	Y	Z
Invested capital	€1,000,000	€ _____	€1,250,000
Income	€ _____	€ 182,000	€ 162,500
Revenue	€2,500,000	€3,640,000	€ _____
Return on sales	4%	_____ %	_____ %
Capital turnover	_____	_____	3
Rate of return on invested capital	_____ %	14%	_____ %

1 Prepare a similar tabular presentation, filling in all blanks.

2 Suppose each division is assessed a capital charge based on a cost of capital of 12% of invested capital. Compute the economic profit for each division.

3 Which division is the best performer? Explain.

10.29 Comparison of asset and equity bases

Laurel Company has assets of €2 million and long-term, 10 per cent debt of €1,200,000. Hardy Company has assets of €2 million and no long-term debt. The annual operating income (before interest) of both companies is €400,000. Ignore taxes.

1 Compute the rate of return on
    (a) assets, and
    (b) stockholders' equity.

2 Evaluate the relative merits of each base for appraising operating management.

10.30 Finding unknowns

Consider the following data:

	Division		
	J	K	L
Income	€280,000	€ _____	€ _____
Revenue	€ _____	€ _____	€ _____
Invested capital	€ _____	€3,000,000	€16,000,000
Return on sales	7%	4%	_____ %
Capital turnover	4	_____	3
Rate of return on invested capital	_____ %	20%	15%
Cost of capital	16%	12%	_____ %
Economic profit	€ _____	€ _____	€ 320,000

1 Prepare a similar tabular presentation, filling in all blanks.
2 Which division is the best performer? Explain.

10.31 Gross versus net asset value

The St Cloud division of Upcraft Company just purchased an asset for €180,000. The asset has a 3-year life. Upcraft's top management evaluates Freida Ramirez, manager of the St Cloud division, based on ROI for this asset. She can choose to measure the asset using either gross asset value or net asset value. Her operating income before depreciation each year is €80,000.

1 What is the St Cloud division's ROI for each of the 3 years using the gross asset value?
2 What is the St Cloud division's ROI for each of the 3 years using the net asset value?
3 If Ramirez expects Upcraft to transfer her to a different division in about a year, which asset valuation policy would she prefer?

10.32 Variable cost as a transfer price

A chair's variable cost is €50 and its market value as a piece of unfinished furniture is €63 at a transfer point from the assembly division to the finishing division. The finishing division's variable cost of sanding and finishing the chair is €28, and the selling price of the finished chair is €85.

1 Prepare a tabulation of the contribution margin per unit for the finishing division's performance and overall company performance under the two alternatives of (a) selling to outsiders at the transfer point and (b) sanding and finishing the chair and then selling to outsiders.
2 As finishing division manager, which alternative would you choose? Explain.

10.33 Maximum and minimum transfer price

Sherwin Company makes bicycles. Various divisions make components and transfer them to the Dayton division for assembly into final products. The Dayton division can also buy components from external suppliers. The Toledo division makes the wheels and it also sells wheels to external customers. All divisions are profit centres and managers are free to negotiate transfer prices. Prices and costs for the Toledo and Dayton divisions are as follows:

Toledo Division

Sales price to external customers	€ 14
Internal transfer price	?
Costs	
Variable costs per wheel	€ 10
Total fixed costs	€320,000
Budgeted production	64,000 wheels*

*Includes production for transfer to Dayton

Dayton Division

Sales price to external customers	€ 170
Costs	
Wheels, per bicycle	?
Other components, per bicycle	€ 85
Other variable costs, per bicycle	€ 45
Total fixed costs	€640,000
Budgeted production	16,000 bicycles

Fixed costs in both divisions will be unaffected by the transfer of wheels from Toledo to Dayton.

1 Compute the maximum transfer price per wheel the Dayton division would be willing to pay to buy wheels from the Toledo division.
2 Compute the minimum transfer price per wheel at which the Toledo division would be willing to produce and sell wheels to the Dayton division. Assume that Toledo has excess capacity.

10.34 Multinational transfer prices

Cambridge International has production and marketing divisions throughout the world. It produces one particular product in Scotland, where the income tax rate is 12 per cent and transfers it to a marketing division in Japan, where the income tax rate is 40 per cent. Assume that Japan places an import tax of 10 per cent on the product and that import duties are not deductible for income tax purposes.

The variable cost of the product is £200 and the full cost is £400. Suppose the company can legally select a transfer price anywhere between the variable and full cost.

1 What transfer price should Cambridge International use to minimise taxes? Explain why this is the tax-minimising transfer price.
2 Compute the amount of taxes saved by using the transfer price in requirement 1 instead of the transfer price that would result in the highest taxes.

PROBLEMS

10.35 Agency theory

The Tamura International Trading Company plans to hire a manager for its division in Nice. Tamura International's president and vice president of personnel are trying to decide on an appropriate incentive employment contract. The manager will operate far from the Tokyo corporate headquarters, so evaluation by personal observation will be limited. The president insists that a large incentive to produce profits is necessary; he favours a salary of ¥150,000 and a bonus of 10 per cent of the profits above ¥1,200,000. If operations proceed as expected, profits will be ¥4,600,000, and the manager will receive ¥490,000. But both profits and compensation might be more or less than planned.

The vice president of personnel responds that ¥490,000 is more than most of Tamura International's division managers make. She is sure that the company can hire a competent manager for a guaranteed salary of ¥400,000. She argued, 'Why pay ¥490,000 when we can probably hire the same person for ¥400,000?'

1 What factors would affect Tamura International's choice of employment contract? Include a discussion of the pros and cons of each proposed contract.
2 Why is the expected compensation more with the bonus plan than with the straight salary?

10.36 Margins and turnover

Accountants often express ROI as the product of two components – capital turnover and return on sales. You are considering investing in one of three companies, all in the same industry and are given the following information:

	Company		
	Abel	Baker	Charlie
Sales	€6,000,000	€ 2,500,000	€37,500,000
Income	€ 600,000	€ 375,000	€ 375,000
Capital	€3,000,000	€12,500,000	€12,500,000

1 Why would you desire the breakdown of return on investment into return on sales and turnover on capital?
2 Compute the return on sales, turnover on capital and ROI for the three companies and comment on the relative performance of the companies as thoroughly as the data permit.
3 Notice that Baker and Charlie have the same income and capital but vastly different levels of sales. Discuss the types of industries that Baker and Charlie might be in.

10.37 ROI by business segment

Multimedia Technology does business in three different business segments: (1) entertainment, (2) publishing/information and (3) consumer/commercial finance. Results for a recent year were as follows (in millions):

	Revenues	Operating income	Total assets
Entertainment	€1,272	€223	€1,120
Publishing/Information	€ 705	€122	€1,308
Consumer/Commercial Finance	€1,235	€244	€ 924

1 Compute the following for each business segment:
   (a) Return on sales
   (b) Capital turnover
   (c) ROI.
2 Comment on the differences in ROI among the business segments. Include reasons for the differences.

10.38 EVA at Hershey

The Hershey Company manufactures, distributes and sells many items with the Hershey brand name. It also has many other brands including Almond Joy, Kit Kat, Milk Duds and Twizzler. Its financial results for two recent fiscal years included the following (in millions):

	Year 2	Year 1
Revenues	$4,836	$4,429
Operating expenses	3,975	3,548
Cash Income taxes	280	237
Average invested capital (total assets less current liabilities)	$2,654	$2,764

1 Suppose that Hershey's cost of capital is 9.5 per cent. Compute the company's EVA for years 1 and 2. Assume definitions of after-tax operating income and invested capital as reported in Hershey's annual reports without adjustments advocated by Stern Stewart or others.
2 Discuss the change in EVA between years 1 and 2.

10.39 Evaluation of divisional performance

As the CEO of Friendly Hardware Company, you examined the following measures of the performance of three divisions (in thousands of euros):

Division	Average net assets based on		Operating income based on*	
	Historical cost	Replacement cost	Historical cost	Replacement cost
Tools	€15,000	€15,000	€2,600	€2,600
Appliances	44,000	55,000	6,750	6,150
Lighting	27,000	48,000	5,000	3,900

*The differences in operating income between historical and replacement cost are attributable to the differences in depreciation expenses.

1 Calculate for each division the rate of return on net assets and the economic profit based on historical cost and on replacement cost. For purposes of calculating economic profit, use 10% as the minimum desired rate of return.

2 Rank the performance of each division under each of the four different measures computed in number 1.

3 What do these measures indicate about the performance of the divisions? Of the division managers? Which measure do you prefer? Why?

10.40 Use of gross or net book value of fixed assets

Assume that a machine shop acquires £600,000 of fixed assets with a useful life of 4 years and no residual value. The shop uses straight-line depreciation. The company judges the shop manager based on income in relation to these fixed assets. Annual net income, after deducting depreciation, is £60,000.

Assume that sales, and all expenses except depreciation, are on a cash basis. Dividends equal net income. Thus, cash in the amount of the depreciation charge will accumulate each year. The plant manager's performance is judged in relation to fixed assets because all current assets, including cash, are considered under central-company control. Assume (unrealistically) that any cash accumulated remains idle. Ignore taxes.

1 Prepare a comparative tabulation of the plant's rate of return and the company's overall rate of return based on
(a) gross (i.e., original cost) assets;
(b) net book value of assets.

2 Evaluate the relative merits of gross assets and net book value of assets as investment bases.

10.41 Profit centres and transfer pricing in a car dealership

A large car dealership in Belgrade is installing a responsibility accounting system and three profit centres: parts and service, new vehicles and used vehicles. Top management has told the three department managers to run their shops as if they were in business for themselves. However, there are interdepartmental dealings. For example,
(a) the parts and service department prepares new cars for final delivery and repairs used cars prior to resale;
(b) the used-car department's major source of inventory has been cars traded in as partial payment for new cars.

The owner of the dealership has asked you to draft a company policy statement on transfer pricing, together with specific rules to be applied to the examples cited. He has told you that clarity is of paramount importance because he will rely on your statement for settling transfer-pricing disputes.

10.42 Transfer pricing

The shocks and struts division of Transnational Motors Company produces strut assemblies for cars. It has been the sole supplier of strut assemblies to the automotive division and charges €45 per unit, the current market price for very large wholesale lots. The shocks and struts division also sells to outside retail outlets, at €57 per unit. Normally, outside sales amount to 25 per cent of a total sales volume of 1 million strut assemblies per year. Typical combined annual data for the division follow:

Sales	€48,000,000	
Variable costs, at €37.50 per strut assembly		€37,500,000
Fixed costs		4,500,000
Total costs	€42,000,000	
Gross margin	€ 6,000,000	

Flint Auto Parts Company, an entirely separate entity, has offered the automotive division comparable strut assemblies at a firm price of €42 per unit. The shocks and struts division of Transnational Motors claims that it cannot possibly match this price because it could not earn any margin at €42.

1 Assume that you are the manager of the automotive division of Transnational Motors. Comment on the shocks and struts division's claim. Assume that normal outside volume cannot be increased.

2 Now assume the shocks and struts division believes that it can increase outside sales by 750,000 strut assemblies per year by increasing fixed costs by €3 million and variable costs by €4.50 per unit while reducing the selling price to €54. Assume that maximum capacity is 1 million strut assemblies per year. Should the division reject intracompany business and concentrate on outside sales?

10.43 Transfer-pricing concession

You are the divisional accountant of the US division of Samtech Electronics. Your division is operating at capacity. The Australian division has asked the US division to supply a sound system (chip and speaker), which it will use in a new model Game Box that it is introducing. The US division currently sells identical sound systems to outside customers at $11.00 each.

The Australian division has offered to pay $7.00 for each sound system. The total cost of the

Purchased parts from outside vendors	$28.10
Sound system from US division	7.00
Other variable costs	17.50
Fixed overhead	10.00
Total	$62.60

Game Box is as follows:

The Australian division is operating at 50 per cent of capacity, and this Game Box is an important new product introduction to increase its use of capacity. Based on a target-costing approach, the Australian division management has decided that paying more than $7.00 for the sound system would make production of the Game Box infeasible because the predicted selling price for the Game Box is only $62.00.

Samtech Electronics evaluates divisional managers on the basis of pretax ROI and dollar profits compared to the budget. Ignore taxes and tariffs.

1 As divisional accountant of the US division, would you recommend supplying the sound system to the Australian division for $7.00 each? Why or why not?

2 Would it be to the short-run economic advantage of Samtech Electronics for the US division to supply the sound system to the Australian division? Explain your answer.

3 Discuss the organisational and behavioural difficulties, if any, inherent in this situation. As the US division accountant, what would you advise the Samtech Electronics president to do in this situation?

10.44 Transfer prices and idle capacity

The Eugene division of Union Furniture purchases lumber, which it uses to fabricate tables, chairs and other wood furniture. It purchases most of the lumber from Shasta Mill, also a division of Union Furniture. Both the Eugene division and Shasta Mill are profit centres.

The Eugene division proposes to produce a new Shaker-style chair that will sell for €95. The manager is exploring the possibility of purchasing the required lumber from Shasta Mill. Production of 800 chairs is planned, using capacity in the Eugene division that is currently idle.

The Eugene division can purchase the lumber needed for one chair from an outside supplier for €72. Union Furniture has a policy that internal transfers are priced at fully allocated cost.

Assume the following costs for the production of one chair and the lumber required for the chair:

Shasta Mill – lumber cost		Eugene Division – chair cost		
Variable cost	€48	Variable costs		
Allocated fixed cost	22	Lumber from Shasta Mill		€70
Fully allocated cost	€70	Eugene division variable costs		
		Manufacturing	€23	
		Selling	6	29
		Total variable cost		€99

1 Assume that the Shasta Mill has idle capacity and, therefore, would incur no additional fixed costs to produce the required lumber. Would the Eugene division manager buy the lumber for the chair from the Shasta Mill, given the existing transfer-pricing policy? Why or why not? Would the company as a whole benefit if the manager decides to buy from the Shasta Mill? Explain.

2 Assume that there is no idle capacity at the Shasta Mill and the lumber required for one chair can be sold to outside customers for €72. Would the company as a whole benefit if the Eugene manager buys from Shasta? Explain.

10.45 Negotiated transfer prices

The Lighting division of Ibex Office Furniture needs 1,200 units of a leaded-glass lamp shade from the fabricating division. The company has a policy of negotiated transfer prices. The fabricating division has enough excess capacity to produce 2,000 units of the lamp shade. Its variable cost of production is €23. The market price of the lamp shade to external customers is €39.

What is the natural bargaining range for a transfer price between the two divisions? Explain why no price below your range would be acceptable. Also explain why no price above your range would be acceptable.

10.46 Transfer prices and minority interests

This chapter discussed transferring profits between divisions of a multinational company. Another situation where transfer prices have a similar effect is when a parent company transfers items to or from a subsidiary when there are minority shareholders in the subsidiary. Consider the Michelin Group and its Polish subsidiary, Stomil Olsztyn, of which Michelin owns 70 per cent. Michelin buys tyres from Stomil Olsztyn at a transfer price. Since Michelin owns a majority of Stomil Olsztyn, it controls the transfer-pricing policy. The holders of the other 30 per cent of Stomil Olsztyn claim that Michelin sets the transfer prices too low, thereby reducing the profits of Stomil Olsztyn. They maintain that Stomil Olsztyn would be more profitable if it were allowed to sell its tyres on the market rather than transfer them to Michelin. In reply, Michelin managers maintain that Stomil Olsztyn is more profitable than other members of the Michelin Group and, therefore, the transfer prices must be fair.

Discuss the incentives for Michelin to transfer tyres at a low price from Stomil Olsztyn to its Michelin parent. What transfer price do the minority shareholders in Stomil Olsztyn favour? Use an example of a tyre that Stomil Olsztyn produces at a variable cost of €20 that is transferred to Michelin for €25. How should Michelin and Stomil Olsztyn establish a fair transfer price?

10.47 Multinational transfer prices

American Medical Instruments produces a variety of medical products at its plant in Minneapolis. The company has sales divisions worldwide. One of these sales divisions is located in Uppsala, Sweden. Assume that the US income tax rate is 34 per cent, the Swedish rate is 60 per cent, and a 12 per cent import duty is imposed on medical supplies brought into Sweden.

One product produced in Minneapolis and shipped to Sweden is a heart defibrillator. The variable cost of production is $400 per unit and the fully allocated cost is $650 per unit.

1 Suppose the Swedish and US governments allow either the variable or fully allocated cost to be used as a transfer price. Which price should American Medical Instruments choose to minimise the total of income taxes and import duties? Compute the amount the company saves if it uses your suggested transfer price instead of the alternative. Assume import duties are not deductible for tax purposes.

2 Suppose the Swedish parliament passed a law decreasing the income tax rate to 50 per cent and increasing the duty on heart monitors to 20 per cent. Repeat number 1, using these new facts.

10.48 Review of major points in this chapter

The European Instruments Company uses the decentralised form of organisational structure and considers each of its divisions as an investment centre. The T division is currently selling 15,000 air filters annually, although it has sufficient productive capacity to produce 21,000 units per year. Variable manufacturing costs amount to $21 per unit, while the total fixed costs amount to $90,000. These 15,000 air filters are sold to outside customers at $40 per unit.

The M division, also a part of European Instruments, has indicated that it would like to buy 1,500 air filters from the T division, but at a price of $37 per unit. This is the price the M division is currently paying an outside supplier.

1 Compute the effect on the operating income of the company as a whole if the M division purchases the 1,500 air filters from the T division.

2 What is the minimum price that the T division should be willing to accept for these 1,500 air filters?

3 What is the maximum price that the M division should be willing to pay for these 1,500 air filters?

4 Suppose instead that the T division is currently producing and selling 21,000 air filters annually to outside customers. What is the effect on the overall Canadian Instruments Company operating income if the T division is required by top management to sell 1,500 air filters to the M division at (a) €21 per unit and (b) €37 per unit?

5 For this question only, assume that the T division is currently earning an annual operating income of €36,000 and the division's average invested capital is €300,000. The division manager has an opportunity to invest in a proposal that will require an additional investment of €20,000 and will increase annual operating income by €2,000. (a) Should the division manager accept this proposal if the European Instruments Company uses ROI in evaluating the performance of its divisional managers? (b) If the company uses economic profit? (Assume a cost of capital of 7 per cent.)

CASES

10.49 Profit centres and central services

Star Manufacturing, manufacturer of Starlite brand small appliances, has a process engineering department (PED). The department's major task has been to help the production departments improve their operating methods and processes.

For several years, Star Manufacturing has charged the cost of consulting services to the production departments based on a signed agreement between the managers involved. The agreement specifies the scope of the project, the predicted savings and the number of consulting hours required. The charge to the production departments is based on the costs to the Engineering Department of the services rendered. For example, senior engineer hours cost more per hour than junior engineer hours. An overhead cost is included. The agreement is really a 'fixed-price' contract. That is, the production manager knows the total cost of the project in advance. A recent survey revealed that production managers have a high level of confidence in the engineers.

The PED department manager oversees the work of about 40 engineers and 10 technicians. She reports to the engineering manager, who reports to the vice president of manufacturing. The PED manager has the freedom to increase or decrease the number of engineers under her supervision. The PED manager's performance evaluation is based on many factors including the annual incremental savings to the company in excess of the costs of operating the PED department.

The production departments are profit centres. Their goods are transferred to subsequent departments, such as a sales department or sales division, at prices that approximate market prices for similar products.

Top management is seriously considering a 'no-charge' plan. That is, production departments would receive engineering services at absolutely no cost. Proponents of the new plan maintain that it would motivate the production managers to take better advantage of engineering talent. In all other respects, the new system would be unchanged from the present system.

1 Compare the present and proposed plans. What are their strong and weak points? In particular, will the PED manager tend to hire the 'optimal' amount of engineering talent?
2 Which plan do you favour? Why?

10.50 Management by objectives

Roger Ravenhill is the CEO of Haida Company. Ravenhill has a financial management background and is known throughout the organisation as a 'no-nonsense' executive. When Ravenhill became CEO, he emphasised cost reduction and savings and introduced a comprehensive cost control and budget system. The company goals and budget plans were established by Ravenhill and given to his subordinates for implementation. Some of the company's key executives were dismissed or demoted for failing to meet projected budget plans. Under the leadership of Roger Ravenhill, Haida has once again become financially stable and profitable after several years of poor performance.

Recently, Ravenhill has become concerned with the human side of the organisation and has become interested in the management technique referred to as 'management by objectives' (MBO). If there are enough positive benefits of MBO, he plans to implement the system throughout the company. However, he realises that he does not fully understand MBO because he does not understand how it differs from the current system of establishing firm objectives and budget plans.

1 Briefly explain what MBO entails and identify its advantages and disadvantages.
2 Does Roger Ravenhill's management style incorporate the human-value premises and goals of MBO? Explain your answer.

CASE STUDY

Empire Glass Company (A)

David F. Hawkins

Peter Small of the Harvard Business School undertook to write case material on the budgetary control system of the Empire Glass Company, a manufacturing company with a number of plants located throughout Canada. In particular, Peter Small was interested in how James Walker, the corporate controller, saw the company's budgetary control system. Therefore, Small focused his research on the budgetary control system in relationship to the company's Glass Products Division. This division was responsible for manufacturing and selling glass food-and-beverage bottles.

Organisation

Empire Glass Company was a diversified company organised into several major product divisions, one of which was the Glass Products Division. Each division was headed by a vice president who reported directly to the company's executive vice president, Landon McGregor. (Figure A shows an organisation chart of the company's top management group.) All of the corporate and divisional management groups were located in British City, Canada.

McGregor's corporate staff included three people in the financial area – the controller, the chief accountant and the treasurer. The controller's department consisted of only two people – Walker and the assistant controller, Allen Newell. The market research and labour relations departments also reported in a staff capacity to McGregor.

All of the product divisions were organised along similar lines. Reporting to each product division vice president were several staff members in the customer service and product research areas. Reporting in a line capacity to each divisional vice president were also a general manager of manufacturing (responsible for all of the division's manufacturing activities) and a general manager of marketing (responsible for all of the division's marketing activities). Both of these executives were assisted by a small staff of specialists. Figure B presents an organisation chart of the Glass Products Division's top management group. Figure C shows the typical organisation structure of a plant within the Glass Products Division.

Products and technology

The Glass Products Division operated a number of plants in Canada, producing glass food-and-beverage bottles. Of these products, food jars constituted the largest group. Milk bottles, as well as beer and soft drink bottles, were also produced in large quantities. A great variety of shapes and sizes of containers for wines, liquors, drugs, cosmetics and chemicals were produced in smaller quantities.

Most of the thousands of different products, varying in size, shape, colour and decoration were produced to order. According to British City executives, the typical lead time between the customer's order and shipment from the plant was between two and three weeks.

The principal raw materials for container glass were sand, soda ash and lime. The first step in the manufacturing process was to melt batches of these materials in furnaces or tanks. The molten mass was then passed into automatic or semiautomatic machines which filled moulds with the molten glass and blew the glass into the desired shape. The 'ware' then went through an automatic annealing oven or lehr where it was cooled slowly under carefully controlled conditions. If the glass was to be coated on the exterior to increase its resistance to abrasion and scratches, this coating – often a silicone film – was applied in the lehr. Any decorating (such as a trademark or other design) was then added, the product inspected again and the finished goods packed in corrugated containers (or wooden cases for some bottles).

Quality inspection was critical in the manufacturing process. If the melt in the furnace was not completely free from bubbles and stones (unmelted ingredients or pieces of refractory material), or if the fabricating machinery was slightly out of adjustment, or moulds

---

Figure A Top management group

were worn, the rejection rate was very high. Although a number of machines were used in the inspection process, including electric eyes, much of the inspection was still done visually.

While glass making was one of the oldest arts, and bottles and jars had been machine-moulded at relatively high speeds for over half a century, the Glass Products Division had spent substantial sums each year modernising its equipment. These improvements had greatly increased the speed of operations and had reduced substantially the visual inspection and manual handling of glassware.

No hand blowing was done in the division's plants; contrary to the early days of the industry, most of the jobs were relatively unskilled, highly repetitive and gave the worker little control over work methods or pace. The mould makers who made and repaired the moulds, the machine repairers and those who made the equipment-setup changes between different products were considered to be the highest-skilled classes of workers.

Wages were relatively high in the glass industry. The rumble of the machinery and the hiss of compressed air in the moulding operation, however, plus the roar of fuel in the furnaces, made the plants extremely noisy. The great amount of heat given off by the furnaces and molten glass also made working conditions difficult. Production employees belonged to two national unions and for many years bargaining had been conducted on a national basis. Output standards were established for all jobs, but no bonus was paid to hourly plant workers for exceeding standard.

Marketing

Over the years, the sales of the Glass Products Division had grown at a slightly faster rate than had the total market for glass containers. Until recently, the division had charged a

Figure B Glass Products Division – Top management and staff

premium for most of its products, primarily because they were of better quality than competitive products. In later years, however, the quality of the competitive products had improved to the point where they matched the division's quality level. In the meantime, the division's competitors had retained their former price structure. Consequently, the Glass Products Division had been forced to lower its prices to meet its competitors' lower market prices. According to one division executive: 'Currently, price competition is not severe, particularly among the two or three larger companies that dominate the glass bottle industry. Most of our competition is with respect to product quality and customer service. In fact, our biggest competitive threat is from containers other than glass.'

Each of the division's various plants to some extent shipped its products throughout Canada, although transportation costs limited each plant's market primarily to its immediate vicinity. While some of the customers were large and bought in huge quantities, many were relatively small.

Budgetary control system

Peter Small interviewed James Walker, who had been the Empire Glass Company's controller for some 15 years. Excerpts from that interview are reproduced in the following sections.

Small: Mr Walker, what is the overall function of your budgetary control system?

Walker: Well, Peter, to understand the role of the budgetary control systems you must first understand our management philosophy. Fundamentally, we have a divisional organisation based on broad product categories. These divisional activities are coordinated by the company's executive vice president, with the head office group providing a policy and review function for the company's executive vice president.

Within the broad policy limits, we operate on a decentralised basis, with each of the decentralised divisions performing the full management job which normally would be inherent in

Figure C Glass Products Division – Typical plant organisation

any independent company. The only exceptions to this philosophy is that the head office group is solely responsible for the sources of funds and the labour relations with those bargaining units which cross division lines.

Given this form of organisation, the budget is the principal management tool used by head office to coordinate the efforts of the various segments of the company toward a common goal. Certainly, in our case, the budget is much more than a narrow statistical accounting device.

Sales budget

Walker and Small discussed the preparation of the sales budget. This was the first step in the budget preparation procedure.

Walker: As early as May 15 of the year preceding the budget year, the top management of the company asks the various product division vice presidents to submit preliminary reports stating what they think their division's capital requirements and outlook in terms of sales and income will be during the next budget year. In addition, corporate top management also wants an expression of the division vice president's general feelings toward the trends in the particular items over the two years following the upcoming budget year. At this stage, head office is not interested in too much detail.

Small: Does the market research group get involved in these forecasts?

Walker: No. What we want is an interpretive statement about sales and income based on the operating executives' practical feel for the market. Since all divisions plan their capital requirements five years in advance and have made predictions of the forthcoming budget year's market when the budget estimates were prepared last year, these rough estimates of next year's conditions and requirements are far from wild guesses.

After the opinions of the divisional vice presidents are in, the market research staff goes to work. They develop a formal statement of the marketing climate in detail for the forthcoming budget year and in general terms for the subsequent two years.

Small: Putting together the sales forecast, then, is the first step in developing the budget?

Walker: Yes. This is an important first step since practically all of the forecasts or estimates used in planning either start with or depend in some way on a sales forecast.

The market research group begins by projecting such factors as the general economic condition; growth of our various markets; weather conditions related to the end uses of our products; competitive effort; and labour disturbances.

Once these general factors have been assessed, a sales forecast for the company and each division is developed. Consideration is given to the relationship of the general economic climate to our customers' needs and Empire's share of each market. Also, basic assumptions as to price, weather conditions and so forth, are developed and stated explicitly.

In sales forecasting, consideration is given also to the introduction of new products, gains or losses in particular accounts, forward buying, new manufacturing plants and any changes in our definition of, say, gross sales.

The probable impact of such information as the following is also taken into account: industry growth trends, packaging trends, inventory carry-overs and the development of alternative packages to or from glass.

This review of all the relevant factors is followed for each of our product lines, regardless of its size and importance. The completed forecasts of the market research group are then forwarded to the appropriate divisions for review, criticism and adjustments.

Small: How would you summarise the role of the head office group in developing these sales forecasts?

Walker: Well, I suppose our primary goal is to assure uniformity between the divisions with respect to the basic assumptions on business conditions, pricing and the treatment of possible emergencies. Also, we provide a yardstick so as to assure us that the company's overall sales forecast will be reasonable and obtainable.

Next, the product division top management goes back to its district sales managers. Each district sales manager is asked to tell his top management what he expects to do in the way of sales during the budget year. Head office and the divisional staffs will give the district sales managers as much guidance as they request, but it is the sole responsibility of each district sales manager to come up with his particular forecast.

After the district sales manager's forecasts are received by the divisional top management, the forecasts are consolidated and reviewed by the division's general manager of marketing. At this time the general manager of marketing may go back to the district sales managers and suggest they revise their budgets. For instance, a situation such as this might arise: We enjoy a very large share of the liquor market. In one year, however, it may be predicted on the basis of the consolidated district sales manager's estimates that we can look forward to a 20–25 per cent increase in sales.

Obviously, this is unreasonable. What has happened is this: each district sales manager has been told by each of his liquor customers that they expect an increase in sales. When all these anticipated individual sales increases are summed, it looks like the market is going to grow considerably. However, this is not going to happen. What is going to occur is that company A will take sales from company B and company C will take sales from company D, and so forth.

Individually, the district sales managers know little of what's happening outside their territory. However, from the headquarters' point of view, we can ascertain the size of the whole market and the customer's probable relative market share. That's where the market research group's studies come in handy.

Let me emphasise, however, even in this case nothing is changed in the district sales manager's budget, unless the district manager agrees. Then, once the budget is approved, nobody is relieved of his responsibility without top management approval. Also, no arbitrary changes are made in the approved budgets without the concurrence of all the people responsible for the budget.

Small: At this point, have the plant managers – or the divisional general managers of manufacturing – been involved in the preparation of the sales budget?

Walker: Not in a formal way. Informally, of course, the plant managers know what's going on. For example, when a plant manager prepares his capital equipment investment programme he is sure to talk to the district sales manager closest to his plant about the district's sales plans.

Next, we go through the same process at the division and headquarters levels. We keep on repeating the process until everybody agrees the sales budgets are sound. Then, each level of management takes responsibility for its particular portion of the budget. These sales budgets then become fixed objectives.

Small: Besides coming up with a realistic sales budget, what other objectives do the divisions have in mind when they review the sales forecasts?

Walker: I would say they have four general objectives in mind: first, a review of the division's competitive position, including plans for improving that position. Second, an evaluation of its efforts to gain either a larger share of the market or offset competitors' activities. Third, a consideration of the need to expand facilities to improve the division's products or introduce new products. Finally, a review and development of plans to improve product quality, delivery methods and service.

Manufacturing budgets

Walker and Small then turned their conversation to the preparation of the manufacturing budgets. According to Walker, each plant had a profit responsibility.

Small: When are the plant budgets prepared?

Walker: Once the vice presidents, executive vice president and company president have given final approval to the sales budgets, we make a sales budget for each plant by breaking the division sales budget down according to the plants from which the finished goods will be shipped. These plant sales budgets are then further broken down on a monthly basis by price, volume and end use. With this information available, the plants then budget their gross profit, fixed expenses and income before taxes.

Small: How do you define gross profit and income?

Walker: Gross profit is the difference between gross sales, less discounts and variable manufacturing costs – such as direct labour, direct material and variable manufacturing overheads. Income is the difference between the gross profit and the fixed costs.

Small: Is the principal constraint within which the plants work the sales budget?

Walker: That's right. Given his sales budget, it is up to the plant manager to determine the fixed overhead and variable costs – at standard – that he will need to incur so as to meet the demands of the sales budget.

In some companies I know of, the head office gives each plant manager sales and income figures that the plant has to meet. We don't operate that way, however. We believe that type of directive misses the benefit of all the field experience of those at the district sales and plant levels. If we gave a profit figure to our plant managers to meet, how could we say it was their responsibility to meet it?

What we say to the plant managers is this: Assuming that you have to produce this much sales volume, how much do you expect to spend producing this volume? And what do you expect to spend for your programmes allied to obtaining these current and future sales?

Small: Then the plant managers make their own plans?

Walker: Yes. In my opinion requiring the plant managers to make their own plans is one of the most valuable things associated with the budget system. Each plant manager divides the preparation of the overall plant budget among his plant's various departments. First, the departments spell out the programmes in terms of the physical requirements – such as tons of raw material – and then the plans are priced at standard cost.

Small: What items might some of these departmental budgets include?

Walker: Let me tell you about the phase of the budget preparation our industrial engineering people are responsible for. The plant industrial engineering department is assigned the responsibility for developing engineered cost standards and reduced costs. Consequently, the phase of budget preparation covered by the industrial engineers includes budget standards of performance for each operation, cost centre and department within the plant. This phase of the budget also includes budget cost reductions, budgeted unfavourable variances from standards and certain budgeted programmed fixed costs in the manufacturing area such as service labour. The industrial engineer prepares this phase of the budget in conjunction with departmental line supervision.

Small: Once the plant budgets are completed, are they sent directly to the divisional top management?

Walker: No. Before each plant sends its budget into British City, a group of us from head office goes out and visits each plant. For example, in the case of the Glass Products Division, Allen [Newell, assistant controller] and I, along with representatives of the Glass Products Division manufacturing staffs visit each of the division's plants.

Let me stress this point: we do not go on these trips to pass judgement on the plant's proposed budget. Rather, we go with three purposes in mind. First, we wish to acquaint ourselves with the thinking behind the figures that each plant manager will send in to British City. This is helpful because when we come to review these budgets with the top management – that is, the management above our level – we will have to answer questions about the budget and we will know the answers. Second, the review is a way of giving guidance to the plant managers as to whether or not they are in line with what the company needs to make in the way of profits.

Of course, when we make our field reviews we do not know what each of the other plants is doing. Therefore, we explain to the plant managers that, while their budget may look good now, when we put all the plants together in a consolidated budget, the plant managers may have to make some changes because the projected profit is not high enough. When this happens we have to tell the plant managers that it is not their programmes that are unsound. The problem is that the company cannot afford the programmes.

I think it is very important that each plant manager has a chance to tell his story. Also, it gives them the feeling that we at headquarters are not living in an ivory tower.

Small: How long do these plant visits take?

Walker: They are spread over a three-week period and we spend an average of half a day at each plant.

Small: I gather the role of the head office and divisional staff is to recommend, not decide. That's the plant manager's right.

Walker: Correct.

Small: Who on the plant staff attends these meetings?

Walker: The plant manager is free to bring in any of his supervisors he wishes. We asked him not to bring in anybody below the supervisory level. Then, of course, you get into organised labour.

Small: What do you do on these plant visits?

Walker: During the half-day we spend at each plant we discuss the budget primarily. However, if I have time, I like to wander through the plant and see how things are going. Also, I go over in great detail the property replacement and maintenance budget with the plant engineer.

Small: After you have completed the plant tours, do the plant budgets go to the respective division top management?

Walker: That's right. About 1 September the plant budgets come into British City and the accounting department consolidates them. Then the product division vice presidents review their respective divisional budgets to see if the division budget is reasonable in terms of what the vice president thinks the corporate top management wants. If he is not satisfied with the consolidated plant budgets, he will ask the various plants within the division to trim their budget figures.

When the division vice presidents and the executive vice president are happy, they will send their budgets to the company president. He may accept the division budgets at this point. If he doesn't, he will specify the areas to be reexamined by division and, if necessary, plant management. The final budget is approved at our December board of directors' meeting.

Small: As I understand it, the district sales managers have a responsibility for sales.

Walker: Specifically volume, price and sales mix.

Small: And the plant manager is responsible for manufacturing costs?

Walker: His primary responsibility extends to profits. The budgeted plant profit is the difference between the fixed sales dollar budget and the budgeted variable costs at standard and the fixed overhead budget. It is the plant manager's responsibility to meet this budgeted profit figure.

Small: Even if actual dollar sales drop below the budgeted level?

Walker: Yes.

Comparison of actual and standard performance

The discussion turned to the procedures and management philosophy related to the periodic comparison by the head office group of the actual and standard performance of the field organisation. In particular, the two men discussed the manufacturing area.

Small: What do you do with the actual results that come in the head office?

Walker: We go over them on the basis of exception: that is, we only look at those figures that are in excess of the budgeted amounts. We believe this has a good effect on morale. The plant managers don't have to explain everything they do. They only have to explain where they go off base.

Small: What cost and revenue items are of greatest interest to you?

Walker: In particular, we pay close attention to the net sales, gross margin and the plant's ability to meet its standard manufacturing cost. Incidentally, when analysing the gross sales, we look closely at the price and mix changes. All this information is summarised on a form known as the Profit Planning and Control Report #1 (see Exhibit 1). This document is backed up by a number of supporting documents (see Exhibit 2).

Small: When you look at the fixed costs, what are you interested in?

Walker: We want to know whether or not the plants carried out the programmes that they said they would carry out. If they have not, we want to know why they have not. Here we are looking for sound reasons. Also, we want to know if they have carried out their projected programmes at the cost they said they would.

Small: Do you have to wait until you receive the monthly PPCR #1 [Profit Planning and Control Report #1] before you know how well the various plants performed during the month?

Walker: No. At the end of the sixth business day after the close of the month, each plant transmits to the head office certain operating variances which we put together on what we call the variance analysis sheet (see Exhibit 3). Within a half-hour after the last plant report comes through, variance analysis sheets for the divisions and plants are compiled. On the morning of the seventh business day after the end of the month, these reports are usually on the desks of the interested top management.

The variance analysis sheet highlights the variances in what we consider to be critical areas. Receiving this report as soon as we do helps us at head office to take timely action. Let me emphasise, however, we do not accept the excuse that the plant manager has to go to the end of the month to know what happened during the month. He has to be on top of these particular items daily.

Small: Is there any way head office can detect an adverse trend in operations before you receive the monthly variance analysis sheet?

Walker: Yes. At the beginning of each month, the plant managers prepare current estimates for the upcoming month and quarter on forms similar to the variance analysis sheets.

Since our budget is based on known programmes, the value of this current estimate is that it gets the plant people to look at their programmes. Hopefully, they will realise that they cannot run their plants just on a day-to-day basis.

If we see a sore spot coming up, or if the plant manager draws our attention to a potential trouble area, we may ask for daily reports concerning this item to be sent to the particular division top management involved. In addition, the division top management may send a division staff specialist – say, a quality control expert if it is a quality problem – to the plant concerned. The division staff members can make recommendations, but it is up to the plant manager to accept or reject these recommendations. Of course, it is well known throughout the company that we expect the plant managers to accept gracefully the help of the head office and division staffs.

Small: When is the monthly PPCR #1 received at British City?

Walker: The plant PPCR #1 and the month-end trial balance showing both actual and budget figures are received in British City at the close of the eighth business day after the end of the month. These two very important reports, along with the supporting reports (PPCR #2 through PPCR #11, described in Exhibit 2) are then consolidated by the accounting department on PPCR-type forms to show the results of operations by division and company. The consolidated reports are distributed the next day.

Sales-manufacturing relations

Small was curious about the relationship between the sales and manufacturing groups, particularly at the plant level.

Small: If during the year, the actual sales volume is less than the budgeted sales volume, what changes do you make in the plant budget?

Walker: This is one of the biggest risks we run with our budget system. If the sales decline occurs during the early part of the year, and if the plant managers can convince us that the change is permanent, we may revise the plant budgets to reflect these new circumstances.

However, if toward the end of the year the actual sales volume suddenly drops below the predicted sales volume, we don't have much time to change the budget plans. What we do is ask the plant managers to go back over their budget with their staffs and see where reduction of expense programmes will do the least harm. Specifically, we ask them to consider what they may be able to eliminate this year or delay until next year.

I believe it was Confucius who said: 'We make plans so we have plans to discard.' Nevertheless, I believe it is wise to make plans, even if you have to discard them. Having plans makes it a lot easier to figure out what to do when sales fall off from the budgeted level. The understanding of operations that comes from preparing the budget removes a lot of the potential chaos and confusion that might arise if we were under pressure to meet a stated profit-goal and sales-decline quickly and unexpectedly at year-end – just as they did this year.

Under these circumstances, we don't try to ram anything down the plant managers' throats. We ask them to tell us where they can reasonably expect to cut costs below the budgeted level.

Small: What happens when a plant manager's costs are adversely affected by the sales group insisting that a production schedule be changed so as to get out an unexpected rush order?

Walker: As far as we are concerned, the customer's wants are primary – our company is a case where sales wags the rest of the dog.

Whenever a problem arises at a plant between sales and production, the local people are supposed to solve the problem themselves. Let's take your example: a customer's purchasing agent insists he wants an immediate delivery and this delivery will disrupt the production department's plans. The production group can make recommendations as to alternative ways to take care of the problem, but it's the sales manager's responsibility to get the product to the customer. The salesmen are supposed to know their customers well enough to judge whether

Figure D Plant display reporting winners of their housekeeping contest
Source: Company document.

Figure E Excerpt from employee magazine
Source: Company document.

or not the customer really needs the product. If the sales manager says the customer needs the product, that ends the matter.

Of course, if the change in the sales programme involves a major expense at the plant which is out of line with the budget, then the matter is passed up to division for decision.

As I said earlier, the sales department has the sole responsibility for the product price, sales mix and delivery schedules. They do not have direct responsibility for plant operations or profit. That's the plant management's responsibility. However, it is understood that the sales group will cooperate with the plant people wherever possible.

Small: I guess cooperation is very important to the success of your system.

Walker: Definitely. We believe the whole budgetary control system works best if we can get cooperation. But, within the framework of cooperation the sales and production groups have very clear responsibilities.

Motivation

Small: How do you motivate the plant managers to meet their profit goals?

Walker: Well, first of all, we only promote capable people. Also, a monetary incentive programme has been established that stimulates their efforts to achieve their profit goal.

Small: What other incentive devices do you use?

Walker: Each month we put together a bar chart which shows, by division and plant, the ranking of the various manufacturing units with respect to manufacturing efficiency.

We feel the plant managers are one hundred per cent responsible for variable manufacturing costs. I believe this is true since all manufacturing standards have to be approved by plant managers. Most of the plant managers give wide publicity to these bar charts. The efficiency bar chart and efficiency measure itself is perhaps a little unfair in some respects when you are comparing one plant with another. Different kinds of products are run through different plants. These require different setups, etc., which have an important impact on a position of the plant. However, in general the efficiency rating is a good indication of the quality of the plant manager and his supervisory staff.

Also, a number of plants run competitions within the plants which reward department heads, or foremen, based on their relative standing with respect to a certain cost item.

Small: While I waited to see you this morning, I read some of the company publications for employees. They all seemed to stress profits and product quality (see Figure E).

Walker: That's true. In my opinion, the number one item now stressed at the plant level is quality. The market situation is such that in order to make sales you have to meet the market price and exceed the market quality. By quality I mean not only the physical characteristics of the product but also such things as delivery schedules.

As I read the company employee publications, their message is that if the company is to be profitable it must produce high quality items at a reasonable cost. This is necessary so that the plants can meet their obligation to produce the maximum profits for the company under the circumstances prevailing.

Small: Do you analyse the sales reports?

Walker: No. It is the sales group's responsibility to comment on the sales activity. They prepare their own reports. They also control their selling costs against budgets prepared by the sales managers.

Initial sales statistics are developed from plant billings summarised by end use and are available on the third business day after month-end. Detailed sales statistics by end use and customer indicating actual and variance to both budget and prior year are prepared by data processing at British City and available on the eighth business day after month-end. Sales and price and mix variances by plant and end use can be obtained from PPCR #1, PPCR #4 and PPCR #6.

The future

Small: Mr. Walker, do you intend to make any changes in your budgetary control system?

Walker: An essential part of the budgetary control system is planning. We have developed a philosophy that we must begin our plans where the work is done – in the line organisation and out in the field. Perhaps, in the future, we can avoid or cut back some of the budget preparation steps and start putting our sales budget together later on in the year than May 15. However, I doubt if we will change the basic philosophy. Frankly, I doubt if the line operators would want any major change in the system – they are very jealous of the management prerogatives the system gives to them.

It is very important that we manage the budget. We have to be continually on guard against it managing us. Sometimes, the plants lose sight of this fact. They have to be made conscious daily of the necessity of having the sales volume to make a profit. And, when sales fall off and their plant programmes are reduced they do not always appear to see the justification for budget cuts. Although, I do suspect that they see more of the justification for these cuts than they will admit. It is this human side of the budget to which we will have to pay more attention in the future.

	MONTH		REF.		YEAR TO DATE		
GAIN (+) OR LOSS (−) FROM		ACTUAL			ACTUAL	INCOME GAIN(+) OR LOSS (−) FROM	
PREV. YEAR	BUDGET					BUDGET	PREV. YEAR
			1	GROSS SALES TO CUSTOMERS			
			2	DISCOUNTS & ALLOWANCES			
			3	NET SALES TO CUSTOMERS			
%	%	/////	4	% GAIN (+)/LOSS (−)	/////	%	%
				DOLLAR VOLUME GAIN(+)/LOSS(−) DUE TO:			
		/////	5	SALES PRICE	/////		
		/////	6	SALES VOLUME	/////		
			6A	TRADE MIX	/////		
			7	VARIABLE COST OF SALES			
			8	PROFIT MARGIN			
				PROFIT MARGIN GAIN(+)/LOSS(−) DUE TO:			
		/////	9	PROFIT VOLUME RATIO (P/V)	/////		
		/////	10	DOLLAR VOLUME	/////		
%	%	%	11	PROFIT VOLUME RATIO (P/V)	%	%	%
	INCOME ADDITION (+)		12	TOTAL FIXED MANUFACTURING COST	INCOME ADDITION (+)		
			13	FIXED MANUFACTURING COST - TRANSFERS			
			14	PLANT INCOME (STANDARD)			
%	%	%	15	% OF NET SALES	%	%	%
	INCOME ADDITION (+) INCOME REDUCTION (−)				INCOME ADDITION (+) INCOME REDUCTION (−)		
%	%	%	16	% PERFORMANCE	%	%	%
			17	MANUFACTURING EFFICIENCY			
	INCOME ADDITION (+)		18	METHODS IMPROVEMENTS	INCOME ADDITION (+)		
			19	OTHER REVISIONS OF STANDARDS			
			20	MATERIAL PRICE CHANGES			
			21	DIVISION SPECIAL PROJECTS			
			22	COMPANY SPECIAL PROJECTS			
			23	NEW PLANT EXPENSE			
			24	OTHER PLANT EXPENSES			
			25	INCOME ON SECONDS			
			26				
			27				
			28	PLANT INCOME (ACTUAL)			
%	%	/////	29	% GAIN (+)/LOSS (−)	/////	%	%
%	%	%	30	% OF NET SALES	%	%	%
			36A				

EMPLOYED CAPITAL

INCREASE (+) OR DECREASE (−)			REF.		INCREASE (+) OR DECREASE (−)		
			37	TOTAL EMPLOYED CAPITAL			
%	%	%	38	% RETURN	%	%	%
			39	TURNOVER RATE			

PLANT _____   DIVISION _____   MONTH _____   19__

Exhibit 1 Profit planning and control report (PPCR) #1

Report	Description
	Individual plant reports
PPCR #2	*Manufacturing expense*: Plant materials, labour and variable overhead consumed. Detail of actual figures compared with budget and previous years' figures for year-to-date and current month.
PPCR #3	*Plant expense*: Plant fixed expenses incurred. Details of actual figures compared with budget and previous years' figures for year-to-date and current month.
PPCR #4	*Analysis of sales and income*: Plant operating gains and losses due to changes in sales revenue, profit margins and other sources of income. Details of actual figures compared with budget and previous years' figures for year-to-date and current month.
PPCR #5	*Plant control statement*: Analysis of plant raw material gains and losses, spoilage costs and cost reductions programmes. Actual figures compared with budget figures for current month and year-to-date.
PPCR #6	*Comparison of sales by principal and product groups*: Plant sales dollars, profit margin and *PN* ratios broken down by end-product use (i.e., soft drinks, beer, etc.). Compares actual figures with budgeted figures for year-to-date and current month.
	Division summary reports
PPCR #7	*Comparative plant performance, sales and income*: Gross sales and income figures by plants. Actual figures compared with budget figures for year-to-date and current month.
PPCR #8	*Comparative plant performance, total plant expenses*: Profit margin, total fixed costs, manufacturing efficiency, other plant expenses and *PN* ratios by plants. Actual figures compared with budgeted and previous years' figures for current month and year-to-date.
PPCR #9	*Manufacturing efficiency*: Analysis of gains and losses by plant in areas of material, spoilage, supplies and labour. Current month and year-to-date actuals reported in total dollars and as a percentage of budget.
PPCR #10	*Inventory*: Comparison of actual and budget inventory figures by major inventory accounts and plants.
PPCR#11	*Status of capital expenditures*: Analysis of the status of capital expenditures by plants, months and relative to budget.

Exhibit 2 Brief descriptions of PPCR #2 through PPCR #11

Notes

During his conversation with James Walker, Small asked him to describe the various items listed on PPCR #1.

Walker: Let's start with reference 3, *net sales to customers*. This is the difference between the gross sales to customers [ref. 1] and any discounts or allowances [ref. 2].

The next line, percentage gain $(+)$/loss $(-)$ [ref. 4], is the increase or decrease in net sales dollars expressed as a percentage of the budget and previous year's actual figures.

Next, we break the cause of the dollar volume gain or loss into its component parts: namely, changes due to sales price, volume and mix.

Variable cost of sales [ref. 7] includes such items as direct materials, operating labour and that part of indirect labour that varies in monthly dollar amounts directly with changes in unit production volume. These costs are constant per unit of production. The amount listed in the budget column is the standard cost of the actual production.

Reference 8, *profit margin*, is the difference between the total net dollar sales and the total variable manufacturing costs of products sold.

Line No.	Division or plant	Budget income	Gross sales	Sales price	Manufacturing cost	Labour	Overtime	Employee benefits	Outside warehouse	Utilities	Overhaul and repair	Depreciation, rent, insurance and taxes	Controllable plant fixed cost	Other fixed cost	Manufacturing efficiency	Cost reduction	Other operating gains and losses	Income from seconds	Wage changes	Price changes	Division expenses	Actual income	Income adjusted by volume
1																							
2																							
3																							
4																							
5																							
6																							
7																							
8																							
9																							
10																							
11																							
12																							
13																							
14																							
15																							
16																							
17																							
18																							
19																							
20																							
21																							
22																							
23																							
24																							
25																							
26																							
27																							
28																							
29																							
30																							
31																							
32																							
33																							
34																							
35																							

Source: Company document.

Exhibit 3 Variance analysis sheet for various divisions and plants

Next, we identify further the causes of the change in profit margin.

The item reference 9, *profit margin gain* (+)/*loss* (−) *due to profit volume ratio* (PIV), is that portion of the profit margin gain or loss resulting from changes in the relationship between the net selling price and the standard variable manufacturing costs of the products sold to customers. This relationship, expressed as a percentage, is known as the PIV ratio [see ref. 11].

The *profit margin gain* (+)/*loss* (−) *due to dollar volume* [ref. 10] is that portion of the profit margin or loss resulting from the changes in dollar volume of net sales to customers, exclusive of changes in PN. It is the algebraic difference between the total profit margin variance and reference 9.

We keep a close check on the P/V ratio because it shows us how much we are making over our variable costs. Of course, volume changes alone never affect the P/V ratio.

Total fixed manufacturing costs [ref. 12] are the costs that should remain unchanged irrespective of fluctuation in volume during the year. Included in this category are depreciation, rent, general insurance, general taxes and most supervision costs. Fixed costs are calculated on an annual basis and each monthly figure is shown as one-twelfth of the annual total.

The next item, *fixed manufacturing cost-transfers* [ref. 13], doesn't apply to the Glass Products Division as they have very little intra or interdivision transfers.

Therefore, in the case of the Glass Products Division [ref. 14] *plant income (standard) is* the difference between profit margin dollars [ref. 8] and total fixed manufacturing costs [ref. 12].

In the *actual* column of reference 16, percentage performance, we enter the ratio of the standard to the actual manufacturing cost expressed as a percentage.

In the *gain/loss* columns for this same item, we enter the difference in percentage points between current performance and budget, and between the current performance and previous year.

In the *actual* column of reference 17, *manufacturing efficiency*, we put the difference between standard and actual manufacturing efficiency dollar costs.

In the *gain/loss* columns of reference 17, we enter the increase or decrease in income resulting from changes in manufacturing dollar savings or excesses.

References 18 through 25 are self-explanatory. In addition to cost savings or excesses resulting from efficiency, special conditions may arise to cause other departures from standard cost. These additional differences are classified according to cause and the more significant ones are shown individually on separate lines in this portion of PPCR #1.

Reference 28, *plant income (actual)*, is the income remaining after adjusting reference 14 for all the departures from standard manufacturing listed on references 18 through 25, inclusive.

Total employed capital (ref. 37) is the value of employed capital at the end of the month and average for the year to date. At the plant level employed capital consists of inventories [mostly work-in-process and finished goods] valued at their standard direct costs plus the replacement value of fixed assets. At the division level, accounts receivable are included in employed capital.

Small: How do you calculate the replacement value of fixed assets?

Walker: We have formulas that give us the current cost of equipment capable of doing the same job as the installed equipment.

Small: Why do you use replacement costs?

Walker: We have two basic reasons. First, within a single division it places all plants on an equal footing from the standpoint of measuring return, since it eliminates distortions arising from the use of widely disparate acquisition costs for similar equipment. Second, it eliminates distortions arising from the use of unrecovered costs which, even though based on comparable replacement values, are heavily influenced by cumulative depreciation charges that vary widely depending upon the length of time a given facility has been in use.

Small: What about the rest of the items on PPCR #1?

Walker: Reference 38 is *plant income (actual)* dollars expressed as a percentage of *employed capital*. Reference 39 is the net sales dollars divided by employed capital and expressed as a multiple of employed capital.

Small: What are the three most important items on PPCR #1?

Walker: The P/V ratio, *plant income (actual)*, and percentage return *(employed capital)*.

Small: Are the budgets prepared on forms similar to the PPCR series?

Walker: Yes. The only major difference is that the budget forms include columns for recording the current year's budget figures and previous year's actual figures. In addition, variances are shown between the proposed budget figures and the current year's estimated actuals' and the previous year's actual figures.

Source: Company documents.

Question

What are the strengths and weaknesses of Empire Glass's planning and control practices? Your response should include arguments for and against treating the manufacturing plants as profit centres and the problems this may create.

Capital budgeting

Learning objectives

When you have finished studying this chapter, you should be able to:

1 Describe capital-budgeting decisions and use the net-present-value (NPV) method to make such decisions.

2 Evaluate projects using sensitivity analysis.

3 Calculate the NPV difference between two projects using both the total project and differential approaches.

4 Identify relevant cash flows for NPV analyses.

5 Compute the after-tax net present values of projects.

6 Explain the after-tax effect on cash received from the disposal of assets.

7 Use the payback model and the accounting rate-of-return model and compare them with the NPV model.

8 Reconcile the conflict between using an NPV model for making decisions and using accounting income for evaluating the related performance.

9 Compute the impact of inflation on a capital-budgeting project (Appendix 11).

Toyota Motor Corporation

In 2008 Toyota Motor Corporation became the largest automobile company in the world, replacing General Motors. Toyota was founded in 1937 by Japanese entrepreneur, Kiichiro Toyoda, to produce and sell Toyoda cars. Almost immediately the name was changed to Toyota because (according to Wikipedia) 'it took eight brush strokes (a fortuitous number) to write in Japanese, was visually simpler (leaving off two ticks at the end) and sounded better with two 't's'. In 1957 Toyota entered the US market with a car called the Toyopet Crown. Unfortunately, US consumers associated these cars with toys and pets, so Toyota quickly dropped the Toyopet name. Nevertheless, the company continued selling Toyotas in the United States. In 1963 Toyota built its first car outside of Japan (in Australia). Now it has production or assembly plants in more than 25 countries.

Toyota was instrumental in developing lean manufacturing and just-in-time production.

Its management philosophy focuses on four areas: (1) long-term thinking, (2) a process for problem-solving, (3) adding value by developing people and (4) organisational learning. This has led to a variety of awards for quality, from the Deming Prize for Total Quality Management in 1965 to recent J.D. Power awards for automobile quality. This reputation for quality was instrumental in Toyota's worldwide growth.

Nearly a decade ago Toyota invested heavily in foreign manufacturing facilities, especially those for full-size lorries and sports-utility vehicles. With the downturn in the economy in 2008 and 2009, Toyota found itself with excess manufacturing capacity. The company moved quickly to shut down two factories for several months each and to switch production in another from the Highlander SUV to the Prius. The investment in production facilities for lorries and SUVs may not have turned out well, but it was based on the best information available at the time. Toyota has 38 'sushas' or chief engineers, who traditionally have been given near-absolute authority. The sushas came under intense pressure during the term of Katsuaki Watanabe, the company's president from 2005–2009, to boost profitability and cut costs aggressively. When the cuts went too deep, customers raised questions about quality issues, but feedback from customers did not reach top management quickly enough. Possibly, sushas did not take the problems to top management for fear of losing face. Toyota is now rebounding and is reinvesting in quality initiatives, but its historical reputation for quality cars has been dented. Every forward-looking company must make long-term investment decisions based on uncertain predictions. All investment decisions will not be perfect, but making good investment decisions is critical to the long-term success of most organisations. This chapter focuses on the analyses that go into such decisions. ■

Capital budgeting for programmes or projects

Major corporations such as Toyota are not the only companies that face decisions about capital investment and expansion. At some time, every company needs to decide where and how to spend its money on major projects that will affect company financial results for years to come. This chapter concentrates on the planning and controlling decisions for programmes or projects that affect financial results over a period longer than just the next year. Such decisions require investments of large amounts of resources – called capital outlays – in anticipation of future benefits that are often uncertain. The term **capital budgeting** describes the long-term planning for making and financing such outlays.

Capital budgeting has three phases: (1) identifying potential investments, (2) choosing which investments to make (which includes gathering data to aid the decision) and (3) follow-up monitoring, or 'post-audit', of the investments. Accountants usually are not involved in the first phase, but they play important roles in phases 2 and 3.

Why are accountants involved in capital-budgeting decisions? They function primarily as information specialists. One of the purposes of a cost-management system is to provide cost measurements for strategic decisions, such as major capital-budgeting decisions.

Accountants gather and interpret information to help managers make capital-budgeting decisions. To help organise volumes of information, accountants rely on capital-budgeting models. Let's take a look at how some of these models work.

Discounted-cash-flow models

The most widely used capital-budgeting models are **discounted-cash-flow (DCF) models**. These models focus on a project's cash inflows and outflows while taking into account the time value of money. They are based on the old adage that a bird in the hand is worth two in the bush – that a euro in the hand today is worth more than a euro to be received in several years. This adage applies because the receipt of money in the future has an opportunity cost – interest income forgone by not receiving the money now and earning interest on it in the interim period. Similarly, borrowing money now to use for a capital expenditure carries a cost for interest expense. More than two-thirds of the large industrial firms in Europe and North America use a DCF model.

Major aspects of DCF

As the name suggests, DCF models focus on expected cash inflows and outflows rather than on net income. They also compute **present values (PV)**, the value today of a future cash flow. Companies invest cash today in order to receive cash in future periods. DCF models compare the value of today's cash outflows with the present value of the future cash inflows.

DCF methods are based on the theory of compound interest. If your knowledge of compound interest and time value of money is a little rusty, be sure to read Appendix B, pages 676–681. Do not try to learn about the DCF methods until you are able to use Tables B1 (p. 677) and B2 (p. 680) in Appendix B.

Net present value (NPV)

We will focus on the most popular version of DCF, the **net-present-value (NPV) method**. The NPV method computes the present value of all expected future cash flows using a minimum desired rate of return. The minimum desired rate of return depends on the risk of a proposed project – the higher the risk, the higher the rate. This minimum rate, called the **required rate of return**, **hurdle rate** or **discount rate**, is based on the cost of capital – what the firm pays to acquire more capital. Using this required rate, managers sum the present values of all expected future cash flows (inflows and outflows, if any) from the project and subtract the initial investment. If this total, the **net present value**, is positive, the project is desirable. If the net present value is negative, the project is undesirable. Why? A positive NPV means that accepting the project benefits the firm because the present value of the project's cash inflows exceeds the present value of its cash outflows. Similarly, accepting a negative NPV project makes the firm worse off financially because its investment is more than the PV of the future benefits. (An NPV of zero means that the present value of the inflows equals the present value of the outflows so the project will make the firm neither better nor worse off.) When choosing among several investments, managers should pick the one with the greatest net present value.

Applying the NPV method

Objective 1
Describe capital-budgeting decisions and use the net-present-value (NPV) method to make such decisions.

To illustrate how DCF models work, we will use the following example throughout the rest of this section: Managers at Toyota's Burnaston plant in the UK are contemplating the purchase of new, more efficient auto painting equipment that they expect will increase efficiency and produce operating savings of £2,000 cash per year. The useful life of the equipment is 4 years, after which it will have a net disposal value of zero. The equipment will cost £5,827 now and the minimum desired rate of return is 10 per cent per year.

To apply the NPV method, you can use the following three steps, which we illustrate in Exhibit 11.1.

1 *Identify the amount and timing of relevant expected cash inflows and outflows.* The right-hand side of Exhibit 11.1 shows how to sketch these cash flows. Outflows are in parentheses. Be sure to include the outflow at time zero, the date of acquisition. You do not have to use a sketch, but sketches can help you to see costs and cost relationships over time.

	Present value of £1, discounted at 10%	Total present value	Sketch of cash flows at end of year				
			0	1	2	3	4
Approach 1: Discounting each year's cash flows separately*							
Cash flows							
Annual savings	.9091	£1,818		£2.000			
	.8264	1,653			£2.000		
	.7513	1,503				£2.000	
	.6830	1,366					£2.000
Present value of future inflows		£6,340					
Initial outlay	1.0000	(5,827)	£(5,827)				
Net present value		£ 513					
Approach 2: Using annuity table†							
Annual savings	3.1699	£6.340		£2.000	£2.000	£2.000	£2.000
Initial outlay	1.0000	(5,827)	£(5,827)				
Net present value		£ 513					

*Present values from Table B1, Appendix B, p. 677.
†Present value of annuity from Table B2, Appendix B, p. 680. (Incidentally, calculators or computers may give slightly different answers than do the tables because of rounding differences.)

Exhibit 11.1 Net-present-value method
Original investment, £5,827. Useful life, 4 years. Annual cash inflow from operations, £2,000. Minimum desired rate of return, 10 per cent. Cash outflows are in parentheses; cash inflows are not. Total present values are rounded to the nearest pound.

2 *Find the present value of each expected cash inflow or outflow.* Examine Table B1 in Appendix B on p. 677. Find the PV factor for each year's cash flow from the correct row and column of the table. Multiply each expected cash inflow or outflow by the appropriate PV factor. For example, the £2,000 cash savings that will occur 2 years hence is worth £2,000 × .8264 = £1,653 today. Be sure to include the initial investment at time zero.

3 *Sum the individual present values.* The sum is the project's NPV. Accept a project whose NPV is positive and reject a project whose NPV is negative.

The value today (at time zero) of the four £2,000 cash inflows is £6,340. The manager pays only £5,827 to obtain these cash inflows. Thus, the net present value is £6,340 − £5,827 = £513, so the investment is desirable.

■ Choice of the correct table

Exhibit 11.1 also shows another way to calculate the NPV, shown as Approach 2. The basic steps are the same as for Approach 1. The only difference is that Approach 2 uses Table B2 in Appendix B (see p. 680) instead of Table B1. Table B2 is an annuity table that provides a shortcut to reduce hand calculations. It gives discount factors for computing the PV of a series of equal cash flows at equal intervals. Because the four cash flows in our example are all equal, you can use Table B2 to make one PV computation instead of using Table B1 to make four individual computations. Table B2 merely sums up the pertinent PV factors of Table B1. Therefore, the annuity factor for 4 years at 10 per cent is[1]

$$.9091 + .8264 + .7513 + .6830 = 3.1698$$

---

[1]Rounding error causes a .0001 difference between the Table B2 factor and the summation of Table B1 factors.

Beware of using the wrong table. You should use Table B1 for discounting individual amounts and Table B2 for a series of equal amounts. Table B1 is the basis for Table B2 and you can use it for all PV calculations if you wish.

You can avoid Tables B1 and B2 entirely by using the PV function on a handheld calculator or the PV function on a computer spreadsheet programme. However, we encourage you to use the tables when learning the NPV method. Using the tables will help you better understand the process of PV computation. Once you are comfortable with the method, you can take advantage of the speed and convenience of calculators and computers.

MAKING MANAGERIAL DECISIONS

For major capital investments, managers usually prepare a detailed NPV analysis. For smaller items, sometimes they make a quick calculation or use intuition. Suppose you are in charge of a company's mail room. An employee has suggested the purchase of a €12,000 letter sorting machine. She says that it will save 1 hour per day for 250 working days a year for an employee making a total of €12 per hour. She indicates that the €12,000 expenditure will save €15,000 over the machine's 5-year life. Should you approve the purchase?

Answers

The employee is right about the €15,000 total savings:

$$1 \text{ hour} \times 250 \text{ days} \times €12 \text{ hour} \times 5 \text{ years} = €15,000$$

However, her quick calculation ignores the time value of money. The €12,000 must be paid immediately and the €15,000 of savings is spread over the next 5 years at €3,000 per year. You know that the present value of the savings is less than the €15,000 total, but the exact amount depends on the required rate of return.

Therefore, you must know the required rate before you can answer the question.

Suppose the required rate is 10 per cent. Then the NPV (using Table B1) is negative, €(627.90):

$$.9091 \times €3,000 + .8264 \times €3,000 + .7513 \times$$
$$€3,000 + .6830 \times €3,000 + .6209 \times €3,000 -$$
$$€12,000 = €2,727.30 + €2,479.20 + €2,253.90 +$$
$$€1,862.70 = €11,372.10 - 12,000 = €(627.90).$$

Using Table B2 it is $3.7908 \times €3,000 - €12,000 = €11,372.40 - €12,000 = €(627.60)$, which differs from the Table 1 result by a rounding error. With a 10 per cent required rate, the investment is not desirable.

Now, suppose the required rate is 5 per cent. Using Table B2, the NPV is positive:

$$4.3295 \times €3,000 - €12,000 = €12,988.50 - €12,000$$
$$= €988.50.$$

In this case, the purchase is warranted. It is important to recognise the time value of money and to apply the right required rate of return.

Effect of minimum rate

The minimum desired rate of return can have a large effect on NPVs. The higher the minimum desired rate of return, the lower the PV of each future cash inflow. Why? Because the higher the rate of return, the more it costs you to wait for the cash rather than having it available to invest today. Thus, higher required rates lead to lower NPVs. For example, at a rate of 16 per cent, the NPV of the project in Exhibit 11.1 would be −£231. That is, £2,000 × 2.7982 = £5,596, which is £231 less than the investment of £5,827, instead of the +£513 computed with a 10 per cent rate. (PV factor 2.7982 is taken from Table B2 in Appendix B on p. 680.) When the desired rate of return is 16 per cent rather than 10 per cent, the project should be rejected.

Assumptions of the NPV model

We make two major assumptions when using the NPV model. First, we assume a world of certainty. That is, we act as if the predicted cash inflows and outflows are certain to occur at the times specified. Second, we assume perfect capital markets. That is, if we need to get extra cash or invest excess cash at any time, we can borrow or lend money at the same interest rate, which is our required rate of return. In a world that meets these assumptions, no model could possibly be better than the NPV model.

Unfortunately, the real world has neither certainty nor perfect capital markets. Nevertheless, the NPV model is usually preferred to other models because the assumptions of most other models are even less realistic. The NPV model is not perfect, but it generally meets our cost-benefit criterion. That is, the benefit of better decisions based on NPV is greater than the cost of applying it. More sophisticated models often do not improve decisions enough to be worth their cost.

Depreciation and NPV

NPV calculations do not include deductions for depreciation. Why not? Because NPV is based on inflows and outflows of cash and not on the accounting concepts of revenues and expenses.[2] Depreciation is not a cash flow. It is a way of allocating the cost of a long-lived asset (which a company usually pays for in cash upon purchase) to different periods. Because a capital budgeting analysis records and accounts for the cash outflow at the time of purchase, deducting depreciation from future cash flows would be like counting this cost twice – once at purchase and again over the asset's life.

Review of decision rules

Be sure that you understand why the NPV method works, not just how to apply it. The decision maker in our example cannot directly compare an immediate outflow of £5,827 with a series of future inflows of £2,000 each because of the time value of money. The NPV model aids comparison by expressing all amounts in today's monetary units (such as dollars, euros or yen) at time zero. The required rate of return measures the cost of using money. At a rate of 14 per cent, the comparison is as follows:

Outflow in today's money	£(5,827)
Inflow equivalent in today's money at 14%	5,827*
Net present value	£ 0

*£2,000 × 2.9137 from Table B2 = £5,827

Therefore, at a required rate of return of 14 per cent, the decision maker is indifferent between having £5,827 now or having a stream of four annual inflows of £2,000 each. If the interest rate were 16 per cent, the decision maker would find the project unattractive because the net present value would be a negative £231. The graph opposite shows the relationship between the required rate of return and the project's NPV.

At 10 per cent the NPV is a positive £513, so the project is desirable. At all rates below 14 per cent, the NPV is positive. At all rates above 14 per cent, the NPV is negative.

Internal rate of return (IRR) model

Another popular DCF model is the **internal rate of return (IRR) model**. This model determines the interest rate at which the NPV equals zero. If this rate, called the IRR, is greater than the

---

[2] Throughout this chapter, our examples often assume that cash inflows are equivalent to revenues and that cash outflows are equivalent to expenses (except for depreciation). If we account for the revenues and expenses on the accrual basis of accounting, there will be leads and lags of cash inflows and cash outflows that a precise DCF model must recognise. For example, we might record a £10,000 sale on credit as revenue in one period but not recognise the related cash inflow in a DCF model until collected, which may be in a second period. We do not make such refinements in this chapter.

*(£2,000 × 3.1699) − £5,827 = £513
**(£2,000 × 2.7982) − £5,827 = £(231)

required rate of return, a project is desirable. If not, it is undesirable. Finance textbooks provide descriptions of the IRR method and we will not go into details here. However, in most cases the IRR method gives equivalent decisions to the NPV method. In our example, the IRR is 14 per cent; that is, the NPV of the equipment is zero using an interest rate of 14 per cent. Thus, at our required rate of return of 10 per cent (or any rate less than 14 per cent) we accept the project. At any required rate above 14 per cent we would reject it. In general, we find the following:

> If IRR > required rate of return, then NPV > 0 and we should accept the project
>
> If IRR < required rate of return, then NPV < 0 and we should accept the project

Because of the equivalence of NPV and IRR models for most investment proposals, we will use the NPV model for all the illustrations in this chapter.

Real options

Whereas the IRR model is generally equivalent to the NPV model, the use of real options is an improvement on NPV. It is more sophisticated and only a few companies are using it for routine capital-budgeting decisions. But it is an important innovation that is sure to grow in popularity. A **real options model** recognises the value of contingent investments – that is, investments that a company can adjust as it learns more about their potential for success. For example, a project that a company can implement in stages, where investment in one stage occurs only if the previous stage was successful, has an advantage over an 'all or nothing' project, one where the entire investment must take place up front. Suppose implementing a project in stages causes the expected NPV to fall because it is not as efficient as implementing it all at once. Staging the project might still be a preferred alternative if the company gains enough information in the early stages to make better decisions in the later stages. A real options model recognises the value of such staging. Like the IRR model, we will leave the details of real options to the finance textbooks.

Sensitivity analysis and risk assessment in DCF models

Objective 2
Evaluate projects using sensitivity analysis.

Because the future is uncertain, actual cash inflows may differ from what was expected or predicted. To quantify this uncertainty, managers often use sensitivity analysis, which shows the financial consequences that would occur if actual cash inflows and outflows differ from those expected. It can answer what-if questions like *What will happen to the NPV if my predictions of useful life or cash flows change?* The best way to understand sensitivity analysis is to see it in action, so let's take a look at an example.

Suppose the Toyota managers know that the actual cash savings in Exhibit 11.1 could fall below the predicted level of £2,000. How far below £2,000 must the annual cash savings drop before the NPV becomes negative? The cash inflow at the point where NPV = 0 is the 'break-even' cash flow:

$$NPV = 0$$

$$(3.1699 \times \text{cash flow}) - £5,827 = 0$$

$$\text{cash flow} = £5,827 \div 3.1699$$

$$= £1,838$$

If the annual cash savings is less than £1,838, the NPV is negative and the managers should reject the project. Therefore, annual cash savings can drop only £2,000 − £1,838 = £162, or 8.1 per cent below the predicted amount, before the managers would change their decision.

Managers like sensitivity analysis because it can give them immediate answers about possible future events. It also shows managers how risky a given project might be by showing how sensitive the decision is to changes in predictions. If a project has a positive NPV that would become negative with only a small change in cash flows, it can be a risky project. Sensitivity analysis can become complicated very quickly and doing all the calculations by hand can be complex and tedious. Fortunately, there is a good deal of sensitivity analysis software available that lets computers do all the calculations, thus, permitting managers and accountants to focus on interpreting the results of the analysis.

The NPV comparison of two projects

Objective 3
Calculate the NPV difference between two projects using both the total project and differential approaches.

So far we have seen how to use the NPV method to evaluate a single project. In practice, managers very rarely look at only one project or option at a time. Instead, managers compare several options to see which is the best or most profitable. We will now see how to use NPV to compare two or more alternatives.

■ Total project versus differential approach

Two common methods for comparing alternatives are (1) the total project approach and (2) the differential approach.

The **total project approach** computes the total impact on cash flows for each alternative and then converts these total cash flows to their present values. It is the most popular approach and we can use it for any number of alternatives. The alternative with the largest NPV of total cash flows is best.

The **differential approach** computes the differences in cash flows between alternatives and then converts these differences to their present values. We cannot use this method to compare more than two alternatives. Often, the two alternatives being compared are (1) invest in a project and (2) do nothing.

Let's compare the differential and total project approaches. Consider a motor that drives one of the assembly lines at Toyota's Burnaston plant. Assume that Toyota purchased the motor 3 years ago for £56,000. It has a remaining useful life of 5 years but will require a major overhaul at the end of two more years at a cost of £10,000. Its disposal value now is £20,000. Its predicted disposal value in 5 years is £8,000, assuming that the company does the £10,000 major overhaul on schedule. The predicted cash-operating costs of this motor are £40,000 annually. A sales representative has offered a substitute motor for £51,000. The new motor will reduce annual cash-operating costs by £10,000, will not require any overhauls, will have a useful life of 5 years and will have a disposal value of £3,000. If the required rate of return is 14 per cent, what should Toyota do to minimise long-run costs, keep the old machine or replace it with the new one? (Try to solve this problem yourself before examining the solution that follows.)

Regardless of the approach used, perhaps the hardest part of making capital-budgeting decisions is predicting accurately the relevant cash flows. Seeing which events will cause money to flow either in or out can be complex, especially when there are many sources of cash flows. However, you cannot compare alternatives if you do not know their cash flows, so the first step for either the total project or differential approach is to estimate the relevant cash flows. Exhibit 11.2 sketches these cash flows for each approach.

Total project approach: For the total project approach we list the cash flows for each project, replace or keep, separately. We then determine the NPV of the cash flows for each individual project and choose the project with the largest positive NPV or smallest negative NPV. Exhibit 11.2 shows that the NPV of replacing the motor, −132,435, is better than the −£140,864 NPV of keeping the old motor. The advantage is £140,864 − £132,435 = £8,429. Most cash flows are negative because these are the costs of operating the motor. The alternative with the lowest cost – the smallest negative NPV – is the most desirable.

Differential approach: For the differential approach, we first list the difference in cash flow for each year. In other words, assume implementation of one of the projects as a baseline (for example, keeping the old machine) and perform a differential analysis as discussed in Chapter 6. Specifically, subtract the cash flows for keeping from the cash flows for replacement for each year. This isolates the advantages (cash inflows or cost savings) and disadvantages (cash outflows) of replacement compared to the baseline, keeping the machine. (Remember that cash inflows are positive numbers, while cash outflows are negative.) Next, calculate the NPV of the differential cash flows. If the NPV is positive, choose replacement; if it is negative, choose to keep the motor. Whereas the total project approach computed the difference in the NPVs of the two projects, the differential method computes the NPV of the difference in cash flows of the two projects. Both give the same total difference, an £8,429 advantage to replacement.

Exhibit 11.2 illustrates that both methods produce the same answer. As a result, you can use these methods interchangeably, as long as you are considering only two alternatives. If our example had more than two alternatives, our only choice would be to use the total project approach.

■ Relevant cash flows for NPV

Objective 4
Identify relevant cash flows for NPV analyses.

As we mentioned earlier, predicting cash flows is the hardest part of capital budgeting. When you array the relevant cash flows, be sure to consider three types of inflows and outflows: (1) initial cash inflows and outflows at time zero, (2) future disposal values and (3) operating cash inflows and outflows.

Initial cash inflows and outflows at time zero

These cash flows include both outflows for the purchases and installation of equipment and other items required by the new project and either inflows or outflows from disposal of any

I. Total project approach	Present value discount factor at 14%	Total present value	Sketch of after-tax cash flows at end of year					
			0	1	2	3	4	5
A. Replace								
Recurring cash operating costs, using an annuity table*	3.4331	£(102,993)		£(30,000)	£(30,000)	£(30,000)	£(30,000)	£(30,000)
Disposal value, end of year 5	.5194	1,558						£3,000
Initial required investment	1.0000	(31,000)	£(31,000)					
NPV of net cash flows		£(132,435)						
B. Keep								
Recurring cash operating costs, using an annuity table*	3.4331	£(137,324)		£(40,000)	£(40,000)	£(40,000)	£(40,000)	£(40,000)
Overhaul, end of year 2	.7695	(7,695)			£(10,000)			
Disposal value, end of year 5	.5194	4,155						£ 8,000
NPV of net cash flows		£(140,864)						
Difference in NPV between the alternatives		£ 8,429						
II. Differential approach								
A–B. Analysis confined to differences								
Recurring cash operating savings, using an annuity table*	3.4331	£ 34,331		£ 10,000	£ 10,000	£ 10,000	£ 10,000	£ 10,000
Overhaul avoided, end of year 2	.7695	7,695			£ 10,000			
Difference in disposal values, end of year 5	.5194	(2,597)						£ (5,000)
Incremental initial investment	1.0000	(31,000)	£(31,000)					
Difference in NPV between alternatives		£ 8,429						

*Table B2, Appendix B.

Exhibit 11.2 Total project versus differential approach to net present value

BUSINESS FIRST
Does DCF apply to technology investments?

Although DCF models are widely used, some have criticised them for leading to overly cautious investment decisions in information technology (IT). The critics maintain that the benefits of IT investments are difficult to quantify and such investments lead to unforeseen opportunities. By ignoring some of the potential benefits and opportunities, companies pass up desirable IT investments.

Such criticisms abated somewhat early this decade. The economic shakeout in 2001 and 2002 identified the winners and losers – and there were plenty of both. Winners (identified by *BusinessWeek*) included Expedia, Amazon, eBay, Yahoo! and Dell. Losers, at least in the short run, included Hewlett-Packard, Barnes & Noble, AOL Time Warner, drkoop.com and many startups. What differentiated winners from losers? Partly it was how they evaluated capital investment decisions. Some were overly cautious in employing technology. But others forgot the basic economics of investment analysis. Instead of focusing on cash flows and DCF analysis, companies touted their revenue per dollar of investment or, even worse, website hits per dollar of investment. They forgot that only net cash flows generate value. Increasing revenues are worthless if related expenses grow faster. No one became rich because of the number of visits to their website.

How did the winners approach capital-budgeting decisions? First, they identified ways to generate cash – either new inflows or savings of outflows – that technology solutions could produce. Their business plans showed at what point the company's technology investments would become profitable and how profitable they would be. Second, the companies did not try to protect current business while simultaneously pursuing new technology. If technology solutions better served customers, companies lagging in technology would lose them anyway. And finally, they used DCF analysis. They realised that money recieved in the future is worth less

than that recieved today, so they needed large future profits to justify investments that would not pay off in the short term.

In the aftermath of the technology crash, many companies focused on how to correctly apply DCF to technology investments. Microsoft developed guides to its software that showed how to apply DCF to investments in technology and developed blogs to allow managers to share experiences applying DCF methods.

Companies also used new developments in finance and accounting to aid in the application of DCF analyses. For example, Scott Gamster of Grant Thornton's Performance Management Practice suggested using activity-based costing (ABC) to better estimate future cash flows. Analyses that focused primarily on how technology reduced direct costs ignored potentially large savings in indirect costs. Because an ABC system focuses on indirect costs, it can help identify other cost impacts of new technology systems. The attention to activities lets managers better assess the various impacts of new systems. For example, an ERP system will transform much of the work in many of a company's activities. Examining each activity in light of the potential implementation of an ERP system will help managers assess the full impact of the new system.

Criticisms of using DCF for investment decisions were primarily criticisms of incorrect or incomplete applications of it. They have led to a better understanding of how to apply DCF to technology investments and to refinements in DCF analysis that are especially useful to investments in technology.

Sources: Adapted from S. Gamster, 'Using activity based management to justify ERP implementations', *Journal of Cost Management*, September/October 1999, pp. 24–33; 'The e-business surprise', *BusinessWeek*, 12 May 2003, pp. 60–68; Microsoft Dynamics, 'Using ROI analysis to prioritize technology purchases', 7 March 2007, http://community.dynamics.com/blogs/articles/archive/2007/03/07/using-roi-analysis-to-prioritize-technology-purchases.aspx

items that are replaced. In Exhibit 11.2, we subtracted the £20,000 received from selling the old motor from the £51,000 purchase price of the new motor, resulting in a net cash outflow of £31,000. If the company could not sell the old motor, we would add any cost incurred to dismantle and discard it to the purchase price of the new motor.

Future disposal values

Assets may have relevant disposal values. The disposal value at the end of a project's life is an increase in the cash inflow in the year of disposal. Errors in forecasting terminal disposal values are usually not crucial because the PV is usually small.

Operating cash flows

The major purpose of most investments is to affect operating cash inflows and outflows. Many of these effects are difficult to measure and three points deserve special mention:

1 The only relevant cash flows are those that will differ among alternatives. Often, fixed overhead will be the same under all the available alternatives. If so, you can safely ignore it. In practice, it is not easy to identify exactly which costs will differ among alternatives.

2 Remember that you are predicting cash inflows and outflows, not revenues and expenses. Therefore, you should ignore depreciation and book values. We recognise the cost of assets by the initial outlay, not by depreciation as computed under accrual accounting. Further, cash inflows may not occur in the same period as the related revenues and cash outflows may not coincide with the related expense recognition.

3 We treat a reduction in a cash outflow the same as a cash inflow. Both signify increases in value.

◼ Cash flows for investments in technology

Many capital-budgeting decisions compare a potential investment with doing nothing. One such decision is investment in flexible organisational technologies such as a flexible manufacturing system with a high degree of automation to replace a traditional system (see Bhimani, 2012). Cash flows predicted for the automated system should be compared with those predicted for continuation of the present system into the future. The latter predictions are not necessarily the current cash flows. Why? Because the competitive environment is changing. If others invest in automated systems, failure to invest may cause a decline in sales and an uncompetitive cost structure. The future without an automated system might be a continual decline in cash flows.

Suppose a company currently has a €10,000 net cash inflow annually using a traditional system. Investing in an automated system will increase the net cash inflow to €12,000. Failure to invest will cause net cash inflows to fall to €8,000. The benefit from the investment is a cash inflow of €12,000 − €8,000 = €4,000, not €12,000 − €10,000 = €2,000. This situation arises in many technology investments such as those described in the Business first box on page 487.

Summary problem for your review

PROBLEM

Review the example shown in Exhibit 11.2, p. 486. Conduct three independent sensitivity analyses as indicated next.

1 Compute the difference in the NPV of the alternatives if the minimum desired rate of return were 20 per cent instead of 14 per cent.

2 Compute the difference in the NPV of the alternatives if predicted cash operating costs of the new motor were £35,000 annually instead of £30,000, using the 14 per cent discount rate.

3 By how much may the annual cash operating savings fall short of the £10,000 predicted amount before the difference in NPV between the alternatives reaches zero? Use the original discount rate of 14 per cent?

SOLUTION

1 You can use either the total project approach or the differential approach. The differential approach shows the following:

	Total present value
Recurring cash operating savings, using an annuity table (Table B2, p. 680): 2.9906 × £10,000 =	£29,906
Overhaul avoided: .6944 × £10,000 =	6,944
Difference in disposal values: .4019 × £5,000 =	(2,010)
Incremental initial investment	(31,000)
Difference in NPV between the alternatives	£ 3,840

2

Difference in NPV value in Exhibit 11.2	£ 8,429
Present value of additional £5,000 annual operating costs 3.4331 × £5,000	(17,166)
Difference in NPV between the alternatives	£(8,737)

With £5,000 less in annual savings, the new motor yields a negative difference in the NPV between the alternatives and therefore is not desirable.

3 Let X = annual cash operating savings and find the value of X so that the difference in NPV between the two alternatives = 0. Then,

$$0 = 3.4331(X) + £7,695 - £2,597 - £31,000$$

$$3.4331(X) = £25,902$$

$$X = £7,545$$

(Note that the £7,695, £2,597 and £31,000 are at the bottom of Exhibit 11.2.)

If the annual savings fall from £10,000 to £7,545, a decrease of £2,455 or almost 25 per cent, the NPV will hit zero.

An alternative way to obtain the same answer would be to divide the NPV of £8,429 (see bottom of Exhibit 11.2) by 3.4331, obtaining £2,455, the amount of the annual difference in savings that will eliminate the £8,429 of NPV.

Income taxes and capital budgeting

Objective 5
Compute the after-tax net present values of projects.

We must consider another type of cash flow when making capital-budgeting decisions: income taxes. Income taxes paid by companies are cash outflows. Their basic role in capital budgeting does not differ from that of any other cash outflow. However, taxes tend to narrow the cash differences between projects. For example, if the cash savings from operations of one project over another were €1 million, a 40 per cent tax rate would shrink the savings to €600,000. Why? Because the company would have to pay 40% × €1 million = €400,000 of the savings in taxes.

In capital budgeting, the relevant tax rate is the **marginal income tax rate**, that is, the tax rate paid on additional amounts of pretax income. Suppose a company pays income taxes of 15 per cent on the first €50,000 of pretax income and 30 per cent on pretax income over €50,000. What is the company's marginal income tax rate when it has €75,000 of pretax income? The marginal rate is 30 per cent, because the company will pay 30 per cent of any additional income in taxes. In contrast, the company's average income tax rate is only 20 per cent (that is, 15% × €50,000 + 30% × €25,000 = €15,000 of taxes on €75,000 of pretax income). When we assess tax effects of capital-budgeting decisions, we will always use the marginal tax rate because that is the rate applied to the additional cash flows generated by a proposed project.

Effects of depreciation deductions

Organisations that pay income taxes generally keep two sets of books – one for reporting to the public and one for reporting to the tax authorities. This practice is not illegal or immoral – it is necessary. Tax reporting must follow detailed rules designed to achieve certain social goals. These rules do not usually lead to financial statements that best measure an organisation's financial results and position, so it is more informative to financial statement users if companies use a separate set of rules for financial reporting. In this chapter, we are concerned with measuring cash payments for taxes. Therefore, we focus on the tax reporting rules, not those for public financial reporting.

One item that often differs between tax reporting and public reporting is depreciation. Recall that depreciation spreads the cost of an asset over its useful life. Income tax laws and regulations generally permit companies to spread the cost over depreciable lives that are shorter than the assets' useful lives. Some tax authorities allow **accelerated depreciation**, which charges a larger proportion of an asset's cost to the earlier years and less to later years. In contrast, an asset's depreciation for public reporting purposes is usually the same each year, called straight-line depreciation. For example, a €10,000 asset depreciated over a 5-year useful life results in straight-line depreciation of €10,000 ÷ 5 = €2,000 each year. In contrast, accelerated depreciation provides more than €2,000 of depreciation per year in the early years and less than €2,000 in the later years.

Exhibit 11.3 shows the interrelationship of income before taxes, income taxes and depreciation for a hypothetical asset owned by Toyota. Assume that Toyota's Burnaston operation purchases for £125,000 cash a machine that produces replacement parts used in Avensis exhaust systems. The machine has a 5-year **recovery period**, which is the number of years over which a company can depreciate an asset for tax purposes and also a 5-year useful life. Using the machine produces annual sales revenue of £130,000 and expenses (excluding depreciation) of £70,000. The purchase cost of the machine is tax deductible in the form of yearly depreciation.

Depreciating a fixed asset creates future tax deductions. In this case, these deductions will total the full purchase price of £125,000. The PV of this deduction depends directly on its specific yearly effects on future income tax payments. Therefore, the recovery period, the depreciation method selected, the tax rates and the discount rate all affect the PV of the tax deduction.

Exhibit 11.4 analyses Toyota's data for capital budgeting, assuming that the company uses straight-line depreciation for tax purposes. The NPV is £40,821 for the investment in this asset. The £125,000 investment really buys two streams of cash: (1) net inflows from operations over the useful life plus (2) savings of income tax outflows (which have the same effect

Traditional annual income statement		
(S)	Sales	£130,000
(E)	Less: Expenses, excluding depreciation	£ 70,000
(D)	Depreciation (straight-line)	25,000
	Total expenses	£ 95,000
	Income before taxes	£ 35,000
(T)	Income taxes at 40%	14,000
(I)	Net income	£ 21,000
	Total after-tax effect on cash is	
	either S − E − T = £130,000 − £70,000 − £14,000 = £46,000	
	or I + D = £21,000 + £25,000 = £46,000	
	Analysis of the same facts for capital budgeting	
	Cash effects of operations:	
(S − E)	Cash inflow from operations: £130,000 − £70,000	£ 60,000
	Income tax outflow at 40%	£ 24,000
	After-tax inflow from operations (excluding depreciation)	£ 36,000
	Cash effects of depreciation:	
(D)	Straight-line depreciation: £125,000 ÷ 5 = £25,000	
	Income tax savings at 40%	10,000
	Total after-tax effect on cash	£ 46,000

Exhibit 11.3 Toyota machine – Basic analysis of income statement, income taxes and cash flows

in capital budgeting as do additions to cash inflows) from the depreciation deduction over the recovery period. The choice of depreciation method will not affect the cash inflows from operations. But different depreciation methods will affect the cash outflows for income taxes. That is, a straight-line method will produce one PV of total tax savings and an accelerated method will produce a different (higher) PV.

■ Tax Deductions, cash effects and timing

Note that we computed the net cash effects of operations in Exhibit 11.4 by multiplying the pretax amounts by one minus the tax rate, or $1 − .40 = .60$. The total effect is the cash flow itself less the tax effect. Each additional £1 of sales also adds £.40 of taxes, leaving a net cash inflow of £.60. Each additional £1 of cash expense reduces taxes by £.40, leaving a net cash outflow of £.60. Thus, the after-tax effect of the £130,000 − £70,000 = £60,000 net cash inflow from operations is an after-tax inflow of £130,000 × .6 − £70,000 × .6 − (£130,000 − £70,000) × .6 = £60,000 × .6 = £36,000.

In contrast, we compute the after-tax effects of depreciation by multiplying the tax deduction of £25,000 by the tax rate itself, or £25,000 × .40 = £10,000. Note that this is a cash inflow because it is a decrease in the tax payment. Without the depreciation deduction, taxes would be higher by £10,000 annually. The total cash effect of depreciation is only the tax-savings effect.

Throughout the illustrations in this chapter, we assume that all income tax flows occur at the same time as the related pretax cash flows. For example, we assume that both the net £60,000 pretax cash inflow and the related £24,000 tax payment occurred at the end of year 1. We also assume that the companies in question are profitable. That is, the companies will have enough taxable income from all sources to use all income tax benefits in the situations described.

	12% discount factors, from appropriate tables	Total preset value at 12%	Sketch of after-tax cash flows at end of year					
			0	1	2	3	4	5
Cash effects of operations, excluding depreciation, £60,000 × (1 − .4)	3.6048	£129,773		36,000	36,000	36,000	36,000	36,000
Cash effects of straight-line depreciation: savings of income taxes, £25,000 × .4	3.6048	36,048		10,000	10,000	10,000	10,000	10,000
Total after-tax effect on cash		165,821						
Investment	1.0000	(125,000)	(125,000)					
Net present value of the investment		£ 40,821						

Exhibit 11.4 **Impact of income taxes on capital-budgeting analysis**
Assume: original cost of equipment, £100,000; 5-year recovery period; 5-year useful life; zero terminal disposal value; pretax annual net cash inflow from operations, £60,000; income tax rate, 40 per cent; required after-tax rate of return, 12 per cent. All items are in pounds except discount factors. The after-tax cash flows are from Exhibit 11.3.

Summary problem for your review

PROBLEM

Consider Toyota's purchase of the £125,000 machine analysed in Exhibits 11.3 and 11.4. Suppose the machine had a useful life of 6 years, but the recovery period remains 5 years. What is the net present value of the investment?

SOLUTION

The present value of the tax savings will not change. Only the recovery period, not the useful life, affects the depreciation deductions. There will be one extra year of operating savings in year 6. Its present value is £36,000 × .5066 = £18,238. Therefore, the net present value is £59,059:

Original NPV (from Exhibit 11.4)	£40,821
Added PV of savings in year 6	18,238
NPV	£59,059

Note especially that the recovery period for tax purposes and the economic useful life of the asset need not be equal. The tax law specifies recovery periods for various types of depreciable assets. The economic useful life of the asset does not affect the recovery period. Thus, a longer useful life for an asset increases operating cash flows without decreasing the PV of the tax savings.

■ Accelerated depreciation

Governments frequently allow accelerated depreciation to encourage investments in long-lived assets. To see why accelerated depreciation is attractive to investors, reconsider the facts in Exhibit 11.4. Suppose that, as is the case in some countries, companies could write off immediately the entire initial investment for income tax reporting. We see that NPV will rise from £40,821 to £54,773.

	Present values	
	As in Exhibit 11.4	Complete write-off immediately
Cash effects of operations	£129,773	£129,773
Cash effects of depreciation	36,048	50,000*
Total after-tax effect on cash	165,821	179,773
Investment	(125,000)	(125,000)
Net present value	£ 40,821	£ 54,773

*Assumes that the tax effect occurs simultaneously with the investment at time zero:
£125,000 × .40 = £50,000.

In summary, the earlier you can take the depreciation, the greater the PV of the income tax savings. The total tax savings will be the same regardless of the depreciation method. In the example, the tax savings from the depreciation deduction is either .40 × £125,000 = £50,000 immediately or .40 × £25,000 = £10,000 per year for 5 years, a total of £50,000. However, the time value of money makes the immediate savings worth more than future savings. The mottoes in income tax planning are 'When there is a legal choice, take the deduction sooner rather than later,' and 'Recognise taxable income later rather than sooner'.

Managers have an obligation to stockholders to minimise and delay taxes to the extent permitted by law. For example, astute managers use accelerated depreciation instead of straight-line depreciation whenever the law permits its use. We call this tax avoidance. Careful tax planning can have large financial payoffs. In contrast, managers must not engage in tax evasion, which is illegally reducing taxes by recording fictitious deductions or failing to report income. Managers who avoid taxes get bonuses; those who evade taxes undergo investigation and often land in jail. For instance, Italian designers Domenico Dolce and Steffano Gabbana have been at the centre of a tax evasion probe totalling almost €1 billion. The designers started their company in 1985. It now employs more than 3,000 people, with a network of 116 stores and 17 factory outlets. It was claimed that Dolce and Gabbana set up a company in

MAKING MANAGERIAL DECISIONS

Why do managers like accelerated depreciation for tax purposes? Consider an investment of £100,000 in an asset with a 10-year economic life. The asset has no salvage value at the end of 10 years. The tax rate is 40 per cent and the required rate of return is 10 per cent. What is the PV of the depreciation tax savings using straight-line (SL) depreciation? Which depreciation method would you choose if you were managing the company – SL or accelerated?

Answers

Straight-line depreciation = £10,000 per year, so tax savings with SL is .40 = £10,000 = £4,000 per year. Thus, the present value of the SL tax savings is £4,000 = 6.1446 = £24,578.40.

A good manager will choose accelerated depreciation in favour of SL as this will minimise taxes and maximise NPV.

Luxembourg through which sales royalties passed and which were taxed at 3 per cent, enabling them to evade higher-rate Italian taxes. Insufficient evidence to support the accusations is viewed by a Milan judge as making the case dismissible.

Proving tax evasion relies on factual records. Once evidence is clear, penalties can be very punitive.

■ Gains or losses on disposal

Objective 6
Explain the after-tax effect on cash received from the disposal of assets.

The disposal of equipment for cash can also affect income taxes. Suppose Toyota sells its £125,000 machine at the end of year 3 after taking 3 years of straight-line depreciation. If Toyota sells it for its net book value, £125,000 − (3 × £25,000) = £50,000, there is no tax effect. If Toyota receives more than $50,000, there is a gain and an additional tax payment. If the company receives less than £50,000, there is a loss and a tax saving. The following table shows the effects on cash flow for sales prices of £70,000 and £20,000:

		£70,000	£20,000
(a)	Cash proceeds of sale	£70,000	£20,000
	Book value: [£125,000 − (3 × £25,000)]	50,000	50,000
	Gain (loss)	£20,000	£(30,000)
	Effect on income taxes at 40%:		
(b)	Tax savings, an inflow effect: .40 × loss		£ 12,000
(c)	Tax paid, an outflow: .40 × gain	£ (8,000)	
	Net cash inflow from sale:		
	(a) plus (b)		£ 32,000
	(a) minus (c)	£62,000	

Confusion about depreciation

The meanings of depreciation and book value are widely misunderstood. Let's review their role in decisions. Suppose Toyota is considering the replacement of some old copying equipment with a book value of £30,000, an expected terminal disposal value of zero, a current disposal value of £12,000 and a remaining useful life of 3 years. For simplicity, assume that Toyota will take straight-line depreciation of £10,000 yearly. The tax rate is 40 per cent.

You should be careful to examine these data in perspective, as Exhibit 11.5 indicates. In particular, note that the inputs to the decision model are the predicted income tax effects on cash. Book values and depreciation may be necessary for making predictions. By themselves, however, they are not inputs to the DCF decision model.

Other models for analysing long-range decisions

Objective 7
Use the payback model and the accounting rate-of-return model and compare them with the NPV model.

Although an increasing number of companies are using DCF models to make their capital-budgeting decisions, some companies still use simpler models, either in place of or in addition to the NPV model. We will examine two such models, the payback and accounting rate-of-return models.

Exhibit 11.5 Perspective on book value and depreciation

■ Payback model

Payback time or **payback period** is the time it will take to recoup, in the form of cash inflows from operations, the initial amount invested in a project. Assume that Toyota spends £12,000 for a forklift that has an estimated useful life of 4 years. Toyota expects annual savings of £4,000 in cash outflows. The payback period is 3 years, calculated as follows:

$$\text{payback time} = \frac{\text{initial incremental amount invested}}{\text{equal annual incremental cash inflow from operations}}$$

$$P = \frac{I}{O} = \frac{£12,000}{£4,000} = 3 \text{ years}$$

We can use this formula for payback time only when there are equal annual cash inflows from operations. When annual cash inflows are not equal, we must add up each year's net cash inflows until they add up to the amount of the initial investment.

Assume the following cash flow pattern for the forklift:

End of year	0	1	2	3	4
Investment	(£12,000)				
Cash inflows		£4,000	£6,000	£5,000	£5,000

The calculation of the payback period is as follows:

		Net cash inflows	
Year	Initial investment	Each year	Accumulated
0	£12,000		
1	—	£4,000	£ 4,000
2	—	6,000	10,000
2+	—	2,000	12,000

In this case, the payback time is slightly beyond the second year. Interpolation within the third year reveals that an additional $\frac{4}{10}$ of a year is needed to recoup the final £2,000, making the payback period 2.4 years:

$$2 \text{ years} + \left(\frac{£2,000}{£5,000} \times 1 \text{ year} \right) = 2.4 \text{ years}$$

Three major weaknesses of the payback model are that (1) it does not measure profitability, which is a primary goal of businesses, (2) it ignores the time value of money and (3) it ignores cash flows beyond the payback period. DCF models recognise all cash flows and allow for the force of interest and the timing of cash flows. The payback model merely measures how quickly a company will recoup its investment dollars. However, a project with a shorter payback time is not necessarily preferable to one with a longer payback time. After all, a company can recoup its entire investment immediately by not investing.

Sometimes managers use the payback period as a rough estimate of the riskiness of a project. Suppose a company faces rapid technological changes. Cash flows beyond the first few years may be extremely uncertain. In such a situation, projects that recoup their investment quickly may be less risky than those that require a longer wait until the cash starts flowing in.

■ Accounting rate-of-return model

The **accounting rate-of-return (ARR) model** expresses a project's return as the increase in expected average annual operating income divided by the initial required investment.

$$\text{accounting rate-of-return (ARR)} = \frac{\text{increase in expected average annual operating income}}{\text{initial required investment}}$$

$$= \frac{O - D}{I} = \frac{\text{average annual incremental net cash in flow from operations} - \text{incremental average annual depreciation}}{\text{initial required investment}}$$

ARR computations dovetail most closely with conventional accounting models of calculating income and required investment and they show the effect of an investment on an organisation's financial statements.

To see how ARR works, assume the same facts as in Exhibit 11.1: investment is £5,827, useful life is 4 years, estimated disposal value is zero and expected annual cash inflow from operations is £2,000. Annual depreciation is £5,827 ÷ 4 = £1,456.75, rounded to £1,457. Substitute these values in the accounting rate-of-return equation:

$$\text{ARR} = \frac{(£2,000 - £1,457)}{£5,827} = 9.3\%$$

Some companies use the 'average' investment (often assumed to be the average book value over the useful life) instead of original investment in the denominator. Therefore, the denominator[3] becomes £5,827 ÷ 2 = £2,913.50:

$$\text{ARR} = \frac{(£2,000 - £1,457)}{£2,913.50} = 18.6\%$$

---

[3]The investment committed to the project would decline at a rate of £1,456 per year from £5,827 to zero; hence, the average investment would be the beginning balance plus the ending balance (£5,827 + 0) divided by 2, or £2,913.50.

The accounting rate-of-return model is based on the familiar financial statements prepared under accrual accounting. Unlike the payback model, the accounting model at least has profitability as an objective. Nevertheless, it has a major drawback – it ignores the time value of money. DCF models explicitly allow for the force of interest and the timing of cash flows. In contrast, the accounting model uses annual averages. It uses concepts of investment and income that accountants originally designed for a quite different purpose, accounting for periodic income and financial position.

The increasing use of DCF models as well as the continued use of payback and accounting rate of return models is described in the Business First box on p. 498.

Performance evaluation

▪ Potential conflict

Objective 8
Reconcile the conflict between using an NPV model for making decisions and using accounting income for evaluating the related performance.

Many managers who are evaluated on the basis of accounting income or an ARR model are reluctant to accept DCF models as the best way to make capital-budgeting decisions. To illustrate, consider the potential conflict that might arise in the example of Exhibit 11.1. Recall that the NPV was £513 based on a 10 per cent required rate of return, an investment of £5,827, cash savings of £2,000 for each of 4 years and no terminal disposal value. Using ARR with accounting income computed with straight-line depreciation, the evaluation of performance for years 1–4 would be as follows:

	Year 1	Year 2	Year 3	Year 4
Cash-operating savings	£2,000	£2,000	£2,000	£2,000
Straight-line depreciation, £5,827 ÷ 4	1,457	1,457	1,457	1,457*
Effect on operating income	543	543	543	543
Book value at beginning of year	5,827	4,370	2,913	1,456
ARR	9.3%	12.4%	18.6%	37.3%

*Total depreciation of 4 × £1,457 = £5,828 differs from £5,827 because of rounding error. Also, the ARR is based on the book value at the beginning of the year as a proxy for the investment.

Many managers would be reluctant to replace equipment, despite the positive NPV, if superiors evaluated their performance by accounting rate of return. They might be especially reluctant if they are likely to transfer to new positions (or retire) within a short time frame. Why? This accrual accounting system understates the return in early years, especially in year 1 when the return is below the required rate and a manager might not be around to reap the benefits of the later overstatement of returns.

As Chapter 6 indicated, managers are especially reluctant to replace assets if a heavy book loss on old equipment would appear in year 1's income statement – even though such a loss is irrelevant in a properly constructed decision model. Thus, performance evaluation based on typical accounting measures can cause the rejection of major, long-term projects, such as investments in technologically advanced production systems. This pattern may help explain why many firms seem to be excessively short-term oriented.

▪ Reconciliation of conflict

The best way to reconcile any potential conflict between capital budgeting and performance evaluation is to use DCF for both capital-budgeting decisions and performance evaluation. Companies that use EVA for performance evaluation, as described in Chapter 10, p. 425, avoid

BUSINESS FIRST
Who uses what capital budgeting model?

Companies are increasingly using formal capital budgeting models and most use more than one model. Of the 1,000 largest US companies, more than 95 per cent use a DCF model for their large investment decisions, although about half of them use such methods only for investments over $500,000. The NPV model is the most popular DCF method, with many also using IRR. However, use of the payback model remains strong, with more than half of the companies using it for at least some decisions.

Many smaller companies also use DCF methods. However, there is a clear relationship between size and capital budgeting methods. The larger the company and the larger the investment, the more likely is the use of DCF methods. Smaller companies use the payback method more often. Companies that have high financial leverage and young, highly-educated CFOs are more likely to use DCF methods. Fast growing companies use the payback method more than similar-sized, low-growth companies.

DCF methods have also made inroads into nonprofit companies. For example, hospitals have huge capital investment decisions. A few years ago the payback model was the dominant capital budgeting model used, but recent studies show that DCF models are used as often as payback. Further, large, multi-hospital systems generally use DCF methods.

More companies in the United States use DCF methods than in other countries, but the usage is nearly as high in the United Kingdom, Australia and the Netherlands. Even in China, nearly 90 per cent of the large companies use DCF methods. However, in China the dominant DCF method is IRR and a larger percentage of companies continue to use the payback method for some investments. As companies become more sophisticated and more dependent on capital markets, they tend to progress from payback to IRR and then to NPV. One study of 321 firms in Canada, France, Germany, Italy, Britain and the United States showed the following usage rates: payback 70 per cent, IRR 69 per cent, NPV 71 per cent and ARR 26 per cent.[1]

Some companies prefer more sophisticated techniques to analyse capital investment decisions. The most popular is sensitivity analysis. Also, the use of real options is growing quickly. In 2002 a quarter of large US companies already used real options, as did a third of Australian firms in 2008.

Sources: G. Truong, G. Partington and M. Peat, 'Cost-of-capital estimation and capital-budgeting practices in Australia', *Australian Journal of Management*, June 2008, pp. 95–121; C. Kocher, 'Hospital capital budgeting practices and their relation to key hospital characteristics: a survey of U.S. manager practices', *Journal of Global Business Issues*, 1 July 2007, pp. 21–30 ; J. Graham and C. Harvey, 'How do CFOs make capital budgeting and capital structure decisions?' *Journal of Applied Corporate Finance*, Spring 2002, pp. 8–23; P. Ryan and G. Ryan, 'Capital budgeting practices of the Fortune 1000: how have things changed?' *Journal of Business and Management*, Winter 2002, pp. 355–364; and N. Hermes, P. Smid and L. Yao, 'Capital budgeting practices: a comparative study of the Netherlands and China', November 2005, available at SSRN: http://ssrn.com/abstract=881754.
[1] Bhimani, A., Gosselin, M., Soonawalla, K. and Ncube, M. (2007) 'The value of accounting information in investment risk', *Cost Managament* 21 (1), pp. 29–35.

some of the conflict. Although EVA has the weakness of using accrual accounting measures of profit and investment rather than cash flows, it has conceptual similarities to the NPV method of capital budgeting. Both EVA and NPV recognise that a firm creates value only after projects cover their cost of capital.

Another way to address this issue is to conduct a follow-up evaluation of capital-budgeting decisions, often called a **post-audit**. Most large companies (76 per cent in a recent survey) post-audit at least some capital-budgeting decisions. The purposes of a post-audit include the following:

1 Seeing that investment expenditures are proceeding on time and within budget.

2 Comparing actual cash flows with those originally predicted, in order to motivate careful and honest predictions.

3 Providing information for improving future predictions of cash flows.

4 Evaluating the continuation of the project.

By focusing the post-audit on actual versus predicted cash flows, we can make the evaluation consistent with the decision process. However, post-auditing of all capital-budgeting decisions is costly. Most accounting systems are best at evaluating operating performances of products, departments, divisions, territories and so on, year by year. In contrast, capital-budgeting decisions frequently deal with individual projects, not the collection of projects that are usually being managed at the same time by division or department managers. Therefore, most companies audit only selected capital-budgeting decisions.

The conflicts between the longstanding, pervasive accrual accounting model and various formal decision models create some of the most serious unsolved problems in the design of management control systems. Top management cannot expect goal congruence if it favours the use of one type of model for decisions and the use of another type for performance evaluation.

Highlights to remember

1 **Describe capital-budgeting decisions and use the net-present-value (NPV) method to make such decisions.** Capital budgeting is long-term planning for proposed capital outlays and their financing. The net-present-value (NPV) model aids this process by computing the present value (PV) of all expected future cash flows using a minimum desired rate of return. A company should accept projects with an NPV greater than zero.

2 **Evaluate projects using sensitivity analysis.** Managers use sensitivity analysis to aid risk assessment by examining the effects if actual cash flows differ from those expected.

3 **Calculate the NPV difference between two projects using both the total project and differential approaches.** The total project approach compares the NPVs of the cash flows from each project, while the differential approach computes the NPV of the difference in cash flows between two projects. Both produce the same results if there are two alternatives. You have to use the total project approach if you have more than two alternatives.

4 **Identify relevant cash flows for NPV analyses.** Predicting cash flows is the hardest part of capital budgeting. Managers should consider four categories of cash flows: initial cash inflows and outflows at time zero, investments in working capital, future disposal values and operating cash flows.

5 **Compute the after-tax net present values of projects.** Income taxes can have a significant effect on the desirability of an investment. Additional taxes are cash outflows, and tax savings are cash inflows. Accelerated depreciation speeds up a company's tax savings. Generally, companies should take depreciation deductions as early as legally permitted.

6 **Explain the after-tax effect on cash received from the disposal of assets.** When companies sell assets for more than their book value, the gain generates additional taxes. When they sell assets for less than their book value, the loss generates tax savings.

7 **Use the payback model and the accounting rate-of-return model and compare them with the NPV model.** The payback model is simple to apply, but it does not measure profitability. The accounting rate-of-return model uses accounting measures of income and investment, but it ignores the time value of money. Both models are inferior to the NPV model.

8 **Reconcile the conflict between using an NPV model for making decisions and using accounting income for evaluating the related performance.** NPV is a summary measure of all the cash flows from a project. Accounting income is a one-period measure. A positive NPV project can have low (or even negative) accounting income in the first year.

Managers may be reluctant to invest in such a project, despite its positive value to the company, especially if they expect to be transferred to a new position before they can benefit from the positive returns that come later. ▪

Appendix 11: Capital budgeting and inflation

Objective 9
Compute the impact of inflation on a capital-budgeting project (Appendix 11).

Capital-budgeting decision makers should also consider the effects of inflation on their cash-flow predictions. **Inflation** is the decline in the general purchasing power of the monetary unit. For example, a euro today will buy only half as much as it did in the late-1980s. At a 5 per cent annual inflation rate, average prices rise more than 60 per cent over 10 years. The UK had double-digit inflation rates in the late 1970s and some countries, such as Brazil and Argentina, have had triple-digit annual inflation rates (that is, average prices more than doubling each year). In the last decade, inflation rates in the UK and most other Western economies have been low – generally around 3 per cent – but it is possible that rates in the future might increase. If a company expects significant inflation over the life of a project, it should specifically and consistently recognise inflation in its capital-budgeting decisions.

▨ Watch for consistency

The key to appropriate consideration of inflation in capital budgeting is consistent treatment of the required rate of return and the predicted cash inflows and outflows. We can achieve such consistency by including an element for inflation in both the required rate and in the cash-flow predictions.

Many firms base their required rate of return on market interest rates, also called **nominal rates**, that include an inflation element. For example, consider three possible components of a 12 per cent nominal rate:

(a)	Risk-free element – the 'pure' rate of interest	3%
(b)	Business-risk element – the 'risk' premium that is demanded for taking larger risks	5
(a) + (b)	Often called the 'real rate'	8%
(b)	Inflation element – the premium demanded because of expected deterioration of the general purchasing power of the monetary unit	4
(a) + (b) + (c)	Often called the 'nominal rate'	12%

Four percentage points out of the 12 per cent return compensate an investor for receiving future payments in inflated money amounts that is, with less purchasing power than those invested. Therefore, basing the required rate of return on quoted market rates automatically includes an inflation element in the rate. Companies that base their required rate of return on market rates should also adjust their cash-flow predictions for anticipated inflation. For example, suppose a company expects to sell 1,000 units of a product in each of the next 2 years. Assume this year's price is €50 and inflation causes next year's price to be €52.50. This year's predicted cash inflow is 1,000 × €50 = €50,000, and next year's inflation-adjusted cash inflow is 1,000 × €52.50 = €52,500. Inflation-adjusted cash flows are the inflows and outflows expected after adjusting prices to reflect anticipated inflation.

Consider another illustration: purchase cost of equipment, €200,000; useful life, 5 years; zero terminal salvage value; pretax operating cash savings per year, €83,333 (in 20X0 terms); income tax rate, 40 per cent. For simplicity, we assume ordinary straight-line depreciation of €200,000 ÷ 5 = €40,000 per year. The after-tax minimum desired rate, based on quoted market rates, is 25 per cent. It includes an inflation factor of 10 per cent.

		At 25%		Sketch of relevant cash flows (at end of year)					
Description		PV factor	Present value	0	1	2	3	4	5
Correct analysis (Be sure the discount rate includes an element attributable to inflation and adjust the predicted cash flows for inflationary effects.)									
Cash operating inflows:									
Pretax inflow in 20X0 terms	€83,333								
Income tax effect at 40%	33,333								
After-tax effect on cash	€50,000								
		.8000	€ 44,000		€55,000*				
		.6400	38,720			€60,500			
		.5120	34,074				€66,550		
		.4096	29,985					€73,205	
		.3277	26,388						€80,526
Subtotal			€173,167						
Annual depreciation €200,000 ÷ 5 = €40,000									
Cash effect of depreciation									
Savings in income taxes at 40% = €40,000 × .40 = €16,000		2.6893	43,029		€16,000†	€16,000	€16,000	€16,000	€16,000
Investment in equipment		1.0000	(200,000)	(€200,000)					
Net present value			€ 16,196						
Incorrect analysis (A common error is to include an inflation element in the discount rate as above, but not adjust the predicted cash inflows.)									
Cash operating inflows after taxes		2.6893	€134,465		€50,000	€50,000	€50,000	€50,000	€50,000
Tax effect of depreciation		2.6893	43,029		16,000	16,000	16,000	16,000	16,000
Investment in equipment		1.0000	(200,000)	(€200,000)					
Net present value			€ (22,506)						

*Each year is adjusted for anticipated inflation: €50,000 × 1.10, €50,000 × 1.10², €50,000 × 1.10³, and so on.

†Inflation will not affect the annual savings in income taxes from depreciation. Why? Because the income tax deduction must be based on original cost of the asset in 20X0 terms.

Exhibit 11.6 Inflation and capital budgeting

Exhibit 11.6 displays correct and incorrect ways to analyse the effects of inflation. The key words are *internal consistency*. The correct analysis (1) uses a minimum desired rate that includes an element attributable to inflation and (2) explicitly adjusts the predicted operating cash flows for the effects of inflation. Note that the correct analysis favours the purchase of the equipment, but the incorrect analysis does not.

The incorrect analysis in Exhibit 11.6 is inherently inconsistent. The predicted cash inflows exclude adjustments for inflation. Instead, they are stated in 20X0 euros. However, the discount rate includes an element attributable to inflation. An analytical mistake like this might lead to an unwise refusal to purchase.

■ Role of depreciation

The correct analysis in Exhibit 11.6 shows that we did not adjust the tax effects of depreciation for inflation. Why? Because income tax laws generally permit a depreciation deduction based on the original amount invested, nothing more.

Critics of income tax laws emphasise that such laws discourage capital investment by not allowing companies to adjust depreciation deductions for inflationary effects. For instance, the NPV in Exhibit 11.6 would be larger if depreciation were not confined to the €40,000 amount per year. The latter generates a €16,000 savings in 20X1 terms, then €16,000 in 20X2 terms, and so forth. Defenders of existing tax laws assert that they encourage capital investment in many other ways. The most prominent example is provision for accelerated depreciation over lives that are much shorter than the economic lives of the assets.

Summary problem for your review

PROBLEM

Examine the correct analysis in Exhibit 11.6. Suppose the cash-operating inflows persisted for an extra year. Compute the PV of the inflow for the sixth year. Ignore depreciation.

SOLUTION

The cash operating inflow would be €50,000 × 1.10^6, or €80,526 × 1.10, or €88,579. Its PV would be €88,579 × .2621, the factor from Table B1 of Appendix B (period 6 row, 25 per cent column), or €23,217.

Accounting vocabulary

accelerated depreciation, p. 490	inflation, p. 500	payback period, p. 495
accounting rate-of-return (ARR) model, p. 496	internal rate of return (IRR) model, p. 482	payback time, p. 495
capital budgeting, p. 478	marginal income tax rate, p. 490	post-audit, p. 498
differential approach, p. 484	net present value, p. 479	present value (PV), p. 479
discount rate, p. 479	net-present-value (NPV)	real options model, p. 483
discounted-cash-flow (DCF) models, p. 478	method, p. 479	recovery period, p. 490
hurdle rate, p. 479	nominal rate, p. 500	required rate of return, p. 479
		total project approach, p. 484

Fundamental assignment material   MyAccountingLab

Special note: In all assignment materials that include taxes, assume, unless directed otherwise, that (1) all income tax cash flows occur simultaneously with the pretax cash flows, and (2) the companies in question will have enough taxable income from other sources to use all income tax benefits from the situations described.

11.A1 Exercises in compound interest: answers supplied

Use the appropriate interest table from Appendix B (see p. 677 or 680) to complete the following exercises. The answers appear at the end of the assignment material for this chapter, p. 516–517.

1 It is your sixtieth birthday. You plan to work 5 more years before retiring, at which point you and your spouse want to take €25,000 for a round-the-world tour. What lump sum do you have to invest now to accumulate the €25,000? Assume that your minimum desired rate of return is
   (a) 5 per cent, compounded annually.
   (b) 10 per cent, compounded annually.
   (c) 20 per cent, compounded annually.
2 You want to spend €2,000 on a vacation at the end of each of the next 5 years. What lump sum do you have to invest now to take the five vacations? Assume that your minimum desired rate of return is
   (a) 5 per cent, compounded annually.
   (b) 10 per cent, compounded annually.
   (c) 20 per cent, compounded annually.
3 At age 60, you find that your employer is moving to another location. You receive termination pay of €100,000. You have some savings and wonder whether to retire now.
   (a) If you invest the €100,000 now at 5 per cent, compounded annually, how much money can you withdraw from your account each year so that at the end of 5 years there will be a zero balance?
   (b) Answer part a, assuming that you invest it at 10%.
4 Two foottball players, LeBron and Kobe, signed 5-year, €60-million contracts. At 16 per cent, compounded annually, which of the following contracts is more desirable in terms of present values? Show computations to support your answer.

	Annual cash Inflows (in thousands)	
Year	LeBron	Kobe
1	€20,000	€ 4,000
2	16,000	8,000
3	12,000	12,000
4	8,000	16,000
5	4,000	20,000
	€60,000	€60,000

11.A2 NPV for investment decisions

A manager of the engineering department of Manchester University is contemplating acquiring 120 computers. The computers will cost £240,000 cash, have zero terminal salvage value and a useful life of 3 years. Annual cash savings from operations will be £110,000. The required rate of return is 14 per cent. There are no taxes.

1 Compute the NPV.
2 Should the engineering department acquire the computers? Explain.

11.A3 Taxes, straight-line depreciation and present values

A manager of Olympic Mutual Funds is contemplating acquiring servers to operate its website. The servers will cost £660,000 cash and will have zero terminal salvage value. The recovery period and useful life are both 3 years. Annual pretax cash savings from operations will be £300,000. The income tax rate is 40 per cent and the required after-tax rate of return is 12 per cent.

1 Compute the NPV, assuming straight-line depreciation of £220,000 yearly for tax purposes. Should Olympic acquire the computers? Explain.
2 Suppose the computers will be fully depreciated at the end of year 3 but can be sold for £90,000 cash. Compute the NPV. Should Olympic acquire the computers? Explain.
3 Ignore number 2. Suppose the required after-tax rate of return is 8 per cent instead of 12 per cent. Should Olympic acquire the computers? Show computations.

11.A4 Gains or losses on disposal

On 1 January 20X1, Brisbane Company sold an asset with a book value of $50,000 for cash.
   Assume two selling prices: $65,000 and $40,000. For each selling price, prepare a tabulation of the gain or loss, the effect on income taxes and the total after-tax effect on cash. The applicable income tax rate is 40 per cent.

11.B1 Exercises in compound interest

Use the appropriate table to compute the following:

1 You have always dreamed of taking a safari in Africa. What lump sum do you have to invest today to have the €16,000 needed for the trip in 3 years? Assume that you can invest the money at
   (a) 4 per cent, compounded annually.
   (b) 10 per cent, compounded annually.
   (c) 16 per cent, compounded annually.
2 You are considering partial retirement. To do so you need to use part of your savings to supplement your income for the next 5 years. Suppose you need an extra €20,000 per year. What lump sum do you have to invest now to supplement your income for 5 years? Assume that your minimum desired rate of return is
   (a) 4 per cent, compounded annually.
   (b) 10 per cent, compounded annually.
   (c) 16 per cent, compounded annually.
3 You just won a lump sum of €1,000,000 in a state lottery. You have decided to invest the winnings and withdraw an equal amount each year for 10 years. How much can you withdraw each year and have a zero balance left at the end of 10 years if you invest at
   (a) 5 per cent, compounded annually?
   (b) 10 per cent, compounded annually?

4 A tennis player is offered the choice of two 4-year salary contracts, contract X for €1.4 million and contract Y for €1.3 million:

	Contract X	Contract Y
End of year 1	€ 200,000	€ 450,000
End of year 2	300,000	350,000
End of year 3	400,000	300,000
End of year 4	500,000	200,000
Total	€1,400,000	€1,300,000

Which contract has the higher PV at 14 per cent compounded annually? Show computations to support your answer.

11.B2 NPV for investment decisions

The head of the oncology department, Karim Sajo, at the Aga Khan Hospital in Nairobi is considering the purchase of some new equipment. The cost KSh is 420,000, the economic life is 5 years and there is no terminal disposal value. Annual cash inflows from operations would increase by KSh 140,000 and the required rate of return is 14 per cent. There are no taxes.

1 Compute the NPV.
2 Should Dr Sajo acquire the equipment? Explain.

11.B3 Taxes, straight-line depreciation and NPV

The president of E-Games, an online gaming company, is considering the purchase of some equipment used for the development of new games. The cost is €400,000, the economic life and the recovery period are both 5 years and there is no terminal disposal value. Annual pretax cash inflows from operations would increase by €130,000, giving a total 5-year pretax savings of €650,000. The income tax rate is 40 per cent and the required after-tax rate of return is 14 per cent.

1 Compute the NPV, assuming straight-line depreciation of €80,000 yearly for tax purposes. Should E-Games acquire the equipment?
2 Suppose the asset will be fully depreciated at the end of year 5 but is sold for €25,000 cash. Should E-Games acquire the equipment? Show computations.
3 Ignore number 2. Suppose the required after-tax rate of return is 10 per cent instead of 14 per cent. Should E-Games acquire the equipment? Show computations.

11.B4 Income taxes and disposal of assets

Assume that the combined federal and state income tax rate for Quixote Company is 40 per cent.

1 The book value of an old machine is €25,000. Quixote sold the machine for €10,000 cash. What is the effect of this decision on after-tax cash flows?
2 The book value of an old machine is €25,000. Quixote sold the machine for €35,000 cash. What is the effect of this decision on after-tax cash flows?

Additional assignment material

MyAccountingLab

QUESTIONS

11.1 Capital budgeting has three phases: (a) identification of potential investments, (b) selection of investments, and (c) post-audit of investments. What is the accountant's role in each phase?

11.2 Why is discounted cash flow a superior method for capital budgeting?

11.3 'The higher the minimum desired rate of return, the higher the price that a company will be willing to pay for cost-saving equipment.' Do you agree? Explain.

11.4 'The DCF model assumes certainty and perfect capital markets. Thus, it is impractical to use it in most real-world situations.' Do you agree? Explain.

11.5 'Double-counting of costs occurs if depreciation is separately considered in DCF analysis.' Do you agree? Explain.

11.6 Does the IRR model make significantly different decisions than does the NPV model? Why or why not?

11.7 What does the real options model recognise that the NPV and IRR models do not?

11.8 'We can't use sensitivity analysis because our cash-flow predictions are too inaccurate.' Comment.

11.9 Why should the differential approach to alternatives always lead to the same decision as the total project approach?

11.10 'The NPV model should not be used for investment decisions about advanced technology, such as computer-integrated manufacturing systems.' Do you agree? Explain.

11.11 Distinguish between average and marginal tax rates.

11.12 'The government should pass a law forbidding corporations to keep two sets of books.' Do you agree? Explain.

11.13 Distinguish between tax avoidance and tax evasion.

11.14 'Companies that try to avoid taxes are unethical.' Do you agree? Discuss.

11.15 Explain why accelerated depreciation methods are superior to straight-line methods for income tax purposes.

11.16 'An investment in equipment really buys two streams of cash.' Do you agree? Explain.

11.17 Why should companies take tax deductions sooner rather than later?

11.18 'When there are income taxes, depreciation is a cash outlay.' Do you agree? Explain.

11.19 'If DCF approaches are superior to the payback and the accounting rate-of-return methods, why should we bother to learn the others? All it does is confuse things.' Answer this contention.

11.20 What is the basic flaw in the payback model?

11.21 Explain how a conflict can arise between capital-budgeting decision models and performance evaluation methods.

11.22 Study Appendix 11. What are the three components of market (nominal) interest rates?

11.23 Study Appendix 11. Describe how internal consistency is achieved when considering inflation in a capital-budgeting model.

CRITICAL THINKING EXERCISES

11.24 Investment in R&D

'It is impossible to use DCF methods for evaluating investments in R&D. There are no cost savings to measure and we don't even know what products might come out of our R&D activities.' This is a quote from an R&D manager who was asked to justify investment in a major research project based on its expected NPV. Do you agree with her statement? Explain.

11.25 Business valuation and NPV

When a company elects to invest in a project with a positive NPV, what will generally happen to the value of the company? What will happen to this value when the company invests in a negative NPV project?

11.26 Replacement of production facilities

A manufacturing company recently considered replacing one of its forming machines with a newer, faster, more accurate model. What cash flows would this decision be likely to affect? List both cash flows that would be easy to quantify and those for which measurement would be difficult.

EXERCISES

11.27 Exercise in compound interest

Chinn Wong wishes to purchase a €600,000 house. She has accumulated a €120,000 down payment, but she wishes to borrow €480,000 on a 30-year mortgage. For simplicity, assume annual mortgage payments occur at the end of each year and there are no loan fees.

1 What are Wong's annual payments if her interest rate is (a) 8 per cent, (b) 10 per cent, and (c) 12 per cent, compounded annually?
2 Repeat number 1 for a 15-year mortgage.
3 Suppose Wong had to choose between a 30-year and a 15-year mortgage, either one at a 10 per cent interest rate. Compute the total payments and total interest paid on (a) a 30-year mortgage and (b) a 15-year mortgage.

11.28 Exercise in compound interest

Suppose Subaru UK Limited wishes to borrow money from UBS. They agree on an annual rate of 10 per cent.

1 Suppose Subaru agrees to repay £500 million at the end of 4 years. How much will UBS lend Subaru?
2 Suppose Subaru agrees to repay a total of £500 million at a rate of £125 million at the end of each of the next 4 years. How much will UBS lend Subaru?

11.29 Exercise in compound interest

Suppose you are a loan officer for a bank. A start-up company has qualified for a loan. You are pondering various proposals for repayment:

1 Lump sum of £500,000 four years hence. How much will you lend if your desired rate of return is (a) 12 per cent, compounded annually, and (b) 16 per cent, compounded annually?
2 Repeat number 1, but assume that the interest rates are compounded semiannually.
3 Suppose the loan is to be paid in full by equal payments of £125,000 at the end of each of the next 4 years. How much will you lend if your desired rate of return is (a) 12 per cent, compounded annually, and (b) 16 per cent, compounded annually?

11.30 Basic relationships in interest tables

1 Suppose you borrow £100,000 now at 12 per cent interest, compounded annually. You will repay the borrowed amount plus interest in a lump sum at the end of 8 years. How much must you repay? Use Table B1 (p. 677) and the basic equation PV = future amount × conversion factor.

2 Assume the same facts as previously except that you will repay the loan in equal install-ments at the end of each of the 8 years. How much must you repay each year? Use Table B2 (p. 680) and the basic equation: PV = future annual amounts × conversion factor.

11.31 Simple NPV

Banerjee Company expects to receive €200 at the end of each of the next 5 years and an addi-tional €1,000 at the end of the fifth year. Therefore, the total payments will be €2,000. What is the NPV of the payments at an interest rate of 8 per cent?

11.32 NPV relationships

Fill in the blanks.

	Number of Years			
	8	18	20	28
Amount of annual cash inflow*	€12,000	€	€ 9,000	€ 8,000
Required initial investment	€	€80,000	€65,000	€27,000
Minimum desired rate of return	14%	20%	€	25%
NPV	€ 5,613	(€13,835)	€ 2,225	€

*To be received at the end of each year.

11.33 New equipment

The Modesto Office Equipment Company has offered to sell some new packaging equipment to the Chavez Company. The list price is €36,000, but Modesto has agreed to allow a trade-in allowance of €15,000 on some old equipment. The old equipment was carried at a book value of €8,700 and could be sold outright for €10,000 cash. Cash-operating savings are expected to be €5,000 annually for the next 12 years. The minimum desired rate of return is 12 per cent. The old equipment has a remaining useful life of 12 years. Both the old and the new equip-ment will have zero disposal values 12 years from now.

Should Chavez buy the new equipment? Show your computations, using the NPV method. Ignore income taxes.

11.34 Present values of cash inflows

City View Restaurant is about to open at a new location. Operating plans indicate the follow-ing expected cash flows:

		Outflows	Inflows
Initial investment now		€235,000	€ —
End of year:	1	€150,000	200,000
	2	€200,000	250,000
	3	€250,000	300,000
	4	€300,000	450,000
	5	€350,000	500,000

1 Compute the NPV for all these cash flows. This should be a single amount. Use a discount rate of 14 per cent.
2 Suppose the minimum desired rate was 12 per cent. Without further calculations, deter-mine whether the NPV is positive or negative. Explain.

11.35 Effect of minimum rate

Zielinsky Company has an opportunity to invest €5,000 in a new automated lathe that will reduce annual operating costs by €1,000 per year and will have an economic life of 7 years.

1 Suppose Zielinsky Company has a minimum desired rate of return of 5 per cent. Compute the NPV of the investment and recommend to Zielinsky Company whether it should purchase the lathe.
2 Suppose Zielinsky Company has a minimum desired rate of return of 12 per cent. Compute the NPV of the investment and recommend to Zielinsky Company whether it should purchase the lathe.
3 How does the desired rate of return affect the NPV of a potential investment?

11.36 NPV and IRR

Czick Company is considering an investment in a machine that costs €36,048 and would result in cash savings of €10,000 per year for 5 years. The company's cost of capital is 10 per cent.

1 Compute the project's NPV at 10 per cent, 12 per cent and 14 per cent.
2 Compute the project's IRR.
3 Suppose the company uses the NPV model. Would it accept the project? Why or why not?
4 Suppose the company uses the IRR model. Would it accept the project? Why or why not?

11.37 Sensitivity analysis

Gupta and Bonini a firm of solicitors, is considering the replacement of its old accounting system with new software that should save £6,000 per year in net cash operating costs. The old system has zero disposal value, but it could be used for the next 12 years. The estimated useful life of the new software is 12 years and it will cost £30,000. The minimum desired rate of return is 10 per cent.

1 What is the payback period?
2 Compute the NPV.
3 Management is unsure about the useful life. What would be the NPV if the useful life were
 (a) 5 years instead of 12 or (b) 20 years instead of 12?
4 Suppose the life will be 12 years, but the savings will be £4,000 per year instead of £6,000. What would be the NPV?
5 Suppose the annual savings will be £5,000 for 8 years. What would be the NPV?

11.38 NPV and sensitivity analysis

Chippewa Hotel currently has its laundry done by a local cleaners at an annual cost of €46,000. It is considering a purchase of washers, dryers and presses at a total installed cost of €52,000. The hotel expects savings of €15,000 per year and it expects the machines to last 5 years. The desired rate of return is 10 per cent.
 Answer each part separately.

1 Compute the NPV of the investment in laundry facilities.
2 (a) Suppose the machines last only 4 years. Compute the NPV.
 (b) Suppose the machines last 7 years. Compute the NPV.
3 (a) Suppose the annual savings are only €12,000. Compute the NPV.
 (b) Suppose the annual savings are €18,000. Compute the NPV.

4 (a) Compute the most optimistic estimate of NPV, combining the best outcomes in numbers 2 and 3.

   (b) Compute the most pessimistic estimate of NPV, combining the worst outcomes in numbers 2 and 3.

5 Accept the expected life estimate of 5 years. What is the minimum annual savings that would justify the investment in the laundry facilities?

11.39 Depreciation, income taxes, cash flows

Fill in the unknowns (in thousands of euros):

(S)	Sales	550
(E)	Expenses excluding depreciation	350
(D)	Depreciation	100
	Total expenses	450
	Income before income taxes	?
(T)	Income taxes at 30%	?
(I)	Net income	?
	Cash effects of operations	
	Cash inflow from operations	?
	Income tax outflow at 30%	?
	After-tax inflow from operations	?
	Effect of depreciation	
	Depreciation	?
	Income tax savings	?
	Total after-tax effect on cash	?

11.40 NPV, ARR and payback

TexaTaco is considering a proposal to invest in a speaker system that would allow its employees to service drive-through customers. The cost of the system (including installation of special windows and driveway modifications) is €36,000. Jessica Declan, manager of TexaTaco, expects the drive-through operations to increase annual sales by €25,000, with a 40 per cent contribution margin ratio. Assume that the system has an economic life of 6 years, at which time it will have no disposal value. The required rate of return is 12 per cent. Ignore taxes.

1 Compute the payback period. Is this a good measure of profitability?
2 Compute the NPV. Should Declan accept the proposal? Why or why not?
3 Using the ARR model, compute the rate of return on the initial investment.

11.41 Weaknesses of the payback model

De Luca Company is considering two possible investments, each of which requires an initial investment of €12,000. Investment A will provide a cash flow of €3,000 at the end of each year for 4 years. Investment B will provide a cash flow of €2,000 at the end of each year for 10 years.

1 Determine the payback period for each investment. Which investment is most desirable using the payback method?
2 Compute the NPV of each investment using a desired rate of return of 5%. Which investment is most desirable using the NPV method?
3 Explain why the payback method does not lead to an optimal decision for the De Luca Company.

11.42 Sensitivity of capital budgeting to inflation

Study Appendix 11. Enrique Mendoza, the president of a Spanish wholesale company, is considering whether to invest €420,000 in new semiautomatic loading equipment that will last 5 years, have zero scrap value and generate cash operating savings in labour usage of €150,000 annually, using 20X0 prices and wage rates. It is 31 December 20X0.

The minimum desired rate of return is 18 per cent per year after taxes.

1 Compute the NPV of the project. Use €150,000 as the savings for each of the 5 years. Assume a 40 per cent tax rate and, for simplicity, assume ordinary straight-line depreciation of €420,000 ÷ 5 = €84,000 annually for tax purposes.
2 Mendoza is wondering if the model in number 1 provides a correct analysis of the effects of inflation. He maintains that the 18 per cent rate embodies an element attributable to anticipated inflation. For purposes of this analysis, he assumes that the existing rate of inflation, 10 per cent annually, will persist over the next 5 years. Repeat number 1, adjusting the cash operating savings upward by using the 10 per cent inflation rate.
3 Which analysis, the one in number 1 or 2, is correct? Why?

PROBLEMS

11.43 Replacement of office equipment

Southampton University is considering replacing some Xerox copiers with faster copiers purchased from Cannon. The administration is very concerned about the rising costs of operations during the last decade.

To convert to Cannon, two operators would have to be retrained. Required training and remodelling would cost £4,000. Southeastern's three Xerox machines were purchased for £10,000 each, 5 years ago. Their expected life was 10 years. Their resale value now is £1,000 each and will be zero in 5 more years. The total cost of the new Cannon equipment will be £50,000; it will have zero disposal value in 5 years.

The three Xerox operators are paid £8 an hour each. They usually work a 40-hour week. Machine breakdowns occur monthly on each machine, resulting in repair costs of £50 per month and overtime of 4 hours, at time-and-one-half, per machine per month, to complete the normal monthly workload. Toner, supplies, and so on, cost £100 a month for each Xerox copier.

The Cannon system will require only two regular operators, on a regular work week of 40 hours each, to do the same work. Rates are £10 an hour and no overtime is expected. Toner, supplies, and so on will cost a total of £3,300 annually. Maintenance and repairs are fully serviced by Cannon for £1,050 annually. (Assume a 52-week year.)

1 Using DCF techniques, compute the PV of all relevant cash flows, under both alternatives, for the 5-year period discounted at 12 per cent. As a nonprofit university, Southampton does not pay income taxes.
2 Should Southampton keep the Xerox copiers or replace them if the decision is based solely on the given data?
3 What other considerations might affect the decision?

11.44 Replacement decision for railway equipment

Suppose the Norfolk Southern Railway is considering replacement of a power jack tamper, used for maintenance of track, with a new automatic raising device that can be attached to a production tamper.

The present power jack tamper cost £24,000 five years ago and had an estimated life of 12 years. A year from now, the machine will require a major overhaul estimated to cost £5,000.

It can be disposed of now via an outright cash sale for £4,000. There will be no value at the end of another 7 years.

The automatic raising attachment has a delivered selling price of £68,000 and an estimated life of 12 years. Because of anticipated future developments in combined maintenance machines, Norfolk Southern management predicts that the company will dispose of the machine at the end of the seventh year to take advantage of newly developed machines. Estimated sales value at the end of 7 years is £7,000.

Tests have shown that the automatic raising machine will produce a more uniform surface on the track than does the power jack tamper now in use. The new equipment will eliminate one labourer whose annual compensation, including fringe benefits, is £30,000.

Track maintenance work is seasonal and the equipment normally works from 1 May to 31 October each year. Machine operators and labourers are transferred to other work after 31 October, at the same rate of pay.

The salesman claims that the annual normal maintenance of the new machine will run about £1,000 per year. Because the automatic raising machine is more complicated than the manually operated machine, it will probably require a thorough overhaul at the end of the fourth year, at an estimated cost of £7,000.

Records show the annual normal maintenance of the power jack tamper to be £1,200. Fuel consumption of the two machines is equal. Should Norfolk Southern keep or replace the power jack tamper? The company requires a 10 per cent rate of return. Compute PV. Ignore income taxes.

11.45 Investment in machine

The Soho Ale Company has an old brewing machine with a net disposal value of £12,000 now and £4,000 five years from now. A new brewing machine is offered for £57,000 cash or £45,000 with a trade-in. The new machine will result in an annual operating cash outflow of £40,000 as compared with the old machine's annual outflow of £50,000. The disposal value of the new machine 5 years hence will be £2,000.

The minimum desired rate of return is 20 per cent. The company uses DCF techniques to guide these decisions.

Should Soho Ale acquire the new brewing machine? Show your calculations. Company procedures require the computing of the PV of each alternative. The most desirable alternative is the one with the least cost. Assume that the PV of £1 at 20 per cent for 5 years is £.40; the PV of an annuity of £1 at 20 per cent for 5 years is £3.

11.46 Replacement decision

Virgin Trains (VT) has included a cafeteria car on the passenger train it operates. Yearly operations of the cafeteria car have shown a consistent loss, which is expected to persist, as follows:

Revenue (in cash)		£200,000
Expenses for food, supplies, etc. (in cash)	£100,000	
Salaries	110,000	210,000
Net loss (ignore depreciation on the dining car itself)		£ (10,000)

The Auto-Vend Company has offered to sell automatic vending machines to VT for £22,000, less a £3,000 trade-in allowance on old equipment (which is carried at £3,000 book value and which can be sold outright for £3,000 cash) now used in the cafeteria-car operation. The useful life of the vending equipment is estimated at 10 years, with zero scrap value. Experience elsewhere has led executives to predict that the equipment will serve 50 per cent more food than the dining car, but prices will be 50 per cent less, so the new revenue will probably be £150,000. The variety and mix of food sold are expected to be the same as for the cafeteria car. A catering company will completely service and supply food and beverages for the machines, paying 10 per cent of revenue to VT and bearing all costs of food, repairs and so on. All dining-car employees will be discharged immediately. Their termination pay will total £35,000. However, an attendant who has some general knowledge of vending machines will be needed for one shift per day. The annual cost to VT for the attendant will be £13,000.

For political and other reasons, the railroad will definitely not abandon its food service. The old equipment will have zero scrap value at the end of 10 years.

Using the preceding data, compute the following. Label computations. Ignore income taxes.

1 Use the NPV method to analyse the incremental investment. Assume a minimum desired rate of return of 10 per cent. For this problem, assume that the PV of £1 at 10 per cent to be received at the end of 10 years is £.40 and that the PV of an annuity of £1 at 10 per cent for 10 years is £6.00.
2 What would be the minimum amount of annual revenue that VT would have to receive from the catering company to justify making the investment? Show computations.

11.46 PV of after-tax cash flows, payback and ARR

Suppose that Mitsubishi Chemical Corporation is planning to buy new equipment to expand its production of a popular solvent. Estimated data are as follows (monetary amounts are in thousands of Japanese yen):

Cash cost of new equipment now	¥400,000
Estimated life in years	10
Terminal salvage value	¥ 50,000
Incremental revenues per year	¥330,000
Incremental expenses per year other than depreciation	¥165,000

Assume a 60 per cent flat rate for income taxes. The company receives all revenues and pays all expenses other than depreciation in cash. Use a 14 per cent discount rate. Assume that the company uses ordinary straight-line depreciation based on a 10-year recovery period for tax purposes. Also assume that the company depreciates the original cost less the terminal salvage value.

Compute the following:

1 Depreciation expense per year
2 Anticipated net income per year
3 Annual net cash flow
4 Payback period
5 ARR on initial investment
6 NPV.

11.47 Investment justification analysis and graphs

Consider a new video game developed by Dynamic Gaming Innovations (DGI). DGI's development team was formed at the end of 2006 and has been working on the development of the game for several years. After spending €175,000 on the development, the team has reached the point in 2010 where it must make a decision on whether to proceed with production of the game. Production of the game will require an initial investment in facilities of €199,500 at the end of 2010. The project has an expected life cycle of 7 years (end of 2010 through 2017). Predicted cash flows for the game are as follows (assuming that all cash flows occur at the end of the year):

End of year	Cash inflow	Cash outflow
2010	€ 0	€199,500
2011	100,000	100,000
2012	220,000	180,000
2013	340,000	260,000
2014	460,000	320,000
2015	470,000	280,000
2016	410,000	200,000
2017	150,000	120,000

DGI's applicable tax rate is 40 per cent and DGI uses straight-line depreciation over the asset's expected life for tax purposes. The salvage value of the facilities will be zero in 7 years. DGI uses two criteria to evaluate potential investments: payback time and NPV. It wants a payback period of 3 years or less and an NPV greater than zero. DGI has a cost of capital of 18 per cent.

1 Prepare a table that shows the after-tax annual net cash flows, cumulative net cash flow and cumulative discounted net cash flow each year.
2 Would DGI invest in production of the game if it uses the payback period?
3 Would DGI invest in production of the game if it uses the NPV model?
4 Use graph paper to prepare a well-labelled line chart that shows the cumulative after-tax net cash flow and the cumulative after-tax discounted net cash flow of this investment over its life cycle. On your chart, clearly identify the payback time and the NPV for the project.
5 Would you recommend that DGI invest in this project? Explain.

11.48 Fixed and current assets; evaluation of performance

Roxbury Clinic has been under pressure to keep costs down. The clinic administrator has been managing various revenue-producing centres to maximise contributions to the recovery of the operating costs of the clinic as a whole. The administrator has been considering whether to buy a special-purpose X-ray machine for €193,000. Its unique characteristics would generate additional cash operating income of €51,500 per year for the clinic as a whole.

The clinic expects the machine to have a useful life of 6 years and a terminal salvage value of €22,000. The machine is delicate. It requires a constant inventory of various supplies and spare parts. When the clinic uses some of these items, it instantly replaces them so it maintains an investment of €15,000 at all times. However, the clinic fully recovers this investment at the end of the useful life of the machine.

1 Compute NPV if the required rate of return is 14 per cent.
2 Compute the ARR on (a) the initial investment and (b) the 'average' investment.
3 Why might the administrator be reluctant to base her decision on the DCF model?

11.49 After-tax NPV

Berradi Ltd is considering the purchase of a new stamping machine to manufacture its product. The following information is available:

New machine	
Purchase cost new	£85,000
Annual increase in cash revenues	60,000
Annual increase in cash operating costs	42,000
Salvage value – 10 years from now	5,000

If Berradi purchases the new machine, it will use it for 10 years and then trade it in on another machine. The company computes depreciation on a straight-line basis, for both taxes and financial reporting purposes. Assume Berradi currently has an old stamping machine with a book value of £30,000 that it can currently dispose of for £8,000 if it buys the new machine. Assume Berradi's cost of capital is 14 per cent and its tax rate is 30 per cent.

Should the new machine be purchased based on the NPV method?

CASES

11.50 Investment in CAD/CAM

Aswega AS is an Estonian manufacturer of electromagnetic flowmeters, heatmeters and calibration equipment located in Tallinn. Suppose that it is considering the installation of a computer-aided design/computer-aided manufacturing (CAD/CAM) system. The current proposal calls for implementation of only the CAD portion of the system. The manager in charge of production design and planning has estimated that the CAD portion of CAD/CAM could do the work of five designers, who are each paid EEK 500,000 per year (52 weeks × 40 hours × EEK 250 per hour), where EEK is the symbol for the Estonian kroon.

Aswega can purchase the CAD/CAM system for EEK 2.8 million. (It cannot purchase the CAD portion separately.) The annual out-of-pocket costs of running the CAD portion of the system are EEK 1.8 million. The company expects to use the system for 8 years. The company's minimum desired rate of return is 12 per cent. Ignore income taxes.

1 Compute the NPV of the investment in the CAD/CAM system. Should Aswega purchase the system? Explain.
2 Suppose the manager was not certain about her predictions of savings and economic life. Possibly the company will replace only four designers, but if everything works out well, it may replace as many as six. If better systems become available, the company may use the CAD/CAM system for only 5 years, but it might last as long as 10 years. Prepare pessimistic, most likely, and optimistic predictions of NPV. Would this analysis make you more confident or less confident in your decision in number 1? Explain.
3 What subjective factors might influence your decision?

11.51 Investment in quality

The Sydney Manufacturing Company produces a single model of a high-quality DVD player that it sells to Australian manufacturers of sound systems. It sells each DVD player for $210, resulting in a contribution margin of $70 before considering any costs of inspection, correction of product defects or refunds to customers.

On 1 January 2011, top management at Sydney is contemplating a change in its quality control system. Currently, the company spends $30,000 annually on quality control inspections for the 50,000 DVD players it produces and ships each year. In producing those DVD players, the company produces an average of 2,000 defective units. The inspection process identifies 1,500 of these and the company spends an average of $85 on each to correct the defects. The company ships the other 500 defective players to customers. When a customer discovers a defective DVD player, Sydney Manufacturing refunds the $210 purchase price.

Many of Sydney's customers build the DVDs into home-entertainment units. As more of these customers change to JIT inventory systems and automated production processes, the receipt of defective goods poses greater and greater problems for them. Sometimes a defective DVD player causes them to delay their whole production line while they replace the DVD player. Companies competing with Sydney recognise this situation and most have already begun extensive quality control programmes. If Sydney does not improve quality, sales volume is expected to fall by 5,000 DVD players a year, beginning after 2011:

	Predicted sales volume in units without quality control programme	Predicted sales volume in units with quality control programme
2011	50,000	50,000
2012	45,000	50,000
2013	40,000	50,000
2014	35,000	50,000

The proposed quality control programme has two elements. First, Sydney would spend $950,000 immediately to train workers to recognise and correct defects at the time they occur. This is expected to cut the number of defective DVD players produced from 2,000 to 500 without incurring additional manufacturing costs. Second, an earlier inspection point would replace the current inspection. This would require purchase of an X-ray machine at a cost of $250,000 plus additional annual operating costs of $60,000 more than the current inspection costs. Early detection of defects would reduce the average amount spent to correct defects from $85 to $50, and only 50 defective DVD players would be shipped to customers. To compete, Sydney would refund one-and-one-half times the purchase price ($315) for defective DVD players delivered to customers.

Top management at Sydney has decided that a 4-year planning period is sufficient for analysing this decision. The minimum required rate of return is 20 per cent. For simplicity, assume that under the current quality control system, if the volume of production decreases, the number of defective DVD players produced remains at 2,000. Also assume that all annual cash flows occur at the end of the relevant year. Should Sydney undertake the new quality control program? Explain, using the NPV model. Ignore income taxes.

Solutions to exercises in compound interest, Problem 11.A1

The general approach to these exercises centres on one fundamental question: which of the two basic tables am I dealing with? No calculations should be made until after this question is answered with assurance. If you made any errors, it is possible that you used the wrong table.

1   From Table B1, Appendix B, p. 677
  (a) €19,587.50
  (b) €15,522.50
  (c) €10,047.50.

The €25,000 is an amount of future worth. You want the PV of that amount:

$$PV = \text{€}20,000 \times \frac{1}{[(1 + i)^n]}$$

The conversion factor, $1/(1+i)^n$, is on line 5 of Table B1. Substituting,

$$PV = \text{€}25,000(.7835) = \text{€}19,587.50$$

$$PV = \text{€}25,000(.6209) = \text{€}15,522.50$$

$$PV = \text{€}25,000(.4019) = \text{€}10,047.50$$

Note that the higher the interest rate, the lower the PV.

2 From Table B2, Appendix B, p. 680
   (a) €8,659.00
   (b) €7,581.60
   (c) €5,981.20.
   The €2,000 withdrawal is a uniform annual amount, an annuity. You need to find the PV of an annuity for 5 years:

$$PV_A = \text{annual withdrawal} \times F, \text{ where F is the conversion factor.}$$

$$PV_A = €2,000(4.3295) = €8,659.00$$

$$PV_A = €2,000(3.7908) = €7,581.60$$

$$PV_A = €2,000(2.9906) = €5,981.20$$

3 From Table B2:
   (a) €46,194.71
   (b) €52,759.31
   You have €100,000, the PV of your contemplated annuity. You must find the annuity that will just exhaust the invested principal in 5 years:

$$PV_A = \text{annual withdrawal} \times F$$

$$€100,000 = \text{annual withdrawal} \times 4.3295$$

$$\text{annual withdrawal} = €100,000 \div 4.3295$$

$$= €23,097.36$$

$$€100,000 = \text{annual withdrawal} \times 3.7908$$

$$\text{annual withdrawal} = €100,000 \div 3.7908$$

$$= €26,379.66$$

4 Amounts are in thousands. From Table B1: LeBron's contract is preferable; its PV exceeds that of Kobe's contract by €43,143 − €35,441 = €7,702. Note that the nearer euros are more valuable than the distant euros.

Year	Present value at 16% from Table B1	Present value of LeBron's contract	Present value of Kobe's contract
1	.8621	€17,242	€ 3,448
2	.7432	11,891	5,946
3	.6407	7,688	7,688
4	.5523	4,418	8,837
5	.4761	1,904	9,522
		€43,143	€ 35,44

Cost allocation

Learning objectives

When you have finished studying this chapter, you should be able to:

1 Describe the general framework for cost allocation.
2 Allocate the variable and fixed costs of service departments to other organisational units.
3 Use the direct and step-down methods to allocate service department costs to user departments.
4 Allocate costs from producing departments to products or services using the traditional approach.
5 Allocate costs associated with customer actions to customers.
6 Allocate the central corporate costs of an organisation.
7 Allocate joint costs to products using the physical-units and relative-sales-value methods.

Haier

Zhang Ruimin became boss of Qingdao Refrigerator Factory in 1984. He did not like what he saw. The factory produced terrible refrigerators. So he had 76 defective ones pulled out from the rest, gave the staff sledgehammers and told them to destroy the refrigerators. With a focus on quality, he led the company into the production of air conditioners, cookers and washing machines. He also started to build the brand of the company: Haier. Haier Group is today a $20 billion organisation with the world's largest market share in white goods.

Zhang reorganised the entire company into self-managed units – 4,100 of them – each of them being divided into a customer or group of similar customers. Employees who are in direct contact with the customers make all the decisions – managers only manage. Zhang notes that 'If the members of a unit don't like the way their manager is performing, they can vote him out.' (Colvin, B. 'The next management icon', *Fortune* 25/7/2011, p. 38) Moreover, each unit is evaluated as an independent unit earning a profit or loss. At Haier, revenues means cash in the till, not orders booked. Costs have to be allocated from manufacturing,

Haier Group has the world's largest market share in white goods.

sales and other functions. Units are burdened with a capital charge for inventory. If a unit's profit exceeds its target, members split the extra.

Cost allocations can affect the evaluation of managers. Haier evaluates managers based partly on the income of the organisational segment they manage. Therefore, both accountants and managers are concerned with how the allocations affect segment income. But as Zhang states: 'The usual accounting statements didn't tell us what we needed, so we had to create something new.'

Just as is the case for Haier, cost allocation is of strategic importance to most businesses. For example, many faculties use a university's computer systems for both teaching and performing government-funded research. How much of the computer systems' costs should we assign to the research projects? Or consider a special London police unit set up to investigate a series of related assaults. What is the total cost of the effort, including various support costs? Finally, suppose a company uses a machine to make two different product lines. How much of the cost of the machine should we assign to each product line? These are all problems of cost allocation, the subject of this chapter. ■

A general framework for cost allocation

Objective 1
Describe the general framework for cost allocation.

As described in Chapter 4, cost-allocation methods comprise an important part of a company's cost accounting system – the techniques it uses to determine the cost of a product, service, customer or other cost objects. Why? Because, for most companies, accountants can directly trace less than 60 per cent of operating costs to products and services. For the rest of a company's costs, accountants must either apply cost-allocation methods or leave costs unallocated. Most managers prefer to allocate these costs rather than leaving them unallocated.

Because of the importance to all organisations of products, services or customers as final cost objectives, we focus on how companies assign direct costs and indirect (allocated) costs to these cost objects. A recent survey of over 400 organisations worldwide reported that companies trace or allocate a majority of costs in all value-chain functions to products or customers:[1]

Value chain function	Costs traced or allocated to products or customers (%)
Research and development	60
Design	70
Production	94
Sales and marketing	68
Distribution	79
Customer service	67
Corporate support	70

Of course, this also shows that, in all functions other than production, significant costs remain unassigned to products or customers.

Companies must assign all production costs and only production costs to products for external financial reporting purposes. They can elect to assign or not assign all other costs for internal management purposes. The significant percentages of unassigned costs reflect the difficulty and cost of developing useful allocation systems across the value chain. Still,

---

[1] W. Stratton, D. Desroches, R. Lawson and T. Hatch 'Activity-based costing – is it still relevant?' *Management Accounting Quarterly*, Spring 2009, Vol. 10, No. 3, pp. 31–40.

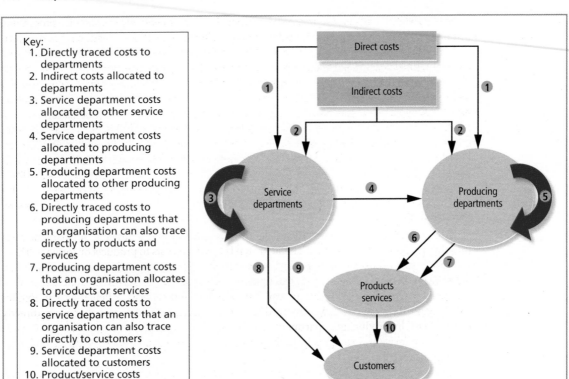

Exhibit 12.1 Framework for cost accounting systems

most companies trace or allocate most value-chain costs to final cost objects. After developing a general framework for allocation, we will take a careful look at how allocation systems are developed and used.

We will use the framework in Exhibit 12.1 to show how cost allocation fits into the overall cost accounting system. Each of the arrows in Exhibit 12.1 represents an assignment of some costs to a cost objective. We show four types of cost objectives – service departments, producing departments, products/services and customers. The cost accounting system first accumulates costs and assigns them to organisational units. We will call each unit a department. There are two types of departments: (1) **producing departments**, where employees work on the organisation's products or services, and (2) **service departments**, which exist only to support other departments or customers. Examples of service departments are personnel departments, laundry departments in hospitals, technical support centres and facility management departments.[2] We can trace the *direct* costs to each department, shown by the arrows labelled 1. In contrast, we have to *allocate* the *indirect* costs, such as rent for facilities used by more than one department. We label these allocations as 2 in Exhibit 12.1.

Assume that a company has now assigned resource costs 1 and 2 to producing and service departments. Suppose some service departments provide services to other service departments. An example is personnel services provided to employees in the facilities maintenance department. Arrow 3 represents the allocation of these costs. After assignments 1, 2 and 3 have been made, managers can evaluate the performance of each service department.

---

[2] There are some costs associated with general (or central) support that we do not consider service department costs. Examples of these are public relations and corporate planning. We will discuss how these central costs are treated later in the chapter.

To evaluate the costs of resources used in producing departments such as machine processing, installation, or assembly, many companies develop allocation methods to assign service department costs to the producing departments. Why? The reason is that managers want to know total costs, both producing-department costs and the costs of using resources from other departments. We show these assignments as 4 in Exhibit 12.1. Sometimes, producing departments transfer items to other producing departments as well as producing products or services. For example, a producing department may process a chemical resulting in several finished products and several products that need to be processed further. We transfer the costs of products that need further processing to other producing departments – labelled as 5 in Exhibit 12.1. Notice that direct service department costs – labelled as 1 – become indirect costs to the producing department when they are part of allocation 4. For example, the salaries of human resources personnel are a direct departmental cost for the human resources department. However, when we allocate these costs, along with all other human resource department costs, to producing departments, they become indirect to the producing department.

At this point, we have accumulated service department and producing department costs into the producing departments. The next step is to assign costs to products or services. There are significant producing department costs that are directly traceable to products and services. We indicate these costs as 6; examples are direct materials and direct labour. The other producing department costs are allocated to products and services, labelled as 7 in Exhibit 12.1. Again, because we have changed the cost objectives, some costs that were directly traceable to the producing departments will be indirect when the cost objective is the various products or services; examples include salaries of production supervisors, supplies and most equipment costs.

All organisations accumulate product- or service-related costs for their products or services. They must do so for financial reporting purposes. Many organisations also accumulated and allocate other value-chain costs. So tracing and allocating costs as shown in arrows 1–7 are common to all organisations. However, an increasing number of organisations also choose to measure and manage the costs and profitability of their customers. Arrows 8–10 demonstrate how they do this.

Some service department activities support customers rather than the production process; examples include order processing and customer service activities. Therefore, we assign the costs of such services to customers rather than to the producing departments. We can trace some of these costs directly to customers – labelled 8 in Exhibit 12.1. Examples are sales commissions and dedicated customer support, such as presales negotiation. We then allocate the other customer-related services, such as order processing – arrow 9 in Exhibit 12.1. The last step shown in Exhibit 12.1 is to assign the cost of products or services to customers who purchase them. After this last assignment, a company can determine customer profitability by subtracting costs 8, 9 and 10 from customer revenue.

Why is it important to directly trace and allocate customer-related service department costs to customers (8 and 9 in Exhibit 12.1) rather than assigning them first to producing departments and then to customers? If we assigned these costs to producing departments and then to products, the allocation to products would be based on production-related output measures that may have little relationship to the cause of customer-service costs. This would cause cost distortions to both the product and customer cost objectives.

Each department will generally trace or allocate most of its direct and indirect costs to its outputs, although it might leave some costs unallocated if there is no logical basis for allocating them. Tracing or allocating these costs requires accountants to identify and measure a department's output and determine the cost-allocation base for the indirect costs. For example, the pediatrics department of a medical clinic might allocate its indirect costs to patients based on docotor time per patient. Or the assembly activity of a manufacturing firm might allocate costs to units assembled based on machine hours used. Or the tax department of a public accounting firm might allocate costs to clients based on professional hours spent.

As indicated in Chapter 4, we would like to use a cost driver as a cost-allocation base because of the driver's logical, cause-and-effect relationship to costs. For example, a logical cost-allocation base for allocating building rent costs to departments is the square feet that each department occupies. Other logical cost-allocation bases include cubic feet for allocating depreciation of heating and air conditioning equipment and total direct cost for allocating general administrative expense. Accountants use many different terms to describe cost allocation in practice. As indicated in Chapter 4, terms such as *allocate, apply, absorb, attribute, reallocate, trace, assign, distribute, redistribute, load, burden, apportion* and *reapportion* are used interchangeably to describe the allocation of costs to cost objectives.

Some individual indirect costs are important enough that we allocate them using obvious cost-allocation bases. For example, we would allocate the cost of professional labour for a law firm to departments, jobs and projects using labour hours used. We pool the other costs that are not important enough to justify being labour individually and allocate them together. Recall that a cost pool is a group of individual costs that we allocate to cost objectives using a single cost-allocation base. For example, building rent, utilities cost and janitorial services may be in the same cost pool because a company allocates all of them on the basis of square footage of space occupied; or a university could pool all the operating costs of its registrar's office and allocate them to its colleges on the basis of the number of students in each college.

The next section looks in detail at allocation of service department costs and the following sections focus on allocation to products or services and to customers.

Allocation of service department costs

Objective 2
Allocate the variable and fixed costs of service departments to other organisational units.

In our general framework shown in Exhibit 12.1, service department allocations are labelled as 3, 4 and 9. Before discussing methods of allocation, we give some general guidelines that managers should consider when designing allocation systems.

■ General guidelines

The preferred guidelines for allocating service department costs are as follows:

1 Establish part or all of the details regarding cost allocation in advance of rendering the service rather than after the fact. This approach establishes the 'rules of the game' so that all departments can plan appropriately.

2 Allocate variable- and fixed-cost pools separately. Note that one service department (such as a computer department) can contain multiple cost pools if more than one cost driver causes the department's costs. At a minimum, there should be a variable-cost pool and a fixed-cost pool.

3 Evaluate performance using budgets for each service (staff) department, just as for each production or operating (line) department. Managers should evaluate the performance of a service department by comparing actual costs with a budget, regardless of how the company allocates costs. From the budget, variable-cost pools and fixed-cost pools can be identified for use in allocation.

Consider an example of a computer department of a university that serves two major users, the school of business and the school of engineering. Exhibit 12.2 shows the allocation system for this service department. Suppose there are two major reasons for the allocation: (1) predicting economic effects of the use of the computer and (2) motivating the individuals in the two schools to use its capabilities more fully. How should the university allocate the costs of the computer department (salaries, depreciation, energy, materials and so on) to the two schools?

We begin by analysing the costs of the computer department in detail. The primary activity performed is computer processing. The university acquired the computer mainframe on a 5-year lease that is not cancellable unless it pays huge penalties. Resources consumed include processing time, operator time, energy, materials and building space. Suppose the university performed cost-behaviour analysis and determined the budget formula for the forthcoming year is €100,000 monthly fixed cost plus €200 variable cost per hour of computer time used. Refer to Exhibit 12.2 as we show how to apply guideline 2 – the topic of the next two sections.

◼ Variable-cost pool

Costs in the variable-cost pool include energy, operator labour costs and materials. The cost-allocation base for the variable-cost pool is actual hours of computer time used. Therefore, the university should allocate variable costs as follows:

$$\text{budgeted unit rate} \times \text{actual hours of computer time used}$$

The cause-and-effect relationship is clear: The heavier the usage, the higher the total costs. In this example, the budgeted cost-allocation rate is €200 per hour, determined by dividing the total budgeted costs of energy, operators and materials by the total budgeted hours of computer time.

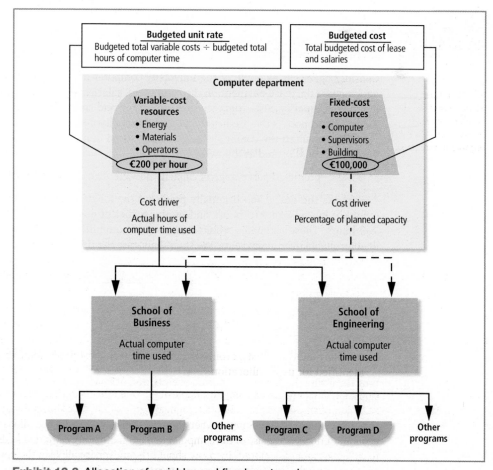

Exhibit 12.2 Allocation of variable- and fixed-cost pools

The use of budgeted cost rates rather than actual cost rates for allocating variable costs of service departments protects the user departments from intervening price fluctuations and also often protects them from inefficiencies in the service departments. When an organisation allocates *actual* total service department cost, it holds user department managers responsible for costs beyond their control and provides less incentive for service departments to be efficient. Both effects are undesirable.

Consider the allocation of variable costs to a department that uses 600 hours of computer time. Suppose inefficiencies in the computer department caused the variable costs to be €140,000 instead of the 600 hours $\times$ €200 = €120,000 budgeted. A good cost-allocation scheme would allocate only the €120,000 to the consuming departments and would let the €20,000 remain as an unallocated unfavourable budget variance of the computer department. This scheme holds computer department managers responsible for the €20,000 variance and reduces the resentment of user managers. User department managers sometimes complain more vigorously about uncertainty over allocations and the poor management of a service department than about the choice of a cost-allocation base (such as direct-labour euros or number of employees). Such complaints are less likely if the service department managers have budget responsibility and the user departments are protected from short-run price fluctuations and inefficiencies.

Consider a car repair and maintenance department for state-owned agencies. Agencies that use the department's service should receive firm prices for various services. Imagine the feelings of an agency head who had an agency car repaired and was told, 'Normally, your repair would have taken 5 hours. However, we had a new employee work on it and the job took him 10 hours. Therefore, we must charge you for 10 hours of labour time.'

■ Fixed-cost pool

Consider again our example of the university computer department. Costs in the fixed-cost pool include the lease payment on the computers, salaries of managers and supervisors, and building occupancy costs (depreciation, insurance and so on). The cost-allocation base for the fixed-cost pool is the predicted amount of capacity needed by the two schools when the university acquired the computer facilities, measured in monthly hours of usage. Therefore, fixed costs are allocated as follows:

predicted percentage of capacity needed $\times$ total budgeted fixed costs

Suppose the deans had originally predicted the long-run average monthly usage by the school of business at 210 hours and by the school of engineering at 490 hours, a total of 700 hours. These estimates resulted in a set of committed fixed costs that remain largely uncontrollable over many years. We should allocate the fixed-cost pool as follows:

	Business	Engineering
Fixed costs per month		
210/700, or 30% of €100,000	€30,000	
490/700, or 70% of €100,000		€70,000

This predetermined lump-sum approach is based on the long-run capacity available to the user, regardless of actual usage from month to month. The reasoning is that long-range planning regarding the expected required overall level of service affects the level of fixed costs, not short-run fluctuations in actual usage.

A major strength of using capacity available rather than capacity used when allocating budgeted fixed costs is that actual usage by user departments does not affect the short-run allocations to other user departments. Such a budgeted lump-sum approach is more likely to have the desired motivational effects with respect to the ordering of services in both the short run and the long run.

In practice, companies often inappropriately allocate fixed-cost pools on the basis of capacity used, not capacity available. Suppose for 2 successive months the computer department's actual fixed costs were exactly the €100,000 budgeted. The university allocated these costs based on actual hours used by the consuming departments. Compare the costs borne by the two schools in the first month when business uses 200 hours and engineering 400 hours.

Total fixed costs incurred, €100,000	
Business: $200/600 \times €100,000 =$	€ 33,333
Engineering: $400/600 \times €100,000 =$	66,667
Total cost allocated	€100,000

What happens if business uses only 100 hours during the following month and engineering still uses 400 hours?

Total fixed costs incurred, €100,000	
Business: $100/500 \times €100,000 =$	€ 20,000
Engineering: $400/500 \times €100,000 =$	80,000
Total cost allocated	€100,000

Engineering's usage was unchanged, but it must bear an additional cost of €13,333, an increase of 20 per cent. Its short-run costs depend on what other consumers have used, not solely on its own actions. This phenomenon is caused by a faulty allocation method for the fixed portion of total costs, a method whereby the allocations are highly sensitive to fluctuations in the actual volumes used by the various consuming departments. We can avoid this weakness by using a predetermined lump-sum allocation of fixed costs based on budgeted usage.

Consider the preceding car repair shop example. You would not be happy if you came to get your car and were told, 'Our daily fixed overhead is €1,000. Yours was the only car in our shop today, so we are charging you the full €1,000. If we had processed 100 cars today, your charge would have been only €10.'

▊ Trouble with using lump sums

Using lump-sum allocations is not without problems, however. If a company allocates fixed costs on the basis of long-range plans, there is a natural tendency on the part of managers to underestimate their planned usage and thus obtain a smaller fraction of the cost allocation. Top management can counteract these tendencies by monitoring predictions and by following up and using feedback to keep future predictions more honest.

In some organisations, there are even definite rewards in the form of salary increases for managers who make accurate predictions. Moreover, some cost-allocation methods provide for penalties for underpredictions. For example, suppose a manager predicts usage of 210 hours and then demands 300 hours. The manager either doesn't get the hours or pays a dear price for every hour beyond 210 in such systems.

▊ Allocating service department costs to producing departments

Recall from Exhibit 12.1 on p. 520 that assignment type 4 is allocating service department costs to producing departments. We now explore methods commonly used for this type of allocation. Suppose a retail display manufacturer assembles parts into custom and standard displays. Exhibit 12.3 is a process map for the facility. There are two producing departments, processing and assembly. There are also two service departments, facilities management (rent, power, insurance, janitorial services and some corporate resources such as administration and engineering) and human resources. In this section of the chapter, we focus on the processing and assembly departments as cost objectives. Let's assume that a single plausible and reliable cost driver serves as a cost-allocation base for each service department and that all resource costs vary in proportion to this cost driver – that is, these are variable-cost resources. Managers have determined that the cost driver for facilities management costs is the square footage occupied and the cost driver for human resources costs is the number of employees. Exhibit 12.3 shows the direct costs for a recent month when the company produced 200 custom and 1,200 standard displays. Exhibit 12.3 shows the area occupied and number of employees for each department. Note that facilities management provides services for the human resources department in addition to providing services for the producing departments and that human resources aids employees in facilities management as well as those in production departments.

There are two popular methods for allocating service department costs to producing departments in such cases: the direct method and the step-down method.

Direct method

Objective 3
Use the direct and step-down methods to allocate service department costs to user departments.

The **direct method** ignores other service departments when allocating any given service department's costs to the producing departments. In other words, the direct method ignores the services that facilities management provides for human resources and the services that human resources provides to facilities management. The direct method allocates facilities management costs based on the relative square footage occupied by the processing and assembly departments only.

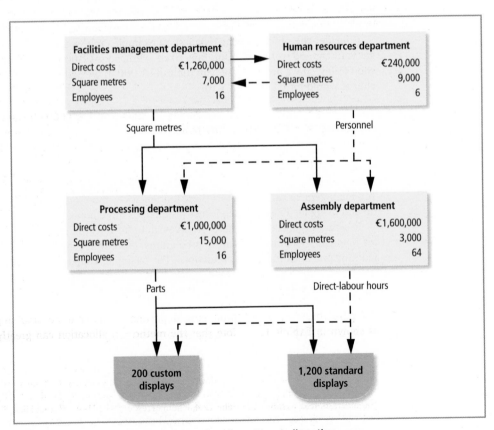

Exhibit 12.3 Processing facility: service department allocation

- Total square metres in producing departments $= 15{,}000 + 3{,}000 = 18{,}000$

- Facilities management cost allocated to processing department $= (15{,}000 \div 18{,}000) \times$ €1,260,000 = €1,050,000

- Facilities management cost allocated to assembly department $= (3{,}000 \div 18{,}000) \times$ €1,260,000 = €210,000

Likewise, human resources department costs are allocated only to the producing departments on the basis of the relative number of employees in the producing departments.

- Total employees in producing departments $= 16 + 64 = 80$

- Human resources costs allocated to processing department $= (16 \div 80) \times$ €240,000 = €48,000

- Human resources costs allocated to assembly department $= (64 \div 80) \times$ €240,000 = €192,000

Step-down method

The **step-down method** recognises that some service departments support the activities in other service departments as well as those in producing departments. To apply the step-down method, we choose a sequence of service department allocations, starting with the service department that renders the greatest service (as measured by costs) to the greatest number of other service departments. The last service department in the sequence is the one that renders the least service to the least number of other service departments. We allocate the costs of one service department at a time, assigning the costs to the producing departments and to the remaining service departments. Once we allocate a department's costs to other departments, we never allocate other service department costs back to it.

In our example, we allocate facilities management department costs first. Why? Because facilities management renders more support to human resources than human resources provides to facilities management.[3] Examine Exhibit 12.4. After allocating facilities management costs, we do not allocate any costs back to facilities management, even though human resources does provide some services to facilities management. The €660,000 human resources costs allocated to the producing departments include the amount allocated to human resources from facilities management (€420,000) in addition to the direct human resources department costs of €240,000.

Examine the last column of Exhibit 12.4. Before allocation, the four departments incurred costs of €4,100,000. In step 1, we deducted €1,260,000 from facilities management and added it to the other three departments. There was no net effect on the total cost. In step 2, we deducted €660,000 from human resources and added it to the remaining two departments. Again, total cost was unaffected. After allocation, all €4,100,000 remains, but it is all in the processing and assembly departments. None was left in facilities management or human resources.

Comparison of the methods

Compare the costs of the producing departments under direct and step-down methods, as shown in Exhibit 12.5. Note that the method of allocation can greatly affect the costs.

---

[3] How should we determine which of the two service departments provides more service to the other? One way is to carry out step 1 of the step-down method with facilities management allocated first and then repeat it assuming personnel is allocated first. With facilities management allocated first, €420,000 is allocated to human resources, as shown in Exhibit 12.4. If human resources had been allocated first, $(16 \div 96) \times$ €240,000 = €40,000 would have been allocated to facilities management. Because €40,000 is smaller than €420,000, facilities management is allocated first.

	Facilities management	Human resources	Processing	Assembly	Total
Direct department costs before allocation	€ 1,260,000	€ 240,000	€1,000,000	€1,600,000	€4,100,000
Step 1					
Facilities management	€ (1,260,000)	$(9 \div 27) \times$ €1,260,000 = € 420,000	$(15 \div 27) \times$ €1,260,000 = € 700,000	$(3 \div 27) \times$ €1,260,000 = € 140,000	
Step 2					
Human resources		€ (660,000)	$(16 \div 80) \times$ € 660,000 = € 132,000	$(64 \div 80) \times$ € 660,000 = € 528,000	
Total cost after allocation	€ 0	€ 0	€1,832,000	€2,268,000	€4,100,000

Exhibit 12.4 Step-down allocation

Processing appears to be a more expensive operation to a manager using the direct method than it does to one using the step-down method. Conversely, assembly seems more expensive to a manager using the step-down method.

Which method is better? Generally, the step-down method.[4] Why? Because it recognises the effects of the most significant support provided by service departments to other service departments. The greatest virtue of the direct method is its simplicity. If the two methods do not produce significantly different results, many companies elect to use the direct method because it is easier for managers to understand.

Costs not related to cost drivers

Our example illustrating direct and step-down allocation methods assumed that we could use a single cost driver as a cost-allocation base for all costs in a given service department. For example, we assumed that we could use area occupied to allocate all facilities management costs. But what if some of the costs in facilities management do not vary proportionately to the cost-driver area? For example, rent often consists of a single sum for the entire plant for a period of time. Another example occurs when the contract for an outside company to perform janitorial services specifies a fixed monthly charge plus an additional charge based on the square metres maintained.

We suggest two guidelines that are helpful in situations where costs are not related to cost drivers:

1 Identify additional cost drivers. Divide facilities management costs into two or more different cost pools and use a different cost-allocation base to allocate the costs in each pool. For example, rent and insurance costs often are fixed but we can allocate them using square metres occupied by the various service departments. Power costs are mostly variable and we can allocate them using a driver such as megawatt hours. The cost of janitorial services as described previously is a mixed cost. The allocation of the variable portion of janitorial services should be allocated based on the same measure used for billing – square metres maintained, for example. The fixed portion may not have a plausible or reliable cost driver and thus might remain unallocated.

---

[4] The most defensible theoretical accuracy is generated by the reciprocal cost method, which is rarely used in practice because it is more difficult to understand. The method uses simultaneous equations and linear algebra to solve for the impact of mutually interacting services.

	Processing		Assembly	
	Direct	**Step-down***	**Direct**	**Step-down***
Direct costs	€1,000,000	€1,000,000	€1,600,000	€1,600,000
Allocated from facilities management	1,050,000	700,000	210,000	140,000
Allocated from personnel	48,000	132,000	192,000	528,000
Total costs	€2,098,000	€1,832,000	€2,002,000	€2,268,000

*From Exhibit 12.4

Exhibit 12.5 Direct versus step-down method

2 Allocate all costs by the direct or step-down method using square metres as the cost-allocation base. In this alternative, we implicitly assume that, in the long run, square metres causes all facilities management costs – even if we cannot easily identify a short-term causal relationship. In other words, the need for more square metres may not cause an immediate increase in all facilities management costs, but eventually management will need to provide more space so the costs will increase.

MAKING MANAGERIAL DECISIONS

Suppose you are on a cross-functional team that is discussing how to allocate the costs of a purchasing department. One team member suggested that 'number of purchase orders issued' is the best cost driver to use as a cost-allocation base. However, a scatter graph of total costs versus number of purchase orders issued shows the following.

Because the data clearly indicate that the single cost driver 'number of purchase orders issued' is not a reliable measure of the work done in the department (because there is too much scatter in the data), the team investigated further. It discovered that a significant amount of work of the purchasing department was certifying new vendors in addition to issuing purchase orders. What alternative method of allocation would you recommend?

Answer

Because a large percentage of the work of the purchasing department is not related to the single cost driver 'number of purchase orders', the team should use a second cost pool with another cost-allocation base, such as 'number of new vendors'.

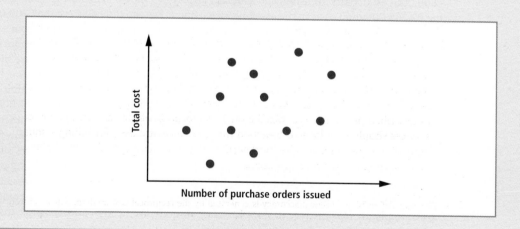

Allocation of costs to product or service cost objects

After the allocation of service department costs, we have all production-related costs residing in the producing departments. All that remains is to allocate those costs to the product or service cost objects. Examples of such cost objects are products such as automobiles, furniture and newspapers, and services such as bank accounts, patient visits and student credit hours. Some accountants use the term **cost application** for the allocation of total departmental costs to the revenue-producing products or services.

■ A traditional approach

The traditional approach to cost allocation is as follows:

Objective 4
Allocate costs from producing departments to products or services using the traditional approach.

1 Divide the costs in each producing department, including both the direct department costs and all the costs allocated to it, into two categories: (1) the direct costs that you can physically trace to the product or service cost objectives and (2) the remainder, the indirect costs.

2 Trace the direct costs to the appropriate products or services. Note that some costs that are direct to the department will be indirect to the product or service cost objectives – for example, depreciation on the department's equipment.

3 Select cost pools and related cost-allocation bases in each production department and assign all the indirect departmental costs to the appropriate cost pool. For example, you might assign a portion of the indirect departmental costs on the basis of direct-labour hours, another portion on the basis of machine hours and the remainder on the basis of number of parts. Be sure to use separate cost pools for fixed and variable costs.

4 Allocate (apply) the costs in each cost pool to the products or services in proportion to their usage of the related cost-allocation base. Apply variable costs on the basis of the actual amount of the cost-allocation base. Apply fixed costs on the basis of the budgeted amount of the cost-allocation base.

Consider our example of the manufacturer's display facility. Exhibit 12.6 shows the process map for the facility assuming that the facility uses the step-down method for allocating service department costs. We now shift our focus from the two operating departments as cost objectives to the two types of displays – the products manufactured by the display facility.

The first step is to determine the operating department costs that we can directly trace to displays. Of the €1,832,000 total costs in the processing department, we can trace the €800,000 cost of parts to custom and standard displays, as shown in Exhibit 12.6. Similarly, of the €2,268,000 total costs in the assembly department, we can directly trace the €200,000 of wages for direct labour to displays. The remaining resources and allocated costs from service departments are indirect costs with respect to the displays and we will assume they are fixed-cost resources. Why is there no direct labour in the processing department? Because this is a machine intensive department with only indirect labour maintaining the machines.

In step 2, we trace the direct costs to the two display types as shown in Exhibit 12.6. Compare the processing department costs in Exhibits 12.3 and 12.6. How did €1,000,000 in direct processing department costs in Exhibit 12.3 decrease to only €800,000 direct costs in Exhibit 12.6? The answer lies in our change in cost objectives. When we were interested only in determining the cost of the processing department, €200,000 of costs such as depreciation on department equipment and costs of supervisors were wholly in support of the department – a single cost object – and did not need to be allocated. When we changed the cost objective to the two displays, these resources became shared. Since we could find no economically feasible way to trace their use directly, we need to allocate their costs.

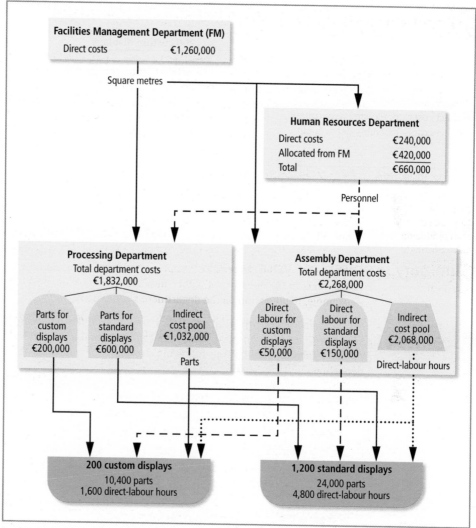

Exhibit 12.6 Display facility: allocation to cost objects using traditional approach and step-down allocation method

Next, in step 3, we select cost pools and related cost-allocation bases for the indirect costs of each department. We assign the remaining €1,032,000 of indirect costs in the processing department to one fixed-cost pool with budgeted number of parts as the cost-allocation base. Similarly, we assign all the remaining €2,068,000 indirect costs in the assembly department to one fixed-cost pool with budgeted direct-labour hours as the cost-allocation base.

Therefore, we allocate indirect departmental costs to the displays as follows:

$$\text{Processing: } €1,032,000 \div (10,400 + 24,000) \text{ parts } = €30.00 \text{ per part}$$

$$\text{Assembly: } €2,068,000 \div (1,600 + 4,800) \text{ direct-labour hours}$$

$$= €323.125 \text{ per direct-labour hour}$$

The total and unit costs of making 200 custom and 1,200 standard displays are as follows:

	200 custom displays		1,200 standard displays	
	Total	**Unit**	**Total**	**Unit**
Parts	€ 200,000	€1,000.00	€ 600,000	€ 500.00
Direct labour	50,000	250.00	150,000	125.00
Indirect costs – processing department	312,000[a]	1,560.00	720,000[b]	600.00
Indirect costs – assembly department	517,000[c]	2,585.00	1,551,000[d]	1,292.50
	€1,079,000	€5,395.00	€3,021,000	€2,517.50

[a] €30.00 × 10,400 parts

[b] €30.00 × 24,000 parts

[c] €323.125 × 1,600 direct-labour hours

[d] €323.125 × 4,800 direct-labour hours

Summary problem for your review

PROBLEM

Nonmanufacturing organisations often find it useful to allocate costs to products or services. Consider a hospital. The output of a hospital is not as easy to define as the output of a factory. Assume the following measures of output in three revenue-producing departments:

Department	Measures of output[a]
Radiology	X-ray films processed
Laboratory	Tests administered
Daily patient services[b]	Patient-days of care (i.e., the number of patients multiplied by the number of days of each patient's stay)

[a] These become the 'product' cost objectives, the various revenue-producing activities of a hospital.

[b] There would be many of these departments, such as obstetrics, pediatrics and orthopedics. Moreover, there may be both inpatient and outpatient care.

Budgeted output for 20X7 is 60,000 X-ray films processed in radiology, 50,000 tests administered in the laboratory and 30,000 patient-days in daily patient services.

In addition to the revenue-producing departments, the hospital has three service departments: administrative and fiscal services, plant operations and maintenance and laundry. (Real hospitals have more than three revenue-producing departments and more than three service departments. This problem is simplified to keep the data manageable.)

The hospital has decided that the cost-allocation base for administrative and fiscal services costs is the direct department costs of the other departments. The cost-allocation base for plant operations and maintenance is square feet occupied and for laundry is kilos of laundry. The pertinent budget data for 20X7 are as follows:

	Direct department costs	Square metres occupied	Kilos of laundry
Administrative and fiscal services	€1,000,000	1,000	—
Plant operations and maintenance	800,000	2,000	—
Laundry	200,000	5,000	—

	Direct department costs	Square metres occupied	Kilos of laundry
Radiology	1,000,000	12,000	80,000
Laboratory	400,000	3,000	20,000
Daily patient services	1,600,000	80,000	300,000
Total	€5,000,000	103,000	400,000

1 Allocate service department costs using the direct method.

2 Allocate service department costs using the step-down method. Allocate administrative and fiscal services first, plant operations and maintenance second and laundry third.

3 Compute the cost per unit of output in each of the revenue-producing departments using (a) the costs determined using the direct method for allocating service department costs (number 1) and (b) the costs determined using the step-down method for allocating service department costs (number 2).

SOLUTION

1 Exhibit 12.7 shows the solutions to all three problems. We present the direct method first. Note that we did not allocate service department costs to another service department. Therefore, we base allocations on the relative amounts of the cost-allocation base in the revenue-producing department only. For example, in allocating plant operations and maintenance, we ignore area occupied by the service departments. The cost-allocation base is the 95,000 square metres occupied by the revenue-producing departments.

 Note that the total cost of the revenue-producing departments after allocation, €1,474,386 + €568,596 + €2,957,018 = €5,000,000, is equal to the total of the direct department costs in all six departments before allocation.

2 The lower half of Exhibit 12.7 shows the step-down method. We allocate the costs of administrative and fiscal services to all five other departments. Because we do not allocate a department's own costs to itself, the cost-allocation base consists of the €4,000,000 direct department costs in the five departments excluding administrative and fiscal services. We allocate plant operations and maintenance second on the basis of square metres occupied. We allocate no cost to the department itself or back to administrative and fiscal services. Therefore, the area used for allocation is the 100,000 square metres occupied by the other four departments.

 We allocate laundry third. We do not allocate cost back to the first two departments, even if they had used laundry services.

 As in the direct method, note that the total costs of the revenue-producing departments after allocation, €1,430,000 + €545,000 + €3,025,000 = €5,000,000, equals the total of the direct department costs before allocation.

3 We label the solutions 3a and 3b in Exhibit 12.7. Compare the unit costs derived from the direct method with those of the step-down method. In many instances, the product costs may not differ enough to warrant investing in a cost-allocation method that is any fancier than the direct method. But sometimes even small differences may be significant to a government agency or anybody paying for a large volume of services based on costs. For example, in Exhibit 12.7 the 'cost' of an 'average' laboratory test is either €11.37 or €10.90. This may be significant for the fiscal committee of the hospital's board of trustees, who must decide on hospital prices. Thus, cost allocation often is a technique that helps answer the vital question, 'Who should pay for what, and how much?'

Allocation base	Administrative and fiscal services	Plant operations and maintenance	Laundry			Daily patient services
	Accumulated costs	Sq. metres	Kilos	Radiology	Laboratory	services
1. Direct method:						
Direct departmental cost before allocation	€ 1,000,000	€ 800,000	€ 200,000	€1,000,000	€400,000	€1,600,000
Administrative and fiscal services	(1,000,000)	—	—	333,333[a]	133,333	533,334
Plant operations and maintenance		(800,000)		101,053[b]	25,263	673,684
Laundry			(200,000)	40,000[c]	10,000	150,000
Total costs after allocation				€1,474,386	€568,596	€2,957,018
Product output in films, tests and patient-days, respectively				60,000	50,000	30,000
3a. Cost per unit of output				€ 24.573	€ 11.372	€ 98.567
2. Step-down method:						
Direct departmental costs before allocation	€ 1,000,000	€ 800,000	€ 200,000	€1,000,000	€400,000	€1,600,000
Administrative and fiscal services	(1,000,000)	200,000[d]	50,000	250,000	100,000	400,000
Plant operations and maintenance		(1,000,000)	50,000[e]	120,000	30,000	800,000
Laundry			(300,000)	60,000[f]	15,000	225,000
Total costs after allocation				€1,430,000	€545,000	€3,025,000
Product output in films, tests and patient-days, respectively				60,000	50,000	30,000
3b. Cost per unit of output				€ 23.833	€ 10.900	€ 100.833

[a] €1,000,000 ÷ (1,000,000 + 400,000 + 1,600,000) = €.33, 1/3 × 1,000,000 = €333,333; and so on.
[b] €800,000 ÷ (12,000 + 3,000 + 80,000) = €8.4210526; €8.4210526 × 12.000 sq. ft. = €101,053; and so on.
[c] €200,000 ÷ (80,000 + 20,000 + 300,000) = €.50; €.50 × 80,000 = €40,000; and so on.
[d] €1,000,000 ÷ (800,000 + 200,000 + 1,000,000 + 400,000 + 1,600,000) = €.25; .25 × 800,000 = €200,000; and so on.
[e] €1,000,000 ÷ (5,000 +12,000 + 3,000 + 80,000) = €10.00; €10.00 × 5,000 sq. ft. = €50,000; and so on.
[f] €300,000 ÷ (80,000 + 20,000 + 300,000) = €.75; €.75 × 80,000 = €60,000; and so on.

Exhibit 12.7 Allocation of service department costs: direct and step-down methods

An ABC approach

The traditional approach to cost allocation focuses on accumulating and reporting costs by department. In the last couple of decades an alternative approach, activity-based costing, as described in Chapter 4, has become popular. It focuses on activities rather than departments. Let's examine how the same facility of the display manufacturer might apply ABC to determine the costs of custom and standard displays.

Assume that management decides to apply ABC only to the producing departments. The service departments will continue to use traditional costing. We will still use the step-down method to allocate the costs of the service departments to the producing departments. First, we allocate facilities management department costs to the human resources department and the specific activities identified in the producing departments. Then, we allocate the human resources department costs, both the direct department costs and the costs allocated from facilities management, to the various activities. Finally, we allocate the producing department activity-cost pools using a two-stage ABC system that uses a four-step procedure. Appendix 12 discusses a multistage ABC allocation system.

To apply ABC we use the following four steps.

Step 1: Determine the key components of the system

The costing objective is to determine the costs of custom and standard displays – the final cost objects for the company. The structure of the service department component of the cost allocation system is unchanged – we still use the step-down method. The major differences are in the producing departments. The ABC accounting system traces the cost of parts and direct labour to each product – this is the same as the traditional approach. During the implementation of ABC, managers often discover ways to improve costing accuracy. In this case, management decided to combine the processing and assembly departments into one new production department with three major activities – design, processing and assembly. The design activity's resources, engineers and CAD equipment, were previously part of the facilities management department. Managers believed that they could more accurately allocate these costs if they accumulate them separately as part of a production department design activity and allocate them using distinct parts as the cost-allocation base. In summary, the cost-allocation bases for design, processing and assembly activities are distinct parts, machine hours and direct-labour hours, respectively.

Step 2: Develop the relationships between resources, activities and cost objects

Interviews with key personnel identified the interrelationships between the two service departments, three activities, resources and final cost objects. Exhibit 12.8 is a process map that depicts these interrelationships. The newly formed production department is depicted by a dashed line in Exhibit 12.8. Why do we use a dashed line? The emphasis in the ABC approach is on allocations to activities without regard to departmental boundaries. Note that the exhibit also shows the cost behaviour for each resource. Understanding the cost behaviour of resources is vital during the planning process.

Step 3: Collect relevant data concerning costs and the physical flow of cost-allocation base units among resources and activities

Using the process map as a guide, accountants collected the required cost and operational data by further interviews with relevant personnel. Data collected are given in Exhibit 12.8.

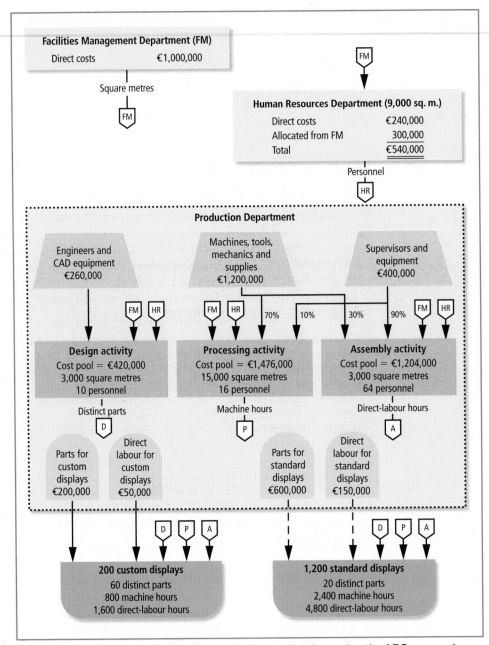

Exhibit 12.8 Display facility: allocation to final cost objectives using the ABC approach

Note that the total costs of the facilities management department is only €1,000,000 instead of the €1,260,000 used under the traditional approach. The difference is the cost of engineers and CAD equipment that is now treated as part of the production department. Each of the three activities shows the total cost pool. For example, the processing activity cost pool is €1,476,000. We calculate this as follows:

Resource supporting the processing activity	Allocation calculation	Allocated cost
Facilities management department resources	€1,000,000 × [15,000 ÷ (9,000 + 3,000 + 15,000 + 3,000)]	€ 500,000
Human resources department resources	€540,000 × [16 ÷ (10 + 16 + 64)]	96,000
Machines, tools, mechanics and supplies	€1,200,000 × 70%	840,000
Supervisors and equipment	€400,000 × 10%	40,000
Total		€1,476,000

Step 4: Calculate and interpret the new ABC information

Exhibit 12.9 shows the last step of allocating the costs of activities to the custom and standard displays. For each activity, the exhibit shows the cost pool of indirect costs that results from allocations of service department costs and the first stage of resource allocations. Then, it shows how to allocate these costs to the displays via the appropriate cost-allocation bases.

Compare the cost per unit figures using the traditional and ABC approaches. There is a substantial difference in the reported cost as shown next:

	Allocated cost	
	Custom displays	Standard displays
Traditional approach	€5,395.00	€2,517.50
ABC approach	€6,175.00	€2,387.50

How important are these differences? Suppose that product costs are 40 per cent of the company's total costs. If the company desires an operating income of 20 per cent of total costs, the required total revenue is [1.2 × product cost ÷ 0.4] = 300% × product cost or three times the product cost. This means that the price for custom displays would be 3 × €5,395 = €16,185 under the traditional approach compared to 3 × €6,175 = €18,525 under the ABC approach. Assuming the ABC cost is the more accurate estimate of actual costs, using the traditional approach would underprice custom displays by €2,340 or 12.6 per cent. The bottom-line

Activity/resource (Cost driver)	Cost pool	Physical flow of cost driver	Cost per driver unit	Custom displays Flow	Custom displays Cost	Standard displays Flow	Standard displays Cost
Design (distinct parts)	€ 420,000	80	€5,250.000	60	€ 315,000	20	€ 105,000
Processing (machine hours)	1,476,000	3,200	461.250	800	369,000	2,400	1,107,000
Assembly (direct-labour hours)	1,204,000	6,400	188.125	1,600	301,000	4,800	903,000
Parts					200,000		600,000
Direct labour					50,000		150,000
Total direct and allocated cost					€1,235,000		€2,865,000
Units					÷ 200		÷ 1,200
Display cost per unit					€ 6,175.00		€ 2,387.50

Exhibit 12.9 Display facility: allocation to final cost objects using the ABC approach

question for the company's decision makers is as follows: Is it worth the cost of maintaining the more expensive ABC system to be able to avoid strategic pricing errors of this magnitude?

The Business First box on p. 539 explains how Dow Chemical used ABC to help implement a new business strategy.

So far, we have seen how to accumulate costs and trace or allocate them to products or services – numbers 1–7 in Exhibit 12.1. This enables the calculation of gross profit for products or services. Many managers recognise that to achieve overall profitability goals, it is necessary to have both profitable products or services and profitable customers. We now consider how organisations measure and manage customer profitability.

Allocation of costs to customer cost objects to determine customer profitability

Objective 5
Allocate costs associated with customer actions to customers.

As shown in Exhibit 12.1, customer profitability depends on more than the gross margin of the products or services purchased. Customer profitability also depends on the costs incurred to fulfill customer orders and to provide other customer services such as order changes, returns and expedited scheduling or delivery. Exhibit 12.10 shows how these two factors determine profitability.

Consider customer type 1. This customer buys a mix of products that have high gross margins yielding a high gross margin percentage, about 70 per cent. Customer type 1 has a low cost-to-serve percentage (cost to serve ÷ sales revenue), about 30 per cent. As a result, customer type 1 will have a high level of profitability, 70% − 30% = 40%. On the other hand, customer type 2 buys products with a lower gross margin and is very costly to serve resulting in a loss to the company of 50% − 70% = −20%. Most of this difference reflects the 40 per cent higher cost to serve. The following list is a profile of low and high cost-to-serve customers.

Low cost to serve	High cost to serve
Large order quantity	Small order quantity
Few order changes	Many order changes
Little pre- and post-sales support	Large amounts of pre- and post-sales support
Regular scheduling	Expedited scheduling
Standard delivery	Special delivery requirements
Few returns	Frequent returns

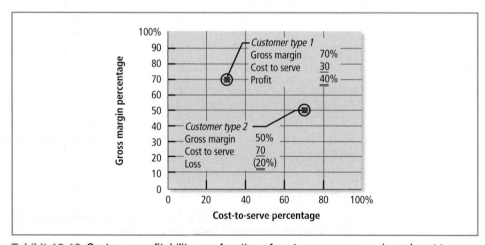

Exhibit 12.10 Customer profitability as a function of customer gross margin and cost to serve

BUSINESS FIRST
Companies use ABC to improve the allocation of service costs and lower the costs to serve customers

Dow Chemical believes that its ABC allocation system is the foundation of its cost-management system. Dow, with annual revenues of more than $54 billion, is the largest chemical company in the United States and number two worldwide. The company has three major business segments: plastics, chemicals and agricultural products. Dow switched from a traditional allocation system to ABC as part of a major shift in its total strategy. It sold its pharmaceutical, energy and consumer products businesses and set a goal to be the number one company in chemicals, plastics and agroscience. Dow believed that, to accomplish its goal, it needed to improve the quality and accuracy of its costing system, including the costs of internal services such as those provided by the human resources and maintenance departments.

Service providers, such as human resources and maintenance, identified the major activities performed, determined the appropriate cost-allocation base for each activity, and computed costs for each activity and service provided to using departments. The focus on activities has led to a better understanding of costs by everyone and better cost control. Another advantage of the ABC system is improved resource planning and utilisation. By focusing on activities and their related

cost-allocation bases, Dow's maintenance department managers can more effectively plan maintenance resource needs and availability. Overall, since the company integrated ABC into its cost management system, it has realised significant benefits.

Another company that used ABC to improve its allocation system is Kemps LLC, a manufacturer of dairy products such as milk, yogurt and ice cream. Kemps' customers range from small convenience stores to large retailers such as Target. When Kemp changed its strategy to focus more on being a low-total-cost provider, it recognised the need to measure and manage the costs to serve its diverse customer base. Using an ABC system it was able to identify customers who had a high cost to serve and thus were unprofitable. Many of these customers ordered in low quantities or made frequent returns. By implementing a menu-based pricing strategy where Kemps charged higher prices for low-volume orders and offered discounts for lowering product returns, Kemps realised significant cost savings.

Sources: J. Damitio, G. Hayes and P. Kintzele, 'Integrating ABC and ABM at Dow Chemical', *Management Accounting Quarterly*, Winter 2000, pp. 22–26; R. Kaplan and S. Anderson, 'Time-driven activity-based costing', *Harvard Business Review*, November 2004, pp. 131–138; and *Dow Chemical Company, 2007 Annual Report*.

■ Measuring and managing customer profitability

In the general framework for cost allocation, we stated that it is important to directly trace or allocate costs associated with customer actions to customers rather than assigning them first to producing departments and then to customers. This is because if we assigned these costs to producing departments and then to products, the allocation to customers would be based on production-related output measures that may have little relationship to the cause of customer-service costs. Such allocations can lead to cost distortions and resulting erroneous customer-profitability measures. Let's consider an example that illustrates this important concept.

Cedar City Distributors (CCD) is a distributor of athletic apparel and sports gear. CCD distributes many products to retail outlets but classifies products into just two product groups – apparel and sports gear.

- Apparel items arrive at CCD in prepackaged cases and CCD ships them to customers in these cases. Examples include shirts, shorts, socks and hats.

- CDD receives sports gear in bulk shipments. CCD must unpack these products and then repack them to meet small order quantities for specific gear. Examples include tennis rackets and balls, cricket bats and gloves and golf clubs and bags.

CCD has two types of customers:

1   *Small stores:* stores that order low volumes (an average of 10 cases per order), the majority being apparel.

2   *Large stores:* stores that order large volumes of both apparel and sports gear.

CCD's management has set a strategic goal to improve both product and customer profitability. A related and necessary subgoal that supports this strategy is to identify profitable products and customers using an accurate cost-accounting system.

CCD currently uses a simple cost accounting system to calculate both product and customer profitability. The only direct costs are the purchase costs of apparel and sports gear products. CCD allocates indirect costs to the product groups using a single indirect cost pool for all indirect costs with 'pounds of product' as the cost allocation base. Cost and operating data accumulated for the most recent year are shown in Exhibit 12.11.

To determine the profitability of a customer, we first calculate the profit margin per case for each product. Then, we use the product mix ordered by each customer to calculate profitability. Exhibit 12.12 shows how to calculate the profit margin per case and the profit margin percentage of both products. Based on the profit-margin percentage, apparel products are more profitable than sports gear. Since small stores' product mix is 75 per cent apparel compared to only 50 per cent for large stores, we expect small store customers have a larger profit margin percentage. We verify this in Exhibit 12.13, which shows customer profitability. Note that customer profitability is based solely on the product mix ordered by a particular customer.

Our analysis indicates that a strategy to increase CCD's overall profitability would involve an emphasis on apparel products and small stores. However, in setting this strategy, CCD's management relied on the accuracy of the cost. CCD's simple cost-accounting system may accurately allocate indirect costs if the single cost allocation base, pounds of product sold, is a plausible and reliable cost driver for all resources in the indirect cost pool. Let's see if that is the case.

Allocation of the costs to serve

We look again at Exhibit 12.11 and ask, 'Is it plausible that all the activities and associated indirect resources included in the indirect cost pool are related solely to the weight of

Product data		
	Apparel	**Sports gear**
Annual demand in cases	1,400	1,000
Average purchase cost per case	€ 80	€ 140
Average weight per purchased case	15 kilograms	25 kilograms
Average sales price per case	€ 570	€ 830

Customer data		
	Small stores	**Large stores**
Apparel demand in cases	600	800
Sports gear demand in cases	200	800
Total annual demand in cases	800	1,600
Orders	80	35

Indirect cost data

A single indirect cost pool consists of resources needed to perform receiving, storing, picking, packing, shipping, order processing and customer service activities. The annual cost of these resources is €690,000. The cost-allocation base used to allocate this pool to the two product groups is kilos of product sold.

Exhibit 12.11 Operating data for cedar city distributors

	Output measure or cost allocation base	Revenue or cost per unit	Apparel		Sports gear	
			Amount of output or cost-allocation base	Total revenue or cost	Amount of output or cost-allocation base	Total revenue or cost
Apparel revenue	Cases	€570.00	1,400	€798,000		
Sports gear revenue	Cases	€830.00			1,000	€830,000
Apparel purchase cost	Cases	€ 80.00	1,400	112,000		
Sports gear purchase cost	Cases	€140.00			1,000	140,000
Indirect cost pool, €690,000	Pounds	€ 15.00[a]	21,000[b]	315,000	25,000	375,000
Total cost				427,000		515,000
Profit margin				€371,000		€315,000
Profit margin per case				€ 265.00		€ 315.00
Profit margin percentage				46.5%[c]		38.0%[d]

[a]€690,000 ÷ (15 lb per case × 1,400 cases) + (25 lb per case × 1,000 cases)
[b]15 kg per case × 1,400 cases
[c]€371,000 ÷ €798,000
[d]€315,000 ÷ €830,000

Exhibit 12.12 Profit margin per case of apparel and sports gear

purchased product?' Might 'number of customer orders' be a more plausible cost-allocation base for some items, like the order processing and customer service activities and related resources?

Let's assume that 'number of orders' was indeed a better cost-allocation base for the order processing and customer service activities. The cost of the resources used by these two activities is €276,000 out of the total indirect cost pool of €690,000. CCD should exclude these costs from the computation of product profit margin. Instead, it should set up an additional cost pool and allocate these costs to customer types. (Note, this is shown as allocation type '9' in Exhibit 12.1 on p. 520)

The partial process map in Exhibit 12.14 shows how we can change CCD's old allocation system to reflect this refinement. Exhibit 12.14 does not contain revenue and direct product costs because they will not change. It shows only the €690,000 of indirect costs, separated into two cost pools. One cost pool is the €276,000 cost of resources used

	Small stores			Large stores		
	Cases	Profit margin per case	Total profit margin	Cases	Profit margin per case	Total profit margin
Apparel	600	€265.00	€159,000	800	€265.00	€212,000
Sports gear	200	315.00	63,000	800	315.00	252,000
			€222,000			€464,000
Total profit margin percentage			43.7%[a]			41.4%[b]

[a]€222,000 ÷ (600 cases × €570 per case + 200 cases × €830 per case) = €222,000 ÷ (€342,000 + €166,000) = €222,000 ÷ €508,000 = .437

[b]€464,000 ÷ (800 cases × €570 per case + 800 cases × €830 per case) = €464,000 ÷ (€456,000 + €664,000) ÷ €1,120,000 = .414

Exhibit 12.13 Customer profitability at cedar city distributors for processing customer orders and providing customer services. We will examine how to allocate this cost shortly. The other cost pool is the €690,000 − €276,000 = €414,000 associated with resources used for receiving, unpacking, storing, packing and shipping that remains in the original indirect cost pool. The allocation of this €414,000 does not change and is still based on pounds of product.

In our refined system, we allocate the €276,000 to the customer cost objectives on the basis of number of orders, an allocation base that represents the cause of the costs much better than does kilos of product. An analysis of the allocation percentages in Exhibit 12.14 reveals how customer profitability will change under the refined allocation system. Consider the allocations of the €276,000 to large stores under both systems. In the old system, large stores receive (32,000 kgs ÷ 46,000 kgs) × €276,000 = €192,000 because shipments to large stores weigh 32,000 kilos out of total shipments of 46,000 kilos. In the refined allocation system, the allocation of the €276,000 is based on the proportion of orders by large stores. Large stores make only 35 out of 115 orders, so the allocation is (35 ÷ 115) × €276,000 = €84,000. The refined cost-accounting system allocates €192,000 − €84,000 = €108,000 less indirect, customer-related costs to large stores and, correspondingly, €108,000 more cost to small stores.

The refined cost-allocation system significantly changes the profitability measures of small and large stores. Exhibit 12.15 shows the calculation of product gross margin, customer gross margin, customer cost to serve and customer profitability.

Contrary to the results based on the simple, existing cost-accounting system (Exhibit 12.13), the refined system shows that large stores are the most profitable customers. Exhibit 12.16 is based on Exhibit 12.15 and depicts both the customer product gross margin and cost

Exhibit 12.14 Cedar City Distributors refined cost-allocation system

Product profitability measures						
			Apparel		Sports gear	
	Output measure or cost-allocation base	Revenue or cost per unit of cost-allocation base	Amount of output or cost-allocation base	Total revenue or cost	Amount of output or cost-allocation base	Total revenue or cost
Apparel revenue	Cases	€570.00	1,400	€798,000		
Sports gear revenue	Cases	830.00			1,000	€830,000
Apparel purchase cost	Cases	80.00	1,400	112,000		
Sports gear purchase cost	Cases	140.00			1,000	140,000
Indirect cost pool, €414,000	Kilos	9.00[a]	21,000	189,000	25,000	225,000
Total cost				301,000		365,000
Product gross margin				€497,000		€465,000
Product gross margin per case				€ 355.00		€ 465.00
Product gross margin percentage				62.3%		56.0%

Customer profitability measures						
	Small stores			Large stores		
	Amount of output or cost-allocation base	Margin or cost per unit of cost-allocation base	Total margin or cost	Amount of output or cost-allocation base	Margin or cost per unit	Total margin or cost
Apparel product gross margin	600 cases	€355.00	€213,000	800 cases	€355.00	284,000
Sports gear product gross margin	200 cases	465.00	93,000	800 cases	465.00	372,000
Gross margin for product mix			306,000			656,000
Cost to serve, €2,400 per order[d]	80 orders	2,400	192,000	35 orders	2,400	84,000
Customer profit margin			€114,000			€572,000
Customer gross margin percentage			60.2%[b]			58.6%[c]
Cost to service percentage			37.8%			7.5%
Customer profit margin percentage			22.4%[e]			51.1%[f]

[a] €414,000 ÷ (15 kgs per case × 1,400 cases + 25 kgs per case × 1,000 cases)

[b] €306,000 ÷ (600 cases × €570 per case + 200 cases × €830 per case)

[c] €656,000 ÷ (800 cases × €570 per case + 800 cases × €830 per case)

[d] €76,000 ÷ (80 orders + 35 orders)

[e] 60.2% − 37.8% or €114,000 ÷ (600 cases × €570 per case + 200 cases × €830 per case)

[f] 58.6% − 7.5% or €572,000 ÷ (800 cases × €570 per case + 800 cases × €830 per case)

Exhibit 12.15 Product and customer profitability measures based on CCD's refined cost-allocation system

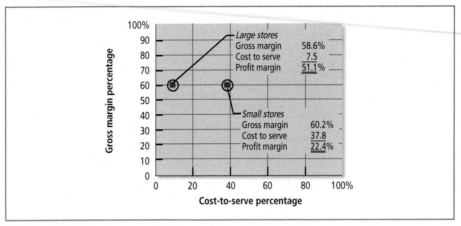

Exhibit 12.16 Customer profitability at Cedar City Distributors

to serve. It is easy to see why large stores are the major source of profit for CCD. The cost to serve is low and the product mix yields a substantial gross margin. This example demonstrates why it is important for accountants to carefully choose and measure cost-allocation bases. The refined system gives managers at CCD more insight into operations and they have a tool to measure and manage customer profitability.

Summary problem for your review

PROBLEM

Consider our example of the manufacturer's display facility. Exhibits 12.8 and 12.9 on p. 536 and 537 show how the company used the ABC approach to determine the cost of goods sold for custom and standard displays. Suppose that management wants to know the profitability of its major customers. Assume that two major customers are Southwest Hardware Stores (SHS) and Southeast Appliance Stores (SAS). SHS orders a mix of custom and standard displays. It also has unique service requirements, orders relatively small order sizes and requires substantial pre- and post-sales support from customer service and corporate staff. In contrast, SAS orders only a few custom displays, has larger order quantities and does not require much customer service or corporate staff support.

Accountants have performed an analysis of customer-related activities and concluded that two activities capture the main differences in cost to serve among the customers – sales activity and customer and corporate support. Both customers use these activities to some extent and it is not economically feasible to directly trace these costs to customers. Therefore, the company allocates these costs to customers. The cost-allocation bases chosen are number of orders for the sales activity cost pool and service and staff labour hours for the customer and corporate support cost pool.

To determine the profitability of the two customers, the company has collected the following data:

Average price of a custom display	€12,000
Average price of a standard display	€ 8,500
Number of custom displays ordered by SHS	180
Number of custom displays ordered by SAS	20
Number of standard displays ordered by SHS	220
Number of standard displays ordered by SAS	980

Cost to serve activity analysis data:

Total sales and marketing cost pool	€3,000,000
Total customer service and corporate support cost pool	€1,150,000

Amount of each cost-allocation base used by each customer:

Cost allocation base	SHS	SAS
Orders	40	20
Hours	6,400	3,600

1 Calculate the gross margin percentage and cost-to-serve percentage for Southwest Hardware Stores and Southeast Appliance Stores.

2 Construct a graph similar to Exhibit 12.16 that depicts customer profitability for Southwest Hardware Stores and Southeast Appliance Stores.

3 Suggest a strategy for profit improvement for both customers.

SOLUTION

1 Exhibit 12.17 shows the calculation of customer gross margin and customer cost to serve.

2 Exhibit 12.18 depicts the profitability of SHS and SAS.

3 You can use Exhibit 12.18 as a guide for setting strategy for profit improvement. SAS is generating much more profit for the company than is SHS. Company managers should protect customers such as SAS from possible competitor actions, perhaps offering discounts to ensure continued business. In addition, the sales department manager should profile this type of customer to make it easier for salespersons to identify profitable new business. SHS is very expensive to serve because of its small order quantities and extensive pre- and post-sales support. Possible actions that would improve its profitability include charging for corporate support, reviewing internal processes within the company's customer service and corporate support function to improve efficiencies and increasing prices for custom displays.

			SHS		SAS	
	Cost-allocation base	Revenue/cost per unit of cost-allocation base	Amount of cost-allocation base	Revenue/cost	Amount of cost allocation base	Revenue/cost
Revenue – custom	Displays	€12,000.00	180	€2,160,000	20	€ 240,000
Revenue – standard	Displays	8,500.00	220	1,870,000	980	8,330,000
Total revenue				4,030,000		8,570,000
Cost of goods sold – custom	Displays	6,175.00[a]	180	1,111,500	20	123,500
Cost of goods sold – standard	Displays	2,387.50[a]	220	525,250	980	2,339,750
Total cost of goods sold				1,636,750		2,463,250
Gross margin				2,393,250		6,106,750

Exhibit 12.17 Contribution to unallocated corporate overhead at display facility

(continues)

Exhibit 12.17 (continued)

	Cost-allocation base	Revenue/cost per unit of cost-allocation base	SHS Amount of cost-allocation base	SHS Revenue/cost	SAS Amount of cost allocation base	SAS Revenue/cost
Cost to serve:						
Sales	Orders	50,000.00[b]	40	2,000,000	20	1,000,000
Customer service and corporate support	Hours	115.00[c]	6,400	736,000	3,600	414,000
Total cost to serve				2,736,000		1,414,000
Contribution to unallocated corporate overhead				€ (342,750)		€4,692,750
Gross margin percentage				59.4%		71.3%
Cost-to-serve percentage				67.9%		16.5%
Customer profit margin percentage				(8.5)%		54.8%

[a] From Exhibit 12.9
[b] €3,000,000 ÷ (40 orders + 20 orders)
[c] €1,150,000 ÷ (6,400 hours + 3,600 hours)

Exhibit 12.18 Display facility: customer profitability using the ABC approach

MAKING MANAGERIAL DECISIONS

Louder Is Better Company makes two speaker models – standard (S) and deluxe (D). The following diagrams show how ABC and traditional allocation systems allocate overhead costs to the deluxe model. The production department has overhead costs of €36,000. Why does the cost allocated to the deluxe type speakers by the ABC system differ from that in the traditional system?

Answer

In the traditional system, the deluxe product receives only 25 per cent of the overhead costs because it uses only 25 per cent of the machine hours. But in the ABC system, it receives 72 per cent of the overhead because it uses 63 per cent of the parts and 83 per cent of the setups.

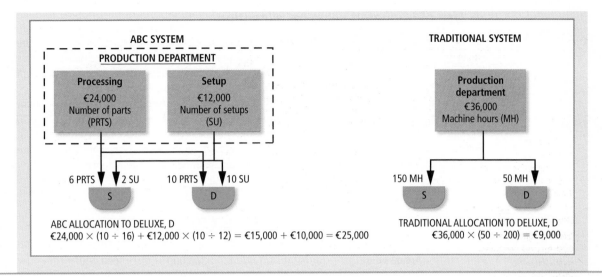

ABC SYSTEM

PRODUCTION DEPARTMENT

Processing
€24,000
Number of parts
(PRTS)

Setup
€12,000
Number of setups
(SU)

6 PRTS   2 SU   10 PRTS   10 SU

S   D

ABC ALLOCATION TO DELUXE, D
€24,000 × (10 ÷ 16) + €12,000 × (10 ÷ 12) = €15,000 + €10,000 = €25,000

TRADITIONAL SYSTEM

Production
department
€36,000
Machine hours (MH)

150 MH   50 MH

S   D

TRADITIONAL ALLOCATION TO DELUXE, D
€36,000 × (50 ÷ 200) = €9,000

This concludes our discussion of service department allocation. We will next consider two specific types of cost allocations: (1) allocation of central corporate costs such as public relations and legal costs and (2) allocation of joint and by-product costs.

Allocation of central corporate support costs

Objective 6
Allocate the central corporate costs of an organisation.

Many managers believe it is desirable to fully allocate all of an organisation's costs, including central corporate support costs, to the revenue-producing (operating) parts of the organisation. Such allocations are not necessary from an accounting viewpoint and usually not useful as management information. For this reason, we do not consider central costs to be part of the value chain in this text. However, when a company allocates such costs, most managers accept them as a fact of life – as long as all managers seem to be treated alike and thus 'fairly'.

Whenever possible, the preferred cost-allocation base for central services is usage, either actual or estimated. But companies seldom allocate the costs of these central services on the basis of usage. They are more likely to choose usage as a cost-allocation base for data processing, advertising and operations research.

Usage is not always an economically viable way to allocate central costs, however. Also, it is difficult to allocate many central costs, such as the president's salary and related expenses, public relations, legal services, income tax planning, company-wide advertising and basic research, on the basis of cause and effect. As a result, some companies use cost-allocation bases such as the revenue of each division, the cost of goods sold by each division, the total assets of each division, or the total costs of each division (before allocation of the central costs) to allocate central costs, even though these bases are not necessarily the cost drivers.

The use of the foregoing cost-allocation bases might provide a rough indication of a cause-and-effect relationship. Basically, however, they represent an 'ability to bear' philosophy of cost allocation. For example, a company might allocate the costs of company-wide advertising, such as the sponsorship of a programme on a PBS station, to all products and divisions on the basis of the revenues in each. But such costs precede sales. They are discretionary costs as determined by management policies, not by sales results. Although 60 per cent of the companies in a large survey use sales revenue as a cost-allocation base for some cost-allocation purposes, it is seldom truly a cost driver in the sense of being an activity that causes the costs.

Use of budgeted sales for allocation

If a company feels it must allocate the costs of central services based on sales, even though the costs do not vary in proportion to sales, it should use budgeted sales rather than actual sales as an allocation base. At least this method means that the fortunes of other departments will not affect the short-run costs of a given department.

For example, suppose the display manufacturer budgets central advertising as 10 per cent of forecasted sales in two countries – Estonia and Kosovo. The forecasted sales are €500,000 in both Countries, so the total advertising budget, a fixed cost, is €100,000. Actual sales in Estonia and Kosovo are €300,000 and €600,000, respectively. How does the company allocate the €100,000 advertising budget if it uses forecasted sales compared to actual sales?

Allocation of €100,000 central advertising budget

	Estonia	Kosovon
Forecast sales	€500,000	€500,000
Allocation based on forecast sales	50,000	50,000
Actual sales	300,000	600,000
Allocation based on actual sales	33,333	67,667

The preferred allocation is based on forecast sales. Why? Because it indicates a low ratio of sales to advertising in Estonia – it directs attention to a potential problem. In contrast, allocation based on actual sales soaks the Kosovon operations with more advertising cost because of the achieved results and relieves Estonian operations despite its lower success. This is another example of the confusion that can arise when cost allocations to one company unit depend on the activity of other units.

Allocation of joint costs and by-product costs

Objective 7
Allocate joint costs to products using the physical-units and relative-sales-value methods.

Joint costs and by-product costs create especially difficult cost-allocation problems. By definition, such costs relate to more than one product and we cannot separately identify them with an individual product. Let's examine these special cases, starting with joint costs.

Joint costs

So far, we have assumed that we could identify cost-allocation bases with an individual product. For example, if we are allocating activity costs to products or services on the basis of machine hours, we have assumed that we can measure the amount of machine time consumed in making each product. However, sometimes we add inputs to the production process before we can separately identify individual products (i.e., before the split-off point). Recall from Chapter 6 (pp. 246–7) that we call such costs joint costs. Joint costs include all inputs of material, labour and head costs that are incurred before the split-off point.

Suppose a department has more than one product and some costs are joint costs. How should we allocate such joint costs to the products? *Allocation of joint costs should not affect decisions about the individual products.* Nevertheless, companies routinely allocate joint product costs to products for purposes of inventory valuation and income determination.

Consider the example of joint product costs that we used in Chapter 6. A department in Lyondell Basell Industries produces two chemicals, X and Y. The joint cost is €100,000 and production is 1,000,000 litres of X and 500,000 litres of Y. X sells for €.09 per litre and Y for €.06 per litre. We want to find a method to allocate some part of the €100,000 joint cost to the inventory of X and the rest to the inventory of Y. Such allocations are useful for inventory purposes only. You should ignore joint cost allocations for decisions such as selling a joint product or processing it further.

There are two conventional ways of allocating joint costs to products: physical units and relative sales values. If a company uses physical units, it would allocate the joint costs as follows:

	Litres	Weighting	Allocation of joint costs	Sales value at split-off point
X	1,000,000	$(10 \div 15) \times €100,000$	€ 66,667	€ 90,000
Y	500,000	$(5 \div 15) \times €100,000$	33,333	30,000
	1,500,000		€100,000	€120,000

This approach shows that the €33,333 joint cost of producing Y exceeds its €30,000 sales value at the split-off point seemingly indicating that the company should not produce Y. However, such an allocation is not helpful in making production decisions. We can produce neither of the two products separately.

A decision to produce Y must be a decision to produce X and Y. Because total revenue of €120,000 exceeds the total joint cost of €100,000, we should produce both. The allocation was not useful for this decision.

The physical-units method requires a common physical unit for measuring the output of each product. For example, board feet is a common unit for a variety of products in the lumber industry. However, sometimes such a common denominator is lacking. Consider the production of meat and hides from butchering a steer. You might use kilos as a common denominator, but kilos is not a good measure of the output of hides. As an alternative, many companies use the relative-sales-value method for allocating joint costs. The following allocation results from applying the relative-sales-value method to the company's department:

	Relative sales value at split-off point	Weighting	Allocation of joint costs
X	€ 90,000	$(90 \div 120) \times €100,000$	€ 75,000
Y	30,000	$(30 \div 120) \times €100,000$	25,000
	€120,000		€100,000

The weighting is based on the sales values of the individual products. Because the sales value of X at the split-off point is €90,000 and total sales value at the split-off point is €120,000, we allocate 90 ÷ 120 of the joint cost to X.

This method might eliminate one problem, but it creates another. Note how the allocation of a cost to a particular product, such as Y, depends not only on the sales value of Y but also on the sales value of X. For example, suppose you were the product manager for Y. You planned to sell your 500,000 litres for €30,000, achieving a profit of €30,000 − €25,000 = €5,000. Everything went as expected except that the price of X fell to €.07 per litre for revenue of €70,000 rather than €90,000. Instead of 30 ÷ 120 of the joint cost, Y received 30 ÷ 100 × €100,000 = €30,000 and had a profit of €0. Despite the fact that Y operations were exactly as planned, the cost-allocation method caused the profit on Y to be €5,000 below plan.

We can also use the relative-sales-value method when we cannot sell one or more of the joint products at the split-off point. To apply the method, we approximate the sales value at split off as follows:

$$\text{sales value at split off} = \text{final sales value} - \text{separable costs}$$

For example, suppose the 500,000 litres of Y requires €20,000 of processing beyond the split-off point, after which we can sell it for €.10 per litre. The sales value at split off would be (€.10 × 500,000) − €20,000 = €50,000 − €20,000 = €30,000.

▇ By-product costs

By-products are similar to joint products. A **by-product** is a product that, like a joint product, is not individually identifiable until manufacturing reaches a split-off point. By-products differ from joint products because they have relatively insignificant total sales values in comparison with the other products emerging at split off. In contrast, joint products have relatively significant total sales values at split off in comparison with the other jointly produced items. Examples of by-products are glycerine from soap making and mill ends of cloth and carpets.

If we account for an item as a by-product, we allocate only separable costs to it. We allocate all joint costs to the main products. We deduct any revenues from by-products, less their separable costs, from the cost of the main products.

Consider a lumber company that sells sawdust generated in the production of lumber to companies making particle board. Suppose the company regards the sawdust as a by-product. In 20X7, sales of sawdust totalled €30,000, and the cost of loading and shipping the sawdust (i.e., costs incurred beyond the split-off point) was €20,000. The inventory cost of the sawdust would consist of only the €20,000 separable cost. The company would allocate none of the joint cost of producing lumber and sawdust to the sawdust. It would deduct the difference between the revenue and separable cost, €30,000 − €20,000 = €10,000, from the cost of the lumber produced.

Highlights to remember

1 **Describe the general framework for cost allocation.** Companies assign direct and indirect costs to various cost objects, including service departments, producing departments, products and customers. All organisations allocate indirect costs to producing departments and to the products or services delivered to customers. These allocations often include the costs of service departments. Some organisations carry cost allocation one more step – to customers.

2 **Allocate the variable and fixed costs of service departments to other organisational units.** Companies should use separate cost pools for variable and fixed costs when allocating service department costs. They should allocate variable costs using budgeted cost rates times the actual cost-driver level. They should allocate fixed costs using budgeted per cent of capacity available for use times the total budgeted fixed costs.

3 **Use the direct and step-down methods to allocate service department costs to user departments.** When service departments support other service departments in addition to producing departments, they can use either the direct or step-down method for allocation. The direct method ignores other service departments when allocating costs. The step-down method recognises other service departments' use of services.

4 **Allocate costs from producing departments to products or services using the traditional approach.** When a company's products or services are the final cost object, it should integrate its service department allocation with the allocation system used to cost final cost objects. A traditional system traces the direct costs in each department to its products or services and allocates indirect costs using a cost-allocation base. The ABC approach uses four steps to assign costs to products or services: (1) Determine key components, (2) Identify resources, activities and cost objects and their relationships, (3) Collect relevant data, and (4) Calculate and interpret ABC information. The ABC approach provides more accurate estimates of product or service costs than the traditional approach but is more costly to maintain.

5 **Allocate costs associated with customer actions to customers.** Customer profitability is a function of product mix and the cost to serve. Activities that can drive up the costs to serve customers include small order quantities, pre-sales work, order changes, returns, special delivery requirements and post-sales work.

6 **Allocate the central corporate costs of an organisation.** Central costs include public relations, top corporate management overhead, legal, data processing, accountant's department and company-wide planning. Often, it is best to allocate only those central costs of an organisation for which measures of usage by departments are available.

7 Allocate joint costs to products using the physical-units and relative-sales-value methods. Companies often allocate joint costs to products for inventory valuation and income determination using the physical-units or relative-sales-value method. However, such allocations should not affect decisions. ■

Appendix 12: Multistage ABC (MSABC) systems

In Chapter 4 we introduced simple two-stage ABC systems. The first stage allocates costs to activities and the second stage allocates the activity costs to products, customers or other cost objectives. They have a financial accounting flavour because the general ledger is at the heart of all the cost data used. While two-stage ABC systems meet the decision-making needs of many organisations, some organisations (such as FedEx, Boeing and Siemens) prefer to design **multistage ABC (MSABC) systems** with more than two stages of allocations and resource cost-allocation bases other than percentages.

There is a distinctive operational flavour to MSABC systems because much of the required data comes from operational data sources, not just the general ledger. Many companies, began their use of ABC by using the two-stage approach. However, they later converted to the multistage approach because of its focus on operations and its tendency to enhance operating managers' understanding of the business. According to one manager, at Pillsbury,

> *Having already completed an ABC model within our organisation using the two-stage ABC approach, my eyes were opened to the importance of the multistage ABC approach and how its scenario-playing capability and flexibility allows an organisation to move past just ABC toward ABM.*

Managers at companies that use MSABC systems believe that their additional complexity yields more accurate costs and a deeper understanding of operations. A deeper understanding of the business leads to better ideas for process improvement. Process improvements, in turn, lead to more satisfied customers and a competitive edge. Three key attributes distinguish MSABC systems from two-stage ABC systems:

1 There are more than two stages of allocation.

2 Cost behaviour of resources is considered.

3 There is a greater use of operational information such as cost-allocation bases and consumption rates.

Let's explore each of these attributes to see why MSABC systems offer so much value to managers.

■ Key attributes of multistage ABC systems

Understanding the relationships between activities, resources, resource costs and cost-allocation bases is the key to understanding MSABC systems and how they facilitate managers' understanding of operations. To gain more insight into how an ABC system actually works, we will look at one of the products produced by Woodland Park Company, a manufacturer of plastic components used in commercial lorries and buses.

One of the components Woodland Park makes, 102Z, is a plastic dashboard casing for the control panel of large trucks. Making 102Z requires resin material and several activities, such as receiving, production scheduling, material handling, setup, moulding machine processing, assembly, inspection, packaging and shipping. We will focus on the set-up and moulding machine processing activities. The resources required by these activities include an injection-moulding machine, operating labour, electrical energy and the plant itself. Exhibit 12.19 shows the relationships between the setup and machine processing activities and the resources used.

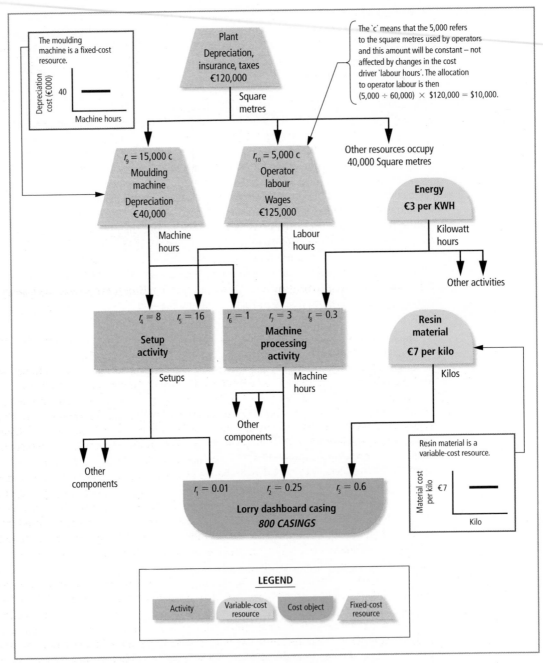

The moulding machine is a fixed-cost resource.

Depreciation cost (€000)   40

Machine hours

Plant
Depreciation, insurance, taxes
€120,000

Square metres

The 'c' means that the 5,000 refers to the square metres used by operators and this amount will be constant – not affected by changes in the cost driver 'labour hours'. The allocation to operator labour is then
$(5,000 \div 60,000) \times \$120,000 = \$10,000$.

$r_9 = 15,000$ c
Moulding machine
Depreciation
€40,000

$r_{10} = 5,000$ c
Operator labour
Wages
€125,000

Other resources occupy 40,000 Square metres

Energy
€3 per KWH

Machine hours

Labour hours

Kilowatt hours

Other activities

$r_4 = 8$ $r_5 = 16$ $r_6 = 1$ $r_7 = 3$ $r_8 = 0.3$
Setup activity

Machine processing activity

Resin material
€7 per kilo

Setups

Machine hours

Kilos

Other components

Other components

$r_1 = 0.01$ $r_2 = 0.25$ $r_3 = 0.6$
Lorry dashboard casing
800 CASINGS

Resin material is a variable-cost resource.

Material cost per kilo   €7

Kilo

LEGEND

Activity   Variable-cost resource   Cost object   Fixed-cost resource

Exhibit 12.19 Relationship between cost object, activities and resources in an ABC system

The first key attribute of MSABC systems is the use of more than two stages of allocation. In Exhibit 12.19, notice that the plant resource costs are allocated to the final cost objective – truck dashboard casings – in three stages. In a two-stage ABC system, plant costs would be allocated to the truck casings in only two stages. In the MSABC system, we assume machine and labour resources consume plant costs as measured by the square feet that each occupies. In a two-stage ABC system, we would ignore the interrelationship between the plant and the machine and labour resources and instead use a percentage to allocate plant costs directly to the setup and machine-processing activities. But this is difficult to interpret and does little to

MSABC process map (partial)   Two-stage ABC process map (partial)

enhance our understanding of operations. MSABC systems overcome this problem, allowing for any number of allocations necessary to accurately describe operations.

The second key attribute of MSABC systems is their extensive use of operational information. Look at the cost objective Lorry Dashboard casing in Exhibit 12.19. It takes 15 minutes of machine time to process each casing. This is shown by the activity-consumption rate, $r_2 = 0.25$ machine hours per casing. Similarly, r_1 gives the consumption rate for setup activity. Each production run produces 100 casings and requires one setup ($r_1 = 0.01$). Each casing requires 0.6 kilos of resin material. Therefore, the annual demand for 800 casings requires a total of 8 setups ($800 \times .01$), 200 processing hours ($800 \times .25$) and 480 kilos of resin (800×0.6).

A similar interpretation can be made for the activities. For example, each hour of machine-processing activity requires (consumes) one moulding machine hour, three operator labour hours and 0.3 kilowatt hours of energy. We can see that the cost-allocation bases are a measure of the activity level (setups and processing hours) and the amount of resources used (machine hours, labour hours and kilowatt hours) to produce casings. The resource-consumption rates (the rs on each activity in Exhibit 12.19) give the rates at which the activity uses resources for each cost-driver unit of the activity.

Two-stage ABC systems differ in the treatment of the consumption of resources by activities. In two-stage ABC, percentages would be used to describe the relationships between resources and activities. Managers who use MSABC believe that resource-consumption rates provide more valuable operational information than percentages. In our example, the managers at Woodland Park Company now have cost and operational information that they can use to manage operations more effectively. For example, consider the portion of the process map shown at the top of this page. There is much more useful operational information in the MSABC map. Operational managers use information, such as the labour hours per machine hour or kilowatt hours per machine hour, to track operational improvements. Using the cost behaviour feature of MSABC, managers can predict the effects on activity costs of such improvements. This is much more difficult – or impossible – using the two-stage approach.

Let's look at an example. Suppose that Woodland Park can increase its sales of lorry casings to an annual total of 900 but does not have the machine time available for the extra 100 casings. It would require an additional 25 hours of processing time to meet this new demand. Management believes that by using special quick-change dies, it can reduce the setup time by 75 per cent. Will this process improvement save enough time to produce the extra 100 casings? The new consumption rate for machine time, $r4$, is 2 hours per setup. So, the total machine time consumed during setups will be 18 hours (900 casings $\times$ 0.01 setups per casing $\times$ 2 machine hours per setup) compared to the current 64 hours (800 $\times$ 0.01 $\times$ 8). Thus, the time savings of 46 hours is more than enough to produce the extra 100 casings. If a two-stage ABC system were being used, it would be much more difficult to analyse this improvement idea because we would not have the consumption rate for machine time. Instead, we would have a percentage based on historical relationships and general ledger data.

The third key attribute of MSABC systems is their recognition of cost behaviour. In Exhibit 12.19, the variable-cost resources – energy and resin material – are modelled by using this symbol ▬. Financial data for these resources are expressed as costs per cost-driver unit. For energy, this is €3 per kilowatt hour. Energy cost varies directly with changes in the processing activity because the power company charges Woodland Park based on the kilowatt hours used. One additional processing hour will require .3 additional kilowatt hours that will increase energy cost by €0.90 (€3.00 $\times$ .3). Thus, energy is a variable-cost resource and it is easy to see that processing hours and kilowatt hours are factors that affect energy costs.

The fixed-cost resources – plant, machines and labour – are modelled by using this symbol ▬. For financial data, we use total costs. The costs of the machine and labour resources are fixed with respect to changes (within the relevant range) in the cost-allocation bases. One additional processing hour requires one additional machine hour and three labour hours, but the costs of the machine (depreciation) and labour (wages) resources do not change as long as machine time and labour time are available. Have we violated our definition of cost driver? Not really. If the number of processing hours increases enough, the required machine hours or labour hours will exceed the capacities of the machine and labour. Management will then decide whether to purchase more machines or to hire additional operating labourers. Costs of fixed-cost resources do not change automatically when the level of a cost-allocation bases change – this involves a management decision.

In simple, two-stage ABC systems, the cost behaviour of resources is usually ignored. This means that planning for future operations is difficult with two-stage ABC because the impact of changes in demand and related cost-driver levels cannot be predicted. For example, if we expect that the demand for casings will increase, a two-stage ABC system will not enable us to predict the increase in variable production costs such as materials and energy, but the MSABC system will correctly predict the variable resin and energy cost increases.

Summary problem for your review

PROBLEM

Refer to the Chapter 4 discussion (Appendix 4, pp. 140–9) of the billing department at a customer care centres. Suppose the billing department has designed an MSABC system. Exhibit 12.20 shows the process map for the MSABC system. Consider the portion of the billing department's process map shown in Exhibit 12.21. Management wants to reduce activities that do not add value for the customer. One idea is to reduce the verification of commercial bills by verifying only 70 per cent of commercial bills (at random) and, further, by verifying only certain parts of each bill. Verifying only part of each bill will reduce the verifying time from 6 minutes to only 3 minutes per bill (account). Management believes that this procedure would not result in any increase in the number of inquiries and that bill accuracy would be unchanged. Since only part of each bill will be verified, the number of computer transactions will also be reduced from 25 to 15 per account. The company's labour agreement specifies that whenever labour utilisation for the combined billing and verification labour pool falls below 70 per cent due to any process improvement, the company may lay off workers until the utilisation level reaches 70 per cent. Currently, billing labour (billing labour plus bill-verifying labour) utilisation is at 85 per cent (actual hours consisting of 1,804 labour hours for billing plus 440 labour hours for verification activity

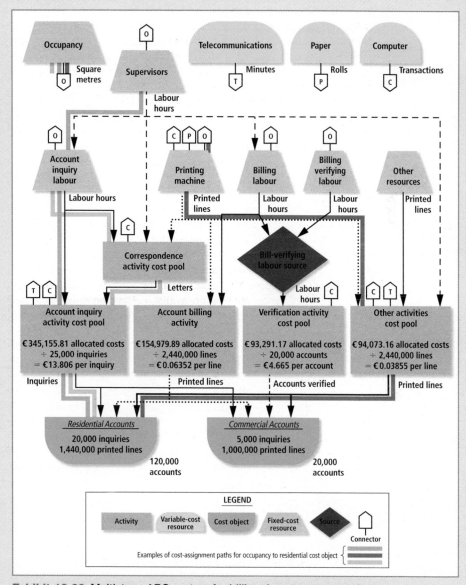

Exhibit 12.20 Multistage ABC system for billing department operations

divided by capacity of 2,640 labour hours = 85 per cent). Wages and benefits are €2,812.50 per month per labourer. Each labourer is available for 110 hours a month. Currently, there are 24 billing labourers, 4 of whom are dedicated to verifying bills – the verification team. Because of the negative impact that layoffs have on employee morale, management is hesitant to implement any layoffs unless the cost savings are significant.

Cost allocation in MSABC systems is complex and requires some form of computer software. To get a feel for this complexity, consider the various cost-allocations required to allocate occupancy cost to the residential accounts. Three of these paths are listed below and are also displayed in Exhibit 12.20.

Allocation Path 1: Occupancy → Account Inquiry Labour → Correspondence Activity → Account Inquiry Activity → Residential Accounts

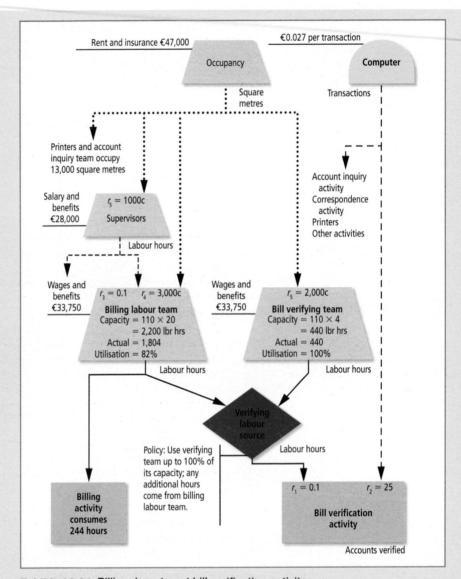

Exhibit 12.21 Billing department bill verification activity

Allocation Path 2: Occupancy → Supervision → Account Inquiry Labour → Account
  Inquiry Activity → Residential Accounts
Allocation Path 3: Occupancy → Printers → Other Activities → Residential Accounts

A computer program, either a spreadsheet or commercial software, would compute the allocations for each step in these paths based on the percentage of cost-allocation bases used. For example, the first set of allocations of the €47,000 occupancy costs are based on the square metres occupied by account-inquiry labour, supervisors, printing machines, billing labour and bill-verifying labour.

1 There are a total of eleven allocation paths to allocate occupancy costs to residential accounts. Give the other eight paths, using the same format shown previously.

2 In Exhibit 12.21, the relationship (indicated by arrows and consumption rates) between the computer resource and activities and resources such as account inquiry, correspondence,

printing machines and other activities is not shown. Explain why it is not necessary to know these relationships in order to determine the incremental billing labour cost savings from the process improvement.

3 Why is 'transactions' a true cost driver for computer costs, whereas supervisor 'labour hours' is not a true cost driver of billing labour costs?

4 Determine the billing labour and computer cost savings from this process improvement. What other potential cost savings may result? What action would you recommend?

SOLUTION

1 The remaining eight cost-allocation paths are as follows:

Allocation Path 4: Occupancy → Account Inquiry Activity → Account Inquiry Labour → Residential Accounts

Allocation Path 5: Occupancy → Supervision → Account Inquiry Labour → Correspondence → Account Inquiry Activity → Residential Accounts

Allocation Path 6: Occupancy → Supervision → Correspondence → Account Inquiry Activity → Residential Accounts

Allocation Path 7: Occupancy → Supervision → Billing Labour → Billing Activity → Residential Accounts

Allocation Path 8: Occupancy → Billing Labour → Billing Activity → Residential Accounts

Allocation Path 9: Occupancy → Supervision → Other Activities → Residential Accounts

Allocation Path 10: Occupancy → Printing Machines → Correspondence → Account Inquiry Activity → Residential Accounts

Allocation Path 11: Occupancy → Printing Machines → Billing Activity → Residential Accounts

We note that the number of stages of allocation for the occupancy resource varies from three (paths 4, 8 and 9) to five (path 5). Two-stage ABC has only two stages of allocations for all paths and there are only three allocation paths. As a manager, you need to decide whether the benefits of increased costing accuracy and operational information exceed the incremental cost to maintain the MSABC system.

2 We can determine how a resource will be affected by an operational change by starting at the point where the change is made and following all possible paths upward through the process map that end at the computer resource. In our case, the starting point is the verification activity. As the number of verified accounts is reduced, the number of computer transactions will also decline, as will computer costs. In this case, there is only one path linking verification to computers and it is shown in Exhibit 12.20. As can be seen from Exhibit 12.20, the cost-driver levels for account inquiry, correspondence, printers and other activities will not be affected by a decrease in the number of accounts verified. No other cost driver links to the computer resource changes so we do not need to show these relationships.

3 Any increase in demand for the computers will result in an immediate and automatic increase in the number of transactions. Since the computer leasing company bills the company on a per transaction basis, the computer costs will 'automatically' decrease in response to the decrease in accounts verified. On the other hand, changes in the number of billing labour hours does not automatically change or drive the cost of this resource. We use the output measure billing labour hours as the cost-allocation basis but it would require a decision by management to change the resource cost. As the number of accounts verified decreases, the number of billing labour hours will also decrease but the total wages paid will stay the same – only the utilisation rate will decrease. If this rate falls below 70 per cent, management can decide whether to reduce the labour pool and hence the labour cost.

4 Exhibit 12.22 shows the calculation of the predicted cost savings from this process improvement – €41,580. Additional cost savings may result from the reduced utilisation of the supervisory resource and the occupancy resource. The space occupied by the eight billing labourers who are let go may either be used for other productive purposes or rented.

Total cost analysis				
Resource	Current cost		Cost with process improvement	
Computer	20,000 acct × 25 trans/ acct × €.027/trans =	€13,500	14,000 accts × 15 trans/acct × €.027/trans = [(14,000 accts × .05 hr/acct) + 244 hr] ÷	€ 5,670
Billing labour	€2,812.50/lbr × 24 lbrs =	€67,500	.7 = desired capacity of 1,349 hr or 1,349 ÷ 110 ≈ 12 lbr*	
			Cost is 12 lbr × €2,812.50 =	€33,750
	Total cost	€81,000	Total cost	€39,420
			Cost savings (€81,000 – €39,420)	€41,580

*Check for utilisation: capacity = 12 × 110 = 1,320; actual = (14,000 acct × .05 hr/acct) + 244 hr = 944hr. Utilisation = 944 ÷ 1,320 = 71.5%. With 13 people, utilisation would be 944 ÷ 1,430 = 66%, so one additional labourer can be laid off.

Exhibit 12.22 Total cost analysis of process improvement in verification activity

Accounting vocabulary

by-product, p. 549
cost application, p. 530
direct method, p. 526
multistage ABC (MSABC) systems, p. 551

producing departments, p. 520
service departments, p. 520
step-down method, p. 527

Fundamental assignment material   MyAccountingLab

12.A1 Direct and step-down methods of allocation; general framework for allocation

Manriquez Tool and Die has three service departments:

	Budgeted department costs
Cafeteria, revenue of €100,000 less expenses of €250,000	€ 150,000
Engineering	2,500,000
General factory administration	950,000

Cost-allocation bases are budgeted as follows:

Production departments	Employees	Engineering hours worked for produc- tion departments	Total labour hours
Machining	120	50,000	300,000
Assembly	540	20,000	720.000
Finishing and painting	60	10,000	120,000

1 Manriquez allocates all service department costs directly to the production departments without allocation to other service departments. Show how much of the budgeted costs of each service department are allocated to each production department. To plan your work, examine number 2 before undertaking this question.

2 The company has decided to use the step-down method of cost allocation. General factory administration would be allocated first, then cafeteria, then engineering. Cafeteria employees work 36,000 labour hours per year. There were 60 engineering employees with 120,000 total labour hours. Recompute the results in number 1, using the step-down method. Show your computations. Compare the results in numbers 1 and 2. Which method of allocation do you favour? Why?

3 Refer to Exhibit 12.1 on p. 520 For each type of cost assignment made in number 2 using the step-down method, indicate the assignment type from Exhibit 12.1.

12.A2 Customer profitability

The following table gives sales, product cost and cost-to-serve data for a company that makes three product lines: E, F and G. The company has two customer types.

	Product E	Product F	Product G
Sales	€5,000	€6,000	€30,000
Cost of sales	4,500	4,800	15,000

	Customer type 1	Customer type 2	Total
Product E sales	€ 500	€ 4,500	€ 5,000
Product F sales	1,000	5,000	6,000
Product G sales	16,000	14,000	30,000
Manager visits	4	16	20

The cost to serve all customers is €12,000 and is allocated to customer types based on the number of manager visits to customer locations for pre- and post-sales support.

1 Determine the gross profit margin percentage of sales for each product. Which product is the most profitable?

2 Determine the gross profit margin and the gross profit margin percentage of sales for each customer type.

3 Determine the cost-to-serve percentage of sales for each customer type.

4 Determine the operating income and operating income percentage of sales for each customer type.

5 Which customer is the most profitable based the following profitability measures:
   (a) Gross margin
   (b) Gross margin percentage of sales
   (c) Operating income
   (d) Operating income percentage of sales.

12.A3 Joint products

San Marino Metals buys raw ore on the open market and processes it into two products, A and B. The ore costs €10 per kilo, and the process separating it into A and B has a cost of €4 per kilo. During 20X7, San Marino plans to produce 200,000 kilos of A and 600,000 kilos of B from 800,000 kilos of ore. A sells for €30 a kilo and B for €15 a kilo. The company allocated joint costs to the individual products for inventory valuation purposes.

1 Allocate all the joint costs to A and B using the physical-units method.
2 Allocate all the joint costs to A and B using the relative-sales-value method.
3 Suppose B cannot be sold in the form in which it emerges from the joint process. Instead, it must be processed further at a fixed cost of €300,000 plus a variable cost of €1 per kilo. Then, it can be sold for €21.50 a kilo. Allocate all the joint costs to A and B using the relative-sales-value method.

12.B1 Allocation of service department costs; general framework for allocation

Slovenia Cleaning provides cleaning services for a variety of clients. The company has two producing departments, residential and commercial, and two service departments, personnel and administrative. The company has decided to allocate all service department costs to the producing departments' personnel on the basis of number of employees and administrative on the basis of direct department costs. The budget for 20X7 shows the following:

	Personnel	Administrative	Residential	Commercial
Direct department costs	€70,000	€90,000	€240,000	€400,000
Number of employees	3	5	12	18
Direct-labour hours			24,000	36,000
Square metres cleaned			4,500,000	9,970,000

1 Allocate service department costs using the direct method.
2 Allocate service department costs using the step-down method. Personnel costs should be allocated first.
3 Suppose the company prices by the hour in the residential department and by the square metre cleaned in commercial. Using the results of the step-down allocations in number 2,
   (a) compute the cost of providing 1 direct-labour hour of service in the residential department.
   (b) compute the cost of cleaning one square metre of space in the commercial department.
4 Refer to Exhibit 12.1 on p. 520. For each type of cost assignment made in number 2 using the step-down method, indicate the assignment type from Exhibit 12.1.

12.B2 Customer profitability

Hogenson Company makes three product lines and has two customer types. The following table gives sales, product cost and cost-to-serve data for Hogenson:

	Product X	Product Y	Product Z
Sales	€2,000	€ 8,000	€20,000
Cost of goods sold	1,000	2,000	14,000
	Customer type 1	Customer type 2	Total
Product X sales	€1,000	€ 1,000	€ 2,000
Product Y sales	5,000	3,000	8,000
Product Z sales	1,000	19,000	20,000
Manager visits	6	4	10

The cost to serve all customers is €10,000 and is allocated to customer types based on the number of manager visits to customer locations for pre- and post-sales support.

1 Determine the gross profit margin percentage of sales for each product. Which product is the most profitable?

2 Determine the gross profit margin and the gross profit margin percentage of sales for each customer type.
3 Determine the cost-to-serve percentage of sales for each customer type.
4 Determine the operating income and operating income percentage of sales for each customer type.
5 Which customer is the most profitable based the following profitability measures:
   (a) Gross margin
   (b) Gross margin percentage of sales
   (c) Operating income
   (d) Operating income percentage of sales.

12.B3 Joint products

Des Moines Milling buys oats at €.60 per kilo and produces CRM Oat Flour, CRM Oat Flakes and CRM Oat Bran. The process of separating the oats into oat flour and oat bran costs €.30 per kilo. The oat flour can be sold for €1.50 per kilo, the oat bran for €2.00 per kilo. Each kilo of oats has .2 kilos of oat bran and .8 kilos of oat flour. A kilo of oat flour can be made into oat flakes for a fixed cost of €240,000 plus a variable cost of €.60 per kilo. Des Moines Milling plans to process 1 million kilos of oats in 20X7, at a purchase price of €600,000.

1 Allocate all the joint costs to oat flour and oat bran using the physical-units method.
2 Allocate all the joint costs to oat flour and oat bran using the relative-sales-value method.
3 Suppose there were no market for oat flour. Instead, it must be made into oat flakes to be sold. Oat flakes sell for €2.90 per kilo. Allocate the joint cost to oat bran and oat flakes using the relative-sales-value method.

Additional assignment material

MyAccountingLab

QUESTIONS

12.1 Why is the cost-allocation method used by an organisation an important part of its cost accounting system?

12.2 In a meeting among company executives and cost accountants, the CEO asked for the product costs for the company's newest product line. The cost accountant replied, 'Product cost depends on the reason for knowing it.' Do you agree? Explain briefly.

12.3 What are the 10 types of cost assignments?

12.4 When determining customer profitability, why is it important to directly trace and allocate customer-related service department costs to customers rather than assigning them first to producing departments and then to customers?

12.5 'The more the better!' was a comment made by the CEO of a major company when asked about allocation of sales, general and administrative costs to products. Do you agree? Explain.

12.6 List three guidelines for the allocation of service department costs.

12.7 Explain how a direct department cost can become an indirect cost.

12.8 Why should budgeted cost rates, rather than actual cost rates, be used for allocating the variable costs of service departments?

12.9 'We used a lump-sum allocation method for fixed costs a few years ago, but we gave it up because managers always predicted usage below what they actually used.' Is this a common problem? How might it be prevented?

12.10 Briefly describe the two popular methods for allocating service department costs.

12.11 'The step-down method allocates more costs to the producing departments than does the direct method.' Do you agree? Explain.

12.12 What is a non-volume-related cost driver? Give two examples.

12.13 How are costs of various overhead resources allocated to products, services or customers in an ABC system?

12.14 'A cost pool for a particular resource is either a variable cost pool or a fixed cost pool. There should be no mixed-cost pools.' Do you agree? Explain.

12.15 Give four examples of activities and related cost-allocation bases that can be used in an ABC system to allocate costs to products, services or customers.

12.16 Name the four steps used to allocate producing department activity cost pools using the ABC approach.

12.17 List several factors that determine whether a customer has a low or high cost to serve.

12.18 Chapter 6 explained that joint costs should not be allocated to individual

products for decision purposes. For what purposes are such costs allocated to products?

12.19 Briefly explain each of the two conventional ways of allocating joint costs of products.

12.20 What are by-products and how do we account for them?

12.21 Suppose Winter Park Company has two plants – the Salem plant and the Youngstown plant. The Youngstown plant produces only three components that are very similar in material and production requirements. The Salem plant makes a wide variety of parts. Which type of costing system would you recommend for each plant (traditional or ABC)? Explain.

12.22 Study Appendix 12. Distinguish between two-stage and multistage ABC systems.

12.23 Study Appendix 12. In Exhibits 12.20 and 12.21, the *r*s represent resource- and activity-consumption rates. Why are these rates important to managers looking for ideas for process improvements?

12.24 Study Appendix 12. Explain the difference between resource-consumption rates and cost per driver unit.

12.25 Why is it necessary to know the profitability of customers? If all the products of a company are profitable, shouldn't its customers also be profitable? Explain.

CRITICAL THINKING EXERCISES

12.26 Allocation and cost behaviour

There are three general guidelines to use when allocating service department (support) costs. One of these guidelines deals with the cost behaviour of support costs. Why do many companies allocate fixed support costs separately from variable support costs?

12.27 Allocation and the sales function

Confusion can arise when cost allocations to one consuming department depend on the activity of another consuming department. 'A commonly misused basis for allocation of central support costs is actual dollar sales.' Explain.

12.28 Allocation and marketing

Many companies are allocating more nonproduction costs because of the increasing magnitude of these value-chain costs. One value-chain function that is receiving more attention is marketing. How should national advertising costs be allocated to territories?

EXERCISES

12.29 Allocation of computer costs

Review the section Allocation of service department costs, p. 522–529, especially the example of the use of the computer by the university. Recall that the budget formula was €100,000 fixed cost monthly plus €200 per hour of computer time used. Based on long-run predicted usage, the fixed costs were allocated on a lump-sum basis, 30 per cent to business and 70 per cent to engineering.

1 Show the total allocation if business used 210 hours and engineering used 390 hours in a given month. Assume that the actual costs coincided exactly with the budgeted amount for total usage of 600 hours.
2 Assume the same facts as in number 1 except that the fixed costs were allocated on the basis of actual hours of usage. Show the total allocation of costs to each school. As the dean of the school of business, would you prefer this method or the method in number 1? Explain.

12.30 Fixed- and variable-cost pools

Newcastle City Council signed a lease for a photocopy machine at £2,500 per month and £.02 per copy. Operating costs for toner, paper, operator salary and so on are all variable at £.03 per copy. Departments had projected a need for 100,000 copies a month. The city planning department predicted its usage at 36,000 copies a month. It made 42,000 copies in August.

1 Suppose one predetermined rate per copy was used to allocate all photocopy costs. What rate would be used and how much cost would be allocated to the city planning department in August?
2 Suppose fixed- and variable-cost pools were allocated separately. Specify how each pool should be allocated. Compute the cost allocated to the city planning department in August.
3 Which method, the one in number 1 or the one in number 2, do you prefer? Explain.

12.31 Sales-based allocations

Johnny's Markets has three grocery stores in the metropolitan Birmingham area. Central costs are allocated using sales as the cost-allocation base. The following are budgeted and actual sales during November:

	Sunnyville	Wedgewood	Capital
Budgeted sales	£600,000	£1,000,000	£400,000
Actual sales	600,000	700,000	500,000

Central costs of £200,000 are to be allocated in November.

1 Compute the central costs allocated to each store with budgeted sales as the cost-allocation base.
2 Compute the central costs allocated to each store with actual sales as the cost-allocation base.
3 What advantages are there to using budgeted rather than actual sales for allocating the central costs?

12.32 Direct and step-down allocations, activity-based allocation and process map

Malta Building Maintenance provides cleaning services for a variety of clients. The company has two producing divisions, residential and commercial, and two service departments, personnel and administrative. The company uses an activity-based allocation system in each of its producing divisions. Previously, the costs of service support departments has been unallocated. However, the company has decided to allocate all service department costs to the producing departments' personnel on the basis of number of employees and administrative on the basis of the direct costs of the activities in each division. Malta uses a process map as part of its activity-based allocation system. The map based on the budget for 20X5 is shown in Exhibit 12.23.

1 Determine the costs allocated to the residential and commercial divisions using the direct method.
2 Determine the costs allocated to the residential and commercial divisions using the step-down method. The personnel department costs should be allocated first.
3 Explain how costs would be allocated to each customer in both the residential and commercial divisions.

12.33 Direct and step-down allocations

Butler Home Products has two producing departments, machining and assembly, and two service departments, personnel and custodial. The company's budget for April 20X7 is as follows:

	Service departments		Production departments	
	Personnel	**Custodial**	**Machining**	**Assembly**
Direct department costs	€32,000	€70,000	€600,000	€800,000
Square metres	2,000	1,000	10,000	25,000
Number of employees	15	30	200	250

Butler allocates personnel costs on the basis of number of employees. Butler allocates custodial costs on the basis of square metres.

1 Allocate personnel and custodial costs to the producing departments using the direct method.
2 Allocate personnel and custodial costs to the producing departments using the step-down method. Allocate personnel costs first.

12.34 Customer profitability; strategy

The table on p. 565 gives the sales, product cost, and cost-to-serve data for a merchandising store. The store has four types of merchandise and three types of customers.

The costs to serve all customers is £140,000 and is allocated to customer types based on the number of units sold.

1 Determine the gross profit margin percentage of sales for each product. Which product is the most profitable?
2 Determine the gross profit margin percentage of sales for each customer type.
3 Determine the cost-to-serve percentage of sales for each customer type.
4 Which customer is the most profitable?
5 Prepare a chart similar to Exhibit 12.18 that shows the customer gross margin percentage and cost-to-serve percentage for the three customers. Recommend a strategy for profit improvement for each customer.

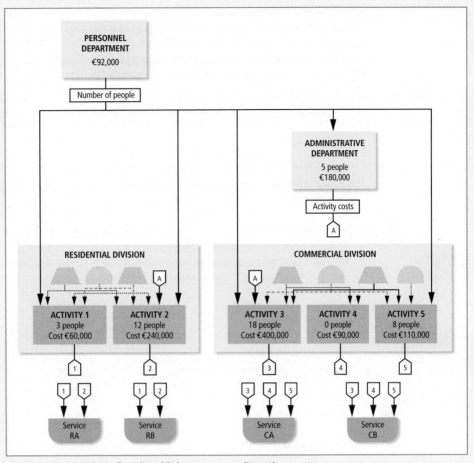

Exhibit 12.23 Malta Building Maintenance – allocation system

Product A		Product B		Product C		Product D	
Sales	£32,000	Sales	£88,000	Sales	£280,000	Sales	£144,000
Cost of sales	20,000	Cost of sales	70,400	Cost of sales	224,000	Cost of sales	81,000

	Customer Type 1	Customer Type 2	Customer Type 3	Total units sold
Product A units	200	2,200	500	2,900
Product B units	100	1,200	3,000	4,300
Product C units	50	400	5,000	5,450
Product D units	400	800	400	1,600
Total units sold	750	4,600	8,900	14,250

12.35 Joint costs

Robinson Chemical Company's production process for two of its solvents can be detailed as follows:

The cost of the joint input, including processing costs before the split-off point, is €300,000. Solvent A can be sold at split off for €30 per gallon and solvent B for €45 per gallon.

1   Allocate the €300,000 joint cost to solvents A and B by the physical-units method.
2   Allocate the €300,000 joint cost to solvents A and B by the relative-sales-value method.

12.36 Joint costs and process map

Hernandez Chemical Company's production process for two of its solvents can be diagrammed using a process map as shown in Exhibit 12.24.

The cost of the joint input, including processing costs before the split-off point, is €400,000. Solvent A can be sold at the split-off point for €25 per litre and solvent B for €50 per litre

1   Allocate the €400,000 joint cost to solvents A and B by the physical-units method.
2   Allocate the €400,000 joint cost to solvents A and B by the relative-sales-value method.

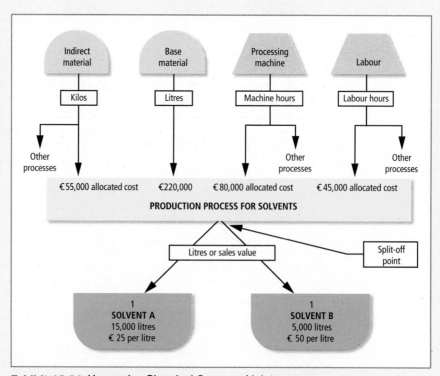

Exhibit 12.24 Hernandez Chemical Company' joint process

12.37 By-product costing

Montenegro Apple Company buys apples from local orchards and presses them to produce apple juice. The pulp that remains after pressing is sold to farmers as livestock food. This livestock food is accounted for as a by-product.

During the 20X7 fiscal year, the company paid €1 million to purchase 8 million kilos of apples. After processing, 1 million kilos of pulp remained. Wenatchee spent €35,000 to package and ship the pulp, which was sold for €50,000.

1 How much of the joint cost of the apples is allocated to the pulp?
2 Compute the total inventory cost (and therefore the cost of goods sold) for the pulp.
3 Assume that €130,000 was spent to press the apples and €150,000 was spent to filter, pasteurise and pack the apple juice. Compute the total inventory cost of the apple juice produced.

12.38 Cost assignment paths

Study Appendix 12, especially the 'Summary problem for your review' on p. 554–558. Exhibit 12.20 shows the MSABC system of the billing department. What costs would be included in the billing labour and bill-verifying labour resources? Compile a list of the cost-allocation paths from these two labour resources to the commercial accounts cost object.

PROBLEMS

12.39 Allocation of car costs

The car pool of a major city provides cars for the use of various city departments. Currently, the car pool has 50 cars. A recent study showed that it costs £2,400 of annual fixed cost per car plus £.10 per mile variable cost to own, operate and maintain cars like those provided by the car pool.

Each month, the costs of the car pool are allocated to the user departments on the basis of miles driven. On average, each car is driven 24,000 miles annually, although wide month-to-month variations occur. In April 20X7, the 50 cars were driven a total of 50,000 miles. The car pool's total costs for April were £19,000.

The chief planner for the city always seemed concerned about her car costs. She was especially upset in April when she was charged £5,700 for the 15,000 miles driven in the department's five cars. This is the normal monthly distance in the department. Her memo to the head of the car pool stated, 'I can certainly get cars at less than the £.38 per mile you charged in April.' The response was, 'I am under instructions to allocate the car pool costs to the user departments. Your department was responsible for 30 per cent of the April usage (15,000 miles ÷ 50,000 miles) so I allocated 30 per cent of the car pool's April costs to you (.30 × £19,000). That just seems fair.'

1 Calculate the city's average annual cost per mile for owning, maintaining and operating a car.
2 Explain why the allocated cost in April (£.38 per mile) exceeds the average in number 1.
3 Describe any undesirable behavioural effects of the cost-allocation method used.
4 How would you improve the cost-allocation method?

12.40 Service department allocation and ABC, product costing

Fancy Fixtures makes displays for retail outlets. The company has three product lines – standard, deluxe and custom. Fancy Fixtures integrates its service department allocation system with its ABC system. There are two service departments – power and facilities management. Fancy allocates its two service department costs to the processing department using the direct method based on megawatt hours and machine hours consumed. There are two activity centres in the processing department – setup/maintenance and assembly. Parts and assembly labour are traced directly to each product. Setup/maintenance costs are allocated based on number of setups and assembly costs are allocated based on machine hours.

Data for a recent reporting period follow:

	Product line		
	Standard	Deluxe	Custom
Units produced and sold	100,000	10,000	1,000
Sales price per unit	£　　20	£　　50	£　250
Total parts costs	£1,003,800	£115,080	£15,980
Total direct-labour costs	£　298,000	£　72,000	£68,000
Setups	20	12	8
Machine hours in assembly	1,000	400	100

			Activity centres' use of driver unit	
Resource/department	Total cost	Driver unit	Setup/maintenance	Assembly
Assembly supervisors	£　90,000	%	2%	98%
Assembly machines	£247,000	Machine hours	400	1,500
Facilities management department	£　95,000	Machine hours	400	1,500
Power department	£　54,000	Megawatt hours	10	80

Prepare a schedule that calculates the gross profit available to cover other value-chain costs for each product and Fancy Fixtures as a whole company.

12.41 Service department allocation and ABC; product profitability; process map

(This problem is the same as problem 12.40, but uses a process map to provide data.) Fancy Fixtures makes displays for retail outlets. The company has three product lines – standard, deluxe and custom. Fancy Fixtures integrates its service department allocation system with its ABC system. There are two service departments – power and facilities management. Fancy allocates its two service department costs to the processing department using the direct method based on megawatt hours and machine hours consumed. There are two activity centres in the processing department – setup/maintenance and assembly. Parts and assembly labour are traced directly to each product. Setup/maintenance costs are allocated based on number of setups and assembly costs are allocated based on machine hours.

Exhibit 12.25 is a process map for operations at Fancy Fixtures.

Prepare a schedule that calculates the gross profit available to cover other value-chain costs for each product and Fancy Fixtures as a whole company.

12.42 Service department allocation and ABC; customer profitability

(This problem should not be assigned unless problem 12.40 or problem 12.41 is also assigned.) Refer to problem 12.40 or problem 12.41. Fancy Fixtures has two types of customers. Customer type 1 purchases mostly standard displays. Customer type 2 purchases

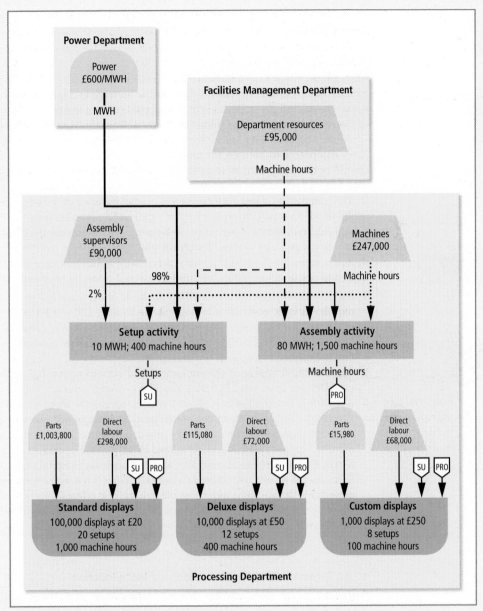

Exhibit 12.25 Allocation of service department costs in Fancy Fixtures' ABC system

all three product lines but is the only customer type that purchases custom displays. Data regarding the product mix for each customer follows:

	Units sold by product line			
	Standard	Deluxe	Custom	Total
Customer type 1	75,000	5,000	0	80,000
Customer type 2	25,000	5,000	1,000	31,000
Total	100,000	10,000	1,000	111,000

Prepare a schedule that calculates the gross profit available to cover other value-chain costs for each customer type.

12.43 Hospital equipment

Many UK boroughs have a hospital commission that must approve the acquisition of specified medical equipment before the hospitals in the borough can qualify for cost-based reimbursement related to that equipment. That is, hospitals cannot bill government agencies for the use of the equipment unless the commission originally authorised the acquisition.

Two hospitals in one borough proposed the acquisition and sharing of some expensive X-ray equipment to be used for unusual cases. The depreciation and related fixed costs of operating the equipment were predicted at £12,000 per month. The variable costs were predicted at £30 per patient procedure.

The commission asked each hospital to predict its usage of the equipment over its expected useful life of 5 years. University Hospital predicted an average usage of 75 X-rays per month, while Children's Hospital predicted 50 X-rays. The commission regarded this information as critical to the size and degree of sophistication that would be justified. That is, if the number of X-rays exceeded a certain quantity per month, a different configuration of space, equipment and personnel would be required that would mean higher fixed costs per month.

1 Suppose fixed costs are allocated on the basis of the hospitals' predicted average use per month. Variable costs are allocated on the basis of £30 per X-ray, the budgeted variable-cost rate for the current fiscal year. In October, University Hospital had 50 X-rays and Children's Hospital had 50 X-rays. Compute the total costs allocated to University Hospital and to Children's Hospital.

2 Suppose the manager of the equipment had various operating inefficiencies so that the total October costs were £16,500. Would you change your answers in number 1? Why?

3 A traditional method of cost allocation does not use the method in number 1. Instead, an allocation rate depends on the actual costs and actual volume encountered. The actual costs are totalled for the month and divided by the actual number of X-rays during the month. Suppose the actual costs agreed exactly with the budget for a total of 100 actual X-rays. Compute the total costs allocated to University Hospital and to Children's Hospital. Compare the results with those in number 1. What is the major weakness in this traditional method? What are some of its possible behavioural effects?

4 Describe any undesirable behavioural effects of the method described in number 1. How would you counteract any tendencies toward deliberate false predictions of long-run usage?

12.44 Direct method for service department allocation

Wheelick Controls Company has two production departments, mechanical instruments and electronic instruments. In addition, there are two service departments, building services and materials receiving and handling. The company purchases a variety of component parts from which the departments assemble instruments for sale in domestic and international markets.

The electronic instruments division is highly automated. The manufacturing costs depend primarily on the number of subcomponents in each instrument. In contrast, the mechanical instruments division relies primarily on a large labour force to hand-assemble instruments. Its costs depend on direct-labour hours.

The costs of building services depend primarily on the square footage occupied. The costs of materials receiving and handling depend primarily on the total number of components handled.

Instruments M1 and M2 are produced in the mechanical instruments department, and E1 and E2 are produced in the electronic instruments department. Data about these products follow:

	Direct-materials cost	Number of components	Direct-labour hours
M1	£74	25	4.0
M2	86	21	8.0
E1	63	10	1.5
E2	91	15	1.0

Budget figures for 20X7 include the following:

	Building service	Materials receiving and handling	Mechanical instruments	Electronic instruments
Direct department costs (excluding direct materials cost)	£150,000	£120,000	£680,000	£548,000
Square metres occupied		5,000	50,000	25,000
Number of final instruments produced			8,000	10,000
Average number of components per instrument			10	16
Direct-labour hours			30,000	8,000

1 Allocate the costs of the service departments using the direct method.
2 Using the results of number 1, compute the cost per direct-labour hour in the Mechanical Instruments department and the cost per component in the Electronic Instruments department.
3 Using the results of number 2, compute the cost per unit of product for instruments M1, M2, E1 and E2.

12.45 Step-down method for service department allocation

Refer to the data in Problem 12.44.

1 Allocate the costs of the service departments using the step-down method.
2 Using the results of number 1, compute the cost per direct-labour hour in the mechanical instruments department and the cost per component in the electronic instruments department.
3 Using the results of number 2, compute the cost per unit of product for instruments M1, M2, E1 and E2.

12.46 ABC allocations, process map, what if analysis

Yamaguchi Company makes printed circuit boards in a suburb of Kyoto. The production process is automated with computer-controlled robotic machines assembling each circuit board from a supply of parts and then soldering the parts to the board. Materials-handling and quality-assurance activities use a combination of labour and equipment. Although a few resources that are used are variable with respect to changes in the demand of boards, these costs are not material compared to the fixed-cost resources that are used.

Yamaguchi makes three types of circuit boards, models 1, 2 and 3. Steps 1–3 of the design process for an ABC system have been completed. Exhibit 12.26 shows the process-based map of Yamaguchi's operations.

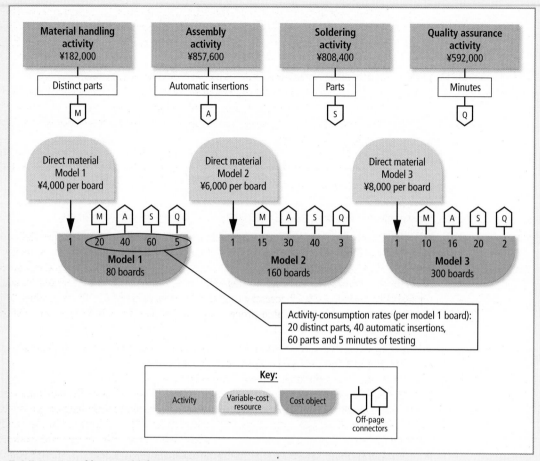

Exhibit 12.26 Yamaguchi Company's two-stage ABC system

1 Compute the cost of production for each of the three types of circuit boards and the cost per circuit board for each type.

2 What if the design of model 1 could be simplified so that it required only 10 distinct parts (instead of 20) and took only 3 minutes of testing time (instead of five). Compute the cost of model 1 circuit boards and the cost per circuit board. Will the costs per circuit board for models 2 and 3 change? You do not need to compute the costs per circuit board for models 2 and 3, only note whether the costs will increase, decrease, remain unchanged or cannot be determined. Explain.

12.47 Activity-based allocations

Louis Wholesale Distributors uses an ABC system to determine the cost of handling its products. One important activity is receiving shipments in the warehouse. Three resources support that activity: (1) recording and record keeping, (2) labour and (3) inspection.

Recording and record keeping is a variable cost driven by number of shipments received. The cost per shipment is €18.

Labour is driven by pounds of merchandise received. Because labour is hired in shifts, it is fixed for large ranges of volume. Currently, labour costs are running €32,200 per month for handling 460,000 kilos. This same cost would apply to all volumes between 300,000 kilos and 550,000 kilos.

Finally, inspection is a variable cost driven by the number of boxes received. Inspection costs are €3.75 per box.

One product distributed by Louis Wholesale Distributors is confectionery. There is a wide variety of confectionery so many different shipments are handled in the warehouse. In July, the warehouse received 500 shipments, consisting of 4,000 boxes weighing a total of 80,000 kilos.

1 Compute the cost of receiving confectionery shipments during July.
2 Management is considering elimination of brands of confectionery that have small sales levels. This would reduce the warehouse volume to 200 shipments, consisting of 3,000 boxes weighing a total of 60,000 kilos. Compute the amount of savings from eliminating the small-sales-level brands.
3 Suppose receiving costs were estimated on a per-kilo basis. What was the total receiving cost per kilo of confectionery received in July? If management had used this cost to estimate the effect of eliminating the 20,000 kilos of confectionery, what mistake might be made?

12.48 Joint costs and decisions

A chemical company has a batch process that takes 1,000 gallons of a raw material and transforms it into 80 pounds of X1 and 400 pounds of X2. Although the joint costs of their production are £1,200, both products are worthless at their split-off point. Additional separable costs of £350 are necessary to give X1 a sales value of £1,000 as product A. Similarly, additional separable costs of £200 are necessary to give X2 a sales value of £1,000 as product B.

You are in charge of the batch process and the marketing of both products. (Show your computations for each answer.)

1 (a) Assuming that you believe in assigning joint costs on a physical basis, allocate the total profit of £250 per batch to products A and B.
  (b) Would you stop processing one of the products? Why?
2 (a) Assuming that you believe in assigning joint costs on a net-realisable-value (relative-s ales-value) basis, allocate the total operating profit of £250 per batch to products A and B. If there is no market for X1 and X2 at their split-off point, a net realisable value is usually imputed by taking the ultimate sales values at the point of sale and working backward to obtain approximated 'synthetic' relative sales values at the split-off point. These synthetic values are then used as weights for allocating the joint costs to the products.
  (b) You have internal product-profitability reports in which joint costs are assigned on a net-realisable-value basis. Your chief engineer says that, after seeing these reports, he has developed a method of obtaining more of product B and correspondingly less of product A from each batch, without changing the per-pound cost factors. Would you approve this new method? Why? What would the overall operating profit be if 40 pounds more of B were produced and 40 pounds less of A?

CASES

12.49 Customer profitability

Distribution Solutions, Inc., (DSI) is a US regional distributor providing logistical support for merchandisers over a three-state area. Its distribution centres have been profitable until recently. DSI provides logistics solutions in industries such as fashion apparel, electronics, housewares, building materials, automotive tools and beverage. Its locations are convenient to major ports and transportation hubs. DSI has an outstanding reputation for customer service.

Profit margins have declined over the past several years due mostly to a weak regional economy and competition from larger merchandisers who use logistic services of larger national distributors. Thus, the market share of merchandisers has declined along with their need for logistics support from DSI.

DSI orders supplies from a variety of manufacturers. All goods processed through the warehouse are stored on pallets and are handled by forklifts driven by forklift operators, who are assisted by warehouse labour. Processing of product consists of unloading at the receiving area (receiving activity), moving to the warehouse storage (put away activity), moving/shifting within the warehouse (warehousing activity), removal from racks (picking activity) and repacking (repacking activity). Customer-specific processing consists of order taking, customer service, order changes, returns, scheduling (regular or expedited) and shipping.

Prices at DSI are set using a cost-plus formula based on the average cost per case delivered during the previous year. Two markups are used. The first markup covers the cost of warehousing and distribution. The second markup covers the costs of general and selling expenses and an allowance for profit. Currently (20X7) this price is $7.25 per case. However, with the various discounts and promotions, this year's actual price averages $4.75 per case for all products.

DSI has six distinct product groups:

1 Regular products are prepackaged arriving and leaving in cases.
2 Fragile products are prepackaged but require care in handling.
3 Bulk products arrive in loose lots in crates or cases and are repackaged in smaller boxes, polybags or small cartons before packing in cases.
4 High-security products must be locked in high-security area.
5 Short shelf-life products are dated products.
6 Singles are received in bundles and will be unbundled and hand-stacked for storage.

Traditionally, the regular prepackaged product has generated both high margins and high volume. Fragile pre-packaged product has high margin but low volume. Bulk products and singles have poor margins but have been part of DSI's offerings because of customer demands for a full-line distributor. As DSI focused on increasing sales, mega stores and local small stores have increased their purchases of bulk products and singles. Until now, no premium has been charged for these products.

DSI has for many years classified its customer base into various types. Prior to 20X2, almost all its customers were mega stores or large local stores. Since 20X2, local small store and specialty store business has been aggressively pursued. The customer types can be described as follows:

- Mega stores (CT1): a few very large stores that order large volumes of all product types (7,680,000 cases annually).
- Local small stores (CT2): many stores that order low volumes of all products for each store (6,000,000 cases annually).
- Local large stores (CT3): many stores that order large volumes of only regular, fragile and bulk products (14,400,000 cases annually).
- Specialty stores (CT4): a few stores that order low volumes of only regular, high-security and short shelf-life products (600,000 cases annually).

Over the past several months, Paul Doxey, accountant, working closely with Jane Stratford, chief marketing officer, and a cross-functional implementation team have been developing the ABC system to include all costs as well as customer profitability. A study has been conducted to determine the key drivers of work associated with the various customer types. These drivers include order frequency, order size, pallets ordered, customer-specific service and order changes.

Key activities associated with serving customers include the following:

- Shipping
- Parcel delivery
- Truck delivery
- Customer support
- Regular scheduling
- Expedited scheduling
- Order processing
- Order changes
- Corporate support.

The implementation team headed by Paul Doxey has completed the activity analysis interviews, prepared a process map, collected data and validated the new model both operationally and financially. The new process map is shown in Exhibit 12.27 on p. 576. In order to link the product and customer models the product mix for each customer is specified giving the gross profit for each customer. Exhibit 12.28 on p. 577 shows the product mix for each of the four customer types. Exhibit 12.29 on p. 577 shows the cost-to-serve data for each driver.

1 Using Excel, construct an exhibit that calculates customer gross margin percentage and customer cost-to-serve percentage for the four customer types. Plot these points along with one for customer type 2 on a graph similar to Exhibit 12.18 on p. 546.
2 For each customer type, recommend a strategy to improve profitability.

12.50 Allocation of data processing costs

The Gibraltar Insurance Co. (GIC) established a systems department to implement and operate its own data processing systems. GIC believed that its own system would be more cost-effective than the service bureau it had been using.

GIC's three departments – claims, records and finance – have different requirements with respect to hardware and other capacity-related resources and operating resources. The system was designed to recognise these differing needs. In addition, the system was designed to meet GIC's long-term capacity needs. The excess capacity designed into the system would be sold to outside users until needed by GIC. The estimated resource requirements used to design and implement the system are shown in the following schedule:

	Hardware and other capacity-related resources	Operating resources
Records	25%	60%
Claims	50	15
Finance	20	20
Expansion (outside use)	5	5
Total	100%	100%

GIC currently sells the equivalent of its expansion capacity to a few outside clients.

At the time the system became operational, management decided to redistribute total expenses of the systems department to the user departments based on actual computer time used. The actual costs for the first quarter of the current fiscal year were distributed to the user departments as shown below.

The three user departments have complained about the cost-distribution method since the systems department was established. The records department's monthly costs have been as much as three times the costs experienced with the service bureau. The finance department is concerned about the costs distributed to the outside user category because these allocated costs form the basis for the fees billed to the outside clients.

Department	Percentage utilisation	Amount
Records	60%	€330,000
Claims	15	82,500
Finance	20	110,000
Outside	5	27,500
Total	100%	€550,000

Exhibit 12.27 Process map for product/customer profitability

	Product mix (%)					
	Regular	Short-lived	Fragile	Bulk	High security	Singles
Customer type 1 mega stores	60	5	5	20	5	5
Customer type 2 local small stores	50	5	5	30	8	2
Customer type 3 local large stores	80	–	10	10	–	–
Customer type 4 specialty stores	10	20	–	–	70	–

Exhibit 12.28 Product mix data for product/customer profitability model

	Cost-to-serve activities								
	Order processing	Customer support	Order changes	Corporate support	Scheduling – regular	Scheduling – expedited	Shipping	Delivery – lorry	Delivery – parcel
Cost driver	Orders	Labour hours	Number of changes	Labour hours	Orders	Orders	Pallets	Deliveries	Deliveries
Cost per driver unit	$27.49	$43.34	$32.63	$51.66	$5.83	$19.44	$6.60	$167.55	$23.89
	Number of driver units (thousands)								
CT1	32	18.7	3.2	0	29	3	416	25.6*	1.6*
CT2	80	100.0	8.0	20	72	8	640	68.0	8.0
CT3	120	70.0	2.4	80	108	12	840	90.0	6.0
CT4	12	30.0	1.2	0	10	2	60	4.8	2.4

* The sum of deliveries (25.6 + 1.6 = 27.2 on average) is less than the number of orders (29 + 3) because a few customers picked up their order at the distribution centre.

Exhibit 12.29 Cost driver data by customer type and cost-to-serve activity

Mostafa Al Rashed, GIC's controller, decided to review the cost-allocation method. The additional information he gathered for his review is reported in Tables 1, 2 and 3 on page 578.

Al Rashed has concluded that the method of cost allocation should be changed. He believes that the hardware and capacity-related costs should be allocated to the user departments in proportion to the planned long-term needs. Any difference between actual and budgeted hardware costs would not be allocated to the departments, but would remain with the systems department.

The costs for software development and operations would be charged to the user departments based on actual hours used. A predetermined hourly rate based on the annual budget data would be used. The hourly rates that would be used for the current fiscal year are as shown on p. 578.

Al Rashed plans to use first-quarter activity and cost data to illustrate his recommendations. The recommendations will be presented to the systems department and the user departments for their comments and reactions. He then expects to present his recommendations to management for approval.

1 Calculate the amount of data-processing costs that would be included in the claims department's first-quarter budget according to the method Al Rashed has recommended.
2 Prepare a schedule to show how the actual first-quarter costs of the systems department would be charged to the users if GIC adopts Al Rashed's recommended method.

Table 1 Systems department cost and activity levels

| | Annual budget | | First quarter | | | |
| | | | budget | | Actual | |
	Hours	Euros	Hours	Euros	Hours	Euros
Hardware and other capacity-related costs	—	€ 600,000	—	€150,000	—	€155,000
Software development	18,750	562,500	4,725	141,750	4,250	130,000
Operations						
Computer-related	3,750	750,000	945	189,000	920	187,000
Input/output-related	30,000	300,000	7,560	75,600	7,900	78,000
Total		€2,212,500		€556,350		€550,000

Table 2 Historical usage

| | Hardware and other capacity needs | Software development | | Operations | | | |
| | | | | Computer | | Input/output | |
		Range	Average	Range	Average	Range	Average
Records	25%	0%–30%	15%	55%–65%	60%	10%–30%	15%
Claims	50	15–60	40	10–25	15	60–80	75
Finance	20	25–75	40	10–25	20	3–10	5
Outside	5	0–25	5	3–8	5	3–10	5
	100%		100%		100%		100%

Table 3 Usage of systems department's services first quarter (in house)

| | Software development | Operations | |
		Computer related	Input/output
Records	450	540	1,540
Claims	1,800	194	5,540
Finance	1,600	126	410
Outside	400	60	410
Total	4,250	920	7,900

Function	Hourly rate
Software development Operations	€ 30
Computer-related	200
Input/output-related	10

3 Explain whether Al Rashed's recommended system for charging costs to the user departments will:

(a) improve cost control in the systems department;

(b) improve planning and cost control in the user departments.

Need more practice? Instant feedback?
Visit www.myaccountinglab.com

MyAccountingLab

Featuring unlimited practice questions, a personalised study plan that identifies the areas where you need to focus for better marks, and interactive material designed to help all kinds of learners, *MyAccountingLab* is a vital tool for maximising your understanding, confidence and success.

Log in at **www.myaccountinglab.com** to see why 92 per cent of students recently surveyed recommend *MyAccountingLab*.

Accounting for overhead costs

Learning objectives

When you have finished studying this chapter, you should be able to:

1 Compute budgeted factory-overhead rates and apply factory overhead to production.

2 Determine and use appropriate cost-allocation bases for overhead application to products and services.

3 Identify the meaning and purpose of normalised overhead rates.

4 Construct an income statement using the variable-costing approach.

5 Construct an income statement using the absorption-costing approach.

6 Compute the production-volume variance and show how it should appear in the income statement.

7 Explain why a company might prefer to use a variable-costing approach.

Dell

Dell is the world's leading direct-sale marketer of made-to-order computer systems. Dell does not manufacture computer components (e.g., circuit boards, hard drives), but instead assembles them into computers on a made-to-order basis.

Dell pioneered the 'direct business model' – selling directly to end users instead of using a network of dealers, which avoids the dealer markup and gives Dell a competitive price advantage. Customers can design their own computer systems to specifications they desire, choosing from among a full complement of options. Before ordering, customers can receive advice and price quotes for a wide variety of computer configurations.

Once an order is taken, Dell assembles it in a manufacturing work cell called a 'mod'. There is a separate mod for each of Dell's lines of business (Dimension Desktop PCs, OptiPlex Desktops for networked environments, Latitude and Inspiron Notebooks, PowerEdge and PowerApp network servers and Precision workstation products). Management considers rapid response to customer orders a key to gaining and maintaining a competitive edge.

Dell takes orders over the phone or over the internet. Dell derives about 50 per cent of its revenues from the company's website, www.dell.com, with daily revenues in excess of $160 million and weekly 'hits' of over 3,000,000. Customers may review, configure and price systems within

Dell sells computers directly to customers around the world.

Dell's entire product line. Dell's website also offers personalised system-support pages and technical services. Customers of all kinds opt for Dell's direct business model, and the internet affords Dell a perfect way to implement this model. They like the immediacy, convenience, savings and personal touches the internet-direct customer experience provides.

Not all customers find satisfaction with Dell. For instance, the *New York Times* reported that 'An unsealed lawsuit indicates Dell hid faults of computers.' (*New York Times*, 18 November 2010) The issues revolved around capacitors in motherboards. Low-quality capacitors bulge when they become too hot and cause devices to malfunction. Documents filed in court include a Dell internal study showing Dell expected a minimum of 12 per cent of its 5×270 Optiplex computers would result in incident reports from customers over a period of 3 years. Within 3 months, Dell raised the minimum incident report forecast to 45 per cent and noted it could run as high as 97 per cent. Dell subsequently took a $300 million charge tied to the cost of fixing or replacing troubled computers.

Why are managers at a highly profitable company such as Dell interested in knowing as much as possible about the cost of their individual product lines and the impact of non-conformance problems? With strong profits being reported over the years, is there a clear need for costs for other management purposes? The answer is yes – most of the reason Dell's profitability has been strong is the strategic and operational decisions its managers make. These decisions are based on detailed cost information. For example, Dell's cost accounting systems supply product costs to managers for evaluating pricing policy and product lines. Dell managers need to know the cost of each kind of computer being produced to set prices, to determine marketing and production strategies for various models and to evaluate production operations. At the same time, product costs appear as cost of goods sold in income statements and as finished-goods inventory values in balance sheets. Although it would be possible to have two product-costing systems, one for management decision making and one for financial reporting, seldom do the benefits of using two completely separate systems exceed the costs. Therefore, both decision-making and financial-reporting needs influence the design of a company's product-costing system.

In Chapter 4, you learned about three types of costs in a manufacturing company, direct materials, direct labour and factory overhead (or indirect manufacturing) costs. You also learned that for many organisations, indirect costs account for as much as 40 per cent of total operating costs. Thus, this is an important area of concern for managers. In this chapter, we focus on overhead. ■

Accounting for factory overhead

Years ago, direct materials and direct labour were the largest costs for most companies. Today, automated companies such as Dell have less direct labour but much larger overhead costs. Thus, methods for assigning overhead costs to the products is an important part of accurately measuring product costs.

■ How to apply factory overhead to products

Objective 1
Compute budgeted factory-overhead rates and apply factory overhead to production.

Managers need to know product costs in order to make ongoing decisions, such as which products or services to emphasise or de-emphasise and how to price each product or service. Ideally, managers would know all costs precisely, including overhead, when they make these decisions. Because accountants directly trace direct materials and direct labour costs to products and services, these costs are available immediately on completion of production and they are known precisely. In contrast, because it is not economically feasible to know all of the indirect manufacturing costs immediately, accountants must estimate them. For this reason, accountants use budgeted (predetermined) overhead rates to apply overhead to jobs.

This makes an estimate of total product cost available for managerial decisions as soon as products or services are completed, if not sooner. When the relative size of the overhead costs is large, we can understand how important it is for companies to have an accurate system for factory overhead accounting.

The size of overhead costs in many manufacturing companies is large enough to motivate companies to search for ways to convert them into direct costs. Dell has increased the accuracy of its product cost information by converting some of its factory-overhead costs from indirect to direct costs. How did the company do this? By dedicating assembly labour and factory equipment to specific product lines. Work cells (mods) do the assembly and software loading for specific product lines. This makes it easier to trace some of the equipment costs to products. Nevertheless, significant overhead costs remain to be allocated. So let's look at how companies such as Dell allocate these overhead costs to products and services.

Budgeted overhead application rates

The following steps summarise how to account for factory overhead:

1   Select one or more cost-allocation bases for applying overhead costs to products or services. In this chapter, we often use the term *apply* instead of *allocate* when assigning overhead costs to a product or service. However, the concept is essentially the same – determining the amount of each cost pool to assign to each cost object. Examples of cost-allocation bases include direct-labour hours, direct-labour costs, machine hours and production setups. The cost-allocation base should be a measure of the amount of overhead resources – a cost or a group of costs such as machinery cost, set-up costs, or energy cost – used by each product. The cost-allocation base(s) should be the most plausible and reliable measure(s) available of the cause-and-effect relationships between overhead costs and production volume.

2   Prepare a factory-overhead budget for the planning period, ordinarily a year. The two key items are (a) budgeted overhead and (b) budgeted volume of the cost-allocation base. There will be a set of budgeted overhead costs and an associated budgeted cost-allocation base level for each overhead cost pool.[1] In businesses with simple production systems, there may be just one set.

3   Compute the **budgeted factory-overhead rate(s)** by dividing the budgeted total overhead for each cost pool by the budgeted cost-allocation base level.

4   Obtain actual cost-allocation base data (such as direct-labour hours or machine hours) used for each product.

5   Apply the budgeted overhead to the products or services by multiplying the budgeted rate(s) in step 3 times the actual cost-allocation base data from step 4.

6   At the end of the year, account for any differences between the amount of overhead actually incurred and overhead applied to products.

Illustration of overhead application

Now that you know the steps in accounting for factory overhead, let's examine how they work in a realistic example. Consider the Enriquez Machine Parts Company.[2] Its manufacturing-overhead budget for 20X0 follows:

---

[1] Cost pools were defined in Chapter 4, pp. 120–1, a group of individual costs that a company allocates to activities or cost objectives using a single cost driver.

[2] If Chapter 14 and job-order costing have been assigned prior to this chapter, you will notice that the chapter illustration of Enriquez Machine Parts Company in both Chapters 13 and 14 are the same, with all data completely compatible.

	Machining	Assembly
Indirect labour	€ 75,600	€ 36,800
Supplies	8,400	2,400
Utilities	20,000	7,000
Repairs	10,000	3,000
Factory rent	10,000	6,800
Supervision	42,600	35,400
Depreciation on equipment	104,000	9,400
Insurance, property taxes, etc.	7,200	2,400
Total	€277,800	€103,200

Enriquez selected a single cost-allocation base in each department, machine hours in machining and direct-labour cost in assembly, for applying overhead. As Enriquez works on a product, it applies the factory overhead to the product using a budgeted overhead rate, computed as follows:

$$\text{budgeted overhead application rate} = \frac{\text{total budgeted factory overhead}}{\text{total budgeted amount of cost driver}}$$

The overhead rates for the two departments are as follows:

	Year 20X0	
	Machining	Assembly
Budgeted manufacturing overhead	€277,800	€103,200
Budgeted machine hours	69,450	
Budgeted direct-labour cost		€206,400
Budgeted overhead rate, per machine hour: €277,800 ÷ 69,450 =	€ 4	
Budgeted overhead rate, per direct labour euro: €103,200 ÷ €206,400 =		50%

Note that the overhead rates are budgeted; they are estimates. Accountants at Enriquez then use these budgeted rates to apply overhead based on actual events. That is, the total overhead applied to a particular product is the result of multiplying the budgeted overhead rates by the actual machine hours or labour cost used by that product. Thus, we would apply €44 of overhead to a product that uses 6 machine hours in machining and incurs direct-labour cost of €40 in assembly:

Machining: 6 actual machine hours × €4 per machine hour	€24
Assembly: €40 of direct-labour cost × 50%	20
Total overhead	€44

Suppose that at the end of the year Enriquez had used 70,000 machine hours in machining and incurred €190,000 of direct-labour cost in assembly. It would have applied a total of €375,000 of overhead to the products produced:

Machining: 70,000 actual machine hours × €4	€280,000
Assembly: €190,000 actual direct-labour cost × 50%	95,000
Total factory overhead applied	€375,000

This €375,000 is an estimate of Enriquez's overhead for the year and it will become part of the cost of goods sold expense on Enriquez's income statement when the units produced are subsequently sold. If the actual overhead costs differ from €375,000, the company will usually charge the difference to expense in the period of production. For example, if Enriquez's actual overhead in 20X0 were €392,000, it would add €392,000 − €375,000 = €17,000 additional expense in 20X0.

This completes our six steps. Next let's go back to step 1 and explore how a company might choose appropriate cost-allocation bases.

▓ Choice of cost-allocation bases

Objective 2
Determine and use appropriate cost-allocation bases for overhead application to products and services.

As you have seen several times in this text, no one cost-allocation base is appropriate in all situations. The accountant's goal is to find the cost-allocation base that best links cause and effect. In the Enriquez machining department, use of machines causes most overhead cost, such as depreciation and repairs. Therefore, machine hours is the most appropriate cost-allocation base for applying overhead costs. Thus, Enriquez must keep track of the machine hours used for each product, creating an added data collection cost. That is, it must accumulate machine hours in addition to direct-materials costs and direct-labour costs for each product.

In contrast, direct labour is the principal cost-allocation base in the Enriquez assembly department because employees assemble parts by hand. Suppose the company records the time each worker spends on each product (or batch of products). Then, all that is needed is to apply the 50 per cent overhead rate to the cost of direct labour already recorded. No additional data are needed.

If the hourly labour rates for workers differ greatly for individuals performing identical tasks, Enriquez might use the hours of labour, rather than the euros spent for labour, as a base. Otherwise, Enriquez would apply more overhead to a product when a €10-per-hour worker works an hour than when an €8-per-hour worker works an hour, even though each employee uses the same facilities and generally consumes the same overhead support. However, sometimes direct-labour cost is the best overhead cost-allocation base even if wage rates vary within a department. For example, higher-skilled labour may use more costly equipment and have more indirect labour support than low-skilled workers. Moreover, many factory-overhead costs include expensive labour fringe benefits such as pensions and payroll taxes. Direct-labour cost rather than direct-labour hours often drive such fringe-benefit costs.

If a department identifies more than one cost-allocation base for overhead costs, it should accumulate a separate cost pool for each cost-allocation base and put each overhead cost into the appropriate cost pool. In practice, such a system is too costly for many organisations. Instead, these organisations select a few cost-allocation bases (often only one) to serve as a basis for allocating overhead costs. We often use the 80–20 rule in these situations – 20 per cent of the cost-allocation bases drive 80 per cent of the overhead costs. For example, suppose a company identifies 10 separate overhead pools with 10 different cost-allocation bases. Often, it can accurately apply approximately 80 per cent of the total overhead cost with only two allocation bases. It may be too costly to devise separate cost pools for the other 20 per cent, so it arbitrarily assigns those costs to the two main cost pools.

Consider Dell. As we mentioned earlier, Dell has converted many of its overhead costs into direct costs. However, two important costs that it cannot directly trace (that is, that remain indirect costs) are facilities and engineering. Facilities costs include occupancy costs such as depreciation, insurance and taxes on the factory. Dell applies these costs using the cost-allocation base 'square footage used by each line of business (assembly line)'. Dell incurs large product and process engineering costs as part of the design phase of the company's value chain. It applies these costs to lines of business using a 'complexity' cost-allocation base such as number of distinct parts in the motherboard. Server computer products, for example, require much more engineering time and effort due to the number of distinct parts in the motherboard (complexity of the product) compared to laptops or PCs. Thus, server products receive a much greater allocation of engineering costs than laptops or PCs.

Another example is Harley-Davidson, which changed from using direct labour as a cost-allocation base to using process hours, as we describe in the 'Business first' box on p. 586.

Problems of overhead application

▨ Normalised overhead rates

Objective 3
Identify the meaning and purpose of normalised overhead rates.

The Enriquez illustration demonstrated what we call the normal costing approach. Why the term *normal*? Because we use an annual average overhead rate consistently throughout the year for product costing, without altering it from day to day and from month to month. The resultant 'normal' product costs include an average or normalised chunk of overhead. Hence, in a **normal costing system** the cost of the manufactured product is composed of actual direct material, actual direct labour and normal applied overhead.

A department's applied overhead will rarely equal the actual overhead incurred. Managers can analyse this variance between applied and incurred cost. The most common – and important – contributor to these variances is operating at a different level of volume than the level used as a denominator in calculating the budgeted overhead rate (for instance, using 100,000 budgeted direct-labour hours as the denominator and then actually working only 80,000 hours). Other frequent causes include poor forecasting, inefficient use of overhead items, price changes in individual overhead items, erratic behaviour of individual overhead items (e.g., repairs made only during slack time) and calendar variations (e.g., 20 workdays in one month, 22 in the next).

Companies generally prefer to use an annual budgeted factory-overhead rate regardless of the month-to-month peculiarities of specific overhead costs. Such an approach is more defensible than, for example, applying the actual overhead for each month. Why? Because a normal product cost is more useful for decisions, and more representative for inventory-costing purposes, than an 'actual' product cost that is distorted by month-to-month fluctuations in production volume and by the erratic behaviour of many overhead costs. For example, the employees of a gypsum plant using an 'actual' product cost system had the privilege of buying company-made items 'at cost'. Employees joked about the benefits of buying 'at cost' during high-volume months, when unit costs were lower because volume was higher, as the following table illustrates:

	Actual overhead			Direct-labour hours	Actual overhead application rate per direct-labour hour
	Variable	Fixed	Total		
Peak-volume month	€60,000	€40,000	€100,000	100,000	€1.00
Low-volume month	30,000	40,000	70,000	50,000	1.40

* Divide total overhead by direct-labour hours. Note that the presence of fixed overhead causes the fluctuation in unit overhead costs from €1.00 to €1.40. The variable component is €.60 an hour in both months, but the fixed component is €.40 in the peak-volume month (€40,000 ÷ 100,000) and €.80 in the low-volume month (€40,000 ÷ 50,000).

▨ Disposition of underapplied or overapplied overhead

The last step on p. 582 dealt with differences between actual and applied overhead. Let's look in more detail at options for accounting for such differences. Recall that in 20X0 Enriquez applied €375,000 of overhead to its products but actually incurred €392,000 of overhead costs. The difference is a €17,000 variance, which we call **underapplied overhead** because the amount applied is less than the amount incurred. The opposite, **overapplied overhead**, occurs when the amount applied exceeds the amount incurred. At year-end, the company needs to produce its financial statements, which require production costs based on the actual costs incurred. To yield this result, it must dispose of any under- or overapplied overhead, either by an immediate write-off to the income statement or through proration between the balance sheet and income statement.

BUSINESS FIRST
Overhead allocation at Harley-Davidson

Milwaukee-based Harley-Davidson, the motorcycle manufacturer, recently celebrated its one hundredth birthday. As happy as everyone at Harley-Davidson is today, it is a bit surprising to some how far the company has come over the past several decades. From near collapse, Harley-Davidson turned its business around during the 1980s and 1990s, and in 1999 captured the number one market position from Honda for the first time in three decades. Harley-Davidson (2010 sales of $4.86 billion) is the only major US-based motorcycle producer. One of the keys to the company's return to competitiveness was the adoption of a JIT philosophy. It is not unusual for a company to discover that a change in an important component of operations requires a corresponding change in the company's accounting system. The main focus of the old accounting system was direct labour, which not only made up a part of product cost itself, but also functioned as an all-purpose base for allocating overhead. However, direct labour was only 10 per cent of total product cost. It certainly did not generate a majority of overhead costs. Although Harley-Davidson's production process had changed, the accounting system remained static.

The JIT system served to emphasise that detailed information on direct-labour costs was not useful to managers. It was costly to have each direct labourer record the time spent on each product or part and then enter the information from these time cards into the accounting system. For example, if each of 500 direct labourers works on 20 products per day, the system must record 10,000 entries per day, which is 200,000 entries per month. The time spent by direct labourers to record the time, by clerks to enter the data into the system, and by accountants to check the data's accuracy, is enormous – and all to produce product

cost information that was used for financial reporting but was useless to managers.

The JIT system forced manufacturing managers to focus on satisfying customers and minimising non-value-added activities. Gradually, accountants began to focus on the same objectives. Accounting's customers were the managers who used the accounting information, and effort put into activities that did not help managers was deemed counterproductive (non-value-added). Therefore, eliminating the costly, time-consuming recording of detailed labour costs became a priority. Harley-Davidson eliminated direct labour as a direct cost and consequently could not use it for overhead application. After considering process hours, flow-through time, materials value and individual cost per unit as possible cost-allocation bases for applying overhead, the company selected process hours. Direct labour and overhead were combined to form conversion costs, which accountants applied to products on the basis of total process hours. This did not result in costs significantly different from the old system, but the new system was much simpler and less costly. The company traced only direct material directly to the product. It applied conversion costs at completion of production based on a simple measure of process time.

Accounting systems should generate benefits greater than their costs. More sophisticated systems are not necessarily better systems. Harley-Davidson's main objective in changing its accounting system was simplification – elimination of unnecessary tasks and streamlining others. These changes resulted in a revitalised accounting system.

Sources: Adapted from W. T. Turk, 'Management accounting revitalized: the Harley-Davidson experience', in B. J. Brinker, ed., *Emerging Practices in Cost Management* (Boston, M A: Warren, Gorham & Lamont, 1990), pp. 155–166; K. Barron, 'Hog wild', *Forbes*, 15 May 2000; and *Harley-Davidson 2010 Annual Report*.

Recall that Enriquez applied €375,000 to the products produced during the period. This amount is part of the cost of goods sold expense for those units that were sold and is included in ending inventory for those units that remain unsold at the end of 20X0. Enriquez still needs to account for the €17,000 variance (which is the amount of actual cost not yet applied to product). Accountants use one of two methods to account for the overhead variance: (1) a simple but imprecise approach is to dispose of the whole amount as a write-off to cost of goods sold and (2) a better but more complex approach is **proration**, which means applying over- or underapplied overhead to cost of goods sold, work-in-process inventory and finished-goods inventory in proportion to the ending balances of each account.

Immediate write-off

The immediate write-off method regards the €17,000 underapplied overhead as a reduction in current income by adding it to the cost of goods sold. By the same logic, we would deduct any overapplied overhead from the cost of goods sold.

The reasoning behind this method is that the company has probably sold most of the goods produced during the period, so that prorating part of the variance to inventory accounts would not produce a materially different result. Another justification is that, if the extra overhead costs result from inefficiencies in the current period, they do not qualify as part of ending inventory costs because they do not represent assets. Because of its simplicity, the immediate write-off method is most commonly used.

Proration among inventories

Proration apportions over- or underapplied overhead among work-in-process (WIP), finished goods (FG) and cost of goods sold. To prorate underapplied overhead means to assign it in proportion to the magnitudes of the ending account balances. Theoretically, if the objective is to obtain as accurate an application of actual costs as possible, we should recompute all the overhead costs of the individual products, using the actual, rather than the budgeted, rates. This approach is rarely feasible, so a practical attack is to prorate on the basis of the ending balances in each of three accounts. Assume that the ending balances for Enriquez are WIP, €155,000; finished goods, €32,000; and cost of goods sold, €2,480,000 (a total of €2,667,000). The results of proration follow:

	(1) Unadjusted balance, end of 20X0	(2) Proration of underapplied overhead	(3) Adjusted balance, end of 20X0
WIP	€ 155,000	$155/2{,}667 \times €17{,}000 = €$ 988	€ 155,988
Finished goods	32,000	$32/2{,}667 \times$ 17,000 = 204	32,204
Cost of goods sold	2,480,000	$2{,}480/2{,}667 \times$ 17,000 = 15,808	2,495,808
Total	€2,667,000	€17,000	€2,684,000

The amounts prorated to inventories are not significant, so proration is probably not cost beneficial here. In actual practice, companies generally prorate overhead variances only when it would materially affect inventory valuations and net income. For simplicity, we will assume for the rest of this chapter that companies immediately write off any over- or underapplied overhead.

◼ The use of variable and fixed application rates

In general the cost of a product or service is the sum of direct costs and allocated costs. As we have seen, overhead application is the most troublesome aspect of product costing.

The presence of fixed costs is a major reason for the costing difficulties. Many companies make no distinction between variable- and fixed-cost behaviours in the design of their accounting systems. For instance, the machining department at Enriquez Machine Parts Company developed the following rate:

$$\text{budgeted overhead application rate} = \frac{\text{budgeted total overhead}}{\text{budgeted machine hours}}$$

$$= \frac{€277,800}{69,450}$$

$$= €4\text{per machine hour}$$

Some companies, though, do distinguish between variable overhead and fixed overhead for product costing as well as for control purposes. Suppose the machining department at Enriquez had made this distinction. Managers determined that rent, supervision, depreciation and insurance were fixed costs and indirect labour, supplies, utilities and repairs were variable costs. The department developed two rates:

$$\text{budgeted variable-overhead application rate} = \frac{\text{budgeted total variable overhead}}{\text{budgeted machine hours}}$$

$$= \frac{€114,000}{69,450}$$

$$= €1.64 \text{ per machine hour}$$

$$\text{budgeted fixed-overhead application rate} = \frac{\text{budgeted total fixed overhead}}{\text{budgeted machine hours}}$$

$$= \frac{€163,800}{69,450}$$

$$= €2.36 \text{ per machine hour}$$

Some companies use such rates for product costing. However, it is more important to make distinctions between variable- and fixed-overhead application rates for control purposes. Why? Because the explanations for over- or underapplied overhead are usually quite different for fixed and variable costs.

After the following summary problem, we will turn our attention to some other issues arising from differences between fixed and variable overhead.

Summary problem for your review

PROBLEM

Review the Enriquez illustration. Suppose Enriquez had sales in 20X0 of €5,000,000. There were no beginning or ending inventories. That is, Enriquez sold everything it produced in 20X0. The company used the budgeted factory-overhead rates on p. 583. Production in 20X0 required 85,000 machine hours in machining and €260,000 direct-labour cost in assembly. The materials used in 20X0 cost €2,400,000, and the total direct-labour cost was €490,000. Actual factory-overhead cost was €455,000. Prepare an income statement for 20X0 through the gross profit line. Include a separate line for the immediate write-off method for overapplied or underapplied overhead.

SOLUTION

See Exhibit 13.1. You can compute the overhead component of cost of goods sold as follows:

Machining: 85,000 machine hours × €4 per machine hour	€340,000
Assembly: €260,000 direct-labour cost × 50% of direct-labour euros	130,000
Total overhead	€470,000

Overapplied overhead is €470,000 − €455,000 = €15,000.

Sales		€ 5,000,000
Cost of goods sold:		
Direct materials	€2,400,000	
Direct labour	490,000	
Factory overhead	470,000	
Total		(3,360,000)
Overapplied overhead		15,000
Gross profit		€ 1,655,000

Exhibit 13.1 Enriquez Machine Parts Company – Income statement, 20X0

Variable versus absorption costing

■ Accounting for fixed-manufacturing overhead

We compare two major methods of product costing in this section: variable costing (the contribution approach) and absorption costing (the functional, full-costing, or financial-reporting approach). You encountered these methods already in Chapter 5, but here we will provide more details. They differ in only one major respect: Fixed manufacturing overhead is excluded from the cost of products under variable costing but is included in the cost of products under absorption costing.

As Exhibit 13.2 shows, a variable-costing system charges fixed manufacturing overhead (fixed factory overhead) as a period cost that is an immediate expense on the income statement – not as a product cost that is added to inventory and charged against sales as cost of goods sold when the company sells the inventory. Note that the only difference between variable- and absorption-costing net incomes is the accounting for fixed manufacturing overhead.[3]

Absorption costing is more widely used than variable costing. Why? Because neither the public accounting profession nor tax authorities approve of variable costing for external-reporting or tax purposes.

However, the growing use of the contribution approach in performance measurement and cost analysis has led to increasing use of variable costing for internal-reporting purposes. Many firms use variable costing as the primary internal format. Why? Because according to

---

[3] Variable costing is sometimes called direct costing. However, variable costing is a more descriptive term, so we will use it exclusively in this text.

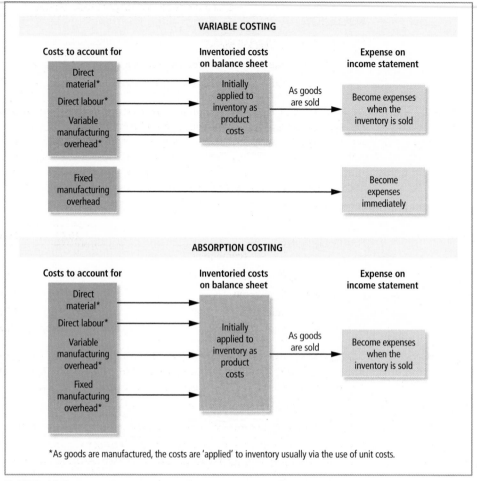

Exhibit 13.2 Comparison of flow of cost

a large proportion of managers, variable costing links manufacturing performance closely with measures of that performance by removing the impact of changing inventory levels from financial results.

Until the last decade or two, use of variable costing for internal reporting was expensive. It requires a company to process information two ways, one for external reporting and one for internal reporting. The increasing use and decreasing cost of computers has reduced the added cost of a variable-costing system. Most managers no longer face the question of whether to invest in a separate variable-costing system. Rather, they simply choose a variable-costing or absorption-costing format for reports. Many well-designed accounting systems used today can produce either format.

Facts for illustration

To see exactly how these two product costing systems work, we will use a hypothetical division of Dell, call it the Desk PC division, as an illustration. The division makes a variety of desktop computers, but for simplicity we will consider all the computers to be identical. The division had the following standard costs for the production of computers:

Basic production data at standard cost

Direct materials	€205
Direct labour	75
Variable manufacturing overhead	20
Standard variable costs per computer	€300

The annual budget for fixed manufacturing overhead (fixed factory overhead) is €1,500,000. Expected (or budgeted) production is 15,000 computers per year, and the sales price is €500 per computer. For simplicity, we will assume that number of computers produced is the single cost-allocation base for the €20 per-computer variable-manufacturing overhead. Also, we will assume that annual budgeted fixed selling and administrative expenses are €650,000 and the only variable selling and administrative cost is a sales commission of 5 per cent of euro sales. Actual product quantities are as follows:

	20X0	20X1
In units (computers)		
Opening inventory	—	3,000
Production	17,000	14,000
Sales	14,000	16,000
Ending inventory	3,000	1,000

There are no variances from the standard variable manufacturing or selling and administrative costs, the actual fixed manufacturing overhead incurred is exactly €1,500,000 each year and the actual fixed selling and administrative cost is €650,000 each year.

Based on this information, we can

1 prepare income statements for 20X0 and 20X1 under variable costing.

2 prepare income statements for 20X0 and 20X1 under absorption costing.

3 show a reconciliation of the difference in operating income for 20X0, 20X1 and the two years as a whole.

■ Variable-costing method

Objective 4
Construct an income statement using the variable-costing approach.

We begin by preparing income statements under variable costing. The variable-costing statement shown in Exhibit 13.3 has a familiar contribution-approach format, the same format introduced in Chapter 5. The only new characteristic of Exhibit 13.3 is the presence of a detailed calculation of cost of goods sold, which is affected by changes in the beginning and ending inventories. In contrast, the income statements in earlier chapters assumed that there were no changes in the beginning and ending inventories.

We account for the costs of the product by applying all variable manufacturing costs to the goods produced at a rate of €300 per computer. This values inventories at standard variable costs. We do not apply any fixed manufacturing costs to products; instead we regard them as expenses in the period they are incurred.

Before reading on, be sure to trace the facts from our Desktop PC division example to the presentation in Exhibit 13.3, step-by-step. Note that we deduct both variable cost of goods sold and variable selling and administrative expenses in computing the contribution margin. However, variable selling and administrative expenses are not inventoriable. Why? They are not incurred in production and so are not considered to be product costs. Only the level of sales, not changes in inventory, affect them.

		20X0	20X1
Sales, 14,000 and 16,000 computers, respectively	(1)	€7,000	€8,000
Variable expenses:			
Variable manufacturing cost of goods sold			
Opening inventory, at standard variable costs of €300		€ —	€ 900
Add: variable cost of goods manufactured at standard, 17,000 and 14,000 computers, respectively		5,100	4,200
Available for sale, 17,000 computers in each year		€5,100	€5,100
Deduct: ending inventory, at standard variable cost of €300		900*	300†
Variable manufacturing cost of goods sold		€4,200	€4,800
Variable selling expenses, at 5% of sales		350	400
Total variable expenses	(2)	4,550	5,200
Contribution margin	(3) = (1) − (2)	€2,450	€2,800
Fixed expenses:			
Fixed factory overhead		€1,500	€1,500
Fixed selling and administrative expenses		650	650
Total fixed expenses	(4)	2,150	2,150
Operating income, variable costing	(3) − (4)	€ 300	€ 650

*3,000 computers at €300 = €900,000.
†1,000 computers at €300 = €300,000.

Exhibit 13.3 Desk PC division – comparative income statements using variable costing, years 20X0 and 20X1 (thousands of euros)

Absorption-costing method

Objective 5
Construct an income statement using the absorption-costing approach.

Exhibit 13.4 shows the standard absorption-costing framework. As you can see, it differs from the variable-costing format in three ways.

First, the unit product cost used for computing cost of goods sold is €400, not €300. Why? Because we add fixed manufacturing overhead of €100 to the €300 variable manufacturing cost. The €100 of fixed manufacturing overhead applied to each unit is the **fixed-overhead rate**. We determine this rate by dividing the budgeted fixed overhead by the expected cost-allocation base activity, in this case expected volume of production, for the budget period:

$$\text{fixed-overhead rate} = \frac{\text{budgeted fixed manufacturing overhead}}{\text{expected volume of production}}$$

$$= \frac{€1,500,000}{15,000 \text{ units}}$$

$$= €1.00$$

Second, fixed factory overhead does not appear as a separate line in an absorption-costing income statement. Instead, the fixed factory overhead appears in two places: as part of the cost of goods sold and as a production-volume variance.[4] A **production-volume variance** (which we explain further in the next section) appears whenever actual production deviates from the expected volume of production used in computing the fixed overhead rate:

$$\text{production-volume variance} = (\text{actual volume} - \text{expected volume}) \times \text{fixed-overhead rate}$$

---

[4] In general, this will be a cost-driver activity variance. In our example, production volume is the only cost driver, so it can be called a production-volume variance.

		20X0	20X1
Sales		€7,000	€8,000
Cost of goods sold:			
Opening inventory, at standard absorption cost of €400*	€ —	€1,200	
Cost of goods manufactured at standard of €400	6,800	5,600	
Available for sale	6,800	6,800	
Deduct: ending inventory at standard absorption cost of €400	1,200	400	
Cost of goods sold, at standard		5,600	6,400
Gross profit at standard		1,400	1,600
Production-volume variance†		200 F	100 U
Gross margin or gross profit, at 'actual'		1,600	1,500
Selling and administrative expenses		1,000	1,050
Operating income		€ 600	€ 450

*Variable cost	€300
Fixed cost (€1,500,000 ÷ 15,000)	100
Standard absorption cost	€400

†Computation of production-volume variance based on expected volume of production of 15,000 computers:

20X0	€200,000 F	(17,000 − 15,000) × €100
20X1	100,000 U	(14,000 − 15,000) × €100
Two years together	€100,000 F	(31,000 − 30,000) × €100

U = Unfavourable, F = Favourable

Exhibit 13.4 Desk PC division – comparative income statements using absorption costing, years 20X0 and 20X1 (thousands of euros)

For example, the production-volume variance for 20X1 is (14,000 − 15,000) × €100 = −€100,000, an under-applied overhead. At €100 per computer, Dell applies only €1,400,000 of fixed overhead to production while actual overhead is exactly equal to its budget of €1,500,000. Assuming it uses the immediate write-off approach, Dell must add the €100,000 to the 20X1 cost of goods sold.

Finally, the format for an absorption-costing income statement separates costs into the major categories of manufacturing and nonmanufacturing. In contrast, a variable-costing income statement separates costs into the major categories of fixed and variable. In an absorption-costing statement, revenue less manufacturing cost (both fixed and variable) is gross profit or gross margin. In a variable-costing statement, revenue less all variable costs (both manufacturing and nonmanufacturing) is the contribution margin. We illustrate this difference by a condensed comparison of 20X1 income statements (in thousands of euros):

Variable costing		Absorption costing	
Revenue	€8,000	Revenue	€8,000
All variable costs	5,200	All manufacturing costs*	6,500
Contribution margin	2,800	Gross margin	1,500
All fixed costs	2,150	All nonmanufacturing costs	1,050
Operating income	€ 650	Operating income	€ 450

*Standard absorption cost of goods sold (16 × €400) plus the production-volume variance (€100).

MAKING MANAGERIAL DECISIONS

When making decisions, it is important for managers to distinguish between gross margin and contribution margin. List the ways in which these two margins differ.

Answer

Among the differences are the following:

- Gross margin appears in an absorption-costing income statement; contribution margin is in a variable-costing income statement.

- Gross margin is revenue less manufacturing cost; contribution margin is revenue less all variable costs.

- Gross margin is based on a categorisation of costs by function (manufacturing versus non-manufacturing); contribution margin separates costs by cost behaviour pattern (variable versus fixed).

- Gross margin is required for external financial reporting; contribution margin is most useful for short-term management decisions and other settings where the variable versus fixed cost distinction is relevant.

Fixed overhead and absorption costs of product

The differences between variable- and absorption-costing formats arise because the two formats treat fixed manufacturing overhead differently. In this and subsequent sections, we explore how to account for factory overhead in an absorption-costing system. We do not further examine this issue under variable costing because its treatment of fixed manufacturing overhead is straightforward – we simply deduct the total amount of actual fixed factory overhead on the current-period income statement.

Variable and fixed unit costs

Continuing our example of the Desktop PC division, we begin by comparing (1) the manufacturing overhead costs in the flexible budget used for departmental budgeting and control purposes with (2) the manufacturing overhead costs applied to products under an absorption-costing system. To stress the basic assumptions behind absorption costing, we will also split manufacturing overhead into variable and fixed components.

Consider the following graphs of variable-overhead costs:

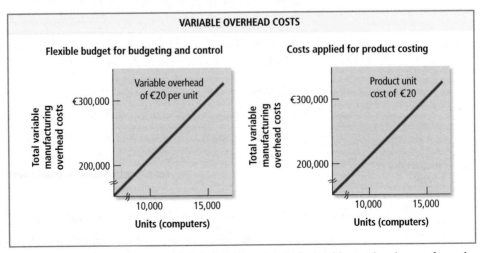

Note that the two graphs are identical. The expected variable-overhead costs from the flexible budget are the same as the variable-overhead costs applied to the products. Both budgeted and applied variable overhead are €20 per computer. Each time we produce 1,000 additional computers, we expect to incur an additional €20,000 of variable overhead, and we add €20,000 of variable-overhead cost to the inventory account for computers. The variable costs used for budgeting and control are the same as those used for product costing.

In contrast, the graph for applied fixed-overhead costs differs from that for the flexible budget:

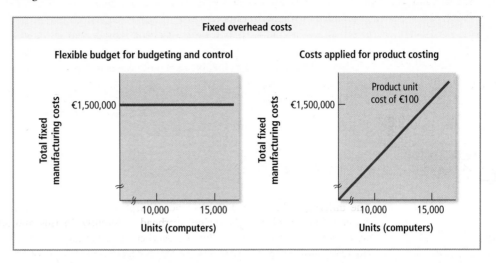

The flexible budget for fixed overhead is a lump-sum budgeted amount of €1,500,000. Volume does not affect it. In contrast, the applied fixed cost depends on actual volume and the predicted volume (denominator level) used to set the budgeted rate for fixed factory overhead.

$$\text{Fixed cost applied} = \text{actual volume} \times \text{fixed-overhead rate}$$

$$= \text{units produced} \times €100$$

Suppose actual volume equals the expected volume of 15,000 computers. Applied fixed overhead would be 15,000 computers × €100 per computer = €1,500,000, the same as the flexible-budget amount. However, whenever actual volume differs from expected volume, the costs used for budgeting and control differ from those used for product costing. For budgeting and control purposes, managers use the true cost behaviour pattern for fixed costs. In contrast, as the graphs indicate, the absorption product-costing approach treats and applies these fixed costs as though they had a variable-cost behaviour pattern. The difference between applied and budgeted fixed overhead is the production-volume variance.

■ Nature of production-volume variance

Objective 6
Compute the production-volume variance and show how it should appear in the income statement.

We calculate the production-volume variance as follows:

$$\text{production-volume variance} = \text{applied fixed overhead} - \text{budgeted fixed overhead}$$

$$= (\text{actual volume} \times \text{fixed-overhead rate})$$

$$- (\text{expected volume} \times \text{fixed-overhead rate})$$

or

$$\text{production-volume variance} = (\text{actual volume} - \text{expected volume}) \times \text{fixed-overhead rate}$$

In practice, accountants often call the production-volume variance simply the **volume variance**. We use the term *production-volume variance* because it is a more precise description of the fundamental nature of the variance. Using production-volume variance also distinguishes it from the sales-volume variance described in Chapter 8. Despite similar nomenclature, they are completely different concepts.

A production-volume variance arises when the actual production volume achieved does not coincide with the expected volume of production used as a denominator for computing the fixed-overhead rate for product-costing purposes:

1 When expected production volume and actual production volume are identical, there is no production-volume variance.

2 When actual volume is less than expected volume, the production-volume variance is unfavourable because usage of facilities is less than expected and fixed overhead is under-applied. It is measured in Exhibit 13.4 for 20X1 as follows:

$$\text{production-volume variance} = (\text{actual volume-expected volume})$$
$$\times \text{ budgeted fixed-overhead rate}$$
$$= (14{,}000 \text{ units} - 15{,}000 \text{ units}) \times €100$$
$$= -€100{,}000 \text{ or } €100{,}000 \text{ U}$$

or

$$\text{production-volume variance} = \text{budget minus applied}$$
$$= €1{,}500{,}000 - €1{,}400{,}000 = €100{,}000 \text{ U}$$

The €100,000 unfavourable production-volume variance increases the manufacturing costs shown on the income statement. Why? Recall that the department incurred €1,500,000 of fixed manufacturing cost, but applied only €1,400,000 to inventory. Therefore, the department will charge only €1,400,000 as expense when it sells the inventory. But eventually it must charge the actual cost of €1,500,000 to the income statement as expense. Recall for simplicity that we assumed any variance is not prorated, so Dell writes off the extra €100,000 to Cost of Goods Sold in the current income statement.

3 When actual volume exceeds expected volume, as was the case in 20X0, the production-volume variance is favourable because use of facilities is better than expected and fixed overhead is overapplied.

$$\text{production-volume variance} = (17{,}000 \text{ units} - 15{,}000 \text{ units}) \times €100 = €200{,}000 \text{ F}$$

In this case, the department will charge €1,700,000 through inventory. Because the department incurs actual costs of only €1,500,000, future expenses will be overstated by €200,000. Therefore, we reduce current period expenses by the €200,000 favourable variance.

The production-volume variance is the conventional measure of the cost of departing from the level of activity originally used to set the fixed-overhead rate. Most companies consider production-volume variances to be beyond immediate control, although sometimes a manager responsible for volume has to do some explaining or investigating. Sometimes, idle facilities caused by disappointing total sales, poor production scheduling, unusual machine break-downs, shortages of skilled workers, strikes, storms and the like are responsible for the failure to reach the expected volume.

There is no production-volume variance for variable overhead. Why? The concept of production-volume variance arises for fixed overhead because of the conflict between accounting for control (by flexible budgets) and accounting for product costing (by application rates) and there is no such conflict for variable overhead costs. Above all, remember that fixed costs are simply not divisible as variable costs are. Rather, they come in large lump sums and are related to the provision of large amounts of production or sales capability, not to the production or sale of a single unit of product.

MAKING MANAGERIAL DECISIONS

Some accountants claim that the production-volume variance is a good measure of how well a company uses its capacity: favourable (unfavourable) variances imply effective (ineffective) use of capacity. As a manager, be careful not to fall into that trap. Why?

Answer

The production volume variance tells you one thing and only one thing – whether actual production was above or below the predicted volume used in setting the fixed overhead rate. Suppose a manager can avoid an unfavourable production-volume variance by lowering the product's selling price to increase sales volume enough to use up the idle capacity. However, if the result is a decline in total contribution margin, this would not be an effective use of the capacity. Similarly, a favourable production-volume variance is not desirable if it occurs because management forces excess production through the facility, despite quality declines or other inefficiencies caused by overburdened production facilities.

■ Reconciliation of variable costing and absorption costing

We can easily reconcile the operating incomes shown in Exhibits 13.3 and 13.4. The difference in income equals the difference in the total amount of fixed manufacturing overhead charged as an expense during a given year. Examine Exhibit 13.5. The total fixed manufacturing overhead incurred (€1,500,000 in 20X1) is always recognised as an expense on a variable-costing income statement. Under absorption costing, fixed manufacturing overhead appears in two places on the income statement: cost of goods sold and production-volume variance.

Under absorption costing, the beginning inventory includes €300,000 of fixed costs incurred before 20X1. During 20X1, accountants added €1,400,000 of fixed manufacturing overhead to inventory, and €100,000 remained in the ending inventory of 20X1 (1,000 units in ending inventory times the €100 fixed factory overhead rate applied to them). Thus, the fixed manufacturing overhead included in cost of goods sold for 20X1 was €300,000 + €1,400,000 − €100,000 = €1,600,000. In addition, the production-volume variance is €100,000, unfavourable. The total fixed manufacturing overhead charged as 20X1 expenses under absorption costing is €1,700,000, or €200,000 more than the €1,500,000 charged under variable costing. Therefore, 20X1 variable-costing income is higher by €200,000.

We can quickly explain the difference in variable-costing and absorption-costing operating income by multiplying the fixed-overhead product-costing rate by the change in the total units in the beginning and ending inventories. Consider 20X1: The change in inventory was 2,000 units, so the difference in net income would be 2,000 units × €100 = €200,000.

Remember that it is the relationship between sales and production that determines the difference between variable-costing and absorption-costing income. Whenever units sold are greater than [less than] units produced, variable-costing income is greater than [less than] absorption-costing income. This means that when inventories decrease [increase], variable-costing income is greater than [less than] absorption-costing income.

■ Why use variable costing?

Objective 7
Explain why a company might prefer to use a variable-costing approach.

Why do many companies use variable costing for internal statements? One reason is that production volume affects absorption-costing income but has no effect on variable-costing income. Consider the 20X1 absorption-costing statement in Exhibit 13.4, which shows operating income of €450,000. Suppose a manager decides to produce 1,000 additional units in December 20X1 even though they will remain unsold. Will this affect operating income? First, note that the gross profit will not change because both revenue and goods sold are based on units sold, not on production volume. However, the production-volume variance will change:

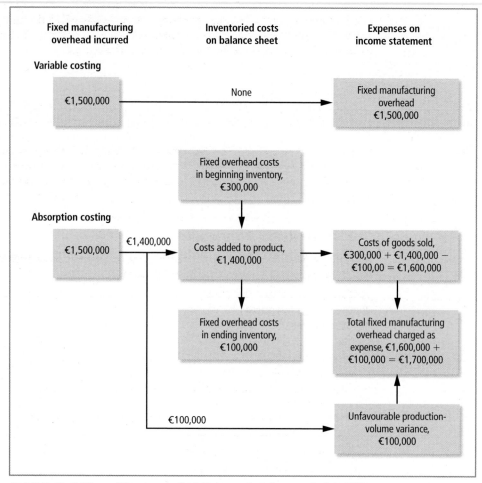

Exhibit 13.5 Flow of fixed manufacturing overhead costs during 20X1

$$\text{If production} = 14{,}000 \text{ units}$$
$$\text{Production-volume variance} = (15{,}000 - 14{,}000) \times €100 = €100{,}000 \text{ U}$$
$$\text{If production} = 15{,}000 \text{ U}$$
$$\text{Production-volume variance} = (15{,}000 - 15{,}000) \times €100 = 0$$

Because there is no production-volume variance when the department produces 15,000 units, the new operating income equals gross profit less selling and administrative expenses, €1,600,000 − €1,050,000 = €550,000. Therefore, increasing production by 1,000 units without any increase in sales increases absorption-costing operating income by €100,000, from €450,000 to €550,000.

How will such an increase in production affect the variable-costing statement in Exhibit 13.3? Nothing will change. Production does not affect operating income under variable costing.

Suppose the evaluation of a manager's performance is based primarily on operating income. If the company uses the absorption-costing approach, a manager might be tempted to produce additional unneeded units just to increase reported operating income. No such temptation exists with variable costing.

Companies also choose variable or absorption costing based on which system they believe gives a better signal about performance. A sales-oriented company may prefer variable costing because the level of sales is the primary effect on its income. In contrast, a production-oriented company, for example, a company that can easily sell all the units it produces, might prefer absorption costing. Why? Because additional production increases the operating income with absorption costing but not with variable costing.

Effect of other variances

So far, our example has deliberately ignored the possibility of any variance except the production-volume variance, which appears only on an absorption-costing statement. All other variances appear on both variable- and absorption-costing income statements. In this section, we will consider these other variances that you encountered in Chapter 8.

▧ Flexible-budget variances

Returning again to the Desktop PC division, we will assume some additional facts for 20X1 (the second of the 2 years covered by our example):

Flexible-budget variances	
Direct materials	None
Direct labour	€ 170,000 U
Variable factory overhead	€ 30,000 U
Fixed factory overhead	€ 70,000 U
Supporting data (used to compute the preceding variances as shown in Appendix 13):	
Standard direct-labour hours allowed for 14,000 units of output produced	87,500
Standard direct-labour rate per hour	€ 12.00
Actual direct-labour hours of inputs	100,000
Actual direct-labour rate per hour	€ 12.20
Variable manufacturing overhead actually incurred	€ 310,000
Fixed manufacturing overhead actually incurred	€1,570,000

As Chapter 8 explained, flexible-budget variances may arise for both variable overhead and fixed overhead. Consider the following:

	Actual amounts	Flexible budget amounts at 14,000 units	Flexible budget variances
Variable factory overhead	€ 310,000	€ 280,000	€30,000 U
Fixed factory overhead	1,570,000	1,500,000	70,000

Exhibit 13.6 shows the relationship between the fixed-overhead flexible-budget variance and the production-volume variance. The difference between the actual fixed overhead and that applied to products is the underapplied (or overapplied) overhead. Because the actual fixed overhead of €1,570,000 exceeds the €1,400,000 applied, fixed overhead is underapplied by €170,000, which means that the variance is unfavourable. The €170,000 underapplied fixed overhead has two components: (1) a production-volume variance of €100,000 U and (2) a fixed-overhead flexible-budget variance (also called the fixed-overhead spending variance) of €70,000 U.

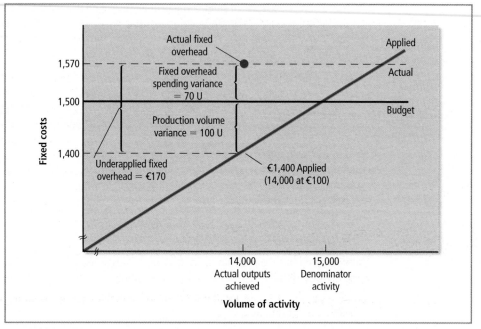

Exhibit 13.6 Fixed-overhead variances for 20X1. (Euro amounts in thousands except per unit amounts.) Data are from Exhibit 13.4

Exhibit 13.7 contains the income statement under absorption costing that incorporates these new facts. These new variances decrease income by 270,000 because, like the production-volume variance, they are all unfavourable variances that are charged against income in 20X1. When cost variances are favourable, they increase operating income.

		(in thousands)
Sales, 16,000 at €500		€8,000
Opening inventory at standard, 3,000 at €400	€1,200	
Cost of goods manufactured at standard, 14,000 at €400	5,600	
Available for sale, 17,000 at €400	€6,800	
Deduct ending inventory at standard, 1,000 at €400	400	
Cost of goods sold at standard, 16,000 at €400		6,400
Gross profit at standard		€1,600
Flexible-budget variances, both unfavourable		
Variable manufacturing costs (€170,000 + €30,000)	€ 200	
Fixed factory overhead	70	
Production-volume variance (arises only because of fixed overhead), unfavourable	100	
Total variances		370
Gross profit at 'actual'		€1,230
Selling and administrative expenses		1,050
Operating income		€ 180

Exhibit 13.7 Absorption costing modification of Exhibit 13.4 for 20X1
(Additional facts are in text)

Summary problem for your review

PROBLEM

1 Reconsider Exhibits 13.3 and 13.4 on pp. 592 and 593. Suppose production in 20X1 was 14,500 units instead of 14,000 units, but sales remained at 16,000 units. Assume that the net variances for all variable manufacturing costs were €200,000, unfavourable. Regard these variances as adjustments to the standard cost of goods sold. Also assume that actual fixed costs were €1,570,000. Prepare income statements for 20X1 under variable costing and under absorption costing.

2 Explain why operating income was different under variable costing from what it was under absorption costing. Show your calculations.

3 Without regard to number 1, would variable costing or absorption costing give a manager more flexibility in influencing short-run operating income through production-scheduling decisions? Why?

SOLUTION

1 See Exhibit 13.8 and Exhibit 13.9. Note that the ending inventory will be 1,500 units instead of 1,000 units.

2 Decline in inventory levels is 3,000 − 1,500, or 1,500 units. The fixed-overhead rate per unit in absorption costing is €100. Therefore, €150,000 more fixed overhead was charged against operations under absorption costing than under variable costing. The variable-costing statement shows fixed factory overhead of €1,570,000, whereas the absorption-costing statement includes fixed factory overhead in three places: €1,600,000 in cost of goods sold, €70,000 U in fixed factory-overhead flexible-budget variance, and €50,000 U as a production-volume variance, for a total of €1,720,000. Generally, when inventories

Sales			€8,000
Opening inventory, at variable			
standard cost of €300	€ 900		
Add: Variable cost of goods manufactured	4,350		
Available for sale	€5,250		
Deduct: Ending inventory, at variable			
standard cost of €300	450		
Variable cost of goods sold, at standard		€4,800	
Net flexible-budget variances for			
all variable costs, unfavourable		200	
Variable cost of goods sold, at actual		€5,000	
Variable selling expenses, at 5% of sales		400	
Total variable costs charged against sales			5,400
Contribution margin			€2,600
Fixed factory overhead		€1,570ᵃ	
Fixed selling and administrative expenses		650	
Total fixed expenses			2,220
Operating income			€ 380ᵇ

ᵃThis could be shown in two lines, €1,500,000 budget plus €70,000 variance.
ᵇThe difference between this and the €650,000 operating income in Exhibit 13.3 occurs because of the €200,000 unfavourable variable-cost variances and the €70,000 unfavourable fixed-cost flexible-budget variance.

Exhibit 13.8 Desk PC division – income statement (variable costing), year 20X1 (thousands of euros)

Sales		€8,000
Opening inventory, at standard cost of €4	€1,200	
Cost of goods manufactured, at standard	5,800	
Available for sale	€7,000	
Deduct: Ending inventory, at standard	600	
Cost of goods sold, at standard	€6,400	
Net flexible-budget variances for all variable		
manufacturing costs, unfavourable	€200	
Fixed factory overhead flexible-budget		
variance, unfavourable	70	
Production-volume variance, unfavourable	50[a]	
Total variances		320
Cost of goods sold, at 'actual'		6,720[b]
Gross profit, at 'actual'		€1,280
Selling and administrative expenses		
Variable	400	
Fixed	650	1,050
Operating income		€ 230[c]

[a] Production-volume variance is €100 × (15,000 expected volume − 14,500 actual production).
[b] This format differs slightly from Exhibit 13.7. The difference is deliberate; it illustrates that the formats of income statements are not rigid.
[c] Compare this result with the €180,000 operating income in Exhibit 13.7. The only difference is traceable to the production of 14,500 units instead in 14,000 units, resulting in an unfavourable production-volume variance of €50,000 instead on €100,000.

Exhibit 13.9 Desk PC division – income statement (absorption costing), year 20X1 (thousands of euros)

decline, absorption costing will show less income than will variable costing; when inventories rise, absorption costing will show more income than variable costing.

3 Absorption costing will give a manager more discretion in influencing operating income via production scheduling. Operating income will fluctuate in harmony with changes in net sales under variable costing, but both production and sales influence it under absorption costing. For example, compare the variable costing operating income in Exhibits Exhibits 13.3 and 13.8. As the second note to Exhibit 13.8 indicates, assorted variances (but not the production-volume variance) may affect operating income under variable costing, but production scheduling per se will have no effect on operating income.

On the other hand, compare the operating income of Exhibits 13.7 and 13.9. As the third note to Exhibit 13.9 explains, production scheduling as well as sales influence operating income. Production was 14,500 rather than 14,000 units. So €50,000 of fixed overhead became a part of ending inventory (an asset) instead of part of the production-volume variance (an expense) – that is, the production-volume variance is €50,000 lower, and the ending inventory contains €50,000 more fixed overhead in Exhibit 13.9 than in Exhibit 13.7. The manager adds €100 to 20X1 operating income with each unit of production under absorption costing, even if the department does not sell the unit.

Highlights to remember

1 **Compute budgeted factory-overhead rates and apply factory overhead to production.**
Accountants usually apply indirect manufacturing costs (factory overhead) to products using budgeted overhead rates. They compute the rates by dividing total budgeted overhead by a measure of cost-allocation base activity such as expected machine hours.

2 **Determine and use appropriate cost-allocation bases for overhead application to products and services.** There should be a strong cause-and-effect relationship between cost-allocation bases and the overhead costs that are applied using these bases.

3 **Identify the meaning and purpose of normalised overhead rates.** Budgeted overhead rates are usually annual averages. The resulting product costs are normal costs, consisting of actual direct materials, actual direct labour and applied overhead using the budgeted rates. Normal product costs are often more useful than true actual costs for decision-making and inventory-costing purposes.

4 **Construct an income statement using the variable-costing approach.** Two major methods of product costing are variable (contribution approach) and absorption costing. The variable-costing method emphasises the effects of cost behaviour on income. This method excludes fixed manufacturing overhead from the cost of products and expenses it immediately.

5 **Construct an income statement using the absorption-costing approach.** The absorption or traditional approach ignores cost behaviour distinctions. As a result, all costs incurred in the production of goods become part of the inventory cost. Thus, we add fixed manufacturing overhead to inventory and it appears on the income statement only when the company sells the goods.

6 **Compute the production-volume variance and show how it should appear in the income statement.** Whenever a company employs the absorption method and the actual production volume does not equal the expected (budgeted) volume that it used for computing the fixed-overhead rate, a production-volume variance arises. When the actual production volume is less than budgeted, the variance is unfavourable; when actual volume exceeds budgeted volume, the variance is favourable. The amount of the variance is equal to the fixed-overhead rate times the difference between the budgeted and actual volume. Companies usually dispose of this variance by adjusting the current-period income. Favourable variances increase current-period income and unfavourable variances reduce current-period income.

7 **Explain why a company might prefer to use a variable-costing approach.** Companies that use operating income to measure results may prefer variable costing. This is because changes in production volume affect absorption-costing income but not variable-costing income. A company that wants to focus managers' energies on sales would prefer to use variable costing, since the level of sales is the primary driver of variable-costing income.

Appendix 13: Comparisons of production-volume variance with other variances

The only new variance introduced in this chapter is the production-volume variance, which arises because companies use fixed-overhead accounting for both control and product-costing purposes. Let's examine this variance in perspective by using the approach originally demonstrated in Exhibit 8.9 of Chapter 8 (p. 351). The results of the approach appear in Exhibit 13.10, which deserves your careful study, particularly the two footnotes. Please ponder the exhibit before reading on.

Exhibit 13.11 graphically compares the variable- and fixed-overhead costs analysed in Exhibit 13.10. Note how the control-budget line and the product-costing line (the applied line) are superimposed in the graph for variable overhead but differ in the graph for fixed overhead.

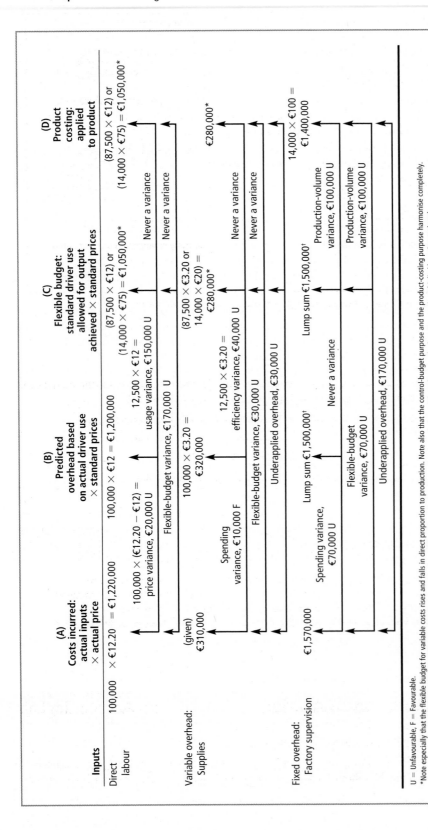

Exhibit 13.10 Analysis of variances (data are from text for 20X1)

U = Unfavourable, F = Favourable.

*Note especially that the flexible budget for variable costs rises and falls in direct proportion to production. Note also that the control-budget purpose and the product-costing purpose harmonise completely. The total costs in the flexible budget will always agree with the standard-variable costs applied to the product because they are based on standard costs per unit multiplied by units produced.

†In contrast with variable costs, the flexible-budget total for fixed costs will always be the same regardless of the units produced. However, the control-budget purpose and the product-costing purpose conflict; whenever actual production differs from expected production, the standard costs applied to the product will differ from the flexible budget. This difference is the production-volume variance. In this case, the production-volume variance may be computed by multiplying the €100 rate times the difference between the 15,000 expected volume and the 14,000 units of output achieved.

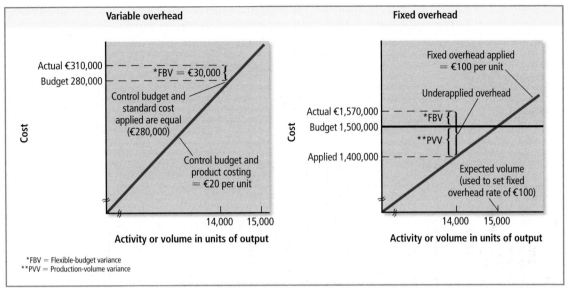

Exhibit 13.11 Comparison of control and product-costing purposes, variable overhead and fixed overhead (not to scale)

Underapplied or overapplied overhead is always the difference between the actual overhead incurred and the overhead applied. An analysis may then be made:

$$\text{underapplied overhead} = \left(\begin{array}{c}\text{flexible-budget}\\\text{variance}\end{array}\right) + \left(\begin{array}{c}\text{production-volume}\\\text{variance}\end{array}\right)$$

for variable overhead = €30,000 + 0 = €30,000

for fixed overhead = €70,000+€100,000 = €170,000

Accounting vocabulary

budgeted factory-overhead rate, p. 582	overapplied overhead, p. 586	proration, p. 587
fixed-overhead rate, p. 592	production-volume variance, p. 592	underapplied overhead, p. 586
normal costing system, p. 585		volume variance, p. 595

Fundamental assignment material   MyAccountingLab

13.A1 Accounting for overhead; budgeted rates

Donald Aeronautics Company uses a budgeted overhead rate in applying overhead to products on a machine-hour basis for department A and on a direct-labour hour basis for department B. At the beginning of 20X0, the company's management made the following budget predictions:

	Department A	Department B
Direct-labour cost	€1,500,000	€1,200,000
Factory overhead	€1,820,000	€1,000,000
Direct-labour hours	90,000	125,000
Machine hours	350,000	20,000

Cost records of recent months show the following accumulations for product M89:

	Department A	Department B
Material placed in production	€12,000	€32,000
Direct-labour cost	€10,800	€10,000
Direct-labour hours	900	1,250
Machine hours	3,500	150

1 What is the budgeted overhead rate that should be applied in department A? In department B?

2 What is the total overhead cost of product M89?

3 If 120 units of product M89 are produced, what is their unit cost?

4 At the end of 20X0, actual results for the year's operations were as follows:

	Department A	Department B
Actual overhead costs incurred	€1,300,00	€1,200,000
Actual direct-labour hours	80,000	120,000
Actual machine hours	300,000	25,000

Find the underapplied or overapplied overhead for each department and for the factory as a whole.

13.A2 Disposition of overhead

Penski Precision Tooling applies factory overhead using machine hours and number of component parts as cost-allocation bases. In 20X0, actual factory overhead incurred was €125,000 and applied factory overhead was €135,000. Before disposition of underapplied or overapplied factory overhead, the cost of goods sold was €525,000, gross profit was €60,000, and ending inventories were as follows:

Direct materials	€ 25,000
WIP	75,000
Finished goods	100,000
Total inventories	€200,000

1 Was factory overhead overapplied or underapplied? By how much?

2 Assume that Penski writes off overapplied or underapplied factory overhead as an adjustment to cost of goods sold. Compute adjusted gross profit.

3 Assume that Penski prorates overapplied or underapplied factory overhead based on end-of-the-year unadjusted balances. Compute adjusted gross profit.

4 Assume that actual factory overhead was €140,000 instead of €125,000, and that Penski writes off overapplied or underapplied factory overhead as an adjustment to cost of goods sold. Compute adjusted gross profit.

13.A3 Comparison of variable costing and absorption costing

Consider the following information pertaining to a year's operation of Blair Company:

Units produced	2,500
Units sold	2,100
Direct labour	€4,000
Direct materials used	€3,000
Selling and administrative expenses (all fixed)	€ 900
Fixed manufacturing overhead	€5,000
Variable manufacturing overhead	€2,500
All beginning inventories	€ 0
Gross margin (gross profit)	€2,200
Direct-materials inventory, end	€ 400
Work-in-process inventory, end	€ 0

1 What is the ending finished-goods inventory cost under variable costing?

2 What is the ending finished-goods inventory cost under absorption costing?

3 Would operating income be higher or lower under variable costing? By how much? Why? (Answer: €800 lower, but explain why.)

13.A4 Comparison of absorption and variable costing

Examine the Trahn Company's simplified income statement based on variable costing. Assume that the budgeted volume for absorption costing in 20X0 and 20X1 was 1,400 units and that total fixed costs were identical in 20X0 and 20X1. There is no beginning or ending work in process.

Income statement Year ended 31 December 20X1		
Sales, 1,260 units at €13		€16,380
Deduct variable costs		
Beginning inventory, 100 units at €7	€ 700	
Variable manufacturing cost of goods manufactured, 1,200 units at €7	8,400	
Variable manufacturing cost of goods available for sale	€9,100	
Ending inventory, 40 units at €7	280	
Variable manufacturing cost of goods sold	€8,820	
Variable selling and administrative expenses	600	
Total variable costs		9,420
Contribution margin		€ 6,960
Deduct fixed costs		
Fixed factory overhead at budget	€4,900	
Fixed selling and administrative expenses	350	
Total fixed costs		5,250
Operating income		€ 1,710

1 Prepare an income statement based on absorption costing. Assume that actual fixed costs were equal to budgeted fixed costs.

2 Explain the difference in operating income between absorption costing and variable costing. Be specific.

13.B1 Disposition of overhead

MacLachlan Manufacturing had underapplied overhead of €40,000 in 20X0. Before adjusting for overapplied or underapplied overhead, the ending inventories for direct materials, WIP and finished goods were €75,000, €150,000 and €100,000, respectively. Unadjusted cost of goods sold was €250,000.

1 Assume that the €40,000 was written off solely as an adjustment to cost of goods sold. Compute the adjusted cost of goods sold.

2 Management has decided to prorate the €40,000 to the appropriate accounts (using the unadjusted ending balances) instead of writing it off solely as an adjustment of cost of goods sold. Would gross profit be higher or lower than in requirement 1? By how much?

13.B2 Application of overhead using budgeted rates

The Bellevue Clinic computes a cost of treating each patient. It allocates costs to departments and then applies departmental overhead costs to individual patients using a different budgeted overhead rate in each department. Consider the following predicted 20X0 data for two of Bellevue's departments:

	Pharmacy	Medical records
Department overhead cost	€225,000	€300,000
Number of prescriptions filled	75,000	
Number of patient visits		50,000

The cost-allocation base for overhead in the pharmacy is number of prescriptions filled; in medical records it is number of patient visits.

In June 20X0, David Li paid two visits to the clinic and had four prescriptions filled at the pharmacy.

1 Compute departmental overhead rates for the two departments.

2 Compute the overhead costs applied to the patient David Li in June 20X0.

3 At the end of 20X0, actual overhead costs were as follows:

Pharmacy	€218,000
Medical records	€321,000

The pharmacy filled 85,000 prescriptions and the clinic had 63,000 patient visits during 20X0. Compute the overapplied or underapplied overhead in each department.

13.B3 Comparison of variable costing and absorption costing

Consider the following information pertaining to a year's operations of Youngstown Manufacturing:

Units sold	1,400
Units produced	1,900

Direct labour	€4,500
Direct materials used	3,500
Fixed manufacturing overhead	2,850
Variable manufacturing overhead	300
Selling and administrative expenses (all fixed)	700
Beginning inventories	0
Contribution margin	5,600
Direct-material inventory, end	800

There are no work-in-process inventories.

1 What is the ending finished-goods inventory cost under absorption costing?

2 What is the ending finished-goods inventory cost under variable costing?

13.B4 Extension of chapter illustration

Reconsider Exhibits 13.3 and 13.4, pp. 592 and 593. Suppose that in 20X1 production was 15,500 computers instead of 14,000 computers and sales were 15,000 computers. Also assume that the net variances for all variable manufacturing costs were €18,000, unfavourable. Also assume that actual fixed manufacturing costs were €1,560,000.

1 Prepare income statements for 20X1 under variable costing and under absorption costing. Use a format similar to Exhibits 13.8 and 13.9, pp. 601 and 602.

2 Explain why operating income was different under variable costing and absorption costing. Show your calculations.

Additional assignment material   MyAccountingLab

QUESTIONS

13.1 Suppose a company uses machine hours as a cost-allocation base for factory overhead. How does the company compute a budgeted overhead application rate? How does it compute the amounts of factory overhead applied to a particular job?

13.2 'Each department must choose one cost-allocation base to be used for cost application.' Do you agree? Explain.

13.3 'Sometimes direct-labour cost is the best cost-allocation base for overhead application even if wage rates vary within a department.' Do you agree? Explain.

13.4 Identify four cost-allocation bases that a manufacturing company might use to apply factory overhead costs to jobs.

13.5 Is the comparison of actual overhead costs to budgeted overhead costs part of the

product-costing process or part of the control process? Explain.

13.6 What are some reasons for differences between the amounts of incurred and applied overhead?

13.7 'Under actual overhead application, unit costs soar as volume increases and vice versa.' Do you agree? Explain.

13.8 Define *normal costing*.

13.9 What is the best theoretical method of allocating underapplied or overapplied overhead, assuming that the objective is to obtain as accurate a cost application as possible?

13.10 'As data processing becomes more economical, more costs than just direct materials and direct labour will be classified as direct costs wherever feasible.' Give three examples of such costs.

13.11 Compare variable and absorption costing regarding the treatment of fixed manufacturing costs.

13.12 Compare variable and absorption costing regarding the treatment of production-volume variance.

13.13 Many companies use variable costing for internal-reporting purposes. These companies must make adjustments to these reports for external-reporting purposes. Explain.

13.14 'With variable costing, only direct materials and direct labour are inventoried.' Do you agree? Why?

13.15 'Absorption costing regards more categories of costs as product costs.' Explain. Be specific.

13.16 'An increasing number of companies are using variable costing in their corporate annual reports.' Do you agree? Explain.

13.17 Why is variable costing used only for internal reporting and not for external financial reporting or tax purposes?

13.18 Compare the contribution margin with the gross margin.

13.19 How is fixed overhead applied to products?

13.20 Name the three ways that an absorption-costing format differs from a variable-costing format.

13.21 'The flexible budget for budgeting and control differs from the costs applied for product costing.' What type of cost is being described? Explain.

13.22 'Variable costing is consistent with cost–volume-profit analysis.' Explain.

13.23 'In a standard absorption-costing system, the amount of fixed manufacturing overhead applied to the products rarely equals the budgeted fixed manufacturing overhead.' Do you agree? Explain.

13.24 'The money amount of the production-volume variance depends on what expected volume of production was chosen to determine the fixed-overhead rate.' Explain.

13.25 Why is there no production-volume variance for direct labour?

13.26 'An unfavourable production-volume variance means that fixed manufacturing costs have not been well controlled.' Do you agree? Explain.

13.27 'The fixed cost per unit is directly affected by the expected volume selected as the denominator.' Do you agree? Explain.

13.28 'Absorption-costing income exceeds variable-costing income when the number of units sold exceeds the number of units produced.' Do you agree? Explain.

13.29 Suppose a manager is paid a bonus only if standard absorption-costing operating income exceeds the budget. If operating income through November is slightly below budget, what might the manager do in December to increase their chance of getting the bonus?

13.30 Why are companies with small levels of inventory generally unconcerned with the choice of variable or absorption costing?

13.31 'Overhead variances arise only with absorption-costing systems.' Do you agree? Explain.

CRITICAL THINKING EXERCISES

13.32 Relationship between cost-allocation bases and factory overhead

'There should be a strong relationship between the factory overhead incurred and the cost-allocation base chosen for its application.' Why?

13.33 Cost application in service firms

'Service firms trace only direct-labour costs to jobs. All other costs are applied as a percentage of direct-labour cost.' Do you agree? Explain.

13.34 Accounting for fixed costs

Applying fixed costs to products seems to cause all kinds of problems. Why do companies continue to use accounting systems that assign fixed costs to products on a per unit basis?

13.35 Marketing decisions and absorption costing

Product pricing and promotion decisions should usually be based on their effect on contribution margin, not on gross margin. Explain how using an absorption costing format for the income statement can provide misleading information on the effect of pricing and promotion decisions.

13.36 Evaluating production using the production-volume variance

The sales-volume variance (see Chapter 8) highlights the effect on income of sales exceeding or falling short of sales targets. Does the production-volume variance provide parallel information for evaluating the effect of exceeding or falling short of production targets? Explain.

13.37 Absorption costing and the value chain

Many costs on a product's value chain, such as R&D and product design costs, are considered period costs and are not assigned to units of product. An absorption-costing system could be expanded to apply such costs to the products. What would be the advantages and disadvantages of doing so? Would this help managers make better decisions?

EXERCISES

13.38 Discovery of unknowns

The Hatch Manufacturing Company has the following budgeted overhead cost and other data for its machining department for the month of December:

Budgeted data:	
Indirect labour and supplies	€ 70,000
Factory rent	€ 19,000
Supervision	€ 84,000
Depreciation on equipment	€139,000
Cost-allocation base for overhead application	Machine hours
Budgeted overhead application rate	€6 per machine hour
Other data:	
Actual machine hours during December	68,000
Actual overhead cost incurred during December	€439,000

Compute the total budgeted machine hours, total applied overhead cost, and indicate how any difference between the actual overhead cost incurred and applied overhead would be treated on Hatch's income statement for the month of December.

13.39 Discovery of unknowns

The Lawson Manufacturing Company has the following budgeted overhead cost and other data for its assembly department for the month of April:

Budgeted data:	
Indirect labour and supplies	€170,000
Factory rent	€ 52,000

Budgeted data:	
Supervision	€ 67,000
Depreciation on equipment	€216,000
Cost-allocation base for overhead application	Direct-labour hours
Total budgeted direct-labour hours	50,000

Other data:	
Total applied overhead costs for April	€616,100
Actual overhead cost incurred during April	€577,000

Compute the budgeted factory overhead rate, actual direct-labour hours, and indicate how the difference between the actual overhead cost incurred and applied overhead would be treated on Lawson's income statement for the month of April.

13.40 Relationship among overhead items

Fill in the unknowns:

	Case 1	Case 2
(a) Budgeted factory overhead	€600,000	€420,000
(b) Cost-allocation base, budgeted direct-labour cost	400,000	?
(c) Budgeted factory-overhead rate	?	120%
(d) Direct-labour cost incurred	570,000	?
(e) Factory overhead incurred	830,000	425,000
(f) Factory overhead applied	?	?
(g) Underapplied (overapplied) factory overhead	?	35,000

13.41 Underapplied and overapplied overhead

Wosepka Welding Company applies factory overhead at a rate of €8.50 per direct-labour hour. Selected data for 20X0 operations are as follows (in thousands):

	Case 1	Case 2
Direct-labour hours	30	36
Direct-labour cost	€220	€245
Indirect-labour cost	32	40
Sales commissions	20	15
Depreciation, manufacturing equipment	22	32
Direct-materials cost	230	250
Factory fuel costs	35	47
Depreciation, finished-goods warehouse	5	17
Cost of goods sold	420	510
All other factory costs	138	204

Compute for both cases

1 factory overhead applied;
2 total factory overhead incurred;
3 amount of underapplied or overapplied factory overhead.

13.42 Disposition of year-end underapplied overhead

Liz's Cosmetics uses a normal cost system and has the following balances at the end of its first year's operations.

WIP inventory	€200,000
Finished-goods inventory	200,000
Cost of goods sold	400,000
Actual factory overhead	413,000
Factory overhead applied	453,000

Compute cost of goods sold for two different ways to dispose of the year-end overhead balances. By how much would gross profit differ?

13.43 Simple comparison of variable and absorption costing

Khalid Company began business on 1 January 20X1, with assets of £150,000 cash and equities of £150,000 capital stock. In 20X1, it manufactured some inventory at a cost of £60,000 cash, including £16,000 for factory rent and other fixed factory overhead. In 20X2, it manufactured nothing and sold half of its inventory for £43,000 cash. In 20X3 it manufactured nothing and sold the remaining half for another £43,000 cash. It had no fixed expenses in 20X2 or 20X3.

There are no other transactions of any kind. Ignore income taxes.

Prepare an ending balance sheet plus an income statement for 20X1, 20X2 and 20X3 under (1) absorption costing and (2) variable costing (direct costing). Explain the differences in net income between absorption and variable costing.

13.44 Comparisons over four years

The Balakrishnan Corporation began business on 1 January 20X0, to produce and sell a single product. Reported operating income figures under both absorption and variable costing for the first 4 years of operation are as follows:

Year	Absorption costing	Variable costing
20X0	€80,000	€60,000
20X1	70,000	60,000
20X2	50,000	50,000
20X3	40,000	70,000

Standard production costs per unit, sales prices, application (absorption) rates and expected volume levels were the same in each year. There were no flexible-budget variances for any type of cost. All nonmanufacturing expenses were fixed and there were no nonmanufacturing cost variances in any year.

1 In what year(s) did 'units produced' equal 'units sold'?

2 In what year(s) did 'units produced' exceed 'units sold'?

3 What is the amount of the 31 December 20X3, finished-goods inventory? (Give absorption-costing value.)

4 What is the difference between 'units produced' and 'units sold' in 20X3, if you know that the absorption-costing fixed-manufacturing overhead application rate is €3 per unit? (Give answer in units.)

13.45 Variable and absorption costing

Chan Manufacturing Company data for 20X0 follow:

Sales: 12,000 units at €18 each	
Actual production	15,000 units
Expected volume of production	18,000 units
Manufacturing costs incurred	
Variable	€120,000
Fixed	60,000
Nonmanufacturing costs incurred	
Variable	€ 24,000
Fixed	18,000

1 Determine operating income for 20X0, assuming the firm uses the variable-costing approach to product costing. (Do not prepare a statement.)

2 Assume that there is no 1 January 20X0, inventory; no variances are allocated to inventory; and the firm uses a 'full absorption' approach to product costing. Compute (a) the cost assigned to 31 December 20X0, inventory; and (b) operating income for the year ended 31 December 20X0. (Do not prepare a statement.)

13.46 Computation of production-volume variance

Osaka Manufacturing Company budgeted its 20X0 variable overhead at ¥14,100,000 and its fixed overhead at ¥26,230,000. Expected 20X0 volume was 6,100 units. Actual costs for production of 5,800 units during 20X0 were as follows:

Variable overhead	¥14,160,000
Fixed overhead	26,340,000
Total overhead	¥40,500,000

Compute the production-volume variance. Be sure to label it favourable or unfavourable.

13.47 Reconciliation of variable-costing and absorption-costing operating income

Blackstone Tools produced 12,000 electric drills during 20X0. Expected production was only 10,500 drills. The company's fixed-overhead rate is €7 per drill. Absorption-costing operating income for the year is €18,000, based on sales of 11,000 drills.

1 Compute the following:
  (a) Budgeted fixed overhead
  (b) Production-volume variance
  (c) Variable-costing operating income.

2 Reconcile absorption-costing operating income and variable-costing operating income. Include the amount of the difference between the two and an explanation for the difference.

13.48 Overhead variances

Study Appendix 13. Consider the following data for the Rivera Company:

	Factory overhead	
	Fixed	Variable
Actual incurred	€14,400	€13,600
Budget for standard hours allowed for output achieved	12,500	11,000
Applied	11,600	11,000
Budget for actual hours of input	12,500	11,400

From the preceding information, fill in the following blanks. Be sure to mark your variances F for favourable and U for unfavourable.

(a) Flexible-budget variance   €_____   Fixed   €_____

                                               Variable   €_____

(b) Production-volume variance   €_____   Fixed   €_____

                                               Variable   €_____

(c) Spending variance   €_____   Fixed   €_____

                                               Variable   €_____

(d) Efficiency variance   €_____   Fixed   €_____

                                               Variable   €_____

13.49 Variances

Study Appendix 13. Consider the following data regarding factory overhead:

	Variable	Fixed
Budget for actual hours of input	€45,000	€70,000
Applied	41,000	64,800
Budget for standard hours allowed for actual output achieved	?	?
Actual incurred	48,100	66,500

Using the preceding data, fill in the following blanks with the variance amounts. Use F for favourable or U for unfavourable for each variance.

	Total overhead	Variable	Fixed
1 Spending variance	_____	_____	_____
2 Efficiency variance	_____	_____	_____
3 Production-volume variance	_____	_____	_____
4 Flexible-budget variance	_____	_____	_____
5 Underapplied overhead	_____	_____	_____

PROBLEMS

13.50 Choice of cost-allocation base at Enriquez Machine Parts Company

Refer to the chapter discussion of Enriquez Machine Parts Company beginning on p. 582. Suppose Enriquez decided to use only one overhead cost pool for both departments with machine hours as the single cost-allocation base.

1 Compute the budgeted overhead application rate for the factory using the budgeted data on p. 583.

2 If Enriquez used 70,000 machine hours during 20X0, what was the total factory overhead applied to products?

3 The applied factory overhead based on separate application rates for the machining and assembly departments was €375,000. Explain why this amount is different than the applied amount from requirement 2.

13.51 Choice of cost-allocation base at Enriquez Machine Parts Company

Refer to the chapter discussion of Enriquez Machine Parts Company beginning on p. 582. Suppose Enriquez decided to use only one overhead cost pool for both departments with direct labour cost as the single cost-allocation base.

1 Compute the budgeted overhead application rate for the factory using the budgeted data on p. 583.

2 If Enriquez incurred €190,000 of direct labour cost during 20X0, what was the total factory overhead applied to products?

3 The applied factory overhead based on separate application rates for the machining and assembly departments was €375,000. Explain why this amount is different than the applied amount from requirement 2.

13.52 Choice of cost-allocation bases in accounting firm

Brenda McCoy, the managing partner of McCoy, Brennan and Cable, a public accounting firm, is considering the desirability of tracing more costs to jobs than just direct labour. In this way, the firm will be able to justify billings to clients.

Last year's costs were as follows:

Direct-professional labour	€ 5,000,000
Overhead	10,000,000
Total costs	€ 15,000,000

The following costs were included in overhead:

Computer time	€ 750,000
Secretarial cost	700,000
Photocopying	250,000
Fringe benefits to direct labour	800,000
Phone call time with clients (estimated but not tabulated)	500,000
Total	€3,000,000

The firm's data processing techniques now make it feasible to document and trace these costs to individual jobs.

As an experiment, in December Brenda McCoy arranged to trace these costs to six audit engagements. Two job records showed the following:

	Engagement	
	Eagledale Company	**Metro Bank**
Direct-professional labour	€15,000	€15,000
Fringe benefits to direct labour	3,000	3,000
Phone call time with clients	1,500	500
Computer time	3,000	700
Secretarial costs	2,000	1,500
Photocopying	500	300
Total direct costs	€25,000	€21,000

1 Compute the overhead application rate based on last year's costs.

2 Suppose last year's costs were reclassified so that €3 million would be regarded as direct costs instead of overhead. Compute the overhead application rate as a percentage of direct labour and as a percentage of total direct costs.

3 Using the three rates computed in numbers 1 and 2, compute the total costs of engagements for Eagledale Company and Metro Bank.

4   Suppose that client billing was based on a 30 per cent markup of total job costs. Compute the billings that would be forthcoming in number 3.
5   Which method of costing and overhead application do you favour? Explain.

13.53 Overhead accounting for control and for product costing

The pickle department of a major food manufacturer has an overhead rate of €5 per direct-labour hour, based on expected variable overhead of €150,000 per year, expected fixed overhead of €350,000 per year and expected direct-labour hours of 100,000 per year.

Data for the year's operations follow:

	Direct-labour hours used	Overhead costs incurred*
First 6 months	52,000	€264,000
Last 6 months	42,000	239,000

*Fixed costs incurred were exactly equal to budgeted amounts throughout the year.

1   What is the underapplied or overapplied overhead for each 6-month period? Label your answer as underapplied or overapplied.
2   Explain briefly (no more than 50 words for each part) the probable causes for the underapplied or overapplied overhead. Focus on variable and fixed costs separately. Give the exact figures attributable to the causes you cite.

13.54 Comparison of variable costing and absorption costing

Simple numbers are used in this problem to highlight the concepts covered in the chapter.

Assume that the Perth Woolen Company produces a rug that sells for €20. Perth uses a standard cost system. Total standard variable costs of production are €8 per rug, fixed manufacturing costs are €150,000 per year and selling and administrative expenses are €30,000 per year, all fixed. Expected production volume is 25,000 rugs per year.

1   For each of the following nine combinations of actual sales and production (in thousands of units) for 20X0, prepare condensed income statements under variable costing and under absorption costing.

	(1)	(2)	(3)	(4)	(5)	(6)	(7)	(8)	(9)
Sales units	15	20	25	20	25	30	25	30	35
Production units	20	20	20	25	25	25	30	30	30

Use the following formats:

Variable costing		Absorption costing	
Revenue	€ aa	Revenue	€ aa
Cost of goods sold	(bb)	Cost of goods sold	(uu)
Contribution margin	€ cc	Gross profit at standard	€ vv
Fixed manufacturing costs	(dd)	Favourable (unfavourable)	
Fixed selling and administrative expenses	(ee)	production-volume variance	ww
		Gross profit at 'actual'	€ xx
		Selling and administrative expenses	(yy)
Operating income	€ ff	Operating income	€ zz

2 (a) In which of the nine combinations is variable-costing income greater than absorption-costing income? In which is it lower? The same?

(b) In which of the nine combinations is the production-volume variance unfavourable? Favourable?

(c) How much profit is added by selling one more unit under variable costing? Under absorption costing?

(d) How much profit is added by producing one more unit under variable costing? Under absorption costing?

(e) Suppose sales, rather than production, is the critical factor in determining the success of Perth Woolen Company. Which format, variable costing or absorption costing, provides the better measure of performance?

13.55 All-fixed costs

The Gibraltar Company has built a massive water-desalting factory next to an ocean. The factory is completely automated. It has its own source of power, light, heat and so on. The salt water costs nothing. All producing and other operating costs are fixed; they do not vary with output because the volume is governed by adjusting a few dials on a control panel. The employees have flat annual salaries.

The desalted water is not sold to household consumers. It has a special taste that appeals to local breweries, distilleries and soft-drink manufacturers. The price, €.60 per litre, is expected to remain unchanged for quite some time.

The following are data regarding the first 2 years of operations:

	In litres		Costs (all fixed)	
	Sales	Production	Manufacturing	Other
20X0	1,500,000	3,000,000	€600,000	€200,000
20X1	1,500,000	0	600,000	200,000

Orders can be processed in 4 hours so management decided, in early 20X1, to gear production strictly to sales.

1 Prepare three-column income statements for 20X0, for 20X1 and for the 2 years together using (a) variable costing and (b) absorption costing.
2 What is the break-even point under (a) variable costing and (b) absorption costing?
3 What inventory costs would be carried on the balance sheets on 31 December, 20X0 and 20X1, under each method?
4 Comment on your answers in numbers 1 and 2. Which costing method appears more useful?

13.56 Semifixed costs

The Plymouth Company differs from the Gibraltar Company (described in problem 13.55) in only one respect: it has both variable and fixed manufacturing costs. Its variable costs are €.14 per litre and its fixed manufacturing costs are €390,000 per year.

1 Using the same data as in the preceding problem, except for the change in production-cost behaviour, prepare three-column income statements for 20X0, for 20X1 and for the 2 years together using (a) variable costing and (b) absorption costing.
2 What inventory costs would be carried on the balance sheets on 31 December 20X0 and 20X1, under each method?

13.57 Absorption and variable costing

The Trapani Company had the following actual data for 20X0 and 20X1:

	20X0	20X1
Units of finished goods		
Opening inventory	—	2,000
Production	15,000	13,000
Sales	13,000	14,000
Ending inventory	2,000	1,000

The basic production data at standard unit costs for the 2 years were as follows:

Direct materials	€22
Direct labour	18
Variable factory overhead	4
Standard variable costs per unit	€44

Fixed factory overhead was budgeted at €98,000 per year. The expected volume of production was 14,000 units so the fixed overhead rate was €98,000 ÷ 14,000 = €7 per unit.

Budgeted sales price was €75 per unit. Selling and administrative expenses were budgeted at variable, €9 per unit sold, and fixed, €80,000 per year.

Assume that there were absolutely no variances from any standard variable costs or budgeted selling prices or budgeted fixed costs in 20X0.

There were no beginning or ending inventories of work in process.

1 For 20X0, prepare income statements based on standard variable (direct) costing and standard absorption costing. (The next problem deals with 20X1.)
2 Explain why operating income differs between variable costing and absorption costing. Be specific.

13.58 Absorption and variable costing

Assume the same facts as in the preceding problem. In addition, consider the following actual data for 20X1:

Direct materials	€ 285,000
Direct labour	174,200
Variable factory overhead	36,000
Fixed factory overhead	95,000
Selling and administrative costs	
Variable	118,400
Fixed	80,000
Sales	1,068,000

1 For 20X1, prepare income statements based on standard variable (direct) costing and standard absorption costing.
2 Explain why operating income differs between variable costing and absorption costing. Be specific.

13.59 Fundamentals of overhead variances

The Durant Company is installing an absorption standard-cost system and a flexible-overhead budget. Standard costs have recently been developed for its only product and are as follows:

Direct materials, 3 pounds at €20	€60
Direct labour, 2 hours at €14	28
Variable overhead, 2 hours at €5	10
Fixed overhead	?
Standard cost per unit of finished product	€ ?

Expected production activity is expressed as 7,500 standard direct-labour hours per month. Fixed overhead is expected to be €60,000 per month. The predetermined fixed-overhead rate for product costing is not changed from month to month.

1   Calculate the proper fixed-overhead rate per standard direct-labour hour and per unit.
2   Graph the following for activity from 0 to 10,000 hours:
    (a) Budgeted variable overhead
    (b) Variable overhead applied to product.
3   Graph the following for activity from 0 to 10,000 hours:
    (a) Budgeted fixed overhead
    (b) Fixed overhead applied to product.
4   Assume that 6,000 standard direct-labour hours are allowed for the output achieved during a given month. Actual variable overhead of €31,000 was incurred; actual fixed overhead amounted to €62,000. Calculate the following:
    (a) Fixed-overhead flexible-budget variance
    (b) Fixed-overhead production-volume variance
    (c) Variable-overhead flexible-budget variance.
5   Assume that 7,800 standard direct-labour hours are allowed for the output achieved during a given month. Actual overhead incurred amounted to €99,700, €62,000 of which was fixed. Calculate the following:
    (a) Fixed-overhead flexible-budget variance
    (b) Fixed-overhead production-volume variance
    (c) Variable-overhead flexible-budget variance.

13.60 Fixed overhead and practical capacity

The expected activity of the paper-making plant of Goldberg Paper Company was 45,000 machine hours per month. Practical capacity was 60,000 machine hours per month. The standard machine hours allowed for the actual output achieved in January were 54,000. The budgeted fixed-factory-overhead items were as follows:

Depreciation, equipment	€340,000
Depreciation, factory building	64,000
Supervision	47,000
Indirect labour	234,000
Insurance	18,000
Property taxes	17,000
Total	€720,000

Because of unanticipated scheduling difficulties and the need for more indirect labour, the actual fixed factory overhead was €747,000.

1 Using practical capacity as the base for applying fixed factory overhead, prepare a summary analysis of fixed-overhead variances for January.
2 Using expected activity as the base for applying fixed factory overhead, prepare a summary analysis of fixed-overhead variances for January.
3 Explain why some of your variances in numbers 1 and 2 are the same and why some differ.

13.61 Selection of expected volume

Rosanne McIntire is a consultant to Georgia Paper Products Company. She is helping one of the company's divisions to install a standard cost system for 20X0. For product-costing purposes, the system must apply fixed factory costs to products manufactured. She has decided that the fixed-overhead rate should be based on machine hours, but she is uncertain about the appropriate volume to use in the denominator. Georgia Paper has grown rapidly; the division has added production capacity approximately every 4 years. The last addition was completed in early 20X0 and the total capacity is now 2,800,000 machine hours per year. McIntire predicts the following operating levels (in machine hours) through 20X4:

Year	Capacity Used
20X0	2,250,000 hours
20X1	2,450,000 hours
20X2	2,700,000 hours
20X3	2,800,000 hours
20X4	2,900,000 hours

The current plan is to add another 500,000 machine hours of capacity in 20X4.

McIntire has identified three alternatives for the application base:
(a) Predicted volume for the year in question
(b) Average volume over the 4 years of the current production setup
(c) Practical (or full) capacity.

1 Suppose annual fixed factory overhead is expected to be €36,400,000 through 20X3. For simplicity, assume no inflation. Calculate the fixed-overhead rates (to the nearest cent) for 20X1, 20X2 and 20X3, using each of the three alternative application bases.
2 Provide a brief description of the effect of using each method of computing the application base.
3 Which method do you prefer? Why?

13.62 Analysis of operating results

Leeds Tool Company produces and sells a variety of machine-tooled products. The company employs a standard cost accounting system for record-keeping purposes.

At the beginning of 20X0, the president of Leeds Tool presented the budget to the company's board of directors. The board accepted a target 20X0 profit of £16,800 and agreed to pay the president a bonus if profits exceeded the target. The president has been confident that the year's profit would exceed the budget target, since the monthly sales reports that he has been receiving have shown that sales for the year will exceed budget by 10 per cent. The president is both disturbed and confused when the controller presents an adjusted forecast as of November 30, 20X0, indicating that profit will be 14 per cent under budget:

Leeds Tool Company
Forecasts of operating results

	Forecasts as of	
	1/1/X0	30/11/X0
Sales	£156,000	£171,600
Cost of sales at standard	108,000*	118,800
Gross margin at standard	£ 48,000	£ 52,800
Over- (under-) absorbed fixed manufacturing overhead	0	(6,000)
Actual gross margin	£ 48,000	£ 46,800
Selling expenses	£ 11,200	£ 12,320
Administrative expenses	20,000	20,000
Total operating expenses	£ 31,200	£ 32,320
Earnings before tax	£ 16,800	£ 14,480

*Includes fixed manufacturing overhead of £30,000.

There have been no sales price changes or product-mix shifts since the 1 January 20X0, forecast. The only cost variance on the income statement is the underapplied manufacturing overhead. This arose because the company produced only 16,000 standard machine hours (budgeted machine hours were 20,000) during 20X0, as a result of a shortage of raw materials while its principal supplier was closed by a strike. Fortunately, Leeds Tool's finished-goods inventory was large enough to fill all sales orders received.

1   Analyse and explain why the profit has declined despite increased sales and good control over costs. Show computations.
2   What plan, if any, could Leeds Tool adopt during December to improve its reported profit at year-end? Explain your answer.
3   Illustrate and explain how Leeds Tool could adopt an alternative internal cost-reporting procedure that would avoid the confusing effect of the present procedure. Show the revised forecasts under your alternative.
4   Would the alternative procedure described in number 3 be acceptable to the board of directors for financial-reporting purposes? Explain.

13.63 Standard absorption and standard variable costing

Schlosser Company has the following results for a certain year. All variances are written off as additions to (or deductions from) the standard cost of goods sold. Find the unknowns, designated by letters.

Sales: 150,000 units, at €20	€3,000,000
Net variance for standard variable manufacturing costs	€ 33,000 unfavourable
Variable standard cost of goods manufactured	€ 11 per unit
Variable selling and administrative expenses	€ 3 per unit
Fixed selling and administrative expenses	€ 650,000
Fixed manufacturing overhead	€ 165,000
Maximum capacity per year	190,000 units
Expected production volume for year	150,000 units
Beginning inventory of finished goods	15,000 units
Ending inventory of finished goods	10,000 units
Beginning inventory: Variable-costing basis	a

Contribution margin	b
Operating income: Variable-costing basis	c
Beginning inventory: Absorption-costing basis	d
Gross margin	e
Operating income: Absorption-costing basis	f

13.64 Disposition of variances

In January 20X0, Lisbon Garden Equipment Company started a division for making grass clippers. Management hoped that these grass clippers were significantly better than most competitors in the market. During 20X0, it produced 100,000 grass clippers. Financial results were as follows:

- Sales: 75,000 units at €18
- Direct labour at standard: 100,000 × €8 = €800,000
- Direct-labour variances: €34,000 U
- Direct materials at standard: 100,000 × €5 = €500,000
- Direct-material variances: $9,500 U
- Overhead incurred at standard: 100,000 × €4 = €400,000
- Overhead variances: €3,500 F

Lisbon uses an absorption-costing system and allows divisions to choose one of two methods of accounting for variances:

(a) Direct charge to income.
(b) Proration to the production of the period; method b requires variances to be spread equally over the units produced during the period.

1 Calculate the division's operating income (a) using method a and (b) using method b. Assume no selling and administrative expenses.
2 Calculate ending inventory value (a) using method a and (b) using method b. Note that there was no beginning inventory.
3 What is the major argument in support of each method?

13.65 Straightforward problem on standard cost system

Study Appendix 13. The Winnipeg Chemical Company uses flexible budgets and a standard cost system.

- Direct-labour costs incurred, 12,000 hours, $150,000
- Variable-overhead costs incurred, $37,000
- Fixed-overhead flexible-budget variance, $1,600, favourable
- Finished units produced, 1,800
- Fixed-overhead costs incurred, $38,000
- Variable overhead applied at $3 per hour
- Standard direct-labour cost, $13 per hour
- Denominator production per month, 2,000 units
- Standard direct-labour hours per finished unit, 6

Prepare an analysis of all variances (similar to Exhibit 13.10, p. 604).

13.66 Straightforward problem on standard cost system

Study Appendix 13. The München Company uses a standard cost system. The month's data regarding its single product follow:

- Fixed-overhead costs incurred, €6,300
- Variable overhead applied at €11 per hour
- Standard direct-labour cost, €44 per hour

- Denominator production per month, 220 units
- Standard direct-labour hours per finished unit, 5
- Direct-labour costs incurred, 1,000 hours, €42,500
- Variable-overhead costs incurred, €10,400
- Fixed-overhead flexible-budget variance, €300, favourable
- Finished units produced, 180

Prepare an analysis of all variances (similar to Exhibit 13.10, p. 604).

CASES

13.67 Multiple overhead rates and activity-based costing

A division of Hewlett-Packard assembles and tests printed circuit (PC) boards. The division has many different products. Some are high volume; others are low volume. For years, manufacturing overhead was applied to products using a single overhead rate based on direct-labour dollars. However, direct-labour has shrunk to 6 per cent of total manufacturing costs.

Managers decided to refine the division's product-costing system. Abolishing the direct-labour category, they included all manufacturing labour as a part of factory overhead. They also identified several activities and the appropriate cost-allocation base for each. The cost-allocation base for the first activity, the start station, was the number of raw PC boards. The application rate was computed as follows:

$$\text{application rate for start station activity} = \frac{\text{budgeted total factory overhead at the activity}}{\text{budgeted raw PC boards for the year}}$$

$$= \frac{\$15,000}{125,000}$$

$$= \$1.20$$

Each time a raw PC board passes through the start station activity, $1.20 is added to the cost of the board. The product cost is the sum of costs directly traced to the board plus the indirect costs (factory overhead) accumulated at each of the manufacturing activities undergone.

Using assumed numbers, consider the following data regarding PC board 37:

Direct materials	$55.00
Factory overhead applied	?
Total manufacturing product cost	?

The activities involved in the production of PC board 37 and the related cost-allocation bases were as follows:

Activity	Cost-allocation base	Factory-overhead costs applied for each activity
1 Start station	Number of raw PC boards	$1 \times \$1.20 = \$1.20$
2 Axial insertion	Number of axial insertions	$39 \times .07 = $?
3 Dip insertion	Number of dip insertions	$? \times .20 = 5.60$
4 Manual insertion	Number of manual insertions	$15 \times ? = 6.00$
5 Wave solder	Number of boards soldered	$1 \times 3.20 = 3.20$
6 Backload	Number of backload insertions	$8 \times .60 = 4.80$
7 Test	Standard time board is in test activity	$.15 \times 80.00 = $?
8 Defect analysis	Standard time for defect analysis and repair	$.05 \times ? = 4.50$
Total		$?

1 Fill in the numbers where there are question marks.
2 How is direct labour identified with products under this product-costing system?
3 Why would managers favour this multiple-overhead rate, ABC system instead of the older system?

13.68 Inventory measures, production scheduling and evaluating divisional performance

The Calais Company stresses competition between the heads of its various divisions and it rewards stellar performance with year-end bonuses that vary between 5 per cent and 10 per cent of division net operating income (before considering the bonus or income taxes). The divisional managers have great discretion in setting production schedules.

The Brittany division produces and sells a product for which there is a long-standing demand but which can have marked seasonal and year-to-year fluctuations. On 30 November 20X0, Veronique Giraud, the Brittany division manager, is preparing a production schedule for December. The following data are available for 1 January through 30 November:

Beginning inventory, 1 January, in units	10,000
Sales price, per unit	€ 400
Total fixed costs incurred for manufacturing	€ 9,350,000
Total fixed costs: Other (not inventoriable)	€10,200,000
Total variable costs for manufacturing	€18,150,000
Total other variable costs (fluctuate with units sold)	€ 4,000,000
Units produced	110,000
Units sold	100,000
Variances	None

Production in October and November was 10,000 units each month. Practical capacity is 12,000 units per month. Maximum available storage space for inventory is 25,000 units. The sales outlook for December–February is 6,000 units monthly. To retain a core of key employees, monthly production cannot be scheduled at less than 4,000 units without special permission from the president. Inventory is never to be less than 10,000 units.

The denominator used for applying fixed factory overhead is regarded as 120,000 units annually. The company uses a standard absorption-costing system. All variances are disposed of at year-end as an adjustment to standard cost of goods sold.

1 Given the restrictions as stated, and assuming that Giraud wants to maximise the company's net income for 20X0, answer the following:
   (a) How many units should be scheduled for production in December?
   (b) What net operating income will be reported in 20X0 as a whole, assuming that the implied cost-behaviour patterns will continue in December as they did throughout the year to date? Show your computations.
   (c) If December production is scheduled at 4,000 units, what would reported net income be?

2 Assume that standard variable costing is used rather than standard absorption costing.
   (a) What would net income for 20X0 be, assuming that the December production schedule is the one in part a of number 1?
   (b) What would net income for 20X0 be, assuming that December production was 4,000 units?
   (c) Reconcile the net incomes in this requirement with those in number 1.

3 From the viewpoint of the long-run interests of the company as a whole, what production schedule should the division manager set? Explain fully. Include in your explanation a comparison of the motivating influence of absorption and variable costing in this situation.

4 Assume standard absorption costing. Giraud wants to maximise her after-income tax performance over the long run. Given the data at the beginning of the problem, assume that income tax rates will be halved in 20X1. Assume also that year-end write-offs of variances are acceptable for income tax purposes. How many units should be scheduled for production in December? Why?

13.69 Performance evaluation

Jens Jensen became president of the Corn Company in 20X0. He is concerned with the ability of his division manager to control costs. To aid his evaluation, Jensen set up a standard cost system.

Standard costs were based on 20X0 costs in several categories. Each 20X0 cost was divided by 1,520,000 cwt, the volume of 20X0 production, to determine a standard for 20X1 (cwt means hundredweight, or 100 pounds):

	20X0 cost (thousands)	20X1 standard (per hundredweight)
Direct materials	£1,824	£1.20
Direct labour	836	.55
Variable overhead	1,596	1.05
Fixed overhead	2,432	1.60
Total	£6,688	£4.40

At the end of 20X1, Jensen compared actual results with the standards he established. Production was 1,360,000 cwt and variances were as follows:

	Actual	Standard	Variance
Direct materials	£1,802	£1,632	£170 U
Direct labour	735	748	13 F
Variable overhead	1,422	1,428	6 F
Fixed overhead	2,412	2,176	236 U
Total	£6,371	£5,984	£387 U

Jensen was not surprised by the unfavourable variance in direct materials. After all, corn prices in 20X1 averaged 10 per cent above those in 20X0. But he was disturbed by the lack of control of fixed overhead. He called in the production manager and demanded an explanation.

1 Prepare an explanation for the large unfavourable fixed-overhead variance.
2 Discuss the appropriateness of using one year's costs as the next year's standards.

13.70 Converting an income statement from absorption costing to variable costing

Holden Corp. has the following income statement under standard absorption costing:

Sales	€1,000,000
Cost of goods sold:	
Beginning inventory	€ 0
Production	€ 975,000
Ending inventory	€ 225,000
Cost of goods sold:	€ 750,000
Less adjustment for variances	€ 95,000

Adjusted cost of goods sold	€ 655,000
Gross profit	€ 345,000
Selling and administrative expenses	
Variable selling and administrative	€ 30,000
Fixed selling and administrative	€ 170,000
Net income	€ 145,000

During the period Holden produced 130,000 units and sold 100,000 units. There was no beginning or ending WIP inventory. Budgeted fixed factory overhead was €150,000, actual fixed factory overhead was €90,000, and denominator level was 100,000 units. Holden does not prorate variances.

Present a variable costing income statement. Be sure to list the amount of any variance in an adjustment for variances.

13.71 Converting an income statement from variable costing to absorption costing

Moseley Corp. currently uses variable costing in its accounting system, with the following selected results (assume there were no variances):

Contribution margin	€ 300,00
Variable selling and administrative	€100,000
Fixed selling and administrative	€ 60,000
Net income	€150,000

During the period Moseley produced 160,000 units and sold 80,000 units. Selling price is €10/unit. There was no beginning or ending WIP inventory and no beginning FG inventory. Moseley is considering a standard absorption costing system. It estimates that if it had used such a system this year, it would have budgeted fixed factory overhead at €100,000, and would have selected a denominator level of 200,000 units. The company also estimates that there would have still been no variances related to direct materials, direct labour and variable factory overhead.

Present a standard absorption costing income statement with proration. Be sure to present the adjustment for variances amount on the income statement.

CASE STUDY

Fiddler Ltd
S. Davidson, M.W. Maher, C.P. Stickney and R.L. Weil

This case compares cost–volume–profit-based calculations to absorption-based costing profit figures. It deals also with standard costing problems. The behavioural issues gain significance in assessing accounting figures validity.

'I just don't understand these financial statements at all!', exclaimed Mrs Alma Spears. Mrs Spears, who was approaching retirement, wished to turn over management of Fiddler Ltd, a division of UK Musical Supplies Plc, to her daughter, Linda, the following month.

Source: Adapted from Davidson, S., Maher, M. W., Stickney, C. P. and Weil, R. L. (1985) *Managerial Accounting.* London: Dryden Press.

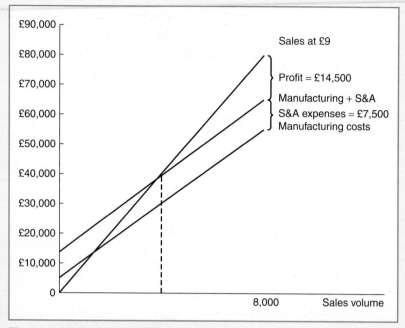

Figure 1 Profit graph for fiddles

Fiddler Ltd manufactures toy stringed musical instruments (referred to by the generic term 'fiddles').

'I am really proud of Linda', she beamed. 'She has shown us all the tricks she learned in business school and, if I say so myself, I firmly believe she is doing rather a good job for us. For example, she has put together this budget for Fiddler, which makes it really easy to see how much profit we'll make at any sales volume (Figure 1). As far as I understand, in March we expected to have a volume of 8,000 units and a profit of £14,500 on our fiddles. But we did much better than that! We sold 10,000 fiddles, so we should have made almost £21,000 on them.'

'Another one of Linda's innovations is this standard cost system', said Mrs Spears proudly. 'She sat down with our production people and came up with a standard production cost per unit (see Table 1). She says that this will tell us how well our production people are performing. Also, she claims it will cut down on our clerical work.'

Table 1 Standard costs*

	Per fiddle
Raw material	
Frame	£3.15
Stringing materials: 20 metres at £0.03 per metre	0.60
Direct labour	
Skilled $\frac{1}{8}$ hour at £9.60 per hour	1.20
Unskilled $\frac{1}{8}$ hour at £5.60 per hour	0.70
Plant overhead	
Indirect labour	0.10
Power	0.03
Supervision[†]	0.12
Depreciation[†]	0.20
Other[†]	0.15
Total standard cost per frame	£6.25

*Based on an estimated volume of 8000 units per month.
[†] These costs are fixed.

Table 2 Profit and loss account for March (actual)

Sales: 10,000 fiddles at £9	£90,000
Standard cost of goods sold: 10 000 fiddles at £6.25	62,500
Gross profit after standard costs	£27,500
Variances	
Material variance	(490)
Labour variance	(392)
Overhead variance	(660)
Gross profit	£25,958
Selling and administrative expenses	7,200
Operating profit	£18,758

Table 3 Actual production data for March

Direct materials purchased and used	
Stringing materials	175,000 metres at £0.025 per metre
Frames	7,100 at £3.15 per frame
Labour	
Skilled (£9.80 per hour)	900 hours
Unskilled (£5.80 per hour)	840 hours
Overhead	
Indirect labour	£ 800
Power	£ 250
Depreciation	£1,600
Supervision	£ 960
Other	£1,250
Production	7,000 fiddles

Mrs Spears continued, 'But one thing puzzles me. My calculations show that we should have shown a profit of nearly £21,000 in March. However, our accountants came up with less than £19,000 in the monthly P&L (Tables 2 and 3). This bothers me a great deal. Now I'm not sure whether the accountants are doing their job properly. It appears to me they're about £2000 short.'

'As you can probably guess', Mrs Spears concluded, 'we are one big happy family around here. I just wish I knew what those accountants are up to – coming in with a low profit figure like that.'

Question

You are required to explain the discrepancy between the profit figures suggested by Linda's profit graph and the accountant's profit and loss account, showing all calculations.

Job-order costing and process-costing systems

Learning objectives

When you have finished studying this chapter, you should be able to:

1 Distinguish between job-order costing and process costing.

2 Prepare summary journal entries for the typical transactions of a job-order costing system.

3 Use an ABC system in a job-order environment.

4 Show how service organisations use job-order costing.

5 Explain the basic ideas underlying process costing and how they differ from job-order costing.

6 Compute output in terms of equivalent units.

7 Compute costs and prepare journal entries for the principal transactions in a process-costing system.

8 Demonstrate how the presence of beginning inventories affects the computation of unit costs under the weighted-average method.

9 Use backflush costing with a JIT production system.

Haribo

Haribo is a major player in the confectionery sector. The German company was founded in 1920 by Hans Riegel of Bonn, hence its acronymous name. Haribo has more than 100 sales offices in virtually

every European country, the US and Australia. Its products include fruit gums, foam-based sweets and liquorice, and it has a growing market of gingerbread pastries, chocolate biscuits and other bakery products through jointly owned corporate interests and acquisitions.

Some of Haribo's well-known products include Goldbear Fruit Gums, Liquorice Wheels, Wine Gums, Starmix, Strawbs and Tangfastics.

How do Haribo's accountants determine the cost of each of the many steps in the production of its products?

How is the cost of flavouring transferred to the sugar-coating process and then to the process that adds a shell? Finally, how are all these processing costs combined to determine the cost of the hundreds of products that are sold worldwide? The answers to these questions enable management to determine the profit of each of the products sold and to set prices. To answer such questions, the accountants at Haribo can use a process-costing system with capabilities that are carefully tailored to meet the decision-making needs of management. ■

Distinction between job-order costing and process costing

Objective 1
Distinguish between job-order costing and process costing.

The two most common systems of product costing are job-order costing and process costing. **Job-order costing** (or simply **job costing**) allocates costs to products that are readily identified by individual units or batches, each of which requires varying degrees of attention and skill. Industries that commonly use job-order methods include construction, printing, aircraft, furniture, special-purpose machinery and any manufacturer of tailor-made or unique goods.

Process costing averages costs over large numbers of nearly identical products. It is most often found in such industries as chemicals, oil, plastics, rubber, lumber, food processing, glass, mining, cement and meatpacking. These industries mass produce homogeneous units that usually pass in continuous fashion through a series of uniform production steps called operations or processes.

The distinction between the job-cost and the process-cost methods centres largely on how they measure product costs. Job costing applies costs to specific jobs, which may consist of either a single physical unit (such as a custom sofa) or a few like units (such as a dozen tables) in a distinct batch or job lot. In contrast, process costing deals with great masses of identical units and computes broad averages of unit costs.

The most important point is that product costing is an averaging process. The unit cost used for inventory purposes is the result of taking some accumulated cost of production (e.g., the sum of production-related activity costs) and dividing it by some measure of production. The basic distinction between job-order costing and process costing is the breadth of the denominator: In job-order costing, the denominator is small (e.g., 1 painting, 100 advertising circulars, 1 special packaging machine or 1 highway bridge); however, in process costing, the denominator is large (e.g., thousands of pounds, gallons or board feet).

Job costing and process costing are extremes along a continuum of potential costing systems. Each company designs its own accounting system to fit its underlying production activities. Some companies use **hybrid costing systems**, which are blends of ideas from both job costing and process costing.

Illustration of job costing

Job costing is best learned by example. But first we examine the basic records used in a job-cost system. The centrepiece of a job-costing system is the **job-cost record** (also called a **job-cost sheet** or **job order**), shown in Exhibit 14.1. The job-cost record contains all costs for a particular product, service or batch of products. A file of job-cost records for partially completed jobs provides supporting details for the work-in-process inventory account, often simply called work in process (WIP). A file of completed job-cost records comprises the finished-goods inventory account.

As Exhibit 14.1 shows, the job-cost record summarises information contained on source documents, such as materials requisitions and labour time tickets. **Materials requisitions** are records of materials used in particular jobs. **Labour time tickets** (or **time cards**) record the time a particular direct labourer spends on each job.

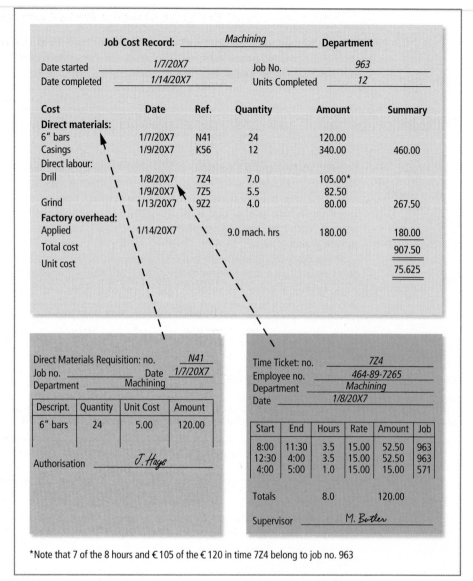

Exhibit 14.1 Completed job-cost record and sample source documents*

Today, job-cost records and other source documents are likely to be computer files, not paper records. With online data entry, bar coding and optical scanning, much of the information needed for such records enters the computer without ever being written on paper. Nevertheless, whether records are on paper or in computer files, the accounting system must collect and maintain the same basic information.

As each job begins, we create its own job-cost record. As units are worked on, we make entries on the job-cost record. We accumulate three classes of costs on the job-cost record as units pass through the departments: materials requisitions are the source of direct-materials costs, time tickets provide direct-labour costs and budgeted overhead rates (a separate rate for each overhead cost pool) are used to apply factory overhead to products. (The computation of these budgeted rates will be described later in this chapter.)

■ Basic records of Enriquez Machine Parts Company

To illustrate the functioning of a job-order costing system, we will use the records and journal entries of the Enriquez Machine Parts Company. The following is a summary of pertinent transactions for the year 20X1:

		Machining	Assembly	Total
1	Direct materials purchased on account	–	–	€1,900,000
2	Direct materials requisitioned for manufacturing	€1,000,000	€890,000	1,890,000
3	Direct-labour costs incurred	200,000	190,000	390,000
4a	Factory overhead incurred	290,000	102,000	392,000
4b	Factory overhead applied*	280,000	95,000	375,000
5	Cost of goods completed and transferred to finished-goods inventory	–	–	2,500,000
6a	Sales on account	–	–	4,000,000
6b	Cost of goods sold	–	–	2,480,000

*We explain the nature of factory overhead applied in Chapter 13, pp. 582–4.

On 31 December 20X0, the firm had the following inventories:

Direct materials (12 types)	€110,000
Work in process	–
Finished goods (unsold units from two jobs)	12,000

Exhibit 14.2 is an overview of the general flow of costs through the Enriquez Machine Parts Company's job-order costing system.[1] The exhibit summarises the effects of transactions on the key manufacturing accounts in the firm's books. As you proceed through the following transaction-by-transaction summary analysis, keep checking each explanation against the overview in Exhibit 14.2 (companies usually make entries as transactions occur but to obtain a sweeping overview, our illustration uses summary entries for the entire 20X1 year). Essentially, we bring into WIP the costs of direct material used, direct labour and factory overhead applied. In turn, we transfer the costs of completed goods from WIP to finished goods. As the company sells goods, its costs become expense in the form of cost of goods sold.

---

[1] Exhibit 14.2 and the following explanation of transactions assume knowledge of basic accounting procedures. We will use the T-account format for a company's accounts. Entries on the left of the *T* are debits and those on the right are credits. Asset T-accounts, such as the inventory accounts, show increases on the left (debit) side and decreases on the right (credit) side of the *T*:

Inventory	
Beginning balance	Decreases
Increases	
Ending balance	

We record transactions affecting the accounts as journal entries. We show debit (left-side) entries flush with the left margin, we indent credit (right-side) entries, and often we include an explanation. For example, we would show a €10,000 transfer from direct-materials inventory to WIP inventory as follows:

WIP inventory 10,000
    Direct-materials inventory 10,000
To increase WIP inventory and decrease
Direct-materials inventory by 10,000.

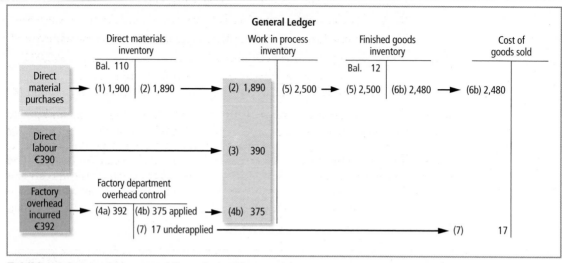

Exhibit 14.2 Job-order, general flow of cost (thousands)

Applying direct materials and direct labour costs

Objective 2
Prepare summary journal entries for the typical transactions of a job-costing system.

The first three transactions in Exhibit 14.2 trace direct materials and direct labour costs to WIP. The entries are straightforward.

1   Transaction: Direct materials purchased, €1,900,000 on account

            Analysis: The asset direct-materials inventory is increased. The liability accounts payable is increased.

        Journal entry: Direct-materials inventory 1,900,000

                       Accounts payable 1,900,000

2   Transaction: Direct materials requisitioned, €1,890,000

            Analysis: The asset WIP inventory is increased. The asset

                       direct-materials inventory is decreased.

        Journal entry: WIP inventory 1,890,000

                       Direct-materials inventory 1,890,000

3   Transaction: Direct-labour cost incurred, €390,000

            Analysis: The asset WIP inventory is increased. The liability accrued payroll is increased.

        Journal Entry: WIP inventory 390,000

                       Accrued payroll 390,000

Applying factory overhead costs

Transactions 4a and 4b deal with factory overhead costs. In transaction 4a we charge the actual factory overhead costs as a debit to a summary account called Factory Department Overhead Control, which we temporarily regard as an asset. Each department will have a variety of detailed overhead accounts to help control overhead, but for our purposes we summarise them all into the Factory Department Overhead Control account.

4a Transaction: Actual factory overhead incurred, €392,000

Analysis: The temporary account Factory Department Overhead Control is increased. Assorted asset accounts are decreased and/or liability accounts increased.

Journal entry: Factory Department Overhead Control 392,000

Cash, Accounts Payable and various other balance sheet accounts 392,000

In transaction 4b we apply factory overhead costs to WIP.[2] While accountants directly trace direct materials and direct labour costs to products (as in transactions 2 and 3), they apply factory overhead costs to WIP via budgeted (predetermined) overhead rates. As described in Chapter 13 (pp. 582–4), to compute the budgeted overhead rates we need the following for each department: (1) cost-allocation base, (2) budgeted overhead costs and (3) budgeted amount of each cost-allocation base. Enriquez allocates overhead based on machine hours in machining and direct-labour cost in assembly, resulting in the following overhead rates:

	Machining	Assembly
Budgeted manufacturing overhead	€277,800	€103,200
Budgeted machine hours	69,450	
Budgeted direct-labour cost		€206,400
Budgeted overhead rate per machine hour: €277,800 ÷ 69,450	4	
Budgeted overhead rate per direct-labour euro: €103,200 ÷ €206,400		50%

Using these rates, the applied overhead for 20X1 is €375,000:

Machining: Actual machine hours of 70,000 × €4	€280,000
Assembly: Actual direct-labour cost of €190,000 × 50%	95,000
Total factory overhead applied	€375,000

The summary journal entry for this application follows:

4b Transaction: Factory overhead applied, €95,000 + €280,000 = €375,000

Analysis: The asset WIP Inventory is increased. The asset Factory Department Overhead Control is decreased.

Journal entry: WIP Inventory 375,000

Factory Department Overhead Control 375,000

▉ Finished goods, sales and cost of goods sold

Transactions 5 and 6 recognise the completion of production and the eventual sale of the goods. When Enriquez completes a particular job, it transfers the costs assigned to that job to finished-goods inventory, and when it sells the job those same costs become expenses on the income statement in the form of cost of goods sold.

---

[2] Refer to pp. 581–4 in Chapter 13 for an expanded discussion of the application of overhead. For our example here, we use the same overhead cost scenario and values for Enriquez Machine Parts Company found on pp. 582–4 in Chapter 13.

5   Transaction: Cost of goods manufactured, €2,500,000

Analysis: The asset Finished-goods inventory is increased. The asset WIP inventory is decreased.

Journal entry: Finished-goods inventory 2,500,000

WIP inventory 2,500,000

6a   Transaction: Sales on account, €4,000,000

Analysis: The asset Accounts receivable is increased. The revenue account Sales is increased.

Journal entry: Accounts receivable 4,000,000

Sales 4,000,000

6b   Transaction: Cost of goods sold, $2,480,000

Analysis: The expense Cost of goods sold is increased. The asset Finished-goods inventory is decreased.

Journal entry: Cost of goods sold 2,480,000

Finished-goods inventory 2,480,000

Finally, transaction 7 in Exhibit 14.2 deals with differences between actual and applied overhead. In 20X1, Enriquez applied €375,000 of overhead to its products but actually incurred €392,000 of overhead costs. We call this difference underapplied overhead because the amount applied is less than the amount incurred. The opposite, overapplied overhead, occurs when the amount applied exceeds the amount incurred. As discussed more fully on pp. 585–7 of Chapter 13, the Enriquez Company disposes of under- or overapplied overhead by some method at year-end. We will assume it uses the immediate write-off method, so it adds the €17,000 of underapplied overhead to cost of goods sold:

7   Transaction: Underapplied overhead, €17,000

Analysis: Cost of goods sold is increased and Factory Department Overhead Control is decreased.

Journal entry: Cost of goods sold 17,000

Factory Department Overhead Control 17,000

MAKING MANAGERIAL DECISIONS

Suppose you are a manager of a manufacturing department. Confirm your understanding of product costing in a job-order environment by indicating the transactions that occurred for each of the following journal entries. Which of these transactions records actual costs versus cost estimates?

1 WIP inventory XXX
      Accrued payroll XXX

2 WIP inventory XXX
      Factory department
      overhead control XXX

3 Cost of goods sold XXX
      Finished goods XXX

Answer

The first entry records the actual cost of direct labour that the accounting system traces to the specific job being costed. We make the second entry to record the application of factory overhead. This is an estimate of the costs of indirect resources used in producing the job. The last entry records the cost of goods sold when the company sells the product from the job. The cost in this transfer from finished-goods inventory to cost of goods sold is a mix of actual costs (direct material and direct labour) and estimated costs (applied factory overhead).

These seven transactions have accounted for all direct materials, direct labour and factory overhead costs incurred during 20X1. As shown in Exhibit 14.2, all these costs ended up in either direct-materials inventory, WIP inventory, finished-goods inventory or cost of goods sold.

Activity-based costing/management in a job-costing environment

Regardless of the nature of its production system, firms will inevitably have resources they share among different products. The costs of these resources are part of the overhead the company must account for. In many cases, the magnitude of overhead is large enough to justify a significant investment in a costing system that provides accurate cost information. Whether companies use this cost information for planning and control or product costing, often the benefits of more accurate costs exceed the costs of installing and maintaining the cost system. As we have seen, ABC usually increases costing accuracy because it focuses on the cause-and-effect relationships between work performed (activities) and the consumption of resources (costs).

■ Illustration of ABC in a job-order environment

Objective 3
Use an ABC system in a job-order environment.

We illustrate an ABC system in a job-order environment by considering Dell. Recall that Dell was the subject of the introduction to Chapter 13, p.580. A few years ago, Dell adopted an ABC job-order costing system. What motivated Dell to adopt ABC? Company managers cite two reasons: (1) the aggressive cost-reduction targets set by top management and (2) the need to understand product-line profitability. As is the case with any business, understanding profitability means understanding the cost structure of the entire business. One of the key advantages of an ABC system is its focus on understanding how work (activity) is related to the consumption of resources (costs). So, an ABC system was a logical choice for Dell. And, once Dell's managers improved their understanding of the company's cost structure, cost reduction through ABM (activity-based management) was much easier.

Like most companies that implement ABC, Dell began developing its ABC system by focusing on the most critical (core) processes across the value chain. These were the design and production processes. After it put the initial system in place, Dell added the remaining phases of the value chain. Exhibit 14.3 shows the functions (or core processes) that add value to the company's products and how Dell assigns the costs of these functions to an individual job under the current ABC system.

To understand product-line profitability, Dell managers identified key activities for the R&D, product design, production, marketing, distribution and customer service phases. Then, they used appropriate cost drivers to allocate activity costs to the produced product lines. While each of the phases shown in Exhibit 14.3 is important, we will focus on the product design and production phases. Product design is one of Dell's most important value-adding functions, providing a defect-free computer product that is easy to manufacture and reliable to use. Engineering costs (primarily salaries and CAD equipment depreciation) account for most of the design costs. These costs are indirect and, thus, Dell must allocate them to product lines using a cost-allocation base.

The production costs include direct materials and factory overhead. Factory overhead consists of six activity centres and related cost pools: receiving, preparation, assembly, testing, packaging and shipping. Facility costs (plant depreciation, insurance, taxes) are considered part of the production function and are allocated to each activity centre based on the area occupied by the centre.

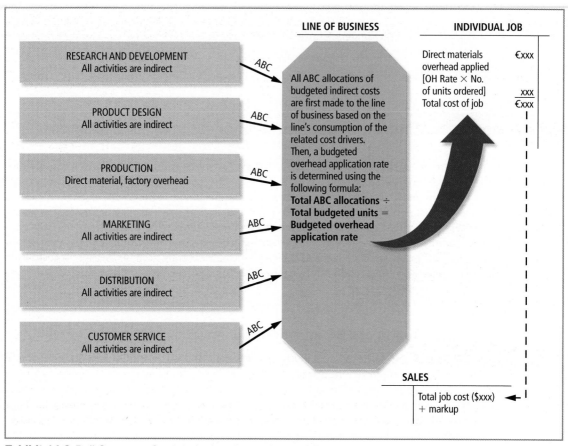

Exhibit 14.3 Dell Computer Corporation's value chain and ABC system

Dell divided the total annual budgeted indirect cost allocated to a product line by the total budgeted units produced to find a budgeted overhead rate. It then used this rate, which is adjusted periodically to reflect changes in the budget, to cost individual jobs.

Dell now breaks down the costs in each activity centre into value added and non-value added and targets non-value-added costs for cost reduction programmes. An example of a non-value-added activity is the preparation activity in the production function.

MAKING MANAGERIAL DECISIONS

Refer to Exhibit 14.3. One of the primary purposes of an ABC system is to increase the accuracy of product costs so that managers can make better cost-based decisions. Assume that you are a manager at Dell and that you have to determine prices for computers by adding a markup to the cost accumulated by the costing system. For example, if the accumulated total job cost is €800, a markup sufficient to 'cover' all unallocated costs and provide a reasonable profit is added. Using the table on p. 639, determine whether the percentage markup under the ABC system is higher or lower than under the previous system. Which system gives you a higher degree of confidence that the price for a computer is adequate to cover all costs and provide a reasonable profit? Why?

MAKING MANAGERIAL DECISIONS (CONTINUED)

Value-chain function	ABC or unallocated Previous costing system	ABC costing system
Research and development	Unallocated	ABC allocations
Design	Unallocated	ABC allocations
Production	Traditional allocation	ABC allocations
Marketing	Unallocated	ABC allocations
Distribution	Unallocated	ABC allocations
Customer service	Unallocated	ABC allocations

Answer

Under the previous costing system, Dell determined prices by marking up only the cost of production. Thus, the markup was relatively high so that the company would cover all the unallocated costs and also achieve a reasonable profit, and managers had a low level of confidence in this cost system. The ABC system provided estimates of all value-chain costs, so the size of the markup was low and the confidence level in the costs provided was high.

Summary problem for your review

PROBLEM

Review the Enriquez illustration, especially Exhibit 14.2 on p. 634. Prepare an income statement for 20X1 through the gross profit line. Use the immediate write-off method for overapplied or underapplied overhead.

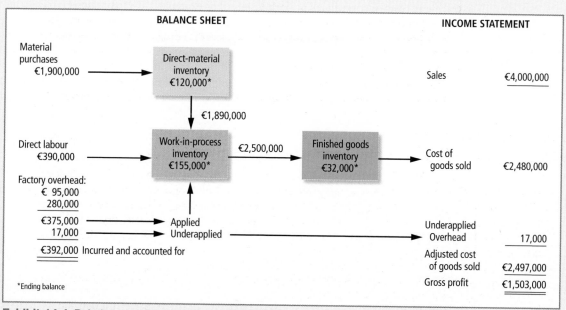

Exhibit 14.4 Relation of costs to financial statements

SOLUTION

Exhibit 14.4 recapitulates the final impact of the Enriquez illustration on the financial statements. Note how the immediate write-off means that we add the €17,000 to the cost of goods sold. As you study Exhibit 14.4, trace the three major elements of cost (direct materials, direct labour and factory overhead) through the accounts.

Job costing in service and nonprofit organisations

Objective 4

Show how service organisations use job costing.

So far, this chapter has concentrated on applying costs to manufactured products. However, the job-costing approach is used in nonmanufacturing situations, too. For example, universities have research 'projects', airlines have repair and overhaul 'jobs', and public accountants have audit 'engagements'. In such situations, the focus shifts from the costs of products to the costs of services, projects or programmes.

Service and nonprofit organisations do not usually call their 'product' a 'job order'. Instead, they may call it a programme or a class of service. A 'programme' is an identifiable group of activities that frequently produces outputs in the form of services rather than goods. Examples include a safety programme, an education programme, or a family counselling programme. Accountants can trace costs or revenues to individual hospital patients, individual social welfare cases and individual university research projects. However, internal departments in service organisations often work simultaneously on many programmes, so the 'job-order' costing challenge is to 'apply' the various department costs to the various programmes. Only then can managers best allocate limited resources among competing programmes.

In service industries – such as repairing, consulting, legal and accounting services – each customer order is a different job with a special account or order number. Accountants can trace just costs, just revenues or both to jobs. For example, car repair shops typically have a repair order for each car worked on, with space for allocating materials and labour costs. Customers see only a copy showing the retail prices of the materials, parts and labour billed to their orders. Meanwhile, accountants trace the actual parts and labour costs of each order to a duplicate copy of the repair order, providing a measure of profit for each job. To get these actual costs, mechanics must enter their starting and stopping times on time tickets for each new order. This is why you might see them stamping a time card each time they start or end a job.

▪ Budgets and control of engagements

In many service organisations and some manufacturing operations, job orders serve not only for product/service costing, but also for planning and control purposes. For example, a public accounting firm might have a condensed budget for 20X1 as follows:

Revenue	€10,000,000	100%
Direct labour (for professional hours charged to engagements)	2,500,000	25%
Contribution to overhead and operating income	€ 7,500,000	75%
Overhead (all other costs)	6,500,000	65%
Operating income	€ 1,000,000	10%

In this illustration,

$$\text{budgeted overhead rate} = \frac{\text{budgeted overhead}}{\text{budgeted direct labour}}$$

$$= \frac{\text{€6,500,000}}{\text{€2,500,000}}$$

$$= 260\%$$

To prepare a budget for each engagement, the partner in charge of the audit predicts the expected number of necessary direct-professional hours. Direct-professional hours are those that partners, managers and staff auditors work to complete the engagement. The budgeted direct-labour cost is the pertinent hourly labour costs multiplied by the budgeted hours. Accounting firms charge partners' time to the engagement at much higher rates than subordinates' time.

How do such firms apply overhead? Accounting firms usually use either direct-labour cost or direct-labour hours as the cost driver for overhead application. In our example, the firm uses direct-labour cost. The budgeted total cost of an engagement is the direct-labour cost plus applied overhead, 260 per cent of direct-labour cost in this illustration, plus any other direct costs.

This practice implies that partners require proportionately more overhead support for each of their hours charged. For example, 1 hour of partner work that has a direct-labour cost of €200 would result in a projected overhead support cost of €520. If this work can be done by a member of staff whose charge rate is only €50, the projected overhead is only €130.

The engagement partner uses a budget for a specific audit job that includes detailed scope and steps. For instance, the budget for auditing cash or receivables on the engagement would specify the exact work to be done; the number of hours; and the necessary hours of partner time, manager time and staff time. The partner monitors progress by comparing the hours logged to date with the original budget and with the estimated hours remaining on the engagement. If the firm quoted a fixed audit fee, the profitability of an engagement depends on whether it can accomplish the audit within the budgeted time limits.

Accuracy of costs of engagements

Managers of service firms, such as auditing and consulting firms, frequently use budgeted costs of engagements as guides to pricing and to allocating effort among particular services or customers. Hence, the accuracy of projected costs of various engagements may affect pricing and operational decisions.

Suppose the accounting firm's policy for price quotes for engagements is 200 per cent of total projected professional costs plus travel costs. The firm projects costs and sets the price on an auditing engagement as follows:

	Projected cost	Price
Direct-professional labour	€ 50,000	€100,000
Applied overhead, 260% of direct-professional labour	130,000	260,000
Total professional costs excluding travel costs	€180,000	360,000
Travel costs	14,000	14,000
Total projected costs of engagement	€194,000	€374,000

Note that costs reimbursed by the client – such as travel costs – do not add to overhead costs and so are not subject to any markups in the setting of fees. Once the client accepts the offer, the firm needs to monitor the assignment of work as well as the overhead incurred to insure control of costs.

Process costing basics

As indicated on p. 631, an alternative to job costing is process costing. Before we examine the procedures of process costing, let's examine a real application. Nally & Gibson Georgetown is a leading producer of limestone products used for industrial and commercial purposes. Limestone is used in highways, high school track beds, concrete sidewalks, buildings, soil enhancement products, residential homes and about a million other places (yes, even in some toothpastes).

The making of limestone products is an excellent example of a process production system. A single raw material – limestone rock – is subjected to several processes that result in finished limestone products. The basic production processes that convert limestone rock into usable limestone are easy to understand and are reasonably simple. Basically, the limestone rock is mined from Nally & Gibson's quarry and mine and transported to the processing facility. There it passes through several stages of crushing and grinding, depending on how fine the finished product needs to be. The ease and homogeneous nature of these processes might make you think that the cost accounting system used to track product costs should also be fairly simple and perhaps even unimportant to the success of the company. However, accurate and timely cost information is critical for both product costing and decision-making purposes at Nally & Gibson.

For example, the accurate allocation of the costs of mining and transporting limestone and then crushing the limestone to form the various products is essential to the success of the company. The company's cost accounting system accumulates the costs of these processes and then calculates an average cost per ton of product using a process-costing system.

One of Nally & Gibson's costs is transporting quarried rock from the mine to plants. Using lorries that have to travel up to 1½ kilometres into the mine and then up a steep gradient is expensive and hazardous. The solution to this transportation problem was provided by the installation of a 1,000-metre conveyor system specially designed for the firm. The accounting system used by the maker of the conveyor system to account for this job is an excellent example of a job-order system. There is a customer-specific product that requires a unique combination of resources.

The result – Nally & Gibson increased its production by up to 50 per cent with increased safety and at a reduced cost. We can see from this example that the cost accounting system a company uses depends on the nature of its products and services. The cost information needed by managers dictates the type of cost accounting system. Some managers need costs for specific products that have unique features. Nally & Gibson's managers, whose product is crushed limestone, have very different cost-information needs.

Companies such as Haribo and Nally & Gibson that produce in a continuous process large quantities of a generic or homogeneous product, such as staples or sliced potato strips for cooking chips, do not use the job-costing techniques that you just learned. Why? Because a method called process costing fits their production process better and so is a more efficient costing system for such companies.

Why doesn't Nally & Gibson use a job-cost system to assign costs to its products? First, because there are no discrete jobs. The company does not wait for a specific customer order before producing the product. The company makes a forecast of the demand for the product and produces to meet this expected demand. Second, it is amazingly difficult (and costly) to trace costs to a specific truckload of limestone. And there would be no benefit in doing so in terms of increased accuracy. So the cost–benefit criterion clearly dictates that the company determines unit costs using much larger quantities – for example, a whole month's production.

As we noted early in this chapter, all product costing uses averaging to determine costs per unit of production. Sometimes those averages apply to a relatively small number of units, such as a particular printing job produced in a job-order production system. Other times, the averages might have to be extremely broad, based on generic products from a continual-process production system, such as limestone road fill. Process-costing systems apply costs to homogeneous products that a company mass produces in continuous fashion through a series of production processes. These processes usually occur in separate departments, although a single department sometimes contains more than one process.

■ Process costing compared with job costing

Objective 5
Explain the basic ideas underlying process costing and how they differ from job costing.

It is easiest to understand process costing if you compare it with something you already know: job costing. Companies use job costing and process costing for different types of products. As mentioned previously, firms in which each unit or batch (job) of product is unique and easily identifiable use job-order costing. However, when there is mass production through a sequence of several processes, such as mixing and cooking, we use process costing. Examples include chemicals, flour, glass, toothpaste and limestone.

Exhibit 14.5 shows the major differences between job-order costing and process costing. Job-order costing has one WIP for each job. In contrast, process costing requires one WIP account for each process. As goods move from process to process, accountants transfer their costs accordingly.

Consider Nally & Gibson's process-costing system. The company's production system has four core processes as shown in Exhibit 14.6. The company first obtains limestone rock from surface quarries or from mines. It then transports the rock to the plant by rail or truck. At the plant, machines crush the rock and screen it to various sizes demanded by customers. The crushed limestone is then stocked in large piles of inventory for shipment. Each process requires resources. The direct-materials resource is the limestone rock itself. All four processes use direct-labour and overhead resources.

The process-costing approach does not distinguish between individual units of product. Instead, it accumulates costs for a period and divides them by quantities produced during that period to get broad, average unit costs. We can apply process costing to nonmanufacturing activities as well as to manufacturing activities. For example, we can divide the costs of giving state automobile driver's license tests by the number of tests given, and we can divide the cost of a post office sorting department by the number of items sorted.

To get a rough feel for process costing, consider Magenta Midget Frozen Vegetables. This company quick-cooks tiny carrots, beans and other vegetables before freezing them. It has only two processes, cooking and freezing. As the following T-accounts show, the costs of cooked vegetables (in millions of dollars) are transferred from the cooking department to the freezing department:

Work in process – cooking			
Direct materials	14	Transfer cost of goods completed to next department	23
Direct labour	4		
Factory overhead	8		
	26		
Ending inventory	3		

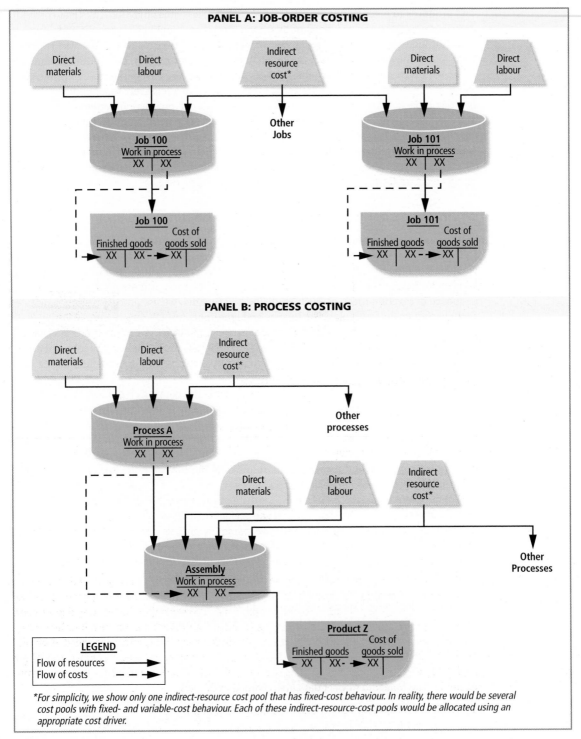

Exhibit 14.5 Comparison of job-order and process costing

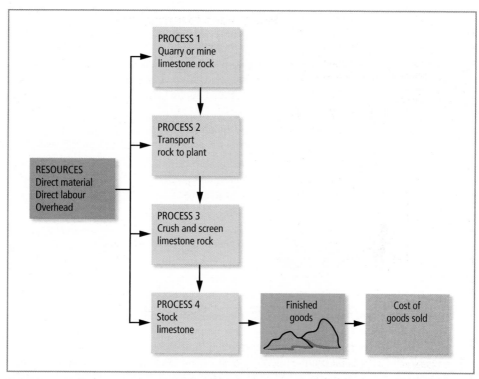

Exhibit 14.6 Process costing at Nally & Gibson

Work in process – freezing			
Cost transferred in from cooking	23	Transfer cost of goods complete do finished goods	21
Direct labour	1		
Factory overhead	2		
	26		
Ending inventory	5		

We determine the amount of cost to be transferred by dividing the accumulated costs in the cooking department by the pounds of vegetables processed. We then multiply the resulting cost per pound by the pounds of vegetables physically transferred to the freezing department.

The journal entries for process-costing systems are similar to those for the job-order costing system. That is, we account for direct materials, direct labour and factory overhead as before. However, now there is more than a single WIP account for all units being manufactured. There is one WIP account for each processing department, WIP – Cooking and WIP – Freezing, in our example. The Magenta Midget data are recorded as follows:

1 Work in Process Work in Process – Cooking 14
         Direct-Materials Inventory 14
      To record direct materials used.

```
2   Work in Process – Cooking ............................................... 4
        Accrued Payroll ...................................................... 4
    To record direct labour incurred.

3   Work in Process – Cooking ............................................ 8
        Factory Overhead ..................................................... 8
    To record factory overhead applied to product.

4   Work in Process – Freezing ......................................... 23
        Work in Process – Cooking ....................................... 23
    To transfer goods from the cooking process; 3 million remains in cooking.

5   Work in Process – Freezing – Freezing ......................... 1
        Accrued Payroll ...................................................... 1
    To record direct labour incurred.

6   Work in Process – Freezing ......................................... 2
        Factory Overhead ..................................................... 2
    To record factory overhead applied to product.

7   Finished Goods ............................................................ 21
        Work in Process – Freezing ...................................... 21
    To transfer goods from the freezing process; 5 million remains in freezing.
```

Process manufacturing systems vary in design. The design shown in panel B of Exhibit 14.5 (as well as Exhibit 14.6) is sequential – units pass from process A to process B and so on until the product is finished. You will find many other designs in practice – each tailored to meet specific production requirements. For example, the firm can operate processes in parallel until final assembly. In this case, process A and process B might occur at the same time to produce different parts of the finished product. Whatever the specific layout, the basic principles of process costing are the same.

The central product-costing problem is how each department should compute the cost of goods transferred out and the cost of goods remaining in the department. If the same amount of work were done on each unit transferred out and on each unit in ending inventory, the solution would be easy. We could simply divide total costs by total units. Then, we would use this unit cost to calculate the total cost of units transferred out and the remaining cost of unfinished units. However, this is not possible because units in ending inventory cannot be complete, which makes them different from the completed units transferred out. Thus, the product-costing system must distinguish between the costs of fully completed units that a department transfers out and the costs of partially completed units that still remain in ending inventory. Let's now see how process costing systems accomplish this.

Application of process costing

To help you better understand our discussion of process costing, we will use the example of Oakville Wooden Toys. The company buys wood as a direct material for its forming department, which processes only one type of toy, marionettes. It inserts all the wood into this department at the beginning of the process. After forming, the company transfers the marionettes to the finishing department where workers hand shape them and add strings, paint and clothing.

The forming department had no beginning inventory and completely manufactured 25,000 identical units during April, leaving no ending inventory. Its costs that month were as follows:

Direct materials		€ 75,000
Conversion costs		
Direct labour	€15,000	
Factory overhead	40,000	55,000
Costs to account for		€130,000

Since there is no ending inventory, the unit cost of goods completed is simply €130,000 ÷ 25,000 = €5.20. An itemisation would show the following:

Direct materials, €75,000 ÷ 25,000	€3.00
Conversion costs, €55,000 ÷ 25,000	2.20
Unit cost of a whole completed marionette	€5.20

But what if not all 25,000 marionettes were completed during April? For example, assume that 5,000 were still in process at the end of April – only 20,000 were started and fully completed. All units – both those transferred out and those still in inventory – have obviously received all the necessary direct materials. However, only the transferred units have received the full amount of conversion resources. Oakville determined that the 5,000 marionettes that remain in process have received, on average, only 40 per cent of conversion resources. How should the forming department calculate the cost of goods transferred and the cost of goods remaining in the ending WIP inventory? The answer lies in the following five key steps:

- Step 1: Summarise the flow of physical units.
- Step 2: Calculate output in terms of equivalent units.
- Step 3: Summarise the total costs to account for, which are the costs applied to WIP.
- Step 4: Calculate cost per equivalent unit.
- Step 5: Apply costs to units completed and to units in the ending WIP.

We now work through each of these five steps. Keep in mind that each step provides managers with data that are useful for product costing and operational control purposes.

Physical units and equivalent units (steps 1 and 2)

Objective 6
Compute output in terms of equivalent units.

Step 1, as the first column in Exhibit 14.7 shows, tracks the physical units of production. How should we measure the output – the results of the department's work? This tracking tells us we have a total of 25,000 physical units to account for, but not all these units count the same in the forming department's output. Why not? Because only 20,000 units were fully completed and transferred out. The remaining 5,000 units are only partially complete and we cannot assign partially completed units the same cost as the completed output. As a result, we have to state output not in terms of physical units but in terms of a different unit measure called an 'equivalent unit'.

Equivalent units are the number of completed (whole) units that the department could have produced from the inputs applied. For example, four units that are each one-half completed represent two equivalent units. Similarly, if each unit had been one-fourth completed, the four together would represent one equivalent unit. So, we determine equivalent units by multiplying physical units by the per cent of completion. This equivalent unit measure correctly equates the completed physical units that are transferred out with the partially completed physical units in ending inventory.

	(Step 1)	(Step 2) equivalent units	
Flow of production	physical units	Direct materials	Conversion
Started and completed	20,000	20,000	20,000
Work in process, ending inventory	5,000	5,000	2,000*
Units accounted for	25,000		
Work done to date		25,000	22,000*

* 5,000 physical units × .40 degree of completion of conversion costs.

Exhibit 14.7 Forming department output in equivalent units – month ended 30 April 20X0

In our example, as step 2 in Exhibit 14.7 shows, we measure the output as 25,000 equivalent units of direct-materials cost but only 22,000 equivalent units of conversion costs. Why? Because direct materials had been fully added to all 25,000 units. In contrast, only 40 per cent of the conversion costs were applied to the 5,000 partially completed units, which would have been sufficient to complete only 2,000 equivalent units in addition to the 20,000 units that were actually completed.

To compute equivalent units, you need to estimate how much of a given resource was applied to units in process, which is not always an easy task. Some estimates are easier to make than others. For example, estimating the amount of direct materials used is fairly easy. However, how do you measure how much energy, maintenance labour or supervision was incurred for a given unit? Conversion costs can involve a number of these hard-to-measure resources, which leaves you estimating both how much total effort it takes to complete a unit and how much of that effort has already been put into the units in process. Coming up with accurate estimates is further complicated in industries such as textiles, where there is a great deal of work in process at all times. To simplify estimation, some companies may decide that all unfinished work in process must be deemed either one-third, one-half, or two-thirds complete. In other cases where continuous processing leaves roughly the same amount in process at the end of every month, accountants ignore work in process altogether and assign all monthly production costs to units completed and transferred out.

Measures in equivalent units are not confined to manufacturing situations. Such measures are a popular way of expressing workloads in terms of a common denominator. For example, radiology departments measure their output in terms of weighted units. Various X-ray procedures are ranked in terms of the time, supplies and related costs devoted to each. A simple chest X-ray may receive a weight of one. But a skull X-ray may receive a weight of three because it uses three times more resources (for example, technicians' time) than a procedure with a weight of one.

Calculation of product costs (steps 3 to 5)

Objective 7
Compute costs and prepare journal entries for the principal transactions in a process-costing system.

Exhibit 14.8 is a production-cost report. It shows steps 3–5 of process costing. Step 3 summarises the total costs to account for (that is, the total costs incurred and applied to WIP – forming). Step 4 obtains unit costs by dividing the two categories of total costs by the appropriate measures of equivalent units. The unit cost of a completed unit – materials cost plus conversion costs per equivalent unit – is €3.00 + €2.50 = €5.50. Why is the unit cost €5.50 instead of the €5.20 calculated on p. 647? Because the €55,000 conversion cost is spread over 22,000 units instead of 25,000 units. Step 5 then uses these unit costs to apply costs to products. The 20,000 finished units are complete in terms of both direct

			Details	
		Total costs	Direct materials	Conversion costs
(Step 3)	Costs to account for	€130,000	€ 75,000	€ 55,000
(Step 4)	Divide by equivalent units		÷ 25,000	÷ 22,000
	Unit costs	€ 5.50	€ 3.00	€ 2.50
(Step 5)	Application of costs			
	To units completed and transferred to the finishing department, 20,000 units at €5.50	€110,000		
	To units not completed and still in process, April 30, 5,000 units			
	Direct materials	€ 15,000	5,000 (€3.00)	
	Conversion costs	5,000		2,000 (€2.50)
	Work in process, April 30	€ 20,000		
	Total costs accounted for	€ 130,000		

Exhibit 14.8 Forming department production cost report – month ended 30 April 20X0

materials and conversion costs. Thus, we can multiply the full unit cost times the number of completed units to determine their costs, which is 20,000 units times €5.50, or $110,000. The 5,000 physical units in ending work-in-process inventory are fully completed in terms of direct materials. Therefore, the direct materials applied to ending work in process are 5,000 equivalent units times €3.00, or €15,000. In contrast, the 5,000 physical units are 40 per cent completed in terms of conversion costs. Therefore, the conversion costs applied to work in process are 2,000 equivalent units (40 per cent of 5,000 physical units) times €2.50, or €5,000. Thus, the total cost of the ending inventory is €20,000.

Journal entries for the data in our illustration would appear as follows:

1   Work in Process – Forming 75,000
      Direct-Materials Inventory 75,000
   Materials added to production in April.

2   Work in Process – Forming 15,000
      Accrued Payroll 15,000
   Direct labour incurred in April.

3   Work in Process – Forming 40,000
      Factory Overhead 40,000
   Factory overhead applied in April.

4   Work in Process – Finishing 110,000
      Work in Process – Forming 110,000
   Cost of goods completed and transferred in April from forming to assembly.

The €130,000 added to the work in process – forming account less the €110,000 transferred out leaves an ending balance of €20,000:

Work in process – forming

1 Direct materials	€ 75,000	4 Transferred out to finishing	€110,000
2 Direct labour	15,000		
3 Factory overhead	40,000		
Costs to account for	130,000		
Bal. April 30	€20,000		

Summary problem for your review

PROBLEM

Consider Nally & Gibson's plant operations in Georgetown. The plant processes limestone rock that is quarried in a nearby mine. Exhibit 14.6 (p. 645) shows the various processing steps. Process 3 is crushing and screening the rock. To produce the crushed limestone, the company starts with limestone rocks from its quarry in Georgetown, Kentucky and puts the rocks through a crushing process. Suppose that during May, the company quarried and shipped to its processing plant 288 tons of rock from its quarry and at the end of the month 15 tons remained in process, on average 20 per cent complete. The cost of rocks from the quarry for the last 5 months has been $120 per ton, so the cost of the limestone rock put into Process 3 is $120/ton times 288 tons, or $34,560. Labour and overhead cost during May in the rock crushing process were $35,880. Assume there was no work in process at the beginning of May.

1 Compute the cost of crushed rock processed and transferred out in May.

2 Compute the cost of the work in process inventory at the end of May.

SOLUTION

Flow of production	(Step 1) Physical units (tons)	(Step 2) Equivalent units in tons	
		Direct materials	conversion
Started and completed	273	273	273
Ending work in process	15	15*	3*
Units accounted for	288		
Work done to date		288	276

*15 × 100% = 15; 15 × 20% = 3.

	Total costs	Details	
		Limestone rock	Conversion costs
(Step 3) Costs to account for	$ 70,440	$ 34,650	$ 35,880
(Step 4) Divide by equivalent units		÷ 288	÷ 276
Unit costs	$ 250.00*	$120.00	$130.00
(Step 5) Application of costs			
To units completed and transferred, 273 tons at $250.00	$ 68,250		
To ending work in process, 15 tons			
Direct materials	$ 1,800	15 × $120.00	
Conversion costs	390		3 × $130.00
Work in process, ending inventory	$ 2,190		
Total costs accounted for	$70, 440		

* Cost per ton ($250) = limestone rock costs ($120) + conversion costs ($130).

Effects of beginning inventories

Objective 8
Demonstrate how the presence of beginning inventories affects the computation of unit costs under the weighted-average method.

So far, our example has been very straightforward because all units were started during the period. In other words, there were no units in beginning inventory. The presence of units in beginning inventory actually complicates matters a great deal.

There are several ways to deal with beginning inventories, but we will describe only the most popular alternative, the weighted-average method. In the next two sections, we will explore this method using the following data from our Oakville example for the month of May. Recall that the ending WIP inventory for April in the forming department was 5,000 units. These units become the beginning inventory for May.

Units

    Work in process, April 30: 5,000 units; 100% completed for materials, but only 40% completed for conversion costs
    Units started in May: 26,000
    Units completed in May: 24,000
    Work in process, May 31: 7,000 units; 100% completed for materials, but only 60% completed for conversion costs

Costs

Work in process, April 30		
Direct materials	€15,000	
Conversion costs	5,000	€ 20,000
Direct materials added during May		84,200
Conversion costs added during May		62,680
Total costs to account for		€166,880*

* Note that the €166,880 total costs to account for include the €20,000 of beginning inventory in addition to the €146,880 added during May.

▪ Weighted-average method

The **weighted-average (WA) process-costing method** determines total costs by adding together the cost of (1) all work done in the current period and (2) the work done in the preceding period on the current period's beginning inventory of work in process. Then, you divide this total cost by the total equivalent units of work done to date, whether that work was done in the current or previous period.

Why do we use the term *weighted-average* to describe this method? Primarily because the unit costs used for applying costs to products are based on the total cost incurred to date, regardless of whether the department incurred those costs in the current period or in the prior period. If costs of materials, labour or overhead changed across periods, essentially the weighted-average method reweights these comingled costs to determine revised unit cost.

Exhibit 14.9 shows the first two steps in this process-costing method, computation of physical units and equivalent units. The computation of equivalent units ignores where the 31,000 units to account for came from, either beginning work in process or those started in May. Exhibit 14.10 presents a production-cost report, summarising steps 3–5 regarding computations of unit product costs and the resulting cost allocations to inventory accounts.

Flow of production	(Step 1) physical units	(Step 2) equivalent units	
		Direct materials	Conversion
Work in process, April 30	5,000 (40%)[a]		
Started in May	26,000		
To account for	31,000		
Completed and transferred out during current period	24,000	24,000	24,000
Work in process, May 31	7,000 (60%)[a]	7,000	4,200[b]
Units accounted for	31,000		
Work done to date		31,000	28,200

[a]Degrees of completion for conversion costs at the dates of inventories.
[b]$60 \times 7,000 = 4,200.$

Exhibit 14.9 Forming department output in equivalent units, weighted-average method – month ended 31 May 20X0

		Totals	Details	
			Direct materials	Conversion costs
(Step 3)	Work in process, April 30	€ 20,000	€15,000	€ 5,000
	Costs added currently	146,880	84,200	62,680
	Total costs to account for	€166,880	€99,200	€ 67,680
(Step 4)	Divisor, equivalent units for work done to date*		÷ 31,000	÷ 28,200
	Unit costs (weighted averages)	€ 5.60	€ 3.20	€ 2.40
(Step 5)	Application of costs			
	Completed and transferred, 24,000 units (€5.60)	€134,400		
	Work in process, May 31, 7,000 units			
	Direct materials	€ 22,400	7,000 (€3.20)	
	Conversion costs	10,080		4,200* (€2.40)
	Total work in process	€ 32,480		
	Total costs accounted for	€166,880		

* Equivalent units of work done. For more details, see Exhibit 14.9.

Exhibit 14.10 Forming department production-cost report, weighted-average method – month ended 31 May 20X0

◼ Transferred-in costs

Many companies that use process costing have sequential production processes. For example, Oakville Wooden Toys transfers the items completed in its forming department to the finishing department. The finishing department would label the costs of the items it receives from the forming department **transferred-in costs** – costs incurred in a previous department for items that have been received by a subsequent department. They are similar to, but not identical to, additional direct-materials costs incurred in the finishing department. Because transferred-in costs are a combination of all types of costs (direct-materials and conversion costs) incurred in previous departments, they should not be called a direct-materials cost in the finishing department.

We account for transferred-in costs just as we account for direct materials that the finishing department adds at the beginning of its process, with one exception: We keep transferred-in costs separate from the direct materials added in the department. Therefore, Exhibit 14.10 includes three columns of costs instead of two: transferred-in costs, direct-materials costs and conversion costs. The total unit cost will be the sum of all three types of unit costs. For an interesting look at how one major snack food company designed its costing system with numerous transferred-in costs, see the 'Business first' box below.

BUSINESS FIRST
Process costing at a snack peanut company

One of the leading producers of snack peanuts is Planters Specialty Products Company, an operating unit of Kraft Foods. Planters markets regular-roast, dry-roast, salted and unsalted peanuts. Processing a peanut snack food involves several activities. Most snack peanuts are blanched (removing the skins) before roasting. Peanuts can be oil-roasted or dry-roasted before being packaged and shipped.

The major activities in the processing of peanuts are shown next. This system not only tracks transferred-in costs between operating departments, such as the 'blanching and frying department' and the 'packing and shipping department,' it also tracks these costs for support (services) departments, such as receiving, moving and storing activities within the overall process costing sequence. This is because Planters incorporates ABC concepts within its process costing environment, designing a system that focuses on tracking and reporting costs by key activities within the system, regardless of traditional operating versus support department boundaries.

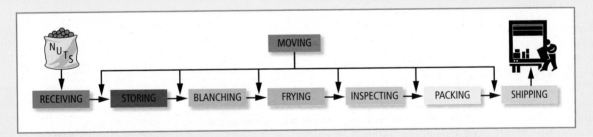

Summary problem for your review

PROBLEM

Consider the cooking department of Middleton Foods, a British food-processing company. Compute the cost of work completed and the cost of the ending inventory of work in process using the weighted-average method.

Units

Beginning work in process: 5,000 units; 100% completed for materials, 40% completed for conversion costs

Started during month: 28,000 units

Completed during month: 31,000 units

Ending work in process: 2,000 units; 100% completed for materials, 50% for conversion costs

Costs

Beginning work in process		
Direct materials	£8,060	
Conversion costs	1,300	£ 9,360
Direct materials added in current month		41,440
Conversion costs added in current month		14,700
Total costs to account for		£65,500

SOLUTION

		(Step 2) equivalent units	
Flow of production	(Step 1) physical units	Material	Conversion
Completed and transferred out	31,000	31,000	31,000
Ending work in process	2,000	2,000*	1000*
Equivalent units	33,000	33,000	32,000

* $2,000 \times 100\% = 2,000$; $2,000 \times 50\% = 1,000$.

Weighted-average method	Total cost	Direct materials	Conversion costs
Beginning work in process	£ 9,360	£ 8,060	£ 1,300
Costs added currently	56,140	41,440	14,700
Total costs to account for	£65,500	£49,500	£16,000
Equivalent units, weighted-average		÷ 33,000	÷ 32,000
Unit costs, weighted-average	£ 2.00	£ 1.50	£ 0.50
Transferred out, 31,000 × £2.00	£62,000		
Ending work in process			
Direct materials	£ 3,000	2,000 (£1.50)	
Conversion cost	500		1,000 (£.50)
Total work in process	£ 3,500		
Total costs accounted for	£65,500		

Process costing in a JIT system: backflush costing

Objective 9
Use backflush costing with a JIT production system.

Tracking costs through various stages of inventory – raw material, work in process inventory for each process (or department) and finished-goods inventory – makes accounting systems complex. If there were no inventories, we could charge all costs directly to cost of goods sold and accounting systems would be much simpler. Organisations using JIT production systems usually have very small inventories or no inventories at all. For them, a traditional accounting system that traces costs through several different types of inventories may be inappropriate or of limited value. Companies that use the JIT production system generally have very low inventory levels and uses **backflush costing**, an accounting system that applies costs to products only when the production is complete. How does backflush costing work? As we shall see, it is a fairly simple costing system.

■ Principles of backflush costing

Backflush costing has only two categories of costs: materials and conversion costs. Its unique feature is an absence of a WIP account. Accountants enter actual material costs into a materials inventory account and they enter actual labour and overhead costs into a conversion costs account. They then transfer costs from these two temporary accounts directly into finished-goods inventories. Some backflush systems even eliminate the finished-goods inventory accounts and transfer costs directly to cost of goods sold, especially if the company does not have a finished-goods inventory but rather sells products before producing them so that it can ship them immediately upon completion. Backflush systems assume that the company completes production so soon after the application of conversion activities that balances in the conversion costs accounts remain near zero as it transfers costs out almost immediately after initially recording them.

■ Example of backflush costing

Sevilia Technology Innovations (STI) produces speakers for luxury car stereo systems. STI recently introduced a JIT production system and backflush costing. Consider the July production for speaker model AX27. The standard material cost per unit of AX27 is €14 and the standard unit conversion cost is €21. During July, STI purchased materials for €5,600, incurred conversion costs of €8,400 (which included all labour costs and manufacturing overhead) and produced and sold 400 units of AX27.

Backflush costing is accomplished in three steps:

1 *Record actual materials and conversion costs.* For simplicity, we initially assume that actual materials and conversion costs were identical to the standard costs. As a company purchases materials, backflush systems add their cost to the materials inventory account:

Materials inventory... 5,600
    Accounts payable (or cash)... 5,600
To record material purchases.

Similarly, we add direct labour and manufacturing overhead costs to the Conversion Costs account when the company incurs them:

Conversion costs... 8,400
    Accrued wages and other accounts............................... 8,400
To record conversion costs incurred.

2 *Apply costs to completed units*. When production is complete, we transfer the costs from Materials Inventory and Conversion Costs accounts to Finished-Goods Inventory, based on the number of units completed and the standard cost of each unit:

Finished-Goods Inventory (400 × €35)........ 14,000
  Materials Inventory.. 5,600
  Conversion Costs.. 8,400
To record costs of completed production.

Because of short production cycle times, there is little lag between additions to the conversion costs account and transfers to finished-goods inventory. The conversion costs account, therefore, remains near zero.

3 *Record cost of goods sold during the period*. We transfer the standard cost of the items sold from finished-goods inventory to cost of goods sold:

Cost of Goods Sold.................................... 14,000
  Finished-Goods Inventory.. 14,000
To record cost of 400 units sold at €35 per unit.

Suppose the company immediately delivers completed units to customers so that finished goods inventories are negligible. We can combine steps 2 and 3 to eliminate the finished-goods inventory account:

Cost of Goods Sold.................................... 14,000
  Material Inventory.. 5,600
  Conversion Costs.. 8,400

What if actual costs added to the conversion costs account do not equal the standard amounts that are transferred to finished-goods inventory? We treat the variances like overapplied or underapplied overhead. Backflush systems assume that account balances for conversion costs are approximately zero at all times. Thus, we charge any remaining balance in the account at the end of an accounting period to cost of goods sold. Suppose actual conversion costs for July had been €8,600 and the amount transferred to finished goods (that is, applied to the product) was €8,400. We would write off the €200 balance in the conversion costs account to cost of goods sold at the end of the month:

Cost of Goods Sold... 200
  Conversion Costs.. 8,400
To recognise underapplied conversion costs.

Summary problem for your review

PROBLEM

The most extreme (and simplest) version of backflush costing makes product costing entries at only one point. Suppose STI had no Materials Inventory account (in addition to no WIP Inventory account). It purchases materials only when it needs them for production. Therefore, STI enters both materials and conversion costs directly into its Finished-Goods Inventory account.

Prepare journal entries (without explanations) and T-accounts for July's production of 400 units. As given earlier, materials purchases totalled €5,600, and conversion costs were €8,400. Why might a company use this extreme type of backflush costing?

SOLUTION

In one step, material and conversion costs are applied to finished goods inventories:

```
Finished-Goods Inventories......................... 14,000
     Accounts Payable........................................................ 5,600
     Wages Payable and Other Accounts.............................. 8,400
```

Finished goods inventories		Accounts payable, wages payable and other accounts	
Materials	5,600		5,600
Conversion costs	8,400		8,400

This example shows that backflush costing is simple and inexpensive. Backflush costing provides reasonably accurate product costs if (1) materials inventories are low (most likely because of JIT delivery schedules), and (2) production cycle times are short, so that at any time a company has incurred only inconsequential amounts of materials costs and conversion costs for products that have yet to be completed.

Highlights to remember

1 **Distinguish between job-order costing and process costing.** Product costing is an averaging process. Process costing deals with broad averages and large volumes of homogeneous units. Job-order costing deals with narrow averages and unique units or a small batch of similar units.

2 **Prepare summary journal entries for the typical transactions of a job-costing system.** The focus of journal entries in a job-order costing system is on inventory accounts. The WIP Inventory account receives central attention. Direct materials used, direct labour and factory overhead applied are accumulated in WIP. In turn, the cost of completed goods is transferred from WIP to Finished Goods.

3 **Use an ABC system in a job-order environment.** ABC can be used for any type of business that has significant levels of shared resources. In a job-order system, ABC helps managers understand the cost structure of the business on a job-by-job basis. Overhead costs are assigned to activity centres and then to jobs based on appropriate cost drivers. ABM uses ABC information and the increased understanding of the organisation's cost structure to control and reduce overhead costs.

4 **Show how service organisations use job costing.** The job-costing approach is used in nonmanufacturing as well as in manufacturing. Examples include costs of services such as auto repair, consulting and auditing. For example, the job order is a key device for planning and controlling an audit engagement by a public accounting firm.

5 **Explain the basic ideas underlying process costing and how they differ from job costing.** Process costing is used for inventory costing when there is continuous mass production of homogeneous units. Process-cost systems accumulate costs by department (or process); each department has its own WIP account. Job-order cost systems differ because costs are accumulated and tracked by the individual job order.

6 **Compute output in terms of equivalent units.** The key concept in process costing is that of equivalent units, the number of fully completed units that could have been produced from the inputs applied.

7 **Compute costs and prepare journal entries for the principal transactions in a process-costing system.** There are five basic steps to process costing:
1 Summarise the flow of physical units.
2 Calculate output in terms of equivalent units.
3 Summarise the total costs to account for.
4 Calculate unit costs (step 3 ÷ step 2).
5 Apply costs to units completed and to units in the ending work in process.

Steps 3 and 5 provide the data for journal entries. These entries all involve the WIP accounts for the various departments (processes) producing products.

8 **Demonstrate how the presence of beginning inventories affects the computation of unit costs under the weighted-average method.** Process costing is complicated by the presence of beginning inventories. The weighted-average method calculates a unit cost that includes the work done in previous periods on the current period's beginning inventory with work done in the current period.

9 **Use backflush costing with a JIT production system.** Many companies with JIT production systems use backflush costing. Such systems have no WIP inventory account and apply costs to products only after the production process is complete.

Accounting vocabulary

backflush costing, p. 655
equivalent units, p. 647
hybrid costing systems, p. 631
job costing, p. 631
job-cost record, p. 631
job-cost sheet, p. 631

job order, p. 631
job-order costing, p. 631
labour time tickets, p. 631
materials requisitions, p. 631
process costing, p. 631
time cards, p. 631

transferred-in costs, p. 652
weighted-average (WA)
process-costing method,
p. 651

Fundamental assignment material   MyAccountingLab

14.A1 Job-order costing, basic journal entries

The following data (in thousands) summarise the factory operations of the Smothers Manufacturing Company for the year 20X1, its first year in business:

(a)	Direct materials purchased for cash		€360
(b)	Direct materials issued and used		325
(c)	Labour used directly on production		130
(d1)	Indirect labour		90
(d2)	Depreciation of plant and equipment		50
(d3)	Miscellaneous factory overhead (ordinarily would be detailed)		40
(e)	Overhead applied: 180% of direct labour		?
(f)	Cost of production completed		625
(g)	Cost of goods sold		425

1 Prepare summary journal entries. Omit explanations. For purposes of this problem, combine the items in part d as 'overhead incurred'.

2 Show the T-accounts for all inventories, cost of goods sold and factory department overhead control. Compute the ending balances of the inventories. Do not adjust for underapplied or over-applied factory overhead.

14.A2 Weighted-average process-costing method

The Magnatto Company manufactures electric drills. Material is introduced at the beginning of the process in the assembly department. Conversion costs are applied uniformly throughout the process. As the process is completed, goods are immediately transferred to the finishing department.

Data for the assembly department for the month of July 20X1 follow:

Work in process, 30 June: €175,500 (consisting of €138,000 materials and €37,500 conversion costs); 100% completed for direct materials, but only 25% completed for conversion costs	10,000 units
Units started during July	80,000 units
Units completed during July	70,000 units
Work in process, 31 July: 100% completed for direct materials, but only 50% completed for conversion costs	20,000 units
Direct materials added during July	€852,000
Conversion costs added during July	€634,500

1 Compute the total cost of goods transferred out of the assembly department during July.

2 Compute the total costs of the ending work in process. Prepare a production-cost report or a similar orderly tabulation of your work. Assume weighted-average product costing. (For journal entries, see Exercise 14.37.)

14.A3 Backflush costing

Digital Controls makes electronic thermostats for homes and offices. The KC Division makes one product, Autotherm, which has a standard cost of €36, consisting of €20 of materials and €16 of conversion costs. In January, actual purchases of materials totalled €45,000, labour payroll costs were €10,000, and manufacturing overhead was €20,000. Completed output was 2,000 units.

The KC Division uses a backflush-costing system that records costs in materials inventory and conversion costs accounts and applies costs to products at the time production is completed. There were no finished goods inventories on 1 January and 20 units on 31 January.

1 Prepare journal entries (without explanations) to record January's costs for the KC Division. Include the purchase of materials, incurrence of labour and manufacturing overhead costs, application of product costs and recognition of cost of goods sold.

2 Suppose January's actual manufacturing overhead costs had been €24,000 instead of €20,000. Prepare the journal entry to recognise underapplied conversion costs at the end of January.

14.B1 Job-order costing, basic journal entries

Consider the following data for Cambridge Printing Company (in thousands):

Inventories, 31 December 20X8	
Direct materials	£ 22
Work in process	27
Finished goods	102

Summarised transactions for 20X9 are as follows:

(a)	Purchases of direct materials	£109
(b)	Direct materials used	90
(c)	Direct labour	140
(d)	Factory overhead incurred	92
(e)	Factory overhead applied, 80% of direct labour	?
(f)	Cost of goods completed and transferred to finished goods	275
(g)	Cost of goods sold	350
(h)	Sales on account	620

1 Prepare summary journal entries for 20X9 transactions. Omit explanations.

2 Show the T-accounts for all inventories, cost of goods sold and factory department overhead control. Compute the ending balances of the inventories. Do not adjust for underapplied or over-applied factory overhead.

14.B2 Basic process costing

Hassan Company produces digital watches in large quantities. The manufacturing costs of the assembly department were as follows:

Direct materials added		€1,750,000
Conversion costs		
Direct labour	€550,000	
Factory overhead	137,500	687,500
Assembly costs to account for		€2,437,500

For simplicity, assume that this is a two-department company, assembly and finishing. There was no beginning work in process.

Suppose 700,000 units were started in the assembly department. There were 400,000 units completed and transferred to the finishing department. The 300,000 units in ending work in process were fully completed regarding direct materials but half-completed regarding conversion costs.

1 Compute the equivalent units and unit costs in the assembly department.

2 Compute the costs of units completed and transferred to the finishing department. Also compute the cost of the ending work in process in the assembly department. (For journal entries, see Exercise 14.34.)

14.B3 Weighted-average process-costing method

The Rainbow Paint Company uses a process-costing system. Materials are added at the beginning of a particular process and conversion costs are incurred uniformly. Work in process at the beginning of the month is 40 per cent complete, while at the end it is 20 per cent complete. One litre of material makes one litre of product. Data follow:

Beginning inventory	600 litre
Direct materials added	8,200 litre
Ending inventory	1,000 litre
Conversion costs incurred	€25,800
Cost of direct materials added	€55,700
Conversion costs, beginning inventory	€ 2,200
Cost of direct materials, beginning inventory	€ 3,700

Use the weighted-average method. Prepare a schedule of output in equivalent units and a schedule of application of costs to products. Show the cost of goods completed and cost of ending work in process. (For journal entries, see Exercise 14.36.)

14.B4 Backflush costing

Audio Components recently installed a backflush-costing system. One department makes 10 cm speakers with a standard cost as follows:

Materials	€ 9.60
Conversion costs	5.40
Total	€15.00

Speakers are scheduled for production only after orders are received and products are shipped to customers immediately on completion. Therefore, no finished goods inventories are kept and product costs are applied directly to cost of goods sold.

In October, 1,600 speakers were produced and shipped to customers. Materials were purchased at a cost of €16,200, and actual conversion costs (labour plus manufacturing overhead) of €6,800 were recorded.

1 Prepare journal entries to record October's costs for the production of 10 cm speakers.

2 Suppose October's actual conversion costs had been €6,000 instead of €6,800. Prepare a journal entry to recognise overapplied conversion costs.

Additional assignment material   MyAccountingLab

QUESTIONS

14.1 'There are different product costs for different purposes.' Name at least two purposes.

14.2 Distinguish between job costing and process costing.

14.3 Describe the supporting details for work in process in a job-cost system.

14.4 What types of source documents provide information for job-cost records?

14.5 State three examples of service industries that use the job-costing approach.

14.6 'Law firms use job-costing to cost engagements. Thus, the markup required to cover overhead costs is not as great as in companies that use a process-costing system.' Do you agree? Explain.

14.7 Give three examples of industries where process-costing systems are probably used.

14.8 Give three examples of nonprofit organisations where process-costing systems are probably used.

14.9 'There are five key steps in process-cost accounting.' What are they?

14.10 Identify the major distinction between the first two and the final three steps of the five major steps in accounting for process costs.

14.11 Suppose a university has 10,000 full-time students and 5,000 half-time students. Using the concept of equivalent units, compute the number of 'full-time equivalent' students.

14.12 Present an equation that describes the physical flow in process costing when there are beginning inventories in work in process.

14.13 How are transferred-in costs similar to direct materials costs? How are they different?

14.14 Explain what happens in a backflush-costing system when the amount of actual conversion cost in a period exceeds the amount applied to the products completed during that period.

CRITICAL THINKING EXERCISES

14.15 Purposes of accumulating job costs

'Job costs are accumulated for purposes of inventory valuation and income determination.' State two other purposes.

14.16 Job-order compared to process costing

'The basic distinction between job-order costing and process costing is the breadth of the denominator.' Explain.

14.17 Cost allocation in service firms

'Service firms trace only direct-labour costs to jobs. All other costs are applied as a percentage of direct-labour cost.' Do you agree? Explain.

14.18 Purpose of product costing in a process production environment

All product costing uses averages to determine costs per unit of product produced. In job-order production systems, the averages are based on a relatively small number of units. In a process production environment, the number of units is much larger. Once the average unit cost is determined, what is the central product-costing problem in process costing?

14.19 Process costing in a JIT environment

Companies using JIT production systems usually have very small inventories or no inventories at all. As a result, a traditional accounting system may be inappropriate. Many of these companies have adopted backflush-costing systems. Do backflush-costing systems work only for companies using a JIT production system? Explain.

EXERCISES

14.20 Job costing in business sectors

Job costing systems are used in all business sectors. For each example listed, indicate whether the company is in the manufacturing, merchandising or service sector:
- (a) Audit engagements by Ernst & Young
- (b) Advertising new products by Target
- (c) Assembly of desktop computers by Dell
- (d) Consulting engagement by McKinsey & Co.

14.21 Direct materials

For each of the following independent cases, fill in the blanks (in millions of euros):

	1	2	3	4
Direct-materials inventory, 31 December 20X0	8	8	5	—
Purchased	5	9	—	8
Used	7	—	7	3
Direct-materials inventory, 31 December 20X1	—	6	8	7

14.22 Use of WIP inventory account

April production resulted in the following activity in a key account of Cheung Casting Company (in thousands):

WIP inventory	
1 April balance	12
Direct materials used	50
Direct labour charged to jobs	25
Factory overhead applied to jobs	55

Job orders A13 and A37, with total costs of €72,000 and €56,000, respectively, were completed in April.

1 Journalise the completed production for April.
2 Compute the balance in WIP inventory, 30 April after recording the completed production.
3 Journalise the credit sale of Job A13 for €101,000.

14.23 Job-cost record

Manchester University uses job-cost records for various research projects. A major reason for such records is to justify requests for reimbursement of costs on projects sponsored by the federal government.

Consider the following summarised data regarding a cancer research project in the Medical School:

- 5 January   Direct materials, various medical supplies, £925
- 7 January   Direct materials, various chemicals, £780
- 5–12 January   Direct labour, research associates, 120 hours
- 7–12 January   Direct labour, research assistants, 180 hours

Research associates receive £32 per hour, while assistants receive £19. The overhead rate is 70 per cent of direct-labour cost.

Sketch a job-cost record. Post all the data to the project-cost record. Compute the total cost of the project through 12 January.

14.24 Analysis of job-cost data

Job-cost records for Ganz Construction contained the following data:

	Dates			
Job no.	Started	Finished	Sold	Total cost of job at 31 May
1	9 April	14 May	15 May	€4,200
2	26 April	22 May	25 May	7,600
3	2 May	6 June	8 June	6,300
4	9 May	29 May	5 June	8,300
5	14 May	14 June	16 June	4,700

Compute Ganz's (1) WIP inventory at 31 May, (2) Finished-goods inventory at 31 May and (3) Cost of goods sold for May.

14.25 Analysis of job-cost data

The Cabrillo Construction Company constructs houses on speculation. That is, the houses are started before any buyer is known. Even if the buyer agrees to purchase a house under construction, no sales are recorded until the house is completed and accepted for delivery. The job-cost records contained the following (in thousands):

	Dates			Total cost of job at	Total construction cost
Job No.	Started	Finished	Sold	30 September	added in October
43	4/26	9/7	9/8	€180	
51	5/17	9/14	9/17	170	
52	5/20	9/30	10/4	150	
53	5/28	10/14	10/18	200	$50
61	6/3	10/20	11/24	115	20
62	6/9	10/21	10/27	180	25
71	7/7	11/6	11/22	118	36
81	8/7	11/24	12/24	106	48

1 Compute Cabrillo's cost of (a) construction-in-process inventory at 30 September and 31 October, (b) finished-houses inventory at 30 September and 31 October and (c) cost of houses sold for September and October.

2 Prepare summary journal entries for the transfer of completed houses from construction in process to finished houses for September and October.

3 Record the cash sale (price = €345,000) and the cost of the house sold for Job 53.

14.26 Discovery of unknowns

DeMond Chemicals has the following balances (in millions) on 31 December, 20X1:

Factory overhead applied	€450
Cost of goods sold	900
Factory overhead incurred	415
Direct-materials inventory	30
Finished-goods inventory	180
WIP inventory	140

The cost of goods completed was €880. The cost of direct materials requisitioned for production during 20X1 was €210. The cost of direct materials purchased was €225. Factory overhead was applied to production at a rate of 150 per cent of direct-labour cost.

Compute the beginning inventory balances of direct materials, WIP and finished goods. Make these computations before considering any possible adjustments for overapplied or underapplied overhead.

14.27 Discovery of unknowns

The Ramakrishnan Manufacturing Company has the following balances (in millions) as of 31 December 20X1:

WIP inventory	€ 14
Finished-goods inventory	175
Direct-materials inventory	65
Factory overhead incurred	180
Factory overhead applied at 150% of direct-labour cost	150
Cost of goods sold	350

The cost of direct materials purchased during 20X1 was €275. The cost of direct materials requisitioned for production during 20X1 was €235. The cost of goods completed was €493, all in millions.

Before considering any year-end adjustments for overapplied or underapplied overhead, compute the beginning inventory balances of direct materials, WIP and finished goods.

14.28 Relationships among overhead items

Fill in the unknowns:

	Case A	Case B	Case C
Budgeted factory overhead	€3,600,000	$?	€1,500,000
Budgeted cost drivers			
Direct-labour cost	€2,000,000		
Direct-labour hours		450,000	
Machine hours			250,000
Overhead application rate	?	$ 5	?

14.29 Process costing in business sectors

Process-costing systems are used in all business sectors. For each example listed, indicate whether the company is in the manufacturing or service sector.

(a) Beverage bottling at Coca-Cola.

(b) Postal delivery of mail by the UK Post Office.

(c) Limestone production at Nally & Gibson.

(d) Processing a life insurance application by Aviva.

14.30 Process map and process costing

Refer to Exhibit 14.5, panel B, on p. 644 Identify an example of (1) a transferred-in cost, (2) a variable-cost resource, (3) a direct fixed-cost resource, and (4) an indirect resource cost for the process-costing system.

14.31 Equivalent

Confirm your understanding of the equivalent units concept by computing the equivalent units for material, direct labour and overhead for the following hypothetical case at Nally & Gibson (refer to Exhibit 14.6).

In Process 3 – crush and screen limestone rock – 400 tons of limestone rock were transported to the plant during March. There was no beginning inventory of rock. During March, 320 tons were crushed, screened and stocked. At the end of March, 80 tons of rock were 40 per cent crushed and screened. Direct labour and overhead are incurred evenly during the crushing and screening process.

14.32 Basic process costing

A department of Jamestown Textiles produces cotton fabric. All direct materials are introduced at the start of the process. Conversion costs are incurred uniformly throughout the process.

In April, there was no beginning inventory. Units started, completed and transferred were 650,000. Units in process on 30 April were 220,000. Each unit in ending work in process was 60 per cent converted. Costs incurred during April were direct materials at €3,654,000 and conversion costs at €860,200.

1 Compute the total work done in equivalent units and the unit cost for April.

2 Compute the cost of units completed and transferred. Also, compute the cost of units in ending work in process.

14.33 Uneven flow

One department of Siena Instruments Company manufactures basic handheld calculators. Several materials are added at various stages of the process. The outer front shell and the carrying case, which represent 10 per cent of the total materials cost, are added at the final step of the assembly process. All other materials are considered to be 'in process' by the time the calculator reaches a 50 per cent stage of completion.

During 20X0, 74,000 calculators were started in production. At year-end, 6,000 calculators were in various stages of completion, but all of them were beyond the 50 per cent stage and, on the average, they were regarded as being 70 per cent completed.

The following costs were incurred during the year: direct materials, €205,520; conversion costs, €397,100. There was no beginning WIP inventory.

1 Prepare a schedule of physical units and equivalent units.

2 Tabulate the unit costs, cost of goods completed, and cost of ending work in process.

14.34 Journal entries

Refer to the in problem 14.B2. Prepare summary journal entries for the use of direct materials, direct labour and factory overhead applied. Also prepare a journal entry for the transfer of goods completed and transferred. Show the posting to the WIP – assembly department account.

14.35 Compute equivalent units

Consider the following data for 20X1:

	Physical units
Started in 20X1	90,000
Completed in 20X1	80,000
Ending inventory, work in process	40,000
Beginning inventory, work in process	30,000

The beginning inventory was 80 per cent complete regarding direct materials and 40 per cent complete regarding conversion costs. The ending inventory was 20 per cent complete regarding direct materials and 10 per cent complete regarding conversion costs.

Prepare a schedule of equivalent units for the work done to date.

14.36 Journal entries

Refer to the data in problem 14.B3. Prepare summary journal entries for the use of direct materials and conversion costs. Also, prepare a journal entry for the transfer of goods completed, assuming that the goods are transferred to another department.

14.37 Journal entries

Refer to the data in problem 14.A2. Prepare summary journal entries for the use of direct materials and conversion costs. Also, prepare a journal entry for the transfer of the goods completed and transferred from the assembly department to the finishing department.

PROBLEMS

14.38 Relationships of manufacturing costs

Selected data concerning the past fiscal year's operations of the Woodson Manufacturing Company are as follows (in thousands):

	Inventories	
	Beginning	Ending
Raw materials	€ 70	€ 90
WIP	75	35
Finished goods	100	120
Other data:		
Raw materials used		€ 468
Total manufacturing costs charged to production during the year (includes raw materials, direct labour, and factory overhead applied at a rate of 80% of direct-labour cost)		864
Selling and general expenses		50

Answer each of the following items:

1 Compute the cost of raw materials purchased during the year.

2 Compute the direct-labour costs charged to production during the year.

3 Compute the cost of goods available for sale during the year.

4 Compute the cost of goods sold during the year.

14.39 Relationship of subsidiary and general ledgers, journal entries

The following summarised data are available on three job-cost records of Red Lake Manufacturing Company, a producer of packaging equipment:

	Job 412		Job 413		Job 414
	April	May	April	May	May
Direct materials	€9,000	€2,500	€12,000	–	€13,000
Direct labour	4,000	1,500	5,000	2,500	2,000
Factory overhead applied	8,000	?	10,000	?	?

The company's fiscal year ends on 31 May. Factory overhead is applied as a percentage of direct-labour costs. The balances in selected accounts on 30 April were as follows: direct-materials inventory, €19,000; finished-goods inventory, €18,000.

Job 412 was completed during May and transferred to finished goods. Job 413 was still in process at the end of May, as was Job 414, which had started May 24. These were the only jobs worked on during April and May.

Job 412 was sold, along with other finished goods, by May 30. The total cost of goods sold during May was €33,000. The balance in Cost of Goods Sold for sales through April 30 was €450,000.

1 Prepare a schedule showing the balance of the WIP Inventory for 30 April. This schedule should show the total costs of each job record. Taken together, the job-cost records are the subsidiary ledger supporting the general ledger balance of work in process.

2 What is the overhead application rate?

3 Prepare summary general journal entries for all costs added to WIP during May. Also prepare entries for all costs transferred from WIP to Finished Goods and from Finished Goods to Cost of Goods Sold. Post to the appropriate T-accounts.

4 Prepare a schedule showing the balance of the WIP Inventory, 31 May.

14.40 Job costing in a consulting firm

Lubbock Engineering Consultants is a firm of professional civil engineers. It mostly does surveying jobs for the heavy construction industry throughout Spain. The firm obtains its jobs by giving fixed-price quotations, so profitability depends on the ability to predict the time required for the various subtasks on the job. (This situation is similar to that in the auditing profession, where times are budgeted for such audit steps as reconciling cash and confirming accounts receivable.)

A client may be served by various professional staff members who hold positions in the hierarchy from partners to managers to senior engineers to assistants. In addition, there are secretaries and other employees.

Lubbock Engineering has the following budget for 20X1:

Compensation of professional staff	€3,600,000
Other costs	1,449,000
Total budgeted costs	€5,049,000

Each professional staff member must submit a weekly time report, which is used for charging hours to a client job-order record. The time report has seven columns, one for each day of the week. Its rows are as follows:

– Chargeable hours
    Client 156
    Client 183
    etc.
– Nonchargeable hours
    Attending seminar on new equipment
    Unassigned time
    etc.

In turn, these time reports are used for charging hours and costs to the client job-order records. The managing partner regards these job records as absolutely essential for measuring the profitability of various jobs and for providing an 'experience base for improving predictions on future jobs.'

1 This firm applies overhead to jobs at a budgeted percentage of the professional compensation charged directly to the job ('direct labour'). For all categories of professional personnel, chargeable hours average 85 per cent of available hours. Nonchargeable hours are regarded as additional overhead. What is the overhead rate as a percentage of 'direct labour', the chargeable professional compensation cost?

2 A senior engineer works 48 weeks per year, 40 hours per week. His compensation is €60,000. He has worked on two jobs during the past week, devoting 10 hours to Job 156 and 30 hours to Job 183. How much cost should be charged to Job 156 because of his work there?

14.41 Weighted-average process costing at Nally & Gibson

Nally & Gibson produces crushed limestone, among other products, used in highway construction. To produce the crushed limestone, the company starts with limestone rocks from its quarry in Georgetown, Kentucky and puts the rocks through a crushing process. Suppose that on 1 May, Nally & Gibson has 24 tons of rock (75 per cent complete) in the crushing process. The cost of that beginning WIP inventory was $6,000. During May, the company added 288 tons of rock from its quarry and at the end of the month 15 tons remained in process, on average one-third complete. The cost of rocks from the quarry for the last 5 months has been $120 per ton. Labour and overhead cost during May in the rock-crushing process were $40,670. Nally & Gibson uses weighted-average process costing.

1 Compute the cost per ton of crushed rock for production in May.
2 Compute the cost of the WIP inventory at the end of May.
3 Suppose the flexible budget for labour and overhead was $16,000 plus $80 per ton. Evaluate the control of overhead and labour costs during May.

14.42 Two materials, basic process costing

The following data pertain to the blending department at Petro Chemicals for April:

Units	
Work in process, March 31	0
Units started	50,000
Completed and transferred to finishing department	40,000
Costs	
Materials	
Plastic compound	$450,000
Softening compound	$ 60,000
Conversion costs	$220,000

The plastic compound is introduced at the start of the process, while the softening compound is added when the product reaches an 80 per cent stage of completion. Conversion costs are incurred uniformly throughout the process.

The ending work in process is 40 per cent completed for conversion costs. None of the units in process reached the 80 per cent stage of completion.

1 Compute the equivalent units and unit costs for April.
2 Compute the total cost of units completed and transferred to finished goods. Also compute the cost of the ending work in process.

14.43 Materials and cartons in basic process costing

A Manchester, England, company manufactures and sells small portable digital voice recorders. Business is booming. Several materials are added at various stages in the assembly department. Costs are accounted for on a process-cost basis. The end of the process involves conducting a final inspection and adding a cardboard carton.

The final inspection requires 5 per cent of the total processing time. All units inspected during the period successfully passed inspection. All materials, besides the carton, are added by the time the recorders reach an 80 per cent stage of completion of conversion.

There were no beginning inventories. During 20X1, 150,000 recorders were started in production. At the end of the year, which was not a busy time, 5,000 recorders were in various stages of completion. All the ending units in work in process were at the 95 per cent stage. They awaited final inspection before being placed in cartons.

Total direct materials consumed in production, except for cartons, cost £2,250,000. Cartons used cost £319,000. Total conversion costs were £1,198,000.

1 Present a schedule of physical units, equivalent units and unit costs of direct materials, cartons and conversion costs.

2 Present a summary of the cost of goods completed and the cost of ending work in process.

14.44 Backflush costing

Adirondak manufactures a variety of measuring instruments. One product is an altimeter used by hikers and mountain climbers. Adirondak adopted a JIT viewpoint with an automated, computer-controlled, robotic production system. The company schedules production only after an order is received, materials and parts arrive just as they are needed, the production cycle time for altimeters is less than one day and completed units are packaged and shipped as part of the production cycle.

Adirondak's backflush-costing system has only three accounts related to production of altimeters: materials and parts inventory, conversion costs and finished-goods inventory. At the beginning of April (as at the beginning of every month), each of the three accounts had a balance of zero. Following are the April transactions related to the production of altimeters:

Materials and parts purchased	€287,000
Conversion costs incurred	€ 92,000
Altimeters produced	11,500 units

The budgeted (or standard) cost for one altimeter is €24 for materials and parts and €8 for conversion costs.

1 Prepare summary journal entries for the production of altimeters in April.

2 Compute the cost of goods sold for April. Explain any assumptions you make.

3 Suppose the actual conversion costs incurred during April were €95,000 instead of €92,000, and all other facts were as given. Prepare the additional journal entry that would be required at the end of April. Explain why the entry was necessary.

14.45 Review of Chapters 13 and 14

Tucson Co. uses normal absorption costing. Factory overhead is applied to production at a budgeted rate based on direct labour cost. At the end of the period, there are two unfinished jobs. Additional information is available as follows:

– Direct materials used = €50,000
– Direct labour = €100,000
– Beginning balance of work in process = €100,000
– Cost of goods manufactured = €150,000
– Finished goods beginning inventory = €140,000
– Finished goods ending inventory = €110,000
– Factory overhead is overapplied by €60,000
– Actual factory overhead = €90,000

Determine the following:

1 The cost of goods sold before disposition of overapplied overhead

2 Ending balance in WIP

3 Budgeted rate for applying factory overhead

4 Assuming the overapplied factory overhead is not prorated, what is adjusted cost of goods sold?

14.46 Review of Chapters 13 and 14

Clark Co. uses normal absorption job order costing. Factory overhead is applied to production at a budgeted rate of 300 per cent of prime costs (direct materials plus direct labour). Clark Co.'s policy is to not prorate any over- or underapplied overhead amounts. All inventory amounts listed next are after disposition of any over- or under-applied overhead:

- Direct labour = €100,000
- Beginning balance of stores (direct materials) = €20,000
- Ending balance of stores = €20,000
- Purchased €50,000 of direct materials during period
- Beginning balance of work in process = €300,000
- Ending balance of work in process = €300,000
- Cost of goods sold = €350,000
- Finished goods beg. inventory = €100,000
- Finished goods ending inventory = €200,000

Determine the following:

1 Direct materials used

2 Factory overhead applied

3 Cost of goods manufactured

4 Actual factory overhead for the period.

Recommended reading

The following section will aid readers who wish to pursue some topics in more depth than is possible in this book. There is a hazard in compiling a group of recommended reading. Inevitably, we will omit some worthwhile books or periodicals. Moreover, such a list cannot include books published subsequently to the compilation date. Although this list is not comprehensive, it includes much excellent reading.

■ Periodicals

Professional journals

The following professional journals are typically available in university libraries and include articles on the application of management accounting:

Accounting Horizons. Published by the American Accounting Association; stresses current practice-oriented articles in all areas of accounting.

CMA Management. Published by CMA Canada; includes much practice-oriented research in management accounting.

Cost Management. Published by Thompson Reuters; stresses cost management tools.

Financial Executive. Published by Financial Executives International; emphasises general policy issues for accounting and finance executives.

Financial Management. Published by the UK-based Chartered Institute of Management Accountants. Includes cutting-edge articles on management accounting practices and issues.

The Journal of Corporate Accounting & Finance. Published by Wiley; directed to corporate accounting and finance executives and outside auditors and accountants working for the corporation.

Harvard Business Review. Published by Harvard Business School; directed to general managers but contains excellent articles on applications of management accounting.

Journal of Accountancy. Published by the American Institute of CPAs; emphasises financial accounting and is directed at the practicing CPA.

Management Accounting Quarterly. An online journal published by the Institute of Management Accountants; practical articles with an academic focus.

Strategic Finance. Published by the Institute of Management Accountants; many articles on actual applications by individual organisations.

BusinessWeek, Forbes, Fortune, The Economist and the *Wall Street Journal.* Popular publications that cover a variety of business and economics topics; often their articles relate to management accounting.

Academic journals

Academic journals that focus most directly on current management and cost accounting research are the *Journal of Management Accounting Research, Management Accounting*

Research and the *Journal of Applied Management of Accounting Research*. *Accounting Review*, the general research publication of the American Accounting Association; *Journal of Accounting Research*, published at the University of Chicago; and *Contemporary Accounting Research*, published by the Canadian Academic Association, cover all accounting topics at a more theoretical level. *Accounting, Organizations and Society* publishes research on a variety of wider accounting research including behavioural aspects of management accounting. The *Journal of Accounting and Economics* covers economics-based accounting research. Equally, the *Review of Accounting Studies* is a top level journal publishing academic research in accounting. *Research on Professional Responsibility and Ethics in Accounting*, published by Emerald Group Publishing, is an annual journal devoted to ethical issues. The *European Accounting Review* also publishes scholarly accounting research.

Books on management accounting

Most of the topics in this text are covered in more detail in the many books on cost accounting, including *Management and Cost Accounting*, 5th edn, by A. Bhimani, C. T. Horngren, S. Datar and M. Rajan (Harlow: Prentice Hall, 2012). You can find more extensive management accounting coverage of managerial and strategic issues in *Strategic Finance* by A. Bhimani (London: Strategy Press, 2012). Current management accounting issues are also discussed in *Issues in Management Accounting* by Trevor Hopper, Robert W. Scapens and Deryl Northcott (Prentice Hall, 2007) and *Contemporary Issues in Management Accounting* by A. Bhimani (Oxford: Oxford University Press, 2006).

Handbooks, general and specialist texts and case books

The books in this list have wide application to management accounting issues. The handbooks are basic references. The textbooks are designed for classroom use but may be for individual study. The case books present applications from real companies.

Adkins, T. C., *Case Studies in Performance Management: A Guide from the Experts,* Hoboken, NJ: John Wiley & Sons, 2006.

Allen, B. R., E. R. Brownlee, M. E. Haskins, L. J. Lynch and J. W. Rotch, *Cases in Management Accounting and Control Systems,* 4th edn, Upper Saddle River, NJ: Prentice Hall, 2004.

Bhimani, A. *Management Accounting Manual,* ABG/ICAEW, 2001.

Bhimani, A. *Management Accounting in the Digital Economy,* Oxford University Press, 2003.

Bierman, H., Jr and S. Smidt, *The Capital Budgeting Decision: Economic Analysis of Investment Projects,* 9th edn, Routledge, 2006. This text expands the capital budgeting discussion from Chapter 11.

Groot, T. and K. Lukka (eds), *Cases in Management Accounting: Current Practices in European Companies,* Harlow: Prentice Hall/Pearson, 2000.

Hopwood, A. G., Unerman, J. and Fries, J. *Accounting for Sustainability,* Earthscan, 2010.

Innes, J., *Handbook of Management Accounting,* 3rd edn, London: CIMA, 2005.

Manning, G. A., *Financial Investigation and Forensic Accounting,* 3rd edn, Boca Raton, FL: CRC Press, 2005.

Pryor, T. *et al.,* *Activity Dictionary: A Comprehensive Reference Tool for ABM and ABC: 2000 Edition,* Arlington, TX: ICMS, Inc., 2000.

Seitz, N. and M. Ellison, *Capital Budgeting and Long-Term Financing Decisions,* Cincinnati, OH: South-Western, 2004.

Shank, J., *Strategic Cost Management: The New Tool for Competitive Advantage,* Free Press, 2008.

Young, S. M., *Readings in Management Accounting,* 5th edn, Upper Saddle River, NJ: Prentice Hall, 2007.

Accounting ethics

An increasing emphasis on ethics and accounting issues has led to a number of books devoted to the subject.

Brooks, L. J. and P. Dunn, *Business and Professional Ethics for Directors, Executives, & Accountants*, Mason, OH: South-Western, 2009.

Cheffers, M. L. and M. Pakaluk, *Understanding Accounting Ethics*, 2nd edn, Manchaug, MA: Allen David Press, 2007.

Duska, R. F. and B. S. Duska, *Accounting Ethics*, Malden, MA: Blackwell Publishing, 2003.

Mintz, S. M. and R. E. Morris, *Ethical Obligations and Decision Making in Accounting: Text and Cases*, New York: McGraw-Hill/Irwin, 2008.

The strategic nature of management accounting

Management accountants realise that cost and performance information is most useful to organizations when it helps define strategic alternatives and assists in the management of resources to achieve strategic objectives. The books in this list, though not necessarily accounting books, provide a valuable foundation to the interaction of strategy and accounting information.

Ansari, S. and J. Bell, *Target Costing: The Next Frontier in Strategic Cost Management*, Mountain Valley Publishing, 2009.

Bhimani, A., *Strategic Finance*, London: Strategy Press, 2012.

Bhimani, A. and M. Bromwich, *Management Accounting: Retrospect and Prospect*, London: CIMA Publishing, 2009.

Carr, L. and A. Nanni Jr, *Delivering Results: Managing What Matters*, Springer, 2009.

Grant, J. L., *Foundations of Economic Value Added*, 2nd edn, New York: Wiley, 2002.

Porter, M., *The Michael Porter Trilogy: Competitive Strategy, Competitive Advantage, the Competitive Advantage of Nations*, New York: The Free Press, 1998.

Small, P., *The Ultimate Game of Strategy: Establish Your Personal Niche in the World of e-Business*, Upper Saddle River, NJ: Prentice Hall, 2001.

Stern, J., J. Shiely and I. Ross, *The EVA Challenge: Implementing Value-Added Change in an Organization*, New York: Wiley, 2003.

Modern manufacturing

The following books provide background on the role of accounting in modern manufacturing environments.

Atkinson, A. A., R. S. Kaplan, S. M. Young and E. M. Matsumura, *Management Accounting*, 5th edn, Upper Saddle River, NJ: Prentice Hall, 2006.

Carriera, B., *Lean Manufacturing That Works: Powerful Tools for Dramatically Reducing Waste and Maximizing Profits*, New York: AMACOM, 2004.

Carreira, B. and B. Trudell, *Lean Six Sigma That Works: A Powerful Action Plan for Dramatically Improving Quality, Increasing Speed, and Reducing Waste*, New York: AMACOM, 2006.

Chase, R., N. Aquilano and F. R. Jacobs, *Operations Management for Competitive Advantage*, Homewood, IL: McGraw-Hill/Irwin, 2005.

Cooper, R. and R. Kaplan, *Design of Cost Management Systems*, 2nd edn, Upper Saddle River, NJ: Prentice Hall, 1999.

Goldratt, E. M., *Theory of Constraints*, Croton-on-Hudson, NY: North River Press, Inc., 2000.

Goldratt, E. M. and J. Cox, *The Goal*, 3rd edn, Croton-on-Hudson, NY: North River Press, 2004. This is a novel illustrating the new manufacturing environment.

Kaplan, R. S. and R. Cooper, *Cost & Effect*, Boston, MA: Harvard Business School Press, 1998.

Morgan, J., *Lean Six Sigma for Dummies*, Indianapolis, IN: Wiley-Blackwell Publishing, 2009.

Pyzdek, T., *The Six Sigma Handbook*, 2nd edn, New York: McGraw-Hill, 2003.

Rubrich, L., and M. Watson, *Implementing World Class Manufacturing*, 2nd edn, Fort Wayne, IN: WCM Associates, 2004.

Management control systems

The topics of Chapters 7–10 can be explored further in several books, including the following:

Anthony, R. N., and V. Govindarajan, *Management Control Systems*, 12th edn, McGraw-Hill/Irwin, 2006.

Arrow, K. J., *The Limits of Organization*, New York: Norton, 1974. [This is a readable classic by a Nobel laureate.]

Gupta, P. and A. W. Wiggenhorn, *Six Sigma Business Scorecard: Creating a Comprehensive Corporate Performance Measurement System*, 2nd edn, New York: McGraw-Hill, 2006.

Kaplan, R. S. and D. P. Norton, *Alignment: Using the Balanced Scorecard to Create Corporate Synergies*, Boston, MA: Harvard Business School Press, 2006.

Kaplan, R. S. and D. P. Norton, *The Balanced Scorecard: Measures That Drive Performance*, Boston, MA: Harvard Business School Press, 1996.

Merchant K. and W. Van der Stede, *Management Control Systems*, Upper Saddle River, NJ: Prentice Hall, 2012.

Niven, P. R., *Balanced Scorecard Step-by-Step: Maximizing Performance and Maintaining Results*, Hoboken, NJ: John Wiley & Sons, 2006.

Simons, R., *Performance Measurement and Control Systems for Implementing Strategy*, Upper Saddle River, NJ: Prentice Hall, 2000.

Solomons, D., *Divisional Performance: Measurement and Control*, New York: Markus Wiener, 1983. [This is a reprint of a 1965 classic that is still relevant.]

Fundamentals of compound interest and the use of present-value tables

▧ The nature of interest

Interest is the cost of using money. It is the rental fee for money, similar to the rental fees charged for the use of automobiles or machinery.

Suppose you invest €10,000 in a savings account in a financial institution. This €10,000 is the *principal*. Interest is the amount you earn on the investment each period. In this appendix, we focus on compound interest, where we add each period's interest to the beginning-of-the-period principal to come up with the principal for the next period. For example, suppose the financial institution promised to pay 10 per cent interest per year on your €10,000 investment. The 10% × €10,000 = €1,000 interest the first year would create a principal of €10,000 + €1,000 = €11,000 at the start of the second year. If you let the amount accumulate for 3 years before withdrawing the full balance of the deposit, the deposit would accumulate to €13,310:

	Principal	Compound interest	Balance, end of year
Year 1	€10,000	€10,000 × 0.10 = €1,000	€11,000
Year 2	11,000	11,000 × 0.10 = 1,100	12,100
Year 3	12,100	12,100 × 0.10 = 1,210	13,310

Because compound interest accumulates on both the original principal and the previously accumulated interest that has been added to principal each period, the 'force' of compound interest can be staggering. For example, the €10,000 deposit would accumulate as follows:

At end of			
3 years	10 years	20 years	40 years
€13,310	€25,937	€67,275	€452,593

Step-by-step calculations of compound interest quickly become burdensome. Therefore, experts have constructed compound interest tables to ease computations. In addition, the computations in these tables are built into many handheld calculators and computer software programs. This appendix explains how to use the two compound interest tables most commonly used in capital budgeting. Both provide measures of *present value*, the value today of a future amount.

Table B.1: Present value of €1

How do you express a future cash inflow or outflow in terms of its equivalent today (at time zero)? Table B.1 provides factors that give the present value of a single, lump-sum cash flow that you will receive or pay at the end of a future period.

Table B.1 Present value of €1

Period	3%	4%	5%	6%	7%	8%	10%	12%	14%	16%	18%	20%	22%	24%	25%	26%	28%	30%	40%
1	.9709	.9615	.9524	.9434	.9346	.9259	.9091	.8929	.8772	.8621	.8475	.8333	.8197	.8065	.8000	.7937	.7813	.7692	.7143
2	.9426	.9246	.9070	.8900	.8734	.8573	.8264	.7972	.7695	.7432	.7182	.6944	.6719	.6504	.6400	.6299	.6104	.5917	.5102
3	.9151	.8890	.8638	.8396	.8163	.7938	.7513	.7118	.6750	.6407	.6086	.5787	.5507	.5245	.5120	.4999	.4768	.4552	.3644
4	.8885	.8548	.8227	.7921	.7629	.7350	.6830	.6355	.5921	.5523	.5158	.4823	.4514	.4230	.4096	.3968	.3725	.3501	.2603
5	.8626	.8219	.7835	.7473	.7130	.6806	.6209	.5674	.5194	.4761	.4371	.4019	.3700	.3411	.3277	.3149	.2910	.2693	.1859
6	.8375	.7903	.7462	.7050	.6663	.6302	.5645	.5066	.4556	.4104	.3704	.3349	.3033	.2751	.2621	.2499	.2274	.2072	.1328
7	.8131	.7599	.7107	.6651	.6227	.5835	.5132	.4523	.3996	.3538	.3139	.2791	.2486	.2218	.2097	.1983	.1776	.1594	.0949
8	.7894	.7307	.6768	.6274	.5820	.5403	.4665	.4039	.3506	.3050	.2660	.2326	.2038	.1789	.1678	.1574	.1388	.1226	.0678
9	.7664	.7026	.6446	.5919	.5439	.5002	.4241	.3606	.3075	.2630	.2255	.1938	.1670	.1443	.1342	.1249	.1084	.0943	.0484
10	.7441	.6756	.6139	.5584	.5083	.4632	.3855	.3220	.2697	.2267	.1911	.1615	.1369	.1164	.1074	.0992	.0847	.0725	.0346
11	.7224	.6496	.5847	.5268	.4751	.4289	.3505	.2875	.2366	.1954	.1619	.1346	.1122	.0938	.0859	.0787	.0662	.0558	.0247
12	.7014	.6246	.5568	.4970	.4440	.3971	.3186	.2567	.2076	.1685	.1372	.1122	.0920	.0757	.0687	.0625	.0517	.0429	.0176
13	.6810	.6006	.5303	.4688	.4150	.3677	.2897	.2292	.1821	.1452	.1163	.0935	.0754	.0610	.0550	.0496	.0404	.0330	.0126
14	.6611	.5775	.5051	.4423	.3878	.3405	.2633	.2046	.1597	.1252	.0985	.0779	.0618	.0492	.0440	.0393	.0316	.0254	.0090
15	.6419	.5553	.4810	.4173	.3624	.3152	.2394	.1827	.1401	.1079	.0835	.0649	.0507	.0397	.0352	.0312	.0247	.0195	.0064
16	.6232	.5339	.4581	.3936	.3387	.2919	.2176	.1631	.1229	.0930	.0708	.0541	.0415	.0320	.0281	.0248	.0193	.0150	.0046
17	.6050	.5134	.4363	.3714	.3166	.2703	.1978	.1456	.1078	.0802	.0600	.0451	.0340	.0258	.0225	.0197	.0150	.0116	.0033
18	.5874	.4936	.4155	.3503	.2959	.2502	.1799	.1300	.0946	.0691	.0508	.0376	.0279	.0208	.0180	.0156	.0118	.0089	.0023
19	.5703	.4746	.3957	.3305	.2765	.2317	.1635	.1161	.0829	.0596	.0431	.0313	.0229	.0168	.0144	.0124	.0092	.0068	.0017
20	.5537	.4564	.3769	.3118	.2584	.2145	.1486	.1037	.0728	.0514	.0365	.0261	.0187	.0135	.0115	.0098	.0072	.0053	.0012
21	.5375	.4388	.3589	.2942	.2415	.1987	.1351	.0926	.0638	.0443	.0309	.0217	.0154	.0109	.0092	.0078	.0056	.0040	.0009
22	.5219	.4220	.3418	.2775	.2257	.1839	.1228	.0826	.0560	.0382	.0262	.0181	.0126	.0088	.0074	.0062	.0044	.0031	.0006
23	.5067	.4057	.3256	.2618	.2109	.1703	.1117	.0738	.0491	.0329	.0222	.0151	.0103	.0071	.0059	.0049	.0034	.0024	.0004
24	.4919	.3901	.3101	.2470	.1971	.1577	.1015	.0659	.0431	.0284	.0188	.0126	.0085	.0057	.0047	.0039	.0027	.0018	.0003
25	.4776	.3751	.2953	.2330	.1842	.1460	.0923	.0588	.0378	.0245	.0160	.0105	.0069	.0046	.0038	.0031	.0021	.0014	.0002
26	.4637	.3607	.2812	.2198	.1722	.1352	.0839	.0525	.0331	.0211	.0135	.0087	.0057	.0037	.0030	.0025	.0016	.0011	.0002
27	.4502	.3468	.2678	.2074	.1609	.1252	.0763	.0469	.0291	.0182	.0115	.0073	.0047	.0030	.0024	.0019	.0013	.0008	.0002
28	.4371	.3335	.2551	.1956	.1504	.1159	.0693	.0419	.0255	.0157	.0097	.0061	.0038	.0024	.0019	.0015	.0010	.0006	.0001
29	.4243	.3207	.2429	.1846	.1406	.1073	.0630	.0374	.0224	.0135	.0082	.0051	.0031	.0020	.0015	.0012	.0008	.0005	.0001
30	.4120	.3083	.2314	.1741	.1314	.0994	.0573	.0334	.0196	.0116	.0070	.0042	.0026	.0016	.0012	.0010	.0006	.0004	.0000
40	.3066	.2083	.1420	.0972	.0668	.0460	.0221	.0107	.0053	.0026	.0013	.0007	.0004	.0002	.0001	.0001	.0001	.0000	.0000

Suppose you invest €1.00 today at 6 per cent interest. It will grow to €1.06 in one year.; that is, €1×1.06=€1.06. At the end of the second year, its value is (€1×1.06)×1.06=€1×(1.06)²= €1.124; and at the end of the third year it is €1 × (1.06)³ = 191. In general, €1.00 grows to $(1+i)^n$ in n years at i per cent interest.

To determine the present value, you reverse this accumulation process. If you will receive €1.00 in one year, it is worth €1 ÷ 1.06 = €0.9434 today at an interest rate of 6 per cent. Stated differently, if you invest €0.9434 today, in one year you will have €0.9434 × 1.06 = €1.00. Thus, €0.9434 is the present value of €1.00 a year hence at 6 per cent.

Suppose you will receive the €1 in 2 years instead of in 1 year. Its present value is then €1.00 ÷ (1.06)² = €0.8900. The general formula for the present value (PV) of an amount S that you will receive or pay in n periods at an interest rate of i per cent per period is as follows:

$$PV = S/(1 + i)^n$$

Table B.1 on p. 677 provides factors computed using this formula. It shows the present value of a single, lump-sum cash flow at the end of a future period at a particular interest rate.

Present values are also called *discounted values*, and the process of finding the present value is called *discounting*. You can think of this as discounting (decreasing) the value of a future cash inflow or outflow. Why is the value discounted? Because you will receive or pay the cash in the future, its value today is reduced or discounted from the future amount to be received.

Assume that a municipality issues a 3-year non-interest-bearing note payable that promises to pay you a lump sum of €1,000 exactly 3 years from the issue date. You desire a rate of return of 6 per cent, compounded annually. How much would you be willing to pay now for the 3-year note? The situation is sketched as follows:

End of year	0	1	2	3
10% PV factor	Present value			Future amount
.7513	€10,000 ←			€13,310

The factor in the period 3 row and 6 per cent column of Table B.1 is 0.8396. The present value of the €1,000 payment is €1,000×0.8396=€839.60. You would therefore be willing to pay €839.60 today for the €1,000 that you will receive in 3 years; €839.60 is the discounted value of the €1,000 future amount.

Compounding can occur more frequently than once per year. Suppose interest is compounded semi-annually rather than annually. In our previous example, the 3 years become six semi-annual interest compounding periods. How much would you be willing to pay, assuming the rate of return you demand per semi-annual period is half the annual rate, or 6% ÷ 2=3%? The factor in the period 6 row and 3 per cent column of Table B.1 is 0.8375. You would be willing to pay €1,000 × 0.8375, or only €837.50 rather than €839.60.

As a further check on your understanding, review the earlier example of your €10,000 investment. Suppose the financial institution promised to pay €13,310 at the end of 3 years. How much would you be willing to deposit at time zero if you desired a 10 per cent rate of return compounded annually? Using Table B.1, the period 3 row and the 10 per cent column show a factor of 0.7513. You multiply this factor by the future amount:

$$PV = 0.7513 \times €13,310 = €10,000$$

A diagram of this computation follows:

Pause for a moment. Use Table B.1 to obtain the present values of

1 €1,700 at 20 per cent at the end of 20 years.

2 €8,300 at 10 per cent at the end of 12 years.

3 €8,000 at 4 per cent at the end of 4 years.

Answers

1 €1,700 × 0.0261 = €44.37

2 €8,300 × 0.3186 = €2,644.38

3 €8,000 × 0.8548 = €6,838.40

Table B.2: Present value of an ordinary annuity of €1

An annuity is a series of equal cash flows spaced equally in time. An ordinary annuity has the equally spaced payments occurring at the end of each period. (We will not discuss the other type of annuity, an annuity due, which has payments at the beginning of each year.) Assume that you buy a note from a municipality that promises to pay €1,000 at the end of each of the next 3 years. How much should you be willing to pay if you desire a rate of return of 6 per cent, compounded annually? This series of payments is a 3-year ordinary annuity. You denote the present value of an ordinary annuity as PV_A.

Before we introduce a computational method to deal with an annuity, note that you can simply treat this as a series of individual amounts and solve the problem using Table B.1. First, you find the present value of each payment and then you add the present values. As shown next, you would be willing to pay €943.40 for the first payment, €890.00 for the second and €839.60 for the third, for a total of €2,673.00:

Payment	End of year Table 1 factor	0 Present value	1	2	3
1	$\dfrac{1}{1.06} = .9434$	€ 943.40	€1,000		
2	$\dfrac{1}{(1.06)^2} = .8900$	890.00		1,000	
3	$\dfrac{1}{(1.06)^3} = .8396$	839.60			€1,000
Total		€2,673.00			

Although you can always treat an annuity as a series of individual amounts, this approach is computationally inconvenient for a long annuity. Instead, the factors in Table B.2 on p. 680 provide a computational shortcut. Let's examine the conceptual basis for Table B.2 using our 3-year annuity. The three present value factors corresponding to the three annuity payments are the first three numbers from the 6 per cent column of Table B.1. Because you

Table B.2 Present value of ordinary annuity of €1

Period	3%	4%	5%	6%	7%	8%	10%	12%	14%	16%	18%	20%	22%	24%	25%	26%	28%	30%	40%
1	.9709	.9615	.9524	.9434	.9346	.9259	.9091	.8929	.8772	.8621	.8475	.8333	.8197	.8065	.8000	.7937	.7813	.7692	.7143
2	1.9135	1.8861	1.8594	1.8334	1.8080	1.7833	1.7355	1.6901	1.6467	1.6052	1.5656	1.5278	1.4915	1.4568	1.4400	1.4235	1.3916	1.3609	1.2245
3	2.8286	2.7751	2.7232	2.6730	2.6243	2.5771	2.4869	2.4018	2.3216	2.2459	2.1743	2.1065	2.0422	1.9813	1.9520	1.9234	1.8684	1.8161	1.5889
4	3.7171	3.6299	3.5460	3.4651	3.3872	3.3121	3.1699	3.0373	2.9137	2.7982	2.6901	2.5887	2.4936	2.4043	2.3616	2.3202	2.2410	2.1662	1.8492
5	4.5797	4.4518	4.3295	4.2124	4.1002	3.9927	3.7908	3.6048	3.4331	3.2743	3.1272	2.9906	2.8636	2.7454	2.6893	2.6351	2.5320	2.4356	2.0352
6	5.4172	5.2421	5.0757	4.9173	4.7665	4.6229	4.3553	4.1114	3.8887	3.6847	3.4976	3.3255	3.1669	3.0205	2.9514	2.8850	2.7594	2.6427	2.1680
7	6.2303	6.0021	5.7864	5.5824	5.3893	5.2064	4.8684	4.5638	4.2883	4.0386	3.8115	3.6046	3.4155	3.2423	3.1611	3.0833	2.9370	2.8021	2.2628
8	7.0197	6.7327	6.4632	6.2098	5.9713	5.7466	5.3349	4.9676	4.6389	4.3436	4.0776	3.8372	3.6193	3.4212	3.3289	3.2407	3.0758	2.9247	2.3306
9	7.7861	7.4353	7.1078	6.8017	6.5152	6.2469	5.7590	5.3282	4.9464	4.6065	4.3030	4.0310	3.7863	3.5655	3.4631	3.3657	3.1842	3.0190	2.3790
10	8.5302	8.1109	7.7217	7.3601	7.0236	6.7101	6.1446	5.6502	5.2161	4.8332	4.4941	4.1925	3.9232	3.6819	3.5705	3.4648	3.2689	3.0915	2.4136
11	9.2526	8.7605	8.3064	7.8869	7.4987	7.1390	6.4951	5.9377	5.4527	5.0286	4.6560	4.3271	4.0354	3.7757	3.6564	3.5435	3.3351	3.1473	2.4383
12	9.9540	9.3851	8.8633	8.3838	7.9427	7.5361	6.8137	6.1944	5.6603	5.1971	4.7932	4.4392	4.1274	3.8514	3.7251	3.6059	3.3868	3.1903	2.4559
13	10.6350	9.9856	9.3936	8.8527	8.3577	7.9038	7.1034	6.4235	5.8424	5.3423	4.9095	4.5327	4.2028	3.9124	3.7801	3.6555	3.4272	3.2233	2.4685
14	11.2961	10.5631	9.8986	9.2950	8.7455	8.2442	7.3667	6.6282	6.0021	5.4675	5.0081	4.6106	4.2646	3.9616	3.8241	3.6949	3.4587	3.2487	2.4775
15	11.9379	11.1184	10.3797	9.7122	9.1079	8.5595	7.6061	6.8109	6.1422	5.5755	5.0916	4.6755	4.3152	4.0013	3.8593	3.7261	3.4834	3.2682	2.4839
16	12.5611	11.6523	10.8378	10.1059	9.4466	8.8514	7.8237	6.9740	6.2651	5.6685	5.1624	4.7296	4.3567	4.0333	3.8874	3.7509	3.5026	3.2832	2.4885
17	13.1661	12.1657	11.2741	10.4773	9.7632	9.1216	8.0216	7.1196	6.3729	5.7487	5.2223	4.7746	4.3908	4.0591	3.9099	3.7705	3.5177	3.2948	2.4918
18	13.7535	12.6593	11.6896	10.8276	10.0591	9.3719	8.2014	7.2497	6.4674	5.8178	5.2732	4.8122	4.4187	4.0799	3.9279	3.7861	3.5294	3.3037	2.4941
19	14.3238	13.1339	12.0853	11.1581	10.3356	9.6036	8.3649	7.3658	6.5504	5.8775	5.3162	4.8435	4.4415	4.0967	3.9424	3.7985	3.5386	3.3105	2.4958
20	14.8775	13.5903	12.4622	11.4699	10.5940	9.8181	8.5136	7.4694	6.6231	5.9288	5.3527	4.8696	4.4603	4.1103	3.9539	3.8083	3.5458	3.3158	2.4970
21	15.4150	14.0292	12.8212	11.7641	10.8355	10.0168	8.6487	7.5620	6.6870	5.9731	5.3837	4.8913	4.4756	4.1212	3.9631	3.8161	3.5514	3.3198	2.4979
22	15.9369	14.4511	13.1630	12.0416	11.0612	10.2007	8.7715	7.6446	6.7429	6.0113	5.4099	4.9094	4.4882	4.1300	3.9705	3.8223	3.5558	3.3230	2.4985
23	16.4436	14.8568	13.4886	12.3034	11.2722	10.3711	8.8832	7.7184	6.7921	6.0442	5.4321	4.9245	4.4985	4.1371	3.9764	3.8273	3.5592	3.3254	2.4989
24	16.9355	15.2470	13.7986	12.5504	11.4693	10.5288	8.9847	7.7843	6.8351	6.0726	5.4509	4.9371	4.5070	4.1428	3.9811	3.8312	3.5619	3.3272	2.4992
25	17.4131	15.6221	14.0939	12.7834	11.6536	10.6748	9.0770	7.8431	6.8729	6.0971	5.4669	4.9476	4.5139	4.1474	3.9849	3.8342	3.5640	3.3286	2.4994
26	17.8768	15.9828	14.3752	13.0032	11.8258	10.8100	9.1609	7.8957	6.9061	6.1182	5.4804	4.9563	4.5196	4.1511	3.9879	3.8367	3.5656	3.3297	2.4996
27	18.3270	16.3296	14.6430	13.2105	11.9867	10.9352	9.2372	7.9426	6.9352	6.1364	5.4919	4.9636	4.5243	4.1542	3.9903	3.8387	3.5669	3.3305	2.4997
28	18.7641	16.6631	14.8981	13.4062	12.1371	11.0511	9.3066	7.9844	6.9607	6.1520	5.5016	4.9697	4.5281	4.1566	3.9923	3.8402	3.5679	3.3312	2.4998
29	19.1885	16.9837	15.1411	13.5907	12.2777	11.1584	9.3696	8.0218	6.9830	6.1656	5.5098	4.9747	4.5312	4.1585	3.9938	3.8414	3.5687	3.3317	2.4999
30	19.6004	17.2920	15.3725	13.7648	12.4090	11.2578	9.4269	8.0552	7.0027	6.1772	5.5168	4.9789	4.5338	4.1601	3.9950	3.8424	3.5693	3.3321	2.4999
40	23.1148	19.7928	17.1591	15.0463	13.3317	11.9246	9.7791	8.2438	7.1050	6.2335	5.5482	4.9966	4.5439	4.1659	3.9995	3.8458	3.5712	3.3332	2.5000

multiply each of these factors by the €1,000 annuity payment, you can sum the factors and then multiply by €1,000 instead of multiplying each factor by €1,000 and then summing. For this example, the sum of the factors is .9434 + .8900 + .8396 = 2.6730, and this is the value that you find in Table B.1 for a three-period annuity with an interest rate of 6 per cent. The present value of the annuity is simply the value from Table B.2, 2.6730, multiplied by €1,000: 2.6730 × €1,000 = €2,673.00. This shortcut is especially valuable if the cash payments or receipts extend over many periods. Consider an annual cash payment of €1,000 for 20 years at 6 per cent. The present value, calculated from Table B.1, is €1,000 × 11.4699 = €11,469.90. To use Table B.1 for this calculation, you would have to perform 20 multiplications and then add the 20 products.

The factors in Table B.2 could be calculated by summing the factors in Table B.1, but they could also be calculated using the following general formula:

$$PV_A = \frac{1}{i}\left[1 - \frac{1}{(1+i)^n}\right]$$

Applied to our illustration,

$$PV_A = \frac{1}{.06}\left[1 - \frac{1}{(1.06)^3}\right] = \frac{1}{.06}(1 - .8396) = \frac{.1604}{.06} = 2.6730$$

Now, use Table B.2 to obtain the present values of the following ordinary annuities:

1 €1,600 at 20 per cent for 20 years

2 €8,300 at 10 per cent for 12 years

3 €8,000 at 4 Per cent for 4 years.

Answers

1 €1,600 × 4.8696 = €7,791.36

2 €8,300 × 6.8137 = €56,553.71

3 €8,000 × 3.6299 = €29,039.20.

In particular, note that the higher the interest rate, the lower the present value.

A

absorption approach (absorption costing) A costing approach that considers all indirect manufacturing costs (both variable and fixed) to be product (inventoriable) costs that become an expense in the form of manufacturing cost of goods sold only as sales occur.

absorption costing *See* absorption approach.

accelerated depreciation A pattern of depreciation that charges a large proportion of an asset's cost to the earlier years and less to later years.

account analysis Classifying each account as a variable cost or as a fixed cost with respect to a selected cost driver.

accounting rate-of-return (ARR) model A non-DCF capital-budgeting model expressed as the increase in expected average annual operating income divided by the initial required investment.

accounting system A formal mechanism for gathering, organising and communicating information about an organisation's activities.

accumulated depreciation The sum of all depreciation charged to past periods.

activity analysis The process of identifying appropriate cost drivers and their effects on the costs of making a product or providing a service.

activity-based budgets Budgets that focus on the budgeted cost of activities required to produce and sell products and services.

activity-based costing (ABC) systems A system that first accumulates indirect resource costs for each of the activities of the area being costed, and then assigns the costs of each activity to the products, services, or other cost objects that require that activity. *See also* Cost allocation.

activity-based flexible budget A budget based on budgeted costs for each activity using the related cost driver.

activity-based management (ABM) Using the output of an activity-based cost accounting system to aid strategic decision making and to improve operational control of an organisation.

activity-level variances The differences between the static budget amounts and the amounts in the flexible budget.

agency theory A theory that deals with relationships where one party (the principal) delegates decision-making authority to another party (the agent).

attention directing Reporting and interpreting information that helps managers to focus on operating problems, imperfections, inefficiencies and opportunities.

avoidable costs Costs that will not continue if an ongoing operation is changed or deleted.

B

backflush costing An accounting system that applies costs to products only when the production is complete.

balanced scorecard (BSC) A performance measurement and reporting system that strikes a balance between financial and nonfinancial measures, links performance to rewards, and gives explicit recognition to the link between performance measurement and organisational goals and objectives.

B2B Electronic commerce from one business to another business.

B2C Electronic commerce from business to consumer.

benchmarking The continuous process of comparing products, services, and activities against the best industry standards.

book value (net book value) The original cost of equipment less accumulated depreciation.

break-even point The level of sales at which revenue equals expenses and net income is zero.

budget A quantitative expression of a plan of action and an aid to coordinating and implementing the plan.

budgetary slack (budget padding) Overstatement of budgeted cost or understatement of budgeted revenue to create a budget goal that is easier to achieve.

budgeted factory-overhead rate The budgeted total overhead for each cost pool divided by the budgeted cost-allocation base level.

budget padding (budgetary slack) Overstatement of budgeted cost or understatement of budgeted revenue to create a budget goal that is easier to achieve.

business process reengineering The fundamental rethinking and radical redesign of business processes to improve performance in areas such as cost, quality, service and speed.

by-product A product that, like a joint product, is not individually identifiable until manufacturing reaches a split-off point, but has relatively insignificant total sales value.

C

capacity costs The fixed costs of being able to achieve a desired level of production or to provide a desired level of service while maintaining product or service attributes, such as quality.

capital budget A budget that details the planned expenditures for facilities, equipment, new products and other long-term investments. *See also* Budget.

capital budgeting The long-term planning for making and financing investments that affect financial results over a period longer than just the next year.

capital charge Company's cost of capital X amount of investment.

capital turnover Revenue divided by invested capital.

cash budget A statement of planned cash receipts and disbursements.

centralisation The process by which organisations concentrate decision making within a particular location or group.

code of conduct A document specifying the ethical standards of an organisation.

coefficient of determination (R²) A measurement of how much of the fluctuation of a cost is explained by changes in the cost driver. *See also* Least-squares regression.

committed fixed costs Costs arising from the possession of facilities, equipment and a basic organisation.

common costs Those costs of facilities and services that are shared by users.

computer-aided design (CAD) The use of computer technology for the design of real or virtual objects.

computer-aided manufacturing (CAM) The use of computer-based software tools in manufacturing or prototyping.

computer-integrated manufacturing (CIM) systems Systems that use computer-aided design, computer-aided manufacturing, robots and computer-controlled machines.

continuous budget (rolling budget) A common form of master budget that adds a month in the future as the month just ended is dropped.

contribution approach A method of internal (management accounting) reporting that emphasises the distinction between variable and fixed costs for the purpose of better decision making.

contribution margin A term used for either unit contribution margin or total contribution margin.

contribution-margin percentage Total contribution margin divided by sales or 100 per cent minus the variable cost percentage.

contribution-margin ratio Contribution margin percentage expressed as a ratio.

control Implementing plans and using feedback to evaluate the attainment of objectives.

controllable cost Any cost that a manager's decisions and actions can influence.

controller (comptroller) The top accounting officer of an organisation who deals mainly with operating matters, such as aiding management decision making.

cost A sacrifice or giving up of resources for a particular purpose. *See also* Variable cost.

cost accounting That part of the cost management system that measures costs for the purposes of management decision making and financial reporting.

cost accounting systems The techniques used to determine the cost of a product, service, customer, or other cost object. *See also* Activity-based costing (ABC) systems; Cost management system (CMS).

cost accumulation Collecting costs by some natural classification, such as activities performed, labour, or materials.

cost allocation Assigning indirect costs to cost objects in proportion to the cost object's use of a particular cost-allocation base. *See also* Activity-based costing (ABC) systems.

cost-allocation base A measure of input or output that determines the amount of cost to be allocated to a particular cost object. An ideal cost-allocation base would measure how much of the particular cost is caused by the cost object.

cost application The allocation of total departmental costs to the revenue-producing products or services.

cost assignment Attaching costs to one or more cost objects, such as activities, departments, customers or products.

cost behaviour How the activities of an organisation affect its costs. *See also* Cost-volume-profit (CVP) analysis; Measurement of cost behaviour.

cost–benefit balance Weighing estimated costs against probable benefits, the primary consideration in choosing among accounting systems and methods.

cost centre A responsibility centre in which managers are responsible for costs only.

cost driver A measure of activities that requires the use of resources and thereby cause costs. *See also* Cost allocation; Cost behaviour; Cost-volume-profit (CVP) analysis; Measurement of cost behaviour.

cost function An algebraic equation used by managers to describe the relationship between a cost and its cost driver(s). *See also* Cost behaviour; Measurement of cost behaviour.

cost management system (CMS) A collection of tools and techniques that identify how management's decisions affect costs. *See also* Activity-based costing (ABC) systems; Cost accounting.

cost measurement Estimating or predicting costs as a function of appropriate cost drivers. *See also* Measurement of cost behaviour.

cost object (cost objective) Anything for which decision makers desire a separate measurement of costs. Examples include departments, products, activities, and territories.

cost of capital The cost of long-term liabilities and stockholders' equity weighted by their relative size.

cost of goods sold The cost of the merchandise that a company acquires or produces and then sells.

cost of quality report A report that displays the financial impact of quality.

cost pool A group of individual costs that a company allocates to cost objects using a single cost-allocation base. *See also* Cost allocation.

cost–volume–profit (CVP) analysis The study of the effects of output volume on revenue (sales), expenses (costs), and net income (net profit). *See also* Break-even point; Cost behaviour.

currently attainable standards Levels of performance that managers can achieve by realistic levels of effort.

cycle time (throughput time) The time taken to complete a product or service, or any of the components of a product or service.

D

decentralisation The delegation of freedom to make decisions. The lower in the organisation that this freedom exists, the greater the decentralisation.

decision making The choice from among a set of alternative courses of action designed to achieve some objective.

decision model Any method for making a choice, sometimes requiring elaborate quantitative procedures.

depreciation The periodic cost of equipment that a company spreads over the future periods in which the company will use the equipment.

differential analysis A decision process that compares the differential revenues and costs of alternatives.

differential approach A method for comparing alternatives that computes the differences in cash flows between alternatives and then converts these differences in cash flows to their present values.

differential cost The difference in total cost between two alternatives.

differential revenue The difference in total revenue between two alternatives.

direct costs Costs that accountants can identify specifically and exclusively with a given cost object in an economically feasible way.

direct-labour costs The wages of all labour that a company can trace specifically and exclusively to the manufactured goods in an economically feasible way.

direct-material costs The acquisition costs of all materials that a company identifies as a part of the manufactured goods and traces to the manufactured goods in an economically feasible way.

direct-material inventory Material on hand and awaiting use in the production process.

direct method A method for allocating service department costs that ignores other service departments when any given service department's costs are allocated to the operating departments.

discounted-cash-flow (DCF) models A type of capital-budgeting model that focuses on cash inflows and outflows while taking into account the time value of money. *See also* Capital budgeting.

discount rate *See* required rate of return.

discretionary fixed costs Costs determined by management as part of the periodic planning process in order to meet the organisation's goals. They have no obvious relationship with levels of capacity or output activity.

discriminatory pricing Charging different prices to different customers for the same product or service.

dysfunctional decision Any decision that is in conflict with organisational goals.

E

e-commerce (electronic commerce) Conducting business online.

economic profit (residual income) After-tax operating income less a capital charge.

economic value added (EVA) Equals adjusted after-tax operating income minus the after-tax cost of invested capital multiplied by the adjusted average invested capital.

effectiveness The degree to which an organisation meets an objective.

efficiency The degree to which an organisation minimises the resources used to achieve an objective.

efficiency variance *See* usage variance.

electronic commerce (e-commerce) Conducting business online.

engineering analysis The systematic review of materials, supplies, labour, support services, and facilities needed for products and services; measuring cost behaviour according to what costs should be, not by what costs have been.

equivalent units The number of completed (whole) units that could have been produced from the inputs applied.

ethics The field that deals with human conduct in relation to what is morally good and bad, right and wrong. It is the application of values to decision making. These values include honesty, fairness, responsibility, respect, and compassion.

expected cost The cost most likely to be attained.

eXtensible Business Reporting Language (XBRL) An XML-based accounting language that helps communicate financial information electronically.

F

factory burden *See* indirect production costs.

factory overhead *See* indirect production costs.

favourable cost variance A variance that occurs when actual costs are less than budgeted costs.

favourable profit variance A variance that occurs when actual profit exceeds budgeted profit.

favourable revenue variance A variance that occurs when actual revenue exceeds budgeted revenue.

financial accounting The branch of accounting that develops information for external decision makers, such as stockholders, suppliers, banks and government regulatory agencies.

financial budget The part of a master budget that focuses on the effects that the operating budget and other plans (such as capital budgets and repayments of debt) will have on cash.

financial planning model A mathematical model of the master budget that can incorporate any set of assumptions about sales, costs or product mix.

finished-goods inventory Goods fully completed but not yet sold.

fixed cost A cost that is not immediately affected by changes in the cost-driver level. *See also* Cost-volume-profit (CVP) analysis.

fixed-overhead rate The amount of fixed manufacturing overhead applied to each unit of production. It is determined by dividing the budgeted fixed overhead by the expected cost-allocation base activity for the budget period.

fixed-overhead spending variance The difference between actual fixed overhead and budgeted fixed overhead.

flexible budget (variable budget) A budget that adjusts to different levels of activity. *See also* Budget.

flexible-budget variance The difference between actual results and the flexible budget for the actual level of output achieved. *See also* Variances.

full cost The total of all manufacturing costs plus the total of all selling and administrative costs.

functional budgeting Budgeting process that focuses on preparing budgets for various functions, such as production, selling and administrative support.

G

generally accepted accounting principles (GAAP) A set of standards to which public companies' published financial statements must adhere.

goal congruence A condition where employees, working in their own perceived best interests, make decisions that help meet the overall goals of the organisation.

Grenzplankostenrechnung (GPK) A German cost accounting system that goes a step further than ABC systems.

gross book value The original cost of an asset before deducting accumulated depreciation.

gross margin (gross profit) The excess of sales over the total cost of goods sold.

gross profit (gross margin) The excess of sales over the total cost of goods sold.

H

high-low method A simple method for measuring a linear-cost function from past cost data, focusing on the highest-activity and lowest-activity points and fitting a line through these two points.

hurdle rate *See* required rate of return.

hybrid costing systems An accounting system that is a blend of ideas from both job costing and process costing.

I

ideal standards *See* perfection standards.

imperfect competition A market in which the price a firm charges for a unit influences the quantity of units it sells.

incentives Rewards, both implicit and explicit, for managerial effort and actions.

incremental analysis An analysis of the incremental (additional) costs and benefits of a proposed alternative compared with the current situation.

incremental benefits The additional revenues or reduced costs generated by the proposed alternative in comparison with the current situation.

incremental costs The additional costs or reduced benefits generated by the proposed alternative in comparison with the current situation.

incremental effect The change in total results (such as revenue, expenses, or income) under a new condition in comparison with some given or known condition.

indirect costs Costs that accountants cannot identify specifically and exclusively with a given cost object in an economically feasible way. *See also* Activity-based costing (ABC) systems; Cost accounting systems.

indirect manufacturing costs *See* indirect production costs.

indirect production costs (indirect manufacturing costs, factory burden, factory overhead, manufacturing overhead) All costs associated with the production process that a company cannot trace to the goods or services produced in an economically feasible way; usually all production costs except direct materials and direct labour.

inflation The decline in the general purchasing power of the monetary unit.

internal auditors Accountants who review and evaluate accounting systems, including their internal controls.

internal controls Policies to protect and make the most efficient use of an organisation's assets.

internal rate of return (IRR) model A capital-budgeting model that determines the interest rate at which the NPV equals zero.

International Financial Reporting Standards (IFRS) Generally accepted accounting principles set by the IASB and applied in the European Union and in more than 120 countries worldwide.

inventoriable costs Capitalised costs associated with the value of goods for sale.

inventory turnover The number of times the average inventory is sold per year.

investment centre A responsibility centre where managers are responsible for investment as well as profits.

J

job costing *See* job-order costing.

job-cost record (job-cost sheet, job order) A document that shows all costs for a particular product, service, or batch of products.

job-cost sheet *See* job-cost record.

job order *See* job-cost record.

job-order costing (job costing) The method of allocating costs to products that are readily identified by individual units or batches, each of which requires varying degrees of attention and skill.

joint costs The costs of manufacturing joint products prior to the split-off point.

joint products Two or more manufactured products that (1) have relatively significant sales values and (2) are not separately identifiable as individual products until their split-off point.

just-in-time (JIT) philosophy A philosophy to eliminate waste by reducing the time products spend in the production process and eliminating the time products spend on activities that do not add value.

K

kaizen costing The Japanese term for continuous improvement during manufacturing.

key performance indicators Measures that drive the organisation to achieve its goals.

key success factor Characteristics or attributes that managers must achieve in order to drive the organisation toward its goals.

L

labour time tickets (time cards) The record of the time a particular direct labourer spends on each job.

lean manufacturing Applying continuous process improvements to eliminate waste from the entire enterprise.

least-squares regression (regression analysis) Measuring a cost function objectively by using statistics to fit a cost function to all the data.

limiting factor (scarce resource) The item that restricts or constrains the production or sale of a product or service.

linear-cost behaviour Activity that can be graphed with a straight line because costs are assumed to be either fixed or variable.

long-range plan Forecasted financial statements for 5- to 10-year periods.

M

management accounting The branch of accounting that produces information for managers within an organisation. It is the process of identifying, measuring, accumulating, analysing, preparing, interpreting, and communicating information that helps managers fulfil organisational objectives.

management by exception Concentrating on areas that deviate from the plan and ignoring areas that are presumed to be running smoothly.

management by objectives (MBO) The joint formulation by managers and their superiors of a set of goals and plans for achieving the goals for a forthcoming period.

management control system A logical integration of techniques for gathering and using information to make planning and control decisions, for motivating employee behaviour, and for evaluating performance.

managerial effort Exertion toward a goal or objective, including all conscious actions (such as supervising, planning and thinking) that result in more efficiency and effectiveness.

manufacturing overhead *See* indirect production costs.

marginal cost The additional cost resulting from producing and selling one additional unit.

marginal income The unit sales price minus the variable cost per unit.

marginal income tax rate The tax rate paid on additional amounts of pretax income.

marginal revenue The additional revenue resulting from the sale of an additional unit.

margin of safety The planned unit sales less the break-even unit sales; it shows how far sales can fall below the planned level before losses occur.

markup The amount by which price exceeds cost.

master budget An extensive analysis of the first year of the long-range plan. It summarises the planned activities of all subunits of an organisation.

materials requisitions Records of materials used in particular jobs.

measurement of cost behaviour Understanding and quantifying how activities of an organisation affect its levels of costs. *See also* Cost behaviour.

mixed costs Costs that contain elements of both fixed- and variable-cost behaviour.

motivation The drive toward some selected goal that creates effort and action toward that goal. *See also* Incentives.

multistage ABC (MSABC) systems Costing systems with more than two stages of allocations and cost drivers other than percentages.

N

net book value The original cost of an asset less any accumulated depreciation.

net operating profit after-tax (NOPAT) Income before interest expense but after tax.

net present value The sum of the present values of all expected cash flows.

net-present-value (NPV) method A discounted-cash-flow approach to capital budgeting that computes the present value of all expected future cash flows using a minimum desired rate of return. *See also* Capital budgeting; Discounted-cash-flow (DCF) models.

nominal rate Quoted market interest rate that includes an inflation element.

non-value-added costs Costs that a company can eliminate without affecting a product's value to the customer.

normal costing system The cost system in which the cost of the manufactured product is composed of actual direct material, actual direct labour, and normal applied overhead.

O

operating budget (profit plan) A major part of a master budget that focuses on the income statement and its supporting schedules.

operating leverage A firm's ratio of fixed to variable costs.

opportunity cost For a resource that a company already owns or that it has already committed to purchase, the maximum available benefit forgone (or passed up) by using such a resource for a particular purpose.

outlay cost A cost that requires a future cash disbursement.

outsourcing Purchasing products or services from an outside supplier.

overapplied overhead The difference between actual and applied overhead when the amount applied exceeds the amount incurred.

P

participative budgeting Budgets formulated with the active participation of all affected employees.

payback period (payback time) The time it will take to recoup, in the form of cash inflows from operations, the initial money invested in a project.

payback time (payback period) The time it will take to recoup, in the form of cash inflows from operations, the initial money invested in a project.

perfect competition A market in which a firm can sell as much of a product as it can produce, all at a single market price.

perfection standards (ideal standards) Expressions of the most efficient performance possible under the best conceivable conditions using existing specifications and equipment.

performance metric A specific measure of management accomplishment.

performance reports Feedback provided by comparing results with plans and by highlighting variances.

period costs Costs that become expenses during the current period without becoming part of inventory.

planning Setting objectives for an organisation and outlining how it will attain them.

post-audit A follow-up evaluation of capital-budgeting decisions.

predatory pricing Establishing prices so low that they drive competitors out of the market. The predatory pricer then has no significant competition and can raise prices dramatically.

present value (PV) The value today of a future cash flow. *See also* Net present value; Net-present-value (NPV) method.

price elasticity The effect of price changes on sales volume.

price variance The difference between actual input prices and standard input prices multiplied by the actual quantity of inputs used.

problem solving The aspect of accounting that often involves a special study to assess possible courses of action and recommends the best course to follow.

process costing The method of allocating costs to products by averaging costs over large numbers of nearly identical products.

process map A schematic diagram capturing interrelationships between cost objects, activities and resources. *See also* Activity-based costing (ABC) systems.

producing departments Departments where employees work on the organisation's products or services. *See also* Cost allocation.

product costs (inventoriable costs) Costs identified with goods produced or purchased for resale.

production-volume variance A variance that appears whenever actual production deviates from the expected volume of production used in computing the fixed overhead rate. It is calculated as (actual volume – expected volume) X fixed-overhead rate.

productivity A measure of outputs divided by inputs.

product life cycle The various stages through which a product passes, from conception and development to introduction into the market to maturation and, finally, withdrawal from the market.

profit centre A responsibility centre in which managers are responsible for revenues as well as costs – that is, profitability.

profit plan *See* operating budget.

proration To assign underapplied overhead or overapplied overhead to cost of goods sold, work-in-process inventory, and finished-good inventory in proportion to the ending balances of each account.

Q

quality control The effort to ensure that products and services perform to customer requirements.

quality-control chart The statistical plot of measures of various product quality dimensions or attributes.

quantity variance The difference between the actual quantity of inputs used and the standard quantity allowed for the good output achieved multiplied by the standard price of the input.

R

rate variance A price variance applied to labour.

real options model A capital-budgeting model that recognises the value of contingent investments – that is, investments that a company can adjust as it learns more about their potential for success.

recovery period The number of years over which a company can depreciate an asset for tax purposes.

regression analysis See least-squares regression.

relevant information The predicted future costs and revenues that will differ among alternative courses of action.

relevant range The limit of cost-driver level within which a specific relationship between costs and the cost driver is valid.

required rate of return (hurdle rate, discount rate) The minimum desired rate of return, based on the firm's cost of capital.

residual income See economic profit.

responsibility accounting Identifying what parts of the organisation have primary responsibility for each action, developing performance measures and targets, and designing reports of these measures by responsibility centre.

responsibility centre A set of activities and resources assigned to a manager, a group of managers, or other employees.

return on investment (ROI) A measure of income divided by the investment required to obtain that income.

return on sales Income divided by revenue.

rolling budget See continuous budget.

S

sales-activity variances The activity-level variances when sales is used as the cost driver.

sales budget The result of decisions to create conditions that will generate a desired level of sales.

sales forecast A prediction of sales under a given set of conditions.

sales mix The relative proportions or combinations of quantities of products that constitute total sales.

Sarbanes-Oxley Act A 2002 US law that requires more top-management oversight of a company's accounting policies and procedures.

scarce resource See limiting factor.

scorekeeping The accumulation and classification of data.

segment autonomy The delegation of decision-making power to managers of segments in an organisation.

segments Responsibility centres for which a company develops separate measures of revenues and costs.

sensitivity analysis In budgeting, the systematic varying of budget data input to determine the effects of each change on the budget.

separable costs Any cost beyond the split-off point.

service departments Units that exist only to support other departments or customers. See also Cost allocation.

service organisations Organisations that do not make or sell tangible goods.

Six Sigma A continuous process improvement effort designed to reduce costs by improving quality.

split-off point The juncture of manufacturing where the joint products become individually identifiable.

standard cost A carefully determined cost that should be attained.

static budget A budget that is prepared for only one expected level of activity.

static-budget variance The difference between actual results and the static budget for the original planned level of output.

step costs Costs that change abruptly at different intervals of activity because the resources and their costs come in indivisible chunks.

step-down method A method for allocating service department costs that recognises that some service departments support the activities in other service departments as well as those in operating departments.

strategic plan A plan that sets the overall goals and objectives of the organisation.

sunk cost A historical or past cost, that is, a cost that the company has already incurred and, therefore, is irrelevant to the decision-making process.

T

target costing Taking a product's market price as given and determining the maximum cost the company can spend to make the product and still achieve the desired profitability.

throughput time See cycle time.

total contribution margin Total number of units sold times the unit contribution margin.

total project approach A method for comparing alternatives that computes the total impact on cash flows for each alternative and then converts these total cash flows to their present values.

total quality management (TQM) An approach to quality that focuses on prevention of defects and on customer satisfaction.

tracing Physically identifying the amount of a direct cost that relates exclusively to a particular cost object.

traditional costing systems Accounting systems that do not accumulate or report costs of activities or processes. They often use a single cost pool for all indirect production costs with a labour-based cost-allocation base.

transfer price The price at which one segment of an organisation sells products or services to another segment of the same organisation.

transferred-in costs In process costing, costs incurred in a previous department for items that have been received by a subsequent department.

two-stage ABC system A costing system with two stages of allocation to get from the original indirect resource cost to the final product or service cost. The first stage allocates indirect resource costs to activity-cost pools. The second stage allocates activity costs to products or services. *See also* Activity-based costing (ABC) systems.

U

unallocated costs Costs that an accounting system records but does not allocate to any cost object.

unavoidable costs Costs that will continue even if a company discontinues an operation.

uncontrollable cost Any cost that the management of a responsibility centre cannot affect within a given time span.

underapplied overhead The difference between actual and applied overhead when the amount applied is less than the amount incurred.

unfavourable cost variance A variance that occurs when actual costs exceed budgeted costs.

unfavourable profit variance A variance that occurs when actual profit falls below budgeted profit.

unfavourable revenue variance A variance that occurs when actual revenue falls below budgeted revenue.

unit contribution margin (marginal income) The sales price per unit minus the variable cost per unit.

usage variance (efficiency variance) Other names for the quantity variance.

V

value-added cost The necessary cost of an activity that cannot be eliminated without affecting a product's value to the customer.

value chain The set of business functions or activities that add value to the products or services of an organisation.

value engineering A cost-reduction technique, used primarily during design, that uses information about all value chain functions to satisfy customer needs while reducing costs.

variable budget *See* flexible budget.

variable-cost percentage Total variable costs divided by total sales.

variable-cost ratio Variable cost percentage expressed as a ratio.

variable cost A cost that changes in direct proportion to changes in the cost-driver level. *See also* Cost; Cost-volume-profit (CVP) analysis.

variable-overhead efficiency variance The difference between actual cost-driver activity and the standard amount allowed for the actual output achieved multiplied by the standard variable-overhead rate per cost-driver unit.

variable-overhead spending variance The difference between the actual variable overhead cost and the amount predicted for the actual level of cost-driver activity.

variances Deviations from plans.

visual-fit method A method in which the cost analyst visually fits a straight line through a plot of all the available data.

volume variance A common name for production-volume variance.

W

weighted-average (WA) process-costing method A process-costing method that determines total cost by adding together the cost of (1) all work done in the current period and (2) the work done in the preceding period on the current period's beginning inventory of work in process, and divides the total by the equivalent units of work done to date.

work-in-process inventory Goods undergoing the production process but not yet fully completed. *See also* Job-order costing.

X

XBRL An XML-based accounting language that helps communicate financial information electronically.

Z

zero-base budget A budget that requires justification of expenditures for every activity, including continuing activities.